HITLER'S MONSTERS

Hitler's Monsters

A SUPERNATURAL HISTORY OF THE THIRD REICH

ERIC KURLANDER

YALE UNIVERSITY PRESS
NEW HAVEN AND LONDON

For information about this and other Yale University Press publications, please contact:

U.S. Office: sales.press@yale.edu   yalebooks.com
Europe Office: sales@yaleup.co.uk   yalebooks.co.uk

Set in Minion Pro by IDSUK (DataConnection) Ltd
Printed in Great Britain by Gomer Press, Llandysul, Ceredigion, Wales

Library of Congress Cataloging-in-Publication Data

Names: Kurlander, Eric, 1973- author.
Title: Hitler's monsters : a supernatural history of the Third Reich / Eric
   Kurlander.
Description: New Haven : Yale University Press, 2017.
Identifiers: LCCN 2017005559 | ISBN 9780300189452 (hardback)
Subjects: LCSH: Germany—Politics and government—1933–1945. |
   Supernatural—Political aspects—Germany—History—20th century. |
   Occultism—Political aspects—Germany—History—20th century. |
   Paganism—Political aspects—Germany—History—20th century. |
   Superstition—Political aspects—Germany—History—20th century. |
   National socialism and occultism—History. | Religion and
   politics—Germany—History—20th century. | Political
   culture—Germany—History—20th century. | Popular
   culture—Germany—History—20th century. | Germany—Social
   conditions—1933–1945. | BISAC: HISTORY / Europe / Germany. | BODY, MIND &
   SPIRIT / Occultism. | HISTORY / Military / World War II. | HISTORY /
   Modern / 20th Century.
Classification: LCC DD256.7 .K87 2017 | DDC 943.086—dc23
LC record available at https://lccn.loc.gov/2017005559

A catalogue record for this book is available from the British Library.

10 9 8 7 6 5 4 3 2 1

CONTENTS

Part Three

ACKNOWLEDGEMENTS

In the eight years I have worked on this book, I have incurred the debt of a great many people and institutions. My research and writing was supported by a 2012 Fulbright Scholar Fellowship, a 2012 Teaching Exchange with the Freiburg Pädagogische Hochschule, four Stetson University Summer Research Grants (2009, 2012, 2013, 2015) and a Spring 2015 Stetson Sabbatical Award. I am extraordinarily grateful to the CIES and the Stetson University Professional Development Committee for this support. Without the expertise and assistance of the outstanding archivists and staff at the German Federal Archives in Berlin, Koblenz, and Freiburg, I could never have assembled the archival research for this book. The same debt of gratitude applies to the staff at the Institute for Contemporary History in Munich and the Institute for Frontier Areas of Psychology and Mental Health in Freiburg.

I am grateful to the wonderful libraries at the University of Cologne, where I conducted much of the preliminary research for this project, and the University of Freiburg, where I spent a semester as a visiting scholar in Spring 2012. Equally valuable was the Berlin State Library (*Staatsbibliothek zu Berlin, Stiftung Preussischer Kulturbesitz*). The exceptional collections at all three institutions provided most of the published primary and secondary sources on which this book is based. I would also like to thank the faculty and staff of the Stetson University Library, notably Barbara Costello and Susan Derryberry, who helped track down and obtain obscure sources online or through interlibrary loan.

A number of of fellow scholars made the research and writing of this book possible. The incomparable David Blackbourn and Geoff Eley supported this project, as they have my earlier projects, with dedication and enthusiasm, as did my Stetson colleagues Grady Ballenger, Paul Croce, Karen Ryan, and Margaret Venzke. I am very grateful to the scholars who invited me to panels, conferences, and colloquia in Germany and the United States, where I was able to present aspects of this project from its earliest stages to the final chapters. These include

Jason Coy, Norbert Finzsch, Bryan Ganaway, Geoffrey Giles, Bernd Grewe, Thomas Pegelow Kaplan, Thomas Lekan, Johannes Mueller, Sylvia Paletschek, Heather Perry, and Richard Wetzell. There are many colleagues who provided helpful feedback on early drafts of chapters, articles, or presentations that I gave in Germany and the United States. These include, but are not limited to, Ofer Ashkenazi, Benita Blessing, Erik Butler, Joel Davis, Michael Fahlbusch, Jamil Khader, Samuel Koehne, Fabian Link, Emily Mieras, Nicole Mottier, Perry Myers, Barry Murnane, Clyde Kurlander, Michele Kurlander, Peter Staudenmaier, Anthony Steinhof, Julia Torrie, Jared Poley, Andrew Port, and George Williamson.

I would also like to thank my co-editors Monica Black, Joanne Miyang Cho, and Douglas McGetchin for collaborating on two edited collections that helped me think through my research, meet like-minded scholars, and develop the arguments put forth in this book. I would like to give special thanks to the late Nicholas Goodrick-Clarke, Peter Fritzsche, Richard Steigmann-Gall, and three other anonymous reviewers for their thorough read of the initial proposal, as well as the finished manuscript. Their helpful suggestions have made this a far better book.

I would be remiss were I not to mention my outstanding editors at Yale University Press, starting with Heather McCallum, who remains one of the most supportive and enthusiastic editors with whom I have worked. Her steady investment in the project, from conception to fruition, was indispensable in making this book happen. I am likewise grateful to Melissa Bond, Samantha Cross, and Rachael Lonsdale for their expertise and assistance. In particular, I want to thank my fantastic copy-editor, Richard Mason, who not only exercised the normal due diligence in finding incomplete references and stylistic errors, but also made a number of helpful editorial suggestions as well.

I would like to express my gratitude to the Stetson History Department's administrative assistants over the past six years, notably Mary Bernard, Jennifer Snyder Hildebrandt, and Chelsea Santoro, for their logistical and editorial support at many stages of the project. Notably, they supervised the efforts of our work-study students in tracking down books and articles, compiling a preliminary bibliography, and performing a number of other helpful tasks. These students include Jesika Butler, John Dieck, Maria Frank, Marissa Hanley, Josh Howard, Katie Nathensen, Andrei Pemberton, and Brett Whitmore. Last but not least, I want to thank my student research assistants, Drew Glasnovich, Noah Katz, Justin McCallister, William Proper, Alex (Matthew) Rafferty, Julie Stevens, and Tabea Wanninger, who helped cull, organize, and analyze hundreds of pages of primary and secondary sources.

Finally, I would like to thank my children, Amélie and Kolya. They have cheerfully accompanied my wife Monika and me to Germany on a half dozen occasions over the past eight years – attending school there for a semester – in order to make the research and writing of this book possible. I dedicate this book to them.

INTRODUCTION

'The success of National Socialism, the unique appearance of the Führer, has no precedent in German History ... The consequence of these historic and unprecedented political occurrences is that many Germans, due to their proclivity for the romantic and the mystical, indeed the occult, came to understand the success of National Socialism in this fashion.'

Alfred Rosenberg, 1941[1]

'Horror always lurks at the bottom of the magical world and everything "holy" is always mixed with horror.'[2]

From a page underscored by Hitler in Ernst Schertel's occult work,
Magic: History, Theory, and Practice (1923)

'Outside a purely secular frame of reference, Nazism [is] felt to be the embodiment of evil in a modern twentieth-century regime, a monstrous pagan relapse in the Christian community of Europe.'

Nicholas Goodrick-Clarke[3]

Early in the blockbuster movie *Captain America: The First Avenger* (2011) a Nazi officer enters a small Norwegian town in search of an ancient relic, the Tesseract, which promises its owner infinite power. We soon find out that the officer, Johannes Schmidt, has imbibed the prototype of a 'supersoldier' serum, developed by a fringe scientist named Abraham Erskine. Intended to give Schmidt superhuman strength and agility, the serum instead causes a monstrous transformation, driving the Nazi officer mad and turning his head into a ghastly red skull. Erskine escapes to America, where he perfects his serum, transfiguring the prototypical 98-pound weakling, Steve Rogers, into our eponymous hero. Captain America has little time to hone his combat skills before confronting the Red Skull and the insidious occult society known as 'Hydra', which, it turns out, pulls the strings behind Hitler and the Third Reich.

Captain America contains all the elements of Nazi supernaturalism in the popular mind: the connection to occult forces, mad scientists, fantastical weapons, a superhuman master race, a preoccupation with pagan religions, and magical relics supposed to grant the Nazis unlimited power. From comic books produced already during the Second World War era to twenty-first-century video games like *Castle Wolfenstein*, from classic science fiction and adventure films such as *Raiders of the Lost Ark* and *The Boys from Brazil* to contemporary horror movies like *Dead Snow* or superhero franchises such as *Captain America*, popular culture is awash with images of the Nazi supernatural.

Of course, few of these comic books, films, or video games are based on reliable primary evidence. Most popular representations of Nazism, even in documentary form, also fail to investigate deeper connections between supernatural thinking and policies and practices in the Third Reich.[4] Rather, the most popular television 'documentaries' generally alternate between making exaggerated claims based on limited evidence and exposing 'revelations' regarding the hidden history of obscure intellectuals or projects whose influence in the Third Reich is dubious at best (a method that comes perilously close to the practice of occultism).

The irony is that the evidence indicating an important link between Nazism and the supernatural has never been greater.[5] In the mid-1920s Hitler almost certainly read Ernst Schertel's parapsychological tome *Magic: History, Theory, Practice*, underlining sentences such as 'Satan is the fertilizing, destroying-constructing warrior' and 'He who does not carry demonic seeds within him will never give birth to a new world.'[6] A few years later Joseph Goebbels hired the famous Weimar horror writer, Hanns Heinz Ewers, to fulfil important propaganda tasks when campaigning for power.

At a seance on the night of 26 February 1933 the clairvoyant Erik Hanussen – a close friend of Nazi stormtroopers – 'predicted' next day's Reichstag fire, which helped justify the Nazi imposition of martial law. In the mid-1930s Hitler's second in command, the Deputy Führer Rudolf Hess, sponsored astrology, 'cosmobiology', and other esoteric medical practices. Hitler's chief of the SS, Heinrich Himmler, pursued similar 'border scientific' doctrines, encouraging research on the Holy Grail, witchcraft, and medieval devil worship ('Luciferianism') as well.

Indeed, there are hundreds of archival documents indicating Nazi attempts to differentiate between occult charlatanry and putatively 'scientific occultism'. During the Second World War, the German Navy, Himmler's SS, and Goebbels' Propaganda Ministry all hired astrologers and pendulum dowsers to obtain military intelligence and conduct psychological warfare. The Gestapo, worried about offending both Hitler and the German public, even banned professional debunkers from revealing the secrets behind 'magic'.

Throughout this period Hitler and Himmler sponsored a fanciful doctrine known as 'World Ice Theory', which posited that history, science, and religion could be explained by moons of ice hitting the earth in prehistoric times. Even in 1945, as the Third Reich was collapsing, the Nazis cobbled together a guerrilla band of Nazi 'Werewolves' to combat Communist partisans, who were in turn accused of vampirism by ethnic Germans fleeing the Russians. Over the past decade I have found ample documentation for these stories and dozens of others.

Based on this evidence, I argue that no mass political movement drew as consciously or consistently as the Nazis on what I call the 'supernatural imaginary' – occultism and 'border science', pagan, New Age, and Eastern religions, folklore, mythology, and many other supernatural doctrines – in order to attract a generation of German men and women seeking new forms of spirituality and novel explanations of the world that stood somewhere between scientific verifiability and the shopworn truths of traditional religion.[7] Certainly no mass party made a similar effort, once in power, to police or parse, much less appropriate and institutionalize such doctrines, whether in the realm of science and religion, culture and social policy, or the drive toward war, empire, and ethnic cleansing. Without understanding this relationship between Nazism and the supernatural, one cannot fully understand the history of the Third Reich.

***

The perception of a deep affinity between Nazism and the supernatural emerged only a few years after the founding of the Nazi Party. Already in the 1920s prominent esotericists were proclaiming that Nazi ideology, iconography, and party apparatus emerged from the Austro-German occult milieu.[8] Numerous critics were equally certain about the supernatural provenance of Nazism. Carl Jung compared Hitler to a 'truly mystic medicine man ... a form of spiritual vessel, a demi-deity', who managed to manipulate the 'unconscious of 78 million Germans'.[9] So too did the defrocked Nazi Hermann Rauschning, who attributed Hitler's success to the fact that 'every German has one foot in Atlantis, where he seeks a better fatherland'.[10] The German political scientist Erich Voegelin likened Hitler to the Egyptian emperor Akhenaten, who changed the old ways 'so that he [might become the guide] to the mysteries of the gods'.[11]

A popular belief in Nazism's supernatural roots became widespread after the outbreak of the Second World War. In 1940 the Munich journalism professor, Gerhard Szczesny, published a dissertation linking the rise of

National Socialism to a proclivity for occult thinking across the German middle classes.[12] The rocket scientist Willy Ley argued similarly that the Third Reich exploited a German tendency 'to resort to magic, to some nonsensical belief which he tries to validate by way of hysterics and physical force'.[13]

Witnesses as disparate as Walter Schellenberg, head of the SS Intelligence service (SD), and Wilhelm Wulff, Himmler's personal astrologer, agreed. Both cited the popularity of esoteric thinking in the uppermost echelons of the Nazi Party. From left-wing writers such as Bertolt Brecht to the Nazi Reich Minister Alfred Rosenberg, from German-Jewish intellectuals such as Theodor Adorno, Siegfried Kracauer, and Lotte Eisner, to more conservative writers like Thomas Mann, Gottfried Benn, and Ernst Junger, scores of artists, scientists, and intellectuals suggested that supernatural thinking helped pave the way for Nazism.[14]

This insistence on an intrinsic connection between Nazism and supernatural thinking was never confined to the German-speaking world. In 1940 the British journalist Lewis Spence published a book-length monograph, *The Occult Causes of the Present War*, which attributed Nazi foreign policy to deep-seated occult and pagan traditions.[15] A few years later, the British historian Hugh Trevor-Roper characterized the Third Reich as the 'history . . . of a savage tribe and a primitive superstition', highlighting stories of astrology and occult belief at the highest levels of the party.[16]

These claims were followed by a number of empirical studies carried out by German-Jewish intellectuals forced into exile by the Third Reich.[17] Siegfried Kracauer's seminal post-war study of Weimar film criticism, *From Caligari to Hitler* (1947), located the cultural and intellectual preconditions for German fascism in the irrational, supernaturally infused 'collective psychology' of the Weimar Republic.[18] In the same year Kracauer's colleague, Theodor Adorno, published his *Theses Against Occultism*, suggesting that the interwar renaissance in occultism – 'the metaphysics of dunces' – made possible the rise of Nazism.[19]

A few years later, in *The Haunted Screen* (1952), the film critic Lotte Eisner observed that the 'mysticism and magic, the dark forces to which Germans have always been more than willing to commit themselves, had flourished in the face of death on the battlefields'. These forces culminated after the First World War, Eisner contended, 'in the apocalyptic doctrine of Expressionism' and 'a weird pleasure . . . in evoking horror . . . a predilection for the imagery of darkness'.[20] These arguments were elaborated in the 1960s by a younger generation of emigré historians, notably Fritz Stern and George Mosse, who argued that the 'irrationalist philosophies of the late nineteenth and early twentieth centuries, including occultism, helped to clear a path for Hitler's rise to power and grounded his barbarous campaign to create a racially pure and powerful Germany'.[21]

The 1960s and 1970s witnessed the birth of a new cottage industry: the crypto-history of Nazi occultism. Epitomized by Louis Pauwels and Jacques

Bergier's *The Morning of Magicians* and Trevor Ravenscroft's *Spear of Destiny*, numerous books, sometimes written by authors with their own occult proclivities, propagated fanciful theories about esoteric cabals, magical runes, and miracle artefacts that ushered in the Third Reich.[22] Some of these books are based on a kernel of truth – a primary source here, an eyewitness account there. But most are so obviously unreliable and unsubstantiated that they cannot be cited with any accuracy.[23]

The best and most nuanced book to examine the relationship between Nazism and the supernatural is Nicholas Goodrick-Clarke's *The Occult Roots of Nazism*.[24] First published in 1985 and updated in 1992, this book examines the influence of the occult doctrine known as Ariosophy on the emergence of National Socialism between the 1890s and 1930s. Goodrick-Clarke shows convincingly that Ariosophy reflected and refracted many of the ideological elements within Nazism. Nevertheless, he concludes that it had little direct influence on Nazi thinking or policy after 1933. For all its strengths, *The Occult Roots of Nazism* makes no attempt to analyse the full range of occult or supernatural phenomena that influenced Nazism. Nor, as the title suggests, does it spend much time on the Third Reich itself.[25]

In the quarter-century since publication of *The Occult Roots of Nazism*, we have seen a trend in the scholarly literature 'toward decoupling occultism and Nazism'.[26] According to historians such as Corinna Treitel and Marco Pasi, for example, there was nothing inherently proto-fascist or illiberal about German occultism. To the contrary, what we now condescendingly dismiss as esoteric or 'pseudo-scientific' practices were highly modern, malleable, and intrinsic to the way educated Europeans negotiated the onrush of modernity. Faced with the 'disenchantment of the world', in the words of Max Weber, and a decline in organized religious devotion, Germans, like many other Europeans, sought alternative forms of knowledge – whether astrology, clairvoyance, spiritualism, or 'natural healing'.[27] The relationship between fascism and the occult, these scholars suggest, was defined by 'escalating hostilities', not ideological affinities.[28]

This revisionist work has provided a welcome corrective to the 'special path' (*Sonderweg*) literature typified by earlier accounts, which overemphasize the anti-modern and illiberal tendencies inherent within German culture. This newer scholarship is also important in highlighting the popularity and persistence of occult, pagan, and border scientific doctrines across German-speaking Central Europe.

But revisionist studies have their own blind spots. German occultism was neither as universally progressive nor as closely interwoven with science as many revisionist scholars suggest.[29] Many natural scientists, journalists, and liberal sceptics were *already* exasperated by – and devastating in their critiques of – occult and border scientific thinking during the first third of the twentieth century. To pretend that professional biologists, chemists, and physicists, both inside and outside Germany, were as prone to occult ideas as amateur 'scientists of the soul' is therefore unhelpful, especially in eliding long-running and heated contemporary debates over occult charlatanry between mainstream and 'border scientists'. Revisionist accounts also tend to understate the reality that National Socialism, even when critical of occultism, was more preoccupied by and indebted to a wide array of supernatural doctrines and esoteric practices than any mass political movement of the interwar period.

In the past decade or so some post-revisionist scholarship, including my own, has begun once again to take seriously the supernatural roots of Nazism. Several German and American scholars have written critical histories of the occult doctrine known as anthroposophy that prevailed from the 1890s through the Third Reich. Equally revealing are a few recent case studies of border sciences such as parapsychology and World Ice Theory.[30] Another group of scholars have produced a series of excellent monographs on the Nazi folklore industry as well as the disciplines of history and political science, psychology, physics, and biology in the Third Reich.[31] Finally, we have witnessed a wave of new research on *völkisch* (racialist) religion and paganism in the period from 1890 to 1945.[32] I have drawn generously on this work in writing *Hitler's Monsters*.

Despite this new research on individual aspects of religion and (border) science in the Third Reich, however, there exists no comprehensive study of the relationship between Nazism and the supernatural. *Hitler's Monsters* is the first book to address this rich, fascinating, often extraordinary relationship from the party's origins to the end of the Second World War.

***

Accustomed to the popular trope of Nazi occultism, the reader might wonder why I chose to write a 'Supernatural' and not an 'Occult History of the Third Reich'. The reasons are twofold. First, 'the occult' tends to connote, by definition, something secret, elitist, and generally obscure. But much of what attracted ordinary Germans and Nazis to the ideas and practices discussed in this book – as the revisionist scholarship has convincingly shown – was eminently public and widely popular.[33] This modern, mass-consumerist orientation of the 'occult' marketplace contrasts greatly with the ostensibly elite, reactionary, obscure nature of occult practice.[34] Indeed, the organizations and publishers that promoted these ideas were politically and ideologically eclectic, as likely to include sexual reformers or New Age gurus in their pages as neo-romantic or *völkisch* conservatives.[35]

Second, early twentieth-century occultism, diverse as it is, constitutes only one cluster of beliefs and practices within the broader German supernatural imaginary.[36] To be sure, under the rubric of occultism we might include a broad range of practices (astrology, clairvoyance, divining, parapsychology, etc.), beliefs (witchcraft, demonology), and syncretic doctrines that share elements of both (Theosophy, Anthroposophy, Ariosophy). Nevertheless, studies of occultism still tend to exclude important 'border sciences' such as World Ice Theory, the Nazi search for 'miracle' technologies, folklore and mythology, and aspects of *völkisch* religion.

Indeed, there is extensive scholarly literature about Nazi religiosity on the one hand, and folklore and ethnology on the other, that has developed independently of the historiography on the occult. We will not get into the details of the various debates on 'political religion' here, except to note that many scholars of fascism highlight the religio-mythical elements at the core of Nazism.[37] Nazism, per those scholars, 'attempted to draw the people into active participation in the national mystique through rites and festivals, myths and symbols which gave a concrete expression to the general will'.[38]

Folklore and mythology facilitated fascism, it is argued, by producing 'national myths, symbols, and stereotypes that made it possible for many men and women to confront the burdens of life: they are the filters through which reality is perceived'.[39] Examining manifestations of this 'longing for myth', this desire for new religious and spiritual experience, is essential to understanding the supernatural roots, character, and legacies of the Third Reich.[40]

Opposite the rise of pagan religion and mythology we have the remarkable growth of 'border science' (*Grenzwissenschaft*) in late nineteenth-century Germany.[41] The *Grenzwissenschaften* included everything from traditional occult disciplines such as parapsychology, cosmobiology, and radiesthesia to World Ice Theory and other doctrines that challenged 'academic scholars ... with a huge number of theories that did not meet the requirements for new scientific knowledge'. Such theories and practices, according to Christina Wessely, 'which appeared both as universal cosmologies and holistic world views [*Weltanschauungen*], explicitly disapproved of the development of modern science, sharing a popular fear that a purely materialistic, abstract science would lead to cultural decline'.[42] It is possibly because of the fact that millions of Germans accepted otherwise dubious border scientific doctrines that revisionist scholars respond quite critically to the idea that there is a clear line to be drawn between mainstream and 'border' sciences.[43] But such lines, then and now, do exist.

The purpose of this book is not to answer the epistemological question of what constitutes science and what constitutes border science.[44] I would nonetheless suggest that many border scientific ideas ardently rejected by intellectuals such as Freud, Adorno, and Einstein were widely popular in Germany and exploited by the Nazi Party.[45] Revisionist scholars who want to rescue occultism,

New Age religion, or border science from the condescension of posterity might condemn Adorno and his colleagues for their hostile attitudes toward supernatural thinking. But we fail to do justice to the period by drawing a false equivalency between mainstream and border science. Nor is it useful to exaggerate the inability of contemporary intellectuals to discern the difference between science and the supernatural, empiricism and faith, or the potentially deleterious sociopolitical consequences of blurring such distinctions.[46]

In short, we must avoid outmoded stereotypes of German backwardness, which presume that the emergence of a quintessentially 'modern' culture and society occurs in inverse relation to the persistence of superstition or occultism.[47] We should be equally wary, however, of a dialectical approach that presumes the inherent irrationality embedded within modern science's claims to rationality or progress.[48] The relative decline or efflorescence of the supernatural – the disenchantment and reenchantment of the world – has more to do with changing social, political, and historical contexts, with culture and ideology, than with the ebb and flow of modernity.[49] Virtually all historians now agree that there was an explosion in new forms of occult, border scientific, and religious thinking in the late nineteenth century. The question is how and whether these kinds of thinking influenced the ideas and practices of Nazism.

***

I have chosen to refer to this vast reservoir of supernatural thinking – the myriad ideas, discourses, and practices covered in this book – as the 'supernatural imaginary'. Scholars have frequently employed the 'notion of imaginary identification' to explain the allure of fascism.[50] But the idea of a 'supernatural imaginary' is most similar to the philosopher Charles Taylor's definition of a 'social imaginary'.

For Taylor, the social imaginary 'is how people imagine their social existence, how they integrate with others, and the deeper normative ideas that influence these expectations'. While political ideology 'is often the acquisition of a small minority', Taylor argues, the social imaginary 'is shared by a whole society or large group; theory is expressed in theoretical terms while imaginary is described by images and legends; the imaginary is the common understanding that creates possible commonplace actions and a sense of legitimacy that is shared among all'.[51] The social imaginary, according to Taylor, 'can never be adequately expressed in the form of explicit doctrines because of its unlimited and indefinite nature. That is another reason for speaking here of an imaginary and not a theory'.[52]

There are important distinctions between Taylor's 'social imaginary' and the concept of a 'supernatural imaginary' employed in this book. Taylor links the emergence of the 'social imaginary' to a post-Enlightenment disenchantment of the world, a response to 'the end of a certain kind of presence of religion or the divine in public space'.[53] Whereas Taylor sees the social imaginary as 'expel[ling] the world of supernatural forces', we employ the premise that the late nineteenth and early twentieth century witnessed a reframing and transposition of supernatural thinking from Christianity to occultism, border science, and alternative religion.[54]

As recent studies have shown, supernatural explanations most readily displace rational, instrumental reasoning in public life when individuals believe themselves to be dealing with 'sacred values'.[55] The political danger point, whether in fomenting religious fanaticism or fascism, appears to be 'when people feel themselves to be completely fused with a group defined by its sacred value'.[56]

Fascism makes sense of sociopolitical reality through the conscious and subconscious use of collective practices, rites, and sacred symbols, a 'network of relationships' that helps create a 'relativization of classical dichotomies: of rational and irrational, left and right, revolutionary and reactionary, modern and anti-modern'.[57] By drawing upon and appealing to an array of supernatural ideas, the Nazis created a space in which existing views – be they liberal, socialist, or traditionally conservative – could be overturned, displaced, or elided to produce a sense of ideological coherence where none otherwise existed.

This strategy proved helpful not only in terms of electoral politics, but in regard to domestic and foreign policy after the Nazi seizure of power in January 1933. By binding Jews, Communists, and freemasons to images of vampires, zombies, demons, devils, spectres, alien parasites, and other supernatural monsters, the Third Reich helped to justify otherwise exaggerated responses to 'an enemy who did not seem to adhere to the same cultural code'.[58]

For most Nazis and many Germans these racial and political 'monsters' became the 'embodiment of difference ... hybrid creatures', who were 'weirdly human and yet terrifyingly other ... abjectly *wrong*, unseemly, unnatural, anathema ... demonic, unholy'. These 'monsters' were 'not created from whole cloth', observes Monica Black, but 'constructed through a recombination of known representations' that were already present in the supernatural imaginary.[59] In this way the supernatural imaginary provided an ideological and discursive space in which Nazism's enemies could be dehumanized, marginalized, and figuratively transformed into monsters requiring physical elimination.

The Afro-Caribbean writer Frantz Fanon may well have been talking about Germany when he discussed the violent consequences of a colonized people believing in 'supernatural, magical powers'. By embracing supernatural thinking, Fanon suggests, the 'settler's powers are infinitely shrunken, stamped with their alien origin' and made into a 'frightening enemy created by myths'. 'Symbolical killings, fantastic rides, imaginary mass murders' – all these fantasies are shared by the colonized people. 'One step further and you are completely possessed,' Fanon continues, immersed in literal and figurative 'séances of possession and exorcism', leading to the representation of your enemies as 'vampir[es] … djinns, [and] zombies'.[60]

Many Germans – and certainly most Nazis – viewed themselves after the First World War as a colonized people, subject to the exterminatory whims and fantasies of the ethnic and political other: whether the Jews, Bolsheviks, and Slavs; the British, French, and Belgians; or the North African troops that briefly occupied the Ruhr.[61] This feeling of subaltern status, biopolitical insecurity, and territorial loss, when combined with supernatural fantasies about race and space, provided a powerful justification for violent action against a variety of 'monsters' in domestic and foreign policy.

At the same time the 'supernatural imaginary' created a discourse in which fantasies of emulation and 'illegal identification' could take place.[62] Alongside the literal and figurative 'demonization' of Jews and Slavs, the supernatural imaginary helped to justify the Nazis' relationship to witchcraft and paganism, pan-Aryan racial brotherhood, and the Third Reich's alliance with Japan.[63]

In this context expressions of sympathy for South Asian or Middle Eastern peoples suffering under British colonial rule cannot be dismissed as pure propaganda. Nor should they be understood as Nazi 'colonial fantasies' presaging imperial designs on the non-European world.[64] Rather, these enthusiastic references to Indo-Aryan peoples reflect the supernatural imaginary's capacity for incorporating esotericism, Eastern religions, and border scientific racial theories in a critique of 'Western' values.[65] Hence, in addition to defining the 'monstrous' racial or political other, the Nazi 'supernatural imaginary' provided a space in which German domestic and foreign policy might be negotiated to justify seemingly cosmopolitan or alternative attitudes toward race, religion, and sexuality.[66]

***

Because of the plethora of non-academic publications in the genre, it is worth taking a moment to discuss my sources and methodology. As indicated in the bibliography, I have relied, as much as possible, on hundreds of Nazi Party and personal papers, government documents, manuscripts, newspapers, and published primary-source accounts drawn directly from the German federal archives located in Berlin (BAB), Koblenz (BAK), and Freiburg (BAM). I have also culled nearly as many documents, personal papers, and published primary sources housed at the Institute for Contemporary History in Munich (IfZG), the Institute for Border Science in Freiburg (IGPP), and the East German Folklore archive (IVDE) in Freiburg. Finally, I have consulted hundreds of published primary and secondary books and articles located at major research libraries in Germany and the United States. Most of the primary research for this book was conducted in German, although I have used a large number of English and in some cases French and Dutch sources.

Despite the impressive amount of documentary evidence, one methodological dilemma in studying the Third Reich is the use of post-war memoirs. Whether written by prominent Nazis, fellow travellers, victims, opponents, or bystanders, the unfathomable crimes of the Third Reich and the unquenchable public fascination with Nazism has made it difficult to take such accounts at face value. Some individuals clearly wanted to profit from their association with the regime, providing sensational or inaccurate accounts. Others wanted to explain or absolve themselves of complicity, fabricating evidence or constructing elaborate conspiracy theories about individuals who were already dead. Still others, often victims or long-time critics, had an interest in portraying the Third Reich as preternaturally evil, insane, or barbaric – ignoring in some cases the utter banality of Nazi evil.

Given these factors, there are always difficulties in parsing the accuracy of first-person accounts, especially those that highlight a Nazi proclivity toward the supernatural. To take one of the most widely cited though problematic examples, we have Hermann Rauschning's *Conversations with Hitler*. As the President of the Danzig Senate and, for a brief time, Nazi Party member, Rauschning met with Hitler perhaps a dozen times in the early 1930s before leaving the party and eventually Germany for the United States in 1936. Rauschning's claims to have talked with Hitler over one hundred times are therefore completely false – a likely attempt to add credence to his *Conversations* at a time when he was devoid of money and on the Anglo-American speaking circuit.[67]

Nevertheless, as Theodor Schieder notes, even Hitler ostensibly admitted that there was 'as much in the book that was correct as there was false'. Goebbels apparently agreed.[68] While Rauschning's *Conversations* is obviously 'not a documentary source from which one can expect the literal transcription of Hitler's sentences', it does represent a 'document of great worth insofar as it contains opinions that arise from immediate insight' based on direct interaction with Hitler and involvement in the Nazi inner circle between 1932 and 1934, as well as the contemplation of those experiences over the following decade.[69]

The same methodological caveat holds, to varying degrees, for other accounts: the memoirs of Himmler's personal masseur, Felix Kersten; Himmler's astrologer Wilhelm Wulff; the head of the SD, Walter Schellenberg; the history of the Thule Society written by its co-founder Rudolf von Sebottendorff; the memoirs of the parapsychologist, Gerda Walther; the post-war analyses of anti-Nazi intellectuals like Konrad Heiden and Willy Ley; the collected letters of Martin Bormann or Hitler's 'table talk', assembled by Bormann's secretaries in the Party Chancellery (*Parteikanzlei*).[70] Although parts of all these sources are no doubt embellished or redacted, they still provide, cumulatively, an important reservoir of evidence for Nazi supernatural thinking.

Finally, I want to comment on the use of secondary sources. As suggested above, we already have an extensive literature, primarily in English and German, on *völkisch* ideology and right-wing parties; folklore, ethnology, and history in the Third Reich; Nazi attitudes toward science and religion; and, to a lesser extent, occultism and border science.

We also have a number of excellent biographies of Hitler, Himmler, Goebbels, and others, not to mention detailed studies of the SS, Gestapo, and SD. Both Peter Longerich's recent biography of Himmler and Michael Kater's classic study of the SS Institute for Ancestral Research (*Ahnenerbe*), for example, are enormously rich in their analysis of the supernatural aspects of the Third Reich. So too is the extensive work of Uwe Puschner, Horst Junginger, and others on the late nineteenth and early twentieth-century *völkisch* movements. On the other hand, we have many dozens of popular, more crypto- or pseudo-historical works that focus on various aspects of Nazi occultism, religion, and science. While I have referenced these sources on a limited basis, I have not relied upon this literature for empirical evidence.

In cases of empirically and methodologically sound if occasionally sensational or popular histories, I have cited them when and where they shed important light on the subject or rely on authentic primary evidence. To take two examples, we have Heather Pringle's *The Master Plan: Himmler's Scholars and the Holocaust* (2006) and Victor and Victoria Trimondi's *Hitler, Buddha, Krishna: An Unholy Alliance from the Third Reich to the Present Day* (2002). Pringle's work, with few exceptions, is based on copious archival research.[71] I have cited her book repeatedly when dealing with substantive issues relating to Himmler's research institute and policies.

The same holds true for the Trimondis' *Hitler, Buddha, Krishna*. There are copious crypto-historical works in the same genre, which the authors themselves criticize. There are also a few specialized academic monographs on the topic of Nazi interest in Tibet, most notably Wolfgang Kaufmann's 900-page dissertation (*Das Dritte Reich und Tibet*, 2009). As Kaufmann rightly observes, the Trimondis' provocative account probably exaggerates the close relationship between Nazism and Tibetan Buddhism. Kaufmann acknowledges, however, that the Trimondis, 'in contrast to sensationalist authors', accept the basic academic standard that 'historical claims of factuality must be provable through sources', and have therefore culled 'the archives relatively thoroughly'.[72] I have tried to apply this nuanced distinction between outright crypto-history and popular history based on sound archival research to all the works I have cited.

∗∗∗

Hitler's Monsters is organized in three chronological parts composed of three chapters each. Part One traces the role of supernatural thinking in the Nazi Party from its intellectual antecedents in the late nineteenth century through its seizure of power in 1933. *Chapter One – The Supernatural Roots of Nazism: Ario-Germanic Religion, Border Science, and the Austro-German Occult Revival, 1889–1914* provides a general introduction to the occult, mythological, and 'border scientific' ideas that permeated Vienna's cafés and Munich's beer halls before the First World War. *Chapter Two – From the Thule Society to the NSDAP: Fashioning the Nazi Supernatural Imaginary, 1912–1924* examines the organizational and ideological connections between late-Wilhelmine occult organizations such as the German Order and Thule Society and the early Nazi Party (NSDAP). *Chapter Three – Exploiting Hitler's Magic: From Weimar's Horrors to Visions of the Third Reich* illustrates how the NSDAP appropriated supernatural ideas in order to appeal to ordinary Germans, enlisting the help of occultists and horror writers in shaping propaganda and political campaigning.

Part Two focuses on the role of supernatural thinking during the first six years of the Third Reich. *Chapter Four – The Third Reich's War on the Occult: Anti-Occultism, Hitler's Magicians' Controversy, and the Hess Action* examines the regime's policies toward occultists in the early to middle years of the Third Reich, including what I call 'Hitler's Magicians' Controversy', a debate regarding the persistence of magic, astrology, and other supernatural practices during the war. *Chapter Five – The Stars Come Down to Frozen Earth: Border Science in the Third Reich* looks systematically at the application of the 'border sciences' promoted by many Nazis, including astrology, World Ice Theory, and 'biodynamic' agriculture between 1933 and 1941. *Chapter Six – Lucifer's Court: Ario-Germanic Paganism, Indo-Aryan Spirituality, and the Nazi Search for Alternative Religions* surveys the Nazis' interest in Germanic paganism, witchcraft, Luciferianism, and Eastern spirituality in their attempt to find a suitable Ario-Germanic alternative to Christianity.

Part Three examines the role of supernatural thinking during the Second World War. *Chapter Seven – The Supernatural and the Second World War: Folklore and Border Science in Foreign Policy, Propaganda, and Military Operations* evaluates the influence of the supernatural imaginary on the Third Reich's conception of foreign policy, investment in fanciful weaponry, and use of astrology, divination, clairvoyance, and telepathy in prosecuting the war. *Chapter Eight – Monstrous Science: Racial Resettlement, Human Experiments, and the Holocaust* illustrates the ways in which science and the supernatural intersected in the Third Reich's approach to anti-Semitism, human experimentation, and ethnic cleansing. Finally, *Chapter Nine – Nazi Twilight: Miracle Weapons, Supernatural Partisans, and the Collapse of the Third Reich* looks at the regime's increasingly desperate if futile investment in 'miracle weapons', partisan warfare, and cataclysmic 'twilight' imagery during the final years of the war, providing a fitting corollary to the disintegration of the Third Reich.

Taking the supernatural elements of Nazism seriously, as we will do throughout this book, does not mean resuscitating outdated arguments about German 'peculiarity'. There was no inherent 'special path' between nineteenth-century occultism or paganism and National Socialism. Astrology, clairvoyance, and paranormal activity, Germanic mythology and fairy tales, pagan religious traditions and folk superstition, alternative healing practices and border science – all these cultural phenomena and practices were remarkably widespread in Germany. They were compatible with many aspects of modernity, mass politics, and consumerism, and never confined exclusively to the racist, proto-fascist right.[73]

This does not mean, however, that all European fascist movements were equally susceptible to or as likely to draw upon supernatural thinking. Nor, in comparison to the Nazis, were German liberals, Socialists, or even Catholics as willing to exploit the 'supernatural imaginary' in propaganda or policy.

In the end, the Nazi movement retained closer ties to the occult, *völkisch*-religious, and border scientific milieu than any other mass party of the Weimar era. If the Nazis sometimes appeared uncertain as to how to navigate supernatural belief and practices, it was because – for all their invocations of 'enlightenment' (*Aufklärung*) and disagreements about the proper role of science and religion in the Third Reich – they recognized the utility, indeed, the necessity, of appealing to post-war Germany's longing for myth and desire for transcendence in making their amorphous racial and imperial visions a reality.[74]

PART I

1

THE SUPERNATURAL ROOTS OF NAZISM
Ario-Germanic Religion, Border Science, and the Austro-German Occult Revival, 1889–1914

'When once the taming talisman, the Cross, breaks in two, the savagery of the old fighters, the senseless Berserker fury of which the Northern poets sing ... will gush up anew ... the old stone gods will rise from the silent ruins, and ... Thor, with his giant's hammer, will at last spring up, and shatter to bits the Gothic cathedrals.'

Heinrich Heine (1834), quoted by Lanz von Liebenfels (1907)[1]

'In Germany, the recovery of the unconscious ... laid the groundwork for the German form of twentieth-century dictatorship. This reaction combined the deep stream of German romanticism with the mysteries of the occult as well as with the idealism of deeds. What sort of deeds these turned out to be is written in blood on the pages of history.'

George Mosse, *Masses and Man* (1987)[2]

One day in August 1909 a young man dropped by the Vienna office of the Austrian occultist, Jörg Lanz von Liebenfels. Pale and shabby in appearance, the man politely introduced himself and asked whether he might order some back copies of Lanz's self-published periodical, *Ostara*. Lanz was central Europe's most ardent proponent of ariosophy, an esoteric doctrine that prophesied the resurgence of a lost Aryan civilization peopled by Nordic 'God Men'. His magazine *Ostara*, per Lanz, was the 'first and only racially scientific journal ... to combat socialist and feminist revolutionaries and preserve the noble Aryan race from decline.'[3] Touched by his visitor's sympathetic appearance and earnest demeanour, Lanz offered the young man back copies of *Ostara* free of charge and two crowns for the streetcar home. The visitor, according to Lanz's 1951 memoir, was Adolf Hitler.[4]

Writing forty years later, Lanz's recollection may be apocryphal. He was proud of his connection to Hitler and, given his occult proclivities, hardly a reliable source. But there is plenty of circumstantial evidence to suggest Lanz's story is true.[5] In perusing any issue of *Ostara* the future Führer would have come across multiple themes that found their way, a decade later, into the programme of the Nazi Party: the importance of 'Nordic' blood purity and the dangers of racial miscegenation; the monstrous perfidy of the 'Jew'; the deleterious effects of socialism, liberalism, and feminism; and the mystical power of the Indo-European swastika. Only strict adherence to arcane religious and eugenic practices, Lanz insisted, including the elimination of the Jews and sterilization of the racially inferior, could trigger a reawakening of Nordic civilization. In order to buttress his case, Lanz filled the pages of *Ostara* with vivid illustrations of muscular Aryan cavaliers defending scantily clad blonde women from the advances of hideous-looking 'ape-men' – all popular tropes in Nazi propaganda of the 1920s and 1930s.[6]

As he scraped by in a tiny apartment on the Felberstrasse, wiling away his time on watercolour postcards, it is easy to imagine a young Hitler eagerly imbibing Lanz's grandiose racialist (*völkisch*) cosmology – a world divided into light and darkness, where blonde, blue-eyed Nordic heroes were locked in an eternal battle with an army of racial 'sub-humans' (*Tschandals*).[7] By 1909 Germany's future Führer was already immersed in the broader *völkisch* subculture to which Lanz belonged. Hitler attended Richard Wagner's operas dozens of times. He devoured the racist and pan-Germanic musings of the Austrian politician, Georg von Schönerer. And he praised the demogogic anti-Semitism of Karl Lueger, the long-serving mayor of Vienna (himself a member of an ariosophic secret society).

Hitler was not atypical in this regard. Much of his generation, which came of age at the turn of the twentieth century, was fascinated by a 'mystical utopian revival'.[8] For this broad cross section of Germans and Austrians, occultism and border science, Nordic mythology and New Age practices, *völkisch* religion and Germanic folklore 'offered a powerfully appealing alternative form of Enlightenment, promising illumination about both the farthest reaches of the cosmos and the innermost depths of the soul'.[9] These supernatural ideas and doctrines were diverse and malleable, finding support among millions of eminently modern, forward-thinking Germans and Austrians in the decades before the First World War.[10]

The purpose of this first chapter is to describe the supernatural ideas and practices that would 'come to be annexed' by Nazism after the First World War.[11] Although these ideas were remarkably fluid and interconnected, they fall loosely into three overlapping subcultures. The first is Ario-Germanic religion, folklore, and mythology. The second is occultism, including the esoteric doctrines of theosophy, anthroposophy, and ariosophy. Third and finally we have the so-called 'border sciences', ranging from astrology, parapsychology, and radiesthesia ('dowsing') to World Ice Theory.

These subcultures played an important role in the rise of Nazism. First, in terms of ideological *content*, all three subcultures circulated and popularized ideas and doctrines that informed the Nazi supernatural imaginary and impressed a broader Nazi constituency. Second, these subcultures legitimized an esoteric and border scientific *approach* to understanding the world that informed Nazi thinking on race and space, science and religion.

We begin below by looking at the renaissance of Ario-Germanic religion, folklore, and Nordic mythology over the 'long nineteenth century', namely the period between 1789 and 1914. We will then turn to the Austro-German occult revival during the last third of the nineteenth century, focusing on the three decades of the 1880s through the 1910s. Finally, we will examine the parallel emergence of border science as a legitimate field of study during this same epoch, tracing the ways in which all three subcultures – Ario-Germanic religion, occultism, and border science – reinforced each other within the emerging Austro-German supernatural imaginary.

Ario-Germanic Religion, Folklore, and Nordic Mythology

In his 1917 lecture on 'Science as a Vocation', Max Weber famously proclaimed, 'The fate of our times is characterized by rationalization and intellectualization, and, above all, by the disenchantment of the world.'[12] This observation is frequently cited as proof of the decline of religion and growing predominance of science by the end of the nineteenth century. Yet scholars often tend to overlook Weber's next sentence: 'Precisely the ultimate and most sublime values have retreated from public life either into the transcendental realm of mystic life or into the brotherliness of direct and personal human relations.'[13]

The modern world may have been defined by a disenchantment with respect to traditional religions. But there emerged simultaneously a renaissance in new forms of everyday religiosity. This longing for myth and renewed belief in fate and miracles occurred outside the framework of traditional religious institutions.[14] If church attendance declined precipitously over the course of the 1800s, Germans and Austrians continued to search for meaning and spirituality in less mediated, sectarian alternatives to mainstream Christianity.[15]

In order to create and consolidate the Second German Reich, intellectuals spent much of the nineteenth century reviving ancient myths and heroes. They explored Indo-European history and religion, seeking a romantic alternative to what many Germans viewed as the overly rationalist culture of the French and phlegmatic pragmatism of the English. As Ernst Bloch argued in the early years of the Third Reich, mythology and *völkisch* religion provided a tool for the fascist manipulation of the population.[16] The political exploitation of these ideas in the 1920s and 1930s by the Nazis would have been impossible if not for their revival, indeed (re)invention, over the course of the long nineteenth century.

The Longing for Myth

Early Romantic writers encouraged the first stirrings of German national feeling. Central to this project was the celebration of German folk traditions and mythology. Johann Wolfgang von Goethe was one of the first Romantic poets to employ as protagonists supernatural figures drawn from German folk-lore, whether the vampire in 'The Bride of Corinth' or the King of the Fairies in 'The Erl-King'. At the same time Goethe would lament, with Friedrich Schiller, the lack of a German fatherland.[17]

Goethe and Schiller's contemporary, Johann Gottfried Herder, sought the roots of the German nation in ancient German folk tales and Norse mythology. 'A poet is the creator of the nation around him,' Herder explained, who 'has their souls in his hand to lead them'.[18] Johann Gottlieb Fichte, in his *Letters to the German Nation,* and Ernst Moritz Arndt, in poems such as 'The German Fatherland', supplemented these ideas with a quasi-mystical idea of ethnicity (*Volkstum*). Friedrich Schelling, for his part, suggested that a spiritual divide differentiated superior races like the Germans from lesser races.[19]

A younger generation of Romantic writers, musicians, and artists, led by the Grimm brothers and Wagner, drew on this growing palette of German nation-alist myths and folk tales for a wider public.[20] Painstakingly assembled by Wilhelm and Jacob Grimm, the roughly two hundred fairy tales they published over four decades helped to reconstruct an authentically 'German' (or 'Aryan') culture, language, and identity. In comparison to French and British fairy tales, the Grimms' stories were more violent, fantastical, and (arguably) racist in tone. They portrayed a world replete with supernatural monsters – cannibalistic witches and scheming magicians, malevolent Jews, vengeful spirits, shapeshifting animals, manipulative demons, and the Devil himself.[21] And yet German nationalists, from the Grimms to Hitler himself, would praise these stories for instilling the foundations of German *völkisch* thinking.[22]

By 1857, Wagner had written the greater part of *Das Rheingold*, the first of four operas comprising *Der Ring des Nibelungen*, which also included *Die Valkyrie, Siegfried*, and *Götterdämmerung*. A loose reconstruction of the Norse sagas, the *Ring* constituted a central moment in the popularization of German national mythology and had a formative influence on Hitler's own vision of Ario-Germanic ideology.[23] In the *Ring*, the hero Siegfried and the gods Wotan and Loge must fend off the dark race of monstrous *Nibelungen*, who steal gold from the Rhinemaidens to create a magic ring with the power to rule the world.[24]

Undergirding the efforts of Wagner and the Grimm brothers to popularize Germanic folklore and mythology was the recovery, and sometimes outright invention, of runic alphabets, dead languages, and ancient texts. Imbued with deeply symbolic, even magical meaning, the Norse sagas, runes, and fairy tales became a crucial expression of the 'roots and essence of the Volk'.[25] The mid- to late nineteenth century would see a general renewal of interest in the medieval Icelandic prose and poetic Edda, for example, which chronicled the exploits of the Norse gods and heroes.[26] By 1900 this Nordic mythological renaissance found expression in dozens of *völkisch* associations and journals with names such as *Odin, Heimdall, Hammer, Irminsul*, the German Order, and the Pan-German Language and Writing Association.[27]

Folklore, mythology, and neo-paganism rushed to fill an important gap in the German spiritual landscape, helping to occupy 'the transcendental realm of mystic life' vacated by Judeo-Christian traditions.[28] Whereas some *völkisch* nationalists attempted to pull German Catholics 'loose from Rome', others sought to unite German paganism with Christianity. A few went so far as to argue that Christianity might be subordinated to 'the cosmic spirit of the world based upon nature'.[29]

This diverse spectrum of 'German Christians', 'German religionists', supporters of the 'German faith movement', and 'new heathens' disagreed on numerous points of doctrine. But such ideas attracted a wide array of 'men and women dedicated to creating a new religion appropriate to the German race'.[30] All such groups shared a common desire to replace traditional Christianity with a religious faith that was more authentically 'German'.[31]

Alongside this interest in folklore, mythology, and an alternative religion there emerged a renewed fascination with werewolves and witches – except these monsters in Christian liturgy now came to be viewed increasingly as positive figures. Willibald Alexis' *Der Werwolf* (1848), appearing in the year of Germany and Austria's national revolutions, and Hermann Löns' *Der Wehrwolf* (1910), published just before the First World War, were both set during the Early Modern wars of religion, when German peasants tried to protect themselves against incursions from the armies of the Counter-Reformation. Such works portrayed 'werewolves' not as monsters – or at least not as evil monsters – but as heroic guerrilla resistance fighters sworn to protect German blood and soil against foreign interlopers.[32]

Medieval and Early Modern witchcraft was also reinterpreted in the new folklore. Instead of being pawns of Satan, German 'witches' became Earth mothers, practitioners of an ancient Indo-Germanic religion that the Catholic Church, whose inquisitors were the true monsters, sought to eradicate.[33] Traditions of magic and witchcraft sometimes merged in nineteenth-century supernatural imaginary with a Manichean strain of German paganism, which saw Lucifer as a positive figure, who had been 'unfairly thrown out of heaven'.[34] Thousands of middle-class Germans flocked to the Brocken Mountains, the location of Walpurgisnacht in Goethe's *Faust*, and pagan sites such as the *Externsteine*.[35] Later occultists as well as many Nazis embraced aspects of this 'Luciferian' tradition.

After 1850 we see a parallel growth of interest in the Early Modern *Vehmgerichte*. Deemed forbidden (*verbotene*) or secret (*geheim*) courts, the *Vehm* were assembled surreptitiously by local notables in specific areas of the Westphalian countryside, with the express purpose of acting as judge, jury, and executioner. The *Vehm* were criticized by Enlightenment reformers and finally outlawed by Jérôme Bonaparte (Napoleon's youngest brother) in the early nineteenth century. But a folkloric interest in these Ur-Germanic secret courts was subsequently revived.[36] Decades later the tradition of secret bands of vigilantes murdering Germany's enemies was put into practice by right-wing fanatics intent on assassinating Jewish and left-wing politicians in the early Weimar period (a practice known as *Fememord*).[37]

In France and Great Britain the vampire came to be viewed as a Gothic literary curiosity, even a tragic Romantic figure. In German-speaking central Europe the vampire became a more malevolent figure.[38] German reports of vampirism from the Slavic hinterlands helped reinforce a supernaturally infused vision of 'Polish [and later Jewish] danger', a physical and mental disease invading 'landscapes of pure Germanic racial origin'.[39] Neighbouring Bohemia was now 'the birthplace of the vampire, Serbia [where tens of thousands of ethnic Germans had settled] the home of barbarism and Poland the school of superstition'. Hence Slavic vampirism became a metaphor for racial degeneration and the political disintegration of the 'transnational relations in the border regions of Prusso-Germany and Austria-Hungary'.[40]

The racially degenerate Slavic (Jewish) vampire met his match in the heroic 'Aryan'.[41] The concept of a superior 'Aryan' race has roots in the early nineteenth-century Indo-European renaissance.[42] It was widely popularized across Europe by the Frenchman Artur de Gobineau and his *Essay on the Inequality of Human Races* (1855). Forty years later the British-born Germanophile, political philosopher, and Wagner's son-in-law, Houston Stewart Chamberlain, lent this idea 'scientific' legitimacy in his two-volume *Foundations of the Nineteenth Century*.[43]

For Chamberlain all European history could be reduced to a struggle for mastery between heroic Aryans and monstrous Semites. 'Aryans' sought higher knowledge and creativity fuelled by their superior 'racial soul', Chamberlain argued. Jews, by contrast, were civilization-destroying materialists who lacked the capacity for transcendence.[44]

An often overlooked element in this supernatural mélange of race, religion, and mythology is Indo-Aryanism.[45] In questioning the classical Judeo-Christian foundations of German culture, many Romantics extolled the virtues of non-Western civilizations. Lessing and Herder were among the first to highlight the 'oriental', pre-Christian roots of German culture in northern India and the Middle East.[46]

Later Romantic thinkers, such as the Schlegel brothers, contrasted Judaism and Christianity unfavourably with the Indo-Germanic Aryans. Hinduism and Islam were more enlightened religions, they argued, than the 'colonizing power' of the Roman Catholic and Evangelical Church.[47] This favourable attitude toward Hinduism and Islam among many German nationalists would span the rest of the nineteenth century, later finding a surprising resonance in the Third Reich.[48]

In time these early Romantic speculations were supplemented by the emerging field of German Indology. Through their study of Indian civilization and religion, German Indologists found evidence for an essentialized idea of Aryan culture and spirituality.[49] The renowned Sanskrit scholar, Leopold von Schroeder, was a devotee of Wagner and supporter of Chamberlain's theories of Aryan civilization and racial degeneration. Schroeder wished to spread Indian culture and religion across Germany, 'dream[ing] of a religion of the future that borrows its predominant characteristics from Buddhism'.[50]

Other Indologists, such as Adolf Holtzmann senior and Holtzmann junior, projected fantasies of a heroic 'Indo-Germanic Epic' ('Ur-epos') on Indian religious texts such as the Mahābhārata and Bhagavad Gita that were largely detached from the textual and philological evidence. By comparing the Mahābhārata to the Nordic Nibelungenlied and ancient India to pre-Christian Germanic civilization, these scholars developed a powerful narrative that the Gita had been 'a pantheistic text reflective of Indo-Germanic views of heroism'.[51]

These selective readings of Hindu and Buddhist religious texts would be advocated more vociferously by Nazi Indologists such as J. W. Hauer and Walter Wust in order to assert the ethnocultural superiority of the Aryan race.[52] Indo-Aryanism, for all its cosmopolitanism, therefore abetted a darker racist and xenophobic trend in Germany's 'mystical utopian revival' and 'longing for myth'.[53]

Consciously integrated into childhood education in Germany, folklore and mythology, Indo-Aryan religion and race theory, became essential elements in instilling a sense of German national and spiritual feeling from an early age.[54] No coincidence, then, that it was a high school history teacher, Dr Leopold Pötsch, who introduced Hitler and his classmates to 'epic periods of German history' replete with Aryan heroes and subaltern monsters, 'the Nibelungs, Charlemagne, Bismarck, and the establishment of the Second Reich'.[55] No longer confined to the obscure musings of a few Romantic-era intellectuals, by the end of the nineteenth century folklore, mythology, and Ario-Germanic religiosity was etched into the consciousness of millions of ordinary Germans.

Germanism, Aryanism, and Geopolitics

As Kris Manjapra has observed, 'there was a possible kinship' between the Indo-Aryan racial theories described above and 'radical anti-colonialism based on what [Ernst] Bloch called the pursuit of false utopias'.[56] Before 1871 Germans lacked a powerful nation state or colonial empire. This nationalist yearning combined with a pre-existing 'longing for myth' to produce a utopian conception of Indo-Aryan racial purity. While seemingly anti-colonial in criticizing Britain's oppression of India, the magical thinking behind this utopian vision of Indo-Aryan brotherhood made it hard for Germans to close the gap between their own racial and colonial fantasies and geopolitical reality. In this way supernatural fantasies about recovering a lost Indo-Aryan civilization produced 'potentials for liberation' but also 'retaliation' and 'genocide'.[57]

To understand the function of this Indo-Aryan 'liberation theology' within the Nazi supernatural imaginary, we need to look at the political gestation of these ideas among fin-de-siècle *völkisch* intellectuals.[58] Perhaps unfairly, the historian Fritz Stern has dubbed the leading practitioners of this late nineteenth century, quasi-religious, race-infused nationalism the 'politicians of cultural despair'. These anti-modern intellectuals, Stern argues, combined a radically racist and nationalist mysticism with a future-oriented utopianism that rejected scientific materialism and industrialization.[59]

The countercultural and pessimistic nature of these intellectuals has been greatly exaggerated. Many progressive reformers, such as Max Weber and Gertrud Bäumer, were equally 'despairing' about the impact of rapid modernization and industrialization on German society. Conversely, the polymath and orientalist Paul de Lagarde and others, for all their *völkisch* musings, were very much part of the cultural establishment.[60] In fact, Lagarde was one of Germany's most widely published and respected scholars of Near Eastern languages and religion, manifesting a fascination with Indo-Aryan culture that we find reproduced across the Austro-German supernatural milieu.[61]

Despite – or perhaps because of – his immersion in 'Indo-Aryan' and Middle Eastern studies Lagarde published a series of works that anticipated the programme of later *völkisch* thinkers: the need for a German national Christianity, a Greater Indo-Germanic Empire founded upon the Aryan race, and a virulently anti-Semitic racial animus, which included, if need be, the physical elimination of the Jews. Needless to say, a number of Nazi race theorists and Indologists like Wüst and H. K. Günther as well as party leaders like Hitler, Himmler, and Alfred Rosenberg, were influenced by Lagarde's works.[62]

In 1890, Lagarde's younger contemporary, the writer and cultural critic Julius Langbehn, published his hugely popular *Rembrandt as Educator*. In it Langbehn laboured to unite a racist vision of pan-Germanic nationalism, inclusive of all 'Aryan' peoples, with his devout if highly unorthodox Catholicism.[63] Langbehn claimed that 'Mysticism was the hidden engine which could transmute science into art', that 'the development of Germany could only progress in opposition to rationalism', and that the 'peasant who actually owns a piece of land has a direct relationship to the centre of the earth'.[64] This mythical apotheosis of the racially and spiritually pure German peasant, embedded in his native homeland (*Heimat*), became a crucial element in fin-de-siècle *völkisch* (and later Nazi) ideology.[65]

Völkisch intellectuals such as Adolf Bartels, Alfred Schuler, and Moeller van den Bruck brought these ideas into the twentieth century. In popularizing the ideas of Lagarde and Langbehn, Bartels became one of the most important *völkisch* publishers in late Imperial Germany, including a collection of sixteen border scientific essays with the simple title *Race*. Bartels also worked with the *völkisch* mystic Friedrich Lienhard to edit the journal *German Heimat*, which promoted *völkisch*-esoteric conceptions of race and space.[66]

As head of the Munich esoteric group known as the 'cosmic circle', Alfred Schuler provided a bridge between Lagarde's Indo-Aryanism, Lanz's occultism, and Langbehn's 'blood and soil' philosophy.[67] For Schuler, one's 'inner life force was equated with the strength of the blood', the mystical purity of which had supposedly degenerated through racial interbreeding. He believed that 'untainted' Aryans with parapsychological and spiritualist powers might restore racial purity under the banner of the 'blood beacon' and holy symbol of the swastika – conducting seances to that effect with the Munich parapsychologist, Albert Schrenck-Notzing (discussed below). Schuler propagated a link between Gnosticism (Manicheanism), the Cathar religious tradition (a Christian heretical sect in fourteenth-century France), and the ariosophic myth of Atlantis. These themes, centred on the mystical power and sanctity of Aryan blood, were taken up by many Nazi thinkers in the 1920s and 1930s.[68]

More vigorously than Schuler, van den Bruck argued for a political revolution founded on a mix of Germanic Christianity and paganism, *völkisch* nationalism, and a German form of socialism. His most famous work, *The Third Reich*, was published in 1923, the same year that Hitler attempted, unsuccessfully, to overthrow the Weimar government.[69] In predicting a cataclysmic future war and civilizational rebirth, van den Bruck's prophetic nationalism intertwined well with late-Wilhelmine science fiction works. Notable among these were *Planet Fire: A Futuristic Novel* (1899) by Max Haushofer, father of the Nazi geopolitical expert Karl Haushofer, and Ferdinand Grauttoff's *1906: The Collapse of the Old Order* (1905), which sold 125,000 copies in its first two years of publication.[70]

The work of pan-Germanic geographers and ethnographers also vacillated between mainstream scholarship and a mystical investment in propagating German race and empire. Perhaps the most influential of these late nineteenth-century geographers and ethnographers was Friedrich Ratzel, the progenitor of the infamous concept of 'living space' (*Lebensraum*).

Like many German intellectuals described above, Ratzel was relatively hostile to overseas colonization along British or French lines.[71] Doing so would have dissipated German ethnonational and territorial integrity, Ratzel believed, inviting millions of racially disparate Africans and Asians into the empire. Ratzel wanted instead to create a contiguous Greater German Empire through the process of 'inner colonization', namely the expansion of German peasant agriculture and folk traditions into eastern European 'living space'.[72]

Ratzel's faith-based concept of *Lebensraum* could not be tested scientifically. But it justified virtually any German intervention into central and eastern Europe. It also provided a template for instrumentalizing German ethnology and folklore in the interests of expansion.[73] By the eve of the First World War, the need for 'living space' was a popular trope among many *völkisch* thinkers.[74]

Indeed, Ratzel's conception of 'living space' helped spawn the popular academic field of 'geopolitics', which his student Karl Haushofer made famous in the last decade of the Second Empire. Haushofer viewed the state as an organic 'life form' that needed to pursue a constantly advancing frontier in order to sustain its racial and cultural life.[75] Through his student at the University of Munich, Rudolf Hess, Haushofer became one of Hitler's early foreign-policy advisors.[76]

All these *völkisch* intellectuals and geopoliticians helped define the border scientific concepts of race and space that inspired Hitler and the Nazi movement.[77] Still, there were subtle differences that help to explain some contradictions within the Nazis' own supernatural imaginary. Chief among these was the tension between *Germanentum* ('Germanness') and *Ariertum* ('Aryanism').

Beginning in the 1890s proponents of *Germanentum*, such as the philologist Andreas Heusler and archaeologist Gustaf Kossina, tended to focus their attention on the cultural genius of north Germanic folklore along the lines of Julius Langbehn. This 'Nordic' conception of Germanness was quite useful in distinguishing racial Germans from Jews and Slavs, and providing a scientific patina to the more 'fantastic elements of *völkisch* thought'. 'Pared by academic Germanists of the more gnostic aspects represented by both Wagner and [Guido von] List', the ideology of *Germanentum* dovetailed well with the 'Nordic racialism of [the later Nazi eugenicist]' H. K. Günther and the 'imperialistic deliberations of the new experts on the East' who collaborated with the Nazi Party after the First World War.[78]

Alongside a racially Nordic *Germanentum*, centered in northern and western Europe, there emerged in the late nineteenth century a broader idea of the 'cultural Aryan ostensibly rooted in comparative Indo-European studies' – a concept inspired by Gobineau, Chamberlain, Lagarde and late nineteenth-century Indologists. To be sure, both 'Aryanism' (*Ariertum*) and 'Germanism' (*Germanentum*) were variations on the same belief in an Ur-Germanic master race. Both concepts, moreoever, were 'symbolically linked by the swastika', as Germanists such as Kossina showed great interest in the Indo-Germanic (Aryan) roots of Nordic civilization.[79]

But Aryanism both transcended and subsumed the narrower concept of Germanism, providing the basis for a more expansive and inclusive conception of Indo-Aryan race and empire. 'By the 1910s, the Aryan, far from being merely an anthropological formulation,' Bernard Mees observes, 'was also being promoted as a cultural identity by some German and Austrian writers. These academics, pseudo-scholarly enthusiasts and even utter fantasists belonged to an Aryanist Grub Street – outright mysticists like [Guido von] List and his followers were merely the most colourful.'[80]

The wholly unscientific distinction between a narrower Germanic mythology of Odin-worshipping Goths and the 'Aryan grub street' would persist into the Third Reich. Such differences of emphasis underlay some of the political and ideological disputes between Nazi border scientists.[81] Still, most Nazis, including Hitler and Himmler, seemed to prefer the broader, more inclusive, more malleable Aryanism of Lagarde to the restrictive Germanism of Langbehn.[82]

These seemingly recondite debates on ancient Germanic race and religion should not obscure their contemporary importance. The late nineteenth-century revival of Ario-German religion, folklore, and mythology, wrote the art historian Fritz Saxl, was akin to the twelfth-century renaissance, a period when 'the Christian religion seemed no longer completely able to satisfy the spiritual side of man, and there was room for paganism to slip in, as we see it doing today'. Carl Jung compared the renewed interest in paganism and mythology – quite presciently as we shall see in Chapter Six – to the proliferating Gnostic heresies of the late medieval era.[83]

Ultimately these proponents of folklore, mythology, and Ario-Germanic religion helped to erect 'a noble and shining faith agreeable to the "soldier soul" of the latter-day Nordic'. In the words of Lewis Spence, they 'foist[ed] upon Germany the whole crude and chaotic mass of the pagan beliefs … found in the twin gospels' of the Elder and Younger Eddas, accompanied by such doctrinal smatterings of their own as might appear to redeem the project from the charge of plagiarism and irrationality'.[84] As we shall see, the Nazis would build upon these strains of folklore, paganism, and mythology in seeking alternatives to Judeo-Christian theology, creating geopolitical alliances in Asia and constructing a racially pure Germanic Empire.

The Austro-German Occult Revival

'The term *occult* derives from the Latin verb *oewlere,* meaning to hide, or conceal,' writes Corinna Treitel, the foremost expert on German occultism. 'It is somewhat ironic, therefore,' she continues, 'that although Germans were certainly fascinated by forces concealed from human sight or reason, there was nothing particularly hidden about the German occult movement itself'.[85] From cosmopolitan Berlin to Catholic Munich, from Saxony to Schleswig-Holstein, thousands of Germans flocked to seances, astrologers, tarot readers, parapsychological experiments, occult bookstores, and even esoteric schools and university courses.[86]

The occult revival was not confined to Germany, of course. We have ample evidence of similar trends in France, Great Britain and the United States.[87] But the sheer size and diversity of the occult marketplace in Germany and Austria suggests that it tapped into a mass consumer culture that was unique in depth and breadth when compared to other European countries. Berlin and Munich alone were home to thousands of spiritualists, mediums, and astrologers who appealed to tens and perhaps hundreds of thousands of consumers.[88]

Importantly, the organizations and publishers that promoted occultism were ideologically eclectic. They incorporated a 'jumble of different political shadings, cultural styles, and social programs' reflecting 'the ferment that accompanied modernist innovation as Germans struggled to accommodate themselves to the exigencies of the new age'.[89] Although, moreover, 'occult and völkisch texts emanated in some cases from the same presses', this does not mean that *all* occultists shared these racial positions or that all racists adopted occult or mystical attitudes.

The fact remains that 'many presses sat at the interface between the occult and völkisch strains of German modernism', a connection that does not appear to have been as prominent, for example, in the British or American context.[90] The quintessentially modern and 'new age' elements that suffused the Austro-German supernatural milieu were interwoven with the bizarre racial theories and Ario-Germanic mythology of Wagner, Langbehn, and Lagarde.[91]

The three decades before the First World War also saw a resurgence of interest in occult-Masonic orders that merged the practices of astrology and spiritualism with neo-pagan religion and politics. The liberal, Anglo-French foundations of freemasonry are generally well known, which explains the anti-Masonic sentiments of Catholics and nationalist conservatives across Europe. Nevertheless, the freemasons, in Germany and elsewhere, were not invariably liberal or cosmopolitan in outlook. Nor was German-speaking central Europe devoid of its own traditions of conservative Masonic and knightly orders, from the Teutonic Knights to Rosicrucianism.[92]

In the wake of the pagan religious and mythological revival described above, *völkisch*-esoteric orders modelled on the Masons sprouted up across Germany and Austria, often growing out of broader occult movements such as theosophy and ariosophy. Some of these secret orders, including the Armanen Order (*Armanen-Orden*), Order of the New Templars (*Ordo Novi Templi*), and German Order (*Germanenorden*) played important roles in the ideological and organizational development of the early Nazi Party.[93]

Theosophy and Anthroposophy

Theosophy, invented by a Russo-German aristocrat named Helena Blavatsky, was the most influential occult doctrine of the late nineteenth century. Inspired by her travels in India and Tibet, Blavatsky founded the first Theosophical Society in New York City in 1875. After more than a decade building up the movement, including sponsoring chapters in Germany and Austria, Blavatsky published her magnum opus, *The Secret Doctrine* (1888).[94] An eclectic two-volume work, *The Secret Doctrine* drew liberally on Darwinism, Hinduism, Tibetan Buddhism, and Egyptian religion. It also plagiarized Edward Bulwer-Lytton's British fantasy novel, *The Coming Race* (1871), which depicted a subterranean master race that could manipulate a magical power source called the *Vril*.[95]

According to Blavatsky's occult theory of human evolution (*anthropogenesis*), there were seven 'root races'. Beginning as a seed of cosmic energy, humanity had moved through different stages of evolution – including the Hyperborean, Lemurean, and Atlantean races – before reaching its current stage of mental and physical development. Due to different branches of humanity retaining different traces of these original root races, modern humanity differed in its biological and spiritual faculties. The Aryan peoples enjoyed pride of place – except they had lost the putative facility for 'magic' still enjoyed by 'oriental peoples'. The invisible leaders or 'Mahatmas' of the theosophic movement, with whom Blavatsky communicated telepathically, were called the 'Great White Brotherhood'.[96]

Theosophy did not espouse a complete rejection of the Enlightenment or 'flight from reason', as some have argued.[97] Typical of much fin-de-siècle occultism, it constituted a genuine attempt to combine natural science and supernaturalism, rationalism and mysticism, in a quintessentially 'modern' answer to the spiritual dilemmas of the industrial age. For all its dubious racialist elements and vulnerability to accusations of charlatanry, theosophy advocated a progressive, cosmopolitan belief in forming 'the nucleus of a Universal Brotherhood of Humanity without distinction of race, creed, sex, caste, or color'.[98] The theosophist movement in Germany sparked an interest in astrology, Gnosticism, and the Jewish Kabbala as well as Christian mysticism and Indian and Tibetan wisdom.[99] Theosophists across Europe and North America were also committed to Indian independence, animal rights, vegetarianism, and sexual liberation – ideas not necessarily associated with conservative nationalism.[100]

Still, the liberal and cosmopolitan aspects of theosophic thought – including feminism, socialism, prison reform, and pacifism – were probably stronger among the British than the Austro-German chapters.[101] Paradoxical as it might seem, an attraction to Indian religions, animal rights, vegetarianism, and sexual liberation were moreover important elements in *völkisch*-esoteric and later Nazi circles.

Theosophy, like other occult doctrines, was malleable and contradictory, mixing 'biological and spiritual notions of race in an often incoherent manner'. 'Theosophists could insist that the race to which one belonged had primarily to do with one's degree of spiritual maturity,' observes Corinna Treitel, 'yet at the same time claim that such biologically understood "races" as the North Indian Aryans had achieved a particularly high degree of spiritual maturity.'[102] Despite its fascination with Eastern religions and claims to 'universal brotherhood', the aim of bringing the 'sixth root race' into existence was central to the theosophic movement, especially in the Austro-German chapters.[103]

Especially relevant here is the role of the lost civilization of Atlantis, or Thule in the theosophic worldview.[104] The lost civilization of Atlantis was considered to be the prehistoric source of divine (possibly extraterrestrial) racial and spiritual perfection. For Blavatsky and her followers Atlantis may have correlated with the mythic Buddhist lands of 'Shambhala' and the capital city of Agarthi in Hindu tradition, ostensibly located under the Himalayas, where the successors of the third root race of Lemurians resided.[105] The later Nazi Tibet expedition (see Chapter Six) had its roots in these geopolitical and historical views, derived from Blavatsky and her amanuensis, Edward Bulwer-Lytton, both of whom emphasized the importance of Tibetan wisdom as well as the evolutionary superiority of races from western China and northern India.[106]

Later Austro-German interpreters of Blavatsky, especially Lanz and List, viewed Atlantis as the North Atlantic island civilization of Thule. As the capital of a proto-Aryan civilization called Hyperborea, its Nordic remnants might be found in today's Helgoland or Iceland. After the destruction of this ancient civilization through a global flood, Lanz and others believed, the few survivors ostensibly migrated to the highlands of the Himalayas, where they founded the secret society of Agarthi.[107] Theosophy's idea of a lost but recoverable Aryan civilization with roots in Indo-European prehistory played an important role in other occult and border scientific theories. Via ariosophy and World Ice Theory, the idea of an Ur-Aryan Atlantis (Thule) found its way, in turn, into Nazi theories on race and space.[108]

Blavatsky's theosophic movement quickly picked up supporters across Germany and Austria, incorporating more racialist and imperialist elements along the way. Wilhelm Hübbe-Schleiden, who founded the German Theosophical Society in 1884, exemplified these tendencies. The son of a solid middle-class Hamburg family, Hübbe-Schleiden became active in colonial commerce as a young man, moving to Africa and opening a trading firm in Gabon in 1875. His mystical preoccupations with race and space, fuelled by his experiences in Africa, inspired him to become an early supporter of both theosophy and German imperialism. In Hübbe-Schleiden's mind theosophy, spread by the German Empire, might provide a vehicle for reforming the world in which 'the living human races – the more evolved Aryan as well as the less-evolved Negro and Mongol races – would learn to work together in a much more united and spiritually sophisticated civilization'.[109]

Typical of late nineteenth-century cultural critics, Hübbe-Schleiden advocated theosophy as a counterpoise to the 'self-decomposition' of the traditional Christian churches, on the one hand, and the 'sensuous materialism and thoughtless pleasure hunting', the 'moral and spiritual decay' of modern life, on the other. Theosophy might provide the basis for a new, less fragmented, more integrated individual – a view of social reform that began with the spirit and not the material conflicts between social classes.[110]

Inspired by a mysterious letter he supposedly received from a powerful Mahatma, Hübbe-Schleiden spent years attempting 'to give the spiritual teachings of Theosophy a scientific grounding'. He filled his apartment with elaborate wire contraptions meant to represent chains of molecules reflecting the transcendent experience of theosophy.[111] In short, Hübbe-Schleiden represented the peculiar mix of cosmopolitan and racist, scientific and esoteric elements that characterized the Austro-German supernatural imaginary.[112]

Franz Hartmann, who founded the first Austrian Theosophical Society in 1887, took a slightly different approach. But his views were no less indicative of the mix of racism and cosmopolitanism, science and the supernatural, that proved so attractive to many Nazis.[113] Like Blavatksy and Hübbe-Schleiden, Hartmann's path to theosophy derived from a genuine desire to find a new doctrine that might unite scientific and supernatural ways of thinking. Like Hitler, Hess, and Himmler, Hartmann was a lapsed Catholic who appreciated the Church's ritual, mysticism, and spirituality but rejected its dogmatism and hierarchy. A trained physician, Hartmann embraced some aspects of modern medicine. And yet he criticized, anticipating many Nazis, medical doctors' over-reliance on treating the biological basis of disease (repudiating, for example, the 'evil practice' of vaccination).[114]

Hartmann became a theosophist after accepting an invitation from Blavatsky to participate in spiritualist experiments in India.[115] Typical of the fin-de-siècle occult milieu, Hartmann's affiliations were eclectic. He possessed close ties to the Jewish occultist and 'life reformer', Friedrich Eckstein. He also admired the radically racist and anti-Semitic ariosophist Guido von List (see below), whose bizarre and unscientific rune studies Hartmann praised.[116]

Hartmann's theosophical colleague, Rudolf Steiner, came to theosophy through the Viennese occult circle led by Eckstein.[117] After years of seeking a path between scientific materialism and religion, he joined the theosophic society because it recognized 'a 'truth' that stands above all religions and the investigation of 'still unexplained natural laws and powers sleeping in human beings', such as spiritualism, clairvoyance, and telepathy.[118] Named General Secretary of the German Theosophical Society in 1902, Steiner dedicated himself to uniting the achievements of natural science with a genuine spiritual awakening compatible with the modern age.[119]

Steiner insisted that theosophy could achieve 'recognition of higher worlds' with the same reliability as the natural sciences. But he eventually rejected the more cosmopolitan approach of theosophists who seemed, in Steiner's mind, too eclectic and too preoccupied with incorporating elements of existing world religions.[120] His more 'scientific' approach and individualist focus on personal enlightenment, as opposed to universal brotherhood, appealed to many German occultists. On the eve of the First World War, Steiner therefore encouraged a group of German theosophists to break away and form the German Anthroposophical Society.[121]

In its attempt to unite spirituality and science, anthroposophy made a nominally greater effort than theosophy to validate its doctrine empirically. In conducting 'aura research', for example, Steiner modelled his 'experiments' on the new techniques of X-rays and the microscope. Nevertheless, his insistence on having 'proven' occult phenomena for which there was no empirical evidence prevented anthroposophy from being accepted within the scientific community. That only changed in the 1930s, when the Third Reich began officially sponsoring elements of Steiner's doctrines, most notably 'bio-dynamic' agriculture.[122]

Anthroposophy was at least as much a religious faith as it was a scientific doctrine. Steiner's teachings and articles, published in his occult journal, *Lucifer-Gnosis*, anticipated the Nazis' own interest in Asian religion, Gnosticism, and Luciferianism. In visiting Hitler's home town of Linz in 1915, for example, Steiner gave a speech titled 'Christ in Relation to Lucifer and Ahriman'. In it Steiner argued that 'Asian religious evolution is the carrier of a Luciferian element' that 'mankind as a whole once possessed but was later forced to abandon'. These 'Luciferian remnants' must be elevated, Steiner concluded, as 'a wise guiding force left behind for the evolution of mankind in general'.[123] Two decades later, Nazi religious theorists would make nearly identical arguments.

The affinities between anthroposophy and the *völkisch* right extended beyond epistemology and religion. Steiner was eager to assert the superiority of white Europeans, claiming 'that in the grand cycle of spiritual evolution, the Germanic race had advanced the furthest'.[124] Steiner's belief in 'cosmic eugenics', to borrow from one of his followers, included a racial model of evolution in which 'that might be destroyed which is not worthy to take part in the ascent of humanity'. 'Humanity has risen by throwing out the lower forms in order to purify itself,' Steiner argued, 'and it will rise still higher by separating another kingdom of nature, the kingdom of the evil race. Thus mankind rises upward.'[125]

Anthroposophists embraced eugenics not primarily because of their faith in modern science, then, but because they thought that spirituality and race were intrinsically linked. 'Human souls develop different cultures on the basis of different racial and ethnic forces,' Steiner contended, whereas 'dark skin is due to demonic interference'.[126] Marriage between Aryans and 'coloured races' or Jews, according to Steiner, was in conflict with Germany's world mission to sponsor positive biological and spiritual evolution. It should come as no surprise that Steiner, along with Hübbe-Schleiden and Hartmann, was affiliated with the racist and anti-Semitic Guido von List Society.[127] For many anthroposophists in fact, 'Jewishness signified the very antithesis of spiritual progress and the epitome of modern debasement.'[128]

Steiner's own attitude towards Jews was complicated, moving, in the words of Peter Staudenmaier, 'from an unreflective embrace of anti-Semitic prejudices, to public denunciation of the excesses of organized anti-Semitism, to an elaborate racial theory of cosmic evolution in which anti-Semitic themes played a prominent part'.[129] Steiner's 'esoteric teachings about the illegitimacy of Jewish life in the modern world', however, combined with 'his portrayal of Jews as a distinct racial group' to facilitate the 'basic premises of non-exterminationist anti-Semitism, the principal mode of anti-Semitic thinking before the rise of Nazism'.[130]

That theosophy and anthroposophy influenced a wide range of Austrian and German intellectuals, including some with liberal and cosmopolitan proclivities, should not divert our attention from its *völkisch* affinities or potentially eliminationist conceptions of race and space.[131] The lure of theosophy and anthroposophy, like many occult doctrines that emerged at the turn of the twentieth century, was precisely their convoluted attempt 'to find new syntheses ... of what they termed *knowledge* [*Wissen*] and *belief* [*Glaube*]', propagating absurd, border scientific racial theories and an eschatological vision of humanity's history and future. While only marginally successful before the First World War, these efforts inspired a range of theories on race and space, something 'that was later co-opted by National Socialism'.[132]

Ariosophy

Theosophy and anthroposophy may have informed the broader supernatural imaginary that helped make Germans susceptible to Nazism. It was their sister doctrine ariosophy, however, developed by Guido von List and Lanz von Liebenfels, that most directly anticipated the Third Reich. Born in 1848 into a wealthy Viennese family, Guido von List was a lapsed Catholic who became obsessed with the pagan religious and folklore revival of the mid-nineteenth century. List's amateur research into Germanic prehistory over the course of the 1870s and 1880s convinced him of the existence of an ancient, pre-Christian cult and runic language of Odin-worshippers ('Wotanists'). He called this ancient cult the 'Armanen', derived from Tacitus's 'Irminones' in his history of the ancient Germanic tribes.[133]

Under Hübbe-Schleiden and Steiner, Austro-German theosophy had already shed many of its universalist trappings. List took their emphasis on race, empire, and anti-Semitism to its (il)logical extreme, 'appropriating Theosophy's invocation of an idealized past and cosmic scheme of racial evolution in order to underpin [his] developing interest in imagining a new social order based on racist and nationalist grounds'.[134] Since the 'Armanen' civilization had been undermined through racial miscegenation with non-Aryans, List argued, only strict adherence to a eugenical program of selective breeding could resuscitate it.[135]

Like Steiner, List viewed himself as a serious (border) scientist, publishing more than two dozen works on sexology, racial and spiritual 'hygiene', and Germanic runes, with picturesque titles such as *Götterdämmerung* (1893) and *Mephistopheles* (1895). Virtually all his works were ignored by mainstream science. On the other hand, some of his books, including his well-known *Secret of the Runes* (1908), helped create the border scientific field of Runic Studies, which became popular in the Third Reich.[136]

Following Blavatsky and Steiner, List attempted to unite Christian, Eastern, and Nordic racial elements in a neo-pagan amalgam that venerated the Norse God Baldur, Jesus, Buddha, Osiris, and Moses – except in List's case all such figures were ostensibly Aryans.[137] In building a Germanic religion, List even created Nordic equinox and Walpurgisnacht celebrations, led his followers through ancient 'Armanist' grottos, and explored shrines called 'Ostara' under the city of Vienna.[138] List also incorporated elements of Masonic Templar, Freemason, and Rosicrucian traditions.

In 1911, List founded his own knightly 'Armanen-Order'. Certainly the pan-Germanic racism and eliminationist anti-Semitism that defined List's Armanen philosophy was incompatible with the initial intentions of Blavatsky or, in some respects, Steiner. It is nonetheless a testament to the malleability and eclecticism of these closely related doctrines that by the eve of the First World War many leading Austro-German theosophists, including the president of the Austrian Theosophists (Hartmann) and the entire chapter of the Vienna Theosophical Society, had joined the vehemently racist and anti-Semitic List Society.[139]

List's younger contemporary, Jörg Lanz von Liebenfels, translated List's Armanism into a fully fledged occult doctrine, which he called 'Ariosophy'. In his book, *The Theozoology or the Science of the Sodom's Apelings and the God's Electrons* and in the pages of *Ostara*, Lanz laid a blueprint for many of the eugenical policies later adopted by the Third Reich. This included banning interracial marriages, selective breeding and polygamy, and advocating the sterilization and elimination of inferior races, from the mentally and physically inferior to the Jews.[140]

Lanz's biological views were rife with the conceptual contradictions and unscientific reasoning typical of fin-de-siècle occultism and later Nazi views on race.[141] Challenged to explain the science behind his distinction between the mass of 'sub-human' Jewry and the heroic genius of Jews such as Karl Kraus, Heinrich Heine, and Baruch Spinoza, Lanz answered that: 'Whoever has seen Karl Kraus will immediately admit that he exhibits the features of neither the Mongoloid nor the Mediterranean type ... He has dark blonde – in his youth undoubtedly light blonde – hair, a well-formed, rectangular skull and other-wise sculpted, heroid [pure Aryan] features.'[142]

The views of Lanz's disciples were just as far-fetched. They claimed that humanity 'was the result of a – forbidden – mixture of angels and animals. Each person has a small percentage of angel and a large percentage of animal.' The greater measure of 'angel' that a race had, the more Nordic the race. The 'inhabit-ants of mountain villages in Norway', the logic went, 'may be as high as one per cent angel'.[143] Lanz's acolytes even believed that 'various races have different smells' – an argument later made by esoterically inclined Nazis such as Julius Streicher ('A fine nose can always smell a Jew').[144]

Lanz also propagated a Gnostic, paganist, Eastern-flavoured religious syncretism that anticipated the Nazi approach to religion.[145] Emulating List's *Armanen*, Lanz founded his own Order of the New Templars (*Ordo Novo Templi*) in 1900. He also purchased a castle, Burg Werfenstein, to establish the religious centre of his new order (much as Himmler would purchase the Wewelsburg thirty years later). There, in 1904, he flew a Swastika flag to cele-brate the pagan winter solstice.[146]

Finally, Lanz was deeply invested in the power of East and South Asian symbols, which he believed to have the same roots as Ario-Germanic runes in Europe. He favoured Hindu concepts such as reincarnation and karma to

Christian ideas of Heaven and Hell, dabbling in the kabbalah (oddly, a common theme among otherwise radical anti-Semites).[147] Even his ubiquitous use of the term 'Tschandals' for subhuman races – a term later invoked by the early Nazi Party – was taken from the Hindu codes of Manu, which derived from 'the Sanskrit term candala (Tschandale), denoting the lowest caste of untouchables'.[148]

If we had to distill List and Lanz's bizarre ideas into a few basic principles, we might emphasize the role of superhuman races whose Aryan golden age had been 'supplanted by an alien and hostile culture' defined by inferior races. This ancient Germanic religion might be restored through 'knowledge in cryptic forms (e.g. runes, myths and traditions)', but such runes and traditions could be 'deciphered ultimately only by their spiritual heirs, the modern sectarians'.[149] This mélange of religious millenarianism and eugenics soon intersected with the popular border scientific fields of 'racial hygiene' and 'racial-breeding' (*Rassenzucht*) popular among mainstream biologists such as Alfred Ploetz.[150]

Hence ariosophy was consistent with the other occult doctrines we have surveyed. Both the theosophists and anthroposophists were preoccupied with bringing the Aryan ('sixth root race') back into existence. Both believed, at least in their Austro-German iterations, that Aryans were superior spiritually and biologically to Jews, Asians, and Africans.[151] Ariosophists experimented with the same astrological and spiritualist practices as theosophists and anthroposophists, contributed to the same journals, and operated in the same Viennese, Munich, and Berlin circles.[152] Just as Hübbe-Schleiden's *Sphinx* and Steiner's *Lucifer-Gnosis* included articles by List and Lanz, Germany's preeminent astrological journal, the *Astrologische Rundschau,* came to be edited by the ariosophist Rudolf von Sebottendorff.[153]

More so than the anthroposophists and theosophists, the ariosophists attracted important *völkisch* politicians and future Nazis to their movement. Hitler's role model in demagogic politics, the populist mayor of Vienna, Karl Lueger, was a member of the Guido von List society.[154] Heinrich Himmler's mentor in ideological and spiritual matters and head of the SS archives, Karl Maria Wiligut, was an ariosophist as well, publishing a number of books on Armanist ('Iriminist') religion and runology. Sebottendorff, the co-founder of the proto-Nazi Thule Society, was a leader of the Armanen's successor organization, the German Order. Even if Hitler never read *Ostara*, as Lanz claims, the occult doctrines permeating Vienna's cafés and Munich's beer halls before the First World War clearly helped to shape the Nazi supernatural imaginary.[155]

Border Science

By the First World War, German academics were 'confronted with an immense number of theories that did not follow the established rules of scientific inquiry'.[156] This efflorescence of ' "a kind of religious" natural science' – what some contemporaries called 'border science' (*Grenzwissenschaft*) – stood on the margins of mainstream science in two respects.[157]

On the one hand, the border sciences examined unseen forces, characteristics or phenomena on the fringes of human perception. These included astrology, graphology, characterology (a form of phrenology often allied with astrology in Germany), chirology ('hand-reading'), mediumism, and radiesthesia. Border science also constituted academically dubious or marginal disciplines, which ostensibly explained how to manipulate esoteric or supernatural forces beyond the understanding of mainstream science. Prominent examples include parapsychology, life reform, telepathy, biodynamic agriculture, and World Ice Theory.

What held all these 'reenchanted sciences' together was the view that the paranormal was a legitimate object of scientific inquiry and power.[158] Astrology, graphology, characterology, and chirology, wrote the prominent border scientist Ernst Issberner-Haldane, are 'just as serious, precise, and intensive' as any other science and just as 'indispensable for economic science and state-building'. Border sciences, per Issberner-Haldane, 'eschew every kind of mysticism, all clairvoyance; today they no longer belong to occultism (the theories of the hidden)' but to the objective sciences.[159]

Parapsychological experiments and border scientific approaches to explaining the natural world were hardly unique to German-speaking central Europe. One of the leading abstract painters, Wassily Kandinsky, was an ardent proponent of spiritualism. Important French and American psychologists, including Charles Richet and William James, experimented with paranormal phenomena as well.[160]

In contrast to Germany, however, few Europeans 'shared the despair of the German Romantics over Newton's contributions to the new modern science' or felt 'that humanity was now condemned to live in a dead, particulate universe devoid of "dryads" or spiritual meaning'.[161] Many German scientists lamented the rise of modern physics and chemistry, which transformed a world of 'color, quality, and spontaneity' into a 'cold, quality-less impersonal realm ... where particles of matter danced like marionettes to mathematically calculable laws'.[162]

Instead of accepting mainstream natural science millions of Germans turned to parapsychology, astrology, 'transcendental physics', and World Ice Theory, among other border sciences.[163] John Reddick speculates that this widespread interest in 'reenchanted' science was a product of Germany's national fragmentation before 1870 and desire for racial and territorial 'wholeness and synthesis, not in the immediately lived realities of the everyday'.[164] Corinna Treitel argues similarly that the special German emphasis on parapsychology might have been a reaction to the loss of political agency in the German states in the wake of the unsuccessful 1848 revolutions.[165] Whatever the reason, one cannot appreciate the Third Reich's attitudes toward politics and society, race or space, without first understanding the depth and breadth of border scientific doctrines within the Austro-German supernatural imaginary.

Parapsychology and Astrology

Parapsychology was probably the most 'legitimate' and all-encompassing 'border science' to emerge in the last decades of the nineteenth century. Early on parapsychology had a decidedly critical edge, as psychologists such as Max Dessoir and criminologists like Albert Hellwig examined 'the psychology of deception and disbelief'. At their most generous, critical parapsychologists worked to explain the prevalence of the esoteric sciences in Germany, as Max Weber would a decade later, in social psychological terms, citing the inadequacy of both traditional religion and scientific materialism in answering pressing ontological questions.

But the goal of critical parapsychologists was not genuinely to 'understand' occultism, and certainly not to prove the existence of occult phenomena. It was to expose mediums, spiritualists, and other occult practitioners as charlatans.[166] Occultism was a 'contagion of the mind', argued Hellwig, to which people without a proper knowledge of science were susceptible: 'Experience shows day after day that countless people are no longer capable of calm and critical thinking as soon as it comes to occult problems. It is truly sad when one sees how even academic men, who have perhaps made their name in a number of fields of science, completely lose all sense of logic and reason.'[167]

A less critical genre of parapsychology, which claimed equal scientific legitimacy, sought to validate the claims of spiritualists, clairvoyants, and astrologers. The most prominent German parapsychologists in this respect were Carl du Prel and Albert Schrenck-Notzing. Inspired by Blavatsky, du Prel drew on biology, spiritualism, and astrology to explain the evolution of human biology and consciousness.[168] Joining the German Theosophical Society in 1884, du Prel collaborated with Hübbe-Schleiden in founding the Psychological Society, which sponsored his border scientific research. He also published many of his 'results' in the theosophical journal, *The Sphinx*.[169]

Schrenck-Notzing, a Munich physician, hypnotist, and protégé of du Prel, joined the Psychological Society in the 1880s, taking his mentor's 'transcendental psychology' even further. Schrenck-Notzing's emphasis on investigating 'the night life of the soul' represented a clearly occult-inspired departure from natural scientific assumptions and explains his popularity in theosophical circles.[170]

In fact, Austro-German esotericists embraced Schrenck-Notzing's 'uncritical' parapsychology enthusiastically. As Franz Hartmann observed, parapsychology 'recovered an entire realm of human experience that had been suppressed during the Enlightenment. This was the realm of the unconscious ... it was too important for scientists and philosophers to leave to the spiritualists'.[171] Epitomizing the new discipline's border scientific credentials was Hübbe-Schleiden's *The Sphinx*, which had 'no pretensions about catering to an exclusively educated audience' and 'carried a jumble of articles and ... sensationalist ... reports on mediumism, astrology, Rosicrucianism, Theosophy, rays, phrenology, and yoga'.[172]

The dubious scientific basis of parapsychology was not lost on mainstream psychologists. Critics noted the preference of parapsychologists for experiments in non-neutral environments, such as their own houses, or the use of dull red light to reduce the ability of observers to make accurate observations.[173] Sigmund Freud, for example, indicated the problems of both the methodology and ideological provenance of parapsychological belief. Methodologically, Freud argued, paranormal belief was a function of unconscious compulsions and complexes that could be easily manipulated by mediums and parapsychologists, themselves often the victims of a delusional 'occult complex'.[174]

As a Jewish liberal and scientific materialist, Freud moreover distrusted occultism's roots in an 'Indic orientalism' that sought to cultivate 'oceanic feeling' and 'claims about [achieving] inner personal harmony'. Infused by Eastern mysticism, parapsychology provided 'false succour' to those already sceptical of science. Parapsychology might be invoked, Freud added, to reinforce fanciful attitudes toward the Jews, a 'race which in the Middle Ages was held responsible for all epidemics and which today is blamed for the disintegration of the Austrian Empire and the German defeat'.[175] Here Freud anticipates the ways in which occultism and parapsychology might provide a dangerous panacea to those already prone to racial scapegoating.

Parapsychologists accused Freud and other critics of being insufficiently 'scientific' in their analysis of occult phenomena. Anyone who believed mediums could influence so many people through trickery or deception, border scientists argued, were themselves suffering from mental illness.[176] Carl Jung was sympathetic to these arguments.[177] Unlike Freud, Jung was 'enveloped in the Aryanism of Central European Orientalists of his day', asserting that 'the Aryan unconscious has a higher potential than the Jewish; that is the advantage and disadvantage of a youthfulness that is not yet totally alienated from the barbarous.'[178]

Supported by 'mainstream' psychologists such as Jung, parapsychologists continued to assert the scientific nature of their methods, accusing their opponents of mental illness and charlatanry. This pattern of mutual recrimination *within* the occult and border sciences and *between* occultists and mainstream natural scientists was endemic to contemporary battles over scientific legitimacy, presaging the tensions between Nazi and mainstream scientists in the Third Reich.[179]

As the French scholar Gustave Le Bon argued in *The Psychology of the Crowd* (1895), even the most intelligent or sceptical individuals in modern society could succumb to suggestion in the presence of less critical or wholly ignorant peers. This phenomenon was especially true of crowds that were influenced by an 'expert', such as a trained medium or a charismatic politician like Hitler.[180]

Le Bon's theories were employed by critical observers to explain the spread of occult belief, whether a small group conducting a putative 'experiment' in Schrenck-Notzing's parlour or as mass phenomena spread through popular media, magazines, and performances. Only by studying the 'neurotic, combative, superficial, absentminded, credulous and charismatic' mind of the parapsychologist, these critics argued, could one gain insight into the psychology of those who promoted scientific occultism.[181] As we shall see in Chapter Three, Hitler seemingly studied Le Bon's theories as well as parapsychology as a means of manipulating the public.[182]

Astrology was, alongside parapsychology, the most popular border science in Germany and Austria. At the most basic level astrologers 'read' the stars in order to produce horoscopes. Horoscopes represented 'an objective statement of astronomical facts' based on a 'geocentric "map" of planetary positions', including 'the Sun and Moon among the planets – in relation to the zodiac'. Horoscopes can be cast for many different things, from people and animals to earthquakes and ship launches. Once the positions of the planets are noted, deductions are made based on the positions on the zodiac in angular relation to one another.[183]

During the first half of the nineteenth century, people in Germany were probably no more interested in astrology than were other Europeans. As Ellic Howe points out, however, the modern German astrological revival coincided with the general renaissance in supernatural and border scientific thinking discussed above.[184] 'Germans suspicious of the hard sciences and their perceived hostility to life' found 'astrology particularly enticing because it offered technical analyses carried out according to intuitive methods. In providing both "logical rigor and emotional warmth" intuitive astrologers 'offered services geared specifically to the psychic needs of private individuals.'[185]

Astrology was *the* supernatural solvent uniting virtually all occult and border scientific practitioners. Hübbe-Schleiden encouraged his protégé at the *Sphinx*, Hugo Vollrath, to create a Theosophical Publishing House to popularize astrology. The actor Karl Brandler-Pracht, inspired by a seance, began publishing

Germany's flagship astrological journal, the *Astrological Rundschau*, in 1905. Co-sponsored by Rudolf Steiner and the new Cosmos Society of German Astrologers, whose official journal was the *Zentralblatt für Okkultismus*, Brandler-Pracht found a ready audience in German theosophical and anthroposophical circles.[186] Both List and Lanz practised astrology. So did Sebottendorff, a future editor of the *Astrological Rundschau*, who contributed six volumes to Vollrath's 'Astrological Library'.[187]

That virtually all occult and border scientific thinkers embraced astrology does not mean they agreed on the finer points of doctrine. Astrologers argued strenuously over whose methods were more 'scientific' and whose were more 'intuitive' – the latter being associated, dismissively, with less rigorous occult doctrines.[188] These divisions represent less a battle between 'irrational' occultists and 'rational' scientists than a conflict over 'science, knowledge, and power' *within* border scientific circles.[189] Deeply embedded in Germany's post-war supernatural imaginary, astrology and parapsychology only increased in popularity and influence in the interwar period.[190]

Radiesthesia, Life Reform, and World Ice Theory

Parapsychology and astrology offered many insights into occult phenomena – the ability to extend mind over matter, the power to manipulate others, the possibility of divining the future. But the closely related border scientific fields of radiesthesia ('dowsing') and cosmobiology, a sub-discipline of astrology, promised broader and more concrete biological and environmental benefits. Because some well-known dowsers and cosmobiologists had advanced degrees in fields such as physics and engineering, many Germans sceptical of popular astrology accepted radiesthesia as 'scientific'. Even a number of medical professionals – usually those with homoeopathic leanings – believed that radiesthesia could provide a way to help purify the body and cleanse the environment of secret influences that modern science could not.[191]

The use of divining rods to locate water and precious metals had been an intrinsic part of folk belief in Europe throughout the Middle Ages. This folk tradition merged in the Early Modern period with the occult belief that one might locate mystical 'energies' along certain landforms (referred to as 'ley lines') and harness invisible 'radiation' under the earth.[192] Subsumed in the early twentieth century under the border scientific rubrics of 'geomancy' and 'radiesthesia', dowsing could be practised in a variety of ways, but usually involved a pendulum composed of a 'small wooden cone suspended ... on a short length of thin thread'.[193]

Dowsers, such as the famous Gustav Freiherr von Pohl, claimed to employ pendulums or more traditional divining rods to locate earth rays and other pathogenic currents (*Reizstreifen*) that carried invisible energies and threat-ened people's health.[194] Radiesthesia could ostensibly locate and treat harmful radiation in ways that neither traditional physics nor biology could (hence the interdisciplinary field of 'cosmobiology').[195] The closely related field of geomancy included *völkisch*-esotericists such as Wilhelm Teudt, who 'postu-lated that prehistoric knowledge over *Ur*-energies' proved 'the superiority of the "Urgermans".'[196] Some dowsers focused on locating radiation and precious metals. Others claimed they could glean secret truths about objects and even interpersonal relationships.[197]

A belief that dowsers could locate unhealthy energies that caused cancer and disease merged well with the movement toward natural healing practices embedded in 'life reform' (*Lebensreform*). A 'middle-class attempt to palliate the ills of modern life', life reform embraced a 'variety of alternative lifestyles – including herbal and natural medicine, vegetarianism, nudism and self-sufficient rural communes'.[198] Many *völkisch* occultists embraced 'natural' (organic) and vegetarian diets, magnetic therapy, and natural healing, practices later adopted by Nazi leaders such as Hitler, Hess, Himmler, and Julius Streicher.[199] Life reform was propagated with particular fervour by the anthro-posophists, who advocated 'a better knowledge of man; Health through natural living; Harmony between blood, soil and cosmos; Life reform as a national aim; Knowledge and Life, The Rule of the Living.'[200]

The principles of life reform helped inspire in turn Steiner's post-war devel-opment of 'biodynamic agriculture' (*biodynamische wirtschaftweise* or BDW), based on restoring the quasi-mystical relationship between earth and the cosmos, 'in which the earth is seen as an organism with magnetic properties of sympathy and attraction that may be damaged by the use of artificial ferti-lizers'.[201] Steiner's BDW would become one of the most prominent and widely accepted border sciences in the Third Reich.[202]

Radiesthesia, life reform, and natural healing emphasized the holistic link between racial and spiritual 'hygiene', between the health of the mind and the body. The two interrelated border sciences repersonalized an increasingly clin-ical medical profession that looked at specific germs, pathogens, and diseases as opposed to the whole person or 'organism'. They also appealed to a transcen-dental worldview, which gained an intuitive and fuller understanding of sick-ness, as opposed to a materialist focus on the etiology of an individual disease.[203]

In rejecting mainstream medical science, border scientists favoured 'a variety of inexpensive and noninvasive techniques (e.g., clairvoyance, the side-real pendulum, physiognomy, graphology, iridology, consultation with séance spirits, and astrology) to achieve an intuitive and fuller understanding of a sickness'. Whereas traditional physicians were careful about making long-term prognoses, radiesthesiologists, natural healers, and life reformers 'had intuitive techniques for making such predictions' and 'determining the proper timing of treatment'.[204]

Certainly homoeopathic medicine and back-to-nature movements (*Wandervögel*) were popular across Europe in the decades before the First World War.[205] Dowsing and life reform tapped into a broader desire for 'reenchanted science' and mind-body holism that was popular across the German middle classes.[206] If life reform included 'apparently liberal and left-wing' elements, however, in Germany and Austria at least, 'there were many overlaps with the völkisch movement'.[207] Just as the Austro-German version of theosophy was more explicitly racist and ariocentric than its French or Anglo-American counterpart, so too were the Austro-German variations on natural healing and border scientific medicine, drawn from anthroposophy and ariosophy, more preoccupied with race and eugenics.[208]

Anthroposophy emphasized the regeneration of the Aryan race through proper cultivation of the land and spirit in connection to the cosmos.[209] Anthroposophists were also typical in arguing that 'racial mixture brings spiritual disharmony' and that only 'racial ethnology could perceive "the true cosmic spirit" lying behind external appearances'.[210] Anthroposophists and ariosophists therefore believed that marriages between 'coloured races', or Jews and Aryans were in conflict with the German world mission.[211]

In helping inspire the faith-based eugenics practices of the Third Reich, this 'reenchanted science' was anything but harmless.[212] There were in fact close ties between leaders of the life reform and back-to-nature movements and *völkisch*-esoteric groups that advocated eugenics. Among the most vocal proponents of the utopian 'garden city' movement, for example, which sought to (re)create a healthy 'greenbelt' in the middle of the modern city, were *völkisch* esotericists such as Theodor Fritsch, Heinrich Pudor, and Phillip Stauff.[213]

Fritsch's colleague, the *völkisch*-esoteric writer Willibald Hentschel, promoted a radically eugenicist return-to-nature ideology as well. Anticipating the Third Reich, Hentschel envisioned vast colonies of pure Aryan peasants practising an ancient Nordic religion. His pre-war plans for 'Thule-settlements' organized by 'Norn-lodges' never came to fruition. They did help to inspire the post-war Artamanen movement, however, to which Heinrich Himmler and Walther Darré belonged, as well as Nazi policies of racial resettlement and ethnic cleansing.[214]

Popular culture in the late-Wilhelmine period was moreover rife with the idea of creating superhuman beings through a combination of biology and sorcery.[215] Paul Wegener's film *Golem* (1915 and 1920) and Hanns Heinz Ewers' novel *Alraune* (1911) were both a product of border scientific thinking, exemplifying this uncanny mélange of science and the supernatural.[216] Before 1914 this supernaturally inspired approach to biology was less overtly monstrous, 'able to accommodate a range of political solutions to the tensions between modernity and nostalgia, mechanism and wholeness, science and spirit'.[217]

But after 1918, in a sociopolitical environment radicalized by war and crisis, this supernaturally infused, holistic approach to biology helped transform the selectively applied practice of eugenics, popular across Europe, into a hugely ambitious and fantastical programme of human experimentation and genocide in Nazi Germany.

Any survey of the border scientific doctrines that informed Nazism would be incomplete without mentioning 'Glacial Cosmogony' or World Ice Theory (*Welteislehre* or WEL). Invented by the Austrian scientist and philosopher Hanns Hörbiger, World Ice Theory was inspired by a dream in which Hörbiger found himself floating in space, observing a giant pendulum swinging back and forth, growing ever longer and eventually breaking. When he woke Hörbiger claimed to know intuitively that the sun's gravitational pull ceased to exert any force at three times the distance of Neptune and that most of the physical universe could be explained through the interplay of the 'antagonistic Ur-substances of ice and fire'.[218]

Lacking even a rudimentary scientific background, Hörbiger enlisted the amateur astronomer Philip Fauth, with whom he collaborated in publishing their 'findings', *Glacial Cosmogony*, in 1912.[219] Their work posited that much of the known universe was created when a small, water-filled star collided with a much larger star, causing an explosion, the frozen fragments of which created multiple solar systems, including our own. Gravity, the rotation of the planets, and various other interstellar phenomena could all be explained through interactions between primordial satellites made of ice. So too could Earth's geological history, as moons made of ice crashed into it in prehistoric times, generating floods, ice ages, and various layers of the earth's crust. Even human and animal biology were explained by World Ice Theory, including the creation of the human race through the impact of a meteor containing 'divine sperma'.[220]

Hörbiger and his supporters proclaimed *Welteislehre* to be a 'scientific revolution'. It provided the foundation of a new 'cosmic cultural history', an 'astronomy of the invisible' founded upon 'creative intuition'.[221] Absurd and totalizing as it was, Hörbiger's 'all-encompassing theory of heaven and earth' promised to solve 'the cosmic riddle between original creation and world collapse'. It explained everything from 'the origins of the sun and species' to 'the earthquake of Messina', Inca religion, and Nordic mythology.[222]

As the supreme 'navigator' of *Welteislehre*, Hörbiger could change its logic, theses, and systems at will, inoculating his theory against any arguments from mainstream science.[223] By providing all the necessary clues to convince his audience that what they saw was truly 'scientific', Hörbiger's doctrine 'produced sensations of authenticity that made the distinction between "serious" scientific work, committed to objectivity and rationality, and mere dramatic banter about it almost impossible, at least for the broader public'.[224] World Ice Theory was therefore a quintessential border science, proudly combining fantasy and reality in ways that delighted spiritually hungry lay people but exasperated scientists.[225]

Indeed, few physicists, astronomers, or geologists gave Hörbiger's theory any credence. According to the astronomer Edmund Weiss, Hörbiger's intuitive methods could just as easily be used to claim the cosmos was made of olive oil as ice. Like most border scientists, Hörbiger merely ignored his critics, accusing them of closed-mindedness or lack of 'faith' in his visions. No formula or numbers could prove *Welteislehre*, Hörbiger argued, because his theory was in flux and alive, a 'new evangelism' and 'global view of salvation' (*erloesendes Weltbild*).[226] He focused instead on convincing lay people of the rectitude of his theories, hoping this would push mainstream science to take his ideas more seriously. He gave hundreds of public lectures, produced World Ice movies and radio programmes, and published World Ice novels and magazines.[227]

In the 1920s a number of amateur scientists and bourgeois intellectuals joined together to form the Cosmotechnical Society (*Kosmotechnische Gesellschaft*) and Hörbiger Institute, creating a virtual cult around Hörbiger and his teachings.[228] His theories also appealed to ariosophists and Germanic paganists such as Chamberlain, List, and Lanz von Liebenfels, who saw in *Welteislehre* 'scientific' proof of their 'fantastic cosmologies and spectacular world views'. In this Ur-Germanic alternative to 'Jewish' physics and 'soulless' natural science, the cataclysmic floods, apocalyptic battles, and heroic Aryan civilization of the Edda appeared to be confirmed.[229]

The popularity of *Welteislehre* is emblematic of the broader renaissance of occult and border science in the first three decades of the twentieth century. Phenomena such as *Welteislehre*, parapsychology, and astrology were neither anachronistic nor marginal. They were popular manifestations of a 'scientific esotericism' that sought legitimacy within the scientific establishment and across a broader public.[230] Despite attacks by state officials, liberals, even conservative religious groups, occultism and border science continued to grow in popularity, becoming 'not only an upstart religion but also an upstart science'.[231] In producing a 'science of the soul', a 'reenchanted science' that transcended both scientific materialism and traditional religion, the border sciences allowed Germans the chance to challenge the authority of both.

***

Hitler may well have read *Ostara*. He might have also visited Lanz von Liebenfels as an aspiring art student. But even if this meeting never took place, the 'links,

both ideological and social, between Hitler and Ariosophical circles' are important.[232] For List and Lanz were hardly marginal figures. Their ideas and goals
had much in common with a range of German and Austrian contemporaries.
From Wagner, Lagarde, and Langbehn to Hübbe-Schleiden, Hartmann, and
Steiner, from du Prel and Schrenck-Notzing to Schuler and Hörbiger, these
individuals should be seen, collectively, as the progenitors of a wider supernatural imaginary shared by millions of Germans and exploited by the Nazi
Party after the First World War.[233]

The second argument of this chapter is that the Austro-German supernatural imaginary propagated an esoteric and border scientific way of thinking
that appeared 'both as universal cosmologies and holistic ideologies'. All these
thinkers were united with millions of Germans in their 'fear that a purely materialistic, abstract science would lead to cultural decline'.[234] Indeed, most of the
doctrines surveyed in this chapter sought to challenge both the monopoly on
knowledge posited by Enlightenment science and the monopoly on spirituality
claimed by the Judeo-Christian tradition.[235]

Many liberals, Marxists, and mainstream scientists were concerned about the
proliferation of such unverifiable border scientific doctrines. Some recognized,
as Freud did, the racist and illiberal tendencies that supernatural thinking might
encourage, especially when combined uncritically with scientific claims.[236]

That does not change the fact that 'the supernatural and extrasensory preoccupied wide swaths of Germany and Austria's intellectual elites'.[237] In concert
with thousands of other astrologers, parapsychologists, dowsers, and World Ice
theorists, theosophists and ariosophists, astrologers and parapsychologists,
the leaders of the Austro-German *völkisch* milieu created a vision of the future
that transcended traditional left and right, religious and scientific, racist and
cosmopolitan – dichotomies that bitterly divided late-Wilhelmine and Weimar
society, culture, and politics.

The 'völkisch milieu in which Nazism evolved', observes Corinna Treitel
quite accurately, was complex. Millions of members of the *völkisch* movement –
whether esotericist, paganist, or border scientist – consistently disagreed about
the 'appropriate means' by which to effect political change. All *völkisch* thinkers
did agree, however, on the need for German renewal.[238] The party that monopo-
lized this supernaturally infused project of German renewal was the NSDAP.

FROM THE THULE SOCIETY TO THE NSDAP
Fashioning the Nazi Supernatural Imaginary, 1912–24

'If anything is unfolkish [*unvölkisch*], it is this tossing around of old Germanic expressions which neither fit into the present period nor represent anything definite ... I had to warn again and again against those *völkisch* wandering scholars ... [who] rave about old Germanic heroism, about dim prehistory, stone axes, spear and shield.'

Adolf Hitler, Mein Kampf (1924)[1]

'It was Thule people to whom Hitler came in the very beginning; it was Thule people who first joined forces with Hitler.'

Rudolf von Sebottendorff (1933)[2]

Near the end of the First World War a twenty-six-year-old art student was discharged from the German Army due to wounds received on the Western Front. Born outside the German Reich, the ambitious young artist developed a passion for pan-Germanic ideology, reading any literature he could find on the history and mythology of the Teutonic people. Shortly after arriving in Munich in late 1917, he co-founded a working group that sought to create a Third German Reich. The group adopted an elaborate array of occult ideas, including ariosophic racism and esoteric symbols like the swastika.[3] Within weeks two members of the young artist's discussion circle founded the German Workers' Party (DAP), which, renamed the National Socialist German Workers' Party (NSDAP), would achieve power fourteen years later.[4]

These biographical details describe almost perfectly the political and ideological trajectory of Adolf Hitler. Except the young artist in question was not Hitler, but Walter Nauhaus, leader of the Germanic Order of the Holy Grail and co-founder, with Rudolf von Sebottendorff, of the proto-Nazi Thule Society.[5]

That the early ideological and organizational trajectories of the occultist Nauhaus and Hitler overlap so closely raises an old question: What were the links between the Austro-German supernatural milieu and the incipient Nazi Party?

The ariosophists and other *völkisch*-esoteric groups recognized the similarities between their pre-war doctrines and National Socialism after 1919. Lanz von Liebenfels and his post-war publisher Herbert Reichstein both insisted that Nazi ideology was a clear expression of the pre-war Austro-German occult milieu. Sebottendorff, as suggested in the epigraph above, argued that the Nazi Party was a direct outgrowth of his ariosophic Thule Society.[6] So too did a broad array of *völksich*-esoteric and *völkisch*-religious leaders welcome the Third Reich, at least initially, as the fulfilment of their 'neo-pagan' beliefs.[7]

For the past thirty years historians have emphasized, instead, the tenuous nature of these connections. Some have seized on Hitler's quote from *Mein Kampf* above as an example of the Nazis' disinterest in occultism and pagan religions. Others point out that the leaders of the Thule Society never went on to play a substantive role in the Third Reich.[8]

This chapter will address the question of the Thule Society's role in shaping the Nazi Party in three ways. First, it re-examines the connection between late-Wilhelmine ariosophic groups such as the German Order and the Thule Society out of which the Nazi Party emerged. Second, it tests Sebottendorff's claim in the epigraph above, tracing the organizational and ideological impact of the Thule Society on the creation of the early Nazi Party.

Third and finally, this chapter interrogates Hitler's epigraph regarding the influence of Ario-Germanic, occult, and border scientific ideas on the early Nazi Party. The organizational and ideological connections between the Wilhelmine *völkisch*-esoteric milieu, the Thule Society, and the early German Workers' Party, this chapter argues, were richer and more substantive than many scholars recognize, helping to inscribe supernatural thinking at the core of the Nazi movement.

From the German Order to the Thule Society

Intent on avoiding service in the multinational Austrian Army, Hitler fled his beloved Vienna for Munich in May 1913. In these last months before the outbreak of hostilities, the *völkisch*-esoteric centre of gravity migrated with Hitler. Guido von List and Jörg Lanz von Liebenfels, Franz Hartmann and Rudolf Steiner, Hanns Hörbiger and Karl Maria Wiligut were Austrian. But their ideas found their greatest political and intellectual expression in Germany.

Beginning in the last years of the Wilhelmine Empire and extending into the first post-war years, hundreds of Bavarians, Saxons, and Silesians created a plethora of ariosophic splinter groups. The Alsace-Lorrainer Rudolf von

Gorsleben founded the Edda Society, continuing List's research into ancient Germanic runes. The Silesian occultist Herbert Reichstein became Lanz's post-war publisher, finding him an audience in Berlin. The Saxon ariosophist and astrologer Rudolf von Sebottendorff moved to Munich and co-founded the Thule Society.[9]

Notable among these ariosophic splinter groups was Theodor Fritsch's Saxon-based German Order (*Germanenorden*). The German Order was a quintessential ariosophic society, replete with occult rituals and bizarre border scientific theories about 'root races'. In founding the German Order, Fritsch decided simultaneously to create a political working group that could dissemi-nate his *völkisch*-esoteric programme to a wider public: the Reich Hammer Association (*Reichshammerbund*).[10] Named after his infamous anti-Semitic publishing company, *Der Hammer*, its goal was to inaugurate an 'Aryan-Germanic' religious revival founded on 'Germanic supremacy over "lower working races"' and an 'inexorable hate for the Jews'.[11]

Like other *völkisch* groups that emerged in the last two decades of the German Empire, Fritsch's German Order/Hammer Association had little polit-ical power or influence before the First World War. But the obscure German Order represented a crucial wartime way station between the late-Wilhelmine *völkisch* milieu and the early Nazi Party. For under the leadership of Nauhaus and Sebottendorff, a renegade Munich chapter of Fritsch's German Order would find new life under a different name: the Thule Society.

The German Order and the First World War

Theodor Fritsch was no novice to *völkisch* politics. One of Germany's first and most vociferous racial anti-Semites, he published Germany's oldest anti-Semitic paper, the *Anti-Semitic Correspondence*. In 1890 he was elected a Reichstag representative for the radically *völkisch* and anti-Semitic German Social Party, subsequently playing an important role on the socially reformist right.[12] Fritsch was nearly as passionate about *völkisch*-esotericism as he was about eliminating Jews from German society, signing some of his pseudony-mous writings 'Fritz Thor' and joining both the Guido von List Society and Lanz's Order of the New Templar (ONT).[13]

Still, it is Fritsch's attempt to combine *völkisch*-esotericism and mass politics in the German Order/Hammer Association that deserves our attention. At first glance the two organizations do not appear that different from the ONT or German Social Party that preceded them. The co-founders of the German Order and Hammer Association, Philipp Stauff and Hermann Pohl, were prominent ariosophists. Stauff was a ranking member of the List Society/Armanen Order and Pohl was head of the local Saxon 'Wotan Lodge'.[14]

Like the ONT, the German Order required its members to meet obscure racial criteria, including an 'Aryan clause' forbidding Jewish ancestry. The German Order also practised secret rites modelled on the Freemasons and published an ariosophic journal entitled *Runen*, replete with a swastika on the cover. The Hammer Association had its own occult trappings. It was directed by a quasi-Arthurian 'Armanen-Rat' or council of twelve individuals borrowed directly from List. Fritsch's use of the term 'Tschandala' to represent Jews and lower races also gives away its debt to List and Lanz's border scientific musings on race.[15]

And yet there were important differences between the German Order/ Hammer Association and earlier *völkisch* parties. The goal of the Hammer Association was to transcend the petty bourgeois character of the Wilhelmine anti-Semitic movement. Anticipating Hitler's NSDAP, the Hammer Association was pan-German in scope, with branches across Austria as well as Germany. It also sought to bring together all 'racist-reformist groups' with 'national' and 'social' values – uniting *völkisch* businessmen with nationalist workers, army officers and professors with peasants and shopkeepers.[16] In working to transcend Germany's ingrained class and confessional milieus, Fritsch urged 'collaboration with Catholics, a broad spread of propaganda to workers, farmers, teachers, officials, and officers, and special activity at the universities'.[17] Eventually, individual chapters of the German Order developed their own youth movement, again anticipating the NSDAP.[18]

Fritsch and Pohl managed to build a remarkably broad coalition of likeminded politicians and intellectuals. The list included the usual suspects such as List, Lanz, and Bernhard Koerner, who signed his letters with runic symbols (and would go on to play a major role in the SS).[19] Sebottendorff was a member as well, enthusiastically recalling a meeting of the German Order near the Quedlinburg castle at the foot of 'the Brocken' in the Hartz mountains, the site of Walpurgisnacht in Goethe's *Faust* (and later Nazi archaeological projects).[20] To these outright *völkisch*-esotericists we must add a number of prominent fellow travellers, including Field Marshall Erich von Ludendorff, the German Conservative leader Alfred Hugenberg, and Heinrich Class, head of the Pan-German League.[21]

Given its ideological antecedents and political proponents, we should hardly be surprised that the Hammer Association programme was steeped in racialist hysteria, premised on an apocalyptic war between Ario-Germanic peoples and lesser races ('Tschandala').[22] At the centre of Fritsch and Pohl's ideology stood a 'pathological brand of anti-Semitism combined with a belief in the inherent superiority of the Germanic or Nordic race'.[23] Two decades before the Third Reich, they advocated the deportation of 'parasitic and revolutionary mob races (Jews, anarchist cross-breeds and gipsies [sic])'.[24]

Anticipating Hitler's infamous prophecy from January 1939, Pohl moreover announced that if the Jews 'prepared to exploit war or revolution', their annihilation would occur through the 'Sacred Vehme', which would 'smite the mass-criminals with their own weapons'.[25]

Here we see both the biomystical racism and apocalyptic justification of political violence that defined the later Nazi supernatural imaginary. Pohl not only advocated the murder of the Jews, but invoked, with little irony, the secret, semi-mythical court that murdered 'criminals' in medieval Westphalia and helped justify political murder in the Weimar Republic.

In an environment of relative economic and political stability, the Hammer Association had trouble attracting supporters. Its elitist structure, highly restrictive racial requirements, and prohibitive dues also limited its membership. The Hammer Association moreover retained all the tendencies toward internal squabbling that had rendered the *völkisch*, anti-Semitic parties ineffectual for thirty years prior to 1912.[26] Hence the Hammer Association represented a kind of halfway house between an occult order and a modern *völkisch* political organization, blending secret rites and bizarre racial theories with an ambitious sociopolitical agenda and geographically diverse, national organization.[27]

When war did break out in August 1914, both the Hammer Association and German Order fell into disarray. Much of this was a result of nearly half the members being called up to military service. But the precarious financial situation, elitist structure, and expensive banquets in the midst of war continued to put off many potential supporters. As Pohl wrote to a colleague in November 1914, 'the war came on us too early, the G.O. was not yet completely organized and crystallized, and if the war lasts long, it will go to pieces'.[28]

Even as it challenged the bourgeois foundations of the German Order, the war opened the way to mass politics. It tore away all convictions and values from the vast majority of ordinary people. To address their 'social and spiritual needs', Germans began to fall 'into the arms of the oldest and most primitive of all human illusions promising wish fulfilment and a more beautiful future ... the sphere of a magical world view and superstition'.[29] Heretofore apolitical occultists now characterized the war as 'cosmically necessary ... [a] manifestation of processes playing out among "the beings of the spirit worlds" ... [a] world of demons and spirits which works through humankind when nations battle one another'.[30] By the last two years of the war, as the death toll exceeded one million, the racial utopian fantasies of the German nationalist right attained a fever pitch.[31]

Fritsch and Pohl tried to capitalize on wartime radicalization to create a broader *völkisch*-nationalist coalition. But the Hammer Association was eventually absorbed into the German Nationalist Protection and Defence

Organization (*Schutz- und Trutzbund*), one of the more powerful nationalist associations in the early Weimar Republic.[32] As most individual chapters of the German Order dissipated or merged with larger nationalist groups, the Munich chapter, led by Pohl, split off to form the *Walvater* chapter of the Holy Grail.[33]

The most important individual to join Pohl's *Walvater* chapter was Rudolf von Sebottendorff. Born Adam Alfred Rudolf Glauer to a modest lower middle-class family in Saxony, Sebottendorff briefly pursued a degree in engineering during the early 1890s.[34] Abandoning his studies, Sebottendorff moved to Egypt and then Turkey. He immersed himself in the study of theosophy, Sufi Islam, and astrology, the latter with a Greek Jew who initiated Sebottendorff into Freemasonry. To make ends meet, Sebottendorff spent time as a tutor at a Kievan Jewish community and even became a Turkish citizen.[35] Despite – or perhaps because of – his immersion in Eastern religions and Freemasonry, Sebottendorff gravitated to ariosophy, citing List, Lanz, and Fritsch as his primary influences.[36]

This transition from a seemingly universalist intellectual to a *völkisch*-esoter-icist makes sense if one views Sebottendorff in the context of a broader Austro-German supernatural imaginary.[37] Sebottendorff displayed the same fascination with 'oriental' mysticism and Eastern religions that influenced Lagarde, Steiner, and Lanz. Typical of these *völkisch*-esotericists, Sebottendorff saw no contradic-tion in merging radically racist and anti-Semitic views with socially progressive, selectively cosmopolitan ideas that drew on Eastern spirituality and the transna-tional brotherhood of Indo-Aryan races. The German Order, Thule Society, and later Nazi movement would all retain this combination of extreme *völkisch* nationalism and Indo-Aryanism.[38]

After his Turkish interlude, Sebottendorff returned to Germany. He soon fell in with a group of Berlin occultists around a newspaper called *The Magic Pages*, where Sebottendorff worked on a manuscript about magical amulets.[39] He also became an expert on astrology, which culminated in him being named editor of Karl-Brandler Pracht's *Astrologische Rundschau* in the early 1920s.[40] After a couple of years in this Berlin demi-monde, Sebottendorff – who had since joined Fritsch's German Order – made his way to Munich.[41] In 1917 he attended a meeting of the new Walvater chapter of the Holy Grail, presided over by Pohl. Impressed by Sebottendorff's *völkisch*-esoteric convictions, Pohl invited the itinerant astrologer to join the Order and entrusted him with renewing the Bavarian chapter.[42]

In most respects Sebottendorff's Walvater chapter of the Holy Grail was not much different from the German Order that preceded it. He envisioned the chapter as a 'social-national organization' that combined a 'pathological brand of anti-Semitism with a belief in the inherent superiority of the Germanic or Nordic race'. Also like the German Order, it was organized along Masonic lines.[43] The society was therefore still 'secret', producing few written documents. When political correspondence did occur, it was often communicated through Germanic runes – hardly an effective basis for mass politics. In fact, Sebottendorff decided to have the Walvater chapter sponsor an occult journal called *Runes* and continued to give lectures on pendulum dowsing and astrology.[44]

None of these decisions appear to have moved the German Order much beyond the organizational cul-de-sac it had entered a year earlier, when Pohl broke away from Fritsch. But the devastating impact of the war began to radicalize even the most obdurate and apolitical members of the Order. By the summer of 1918, as Germany's prospects of victory dimmed, Sebottendorff decided it was time to enter politics.[45]

The Thule Society

Sebottendorff met his 'kindred spirit', Walter Nauhaus, during recruiting efforts for the Walvater chapter of the German Order. Nauhaus was a sculptor by training, fascinated, like many *völkisch* intellectuals, by 'the esoteric side of the Cabala' as well as Egyptian and Hindu religious beliefs. With his friend Walter Deicke, Nauhaus had already formed a discussion group on New Year's Day 1918 to explore such ideas. They called it the Thule Society.

At the time Nauhaus's small discussion group was entirely apolitical and had no connection to the German Order.[46] That gradually changed after Sebottendorff appointed Nauhaus the Walvater chapter's deputy recruiter. By the summer of 1918, Sebottendorff and Nauhaus were hosting frequent meetings of the German Order at the Four Seasons hotel in Munich. As the Order became more politicized, Nauhaus seized upon the idea of substituting the innocuous-sounding 'Thule Society' for the Walvater chapter as a cover for their activities. On 17 August 1918, as Ludendorff's last offensive dissipated on the Western Front, Sebottendorff merged the Bavarian Walvater chapter of the Germanic Order with Nauhaus's nascent 'Thule Society'.[47]

As we saw in Chapter One, the concept of a lost civilization of Hyperborea or Thule derived from the theosophist preoccupation with Atlantis. It then found a way, in more racialized form, into ariosophy, the principles of which Nauhaus and Sebottendorff embraced as the basis of their organization.[48] Hence the Thule Society retained all the trappings of its ariosophic predecessor organizations, propagating a 'unique mixture of occult-mythological window-dressing and natural scientific theories' and promising a utopian future in the final months of an apocalyptic war.[49]

The fact that the war was not yet lost was important in determining the initial trajectory of the group. At a meeting two weeks after its founding Sebottendorff still found time for an extended peroration on 'The Pendulum' as an 'instrument for radiesthetic experiments or alleged medical diagnosis'. In typically bourgeois, esoteric fashion newly initiated male Thulists were encouraged to wear a bronze pin adorned with a swastika and two spears while women were given a golden swastika.[50] Important here is not the fact that Sebottendorff wasted the Society's time on initiation pins or the health benefits of divining rods. When Hitler came to power, he too would have a dowser scour the Reich chancellery for cancerous 'death rays' and Himmler would order his chief occult advisor, Wiligut, to develop all sorts of *völkisch*-esoteric runes and insignia.

What makes his lectures and initiation practices interesting is Sebottendorff's attempt to attract women members – a significant change from the overtly chauvinist nature of Liebenfels' New Templar, List's Armanen, and Fritsch's German Order.[51] The Thule Society's focus on occult and border scientific thinking was also leavened by a greater instinct for mass politics than its precursors. Finally, Sebottendorff sought and gained support from remnants of the German Order in Berlin, an attempt to branch off into northern Germany that had not worked well for Fritsch and his predecessors.[52]

In many respects the Thule programme was the same as its *völkisch*-esoteric predecessors. The Thulists wanted a Greater Germany devoid of Jews, Freemasons, and Communists, and proposed a set of progressive social 'reforms' to help unite the forces of labour and capital.[53] In other ways, the 'social-national' elements were more strongly represented in the Thule Society than the German Order. Sebottendorff's apparent hostility to capitalism and sympathy for workers was not 'Marxist' or Socialist, he argued, but quintessentially 'German'. He wanted to eliminate 'Jewish' capitalism so that honest German workers and small businessmen could thrive. Such arguments were virtually identical to early iterations of Hitler's National Socialism.[54] This socially and economically progressive programme is particularly interesting given the solidly bourgeois character of the Thule's early membership.[55]

After founding the Thule Society, Sebottendorff and his colleagues made two important decisions in the early autumn of 1918. First, Sebottendorff purchased a newspaper, the *Munich Observer* (whose masthead read 'Independent Paper for National and Racial Politics'). In masquerading as a sports paper (*Sportblatt*), the *Observer* would fly under the radar of liberal and Socialist opposition, Sebottendorff reasoned, since 'A Jew is only interested in sport if it shows a profit'.[56] Within a year the *Observer* would change its name to the *Racial Observer* (*Völkischer Beobachter* or *VB*), becoming the principal press vehicle for the Nazi Party.

Second, the *Munich Observer*'s head sportswriter and new political editor, Karl Harrer co-founded, in October 1918, the 'Political Workers' Circle' (*Politische Arbeiter-Zirkel*), with his fellow Thule Society colleague, Anton Drexler. It was Drexler who would suggest changing the group from a 'circle' to the German Workers' Party (*Deutsche Arbeiterpatei* or DAP) a few weeks later.[57]

Sebottendorff did not personally spearhead this 'working class' initiative. But his associates recall that he had begun to reach out to younger members of the German Order outside the framework of the bourgeois Thule Society. He and Harrer both recognized that the Society needed more working-class support to gain political influence.[58]

At the time Sebottendorff would insist that the Thule Society was apolitical, focused primarily on occult activities typical of Theodor Fritsch's pre-war German Order. Some historians have accepted Sebottendorff's claims as evidence of the gap between the occult-based Thule Society and politically oriented Nazi Party. As previously suggested, however, the late-Imperial German and early Weimar governments were closely monitoring extremist political organizations, which is why Nauhaus and Sebottendorff created the cover of the Thule Society and portrayed the *Munich Observer* as a 'sports paper.'[59] Their relative freedom from surveillance probably explains why the politically revolutionary Thule Society was able to meet openly at the Four Seasons hotel and draw such an eclectic crowd of pan-Germans, *völkisch* intellectuals, and future Nazis, even as other right-wing groups were persecuted.[60]

Still, the Thule Society would have likely remained a small, mostly harmless *völkisch* splinter group if not for the outbreak of left-wing revolution and the military catastrophe of Germany's defeat in the First World War. Beginning in late-October 1918 the centre-left governing coalition of liberals, Catholics, and Social Democrats encountered increasing opposition from striking workers and mutineering soldiers. Worker demands were soon taken up by new, more radical Independent Socialists (USDP) and an incipient Communist (Spartacist) Party (KPD) that wanted an immediate end to the war and eradication of the monarchy. These left-wing revolutionaries would have their earliest success in the state of Bavaria, where Kurt Eisner's Independent Socialists managed to overthrow the Wittelsbach monarchy and declare a Socialist Republic on 8 November 1918, just a day before the armistice.

For 'believers in racial apocalypse' like Sebottendorff, the experience of Eisner's Socialist Republic, followed by armistice, defeat, and the disintegration of the German Empire, was catastrophic. Endemic in *völkisch*-esoteric circles before 1914, apocalypticism now became 'a staple of culture and of some strands of religious discourse – not to mention German war propaganda'. Faced with defeat and left-wing revolution, Germans of an 'eschatological outlook', such as Sebottendorff and his *völkisch*-nationalist colleagues, were 'confirmed in their view that the end of days was upon them'.[61] As one soldier put it in the early weeks of the Weimar Republic:

> Jews and ... profiteers became rich, feasting and living at the cost of the
> Volk as if in a 'Promised Land' ... Germany appeared lost. Resigned,

the Front soldier attempted to safeguard his family from ruin and hunger . . . Strikes and revolts in all districts, Germany's fate appeared sealed . . . [the] world turned upside down! . . . The Front soldier and the decent part of the population led a nearly hopeless struggle against this epidemic. Parliamentarianism was celebrated like an orgy. Roughly thirty-five parties and factions arose and confused the volk. A pure witch's Sabbath! The German Volk, devoid of political acumen, staggered toward the diverse will-o'-the-wisps, sick in body and soul.[62]

Such impressions were prevalent to some extent within *völkisch* circles before 1914. But the idea of an apocalyptic racial struggle against liberals, Socialists, and Jews made 'conspicuously little headway in Münich and Bavaria until war, revolution, the Münich Soviets, and the killing of the hostages provided the festering soil for them to grow in'. Only in the wake of the First World War and ensuing left-wing revolutions did 'violent racist anti-Semitism become "popular" in Bavaria, only then could Münich become the logical centre for national socialism'.[63]

On 8 November 1918 – the day Eisner declared his Socialist Republic in Bavaria – Sebottendorff called a meeting of the Thule Society. 'Yesterday we experienced the collapse of everything which was familiar, dear and valuable to us', he explained. 'In the place of our princes of Germanic blood rules our deadly enemy: Judah. What will come of this chaos, we do not know yet. But we can guess. A time will come of struggle, the most bitter need, a time of danger . . . As long as I hold the iron hammer [a reference to his Master's hammer], I am determined to pledge the Thule to this struggle.'[64]

If there was any doubt about the Thule Society's political purpose before 8 November 1918, its future path was now clear. The Society could no longer afford to sit idly by in the Four Seasons hotel, discussing Germanic runes and divining rods. To reverse the consequences of the country's defeat and restore a racially pure German Empire, the Society would need to take up arms against 'Juda'.[65] They would soon be accompanied in this mission by a young Austrian corporal, who returned to his adopted home of Munich barely two weeks after Sebottendorff's declaration of war: Adolf Hitler.

From the Thule Society to the NSDAP

In late-November 1918 the new centre-left government of Social Democrats, Catholic Centrists, and Liberal Democrats faced a nearly impossible situation. They were bedevilled by extremist opposition on the far left and right. They also faced a situation of widespread starvation, an influenza epidemic claiming hundreds of thousands of lives, and millions of decommissioned soldiers streaming back to Germany to find their homes, families, or livelihoods destroyed. Forced to take extreme measures to defend the Republic, the provisional Weimar government made two fateful decisions. The first helped ensure that the Thule Society would evolve into the incipient German Workers' Party (DAP). The second facilitated Hitler coming into contact with this party a few months later.

The first decision was made by Gustav Noske, Socialist Minister of Military Affairs, who founded the paramilitary 'Free Corps' (Freikorps) in January 1919. The Freikorps enlisted bands of decommissioned soldiers to combat the far left on behalf of the Republic. Those who joined Noske's paramilitary most enthusiastically were rabid *völkisch*-nationalists, some of whom were too young to see much action during the war.[66] Among the roving bands of Freikorps that Noske deputized was Rudolf von Sebottendorff's *Kampfbund* ('Fighting Association'), later renamed the *Freikorps Oberland*, a breeding ground for future Nazis.[67]

The second fateful decision occurred a few weeks later, when the German Army or *Reichswehr* appointed Hitler to be his company's government liaison (*Vertrauensleute*). By enlisting Hitler to convey 'educational material to the troops' and work as an 'anti-Bolshevist' informant, charged with infiltrating radical parties in Bavaria, the *Reichswehr* gave the politically inexperienced Hitler the keys to the proverbial hen house.[68] As Sebottendorff put it, 'Even in the Social Democratic Party, especially the Bavarian branch, one could see many signs of the emerging realization that the [Jews], the racially foreign elements, bore the greatest responsibility for the whole "swine pen".'[69] It was in this politically radicalized, militarized, and hyper-nationalist environment that Hitler first came into contact with the German Workers' Party.

The Emergence of the DAP

Beginning in November 1918, Sebottendorff and his Thule colleagues began conspiring against the Bavarian Republic. In December the Thule Society devised a plan to kidnap Eisner. It failed miserably. So did a scheme to infiltrate the civilian militia for counter-revolutionary aims. The latter plan resulted in the arrest of multiple Thule members and public denunciation in the regional parliament.[70] By March 1919 the Thule Society was under constant surveillance. In order to avoid arrest Sebottendorff had to resort to dissembling and tips from contacts in the Bavarian police.[71]

One particular incident provides insight into the Thule Society's approach to political action. It occurred when Bavaria's Socialist Police Commissioner visited the Thule headquarters in search of 'anti-Semitic propaganda'. Alerted the night before by a sympathetic official, Sebottendorff urged all the women

members to assemble the following morning for a 'choral hour'. When the
police commissioner arrived he was greeting by Countess Heila von Westarp,
the Thule Society secretary, leading a number of other women in singing a
nationalist hymn. Puzzled, the police commissioner, according to Sebottendorff,
asked 'What kind of association is this?', to which Sebottendorff replied, 'This is
an association for the elite breeding [*Höherzüchtung*] of the Germanic race.'
Nonplussed, the police commissioner pressed him with 'Yes, but what are you
really up to?', to which Sebottendorff replied, 'You can hear it, we are singers.'[72]

Frustrated at Sebottendorff's dissembling, the police commissioner insisted
on continuing with a house search for anti-Semitic propaganda. Sebottendorff's
response is chilling, 'If you . . . arrest me or one of my people . . . then my people
will nab a Jew, wherever they find one, and drag him through the streets and
insist that he has stolen the [Christian] Host. Then, Herr Police President, you
will have a pogrom on your hands that will sweep you aside as well.'[73]

Indeed, during the first few months of 1919, Sebottendorff employed the
Munich Observer to publish a constant barrage of anti-Bolshevik and anti-
Semitic propaganda meant to undermine Eisner's Republic. The *Observer*
carried dozens of articles on how the 'Jew Eisner' and representatives of 'Israel
in Germany' were attempting to destroy the German race through 'Russian
Bolshevism' and 'Bolshevist Education'. Needless to say, these articles received
considerable attention from local republican authorities and caused a temporary ban of the *Observer* in early April 1919.[74]

Sebottendorff's focus was not on building a party organization in the
interest of achieving power. It was to overthrow the Socialist government
through violent counter-revolution – a pattern Hitler would follow four years
later in his Beer Hall Putsch (9 November 1923). The most sensational of these
plots, developed by Sebottendorff only days after the regime banned the
Observer, was a coup d'état against the Bavarian Soviet Republic. Its planning
and outcome are eerily similar to Hitler's Beer Hall Putsch. Thinking that he
could rally all nationalist forces in Munich against Eisner, Sebottendorff
approached local militia in an effort to raise a 6,000-man army, take Munich by
surprise, and arrest the Communist authorities – all in the course of twenty-
four hours.[75]

Before Sebottendorff's ill-conceived putsch could be initiated, the Bavarian
'Red Army' uncovered the plot. Seven conspirators, including Nauhaus and
Countess Westarp, were arrested and summarily executed. The murder of these
seven 'hostages' burnished the Thule Society's reputation in radical nationalist
circles, much as the Beer Hall Putsch raised the profile of the NSDAP. But
unlike Hitler, who used his trial as a national platform, Sebottendorff found
himself discredited in *völkisch* circles, blamed for leaking the names of the
conspirators.[76]

After these strategic blunders and lost opportunities, Sebottendorff's role in the Thule Society and the *Bund Oberland* diminished.[77] He was clearly not the right individual to translate the völkisch-esoteric ideas that defined the pre-war German Order into a mass political movement. Nor was the bourgeois, conspiratorial Thule Society the appropriate vehicle for such a movement.

The first of Sebottendorff's colleagues to recognize the need for an independent party-political counterpart to the Thule Society was Karl Harrer. In October 1918, as we have seen, Harrer co-founded a 'political workers' circle' with the railroad locksmith, Anton Drexler. Its goal was to attract nationalist members of the labouring classes to the *völkisch* movement. Two months later, on 5 January 1919, Drexler joined with Harrer, the economist Gottfried Feder, and the right-wing poet Dietrich Eckart to form the German Workers' Party (DAP).[78]

From the beginning, there were subtle differences between the occult-inspired Thule Society and the nascent DAP. The Thule Society, similar to the German Order, represented a largely bourgeois constituency, which had the leisure time and means to spend afternoons listening to lectures on Germanic runes, astrology, and divining rods. The DAP, on the other hand, was more lower middle and working class in composition. It met not in the upscale Four Seasons hotel, but in a local tavern. In terms of political strategy, the DAP was also more pragmatic than the Thule Society, focusing on building a party as opposed to fomenting revolution.[79]

Despite these differences, it is hard to imagine the development of the early DAP without its Thule foundations. The DAP braintrust, including Harrer, Drexler, Eckart, Feder, Alfred Rosenberg, Hans Frank, and Rudolf Hess, were all Thule members or associates. Harrer was the editor of the *Munich Observer*. Friedrich Krohn, another Thule member, would go on to design the swastika flag for Hitler.[80]

To be sure, the *Munich Observer* was initially sympathetic to the German Socialist Party (*Deutschsozialistische Partei* or DSP), which was created by Sebottendorff in May 1919 as an alternative to the DAP.[81] In August 1919, however (as noted earlier), the paper changed its name to the *Racial Observer* (*Völkischer Beobachter* or VB), and moved its offices to Franz Eher Verlag, the official Nazi publisher.[82] Within a few weeks – coincident with Hitler joining the party – the VB would start reporting regularly on the DAP.

Hence the 'Thule Society', in the words of Richard Evans, 'would prove to be a major staging-post for many later leading Nazi activists on their way to commitment to Hitler and his movement'.[83] As Sebottendorff recalled with only slight embellishment, 'Apart from the Thule itself, the future Führer's armoury consisted of the *Deutsche Arbeiter Verein* [DAP], which was founded in the Thule Society by Brother Karl Harrer, also the Deutsch-Sozialistische

Partei, which was led by Hans George Grassinger, and whose official organ was the *Völkischer Beobachter*.[84] Without Sebottendorff's Thule Society, without Harrer's Political Workers' Circle, and without the infamous newspaper they purchased to promote their worldviews, the Nazi Party would almost certainly not have been born.[85]

The DAP also inherited the Thule Society's rabid anti-Semitism and anti-Communism, fanatical hatred of democracy, and dedication to overthrowing the Republic. The 'angry nationalists and wounded veterans' who joined the DAP looked 'down with contempt on a civilian society, that was trapped in a life of mere surface events, unable to share the soldier's quasi-religious experiences of transcendence and eternity'.[86] In the middle of this *völkisch*-esoteric cosmology emerged the 'fantasy figure of a saviour … [who] acted as a kind of psychological linchpin holding together the radical nationalist's character armour'.[87] After many false messiahs, from List and Fritsch to Sebottendorff, the DAP would now find their 'saviour'.

Hitler Takes the Reins

The DAP's distancing from the Thule Society was never a clean break. Conditioned by changing political circumstances, the DAP's evolution out of the Thule Society was just as organic as the Society's emergence from Fritsch's German Order before it.[88] The 'professional' astrologer and pendulum dowser Sebottendorff may have been out. But the amateur astrologer and pendulum dowser, Wilhelm Gutberlet, was now in. A Munich doctor, Gutberlet was an 8.5 per cent share-holder of the *Völkischer Beobachter* and one of the DAP's most important finan-ciers. He was present at the first DAP meeting that Hitler attended in September 1919. A quarter-century later, Gutberlet was still active in the NSDAP – invited by the Nazi intelligence chief, Walter Schellenberg, to consult on the viability of employing astrology and divining in wartime intelligence.[89]

The point is that Nauhaus and Sebottendorff's interest in Ario-Germanic religion, occultism and border science far outlived the Thule Society's associa-tion with the DAP.[90] Moreover, virtually all the early DAP leaders – including Drexler, Harrer, Eckart, Hess, Rosenberg, and Frank – expressed interest in Ario-Germanic religion, occultism, and/or border science.[91] It was not the DAP's embarrassment about the Society's supernatural proclivities that explains Sebottendorff's marginalization. It was his amateurish approach to politics and his decision in May 1919 to found the rival German Socialist Party (which had virtually an identical programme and therefore merged with Hitler's NSDAP a couple of years later).[92]

But for the time being, the DAP was only one small party among dozens of *völkisch* organizations. It required another element in order to become a national movement, a charismatic leader. On 12 September 1919 Eckart was slated to give a speech at a meeting of the DAP. Having fallen ill, he was replaced at the last minute by another Thule Society member and DAP co-founder, Gottfried Feder, whose penchant for colourful, anti-Semitic tirades against 'Mammonism' and 'interest slavery' made him extremely popular in *völkisch* circles.

It so happens that Hitler, in his capacity as an inspector for the *Reichswehr*, decided to attend this meeting. He was not particularly impressed by Feder's speech and was leaving the meeting when another DAP member made a plea for Bavaria to secede from the Reich. As a young Austrian who fantasized his entire life about a Greater German Reich, Hitler was incensed. He responded with an impassioned speech in favour of pan-Germanic racial unity that clearly won the day. Impressed by Hitler's impromptu intervention, Drexler provided him with some political literature and asked him to join the party.[93]

Shortly thereafter the *VB* reported on a meeting of the DAP for the first time, including a speech by one 'Herr Hitler' attacking the Jews. By early 1920 it became clear that the *VB* was paying increasing attention to the newly christened National Socialist German Workers' Party (*Nationalsozialistische Deutsche Arbeiterpartei* or NSDAP) and its rising star, Adolf Hitler.[94]

Given Hitler's dismissive comments about '*völkisch* wandering scholars', it is tempting to assume that subsequent changes in the NSDAP party organization had to do with purging its occultist elements. And yet the intra-party conflicts that emerged after Hitler took the reins had relatively little to do with occultism or paganism. They had to do with the widespread conviction that the DAP had attracted people who, due to their elitist background and preference for abstruse discussion groups, were ill-equipped to achieve power.[95]

This tension between the culture of an esoteric discussion group and creating a mass political organization was endemic to the *völkisch* movement before the DAP's break from the Thule Society.[96] It was inherent in the failure of the Wilhelmine anti-Semitic parties as well as the marginal political influence of the Armanen, List Society, and German Order/Hammer Association. Sebottendorff cited these tensions in his own decision to create a political successor organization to the Walvater chapter of the German Order. As everyone from Drexler and Harrer to Hitler and Goebbels lamented but could not immediately resolve, it was petty infighting among *völkisch* groups that prevented Germans from coming together against Jews and Communists.[97]

Such political and strategic tensions played out in the pages and editorial meetings of the *Völkischer Beobachter*. For eight months the *VB*, under Harrer's redaction, tried to avoid favouring the DAP exclusively over the DSP.[98] But in the spring of 1920, Hitler forced Harrer out and insisted that the *VB* devote its attention to the NSDAP.[99] At the end of 1920, Hitler sought to purchase the

Völkischer Beobachter for the exclusive use of the NSDAP. Decisive here was the role of Hitler's friend, the paramilitary leader Ernst Röhm, himself a devotee of astrology. Convinced that Hitler was the right man for the job, Röhm encouraged his commanding officer, Ritter von Epp, to purchase the *VB* as a vehicle for Hitler and the NSDAP.[100]

Eckart and Rosenberg – both Thule Society members with esoteric leanings – took over the running of the *VB* and the party's propaganda activities.[101] This transition from the relatively pragmatic Harrer to the pagan religious dilettante Rosenberg and *völkisch* mystic Eckart can hardly be seen as a break with supernatural thinking. It was part of the continuing political evolution of the DAP, including Hitler's growing dominance within the wider *völkisch* movement.[102]

By 1922 the NSDAP had absorbed Sebottendorff's German Socialist Party (DSP) as well as the Thule-affiliated paramilitary *Bund Oberland*.[103] Included in this merger were a number of 'völkisch wandering scholars'. Among them were the old Wilhelmine anti-Semitic leaders, Ernst von Reventlow, who would help lead the pagan German Faith movement after 1933, and Theodor Fritsch, whose iconic status would be immortalized in numerous party schools and street names in the Third Reich.[104] Also abandoning the DSP for the Nazis was Julius Streicher, who claimed to possess the rare 'power' to 'smell' Jews from many metres away. The NSDAP attracted Artur Dinter as well, whose radically anti-Semitic, superstition-fuelled fantasy novel, *The Sin Against the Blood* (1917), sold hundreds of thousands of copies.[105] To these prominent *völkisch* leaders we need to add the paganists Hugo Christoph Heinrich Meyer, Ernst Hunkel, and Ernst Freiherr von Wolzogen, as well as prominent ariosophists such as Johannes Dingfelder, Franz Schrönghamer-Heimdal, Hermann Wirth, and Frenzolf Schmid.[106]

Given this growing stable of *völkisch*-esotericists, it is no wonder that the *VB* continued to feature articles by Ario-Germanic paganists and ariosophists well after Harrer's departure. Such articles were peppered with concepts such as 'Tschandalen', 'Halgadome' (a sacred place), 'the church of Wotan or the Armanen', 'racial soul', and 'Aryan religions of light'.[107] In December 1920, the NSDAP co-sponsored a pagan winter solstice festival that 'publicly proclaimed its link to the *völkisch* ideas of Guido von List'. The terrible crisis of the early years of the Republic, reported the *VB*, had been 'prophesied' in 'the Edda and the teachings of the Armanen'. The report concluded that one 'day more happy times will come for the Aryan race – a new Idafeld'.[108] In the summer of 1921 the NSDAP sponsored another solstice festival, replete with nods to 'Baldur, the sun-god' and the 'sun-hero and son of god Siegfried'.[109] Again in 1922 we find a pagan Nazi Christmas celebration, a 'Yule festival', accompanied by an approbatory article by Rosenberg.[110]

The Nazi battle cry prior to the Beer Hall Putsch of 9 November 1923, as Samuel Koehne reminds us, 'featured concepts derived from Madame Blavatsky and popularized by Theodor Fritsch'. If the Nazi revolution was successful, the party publication argued, the 'horrific Marxist episode, this devilish product, the result of the crossing of Talmudic spirit and materialistic insanity' would vanish 'before the Christian-Germanic worldview, which, in one quick movement, breaks the chains that had been forged when darkness ruled'. 'The eternal struggle between Ormuzd and Ahriman, between light and darkness,' the article continued, 'has once again ended in the victory of the sun, whose symbol is the ancient Aryan sign of salvation: the swastika.'[111] The November 1923 coup failed miserably, to be sure. But the supernatural sentiments and expectations of many party members are clear.

Indicating just how little stake we can put in Hitler's dismissive comments regarding *völkisch* wandering scholars is the fact that he subsequently made Streicher regional party leader (*Gauleiter*) of Lower Saxony and Dinter *Gauleiter* of Thuringia.[112] Streicher would remain a major party leader until the end of the war. Dinter was eventually expelled from the party in 1928. But this was due primarily to his unwillingness to follow Hitler's 'leader principle' (*Führerprinzip*), including the pursuit of independent political alliances and propagation of his specific *völkisch*-esoteric religion.[113]

In showing little tolerance for political or ideological independence, Hitler was no different than Fritsch, Sebottendorff, and other *völkisch*-esotericists. All *völkisch* leaders recognized the need to unite their movement behind one leader.[114] As Sebottendorff later acknowledged, Hitler deserved all the credit for bringing the *völkisch* movement together within the NSDAP. The 'German needed a Führer that admonished him,' Sebottendorff observed, 'to fix his gaze only on the goal and not on the path'.[115] The party did not expel loyal *völkisch*-esotericists so much as convince them to accept a hierarchical, nationally unified, Hitler-centric NSDAP.[116]

A few years after this 'refoundation' of the party in 1925, Goebbels admitted that the NSDAP 'is often accused of losing its character as a movement ... of taking the vast, broad and ever-moving system of thought of the *völkisch* movement and forcing it into a Procrustean bed'. But 'the *völkisch* movement ran aground on this matter,' he continued. 'Each declares his own particular interest central to the *völkisch* movement, and accuses anyone who does not share his views of being a traitor to the cause. That is the way the *völkisch* movement was before the war ... If a *völkisch* organizer had understood how to form a great movement – it is a question of life or death for our nation – the *völkisch* idea, not Marxism, would have won.'[117] Hitler and the NSDAP's decision to break with the Thule Society was not primarily related to its occult and border scientific views, Goebbels suggested, but its desultory approach to politics.[118]

Decades after the NSDAP's break from the Thule Society, Nazi 'old fighters' would still lament Hitler's lack of feeling for 'the romantic-based *völkisch* idea'.[119] But Hitler's apparent rejection of *völkisch*-esotericism must 'be seen in light of his conceptualization of the party as a "movement" that rejected the old conspiratorial approach epitomized by groups like the Thule Society'.[120] The 'period from 1920 to 1923 was a distinct era in the life of the Nazi Party, an era during which it transformed itself from a small and obscure organization – which Adolf Hitler described as a "tea club" – into a revolutionary movement'. Although abandoning the 'tea club' approach to politics, the Nazis remained 'closely connected to their roots in the *völkisch* movement'.[121]

The Nazi Supernatural Imaginary

The first four years of the Weimar Republic – the formative years of the Nazi Party – were a time of rampant political terror, paranoia, and revolution. From the wave of left-wing uprisings in early 1919 to the right-wing Kapp Putsch in March 1920 and Hitler's Beer Hall Putsch in November 1923, paramilitary radicals fought each other in the streets, assassinating politicians and staging violent anti-government actions. All across Germany families were struggling to come to terms with millions of dead and wounded. Then, in response to the Weimar government's default on reparation payments, French and Belgian troops occupied Germany's industrial heartland, the Ruhr valley. The Ruhr occupation initiated a bout of hyperinflation in January 1923 that left millions of Germans impoverished.

Among right-wing groups much of this violence and crisis was perceived in supernatural fashion. The Saxon communist and revolutionary Max Hoelz, for example, led two violent insurrections in 1919 and 1920, escaped capture and eventually disappeared across the Czechoslovak border. But stories of Hoelz, who was referred to as 'the invisible one . . . the evil spirit', continued to circulate among his *völkisch* and right-wing opponents in Saxony. Even the local police talked of the 'phantasmagoria' associated with Hoelz's superhuman actions, which suggests the importance of supernatural thinking in framing right-wing political views.[122]

The popular response to Hoelz in Saxony – the home base of Fritsch's German Order – is merely one example of the sociopolitical currency and spread of supernatural motifs 'at the peak of the inflation and during the subsequent period of upheaval'.[123] These elements, as we have seen, were present across Germany and Austria in some form for decades. But they gained popular momentum in the wake of war and revolution, exemplified by the right-wing paranoia surrounding Hoelz.[124] The Nazi Party emerged from this same '*völkisch* subculture' whence 'neither paganism nor the esoteric was excluded'.[125]

As the German journalist Konrad Heiden observed, National Socialism incorporated elements of 'every kind of political theory, from the most reactionary monarchism to pure anarchy, from unrestricted individualism to the most impersonal and rigid Socialism'.[126] The only thing consistent was Nazism's rejection of liberal and materialist 'notions of objectivity or of causality ... a world in which causal links work themselves out independently of transcendent forces'.[127] After breaking with the Thule Society, the NSDAP developed a malleable discourse that drew on elements of pre-war occultism, paganism, and border science but was also ideologically eclectic and politically accessible – what I call the Nazi supernatural imaginary.

Supernatural Thinking in the Early Nazi Party

On his deathbed in 1923 Dietrich Eckart is supposed to have said, Hitler 'will dance, but it is I who will call the tune'.[128] Apocryphal or not, this story was widely circulated. For Eckart was one of the most important early influences on Hitler and a model for future Nazi leaders. In his periodical, *Auf Gut Deutsch*, Eckart combined a keen intellect and pragmatic approach to politics with a genuine enthusiasm for Nordic folklore and the mystical roots of Germanic religion.[129] In articles such as 'The Midgard Serpent' and 'Jewry über alles', Eckart propagated ariosophic principles and fantastical theories about the 'blood-sucking caste' of 'Jewish wire pullers', with Hitler as both his muse and acolyte.[130]

Eckart was a strong believer in the power of religion and mythology as an ideological tool.[131] In early conversations with Hitler, he frequently invoked the Manichean, dualistic role of good and evil, God and the (Jewish) Devil – a quasi-Christian, quasi-pagan Gnosticism typical of ariosophy and later Nazi approaches to religion.[132] Eckart argued, echoing Lagarde and Chamberlain, that the racially superior 'Indo-European people' had been corrupted by the 'Jewish desert spirit' embedded in mainstream Christianity.[133] 'Diametrically opposed' to Christianity was 'the wisdom of India', which moved beyond nature to recognize the connectivity of everything to the 'world soul'.[134] Here Eckart provided Hitler with a crash course in Indo-Aryan mysticism and *völkisch-esoteric* religion not dissimilar from the Armanism of List and Lanz.[135]

Alfred Rosenberg helped synthesize Eckart's 'völkisch-redemptive views of German spiritual and racial superiority' with 'conspiratorial-apocalyptic ... conceptions of international Jewry as a malevolent force that strove for world domination through dastardly means'.[136] In his most important work, *The Myth of the Twentieth Century*, Rosenberg introduced an eclectic mix of border scientific racism and Indo-Germanic paganism into the Nazi supernatural imaginary.[137] Echoing the ariosophists and Ario-Germanic religionists, Rosenberg claimed that ancient Aryans from northwest India and Persia had founded all the great civilizations before declining due to intermingling with lesser races and the deleterious influence of Judeo-Christianity.[138]

According to Rosenberg, the new mythology of the twentieth century 'is the myth of the blood, which under the sign of the Swastika, released the world revolution. It is the awakening of the soul of the race.'[139] Rosenberg was keen on pushing this biomystical concept of the 'racial soul' as the motor of world history. But he was careful to avoid privileging any particular religious doctrine.[140] In appealing to the German longing for myth, Rosenberg believed the NSDAP must draw on a variety of Ario-Germanic religious and *völkisch*-esoteric traditions.[141] The redemptive 'myth of the blood' and idea of 'awakening the soul of the race' anew was popular across the post-war *völkisch* milieu.[142] But no party took more seriously the 'holy sacrifice' of dead soldiers or made greater efforts to redeem their deaths, reflecting the NSDAP's 'cosmological impulse ... [to] remake the world on wholly new terms'.[143]

Through the National Socialist movement, wrote the Nazi labour leader Robert Ley, the living and the dead 'have found the road to eternity.'[144] Nazi fellow travellers published books that 'illustrated more than 700 "shrines of honour" [*Ehrenhaine*]'. These dead were 'not really dead ... but climb out of their graves at night and visit us in our dreams'.[145] In this way the Nazis adopted 'the two million German dead, who had entered into the Valhalla of the race-soul'. By claiming to represent undead soldiers, the Nazis appeared more in tune than traditional conservatives with the mystical 'race-soul' shared by living and dead soldiers alike.[146]

Invoking the living or undead could also be used negatively. Hitler, Himmler, Rosenberg, and other early Nazi leaders refer frequently to monsters – demons, devils, vampires, mummies, and other supernatural tropes – in articulating their views. In criticizing Communism, for example, Hitler declares 'the original founders of this plague of nations must have been veritable devils; for only within the brain of a monster – not that of man – could the plan of an organization assume form and meaning'. One 'cannot drive out the Devil with Beelzebub', Hitler explained elsewhere. Fighting Jews and Communists meant developing a hostile attitude toward the Soviet Union and avoiding bourgeois political meetings 'as the devil [avoids] holy water'.[147] Feder blamed the Weimar Republic for turning Germans 'into zombies'.[148] For their part, Rosenberg, Himmler, and Hitler repeatedly associated Jews with demons and vampires.[149] This brings us back to the Nazis' mystical obsession with the 'transformative power passed from generation to generation through blood'.[150] For the Nazis, German soil was 'soaked in the unforgettable, heroic blood of the martyrs', whether they had fallen in the First World War or were party members during its early 'times of struggle'. As one Nazi poet put it, the German soil was still 'alive' with 'the blood of the dead'.[151] We see this biomystical preoccupation with blood, in a positive sense, in Rosenberg's *Myth of the Twentieth Century*. Conversely, it is expressed in negative terms in Artur Dinter's supernatural fantasies about Jewish corruption in *The Sin Against the Blood.*

Before dismissing these supernatural tropes as purely rhetorical in nature, we must recall the degree to which high-ranking Nazis *subscribed* to occult and border scientific doctrines. Born and educated partly in Egypt, Rudolf Hess returned to Germany as a teenager and volunteered in the First World War. After the war, Hitler's future Deputy Führer went to Munich to study history and geopolitics under Karl Haushofer, whose border scientific approach to geopolitics we noted in Chapter One.[152] Galvanized by the experience of war, defeat, and revolution, Hess was drawn to the Thule Society in early 1919.[153] Although he broke with the Society because of his devotion to Hitler, Hess never relinquished his interest in *völkisch*-esotericism.[154] He continued to sponsor astrology, anthroposophy, Buddhism, Hinduism, and Tibetan mysticism, even consulting an astrologer before his infamous flight to England in May 1941.[155]

Born in Munich, Heinrich Himmler was training as an agricultural assistant at a chemical factory when he met the SA leader Ernst Röhm in 1922. Joining the Nazi Party in August 1923, Himmler quickly rose through the ranks, becoming a part of Hitler's inner circle.[156] As a young adult, Himmler devoured the works of Theodor Fritsch, about whom he said, 'One suddenly begins to understand things that one couldn't grasp as a child about what quite a lot of biblical stories are worth ... the terrible scourge and danger of religion by which we are being suffocated'.[157] By 'religion', of course, Himmler meant Christianity, which, according to Fritsch and other ariosophists, had attempted to replace the Edda and the *Nibelungenlied*, 'the magical world of Thor, Freya, Loki, and other Norse divinities'.[158] Himmler invested heavily in Eastern religion and esotericism as well, carrying around with him, alongside the Edda, the Vedas and *Bhagavad Gita*, and the speeches of Buddha.[159]

Besides Nordic paganism and Eastern religions, Himmler read widely in border scientific areas that in his view, dealt with occult phenomena in a serious 'scholarly' way; for example, a book about 'Astrology, Hypnosis, Spiritualism, Telepathy', and monographs on pendulum dowsing. He also studied the 'transmigration of souls' and believed that 'it was possible to communicate with the souls of the dead'.[160] Himmler was fascinated by the freemasons and the history of secret Orders, which he drew upon in developing the SS.[161] By 1923 Himmler had 'developed a coherent voelkisch vision, involving ... occult beliefs and Germanophile enthusiasms; from these elements arose an ideology that was a mixture of political utopia, romantic dream world, and substitute religion'.[162]

The supernatural imaginary of Himmler and other Nazis included a fascination with werewolves. According to one of Alfred Rosenberg's subordinates, unlike in France or the Slavic East, where werewolves were associated with 'witchcraft and the power of the devil', werewolves played a largely positive role in pagan German tradition.[163] Even in present-day Germany, Rosenberg's associate argued, there are many cases of 'the good werewolf' who accompany 'evening wanderers' in Westphalia and protect the homes of peasants against the common 'wood wolves' in East Prussia.[164] Alongside the Germanic folklore revival, the 'uncanny word [werwolf] was resuscitated in Germany' by Hermann Löns' revenge fantasy, The Werwolf, which was read almost as widely in the interwar period as Dinter's The Sin of the Blood.[165]

Werewolf-inspired revenge fantasies found their most concrete political and intellectual expression in Fritz Kloppe's paramilitary Organisation Wehrwolf. Founded in early 1923, in response to the French occupation of the Ruhr, the Wehrwolf fashioned themselves as a 'dreaded … pack of wolves hunting down their victims in the dark of the night; and that is exactly what these counter-revolutionary conspirators did.'[166] As one Wehrwolf pamphlet explained: 'Why do we fight? Quite simply because so much Nordic blood pulses through us that we cannot live without fighting.' The 'contemporary church can no longer meet the spiritual needs of the people', the Wehrwolf pamphlet continued. Only 'we, the racial-bundish movement, we the werewolves, will clarify and shape … the articles of faith of the coming time.'[167]

The Wehrwolf's broad investment in border scientific racial theories and völkisch religion was reinforced by Kloppe's interest in J. W. Hauer's German Faith movement as well as the ariosophic writings of the 'Atlantis' scholar and future SS leader, Hermann Wirth, and the rune researcher, Siegfried Kummer.[168] The Wehrwolf likewise developed ties to Field Marshall Erich Ludendorff's esoterically inclined Tannenberg Association and the Thule-inspired Bund Oberland. Kloppe even set up a Jung Wehrwolf division for youths under seventeen, replete with 'Death's Head' insignia (later appropriated by the SS).[169]

'The Wehrwolf stands on racialist soil', Himmler wrote in July 1924. 'It desires from every member or new initiate the unconditional commitment to patriotic and racialist [völkischen] Germanness.'[170] Due to the Wehrwolf's constant surveillance by the Weimar police – which the NSDAP could ill afford in the wake of Hitler's arrest following the Beer Hall Putsch – Himmler was afraid to join Kloppe.[171] But the future SA Chief and Nazi Police Commissioner of Berlin, the appropriately named Wolf Graf von Helldorff, did become a Wehrwolf leader.[172] Helldorff and Ernst Röhm, both immersed in völkisch-esoteric doctrines, were merely two of the most important Nazi leaders among the 'patriotic paramilitary associations', eventually bringing thousands of their 'Werewolf' and other völkisch groups into the ranks of the Brownshirts or stormtroopers (SA).[173]

Early Nazi leaders found additional inspiration for their supernatural musings on race and space in the interwar Artamanen movement.[174] The

Artamanen was a racist and imperialist organization founded in 1924 by August Georg Kenstler, an ethnic German emigré from, of all places, Transylvania, and a future Nazi. The Artamanen's overarching goal was to restore German racial and territorial superiority in eastern Europe by obtaining 'living space' and creating 'eastern settlements'.[175] In 1926 the Artamanen had approximately six hundred members working on sixty farms, mostly in eastern Germany. Four years later they had nearly two thousand members working on three hundred farms.[176]

Beyond the practical goal of eastern expansion, the Artamanen propagated 'esoteric preconceptions' and 'ariosophic and theosophic ideas' that defined many Nazis' views on race and space.[177] Echoing the life-reform movement, the Artamanen sought to create 'a community of young, racially conscious' men and women 'who wanted to remove themselves from the unhealthy, destructive and superficial life of the cities . . . [and] return to a healthy, hard but natural lifestyle in the countryside. They abjured alcohol and nicotine, indeed every-thing that did not serve the healthy development of the mind and body'.[178] They staged night-time celebrations involving 'fire- and sword play', employed ancient Germanic runes, and paraded the swastika as a holy 'symbol of the sun' and 'Germanic holy symbol of German divinity, blood purity and spirit'.[179]

In a negative sense, the Artamanen combined 'anti-Slavicism, anti-urbanism' and 'anti-Polish xenophobia' with an extreme anti-Semitism.[180] Emulating the ariosophists, the Artamanen warned against the dangers of race-mixing, in which the 'un-Nordic part of the blood resurfaces ever again in its attempt to attack the Nordic man'.[181] In this *völkisch* cosmology, the Jew appeared as the monstrous 'symbol of the corrupt city', vampiric parasites that grew on the racial body like a tumour and must be removed in the same way.[182]

The Artamanen helped pave the way for the fundamental principles of the 'National Socialist faith' and the organizational foundations for eastern settle-ment work.[183] Himmler joined the Artamanen and became Gauführer of Bavaria in the mid-1920s, where he met a number of other future Nazi leaders, including Alfred Rosenberg, the SS official Wolfram Sievers, the Nazi Youth Leader Baldur von Schirach (who used Artamanen runes in Hitler Youth cere-monies), and Rudolf Höss, whom Himmler later named Commandant of Auschwitz.[184] It was also through the Artamanen that Himmler met Walther Darré, the future chief of the SS Race and Settlement Office (RuSHA).[185]

As a young man Darré had been immersed in the Austro-German super-natural milieu, reading Langbehn's *Rembrandt as Educator* and Rudolf Steiner's anthroposophic works with alacrity.[186] Darré was also positively inclined toward Eastern religions and the 'Irminglauben' (Armanist religion) made popular by List and Liebenfels.[187] According to Darré, Nordic Germans had to reject Christianity because it failed to 'recognize blood and race . . . [Only] Folk tales and myths, seldom written down, but passed from the wise to the faithful, kept the Ur-faith in the Ur-mother awake.'[188]

In a series of books and pamphlets published throughout the interwar period, Darré elevated the mystical idea of blood and soil to a kind of ersatz religion.[189] Through Darré, German territory was reconceived, in the words of one Nazi poet, as the 'mother-soil for the mystic "folk" ... the living and the dead', an 'eternally fruitful womb' that 'suckles [Germany] from an unending source'.[190] 'Lost, uprooted from you, I lie fallow', the poem continued, 'I am coming home, o Mother, take me back again/At that the stream of old blood was awakened ... And from clods torn out of the earth's heart/The blood broke free, hotly, and foamed with fruit and deed ... And flying red, the flag of the new seed ... Thus the new Reich grew from blood and soil.'[191] Through the mysticism of blood and soil, Darré insisted, the Nordic idea became 'a light in the darkness of the epoch', a recognition of the 'divine law of preserving and propagating the race'.[192]

As the NSDAP increased in strength, gathering *völkisch* splinter groups under one banner, most members of the Thule Society, the *Wehrwolf*, and the Artamanen were absorbed into the party.[193] During the early to middle years of the Weimar Republic, however, these *völkisch*-esoteric groups functioned as a political and cultural laboratory, entertaining fantasies of racial utopia and eastern colonization and helping to fashion the Nazi supernatural imaginary.[194]

Hitler's Supernatural Imaginary

Hitler may have been less enamoured of traditional occult doctrines than his peers, but his preoccupations with the supernatural were authentic.[195] When he left his home town of Linz for Vienna in 1908, Hitler already possessed a strong appreciation of Norse mythology and Germanic folklore.[196] In Vienna he attended dozens of performances of Wagner's operas, attempting to compose his own opera based on elements drawn from Norse mythology and Goethe's *Faust*.[197] Hitler also encountered the border scientific racial doctrines and anti-Semitic demagogy of Georg von Schönerer and Karl Lueger, a member of the Guido von List Society whom Hitler called the 'greatest German mayor of all time'.[198]

Whether or not he read Lanz von Liebenfels' periodical *Ostara*, Hitler almost certainly consulted ariosophic works at this time. By the end of the First World War he had somehow picked up the 'manichaean comic-book dualism of blonds and darks, heroes and sub-men, Aryans and *Tschandalen*, described in the *Ostara* of Lanz von Liebenfels'.[199] Throughout the 1920s Hitler also referred positively to Langbehn's *Rembrandt as Educator* and Dinter's best-seller, *The Sin Against the Blood*.[200]

These supernatural tastes did not dissipate with age. Hitler's library at

Berchtesgarden, discovered by the 101st Airborne Division in a salt mine in 1945, included almost no works on political theory or philosophy.[201] But Hitler did own many books 'on popular medicine, miraculous healing, cooking, vegetarianism and special diets' and dozens 'about Wotan and the gods of German mythology ... magic symbols and the occult'. Among these volumes were Ernst Schertel's *Magic* and Lanz von Liebenfels' *The Book of German Psalms: The Prayerbook of Ariosophic-Racial Mystics and Anti-Semites*.[202]

Hitler did not hide these influences after he entered politics. In February 1920 he gave a speech that relied openly 'on *völkisch* writers such as Guido von List and Theodor Fritsch'. He began with a gloss on List, arguing that the 'Aryan, during the ice age, engaged in building his spiritual and bodily strength in the hard fight with nature, arising quite differently than other races who lived without struggle in the midst of a bountiful world ... We know that all of these people held one sign in common, the symbol of the sun. All of their cults were built on light, and you can find this symbol, the means of the generation of fire, the Quirl, the cross. You can find this cross as a swastika not only here [in Germany], but also exactly the same [symbol] carved into temple posts in India and Japan. It is the swastika of the community (*Gemeinwesen*) once founded by Aryan culture (*Kultur*).'[203] 'The old beliefs will be brought back to honour again,'[204] Hitler ostensibly told Hermann Rauschning, through 'order castles' where Aryan youths would learn the principles of 'the magnificent, self-ordaining god-man'.[205]

In *Mein Kampf*, Hitler again echoed ariosophy in describing his theories of race and history. 'Human culture and civilization on this continent are inseparably bound up with the presence of the Aryan,' he explained. 'If he dies out or declines, the dark veils of an age without culture will descend on this globe.'[206] Racial miscegenation would lead to 'monstrosities halfway between man and ape,' Hitler asserted, aping Lanz's 'theozoology', while 'the personification of the devil as the symbol of all evil' would assume 'the living shape of the Jew'.[207] 'The Aryan gave up the purity of his blood and, therefore, lost his sojourn in the paradise which he had made for himself,' he argued elsewhere. 'He became submerged in the racial mixture, and gradually ... lost his cultural capacity, until at last, not only mentally but also physically, he began to resemble the subjected aborigines more than his own ancestors ... Blood mixture and the resultant drop in the racial level is the sole cause of the dying out of old cultures.'[208]

Hitler would later remove some comments from *Mein Kampf* that suggested his indebtedness to '*völkisch* wandering scholars' and 'so-called religious reformers'.[209] In self-censoring himself, however, Hitler was not rejecting the 'mystical nationalism of these groups'.[210] Six years after the publication of *Mein Kampf* he still had not dispensed with the mystical, border scientific foundations of his ideology. 'We do not judge by merely artistic or military standards or even by purely scientific ones,' Hitler explained in 1931. 'We judge by the spiritual

energy which a people is capable of putting forth ... I intend to set up a thousand-year Reich and anyone who supports me in battle is a fellow fighter for a
unique spiritual – I would almost say divine – creation. At the decisive moment
the decisive factor is not the ratio of strength but the spiritual force employed.[211]

In tempering his overt references to *völkisch*-esotericism, Hitler was expressing
a desire to differentiate his nascent movement from 'the failed, impotent, often
Germano-maniacal, antiquarian-enthusing old right'.[212] Hitler wanted to fashion
a broader and more inclusive supernatural imaginary, one that extended far
beyond the 'academic, *völkisch*-esotericism of the day'.[213] National Socialism was
for him something greater and more universal; a way of thinking that drew on an
eclectic array of influences, including Indo-Aryan religion and mythology.[214]
That the 'leader of a party, which so strongly emphasized the superiority of
Nordic blood, indeed, that wanted a Germanic rebirth, was preoccupied so extensively with oriental and Asian magic, is hard to understand. But it is nonetheless
a fact'.[215]

Indeed, with respect to perhaps the core element of occultism – magic –
Hitler's fascination was clear. Only recently has it come to light that he probably
read a book on practising 'magic', the parapsychologist Ernst Schertel's 1923
occult masterpiece, *Magic: History, Theory, Practice*.[216] In this book Hitler appears
to have underlined many passages that give us unique insight into his views
about border science, occultism, and 'magical thinking' more generally. In the
first section Hitler underscored the line: 'All men of genius' possessed the ability
to harness 'para-cosmical (demonic) forces', which 'can be combined with a lot of
misery and misfortune but always leads to a consequence with the deepest
meaning'.[217]

Hitler agreed with Schertel that the modern European was preoccupied by
'materialism and rationalism', lacking 'every sense for the deeper meaning' of the
world.[218] Another consequence of the displacement of older magical traditions
with monotheistic religions, according to Hitler (via Schertel), was 'the establishment of an absolute "morality", which was seen as equally applicable for all people'.
Fortunately, the pre-Christian era rejected universal morality in favour of the
'rule of life' given by 'folkish "custom"' and 'the will of the tribal god'. The god or
his vessel on earth could govern in 'utterly autocratic' fashion, 'giving orders at his
discretion' and demanding 'blood and destruction'. Pagan morality, grounded in
magic, had 'nothing to do with "humaneness", "brotherly love", or an abstract
"good"'. The only relevant 'rule of life', Schertel adds in a passage cited by Hitler, is
'limited to the individual nation and this nation conceives it as completely
natural'.[219]

The passages Hitler cited in regard to 'theory' likewise help us to understand
his supernatural imaginary. The 'emerged imagination' (the subconscious),
Schertel explained, might be 'projected onto the outside world and appear as
either hallucination or reality'.[220] The modern man 'resists these insights ... raves

about "empiricism"' and 'rejects all "imaginations"' as hallucination. But he fails to realize, Hitler noted, that 'his empirical worldview, in which he takes great pride, also ultimately rests on imagination', because 'every worldview is built on an imaginative basic-synthesis'.[221] 'The man with the greatest force of imagination,' Hitler underscored, 'is commanding of the world and creates realities according to his will instead of being the slave of an unsubstantial, bodiless empiricism.' Whereas the 'pure empirical man is the entropic type, which leads to the complete devaluation of cosmic energy, the imaginative man instead, the magician, is the actual focus of the ectropic, the renewal of the world, remodelling of the world, [and] the new birth of being'.[222]

After highlighting passages related to the manipulation of cosmic forces, of one's 'god' or 'demon', Hitler picked up on Schertel's assertion that 'Every demonic-magical world is centred towards the great individuals, from whom basic creative conceptions spring. Every magician is surrounded by a force field of para-cosmic energies.' Individuals 'infected' by the magician would henceforth form a 'community' or his 'people' (Volk) and 'create a complex of life of a certain imaginative framework which is called "culture"'.[223] To harness these 'para-cosmic energies', Hitler observed, the 'great individual' needed to make a sacrifice to the *völkisch* community.[224] As we shall see in Chapter Three, Hitler seemed particularly interested in Schertel's passages on 'Practice' – on wielding one's para-cosmic energies, one's 'magic', to manipulate others.[225]

I do not mean to suggest that Hitler had the same unqualified investment in occult and border scientific thinking as Himmler, Hess, or Darré. Hitler's interest in the supernatural was both less doctrinaire and more utilitarian, embedded in 'his conviction that man exists in some kind of magic association with the universe'. Hitler studied occult doctrines because they provided material for his political propaganda and manipulation of the public.[226]

Unlike many Nazis, for example, Hitler expressed relatively little interest in the dangers of freemasonry. But he did admire their 'esoteric doctrine', according to Rauschning, 'imparted through the medium of symbols and mysterious rites in degrees of initiation. The hierarchical organization and the initiation through symbolic rites, that is to say without bothering the brains but by working on the imagination through magic and the symbols of a cult.'[227] Whatever his reservations regarding '*völkisch* wandering scholars', Hitler recognized the power of the supernatural imaginary in appealing both to his party colleagues and ordinary Germans.[228]

***

The political and organizational debt owed by the Nazi Party to the *völkisch*-esoteric movement should not be underestimated. Fritsch's German Order and Hammer Association were themselves populist manifestations of List's

Armanen and Lanz's Order of the New Templar. Hermann Pohl broke away from Fritsch's German Order for the same political and organizational reasons that Sebottendorff later worked to distinguish the Thule Society from Pohl's Walvater Order of the Holy Grail. The DAP's break from the Thule Society was just another step in the evolution of the *völkisch*-esoteric movement from a collection of impotent splinter associations into a mass party capable of drawing support from across the entire social spectrum of the Weimar Republic.

Despite these important transformations, the Thule Society and early Nazi movement shared a supernatural imaginary that transcended the particulars of their internal political and organizational differences.[229] Fritsch, Sebottendorff, and Nauhaus, Eckart, Rosenberg, and Hitler, Himmer, Hess, and Darré were all, to varying degrees, fascinated by Nordic mythology and Germanic paganism, occult doctrines such as ariosophy, and border scientific theories of race ('blood'), space ('soil'), and psychology ('magic').[230]

'Nazism emerged from German culture,' Monica Black reminds us. 'Its repertoire of symbols and images was in many ways rooted in the past.' The 'recasting of old symbols' gave Nazi ideas 'a familiarity that made them seem less revolutionary than prosaic.'[231] As an ideology National Socialism, like fascism more generally, was always 'vague, imprecise, and deliberately left the greatest possible scope for irrational needs. Its followers owed allegiance less to the orthodoxy of a doctrine than to the person of the Führer.' But this lack of clarity in Nazism's 'ideological reference-points has no bearing on the intensity of the emotions called for or aroused.'[232]

If Nazism's supernaturally infused approach to politics alienated liberals and social democrats, it proved attractive to Germans who denied 'objective experience' and disparaged 'reason and intellect in favour of instinct and intuition', unconsciously erasing 'the boundary between fantasy and reality.'[233] Devastated by a lost war, revolution, and a sociopolitical crisis, millions of Germans 'dismissed what was for them an overly complex, difficult, and demoralizing reality and indulged in elaborating fantasies.'[234] Instead of viewing interwar politics 'from a rational perspective', in the words of Peter Fisher, Germans perceived political and historical events 'as part of a state of flux ultimately determined by the supernatural'. Political and social reality was 'transposed to a conceptual realm framed by notions of heaven-inspired retribution and miracles, of collective crucifixion and resurrection.'[235]

In contrast to the mainstream parties that dominated the first decade of the Weimar Republic, the NSDAP drew upon a broader supernatural imaginary which spoke to a diverse social milieu that had lost faith in secular liberalism, traditional Christian conservatism, and Marxist socialism. Like the Germans themselves, many Nazis, living in a society riddled by crisis, increasingly viewed popular aspects of occultism, paganism, and border science as fundamental to negotiating the complexities of modern life.[236] The nascent Nazi Party may have broken from the Thule Society in 1919, but its leaders continued to exploit a shared supernatural imaginary in both eliding and transcending the sociopolitical divisions of Weimar democracy.[237]

EXPLOITING HITLER'S MAGIC
From Weimar's Horrors to Visions of the Third Reich

'Unemployed officers and soldiers, intellectuals, and workers ... [were] the generation in which National Socialism took root. The best of them ... warmed themselves at a fire whose flickering light distorted the gloomy conditions of contemporary Germany. Thus there developed among them ... the "mysticism of a political movement" ... In almost no other land were so many "miracles" performed, so many ghosts conjured, so many illnesses cured by magnetism, so many horoscopes read, between the two World Wars. A veritable mania of superstition had seized the country, and all those who made a living by exploiting human stupidity thought the millennium had come.'
Konrad Heiden (1945)[1]

'The German tends to resort to magic, to some nonsensical belief which he tries to validate by way of hysterics and physical force. Not every German, of course. Not even a majority, but it seems to me that the percentage of people so inclined is higher in Germany than in other countries. It was the willingness of a noticeable proportion of the Germans to rate rhetoric above research and intuition above knowledge, that brought [the Nazis] to power.'
Willy Ley (1947)[2]

In 1945, Konrad Heiden began his preface to the memoirs of Himmler's masseur, Felix Kersten, with a 'peculiar report from the world of these occult sciences'. The report 'asserted that in the early twenties a society of Asiatics, who lived in Paris and were versed in occultism, had decided to destroy European civilization by means of secret forces. For this purpose someone had to be found who was possessed with a demoniacal mania for annihilation ... we will say only that the initials of the great evildoer were A.H.'[3]

Without accepting the veracity of this report, Heiden cites it as an example of Germany's frame of mind in the interwar years. Germans shared a mentality that made them susceptible to a 'man who became their flag and fire', who 'towered above them and illuminated them; who with magic eloquence ... expressed what they thought'. 'The mystic spell that Hitler cast over millions and millions,' Heiden observed, 'has often been compared with hypnotism; and as an analogy that may be apt. At least, mental compliance is a prerequisite to being hypnotized – no matter how hidden that compliance may be.'[4]

Heiden was not alone among Weimar intellectuals in noting Nazism's appeal to mystical or 'demonic' elements in the German collective unconscious, a preoccupation with the macabre that spoke to a generation battered by war, violence, and sociopolitical dislocation. The post-war explosion in supernatural thinking, observed the Weimar sociologist Theodor Adorno, directly facilitated 'fascism, to which [occultism] is connected by thought patterns of the ilk of anti-Semitism'. In her post-war analysis of Weimar film, *The Haunted Screen*, the film critic Lotte Eisner blamed the rise of Nazism on the 'mysticism and magic, the dark forces to which Germans have always been more than willing to commit themselves'. 'German man is the supreme example of demoniac man,' added the philosopher Leopold Ziegler – demoniac in terms of the politico-psychological 'abyss which cannot be filled, the yearning which cannot be assuaged, the thirst which cannot be slaked'.[5]

None of these intellectuals was naive enough to blame ideas alone. The Weimar Republic would not have collapsed without having to face the consequences of millions of battlefield casualties and hundreds of thousands of deaths caused by famine and disease; without the widely detested Versailles Treaty, the destabilizing hyperinflation of 1923 or the Great Depression six years later; without the 'explosive spiritual vacuum' generated by military defeat, the disintegration of the German Empire, and the decline of traditional religion.[6] In short, the Nazis could not have come to power without the remarkable conflation of politico-diplomatic challenges and socioeconomic crises faced by the Weimar Republic between 1918 and 1933.[7]

At the same time we cannot ignore the dynamic nature of Hitler and the Nazi movement. In comparison to other *völkisch* parties with similarly nationalist, illiberal, and anti-Communist programmes, Hitler and the NSDAP were far more effective at the level of grassroots organizing. They were superior when it came to political messaging and utilizing modern propaganda techniques. And they possessed a wild card that trumped all other *völkisch* movements: the political genius and charisma of Adolf Hitler.[8] Certainly we cannot assert that supernatural thinking alone produced the Third Reich.

Despite these important caveats, I want to argue in this chapter that the Third Reich would have been highly improbable without a widespread penchant for supernatural thinking – exacerbated by war and crisis – which Hitler and the Nazi Party rushed to exploit.[9] National Socialism may not have been the first movement to take advantage of people's faith for political purposes. But Hitler's NSDAP was far more effective than other parties in drawing so deliberately on the supernatural imaginary in the interest of achieving power.

Chapter Three elaborates on this argument through three case studies. The first examines Hitler's approach to politics through his reading of Ernst Schertel's 1923 occult treatise, *Magic: History, Theory, Practice*.[10] The second looks at the NSDAP's propaganda collaboration with the horror writer, Hanns Heinz Ewers. The third delves into the relationship between the NSDAP and Weimar's most popular 'magician', Erik Hanussen.

The Occult Public and Hitler's Magic

Ernst Schertel was one of Germany's most prominent esotericists. A student of the historian Rudolf Eucken at Jena, Schertel was also an admirer of the Expressionist poet and 'prophet', Stefan George (to whom Goebbels later offered the presidency of the Third Reich's Academy of Fine Arts).[11] Shortly before the First World War, Schertel embarked on a career as a novelist, weaving in themes such as parapsychology, life reform, and Eastern spirituality. He supported himself as a high-school teacher, whose unconventional methods included staging Asian dance festivals scored by atonal music.[12]

After encouraging his students to explore the 'cultural benefits' of 'man-on-man love', Schertel was dismissed from his teaching position in 1918. But he used the extra time to publish a series of controversial books and articles on everything from parapsychology to homosexuality.[13] With picturesque titles such as *Magic, Flagellation as Literary Motif,* and *The Erotic Complex*, these works drew scrutiny even from the liberal Weimar government. Schertel nonetheless developed personal and professional relationships with a vast range of central European intellectuals, including Jewish liberals like Freud and the sexual reformer Magnus Hirschfeld, as well as *völkisch*-esotericists such as Stefan George.[14]

Given Schertel's background, it is perhaps surprising to learn that Hitler had a copy of *Magic* in his library.[15] The promotion of gay rights, sadomasochism, and world music are areas we tend not to associate with the Führer of the Nazi movement. Yet Schertel's occult proclivities and scandalous public persona hardly discouraged Hitler from reading and annotating *Magic* thoroughly, including thick pencil lines next to passages such as: 'He who does not carry demonic seeds within him will never give birth to a new world.'[16]

In light of what we learned in Chapter Two, Hitler's interest in Schertel's *Magic* makes sense. Schertel's occult primer blended elements of parapsychology and paganism with border scientific musings on race, eugenics and politics – themes already pervasive in Hitler and the NSDAP's supernatural imaginary. Understanding 'magic' was moreover helpful, perhaps indispensable in Hitler's mind, in appealing to Weimar's 'occult public'.[17]

'Even those who find occultism detrimental,' observed one Weimar sceptic, could not dismiss its impact because the 'occult movement of our times has very deep roots in the necessity of a humanity that has become disillusioned with the outside world'.[18] With German society and values profoundly destabilized by dislocation and defeat, the Weimar Public was particularly susceptible to charismatic 'leaders' capable of manipulating supernatural thinking in order to undermine rationalism and democracy.[19] No party leader in this period was better at exploiting magic for political purposes than Hitler.

The Occult Public

In 1940, Gerhard Szczesny submitted a dissertation on occult periodicals to the faculty at the University of Munich. Comparing Germany to other Western countries, Szczesny noted the remarkable size of Germany's 'occult public' in the wake of the First World War. Unlike France or Great Britain 'the continuum from scientific to pseudo-scientific to the popular sphere' was 'more fluid' in Germany.[20] This lack of clear boundaries between science and border science, Szczesny suggested, made Germans more susceptible to occult ideas well before 1914. But the 'period from after the World War to the Nazi seizure of power' required special consideration. The 'general cultural and economic collapse, inflation and the ensuing big political and social crises,' Szczesny averred, 'prepared the way for the occult in its lowest forms and created a whole new genre in terms of [occult] periodicals' drawn from 'the murkiest sources'.[21]

Szczesny was not an outright sceptic. He conceded that pre-war occultism was generally authentic in attempting to address 'humanity's weal and woe' in ways that conventional science and traditional religion could not. But he was profoundly troubled by the proliferation of vulgar, popular occultism in the wake of the First World War, which found a new audience for its 'magical worldview and superstition' by exploiting a German desire for social and spiritual succour and appealing to people's most primitive instincts. 'Almost overnight,' Szczesny wrote, 'occultism has been transformed from an object of scientifically driven research, from a faith-based preoccupation of religiously inclined souls to a petty bourgeois sensationalism of the street, to the most primitive superstition and profane mode.' In searching to convert as many people as possible, occultism had 'reached the broadest spectrum of the masses, but also the lowest level of degradation, becoming a manifestation of decline, a symbol of crisis and mark of Cain for a chaotic time'.[22]

The shock of the war, Szczesny explained, and the 'social and spiritual distress of the years thereafter', pushed 'the average person into the warm arms of the oldest and most primitive of all human illusions of wish fulfillment, [the] exciting, feverish spell of the magical world view and superstition'.[23] As 'ubiquitous corruption and dirty dealing exploded with the final peace' of Versailles, esotericism and border science 'promised to be good for business'. For these doctrines reflected 'perfectly the interweaving of occultism, mysticism, life reform, vegetarianism and all possible other religious, ethical and enthusiastic efforts that were indicative of the entire period and an intellectual historical indication' of Weimar's 'weak and degenerate culture'.[24]

Within a few years, said Szczesny, 'one paper after the other shot out of the ground and displaced the other with still less tasteful global diagnoses and more unabashed revelations of ponderous and infinite wisdom. ... Nearly inexplicable in regard to normal sensibilities in a healthy time is how there could be more than 100,000 copies of such papers, how thousands of people from all social circles and population groups returned every week to the monstrous foolishness and thinking'.[25] Occult papers such as *The Fist of the Masters, The House of Spirits, The Other World,* and *The Vampire* had a significant 'influence on the half-educated youth', helping satisfy their 'unclear thirst for knowledge, hunger for power, and self-centredness'. The occult turned people off from 'the effort of learning real science' and 'legitimate' periodicals, offering 'more comfortable and exciting ways' to obtain 'wisdom and capabilities' with which one could 'master the difficulties of this world'.[26]

Szczesny's diagnosis of this new 'occult *Publicistik*' is remarkably similar to contemporary Nazi, liberal, and socialist appraisals of Weimar's occult public.[27] Except Szczesny probably exaggerates the predominance of the 'half-educated'. After all, even political and military elites such as Field Marshall Erich von Ludendorff, Heiden reminds us, 'tried to produce gold with the assistance of a swindler'. And there was 'scarcely a folly in natural or world history to which the great commander-in-chief did not lend credence'. When the Weimar government had railway crossings painted with republican colours, Ludendorff 'declared that the Jews in the government were doing this because Moses had led the Jews through the desert under these colours'.[28] Another high-ranking general 'was convinced that he possessed the secret of the death ray ... that he could halt airplanes in their flight and stop tanks in their tracks'.[29]

A dizzying array of occult associations and esoteric institutes sprung up to satisfy this demand for border scientific knowledge across all social strata. Those who could not afford to take classes or subscribe to esoteric journals flocked to the thousands of tarot readers, clairvoyants, and astrologers who lined the streets of Berlin and Munich.[30] A steamship company dismissed its managing director because 'his handwriting had displeased a graphologist'.

Motorists avoided a road between Hamburg and Bremen, Heiden observed, because of rumours about 'certain mysterious "terrestrial rays", which provoked one accident after another':

> A miracle worker, who had the faculty of making the dead Bismarck appear during his mass meetings and who healed sickness by application of white cheese, had enough followers to establish a city: another crackpot was almost elected to the Reichstag; and still a third, who also barely missed election, promised to perform the greatest miracle of all by undoing the German inflation ... Among Hitler's intimates was a man on whose visiting card appeared the word 'magician' to indicate his profession [most likely Gutberlet].

'And of course,' Heiden notes, 'many were firmly convinced that the course of world history was the sinister result of the ministrations of ancient secret societies, such as those of the Masons, the Jews, and the Jesuits.'[31]

Mainstream scientists and the traditional 'churches of all denominations raged against this fraudulent "substitute for religion", which, with stupid hocus-pocus, was designed to assuage man's craving for the supernatural and the divine'. But the admonishments of scientists, the mockery of liberal intellectuals, and the metaphysical frustration of the churches proved powerless, Heiden concluded, in the face of so many 'astrologers, quacks, necromancers, and fake radiologists of witchcraft and sorcery ... [who] replied indignantly that they occupied themselves with science – naturally, a science that the "experts" did not understand, for it was the science of the future, perhaps a science predicated on experiments that were still imperfect'.[32]

A crucial factor in energizing this occult public was Weimar's crisis-ridden environment. 'Representatives of all these groups existed in Germany before World War I,' Willy Ley recalls, but only 'began to flourish during World War I.' Occult and border scientific doctrines 'kept flourishing during the inflationary period,' he suggested, 'received a slight setback during the few years of mild prosperity in the twenties, and flourished again during the years leading up to Hitler'.[33] Critical observers such as Heiden and Ley acknowledged that occultism alone could not have destabilized the Republic. It was political and socioeconomic dislocations working hand in hand with supernatural thinking that 'long permeated German political culture', which provided 'an intellectual foundation for the drift to an unreflective, emotionalized politics and a reckless brand of militant nationalism'.[34]

German willingness to surrender to the Nazis, added the Weimar sociologist Siegfried Kracauer, 'was based on emotional fixations rather than on any facing of facts'. Behind the 'overt history of economic shifts, social exigencies and political machinations', he explained, there ran 'a secret history involving the inner dispositions of the German People ... [which] may help in the under-standing of Hitler's ascent and ascendancy'.[35] Nor was the 'paralysis of mind' spreading throughout Germany between 1924 and 1929 'specifically German'. Under similar circumstances a similar 'collective paralysis' might occur else-where. But the fact that it *could* happen elsewhere, Kracauer insisted, did not mean that scholars should dismiss the unique interplay, in interwar Germany, between sociopolitical crisis and supernatural thinking. These two factors working in concert, Kracauer concluded, had 'something important to say about the larger socio-cultural context that produced some of the most egre-gious crimes of the twentieth century'.[36]

A central feature of interwar occultism that brings together mass politics and Hitler's reading of Schertel's *Magic* is parapsychology.[37] The main purpose of modern parapsychology, according to the *Journal of Critical Occultism*, was to investigate 'the relationship of religious-mystical ideas to ... human beings living in the natural world' as well as 'border questions regarding the life of the soul [*Grenzfragen des Seelenlebens*]', namely the interaction of the subconscious or unconscious with the the conscious self.[38]

Less critical parapsychologists went a step further, accepting the existence of 'magic' and its power to influence the subconscious of others. What they debated was the methodology for confirming magical phenomena.[39] Although both critical and uncritical occultists attempted to discredit each other's claims, both agreed on the remarkable potential of (para)psychology in manipulating the public.[40] Both groups also heralded parapsychology's insights into the 'subconscious' (*Unterbewusstsein*), which had ostensibly been 'lost to science because [it was] defined as mythological, as possession by spirits and demons'.[41]

When Weimar (para)psychologists spoke of the 'sub/unconscious', they meant something slightly different than the 'unconscious' in a Freudian sense. Freud, who rejected parapsychology out of hand, saw the 'unconscious' as a layer of consciousness that had its own will and purpose that needed to be uncovered through psychoanalysis. For Jung and many parapsychologists, the subconscious or 'unconscious' was a different psychological terrain, where primeval thoughts, feelings, and powers of perception resided that the conscious mind was not capable of processing. This distinction is useful in differentiating not only between Freud and Jung, but between mainstream psychology and parapsychology.[42]

The central problem in the collective psychology of the German people, Jung believed, was the integration of opposites within the unconscious – in particular the 'integration of Satan'. So long as 'Satan is not integrated,' Jung argued, 'the world is not healed and man is not saved ... The ultimate aim ... cosmic salva-tion'.[43] Like Steiner, Schertel, and many esotericists, Jung emphasized here the fruitful role of one's 'demons' in 'reactivating archaic images stored in the unconscious from past historical eras'.[44]

The famous psychologist of German culture and ethnicity (*Völkerpsychologe*), Willy Hellpach, writing during the final years of the Third Reich, agreed. Germany's violent divisions (*Zerissenheit*) since the Middle Ages, followed by the emotional trauma of the First World War, had made 'ordinary' Germans peculiarly susceptible to manipulation by a 'genius' or 'leader'. For individuals such as Hitler to be successful, their 'creative powers' and 'will formation' had to feed upon the 'average human environment' of their 'racial tribe'.[45]

For Jung and Hellpach the occult phenomena that parapsychologists claimed to control were not necessarily real but rather an important 'projection of a drama both cosmic and spiritual in laboratory terms'. What occultists 'called "matter" was in reality the [unconscious] self'.[46] For Schertel and practising parapsychologists, however, recovering this unconscious allowed one to tap into long-lost paranormal powers ('magic') akin to those that Blavatsky, Steiner, and Lanz claimed were lost when the ancient Aryans mated with lesser races. Occultism offered a way of channeling primordial magic, the 'mana' or 'demonic' power that dwelt naturally in both animals and humans.[47] Magicians or 'shapers of mana', Schertel admitted, possessed traits that might be considered as 'psychopathic' under normal circumstances. But they also had very strong characters and leadership capabilities, which is why 'the Magician is in all earlier times identical with Ruler'.[48]

Hitler's Magic

As the border science *par excellence*, parapsychology experienced a renaissance in the Weimar Republic. No wonder that Hitler apparently read Schertel's parapsychological tome, *Magic*, which explained how to manipulate people in achieving power.[49] In his reading of Schertel, Hitler seized immediately on one of the central tenets of parapsychology: the power of the will in appealing to the collective unconscious. The magician did not seek the support of a ' "people" (Volk) whose "good" he would have to 'serve', Hitler underscored, but in order to garner power ('an enlargement of his I-sphere'). Should people 'not seem reactive enough', should they lose faith in their leader, Schertel added, the magician had every right to abandon them as Christ abandoned the Jews.[50]

Practising magic required 'getting in touch with what modern man considered "irrational" by invoking one's intuition', which facilitates a 'divinization of the body'.[51] This 'hallucinatory-suggestive process [was] fostered in ancient times through gods and concrete ceremonies', a 'whole cult with its temples and underground vaults, his idols, his sacred groves, gardens, lakes and mountains, his whole magic pomp and solemn ritual.'[52] Hitler generated the same energies by shifting his venue from Munich beer halls to massive rallies, ceremonies, and parades.

Hitler's reading of Schertel anticipates the Nazi approach to propaganda often attributed to by Goebbels: 'If you repeat a lie a thousand times, people are bound to start believing it.' 'All reality is only Phantoms,' Hitler noted, 'even if the reality of this demon image is a "deception" to dismiss. False images are necessary for the recognition of truth.'[53] There was in fact 'no fundamental difference' between ' "fantastical perceptions" ("imaginations") and "objective observations".' 'Imagination and observation are to the same extent products of the cosmic dynamic and of inner-bodily forces and as such "real", provided that the notion of "reality" still has any meaning at all', Schertel's text continued, for 'no perception can per se be described as "true" or "wrong", as "right" or "false", as "real" or "illusory".'[54]

Because of the revolutionary nature of these efforts at enlightenment, failure to sway the public was initially unimportant. 'We must not be despondent when concerned that the world is against us and the strongest spell remains ineffective,' Schertel writes in the final passage underlined by Hitler. 'Our demon is struggling, and he is struggling in pain and hardship. We must suffer with him to share victory with him.'[55] During the NSDAP's wilderness years in the mid-1920s this passage must have lent Hitler encouragement.

Was Hitler's reading of Schertel an isolated occurrence? Or does it reflect a pattern of interest in parapsychology that helps to explain the NSDAP's approach to politics. We know that Hitler read other works on mass psychology, including Gustav le Bon's *Psychology of Crowds*.[56] Le Bon based his theories on Theodule Ribot, who argued that a great mental disturbance, such as the French Revolution (or First World War), could cause psychological dissolution and mass reversion to an earlier stage of evolution where human beings had less willpower and more impulsiveness.[57] Le Bon subsequently theorized that civilized individuals can return to a savage state, similar to mass hypnosis, under certain circumstances. Those capable of manipulating the masses in this way, Le Bon argued, tended to be mentally abnormal, neurotic, combative, and charismatic – all traits generally ascribed to Hitler (and traits that Schertel describes, positively, as 'psychopathic').[58]

Hitler himself expressed a profound appreciation for magical thinking. 'In the late 1920s', according to Hermann Rauschning, Hitler 'discussed at some length the supposed fact that the magical forces of nature break through in man's dreams, though his culture has falsely sublimated them. Knowledge must once again take on the characteristics of a "secret science". A 'new age of magic interpretation of the world is coming,' Hitler reasoned, which would focus on 'the will' and not 'intelligence'.[59]

Hitler, George Mosse argues, may have 'kept his "secret science" to himself or at most discussed it with his intimates'.[60] But we have every reason to believe that Hitler, impressed by his reading of Schertel and Le Bon, accepted the existence of 'occult power' that was 'capable of being channelled, controlled, and directed by man'. This magical tradition, per Hitler, had 'very deep roots in the human past' and was 'an essential part of political life, because its primary purpose was to give human beings power'.[61]

Numerous witnesses compared Hitler to a medium, magician, or medicine-man, who could, in the words of the Nazi Party leader Robert Ley, manipulate 'mystical forces, which humans cannot avoid'.[62] In 1924 the astrologer Elsbeth Ebertin observed that Hitler is 'only in his element when he has a crowd in front of him ... On the platform he is more like a medium, the unconscious tool of higher powers'.[63] The liberal journalist Rudolf Olden agreed. Hitler was a master magician, for whom other Nazi leaders were merely lower-level ' "mediums", middle men of a power located in the Führer'.[64] Rauschning too would argue that Hitler was a 'medium' whose 'genuinely daemonic powers' made 'men his instruments'.[65] Of the 'two kinds of dictators [the] chieftain type and the medicine-man type', Jung explained, 'Hitler is the latter. He is a medium.' German policy was not made, Jung suggested, but 'revealed through Hitler. He is the mouthpiece of the gods as of old.'[66]

Critics and supporters alike felt the same magical power in Hitler's presence. In 'Hitler's company', Rauschning recalls, 'I have again and again come under a spell which I was only later able to shake off, a sort of hypnosis.' He was a 'medicine-man', who could take one back 'toward the savage state ... the Shaman's drum that beats round Hitler'.[67] 'Like a record in a groove,' recalled Albrecht Haushofer, the son of Hitler's foreign policy advisor Karl Haushofer, 'Hitler could channel his remarkable energy.' When he became 'absolutely exhausted', he 'just sat down once more a simple and nice man'.[68] Otto Strasser described Hitler as a 'clairvoyant' who went into a trance when 'face-to-face with his public'. 'That is his moment of real greatness,' Strasser explained, 'carried away by a mystic force, he cannot doubt the genuineness of his mission.'[69] Like a wireless receiving set, Hitler was able 'with a certainty with which no conscious gift would endow him, to act as a loudspeaker, proclaiming the most secret desires, the least admissible instincts, the sufferings and personal revolts of a whole nation'.[70]

Like any shaman or magician, the spoken word was essential to Hitler's magic. But it was not the rhetorical or political content of his speeches that mattered. 'Hitler's speeches were probably the greatest example of mass sorcery that the world has heard in modern times,' Heiden observed. 'And yet it is hard to find in this stream of words ... even one or two that will live.' 'Never in all his flights of rhetorical fire,' Heiden conceded, did Hitler 'succeed in coining such a ringing phrase as "cross of gold" or "blood, sweat, and tears".' And yet, great statesmen such as William Jennings Bryan and Winston Churchill were never 'as close to the masses as Hitler', who 'uttered entire paragraphs in which each sentence seemed to have the resonance and rhythm of an unforgettable composition'.[71]

As Hitler wrote of his idol Karl Lueger, 'The power to bring together the great historical avalanches of religious and political nature has always been possible only through the magical power of the spoken word. Whoever eschews emotion and keeps their mouth closed will not be able to employ heaven as the proclaimer of his will.'[72] Hitler believed, like a 'magician delivering an incantation', that repeating the same message over and over would make it become reality.[73] Heiden agreed that Hitler had an 'ability to simplify intricate ideas ... [to] certain phrases, repeated again and again by his propaganda mill without losing their banality'.[74]

Hitler's powers of suggestion rendered the incoherent Nazi Party programme moot. The NSDAP programme, observed Olden, 'originated long after the movement and was given up long before the victory ... The decisive factor is the influence of the Führer on the masses.' Wise people might laugh at the idea that Hitler exercised powers of suggestion. 'Only, what is suggestion?' Olden continued. 'Why does [the democrat] August Weber or [liberal Eduard] Dingeldey not succeed, but Adolf Hitler clearly does?' It was because practical social and political matters that had to do 'with cause and effect' became unnecessary. All that remained was 'the miraculous'. Hitler was not a conventional politician or statesman, but a 'prophet regularly in a state of narcissistic conviction, which he attributes to his call to the salvation of his supporters'.[75] Olden wrote this in 1932, just a year before the Nazi seizure of power.

For the left wing of the Weimar government, for many liberals, and for most foreign observers, the content of Hitler's speeches, his words, his gesticulations, were laughable.[76] For his 'magic' to work, as Schertel and Le Bon suggested, Hitler needed 'a receptive audience whose members believe in its efficacy'.[77] Why did Hitler, whom most Germans seem to worship, produce 'next to no impression on any foreigner?' Jung asked rhetorically. 'It is because Hitler is the mirror of every German's unconscious', while he 'mirrors nothing from a non-German'.[78] 'There is such a force as the collective unconscious of a nation,' Jung continued. Hitler had 'an uncanny power of being sensitive to that collective unconscious ... [as if] he knows what the nation is really feeling at any given time'.[79] 'You can take a hundred very intelligent men,' Jung concluded, following Le Bon. But 'when you have them all together they may be nothing more than a silly mob', susceptible to mass suggestion.[80]

Hitler's magical impact on his audience – at least his German audience – is well documented. In observing Hitler dozens of times, Heiden was less fascinated by Hitler than his audience. No matter how ridiculous his statements,

Heiden recalled, 'the listeners sat rooted to their chairs [with] a blissful expression that had no connection whatever with the theme of the speech but reflected instead the deep beatitude of a thoroughly muddled soul'.[81] Hitler was able to 'hear a voice', Jung added, which represented the 'collective unconscious' of his own race. 'It is this fact that makes dealing with Hitler such a problem. He is virtually the nation.'[82] Ultimately, Hitler became 'the loudspeaker that magnifies the inaudible whispers of the German soul until they can be heard by the German's unconscious ear'. His power was 'not political; it is magic'.[83]

As Jung and Heiden suggest, Hitler benefited from a reservoir of Germans whose 'longing for harmony' facilitated his ability 'to harness the raw power embodied in the frustrated masses'.[84] After the First World War objective reality had for many Germans 'collapsed into a psychic disorder of apocalyptic proportions', which rendered millions of people susceptible to 'some higher power or charismatic messiah/guru', an idea, a movement, or an individual that 'elicited the conversion experience and the sense of liberation that comes with it'.[85] For those who were 'starving for the unattainable', who have been 'unsuccessful in the battle of life', National Socialism was the 'great worker of magic'. By translating the 'religious mysteries of Nazism' for the German people, Hitler became 'the master-enchanter and the high priest', the nation's supreme magician.[86] By exercising his magic on the desperate masses, immersed in fantasies of civil war and apocalyptic imagery, Hitler was able to attract thousands of converts.[87]

According to many converts Hitler's attraction 'seemed almost supernatural'. As one witness reports, after hearing Hitler for the first time, 'instantly I came to a decision, and I said to myself, that only this party can save Germany'. Hitler's speech 'drew me to it [the NSDAP], so to speak, with magical power'.[88] Kurt Ludecke recalls, after hearing Hitler, that his 'critical faculty was swept away' by the 'intense will of the man, the passion of his sincerity seemed to flow from him into me. I experienced an exaltation that could be likened only to a religious conversion. I felt sure that no one who had heard Hitler that afternoon could doubt that he was a man of destiny, the vitalizing force in the future of Germany'.[89] For another witness the profound uncertainty and doubt he felt was dissipated in 'sudden revelation . . . It was for me as if he had spoken to me personally . . . I was a National Socialist . . . A joyful knowledge, a bright enthusiasm, a pure faith – Adolf Hitler and Germany'.[90] Even General Ludendorff, a man who had commanded millions, 'trembled with emotion' when he first heard Hitler.[91]

If Hitler's magic manifested itself early on, it attracted relatively few followers during the first decade of the Weimar Republic. Before 1929, Hitler's powers of suggestion tended to be limited to those already receptive to *völkisch*-esoteric thinking – disillusioned nationalists, unemployed veterans, and other members of the traditional petty bourgeois right.[92] It required more than magic for

Hitler to be acknowledged Führer over all Germany.[93] First, Hitler needed a strong enough party and propaganda apparatus to distil the lessons of Schertel and Le Bon for the masses.[94] A decade of social and political crisis was equally necessary in catalyzing the 'conversion' of Germans who didn't yet recognize Hitler or the NSDAP as the logical vehicle for their hopes and aspirations.[95] Nothing exemplifies better the interplay of supernatural thinking with these two other factors, the party propaganda apparatus and sociopolitical crisis, than the NSDAP's relationship with the horror writer, Hanns Heinz Ewers.

Hanns Heinz Ewers and Nazi Propaganda

In 1928, just before the NSDAP began to make electoral breakthroughs in regional elections, Goebbels gave a speech titled 'Knowledge and Propaganda' to an audience of National Socialist functionaries. The *völkisch* movement that culminated in Nazism, Goebbels explained, had rightly sought to conquer the state and carry out practical political activity. Too many *völkisch* thinkers, however, worried about impractical matters like border science and New Age medicine. 'I have often met the kind of wandering apostle,' Goebbels remarked sardonically, who says "Well, everything you say is good, but you must have a point in your program that says allopathy is dangerous, and you must support homoeopathy." If the NSDAP had dispensed with the *völkisch* movement's more overt esoteric trappings, of its "romantic magic", Goebbels reasoned, it had done so for its own good. If 'someone had had the courage to strip the *völkisch* idea of its romantic mystery' before the First World War, 'it would have kept millions of German children from starving.'[96] 'It is not the task of a revolutionary fighting movement to settle the dispute between allopathy and homoeopathy,' Goebbels explained. Its 'task is to take power.'[97]

On the other hand, Goebbels pointed out, it was not his goal to eliminate esoteric debates over homoeopathy from the *völkisch* movement altogether. 'The important thing,' he continued, 'is not to find people who agree with me about every theoretical jot and tittle.' The only thing that matters is whether propaganda was effective:[98]

> You will never find millions of people willing to die for a book. But millions of people are willing to die for a Gospel, and our movement is becoming more and more a Gospel ... No one is willing to die for the eight–hour day. But people are willing to die so that Germany will belong to the Germans ... The time is coming when people will not ask us what we think about the eight–hour day; but rather when Germany is seized with desperation they will ask: 'Can you give us back faith?'[99]

Resolving specific programme points was less important than tapping into ideas that people *already* share but have yet to hear articulated.[100] 'Was Christ any different? Did he not make propaganda? Did he write books, or did he preach? Was Mohammed any different? Did he write learned essays, or did he go to the people and say what he wanted to say? Were not Buddha and Zarathustra propagandists?'[101] Had 'the *völkisch* movement had such agitators at its disposal,' Goebbels concluded, 'its stronger intellectual foundations would surely have led it to victory'.[102]

One such agitator, hand picked by Goebbels and Hitler, was Hanns Heinz Ewers.[103] Ewers was born in 1871, in Düsseldorf, into a middle-class family of artists.[104] He began writing fairy tales and short stories as a young adult and later collaborated on scripting two early 'horror movies', *The Picture of Dorian Gray* (1910) and Paul Wegener's *The Student of Prague* (1913).[105] Ewers also travelled widely in the East, developing, like many Nazis, a fascination with Indo-Aryan esotericism.[106] His classic 1911 horror novel *Alraune*, reprinted numerous times and filmed on at least five occasions, was a modern refashioning of Mary Shelley's *Frankenstein*. It told the story of a female homunculus with vampiric tendencies, conceived when Ewers' literary alter ego, Frank Braun, helps his scientist-uncle impregnate a prostitute with semen from a hanged murderer.[107]

As a master of the macabre, Ewers was accustomed to exploiting the fantastic, the monstrous, and the occult in order to evoke feelings of horror among his readers. The range of monsters that filled Ewers' horror stories – from the witches, devil worshippers, and homunculi of his pre-war efforts to his later *Vampire* (1921) and *Rider in the German Night* (1932) – moreover reflected German anxieties about colonialism and territorial loss, military defeat and the racial other.[108] In Hitler and Goebbels, Ewers found enthusiastic co-conspirators in exploiting Weimar's horrors in 'a propagandistic call for militant nationalism and engagement in anti-republican politics'.[109]

Weimar's Horrors

Weimar is virtually synonymous with modernity in the arts, indeed, a quintessentially avant-garde and experimental culture that brings to mind Expressionism, Bauhaus, and the cabaret. But the creative unconscious that inspired Weimar culture included important elements of supernatural thinking.[110] 'Occult beliefs and practices permeated the aesthetic culture of modernism,' writes the foremost expert on German esotericism, Corinna Treitel. There was a shared expectation that the 'new art speaks to the soul' by drawing 'heavily on fin-de-siècle German theosophy and its deeply psychological understanding of a spiritual reality that lay beyond the reach of the five senses'.[111] Art created during the Weimar Republic, in fact, could be seen as 'an outgrowth of a Zeitgeist in which the psychological experiences and metaphysical concerns so common in occult circles occupied a dominant place'.[112]

Weimar artists craved direct 'intuitive experience' and 'mystical self-deification' grounded in the occult.[113] Hanns Ewers, his fellow horror writer Gustav Meyrinck, and the poet Rainer Maria Rilke all drew on occultism for creative inspiration.[114] Some experimented with Steiner's eurhythmy, an occult-based meditative dance akin to Schertel's unconventional high-school curriculum mentioned above.[115] Others, like Meyrinck, preferred theosophy. So did the German painter and poet, Joseph Anton Schneiderfranken (otherwise known as 'Bo Yin Ra'), who claimed to have met the spirit of Jesus after 'years of training his mental powers'. Even the great Expressionist Russian painter Kandinsky read occult literature such as Hübbe-Schleiden's theosophical journal *Sphinx* in seeking to tap into a creative unconscious that offered something 'less suited to the eye than the soul'.[116]

Given occultism's broad impact on Weimar culture, including a number of left-wing and Jewish artists, it would be inaccurate to suggest that occultism was inherently racist or fascist.[117] A renewed interest in the occult nonetheless interacted with Expressionism, according to many critics, helping to articulate the underlying socio-psychological pathologies experienced by Germans in the wake of the First World War.[118] The trauma of that conflict, according to Lotte Eisner, nourished 'the grim nostalgia of the survivors', reviving the 'ghosts that had haunted the German Romantics' within Weimar culture, 'like the shades of Hades after draughts of blood'. This 'eternal attraction towards all that is obscure and undetermined', Eisner concludes, 'culminated in the apocalyptic doctrine of Expressionism'.[119]

Indeed German film, more than any contemporary medium, explored 'the creative possibilities of the occult'. Horror films such as Robert Wiene's *The Cabinet of Dr Caligari* (1920), Paul Wegener's *The Golem* (1920), and Friedrich Wilhelm Murnau's *Nosferatu: A Symphony of Terror* (1922) played on prominent esoteric themes and included occultists in the production crew. Ewers worked on *The Golem*, while Murnau consulted astrologers and read theosophical texts. His producer and set designer, Albin Grau, was a spiritualist.[120]

The occult themes that pervaded Expressionist film were hardly politically neutral. Most such films contain symbolic representations of evil doctors, magicians, and psychopaths with the ability to manipulate the public. Kracauer cites Wiene's Dr Caligari and Fritz Lang's criminal mastermind Dr Mabuse in particular as representative of Germany's 'collective soul' wavering between 'tyranny and chaos'.[121] Expressionist filmmakers, according to critics, seemed to take a 'weird pleasure . . . in evoking horror . . . a predilection for the imagery of darkness'.[122]

Some Expressionist films anticipated the Nazi preoccupation with occult-infused eugenics as well. *Alraune* (1913) and the *Student of Prague* (1913, 1926) – based on Ewers' scripts – invoked a tantalizing combination of religion and border science, eugenics and magic.[123] Wegener's *Golem* played off the darker elements in Jewish mysticism, emphasizing the desire to create a vengeful monster out of magic. For some right-wing, anti-Semitic viewers the *Golem* therefore highlighted 'the Jew as a problematic figure'.[124] Hitler himself admired Lang's 1924 films, *Die Nibelungen: Siegfried's Death* and *Die Nibelungen: Kriemhild's Revenge*, which portrayed Aryan Germans in an existential struggle with evil dwarves (or Jews, according to some critics) who turned to stone when defeated.[125]

Murnau's *Nosferatu* constitutes a brilliant work of Expressionism as well as a rumination on the Jewish (East European) other. It doesn't take a huge leap of imagination to see the relationship between Murnau's thinly veiled representation of Bram Stoker's *Dracula* and the 'Jewish enemy' in the Nazi supernatural imaginary.[126] Like the infamous Caligari or Mabuse, the vampire Count Orlok possesses malevolent powers of hypnotism, suggestion, and seduction.[127] For many Germans immersed in the supernatural imaginary, Murnau's Nosferatu simultaneously became the embodiment of racial (Jewish) difference, 'weirdly human and yet terrifyingly other … abjectly *wrong*, unseemly, unnatural, anathema'. Orlok's vampiric practices – bringing plague, drinking Aryan blood, or corrupting German women – were inherently demonic and unholy.[128] Hence Weimar films, even those produced by anti-fascist or Jewish directors, expressed the dangers of race mixing and the degeneracy of foreigners.

If left-wing social critics viewed vampires, magicians, and other occult 'tyrants' in terms of Weimar's susceptibility to fascism, *völkisch* intellectuals embraced the supernatural discourse and culture of horror.[129] As the Nazi 'prophet' Josef Fischer-Haninger put it in 1932, all the vampires on the German national body [*Völkskörper*] fear a dictator, whereas the honest working people yearn for a father of the poor, for a prince of justice like Hitler.[130] 'Expressionist film and literature facilitated Nazism,' writes Linda Schulte-Sasse, because it 'was packaged in a medium that guarantees a pleasurable illusion of wholeness.'[131] By propagating a particular supernatural imaginary, Expressionist film reflected and refracted the sociopolitical anxieties that facilitated Nazism.[132]

The emotional power of film and mass culture was not lost on the Nazis. Cultic plays and folklore festivals, according to the future chief of the Third Reich's Literary Chamber, Hanns Johst, helped create a community of faith. Well before 1933 the Nazis had embraced the idea of a 'people's theatre', which incorporated German mythology and required a new kind of monumental space accommodating a mass of spectators. The model for this kind of theater was the so-called 'Thing' play, drawn from Germanic folklore and traditionally performed in an outdoor setting in which the audience was encouraged to become involved.[133] In the interest of 'mass manipulation' the Nazis 'degraded the mythic', exploiting folklore and mythology, paganism and the occult, to create a variety of spectacles accessible to the broader public.[134]

The explosion of fantastical literature was an equally powerful component of the Weimar supernatural imaginary. Interwar Germany was replete with pulp novels and science fiction that 'blended politics and wish-fulfilling fantasies' about overthrowing the Versailles Treaty and exacting revenge on the Allies.[135] These works, notes Peter Fisher, provide great insight into the 'ideological and psychological roots of the Weimar Republic's highly emotionalized politics, especially some of its uglier racist and Messianic strands'. The preference on the right 'for the world of fantasy over reality' abetted 'a cultural drift toward irrationalism that manifested itself politically in the call for dictatorship'.[136] Unsurprisingly, *völkisch* writers, from the popular Weimar author Fanny Reventlow to the best-selling Artur Dinter, took esoteric topics as their primary themes.[137]

This fantastical literature was not merely the 'self-serving fabrication' of right-wing fanatics. According to Fisher, by the end of the Weimar Republic, the 'dreams, daydreams, and semireligious entrancement' of the *völkisch* right, its 'visions of revenge and renewal', had been 'converted into a literature of mass consumption'. Often 'a quirky mixture of adventure story, fairy tale, millenarian vision, and political program', such fantasy literature 'was intended to act as a catalyst inflaming the same type of emotions among the readers that originally elicited the fantasies in the minds of their creators'.[138]

Initially the province of fringe thinkers, by the early 1930s this science fiction and fantasy literature had transformed 'into a psychological tool, a propagandistic call for militant nationalism and engagement in anti-republican politics'.[139] Even the putatively scientific journal, *Archive for Race and Sociobiology*, recognized the propaganda value of the anti-Semitic fantasy *Deutschland ohne Deutsche* (*Germany without Germans*, 1930). 'Science can win over the mind,' the Nazi reviewer explained, 'but not the soul – the whole person. In this respect novels are more successful, especially among the masses who cannot make heads or tails of "exact science".' As a 1932 article in the liberal *Frankfurter Zeitung* lamented, 'an edgy, anxiety-ridden public was very susceptible to the messages and psychological manipulation' of this fantastical literature.[140] What better context for the bizarre political marriage between the horror writer Hanns Heinz Ewers and the NSDAP.

Ewers and the NSDAP

Until the end of the First World War, Ewers' life and literary opus reflected a generally cosmopolitan, quintessentially modern view of the world typical of many Weimar artists. After working for German intelligence and getting imprisoned in the United States for the duration of the conflict, however, Ewers returned to a Germany politically transformed and psychologically trauma-tized.[141] In 1921 he published the third instalment in the semi-biographical Frank Braun horror series, *Vampire*. Loosely based on Ewers' experiences in the United States and Mexico during the war, the tone had changed considerably from his earlier works. Rather than celebrate cosmopolitanism and ethno-sexual difference, *Vampire* suggested that Braun becomes a blood-sucking monster as a result of sexual congress with the racial other and detachment from the fatherland.[142] Written a year after the Versailles Treaty, *Vampire* encap-sulates the anxieties of millions of Germans, who had become more susceptible to emotional nationalism and border scientific thinking.[143]

Essential in catalyzing Ewers' transition from tepid liberal to Nazi fellow traveller were two experiences: the 1923 Franco-Belgian occupation of the Ruhr, which employed French and African troops, and the 1929 Great Depression. These two events combined to inspire Ewers' first (unofficial) work of pro-Nazi propaganda, *Rider in the German Night* (1932), a patriotic counterpoise to Erich Maria Remarque's antiwar novel, *All Quiet on the Western Front* (1929). Ewers even chose the Nazi Freikorps leader and SA man, Paul Schulz (aka Gerhard Scholz), as his protagonist. Schulz was a leader of the secret 'black army' (*Schwarze Reichswehr*), based on the esoteric tradition of the *Vehm* (*Feme*). He garnered the nickname 'Feme-Schulz' due to his reputation for organizing revenge murders against left-wing politicians. Convicted of murder in 1927, Schulz was released three years later, rising quickly in the ranks of the NSDAP.[144]

That the libertine Ewers chose Schulz as his protagonist appears remarkable – until one recalls that many Nazi stormtroopers emerged from the same Berlin demi-monde of street violence, sexual experimentation, and esotericism that defined Ewers' life and art.[145] This milieu included the Nazi doctor, astrologer, and gay rights advocate Karl Heimsoth.[146] Heimsoth, who was also advisor and confidant to the SA leader Ernst Röhm, studied (para) psychology and belonged to the 'Academic Society for Astrological Research'.[147] Drawing on esoteric research, Heimsoth argued that paramilitary groups like the SA, Wehrwolf, and NSDAP were cemented together through homosocial bonds based on common 'characterological' factors.[148]

This paramilitary milieu included SA members such as Schulz, Röhm, and the *Werewolf* leader Wolf-Heinrich Graf Helldorff, who had close ties to the esotericists Heimsoth and Hanussen (more on him below).[149] Other once and future Nazi leaders who belonged to the *völkisch*-esoteric circles illuminated by Ewers in *Rider in the German Night* were Erich von Ludendorff and his Tannenberg Association, Friedrich Weber and the Thule-inspired *Bund*

Oberland, and Edmund Heines, leader of the so-called Rossbach group.[150] Given these connections between Ewers and the *völkisch*-esoteric paramilitary milieu, we should hardly be surprised that Heimsoth and Röhm appear positively (albeit by pseudonym) in *Rider*.[151]

Rider epitomized a moment of remarkable convergence between nationalist paramilitary groups behind the NSDAP.[152] By the time Ewers finished *Rider* in 1931, most members of the *völkisch* movement, in the words of Helldorff's Werewolf, 'viewed a revolution under the leadership of National Socialism with joy. With their march into the Third Reich, they could no longer be treated as peons.'[153] Or as the Artamanen put it in the prelude to the September 1930 Reichstag election: 'no hour should be wasted until 14 September. Hurry from town to town, house to house, into the last farmer's cottage . . . Carry with you the faith in our mission, the faith in the Third Reich. We recognize in this moment that we are intrinsically bound to the leader of the German liberation movement: Adolf Hitler!'[154]

In drawing on supernatural themes for propaganda purposes, Ewers emulated a technique perfected by Hitler and Goebbels over the previous decade. The supernatural tropes in *Rider* were embedded, like much Nazi propaganda, in the recognition of Weimar's political and social crisis.[155] Unlike the work of left-wing writers such as Remarque and Döblin, Ewers abandoned any pretensions at portraying empirical reality in favour of fantastical themes and heroic individuals that evoked an emotional response. Ewers employed Nazi occultists like Heimsoth as main characters, invoked the work of Lanz von Liebenfels, and represented his chief protagonist, the cold-blooded murderer Schulz, as the Grail Rider Sir Galahad.[156] Instead of confronting Weimar's complex challenges, *Rider* denied 'objective experience' and disparaged 'reason and intellect in favour of instinct and intuition'. It thereby erased 'the boundary between fantasy and reality' and indulged in 'elaborating fantasies of a victorious war of revenge'.[157]

In times of national revolution, observed the pro-Nazi writer Gottfried Benn, 'there tended to be a regression in intellectual advances while those grasping for power – or seeking to legitimize it – reached backwards in search of mythical continuity.[158] *Rider* did exactly that for the Nazi Party. It appealed to 'the most militant nationalists' for whom 'the war dead were as much a galvanizing force for future action as a source of pain'. Ewers and the 'Nazis seem to have understood what a lot of Germans felt' better than other parties. 'They offered a compelling mythos that claimed inviolability for the war dead and invested their "sacrifice" with the pageantry, ceremony, even majesty' that Germans craved.[159]

Here *Rider* played on German resentments over the Versailles Treaty and racially and sexually charged revenge fantasies against the French (and North

African) 'colonizers' in the Ruhr. Many passages in *Rider* recall the Afro-Caribbean revolutionary Frantz Fanon's description of North African reactions to French colonial occupation. In Ewers' portrayal of Schulz's battle against Franco-British oppression, 'supernatural, magical powers reveal themselves as essentially personal'. Ewers' *völkisch* protagonists, like the North Africans in Fanon's *Wretched of the Earth*, appear 'lost in an imaginary maze, a prey to unspeakable terrors yet happy to lose themselves in a dreamlike torment'. Becoming 'unhinged', the *völkisch*-nationalists around Schulz, Röhm, and the NSDAP finally 'reorganize' themselves 'and in blood and tears' give 'birth to very real and immediate action'.[160]

Although Ewers still enjoyed a reputation as an irresponsible libertine in 1932, Nazi party members lauded his first foray into political propaganda. In the run-up to the April 1932 presidential elections, Goebbels promoted *Rider in the German Night* as a 'flaming accusation' against the republican parties, 'a ghostly procession [*Geisterzug*] out of the darkest chapter of the post-war era' that 'should be disseminated as widely as possible'. In 'spite of the crassness of some of the erotic situations', Goebbels conceded, Ewers has 'claimed an honourable place in the row of nationally conscious writers'. Röhm was even more unqualified in his praise: 'Your wonderful book has affected and aroused me deeply. I know that I speak for all my SA comrades when I extend my hand to you in thanks and I am happy that I might have given the impetus to creating this heroic song'.[161]

Ewers, for his part, was eager to join the Nazi movement. In early November 1931 he asked one of his many Nazi friends, Putzi Hanfstaengl – Hitler's chauffeur – to alert Röhm and Rudolf Hess that his 'only wish for his 60th birthday would be to meet the Führer and be able to shake his hand'. The next day Ewers received a telegram inviting him to Nazi headquarters, the *Braunes Haus* in Munich, on 3 November – his birthday. Upon arrival the prudish Rosenberg 'acted coolly' and 'expressed his misgivings over the book *Vampir*'. Ewers nonetheless received his audience with Hitler, which lasted for perhaps three-quarters of an hour.[162]

Over Rosenberg's objections, Goebbels and Röhm apparently convinced Hitler that Ewers 'might attract new circles to the party'.[163] During their meeting, Hitler complimented Ewers on his work and urged him to write a novel about the Nazi movement from a stormtrooper's perspective, for which Hitler offered Ewers the use of the party archives. Eyewitness accounts vary on the details. But Hitler ostensibly closed the discussion by extending Ewers a personal invitation to join the NSDAP, sealed with a handshake. Ewers left the *Braunes Haus* ecstatic, exclaiming to Hanfstaengl, 'That was really fine, Putzi! I could not think of a nicer gift for my 60th birthday'.[164]

That Ewers chose Horst Wessel, the Nazi martyr, as the subject of his book was no accident. It is likely that Röhm himself suggested the idea of the young

SA-Man, who had been murdered by Communists in February 1930. Ewers may have already known Wessel from the Friedrichs-Wilhelms University in Berlin, where they had both studied law and were brothers in the same fraternity (some decades apart). Wessel and Röhm probably also bumped into each other on the set of the Expressionist horror film, *Student of Prague* (1926), which Ewers helped write and in which Wessel acted as an extra.[165]

Wessel was, like Ewers, a rake, well acquainted with the seedier side of Berlin street life. Wessel had a reputation for spending money freely on alcohol and prostitutes – and instigating fights with Communists. Despite his penchant for illicit sex and violence, Wessel became head of the local SA in Friedrichshain in 1929, writing the Nazi marching song 'Die Fahne hoch!' before being murdered by Communists, allegedly over a financial dispute, a few months later.[166] After writing a hagiography of the rabid anti-Semite and murderer Paul Schulz, Ewers must have found Wessel even easier to mythologize. He was assisted by Nazi efforts to whitewash and beatify the young martyr in every way possible. Even Wessel's burial was made into a propaganda film, helping create a cult that led to multiple sites of remembrance and a Christ-like narrative of his life and death.[167]

In Ewers' biography of Wessel, Nazi ideology is expressed in vague, contradictory, and mystical terms.[168] 'To be German is a phenomenon that cannot be explained rationally', Wessel says to an American associate, echoing Thomas Mann's quote that 'the German soul possesses something profound and irrational ... an element of the demonic and heroic'.[169] Like Schertel's *Magic*, Ewers' *Wessel* appealed to an emotional longing that transcends specific political programme points; even anti-Semitism and anti-Communism are played down in favour of myth and spirituality.[170] Once again overlooking its salacious elements, many Nazi leaders, including Goebbels and the Nazi Youth leader Baldur von Schirach, praised the book as 'a monument to all our dead ... to our immortal Horst Wessel ... It is the myth of the nameless SA-Mann'.[171]

In concert with Ewers' forthcoming biography, the Nazis decided to unveil a 'monument for German-conscious youth' at Wessel's gravesite in November 1932. Due to police restrictions the event was delayed repeatedly until 22 January 1933, merely eight days before President Hindenburg decided to name Hitler Chancellor of the Weimar Republic. The procession began with Ewers' friend Röhm assembling 16,000 Nazi stormtroopers in the middle of Berlin, who then slowly filed by Adolf Hitler on the way to the Nikolai Cemetery, where another 500 stormtroopers stood waiting with 300 Nazi civilians. Prominent Nazi leaders, featuring Röhm, Goebbels, and Hitler, next gave a series of speeches, culminating in laying a wreath on Horst Wessel's grave.[172]

After Hitler and his associates gave their perorations, Ewers took the stage. He proceeded to deliver a rousing speech in the name of all German youth 'united by a narrow, unbreakable bond of love and camaraderie . . . Horst Wessel had made the word of the Führer reality: Forget everything – class, profession, origin! Forget confession and education! Only never forget Germany!' Ewers speech was followed by drums and then another procession of SA, SS, and Hitler Youth, and culminated in a commemorative ceremony in the Berlin Sports Palace. It was keynoted by Hitler and the SA leader Helldorff, whose esoteric convictions and personal connections to the clairvoyant Hanussen we will discuss below.[173]

In contrast to the NSDAP, the left-wing press was disgusted by Ewers' brazen mixture of mysticism and demagoguery. According to one reviewer, Ewers had created a 'national Socialist Vampire' in Wessel, the culmination of a perverse career. For decades Ewers had toiled away, mixing 'blood with barf and sperm with Henna in his *Alraune, Vampire, Possessed*, and *Sorceror's Apprentice*' until he was rescued by 'the chosen one of the people [Hitler]' and 'entrusted with the worthy task' of writing Wessel's biography. 'Frank Braun, the behind-the-scenes hero of "Vampire" and "Alraune"', observed another left-wing paper, 'has been transformed into Horst Wessel' whose 'fabled characters now represent Hitler and Goebbels'. 'In order to produce the definitive biography of the young hero', observed Bertolt Brecht, 'Goebbels [has] turned to a successful pornographer', who 'has written, among other things, a book in which a corpse is dug up and raped'. Ewers was 'strikingly suitable as the one to write the life story of the dead Horst Wessel', Brecht concluded, since there 'were not two people with so much fantasy in Germany' – the 'pornographer [Ewers] and the doctor of propaganda [Goebbels]'.[174]

Turning to the bizarre ceremony at Wessel's grave, the Socialist *Wahrheit* remarked upon its 'demonic' elements. Going further, the Communist *Red Post* published a series of articles lamenting the 'new German mysticism', 'political irrationalism', and 'superstition' exemplified by Ewers' role as propagandist in the Nazi movement.[175] Unfortunately, petty bourgeois and middle-class voters preferred this 'superstition' and 'mysticism' to people from the left. All Weimar's 'forlorn liberals and pacifists could do' was 'watch the irrationalist storm as it unleashed its fury on the republic'.[176]

By articulating Weimar's horrors, Ewers helped convert Nazi visions into political reality.[177] Ignoring the concrete reasons for Weimar's many challenges, he portrayed German politics and society in a 'state of flux ultimately determined by the supernatural'. Social and political crisis was 'thus transposed to a conceptual realm framed by notions of heaven-inspired retribution and miracles, of collective crucifixion and resurrection'.[178] In Schulz and Wessel, Ewers brought to life two 'national saviours . . . fictive superhumans . . . meant to symbolize and foreshadow the materialization of a powerful and real saviour', Adolf Hitler.[179] While Ewers elucidated Weimar's horrors – the omnipresent trauma of defeat, occupation, and ethnonational disintegration – Erik Hanussen would help sell Nazi visions of the Third Reich.

Erik Hanussen and the Nazi Seizure of Power

In January 1932, Erik Hanussen, Germany's most flamboyant clairvoyant, reported on an outing with his new associate, Hanns Ewers. Hanussen had met Ewers through their mutual Nazi acquaintance, Alfons Sack, Hanussen's personal attorney and a close friend of Hermann Göring.[180] Over the course of that chilly January evening, Ewers mentioned two book projects. The first, about the German nationalist resistance to the Ruhr Occupation, would turn out to be *Rider in the German Night*. The second book, which was never written, had to do with a famous clairvoyant who meets a tragic end.

Nevertheless, in conceiving the plot of the second book, Ewers turned out to be more prescient than his friend Hanussen, the professional clairvoyant. For Ewers had anticipated Hanussen's own career trajectory over the next twelve months. By exploiting the occult in the wake of the Great Depression, Hanussen's star rose exponentially, paralleling the ascendancy of the Nazi Party.

Hanussen exploited the political and cultural *Zeitgeist* more effectively than his occult contemporaries. He became friends with leading Nazis. He evinced a charisma and facility for crowd manipulation that rivalled Hitler himself. Hanussen's occult periodicals, which extolled the coming Third Reich, exercised a considerable influence on public opinion. Finally and most ominously, he 'predicted' the Reichstag fire on 27 February 1933 that would help the Nazis to seize power – only to be murdered a few weeks later (see Chapter Three).

At first glance the intimate relationship between the Jewish clairvoyant Hanussen and the NSDAP is astounding. Like other stories in this book, however, it makes sense in the context of the supernatural imaginary, which the Nazis shared with Hanussen and exploited for political gain. If Schertel inspired Hitler's magical approach to politics and Ewers' articulated the horrors on which Nazism drew for its propaganda, Hanussen represented the 'barefoot prophet', who foresaw the coming Third Reich. Hanussen's intimate relationship with the NSDAP and occult-inspired propaganda, consumed by thousands of Germans, illustrates the affinities between supernatural thinking and the rise of the Third Reich.

Predicting the Third Reich

'Our contemporary distress elicits a growing desire for forecasts and predictions of the future,' wrote one critic during the last years of the Weimar Republic. '[P]rophets, wise men, and swindlers – driven either by spiritual calling or by the scent of money – compete against one another for a chance to console or strike fear into the multitude of troubled souls, for an opportunity to bring illumination or still more confusion to the confused many.' In the 'chaos of opinions, views, and demands . . . superstition flourishes'.[181]

The Nazi ideological czar, Alfred Rosenberg, agreed. 'Already soon after coming to power,' he observed, many Germans 'stamped the Führer as a messiah and ascribed the great results of the struggle to otherworldy powers'. 'Astrology made a special effort', Rosenberg noted, 'to exploit this ideological situation for themselves and obscured the achievements and goal of National Socialism with prophecies and soothsaying of the most primitive kind'.[182]

'Even the blind,' added the liberal journalist Rudolf Olden, on the eve of Weimar's final free election, 'must see the monstrous swing from rational to irrational in the short history of the Republic.' 'Naturally there is no political party that would survive without the help of irrationalism,' he conceded. But most 'decisive and irrefutable' in coming to terms with the rise of Nazism was the fact that 'our people have turned away from rationality and openly declared themselves for miracles'.[183]

Whether liberal, socialist, or Nazi, most contemporaries acknowledged the remarkable success that 'many occult "sects"' were having 'with a Protestant constituency' – the same middle-class Protestant constituency that overwhelmingly favoured the NSDAP – and the ways in which this success reinforced Nazism.[184] From 'a political standpoint', Gerhard Szczesny explained, the majority of 'occult-astrological periodicals and their editors' represented 'nationalist and especially racist thoughts out of a conviction that derived from ideological principles that lay not too far' from occultism. No surprise that their 'circle of readers, if not entirely National Socialist, was nonetheless national'.[185]

The onset of the Great Depression 'brought "barefoot prophets" and "inflation holy men" to the streets', who preached 'the end times and styl[ed] themselves as redeemers. Hitler was, in a sense, one of them.' Millions of Germans, especially those immersed in the Weimar supernatural imaginary, would 'see his rise and the coming of the Third Reich as veritable signs that history was moving not meaninglessly or randomly, but with all the purpose of destiny and divine grace'.[186]

The belief that one could glean knowledge from reading the stars or uncovering hidden forces operating in everyday life was remarkably widespread in interwar Germany. By the mid-1920s astrology in particular had experienced an expansion in popularity, followed by a mainstreaming of astrological periodicals, institutes, and organizations.[187] More than two dozen astrological journals and manuals alone competed for readers during a period of expanding interest in the occult.[188]

Academic institutions followed suit. In 1930 one local university offered a course given by the astrologer Heinz Artur Strauss. In 1932 the occult information centre known as *Eclaros* sponsored a public exhibition highlighting 'astrology, characterology, and graphology; the pendulum and the divining rod; anthroposophy and theosophy; spiritualism, hypnotism, and magnetism; and cabala, mysticism, and Buddhism'. In 1933, the year of the Nazi seizure of power, the Astrological Central Office 'established an accreditation exam, for which aspiring astrologers could prepare by enrolling in one of the fee-based astrological training courses'.[189]

With the renaissance in both popular and 'scientific' occultism, critics worried about the use of astrology in terms of mass suggestion and political manipulation.[190] The more 'primitive a person is in terms of material conditions,' wrote one critical occultist, 'all the easier it is to read his future, for he will follow any suggestions ... whether or not they help or hinder him'. Thus fortune-telling invariably found greatest success among individuals who were 'less sophisticated in nature'.[191] The problem was that not 'every medium which claims to be able to see the future is ill-intentioned', suggested the debunker Albert Hellwig. Many clairvoyants believed in their 'own supranormal capabilities', making their prosecution all the more difficult.[192]

Attempting to combat occultists empirically was equally problematic, since it was increasingly difficult for critics of this 'field of research' to publicize their views. Supported by a massive interest in the occult, proponents of occultism could discredit critics 'for a lack of knowledge, intellectual capability, a priori negative prejudice, for ideological reasons or merely evil intentions and dishonesty'.[193] Nor was the public particularly interested in parsing the methodological differences between 'scientific' and popular astrology, much less mainstream and border science. Even 'scientific' astrologers were alarmed by the uncritical fashion in which visions of the future were produced and consumed by many Germans. In language remarkably similar to Hitler's criticism of '*völkisch* wandering scholars', scientific occultists cautioned against 'astrologically oriented wandering speakers' who 'travel the country and speak primarily about political problems ... about which they have not the slightest idea'.[194]

Many Nazis shared these concerns. But we should not confuse the NSDAP's antipathies toward *other* people wielding astrology to manipulate public opinion, unscientifically or otherwise, with a blanket rejection of occult thinking. Many members of the Thule Society and early Nazi Party, including Walter Nauhaus and Rudolf von Sebottendorff, were fascinated by the occult.[195]

Early Nazis such as Herbert Volck, Wilhelm Gutberlet, and Karl Heimsoth were card-carrying astrologers as well.[196] Heimsoth's friend and confidant, the SA chief Ernst Röhm, eagerly solicited astrological advice, while Röhm's subordinates Karl Ernst, Helldorff and Friedrich Wilhelm Ohst attended seances and consulted astrologers.[197] Of course, Himmler and Hess were fascinated by the occult, which becomes evident in the dozens, perhaps hundreds, of occultists and border scientists enlisted by Himmler's SS and Hess's Party Chancellery after 1933.

The political interplay between (perceived) Nazi esotericism and a broader interest in the occult expressed by the public preceded the Great Depression. The well-known astrologer Elsbeth Ebertin had made political prognostica- tions about Hitler even before he became a household name in 1923: 'According to the stars, the man must be taken very seriously indeed,' Ebertin's horoscope concluded; 'He is destined to play a significant Führer-role in future battles.'[198] Ebertin's later book-length horoscope, *A Look into the Future* (1924), published after the Beer Hall Putsch, argued that the 'National Socialist movement', as a result of Hitler's leadership, 'will have historic consequences'. It sold a very respectable 20,000 copies in the mid-1920s.[199] There was also no dearth of political discussion in occult journals throughout the mid- to late 1920s.[200]

With the Great Depression and the Nazis' impressive showing in the September 1930 Reichstag elections, a growing number of astrologers began to hitch their star to the NSDAP.[201] The main astrological journal, *Zenith*, now regularly produced favourable horoscopes of Hitler (as well as Goebbels, Göring, Strasser, and Röhm), referring back to Ebertin's now famous 1923 and 1924 predictions as omens of Hitler's success. 'Adolf Hitler makes the plan', according to one April 1931 horoscope, 'because he thinks more consciously in a cosmic fashion than many other German politicians.' 'He has a heart in his breast that feels the inter- relationship with the cosmos more distinctly than speculative Sophists', the horo- scope continued. Hitler possessed 'heroism and willingess to suffer. He needs to remain a fighter, in order to make his claim, just like Mussolini in Italy.'[202]

Not all astrologers were in the Nazi camp.[203] But the majority of popular astrological journals ranged from printing cryptic promises of a future Führer and critical screeds against the Weimar government to open support for Hitler and the NSDAP.[204] Although bitter rivals, both the founder of the *Astrologische Rundschau*, Hugo Vollrath, and the head of the Astrological Society in Germany (AsiG), Hubert Korsch, were clear about the chances for 'renewal' promised by the NSDAP. 'Despite all obstacles our Führer has completed his struggle in defence of the German racial soul [*Volksseele*] in victorious and in legal fashion,' Korsch exclaimed. 'The national renewal has begun in all corners of the Reich ... A new German era has begun!' Just as 'the national government' seeks racial purity and 'opposes all corruption with an iron fist', so would they support 'the struggle for purity in practising astrology.'[205]

Occult pracitioners and sceptics alike acknowledged the political and ideo- logical convergence between Nazism and occultism.[206] Many prominent occultists simply assumed, from Nazi rhetoric, that the NSDAP shared their supernatural approach to the world.[207] The ariosophists were ecstatic, describing Nazism as the culmination of their pre-war doctrines. So too were many anthroposophists and theosophists, who viewed the NSDAP as a party that united material and spiritual, eugenical and racial theories and ideas of organic brotherhood.[208] As Fritz Quade, head of the German Society for Scientific Occultism (*Deutsche Gesellschaft für wissenschaftlichen Okkultismus* or DGWO) put it, the NSDAP was the first party to put into practice the unity between occult and *völkisch* thinking based on recognition of the material world as well as the beyond.[209]

'It is one of the astounding facts in the typology of occult periodicals,' wrote the more sceptical Szczesny, 'that they all, without exception, took a national and racial [*völkisch*] standpoint.' Even 'the Jewish "Bunte Wochenschau" [*Illustrated Weekly*] of Hanussen', Szczesny continued, became in the 'year before the seizure of power a true official organ of the National Revolution and outdid itself in prophecies about "World Turning" and "Third Reich" '. 'If one dispenses with the idea that these journals knew the future due to their magical abilities,' Szczesny remarked sarcastically, 'then one has to explain why almost all of these occult magazines were pro-Nazi after 1931.'[210]

There was no such relationship between politics and occultism on the left. 'Communist or left and internationally inclined workers,' Szczesny admitted, 'did not belong to those' who bought these *völkisch*-esoteric periodicals or patronized occult establishments. 'The workers had hunger, unemployment and despair that was far too real staring them in the face,' he reasoned, 'to waste a single serious thought to the blasphemous nonsense and irrationality of occult teachings.' It was rather the 'half-educated circles of the bourgeoisie' that comprised the readership of these occult periodicals and were, 'if by no means always National Socialist', certainly nationalist. 'Although it is hardly a reputable chapter in the history of the bourgeoisie', it must 'be acknowledged that it was precisely these Germans who, in the chaos of the post-war crises, fell into the hands of Boulevard occultism.'[211]

The far left may have discussed the need for dictatorship of the proletariat, but the Communists never relied on *völkisch*-esoteric fantasies or prophecies to justify it. 'Right-wing visionaries', on the other hand, invoked the supernatural imaginary at every turn, propagating *völkisch* fantasies that helped 'catalyze the integration of the popular will with that of an anticipated Führer, and to reassure the readers that His arrival was indeed imminent . . . a single prophet who preserved the German essence against all odds'.[212] 'Upon the one path a man travels,' wrote one Nazi in describing his vision of the Third Reich,

> with head erect, in front of the Volk, indicating the destination – the sunlit mountain peak. Again and again he summons a vacillating people, despite

disappointments and persecution, through the wasteland and the false paths, to the right path ... more and more the seduced and wrongly guided Volk awakens to the perception: 'That which summons you, you German Volk, can alone lead you on the path away from the quagmire, from the misery and destitution, safely to the light – to freedom and to honour – your Volk's Führer, your Führer! All of this is no longer an image, but a reality, a miracle, God's hand over our Führer and our Volk!'[213]

'Thousands, hundreds of thousands, imagine him,' wrote the Nazi military officer Kurt Hesse, 'millions of voices call for him; a single German soul searches for him. No one can predict from where he will come ... Yet everyone will know: he is the Führer. All will cheer him on, all will obey him. Why? Because he exercises a power that he alone possesses. He is a ruler of souls!'[214]

In 1932, Hitler himself prophesied a 'new order'. He would create 'a thousand-year Reich', fuelled by 'the spiritual energy which a people is capable of putting forth'. Anyone 'who supports me in battle,' Hitler promised, would become 'a fellow fighter for a unique spiritual – I would almost say divine – creation'.[215] Among the millions of Hitler's fellow fighters for a thousand-year Reich none is more interesting than Erik Jan Hanussen.

Hanussen and the Nazi Seizure of Power

Erik Hanussen was born Hermann Steinschneider in 1889, the same year as Hitler, to a family of Jewish artists in Vienna. Hanussen's talent for deception became apparent in his teen years, when he forged an anthology of poems and songs to finance a theatre trip. He then joined the 'Oriental Circus', where he participated in reenactments of the Passion of Christ. He moved on to working with the trapeze arts, eating glass and swords, fire-breathing, and other magical tricks.[216]

Hanussen's explanation of his conversion to occultism is similar to Hitler's explanation of becoming an anti-Semite. According to Hanussen, 'I was an anti-occultist through and through, a realist.' 'But the more I read the available periodicals attacking the occult, the more I felt the need to discover their meaning for myself,' he continued. Although he tried to suppress his emerging powers of clairvoyance, Hanussen claimed that he could no longer 'read a letter without immediately seeing the face of the author'.[217]

During the First World War, Hanussen conducted his first seance before an audience of Russian POWS. He eventually performed for the Austrian royal family, before getting arrested for desertion (Hitler too would desert the Austrian Army).[218] Typical of most esotericists and many Nazis, Hanussen was fascinated by the Orient ('the home of the occult'), where he travelled extensively. In Ethiopia he learned the 'Lebascha System' of muscle reading and in Belize he discovered how to use a divining rod.[219] Returning to Europe after the war, Hanussen settled in the new capital of astrology, Berlin, establishing his reputation as a powerful 'magician'.[220]

Hanussen was open about his desire for power, wealth, and fame. He was less interested in proving the existence of the supernatural than employing the newest parapsychological techniques to manipulate people for his own purposes. 'Anyone claiming to be the miracle man,' he argued, 'will always have more success than the one who wants to convince them of the impossibility of miracles.'[221] 'What is magic?' Hanussen asked rhetorically: 'Not to undermine but to encourage people in their beloved beliefs in the miraculous.'[222] Hanussen was equally quick to accuse his occult rivals of 'deception' (*Betrug*), explaining the 'scientific' basis of occultism by referring to theories drawn from Mesmer, Schrenck-Notzing, and Freud.[223]

And yet Hanussen ultimately recognized that Germans *wanted* to believe and chose to encourage his audience that he possessed access to magical forces. Increasingly his performances incorporated different forms of divination, from graphology and telepathy to clairvoyance.[224] Despite his claims to scientific legitimacy, Hanussen was accused by Weimar authorities of charlatanry and deception on multiple occasions, including a famous December 1928 trial.[225] Yet many reporters left the proceedings believing that Hanussen was innocent since the court was unable to prove that he did *not* have supernatural powers. Another sceptical observer was far more impressed. 'We arrived as critics and doubters,' he reported, and left 'convinced of his occult abilities'.[226]

In the wake of the Great Depression, Hanussen turned more consciously to politics and finance, portraying himself as an 'expert for the occult fields of domestic and foreign affairs'.[227] He built a large audience by organizing major publicity stunts and starting his own occult periodicals, *The Other World* (*Die Andere Welt*) and *Illustrated Weekly*.[228] A combination of American pulp fiction and border science, *The Other World* included first-hand accounts of paranormal experiences ('A ghostly experience from my time as an Artist'), love advice ('Graphology: Marry Graphologically!'), popular occult techniques ('You could read hands. In five minutes . . .'), and features such as 'Séance of the Month' and free psychographic readings. To increase his scientific legitimacy, Hanussen solicited articles by famous occultists such as Ernst Issberner-Haldane ('Chyromantie: When is the Best Time for Love?) and Walther Kröner, who related 'spook appearances' to women's menstrual cycles. Hanussen even recruited the star of *The Cabinet of Dr Caligari* (and later *Casablanca*), Conrad Veidt, who contributed a Schertelesque if tongue-in-cheek rumination: 'Am I Demonic?'[229]

All this might appear harmless if not for the size and seriousness of Hanussen's audience.[230] He had aligned himself with the NSDAP already in

March 1930, for example, six months after the Great Depression, but six months before the NSDAP's first great electoral triumph. This suggests, if we discount any real ability at prognostication, that Hanussen believed the Nazis were the perfect vehicle for his venture into politics in a time of growing desperation.[231] According to his assistant Geza von Cziffra, Hanussen told his NSDAP colleagues that he started *The Other World* in 1931 explicitly to propagate Nazi ideas on an occult basis.[232]

Hanussen's political commentary could not have been more helpful to the NSDAP. In September 1931, *The Other World* carried a front-page article entitled 'Hope for Germany's Rise: Hindenburg–Hitler Union and Two Horoscopes (one for Germany, the other for the Reichstag), Predicting Communism's Decline and National Socialism's Triumph'.[233] He also questioned Chancellor Heinrich Brüning's ability to manage the Reichstag and produced a 1932 sound recording warning Germans that 'Bolshevism would make its most concerted attempt to seize power'.[234] On the day Hitler was named Chancellor, Hanussen published an open letter praising the Führer's greatness.[235] 'Apparently Hanussen really had the ambition to become that of which he was accused by the left-wing press,' Szczesny observed, a shill for the coming Third Reich.[236]

Hanussen's dozens of predictions indicating the inevitable rise of Hitler between March 1930 and March 1933 were abetted by his close relationship with leading stormtroopers.[237] Unaware of or indifferent to rumours of Hanussen's Jewish background, Nazi party members were attracted to the popular and charismatic magician. These included the Nazi Reichstag representative, SA General, and Police President of Berlin, Wolf Graf von Helldorff; Nazi Reichstag representative and leader of the Berlin SA, Karl Ernst; and SA General and Police President of Breslau, Edmund Heines.[238]

Hanussen's personal relationship with Ernst and Helldorff appears particularly ironic, given that it emerged around the time the two SA leaders organized the infamous Kürfurstendamm anti-Jewish pogrom. On Rosh Hoshannah 1931, Goebbels, Helldorff, and Ernst ordered the SA to attack Jews exiting the synagogues in the Berlin neighbourhood of Charlottenburg, initiating a nationwide scandal. Helldorff and Ernst were arrested and subsequently defended in a sensational trial by a team of Nazi lawyers that included the former Thule Society member Hans Frank and Alfons Sack, Hanussen and Ewers' mutual acquaintance.[239]

That Berlin's highest-ranking Nazi politicians and stormtroopers would embrace the country's most famous occultist is odd enough. Hanussen's emerging relationship with the NSDAP appears all the stranger, however, given his rumoured Jewishness – rumours encouraged by the liberal and socialist left.[240]

The left-leaning Jewish journalist, Bruno Frei, was particularly hostile. Frei recognized that Hanussen's political predictions, which earned him the nickname 'Hitler's prophet' in the press, were exceedingly dangerous. Because Hanussen displayed 'a marked contempt for the critical faculties of the masses', Frei felt he was 'leading Germany's "little man" astray'. His 'astrological predictions about Hitler's rise', Frei warned, 'were an attack on European civilization and its rational traditions'. 'Have we laboured to attain the scientific worldview', Frei asked, 'or are we willing to allow today's masses – a political rabble that make a business out of barbarism – to steal it from us?'[241]

Frei carried out an aggressive campaign against Hanussen, titled 'A Charlatan Conquers Berlin', in the pages of the liberal *Berlin am Morgen*. Frei did not shrink from reporting Hanussen's orgiastic parties with Nazi leaders on his yacht – named after 'the Indian goddess of love', the 'Aryan Schakti' in 'service of the [formless goddess] Shiva'. 'They worshipped in holy ecstasy of the linga, the divine phallus', Frei reported, and Hanussen acted as a 'priest of the devil ritual'.[242] Frei hoped his series of sensational editorials would provoke Hanussen to accuse him of slander, providing the opportunity to expose the Nazi charlatan in court. Instead, Hanussen managed to get the Berlin authorities to put an injunction on Frei's paper under threat of fines or arrest.[243] Hence, like Ewers, Hanussen proved immune to left-wing criticisms, shielded by those who believed in occult practices.

Hanussen's Nazi friends meanwhile were too enamoured of his political and financial largesse to give Frei's accusations much thought.[244] Hanussen threw lavish parties and was extremely generous with his SA colleagues, ostensibly loaning Helldorff 150,000 marks to pay off gambling debts and offering his Cadillac for stormtrooper rallies. In return for these favours and his public support of the NSDAP, Hanussen enjoyed unofficial SA protection.[245]

For a brief time at least, Hanussen's connections extended into the highest ranks of the NSDAP. In 1932, for example, he managed to get an audience with Hermann Göring.[246] According to some accounts – for which there is no hard evidence – Hanussen met with Hitler as well, possibly to provide advice on manipulating the public.[247] Whether or not Hanussen met the Führer personally, the clairvoyant's personal and political association with the Nazi Party is clear.[248] When Hanussen opened a 'Palace of Occultism' near the same Kürfurstendamm where his fellow German Jews had been attacked by the SA a year earlier, Helldorff, Sack, and Ewers featured at the top of the guest list.[249]

Nevertheless, it is Hanussen's role in 'predicting' the infamous 27 February 1933 Reichstag fire that indicates the remarkable extent – and limits – of the Jewish clairvoyant's intimacy with the Nazi Party. Most scholars agree that the Reichstag fire was set by a Dutch communist, Marinus van der Lubbe, who was found at the site and confessed to the Gestapo under duress. A small number of historians give credence to the idea, popular at the time, of direct Nazi complicity.[250]

Hanussen, in any event, appeared curiously prescient regarding the likelihood of someone setting fire to the Reichstag. Earlier in 1932 he had 'predicted' a 'sensational action by an extreme party', which caused some observers to speculate that the idea for the Reichstag fire was circulating among the Nazi rank and file before February 1933.[251] On 8 February 1933, barely two weeks before the fire, the *Hanussen-Zeitung* published an article titled the 'Death Horoscope of the German Reichstag', in which it claimed that the Communist Party would attempt some form of violence in anticipation of the Reichstag elections on 5 March. Finally and most remarkably, in a seance at his Palace of Occultism on the night of 26 February, Hanussen 'predicted' that a fire would occur at the Reichstag.[252]

There is no concrete evidence that Hanussen found out about the plan from his Nazi associates. Nor is there any proof behind the more fanciful rumour that he hypnotized the communist van der Lubbe into performing the deed.[253] It is nonetheless important to note that Ewers, Helldorff, and Ohst – the latter two SA leaders being closely attached to rumours about setting the Reichstag fire – were among the small group who attended the seance. Also present were Hanussen's private secretary Dzino and the mediums Maria Paudler and Paul Marcus, who agreed that Hanussen spoke distinctly of seeing 'flames arising from a large house'. Writing in the *Hanussen-Zeitung* ten days after the fire, Dzino insisted that Hanussen must have known about the fire in advance. Whether Ernst, Ohst, or Helldorff informed Hanussen remains unclear. Equally suggestive is the fact that Hitler relieved Helldorff of his SA leadership post three weeks after the fire, around the same time that Helldorff's colleagues murdered Hanussen (see Chapter Four).[254]

Whether Hanussen knew about the fire in advance or not, he and his occult-inspired colleagues convinced millions of Germans that they were the 'Chosen People and that the downfall of 1918 would be reversed' by Hitler's ability to make 'the impossible possible'.[255] The Nazis certainly might have come to power without Hanussen. But it is unlikely they could have succeeded without exploiting Weimar's supernatural imaginary in ways exemplified by the country's greatest occultist. At a time when millions were agitated about their futures, recalled Cziffra, it was 'comfortable and easy to believe' in prophets like Hanussen and Hitler, who 'gave millions a false belief in a new saviour'.[256]

Conditioned by Hanussen and other 'barefoot prophets' to accept the role of 'supernatural ability' in shaping Weimar's future, Germans agreed that Hitler too 'possessed magic'. Like Hanussen, he appeared to the 'devotees of the [coming] Third Reich as something more than mere man,' Jung recalled. Hitler emerged rather as a 'prophet under the banners of wind and storm and whirling vortices'.[257] With Hanussen's help, and supported by millions swept up 'in a hurricane of unreasoning emotion', Hitler created 'a mass movement' that careened toward 'a destiny that perhaps none but the seer, the prophet, the Führer himself [could] foretell'.[258]

***

In 1932 the liberal journalist Rudolf Olden published a collection of essays titled *Prophets in the German Crisis: The Miraculous or the Enchanted*. With contributions by leading Weimar intellectuals, the volume was as clear as any contemporary publication in linking the rise of National Socialism to a German preoccupation with the supernatural, exacerbated by war, defeat, and depression. In his introduction Olden did not pull any punches. Politics was 'an eternal struggle between rationality and the miraculous'. Unfortunately when 'rationality comes under pressure', as it had by the crisis-ridden years of the Weimar Republic, its weapons are rendered 'mute, it is eaten by doubt, it emigrates or is restricted'.[259] It was the unfortunate 'fate of our times', Olden continued, that in the realm of 'politics, the predominance of miraculous forces' had marginalized 'everyone that wants to think rationally'.[260]

To be sure, Hitler's magical thinking only affected 'one half of the people; the other half are disgusted, find him laughable, grotesque'.[261] But this first half of the population, the ones that followed Hitler, were conditioned to support Nazism by thousands of 'small' prophets both inside and outside the NSDAP. Such prophets included 'the theosophists, the anthroposophists, the miracle rabbis ... the death rays, the three thousand magicians who live in Berlin alone ... the diviners ... the astrologers ... the miracle doctor Steinmeyer in Hahnenklee ... the Buddhists in Frohnau, the many sects, political and medical miracle makers'. Even 'the belief in witchcraft is growing', Olden lamented. 'With sickness of men and cattle the master witches from the old country ... are being brought in! ... a few kilometres from the cosmopolitan city of Hamburg.'[262] Millions of Germans sought salvation in these 'parapsychologists', the 'proponents of esoteric sciences' and 'the occultists, who speak of unknown powers ... that stream out of the Führer'.[263] Liberal intellectuals wanted to dismiss this supernaturally inspired relationship between Hitler and the masses as 'saviour-neurosis' (*Erlöser-Neurose*), Olden concluded. But that would not make it any less palpable.[264]

As we have seen throughout this chapter, Olden was absolutely correct in his diagnosis, delivered only months before the Nazi seizure of power. Nazism's appeal lay in the spiritual and metaphysical solution it seemed to offer to the contemporary sociopolitical crisis.[265] When Nazis and their supporters referred to a 'Thousand-Year Reich, they not only gave themselves a name with deep biblical overtones and the power of magic numbers', writes Monica Black, 'but also predicted the future'. In the Nazi version of history and politics, Hitler 'figured as a redeemer who would save the German nation and lead a godly realm to an ultimate triumph over evil, light over darkness'. By exploiting the supernatural imaginary, Hitler tied his political mission into something out of the Book of Revelation, as one 'divinely chosen' to create the Third Reich.[266]

The power of National Socialism was not in resuscitating 'mythical-magical thinking', observes Wolfgang Emmerich, 'and even less so the various contents of myths'. Supernatural thinking was already prevalent in the Weimar Republic. Hitler's genius lay in 're-functionalizing the mythical in the sense of fascist rule'.[267] Interwar Germany, a place where 'unrealistic perceptions and unsubtle modes of thought' found wide acceptance, where mentalities that were out of touch with reality were believed capable of changing reality, was the perfect place to carry out this project.[268] In coopting Schertel's magic, enlisting Ewers, and forming an alliance with Hanussen, the Nazis diverted the masses from objective reality and toward the coming Third Reich.

PART II

4

THE THIRD REICH'S WAR ON THE OCCULT
Anti-Occultism, Hitler's Magicians' Controversy, and the Hess Action

'Unclear mythical concepts ... must disappear from the German press where they are used in conjunction with the essence and idea of National Socialism ... Concepts such as *Thing* [folk gathering] and cult simply remind us of those pure German prophets about whom the *Führer* says in his book *Mein Kampf* that most of all they would like to clothe themselves in bearskins, and who maintain further that they created National Socialism some forty years before he did. The National Socialist movement is too close to reality and life to deem it necessary to drag forth outmoded and dead concepts from the dark past, concepts which in no way are able to support the difficult political battle of today, but just weigh it down'.

Joseph Goebbels (1935)[1]

'Already in 1937, as the first measures were taken ... against the over-weening spread of astrology for profit, Comrade Rudolf Hess [asked] ... whether "scientific astrology" would be spared from this measure. Thereafter it became increasingly clear that ... the ... struggle [against occultism] ... faced a consolidated group [within the Nazi Party] for the sponsorship of astrology and occultism'.[2]

Enclosure sent from Alfred Rosenberg's office, the Amt Rosenberg, to Martin Bormann (28 May 1941)

'The whole background of the ban on astrology and its ... partial persistence is interesting not only as an individual case, but speaks to the manifold contradictions within National Socialism of which I have often spoke'.[3]

Interview with the Nazi historian, Ernst Anrich (1960)

On 7 May 1941, Martin Bormann sent an important circular to Nazi officials on behalf of the Party Chancellery.[4] 'Confessional and occult circles,' he wrote, 'have attempted to spread confusion and insecurity amongst the people through the conscious dissemination of miracle stories, prophecies, astrological predictions of the future.' 'Hell and the devil, purgatory and apocalypse are systematically portrayed in all their horrors to the population; fabulous visions and miracle cures are spread and religious prophecies regarding the supposed political and military future travel across the population through whisper campaigns.' 'The use of holy pictures, medallions and amulets for personal use against dive-bombers spreads,' Bormann continued, while 'soothsayers, clairvoyants, palm-readers and tarot practitioners are exploiting the understandable tension.' 'These events,' he concluded, 'show how important ideological education and enlightenment is, precisely during the war.'[5]

Bormann was concerned not only about the persistence of occult and magical thinking among the general German population. 'National Socialist ideology is built upon the scientific knowledge of racial, social and natural laws,' he observed, and 'must not allow such intentional attempts at poisoning by our enemies.' We 'have to be careful,' Bormann added, 'that no party members, especially in rural areas, take part in the propagation of political fortune telling, confessional belief in miracles or superstitions as well as occult miracle making'. 'The party can and will not tolerate it if irresponsible elements attempt to influence the trust of the people in the political leadership through medieval methods.'[6] In other words, Bormann suggested, high-ranking Nazis needed to stop sponsoring occult tendencies.

Which prompts the question: after eight years in power, why hadn't the Third Reich moved more aggressively to curb occultism? And why did the ensuing police measures sponsored by Bormann, Heydrich, and the Gestapo (the so-called 'Hess Action' of June 1941), ultimately prove so modest in comparison to the regime's treatment of other ideological enemies? Chapter Four begins to answer this question by surveying Nazi attempts to police or 'coordinate' the occult during the first four years of the Third Reich. It then turns to the regime's more concerted efforts to combat occultism and promote 'enlightenment' after 1937, culminating in what I call 'Hitler's Magicians' Controversy' – a debate over whether to allow professional anti-occultists to debunk 'magic' and occultism. The chapter concludes with an analysis of the 'Hess Action' against the occult and its longer-term consequences.

I will argue that the 'zigzag course' in Nazi policies toward the occult can be explained by the fact that the Nazis embraced many elements of occult and border scientific thinking.[7] When the regime worked to repress or 'coordinate' esoteric groups, it had more to do with controlling than eliminating occult ideas. Indeed, like border scientists generally, many Nazis worked carefully to distinguish between commercial and popular occultism on the one hand and 'scientific' occultism on the other. While the Nazis indicated considerable hostility toward commercial occultism, practitioners of the scientific variety, as we shall see, enjoyed remarkable latitude, even sponsorship, by the Third Reich.

Occultism in Everyday Life and the Nazi Response, 1933–7

In early April 1933, Erik Hanussen's dead body was discovered by workers in the Berlin suburb of Zossen. All evidence suggests that he was shot on 24 or 25 March, a day after the Enabling Law that secured the Nazi dictatorship. The perpetrators were a group of Nazi stormtroopers, including his old friends Helldorff and Ernst, head of the Berlin-Brandenburg SA. The traditional explanation for Hanussen's assassination is that the anti-occultist Third Reich was not ready to tolerate a prominent – much less Jewish – clairvoyant in its midst. In this reading of events, Hanussen's murder was merely the first salvo in an escalating fuselage directed against the occult.[8]

But if Hanussen's murder had primarily to do with the new government's hostility to occultism, then how do we explain the intimate relationship between Hanussen and the Nazi Party, including his own murderers, before his killing?[9] As we saw in Chapter Three, neither accusations of charlatanry, nor debauchery, nor even the revelation that he was Jewish had undermined Hanussen's reputation among his Nazi colleagues.[10] It was the left-wing and liberal elements in the Weimar Republic that had attacked Hanussen most vociferously, both for propagating charlatanry and for abetting the rise of fascism.

The chief difference between the Third Reich and Weimar Republic was not the Nazis' greater scepticism toward supernatural thinking. To the contrary, the Third Reich 'redefined the issue of occultism', in the words of Corinna Treitel, 'not in epistemological but in ideological terms'.[11] In other words, the Nazis did not oppose occultism on primarily scientific grounds, as did the liberal and left-wing sceptics who dominated the Weimar Republic. The Third Reich wanted rather to control or repress any groups – occult or otherwise – that failed to share Nazi ideology or conform to the norms of the 'racial community' (*Volksgemeinschaft*). To the extent that they were sympathetic to Nazism, however, occultists found a surprising level of tolerance during the first four years of the Third Reich.

Nazi Anti-Occultism 1933–7

When Hitler was named Chancellor of the Weimar Republic on 30 January 1933, the Third Reich inherited a German public that was highly receptive to occultism.

From Vienna, Munich, and Frankfurt to Berlin, Hamburg, and Leipzig, hundreds of thousands of Germans and Austrians continued to purchase occult and New Age literature, read border scientific journals, and participate in astrological and theosophical societies, seances, and spiritualist experiments.[12]

The Third Reich also inherited an 'evolving pattern of ambivalence' when it came to policing the occult.[13] The complexity of determining what was occult charlatanry and what was legitimate border science had forced the Weimar Republic to rely on scientists, medical professionals, and putative experts.[14] As occultism became 'part of the era's increasingly scientific orientation to social problems', however, many such experts, as well as the legal authorities that relied on them, found it 'increasingly difficult to reject the occult sciences wholesale'.[15]

The Third Reich did introduce some new restrictions against occultism between 1933 and 1937. But their general approach was to reinforce this Weimar-era pattern, which focused on eradicating fraud and exploitation.[16] On 13 August 1934, for example, the regime merely tightened a June 1931 law against clairvoyants and tarot readers who attempted to make money through information that is 'not possible to know through natural means'.[17] In other cities and states, bans against commercial occultism were enhanced and better enforced, though no new laws were passed.[18]

It did not help policing efforts that the Third Reich inherited a group of professional occultists who developed effective strategies for circumventing the law in the Weimar Republic – usually by asserting their belief in the ('scientific') efficacy of what they practised and without seeking profit.[19] This strategy worked in Weimar not because republican authorities acknowledged the authenticity of occultism, but due to legal niceties inherent to a liberal republic. Before 1933 even highly sceptical legal experts felt a juridical obligation to distinguish between charlatans seeking commercial gain and those exercising their beliefs in 'good faith'.[20] 'Fee-charging occultists' soon learned to exploit this legal 'loophole'.[21]

Occultists continued these practices in the Third Reich, though on very different premises. The Nazis were far less tolerant of dissenting beliefs than the Weimar Republic and far less concerned about juridical niceties. And yet occultists could now take advantage of an epistemological environment that openly acknowledged esoteric forces and embraced border scientific thinking.[22] As the SS paper, the *Schwarze Korps*, explained in 1936: 'We want in no way to deny that there are things which are invisible to our natural faculties. We also do not want to oppose a science that occupies itself with research on such matters ... What we reject unequivocally is any obvious swindle that is based on deception and exploitation of stupidity and therefore constitutes criminal activity.'[23] Provided that the occult doctrine or practitioner was sufficiently 'scientific' in character, the Third Reich appeared reluctant to carry out any police action.

Hence the German Society for Scientific Occultism (DGWO) negotiated the first few years of the Third Reich fairly easily.[24] So did the major astrological associations and journals. They were generally allowed to police themselves in terms of practising 'scientific' occultism – provided they promised to stop publishing horoscopes of Nazi leaders.[25] Hitler even sent a note thanking the president of the German Astrological Association (DAZ), Hubert Korsch, for organizing the 1935 Astrologer's Conference taking place in Wernigerode.[26]

On both the legal and cultural front, the Interior Minister Wilhelm Frick and Joseph Goebbels' Reich Literature Chamber (RSK) intervened to defend research having to do with 'pure scientific' astrology. They also allowed open discussions in the media of Hans Bender's experiments in parapsychology.[27] When the Reich Office for Public Health intervened, accusing Bender of fraud, Goebbels' Propaganda Ministry (RMVP) and the *Völkischer Beobachter* defended Bender's assertion that the news coverage 'had not differentiated between his scientific approach' and that of popular occult practitioners. Bender's argument also 'found full support among officials in Berlin'.[28]

The Third Reich was surprisingly accommodating toward occult societies with a more political bent as well.[29] In 1933 the opportunistic Rudolf von Sebottendorff returned to Germany, joined the NSDAP, and refounded the Thule Society.[30] He then published a memoir, *Before Hitler Came*, arguing that the Society had produced National Socialism and laid the foundation for the Third Reich. In March 1934 the regime finally decided to proscribe the book and expel Sebottendorff from the party for writing a sensationalist account that gave 'chief credit for the national renewal of Germany to the Thule Society'.[31] But the Society survived Sebottendorff's expulsion and continued publishing his *Thule-Bote* for a number of months.[32] When the Society disbanded, it was due to their members' own feeling of redundancy in a regime that fulfilled so many of its aspirations.[33]

The same pattern holds for the Artamanen.[34] In 1930 the association endorsed the NSDAP because it 'maintained the belief in our mission, the belief in the Third Reich'. It further proclaimed that the Artamanen were 'intrinsically connected with the leader of the German freedom movement, Adolf Hitler'.[35] Upon absorbing the Artamanen into the Hitler Youth a few years later, Baldur von Schirach agreed, declaring that the 'association of Artamanen carried out pioneering work for National Socialism ... its leaders were national socialist fighters'.[36] The Wehrwolf were absorbed into the SA in relatively seamless fashion as well.[37]

This pattern of integrating ariosophic groups into the party or state was endemic to the regime's approach to ideological policing. It focused on eliminating political and ideological sectarianism, not eradicating occultism per se. The primary responsibility for policing sectarianism fell to Reinhard Heydrich's Security Service (SD), part of the Reich Security Main Office (RSHA) built up by Himmler during the first six years of the Third Reich.[38] The SD treated occult groups as they did any other 'sectarian' associations and 'worldview sects'. They pursued aggressively those that 'espoused an independent belief system and obstinately maintained their separation from the state ... a distinct barrier to the creation of a united *Volksgemeinschaft*.'[39]

This explains why the regime's treatment of ariosophists was vastly different than that of Jehovah's Witnesses.[40] The SD acknowledged, for example, that many ariosophists viewed Nazism as the culmination of their doctrine. 'Ariosophists are not influenced by Freemason-pacifistic tendencies,' Heydrich's SD conceded, but '*völkisch* ideology.'[41] Asked to conduct a background check on a former member of the German Order, the SS responded that 'The 'German Order' belongs to the *völkisch* orders that sought the renewal of Germany and had as their mission anti-Freemason and anti-Church goals', which is why 'the highest party court has determined that erstwhile members of the "German Order" may be party comrades without any restrictions'.[42] A member of the ariosophic-inclined Skalden Order was accepted into the party because the Skalden 'belonged to the *völkisch* lodges and orders' on which 'the Upper Party Court had ruled positively'. It is important to 'differentiate between Freemason lodges', which were hostile to Nazism, Heydrich's SD continued, and 'lodges, Orders or associations that especially prior to the war preserved a German tradition which was taken from German prehistory and that strived for an empowerment of the German people'.[43]

So long as their leaders indicated 'solidarity with Hitler's anti-materialism, on the one hand, and aggressive nationalism, on the other', many theosophic and anthroposophic groups were permitted to continue as well.[44] Admittedly, the Gestapo declared the Anthroposophic Society a danger to the state in late-1935. The SD was clear, however, that the danger had little to do with occultism. More problematic was the Society's loyalty to an alternative Führer – Rudolf Steiner – whose politics were linked to the unholy trinity of Marxism, Masonry, and Jewry.[45] Anthroposophic doctrines and institutions, on the other hand, including Steiner's 'Christian Community' (*die Christengemeinschaft*), Waldorf Schools, and biodynamic agriculture, survived into the period of the Second World War, sponsored by prominent Nazi leaders (see Chapter Five).[46]

Even with respect to Freemasonry, Nazi policies were remarkably loose and inconsistent. For Hitler the most 'dangerous element' in Freemasonry, according to Hermann Rauschning, was not the 'skeletons and death's heads, the coffins and the mysteries'. It was the fact that they formed 'a sort of priestly nobility ... imparted through the medium of symbols and mysterious rites in degrees of initiation'. 'The hierarchical organization and the initiation through symbolic rites without bothering the brains but by working on the imagination through magic and the symbols of a cult,' Rauschning observed, is what Hitler both emulated and feared.[47] Himmler's masseur, Felix Kersten, made virtually identical statements regarding his master's ambivalent attitude toward Masonry.[48]

The Masons garnered attention from Himmler and Rosenberg not because of their historical links to esotericism per se. It was because of the Masons' ostensible participation 'in an international conspiracy against German culture' and 'dangerous cosmopolitanism that led to Jewish emancipation in the nineteenth century'.[49] When it came to policing individuals, the regime's ban forbidding former Masons from joining the party or the army was rarely enforced.[50] In fact, many Nazis in charge of surveillance of the occult, including J. W. Hauer and Gregor Schwarz-Bostunitsch, stood, in the words of Heydrich's SD, 'very near to theosophy and anthroposophy', and continued to draw on 'Indian philosophy and eastern ways of thinking'.[51]

This brings us back to Hanussen's murder.[52] Besides the rumours of his Jewishness, the famous clairvoyant knew far too much about the personal and financial matters of leading party members, including Helldorf, Röhm, and Ernst.[53] Hanussen had furthermore bragged about predicting the Reichstag fire, which implicated his SA colleagues in having committed a premeditated crime.[54] Finally, Hanussen's popularity undermined the Nazi obsession with controlling public opinion and 'corresponding fear that charismatic individuals beyond the regime's ken could sway it'. Hanussen was not murdered because he was an occultist. He was murdered because he had become too great a political liability and 'public-relations threat' – elements that doomed many Nazi Party members in the period from the Enabling Law of March 1933 to the infamous 'Night of the Long Knives' in June 1934.[55]

In comparison to the Weimar Republic, there was certainly increased surveillance and repression after 1933. When gauging Nazi anti-occultism, we nonetheless need to recognize that, first, the Third Reich kept watch on and murdered hundreds of members of its own party in this period and, second, that it was *less repressive* toward occultists than any other sectarian group (much less Jews or Communists).[56] According to the SD's own numbers, there were by 1937 more than three hundred existing sects, some of which contained several thousand members. In fact, the SD found itself lamenting the 'dismal legal tools available to wage the war against occultism' because of gaps in the law that the regime had not 'bothered to close'.[57]

According to one frustrated anti-occultist, writing in the pages of the *Racial Observer* in 1937, 'it is regrettable that the proclivity for superstition and mysticism has been systematically fomented' in the Third Reich. After four years in power 'nearly 80 per cent of Germans are still in some form

susceptible to this nonsense'.[58] Far from inaugurating a 'war on the occult', the
years 1933–7 had witnessed an efflorescence of occult and supernatural
thinking. For sceptics and debunkers, both inside and outside the NSDAP, the
situation was untenable.

The Spring 1937 Action Against the Occult

Because the Third Reich's efforts to combat occultism were so underwhelming,
a number of Weimar-era anti-occultists took it upon themselves to weed out
the 'vampire of superstition'.[59] At the forefront of these efforts was the so-called
'Ludendorff circle', loosely centred on the former Field Marshall Erich
Ludendorff and his second wife, Mathilde Ludendorff. A sometime Nazi fellow
traveller, sometime critic, Mathilde was a trained psychiatrist who began her
career by dissecting the work of the famous Munich parapsychologist Albert
von Schrenck-Notzing in the mid-1920s.[60]

The Ludendorff circle attracted a broad range of anti-occultists before 1933,
including the Nazi Police Commissar Carl Pelz, the chemist Albert Stadthagen,
and Albert Hellwig, editor of the *Journal for Critical Occultism*.[61] Ludendorff's
publications attacked everyone from Hanussen, to whom they referred as
'Hitler's Jewish prophet', to respected border scientists such as Hans Driesch
and H. H. Kritzinger, who later worked for the Third Reich.[62]

Initially, the Ludendorff circle held out hope that the Third Reich would
embrace 'the struggle against particular exploiters of need and distress, against
undeniable deceivers in the sphere of superstition'.[63] In his 1935 book *Vampire
of Superstition*, Carl Pelz, writing under a pseudonym, argued that the rise of
Hitler was the opportune time to attack 'racially foreign' clairvoyants such as
Hanussen, who used their 'powers' to exploit people desperate from the war,
inflation, and Great Depression.[64] Not much was done during the first two
years of the Third Reich, Pelz conceded. Still, he hoped that 'all the psychological preconditions for popular ignorance and mass deception' might soon
disappear through government and police action.[65]

Upon close inspection, the motivations of the Ludendorff circle in
combating occultism reflect the same esoteric predispositions we see in the
Nazi Party at large. In a series of books and pamphlets with picturesque titles
– such as *Christian Terror Against Women* (1934), *The Jewish Power: Its Essence
and End* (1939), *The Creeping Poison: Occultism, its Teachings, World View, and
Combating it* (1935) – and Pelz's *Vampire of Superstition* (1935; under the pseudonym of Fred Karsten), the Ludendorff circle argued that Jews, Christians,
and Masons had infiltrated the upper echelons of European society in an effort
to destroy the Ur-Germanic race and religion. The members of the Ludendorff
circle were partial to their own *völkisch*-esoteric religion as well, the 'Society for

the Knowledge of a German God' (*Bund für deutsche Gotteserkenntnis*), based on racial border science, fanatical anti-Semitism, and Germanic paganism.[66]

The Ludendorff circle did not reject the existence of esoteric forces. 'To the objection that clairvoyance, telepathy or other supernatural powers are not a pure swindle,' Pelz explained, 'we respond that this has never been the claim. It should not be denied that there are sensible people who in some cases are capable of manifesting clairvoyance or telepathic not to mention other mysterious powers. But these people – and that is the decisive point – do not attempt to profit from their abilities.'[67] Pelz and his colleagues in the Ludendorff circle merely sought to root out the 'vampire of superstition' propagated by charlatans. This included religious sectarians, foreigners, and Jews like Hanussen (a common bugbear of anti-occultists), who attempted to 'profit from their abilities' by exploiting the German people.[68]

The fact that 'so many members of the Ludendorff circle were themselves immersed in fanciful visions of Germanic paganism and Jewish world conspiracy hardly reinforces their "Enlightenment" claims'.[69] In her 1933 book, *The Deception of Astrology*, for example, Mathilde Ludendorff extolled 'the primarily German belief in universal spirituality of the divine'.[70] Across Babylonia, Persia, India and Europe, Ludendorff opined, all Indo-Aryan peoples had embraced 'cosmic awareness, the living unity with the entirety of the universe as a spiritual manifestation of an Ur-Germanic living God. We share this with our ancestors, with some astrologers of our blood'.[71] This authentic German belief in cosmic forces was threatened, Ludendorff argued, by the 'kismet'-obsessed Semitic people – whose astrological pronouncements focused on everyday distractions like love, sports, character, and money instead of the supernatural powers of God, the Norns, the Edda and Nordic religion.[72] In this respect Ludendorff was similar to Nazi 'anti-occultists', such as Kurd Kisshauer and Alfred Rosenberg, who propagated the 'cosmic laws' of Germanic paganism, though they warned against 'oriental . . . star-reading' and 'sorcerous magic of the Orient and Africa'.[73]

Much of the Ludendorff circle likewise argued that there was a secret conspiracy of 'Asiatic priests' living in Tibet. Led by the Dalai Lama, these priests were 'prepared to use any methods in championing their claim to world domination – including monstrous genocide'.[74] Erich Ludendorff himself, ostensibly a vocal anti-occultist, was swindled by an alchemist and believed that a cabal of Masons and Jews stood behind the Weimar Republic.[75] His colleague Hermann Rehwaldt insisted that the British made 'secret alliances' with African occultists to prop up their empire.[76] Not surprisingly, Heydrich's SD, which had members of the circle under surveillance, found it impossible to determine whether the Ludendorff circle were occultist or anti-occultist in nature.[77]

Despite their crypto-esoteric agenda, the Ludendorff circle continued to view themselves as pro-enlightenment crusaders fighting an existential struggle against occultism.[78] Frustrated by the Third Reich's dearth of anti-occultist policies, the Nazi Police Commissar Pelz therefore submitted a long report on the persistence of occultism to Reinhard Heydrich and his chief of the criminal police (*Kripo*), Arthur Nebe.[79] Impressed by Pelz's analysis, Heydrich instructed Nebe to come up with a set of parameters for combating occultism on a Reich level and to forward his recommendations to Himmler.[80]

Following the Nazis' nuanced approach, Nebe's instructions were careful to differentiate 'from a policing perspective' between 'the investigation of all the occurrences which are inaccessible through natural human perception (scientific occultism)' and 'on the other hand every activity that rests on and exploits superstition'. 'Scientific occultism,' Nebe emphasized, 'remains beyond our purview from a policing standpoint.' In contrast, 'unscientific and pseudoscientific occultism requires the sharpest police oversight and countermeasures, especially insofar as it is done for commercial reasons'.[81]

The distinction Nebe makes between 'scientific occultism' and the commercial exploitation of 'unscientific' occultism is essential to understanding the *seeming* contradictions in Nazi attitudes toward border science. This episode is important, however, in two other respects. First, it suggests that efforts by the SD and Gestapo to police the occult in the spring of 1937 were generated not by Himmler or Heydrich, but by a professional debunker (Pelz) who was frustrated at the Third Reich's lack of activity. In the polycratic Nazi state it was not unusual for the Gestapo to implement policy based on unsolicited reports from lower-level functionaries or civilian informers.[82] Nevertheless, the fact that the Gestapo's first coordinated effort to police occultism emerged from Pelz's report says much about the regime's general disinterest in eradicating supernatural thinking.

Second, this episode provides insight into the highly differentiated responses of individual leaders *within* the Nazi police apparatus. It is no coincidence that Heydrich used the occasion of receiving an unsolicited report from an obscure police commissar (Pelz) to initiate a campaign against the occult. As chief of the SS intelligence service (SD), Heydrich's primary task was to uncover ideological opposition.[83] Moving against occultism was part of a wider purge of 'sectarian tendencies' in preparation for war between the summer of 1937 and that of 1938.[84]

It is also no coincidence that, four years into the Third Reich, Himmler and the SS had yet to develop a coordinated campaign against occultism. Nor is it surprising that it took weeks – requiring a second letter from Nebe – for Himmler to respond to Pelz's report. For Himmler was deeply invested in occult and border scientific thinking and saw no incompatibility between policing commercial occultism and appropriating 'scientific occultism' for the purposes of the Third Reich.[85] These differences within the upper echelons of the SS and police administration might explain why Nebe, as head of the Kripo, proposed a middle way that would preserve a space for 'scientific occultism' while moving with all seriousness against 'every activity that rests on and exploits superstition'.

Responding to Nebe's recommendations, the SD and Gestapo began a campaign of surveillance and repression aimed at 'sectarian' tendencies in the spring of 1937.[86] Instead of attacking occultism *tout court*, the SD focused selectively on occult groups that promoted 'corrosive individualism and dangerous internationalism' and 'whose charismatic proponents threatened to lead the public astray'.[87] Notably, practising 'occultism' per se did not figure in the SD's list of suspect activities: egocentrism, Communist agitation, internationalism, failure to give the Hitler salute, refusal to do military service, failure to accept absorption into Nazi Party associations, refusal to work in military industries, promotion of faith healing, promotion of ignorance, homosexuality, and/or the denial of racial teachings of Nazism.[88]

After years of piecemeal legal restrictions, the regime did institute a universal ban on commercial forms of astrology. By 1938 the major German astrological societies and periodicals had also been dissolved or suspended.[89] Where banned organizations continued to practise with impunity, surveillance and legal bans were occasionally transformed into fines, warnings, or even the occasional tenure in jail for the ringleader.[90]

Also beginning in the summer of 1937, the SS paper *Die Schwarze Korps* ran a series of articles entitled 'Dangerzone Superstition'. The purpose of the short-lived series was to promote 'public enlightenment', citing rational explanations for occult events similar to articles run in critical occultist publications during the Weimar Republic. Still, the emphasis on enlightenment was always secondary to the typical Nazi insistence that occult (and other sectarian) forces were exploited by Jews, Masons, and Catholics.[91]

The Reich Office for Public Health (RVG), headed by Dr Bernhard Hörmann, joined these 'pro-enlightenment' efforts in the spring of 1937.[92] In a May 1937 article in *The People's Health Watch* (*Die Volksgesundheitswacht*), Hörmann drew the typical Nazi distinction between scientific occultism and those 'obvious deceivers and conscienceless exploiters' of people's 'lack of knowledge and helplessness'. The danger of occultism, Hörmann argued, was its 'international' flavour, the 'people-disintegrating international occult movement, led by Jews and Freemasons' that threatened 'Nordic human beings'.[93]

In short, what made occultism dangerous 'was not so much ideological distance as ideological proximity'. Nazi anti-occultists 'discerned a menacing potential in esoteric discourse on themes central to Nazism's own self-understanding, above all the intertwined topics of nation and race'. Because they feared a 'prospective challenge to the hegemony of strict National Socialist teachings as they defined them', the Nazis infiltrated and banned occult groups that departed from the party line in areas 'that shared significant theoretical overlap with Nazi imagery and ideals'.[94] Because of these same ideological and epistemological affinities, however, the Nazis remained careful not to dismiss scientific occultism out of hand.[95] It remains to be seen how effective this coordinated, if highly nuanced, attack on occultism would be.

The Limits of Enlightenment and Hitler's Magicians' Controversy, 1937–41

On 14 January 1941 the professional debunker, Albert Stadthagen, received a terse letter from the president of the Reich Magicians' Association, Helmut Schreiber. According to Schreiber, Stadthagen and his Nazi associate, the Police Commissar Carl Pelz, were undermining illusionists everywhere by publicly demonstrating the 'scientific' basis of magic. Insisting that such performances contradicted 'a point of view expressed at the highest level', Schreiber advised Stadthagen and Pelz to 'follow up with the Führer's adjutant, Herr SS-Gruppenführer Schaub, should they have any doubt about what that meant'.[96] Within two weeks of Schreiber's letter, Pelz received a direct order from the Gestapo to cease his campaign of public 'enlightenment'.[97]

As a good National Socialist, Pelz turned to his most frequent sponsor, the 'Strength Through Joy' (*Kraft durch Freude* or KdF) division of the German Labour Front (*Deutsche Arbeiterfront* or DAF) headed by Dr Robert Ley. The KdF found Pelz and Stadthagen's presentations as entertaining as they were enlightening, employing the debunkers to perform occult-based 'demonstrations' before explaining the science behind the supernatural. Except when the KdF dutifully protested the ban, the Gestapo official's response was unambiguous, 'I note that the Führer has personally ordered these measures against Pelz and that any lifting of or change in these measures is only possible with the agreement of the Führer . . . in the mean time, Pelz must be stricken [from your list] as a potential speaker'.[98]

This fascinating episode, at the heart of what I call 'Hitler's Magicians' Controversy', typifies the Third Reich's complicated attitude toward occultism.[99] As the experiences of Pelz and Stadthagen make clear, the 1937 'crackdown' had already begun to dissipate before the Second World War. Indeed, while the war led to greater persecution of most of the Third Reich's enemies, it seemed to have the reverse effect in regard to practising magicians. So long as magicians – or other purveyors of occult and supernatural ideas – played by the rules, whether in terms of providing occult-based popular entertainment or pursuing 'scientific occultism', they stood a chance not only of avoiding arrest but of plying their trade for the enjoyment and utility of the Reich.

The Limits of Enlightenment

The May 1937 salvo against occultism was a clear departure from the uneven approach during the first four years of the Third Reich.[100] New, more restrictive laws against practising astrology and palm-reading were passed. Many occult organizations were banned. Nevertheless, as suggested above, scientific occultists were permitted by the SD and Gestapo to proceed with their astrological and parapsychological 'experiments'.[101] In the few cases where leading astrologers were put under surveillance or persecuted, it was often due to something other than astrology. In Hubert Korsch's case, his permission to publish was abrogated due to moral turpitude ('evidence' of homosexuality) and political unreliability. These rumours had been around since the Nazi seizure of power. But the Gestapo had not determined to investigate them until 1938.[102]

The SD and Gestapo also commissioned dozens of well-intentioned reports and peer reviews aimed at differentiating 'scientific occultism' from charlatanry.[103] As a result, Heydrich confirmed in June 1938 that while 'commercial astrology' should finally be banned, 'astrology as a research field' should 'not be prevented, per request of the Reichsführer'.[104] To be sure, when Hitler gave a speech in August 1938 denying that the Nazi movement was tied to mystical influences, it set off a flurry of debates within the SS regarding the viability of 'scientific occultism'. Ultimately, Himmler and others determined not to interpret Hitler's general comments as a blanket attack on the occult.[105] 'As you know,' the Reichsführer explained to Heydrich in January 1939, 'I do not consider astrology to be pure humbug, but believe that there is something behind it ... We must do much more to restrict [charlatans] in a way that we only allow specific communities of research in this sphere.'[106]

The same pattern of ambivalence – or more precisely, the same distinction between popular and scientific occultism – appears in the attitude of the Reich Office of Public Health (RVG) under Bernard Hörmann. Hörmann's RVG was arguably the second most important office, after the SD and Gestapo, in policing occultism and enlightening the population. After a long 1937 diatribe ('Protection of Serious Science') explaining the need to move against occultism, however, Hörmann conceded that 'medical science is often wrong' and 'there are still many things between heaven and earth of which our school wisdom could not dream'.[107] Another article, 'The Twilight of Occultism', agreed that it would be unfair to dismiss all occult sciences 'summarily as superstition'. One had to accept the existence of 'extrasensory' phenomena' that had been 'referred to earlier as "supernatural"'.[108]

To help determine the line between serious 'border science' and charlatanry, Hörmann sponsored experiments by 'scientific' astrologers, cosmobiologists, and anthroposophists.[109] At the same time he employed 'speakers who were "experts" on occultism to give lectures designed to "enlighten" the public about outmoded "superstition" that endangered the Reich' and who published 'books that took a critical approach to occultism'.[110] Hörmann hired Pelz and Stadthagen not to debunk border science in all its forms. Their goal was to enlighten the population as to the deception behind popular or commercial occultism.[111]

It makes sense that Pelz and Stadthagen were employed most frequently by the Strength Through Joy (KdF) division of Dr Ley's Reich Office for German Public Education (Reichsamt Deutsches Volksbildungswerk or RDVW). Their scientific demonstrations were mostly entertainment. They began with many of the famous acts performed by Hanussen and others, dazzling the crowd with occult-inspired tricks. Only in the second act would they attempt to explain their methods. Pelz and Stadthagen simply didn't see – or conveniently overlooked – the irony. While they believed they were 'enlightening' Germans regarding the scientific basis of magic, the reality was that they were providing cheap, occult-inspired entertainment to thousands of workers and troops.[112]

That the SS, RVG, and DAF took the lead in commissioning pro-'enlightenment' demonstrations did nothing to dampen Himmler, Ley, or Hörmann's personal interest in esotericism.[113] Nor did it mean an end to popular occultism. In the spring of 1937, even as the first coordinated wave of anti-occultist policies began, the Völkischer Beobachter (VB) published an article 'From the Journal of a Sorcercer's Apprentice: From Abracadabra to Magic Circle'. 'Certainly the magical art is deception,' the article reported, but 'the world wants to be deceived.'[114] The Nazis were in fact 'surprisingly reticent to publicize its suppression of occultism to the masses', preferring a more gentle message of 'enlightenment' or increasingly 'studious silence'.[115] The Reich Literary Chamber (RSK), which operated under the umbrella of Goebbels' RKK, was genuinely uncertain about what constituted popular occultism. An official in the RSK wrote to the RMVP repeatedly, beginning in late-1937, recommending a ban of Hertha Kokott's book The Magical Power of the Stars and Love Life: Astrological Observations on Love, Marriage, and Friendship.[116] The book had been confiscated by the police six months earlier, around the time of the spring 1937 action. The publisher protested the ban, however, leading the RSK to enlist an 'expert', Dr Curt Rosten, to conduct a peer review of the book.[117]

'Based on form and content,' Rosten wrote, 'this is one of the most despicable books published on this theme.'[118] The 'author attempts to give their expositions a certain scientific sheen', Rosten continued, and failed because of insufficiently rigorous astrological training.[119] The only places where the book appears at all competent is where the 'author copies the works of [the respected astrologer] Karl Brandler-Pracht verbatim in an irresponsible fashion', as if they 'were her own ideas'.[120] In short, the Nazi expert was criticizing the book not for its occult premise, but for its lack of astrological rigour. And yet, even this negative review by a scientific occultist was not sufficient to convince the RSK to ban the book. Were the author to publish a new addition, wrote the RMVP, she would need to revise it substantially in the more scientific direction recommended by Rosten. Until then the matter was closed.[121]

In March 1939 the specific office dealing with astrological and related matters within Goebbels' RSK was eliminated. Its responsibilities were incorporated into Philip Bouhler's Official Party Examining Commission for the Protection of National Socialist Publications (*Parteiamtliche Prüfungskommission zum Schutze des national-sozialistischen Schrifttums* or PPK). The PPK's 'experts' included an erstwhile member of Sebottendorff's *Bund Oberland*, Karl Heinz Hederich, and a professional astrologer, Dr Werner Kittler, whose specialization was 'cosmobiology'.[122] Kittler and Hederich subsequently used their position in the PPK 'to bring National Socialist ideology and the worldview of astrology together in harmony'.[123]

Encouraged by Hederich and Kittler, Hitler's Chancellery intervened more vigorously on behalf of occultists.[124] In August 1938 the PPK approved Elsbeth Ebertin's 1939 astrological calendar because of its rigorous 'cosmobiological' basis.[125] As the PPK's resident 'Expert for Cosmobiology', Kittler recruited dozens of famous astrologers, dowsers, and parapsychologists to study the potential benefits of various border sciences.[126] Not only were numerous astrological and 'moon' calendars approved and defended by the PPK.[127] According to one official in Alfred Rosenberg's office, the Amt Rosenberg, the PPK 'was trying to make decisions in regard to official party ideology with the help of an obscure astrologer' (namely Kittler).[128]

With the outbreak of war in September 1939, Rosenberg urged the PPK to ban astrological calendars because they could be used to manipulate public opinion.[129] Hederich agreed that it was important to prevent 'every political misuse and every comment on National Socialists'. This is why he had 'fundamentally forbidden all prophecies that had to do with the leading personalities of contemporary political life' as well as restricting 'political prognoses' – a restriction that had been on the books since 1934. Hederich nonetheless insisted the regime permit occult publications on 'harmless things that have a positive effect on people who are open to astrological speculation'.[130] Rosenberg's 'approach, which suddenly introduces a ban, promised no success', Hederich argued, and would merely lead to the proliferation of smaller, private, less ideologically loyal astrological groups. On 14 October 1939 he recommended that the RSK continue to allow the publication of astrological literature.[131]

Exasperated, Rosenberg wrote to Goebbels personally to ask him to intervene.[132] According to Rosenberg, his office did not intend to 'hinder' the practice of serious 'astrological research'. 'If [Bouhler] believes this research needs to be published in a scientifically oriented book,' Rosenberg added, 'we do not plan to cause him any problems.' But 'astrological calendars' were something else entirely since 'the only purpose of them was to make our actions dependent on uncontrollable constellations of stars and thereby rob us of our impartiality of judgement. If a political operation or agricultural enterprise became dependent on those kind of prophecies then it would lose any kind of personal responsibility.' Regardless of the scientific validity of astrology, Rosenberg concluded, the calendar needed to be prevented for 'purely practical reasons'.[133] Goebbels either did not see the urgency or, more likely, genuinely worried about moving against a practice as popular as astrology in the midst of war. Whatever the reason, the Propaganda Minister did not intercede.[134]

Hence, by the outbreak of the Second World War, nearly every Reich office charged with *combating* occultism – whether Bouhler's PPK, Hörmann's RVG, Ley's DAF, Goebbels' RMVP (RKK), Himmler's SS, or even Heydrich's SD and Gestapo – appeared to take the same approach and make the same concessions. They pronounced the evils of 'sectarian' tendencies and occult charlatanry while simultaneously permitting and in some cases sponsoring 'scientific occultism'.[135] This nuanced approach to policing the occult was not what Pelz had envisioned when he wrote to the Kripo two years earlier. Enormously frustrated, he admonished Hörmann to move more aggressively against 'occult teaching that promoted popular stupidity'.[136]

Any disappointment that Pelz and Stadthagen might have felt about the Third Reich's lack of seriousness was exacerbated by the outbreak of war in 1939. For the war would make the enviroment *more* hostile for debunkers – and for the same reason that Pelz and Stadthagen received so many opportunities to perform their acts of 'enlightenment'. By meeting the need for popular occult-based entertainment, Pelz and Stadthagen's 'demonstrations' brought them into the crosshairs of the most unapologetic of commercial occultists: professional magicians.

Hitler's Magicians' Controversy

In February 1940 the above-mentioned president of the Magic Circle, Helmut Schreiber, sent a frustrated letter to the Amt Rosenberg. Pelz and Stadthagen's debunking activities, Schreiber complained, by revealing the tricks of the trade, were undermining the livelihood of magicians – and no doubt drawing away their audience through state-subsidized 'demonstrations'. These performances, Schreiber argued, had to stop.

One might assume that the Nazi regime, in the name of 'public enlightenment', would come down unequivocally on the side of their favourite debunkers. Nevertheless, after some debate, the KdF and the Amt Rosenberg, the offices most sympathetic to Stadthagen and Pelz, agreed to a modus vivendi with the Reich Artists' Union (*Reichsfachschaft Artistik*), which represented a number of occult performers, including the Magic Circle. The Reich Artists' Union would allow Pelz and Stadthagen to 'perform' provided they focused on debunking general occult phenomena and not specific 'magic' tricks. Pelz and Stadthagen were dubious about their ability to do one without the other. Still, they accepted the modus vivendi with the caveat that 'the gentlemen are in agreement to clear up any questions in borderline or doubtful cases bilaterally and collegially'.[137]

Only three months later, in May 1940, the Reich Artists' Union appealed to the same authorities – this time including the Reich Press Office, the Reich Film Chamber, and Hitler's Chancellery. At issue was Stadthagen's bread-and-butter presentation, 'Apparent Miracles of Occultism', which revealed various secrets behind clairvoyance, telepathy, and other traditional occult practices – much of which apparently overlapped with the province of 'magic'.[138] Finding little support from his ostensibly anti-occultist sponsors, Stadthagen promised to modify his act accordingly.

But on 14 January 1941 the Magic Circle renewed its complaints, first against Pelz, then Stadthagen, for revealing 'card tricks' that contradicted the May 1940 agreement.[139] This January 1941 complaint led to a Gestapo ban on Pelz's performances, followed shortly thereafter by an acrid letter to Stadthagen threatening a similar ban if he didn't modify his act.[140]

On 16 March Stadthagen responded, copying his sponsor Hörmann in the RVG. As one of the '*oldest* pioneers of the struggle against occultism', who has fought for decades '*against* attempts to deceive the public with supernatural activities', Stadthagen's 'scientific conscience' would not allow him to 'stand by patiently and watch as frivolous conjurers pretend that their tricks are *scientific achievements* [his emphasis]'. It was precisely this attempt to pass off a well-known card trick as 'proof of occult phenomena' that 'exploits the uncertainty and gullibility of our fellow human beings'.[141]

'Since an immense number of our comrades have been brought over to superstitious beliefs through fraudulent manoeuvres and still hold for real today what in truth is only a lie and deception,' Stadthagen continued, it is '*in the interest of the people* that the supporter of enlightenment must intervene – in order to dispel this nonsense. For superstition is ultimately the worldview of the intellectually inferior, of fatalists. No state could tolerate this state of affairs, least of all our Third Reich!'[142] After twenty years of battling 'occult swindlers, Jewish Masons and Jesuits' and withstanding the attacks of 'the Jewish press mob ... and other degenerates', Stadthagen found it infuriating that his work was now being threatened by charlatans and 'supersensory'-oriented professional magicians who 'have not only dabbled in numerous, supposedly "occult matters" but even endorse them.[143]

Although Stadthagen directed most of his bile toward Schreiber, he was obviously frustrated with Hitler's Chancellery and the Gestapo's role in generating the controversy. The Magic Circle 'could never have obtained [the ban],' Stadthagen reminded Schreiber, 'if the authorities ... had any inkling ... that the orders that are supposed to protect the magician's craft would be employed against popular enlightenment, which is viewed by the Third Reich as unconditionally necessary in an ideological sense and has been ordered and sponsored by the highest authorities.'[144] Except the Gestapo *did* realize the ban was preventing enlightenment presentations in favour of commercial occultism ('magic') and did nothing to reverse it.

Implicitly recognizing the firm position of the Reich Magician's Association, Stadthagen urged a return to the terms of the 1940 modus vivendi. My 'enlightenment work ... has always been directed expressly against superstition and occult nonsense,' Stadthagen explained. 'In that respect there can be no discussion about whether I reveal artistic talents and "works of magical arts" and thereby deprive artists of their opportunities for subsistence.' In closing Stadthagen attempted to pull rank, reminding Schreiber that his and Pelz's anti-occultist demonstrations had been approved by Goebbels' RMVP every year since 1935 and that they had since worked almost exclusively for Ley's KdF.[145]

Taken in isolation, this controversy appears typical of many conflicts over competency in the Third Reich. In the absence of clear policy and competing party-state bureaucracies, apparently minor issues – such as whether to allow horse-racing during the war – could escalate into larger controversies requiring Hitler's direct intervention.[146] Stadthagen recognized that he was complicit in this process of 'working toward the Führer'. He betrayed some reticence at bringing in higher authorities to adjudicate a dispute that should have been resolved collegially at a lower level. Since Schreiber had invoked the big guns, however, involving both Hitler and the Gestapo ('*This is how far it has gone!*'), Stadthagen felt he had no choice but to enlist his own high-ranking allies.[147]

More importantly, Stadthagen, like Pelz, was keenly aware of the larger ideological and epistemological context in which this seemingly minor dispute over the practice of 'magic' was taking place. According to Stadthagen, the issue was not about revealing magic tricks. It represented a bellwether in gauging the Third Reich's seriousness in eliminating occultism eight years after the seizure of power. Not only did the ban prevent Germany's most talented debunkers from combating occultism; it elevated a group of known charlatans 'into the position to silence [pro-enlightenment] opponents in such an uncomfortable fashion. And this in the 20th Century!'[148]

This defence of free speech and scientific inquiry might seem odd coming from a Nazi fellow traveller during the most brutal war in history. And yet Stadthagen was genuinely surprised at the Reich's highest authorities acceding to a back-room request for police repression in favour of commercial occultism. As Stadthagen wrote to Hörmann, his unwillingness to accept this state of affairs had nothing to do with a lack of 'party discipline'. After working toward enlightenment for thirty years, how could he or Pelz stomach the Magic Circle's exploitation of ignorant Reich authorities (including Hitler's Chancellery) to obtain 'well-meaning protective bans' that are misused for the purposes of 'violating the truth and maintaining the people in a state of superstition'?[149]

Hörmann was sympathetic if realistic. There were limits to what he could do to reverse a Gestapo ban, especially one ordered personally by Hitler. Hörmann's advice was to 'direct his enlightenment work exclusively against superstition and occultism' so that there could 'be no question of unveiling artistic achievements and magic tricks'.[150] Frustrated by this unhelpful response, Stadthagen decided to accept Schreiber's challenge and telephone Hitler – or at least Hitler's adjutant Schaub – directly.[151] On 22 February 1941, Stadthagen followed up with a long letter to Dr Brümmel in Hitler's Chancellery, indicating frustration at his 'Enlightenment work being hindered by a small cabal of artists practised in deception'. Stadthagen wanted an assurance from Hitler's Chancellery that the Gestapo would not move against him as they had against his colleague Pelz.[152]

Pelz, meanwhile, was fighting for his professional life. In early February 1941 he sent a detailed letter and curriculum vitae to the KdF to enlist their help in lifting the ban. As a long-time Nazi who had worked against 'occult swindlers' for many years, Pelz could not understand why his Gestapo colleagues would enforce such a ban.[153] The day after the DAF received Pelz's letter, the Gestapo nevertheless reiterated the fact 'that the Führer had personally ordered the measures affecting Pelz and that lifting or modifying these measures would therefore be possible only through the approval of the Führer'.[154]

That Pelz had been banned specifically by Hitler's office and was now under surveillance by the Gestapo was a matter of some consternation in the offices of the KdF.[155] Reticent to lose one of their top performers, the KdF composed a letter on Pelz's behalf. 'Enlightenment lectures on occultism, spiritualism, clairvoyance, telepathy and other spheres,' the KdF explained, 'were for years organized by us precisely due to the wish of the Reich Office Rosenberg and the Reich Office against Nuisances in Public Health, and the demand for these lectures was always exceptionally great, while only very few lecturers were available for this purpose.' The KdF then noted: 'In addition to Party Comrade

Pelz we have had only Party Comrade Wilhelm Gubisch, Dresden, and Party Comrade Albert Stadthagen', and 'these speakers are not sufficient to meet the demand'.[156]

The key word in understanding the KdF's willingness to lobby the Gestapo is 'demand'. Pelz, the KdF emphasized, was an outstanding speaker and performer.[157] For dramatic effect he had developed a technique of pretending to be a clairvoyant, telepath, or card-reader during the highly entertaining first half of his performance, only revealing the mechanics behind his tricks in the second half, where he took a more sober, scientific tone. Pelz himself conceded that one could not reveal these basic methods without demonstrating how magicians carried out 'a whole row of definitive tricks and methods' that were after all 'first discovered and utilized by occult and spiritualist swindlers'.[158] 'Obviously we support the view,' the KdF continued, 'that there is nothing objectionable with the entertaining art of magic that is employed by magicians, but that the deceptive use of a few tricks in the sphere of occultism, etc. must be combated with all severity.'[159] For these reasons the KdF requested 'that the ban against Carl Pelz be lifted as soon as possible', before his 'truly important enlightenment work is undermined'. It then concluded: 'We would consider it appropriate, were the Reichsleiter Party Comrade Rosenberg to request a change in the ban from the Führer directly.'[160] Although Rosenberg apparently did intervene with Hitler, the ban remained in effect.[161]

To add insult to injury, at the same time that Pelz and Stadthagen were appealing to Reich authorities to allow them to reveal occult tricks, in April 1941 Hitler's Chancellery overruled existing 'bans against undesirable litera-ture of soothsaying and astrology for carefully considered reasons related to the importance of the war effort'. Backed by Hitler, the Chancellery 'invoked its own recently acquired competency to lift a series of book bans' decreed by Rosenberg's Office as well.[162] Hitler himself intervened with the Gestapo in 1938 to grant amnesty to members of Masonic organizations, including theos-ophy and anthroposophy.[163] In the autumn of 1939, just weeks into the war, Heydrich's SD agreed that the regime should not interfere with those who researched 'cosmic' forces with 'scientific methods'.[164] More than eight years after the Nazi seizure of power, the debunkers Pelz and Stadthagen had been silenced. The occult practice of magic was alive and well.[165]

The Hess Action and its Consequences 1941–5

On 10 May 1941 Hitler's Deputy Führer, Rudolf Hess, climbed into a small plane at an airfield outside Augsburg (Bavaria) and crash-landed in Scotland, intent on brokering peace between the Third Reich and British Empire. When it became clear that Hess was not acting in an official capacity, the British authorities imprisoned and interrogated him. So began a forty-six-year prison sentence that ended with Hess's likely suicide on 17 August 1987.

Hess did consult his personal astrologer before leaving.[166] He also suggested to British interlocutors that the idea for the flight had been inspired 'through a dream by supernatural powers'.[167] Hess had pragmatic motivations as well. He was concerned about Hitler's plans to invade the Soviet Union, which threatened to engulf the Third Reich in an unwinnable two-front war. Progressively marginalized in decision-making, Hess saw this bold move as a way of restoring his standing with Hitler.[168]

Unfortunately for Hess the plan backfired. That Hitler's designated successor should flee Germany for unsanctioned peace talks was unfortunate under any circumstances. It was particularly embarrassing at this critical turning point in the war, when the Third Reich was about to unleash the greatest military offensive in history, against the Soviet Union.

Hitler was beside himself with rage, demanding to know what had gone wrong with his Deputy Führer. Rosenberg and Bormann had a ready answer: Hess's penchant for 'political fortune-telling'.[169] Goebbels agreed, writing in his diary that the 'whole obscure swindle is now finally rooted out. The miracle men, Hess's darlings, are going under lock and key.'[170]

Sure enough, within days Hitler approved the Third Reich's first coordinated attempt to expose and arrest all practitioners of the occult in Germany.[171] Launched on 9 June 1941, Heydrich's 'Action Against Occult Doctrines and so-Called Occult Sciences' (also referred to as 'The Hess Action') took into its ambit many occult doctrines, hundreds of individuals, and thousands of publications.[172]

Except this programme of repression became subject almost immediately to the same contradictions we saw above.[173] Within weeks most occultists were released.[174] Within months the regime had retreated from its stated policy of eradicating occultism. The perfunctory nature of the Hess Action and its ambivalent consequences therefore reinforce our overall impression of an underlying connection between Nazism and the occult – a relationship that would in fact deepen after the Hess Action.[175]

The Hess Action, May–June 1941

That Hess's flight occurred only three days after Bormann's 7 May anti-occult circular, discussed at the outset of this chapter, is no accident. Both Nazi leaders were influenced in their actions by the impending invasion of the Soviet Union ('Operation Barbarossa'), but in different ways.[176] As already noted, Hess saw the invasion as a mistake that would mire Germany in a two-front war even more unwinnable than in 1914. Bormann, on the other hand, refused to question Hitler's military strategy. Rather, in eager anticipation of the Third Reich's final reckoning with 'Judeo-Bolshevism' – which included secret orders to murder Bolsheviks and 'Jews in party and state employment' – Bormann saw a political opportunity. He could move once and for all against occultism and the churches.[177] Heydrich and Rosenberg agreed.[178] After years of handling occultism with kid gloves, they saw Hess's flight as an opportunity to unleash the full fury of the Nazi police state against 'sectarian tendencies' – including occultists within the party.[179]

On 4 June 1941, barely two weeks before the invasion of the Soviet Union, Heydrich notified all Gauleiter and regional governors that the Third Reich was about to embark on a coordinated 'action against occult teachings and so-called "occult sciences"'.[180] Heydrich explained that it was essential, in light of the pending existential struggle against the Soviet Union, that the Third Reich preserve the people's mental and physical powers. Any teachings that pretend humanity's fate is 'dependent on magical, esoteric forces' had to be combated with the 'sharpest immediate measures'. Echoing Bormann's circular, Heydrich further indicated that the measures would be directed at 'astrologers, occultists, spiritualists, supporters of occult radiation theories, soothsayers (regardless of what kind), faith healers' and 'supporters of anthroposophy, theosophy, and ariosophy'.[181] In a parallel effort, Heydrich asked his subordinate, Hinrich Lohse, to encourage Gestapo and SD speakers to promote 'suitable enlightenment and propaganda' measures that might combat the influence of the occult.[182]

Strictly speaking, the 'Hess Action' was more systematic than any previous measures taken by the Third Reich against sectarian thinkers or esoteric groups. Hundreds of occultists were detained or arrested. Thousands of books and esoteric paraphernalia were confiscated.[183] Even many individuals or groups that had managed to survive earlier campaigns against popular occultism were now arrested or outlawed.[184] The authorities focused in particular on rounding up well-known astrologers, especially those with ties to Hess. This included Hess's personal advisor, Ernst Schulte-Strathaus, who spent almost two years in a concentration camp.[185] Many anthroposophists felt the brunt of the action as well.[186] In rare cases, such as Johannes Verweyen, the Hess Action resulted in detainees perishing in a concentration camp.[187] It is important to note, however, that Verweyen was a persistent critic of the regime, who was nonetheless allowed to pursue his occult-religious activities and publish legally until 1938.[188] When Verweyen was arrested, it was due as much to his 'pacifism, internationalism, and anti-fascism' as it was to his occultism.[189]

In fact, the Hess Action was remarkably moderate in comparison to measures taken against other 'enemies of the Reich'. Whereas Bolsheviks, Jews, individuals deemed 'asocial', and the disabled were arrested and murdered with growing intensity after September 1939, most of those detained in the Hess

Action were released.[190] Instead of eliminating thousands of occultists outright, Heydrich's RSHA preferred to send 'experts' to give lectures designed to 'enlighten' the public and promote the publication of books with a critical approach to occultism.[191] That is, despite the repeated association of occultism with 'sectarianism', measures against the occult, even in the context of Hess's flight and Operation Barbarossa, were remarkably modest.

Long accustomed to his colleagues accommodating the occult, Rosenberg wrote to Bormann in late May to suggest a greater sense of urgency. While Bormann's directive of 7 May was good, Rosenberg explained, it lacked concrete explanations for why the Gauleiter must fight occultism with 'clear and systematic' arguments based in natural law and science. Such 'rather complicated ideological questions could not be resolved simply by sending out a circular'.[192]

'The success of National Socialism and the unique appearance of the Führer,' Rosenberg observed, 'has no precedent in German history. The consequence of these historic and unprecedented political events is that many Germans, due to their proclivity for the romantic and the mystical, indeed the occult, came to understand the success of National Socialism in this fashion.'[193] He continued: 'Already soon after coming to power', many Germans 'stamped the Führer as a messiah and attributed the great results of the struggle to otherworldly powers. Astrologers made a special effort to exploit this ideological situation for themselves and obscured the achievements and goals of National Socialism with prophecies and soothsaying of the most primitive kind.'[194]

Instead of taking the war as an opportunity to settle scores with occultism, Rosenberg continued, the party had *lifted* bans on occult publications (and instituted bans on debunkers). Reich officials were particularly lax toward astrologers, the quintessential 'border scientists', whom Goebbels' RMVP refused to attack with consistency (unsurprising since Goebbels was employing professional astrologers to produce anti-Allied propaganda).[195]

According to Rosenberg, such backsliding on occultism and superstition was nothing new. From the moment the SD and Gestapo issued the first concrete measures against astrology, in 1937, Hess (and Himmler) had insisted that 'scientific astrology' be excepted. Little had changed in the intervening years, Rosenberg noted, submitting to Bormann an enclosure indicating a large cohort of Nazis, who have 'employed all means to anchor harmful and alien astrology as well as the entire sphere of occultism firmly and to spread it throughout the German people, in contradiction to every principle of the National Socialist worldview'.[196]

Chiefly to blame for the lack of decisive action, according to Rosenberg, were Philip Bouhler, head of Hitler's Personal Chancellery, and Goebbels himself, who seemed studiously disinterested in carrying out Bormann's directives against occultism. This sponsorship of occultism was made worse, Rosenberg observed, insofar as Hess had set the precedent of Hitler's Chancellery deciding ideological questions that should have been left to the Führer. Now that Hess was gone, Bormann had the opportunity to reverse this trend.[197]

Rosenberg concluded by offering Bormann a policy paper, which he hoped Bormann would deliver to Hitler. The distinction between scientific and popular occultism made sense, Rosenberg conceded. Even were the Third Reich to accept scientific occultism as legitimate, however, the regime had not moved effectively against the latter. '[E]very human being should investigate whatever his research requires,' Rosenberg opined. The 'propagandistic action of astrologers and occultists with their tens of thousands of calendars' nonetheless 'hinders the ability of men to make decisions and makes them dependent on uncontrollable influences'. If Bouhler, Goebbels, and others agreed with this principle, then why was their first act as censors of occult activity to lift the ban on 'trashy astrological brochures'?[198]

Although usually dismissive of Rosenberg, whose influence had waned by May 1941, Bormann was equally frustrated by indifference in matters of occultism. He indicated as much in a letter to Goebbels several weeks after the Hess Action. According to Bormann, Hess's flight had *finally* inspired Hitler to combat the occult with the 'sharpest means' possible. Heydrich, Bormann wrote, had done his part to fulfil the Führer's intentions with the Hess Action. 'However, police measures can only be decisive,' Bormann insisted, 'if a practical policy of enlightenment is simultaneously employed to prevent wide circles of the population from becoming confused by occult teachings in the future. It has been reported to me that you have indicated the need to pull back from this kind of enlightenment.'[199] Here Bormann was referring to Hörmann's anti-occultist *Volksgesundheitswacht*, which Goebbels had discontinued in the autumn of 1939, ostensibly due to paper shortages. Bormann urged Goebbels to renew the publication of this magazine, 'perhaps in greater distribution across as wide circles of the population as possible in order for it to have an enlightening effect'.[200]

Goebbels' response four days later typified the more nuanced attitude toward occultism shared by most Nazi leaders. The propaganda minister began by reassuring Bormann that he shared his antipathies to popular occultism, citing the RMVP's own 15 May directive '[forbidding individuals] to perform in public occultist, spiritualist, clairvoyant, telepathic, astrological and similar displays as well as hypnotic experiments'. Still, Goebbels was careful to include the important caveat, clearly inspired by Hitler's orders from January 1941, that 'Artistic practice of magic is not to be included in this directive.'[201]

So why, after his snide remarks about 'Hess's darlings' going 'under lock and key', did Goebbels fail to move against occultism? In his response to Bormann, Goebbels cited 'tactical reasons'. In the midst of war, it simply didn't make sense to push the anti-occultist agenda too far. A full-scale propaganda barrage might have the paradoxical effect of strengthening the public's perception of the links between Hess, the Nazi regime, and the occult and create even greater interest in the affair. For the time being, Goebbels argued, the limited radio and press space available to the Propaganda Ministry should be devoted to anti-Communist and wartime propaganda. But 'as soon as the suitable moment arrives and a somewhat lighter burden is required of our public means of prop-aganda,' Goebbels promised his colleague, 'I am ready to realize the suggestions for enlightenment work in the widest possible fashion, especially in terms of founding a magazine' (as if re-founding an anti-occultist magazine would suffice!).[202] The suitable moment never arrived.[203]

The Consequences of the Hess Action

So how important was the Hess Action in the long-term process of eliminating occultism? As suggested above, the summer months of 1941 saw a brief flurry of arrests, followed by a series of compromises between the purveyors of 'enlightenment' and apologists for the occult. Only in September 1941, after four months of haggling with the Gestapo and Magic Circle, did Pelz and Stadthagen receive permission from Hitler's Chancellery to renew their public education efforts.[204] The two long-time debunkers were nevertheless still required to sign a statement promising to consult the Magic Circle regarding any 'experiments' related to 'magic'. The wording was telling: 'I am hereby duty bound to exclude any explanation of the magical arts in my enlightenment presentations on pseudo-occultism.'[205] The implication: attacking authentic occultism (as opposed to 'pseudo-occultism') lay outside the purview of Pelz or Stadthagen.

Heydrich might continue to harangue his colleagues about the dangers of anthroposophy and astrology.[206] But Himmler and other high-ranking SS offi-cials once again raised concerns about a *general* action that might attack 'scien-tific occultism' indiscriminately, insisting the SD and Gestapo leave room for 'legitimate research on astrological questions' and other occult doctrines.[207] In September 1941 the Nazi Minister of the Interior, Wilhelm Frick, and the Nazi Minister of Health, Dr Leonard Conti, gave a keynote address opening the Salzburg Paracelsus Festival – a festival celebrating Germany's most famous occultist. Although Heydrich's SD was nonplussed, they could do nothing about it.[208]

Most illustrative of the Hess Action's failure is the case of Eduard Neumann (aka Rolf Sylvéro). Neumann had been on the regime's radar since at least June 1939, when Hörmann in the RVG received a report that the professional magician had been advertising powers of 'telepathy, clairvoyance and hypnosis'.

In practising commercial fortune-telling, which had been banned in 1934, Neumann tried to avoid trouble by calling it 'thought power' – a transparent ruse, the report suggested.[209] Yet Neumann continued to perform with impunity, even as Pelz and Stadthagen faced increasing restrictions. Only in July 1941, in the aftermath of the Hess Action, did the regime decide to intervene.[210]

Suddenly dropped from a number of engagements, Neumann contacted the Bavarian division of Goebbels' RMVP. The ministry responded in early August that they were forwarding Neumann's inquiry to higher authorities since there was a lively internal discussion regarding 'similar presentations of this kind'. In the interest of clarifying matters, the RMVP official asked whether Neumann could indicate the nature of his 'experiments' in greater detail, 'in particular whether they contain occultist, clairvoyant, spiritualist or similar displays'.[211]

Aware of the fine line between practising occultism and enlightenment in the form of occult-based entertainment, Neumann petitioned the RMVP on 7 August for permission to perform 'anti-occult experimental lectures'.[212] In his letter to the RMVP, he denied practising magic or the occult arts. Rather, he emphasized the 'enlightened' nature of his show, beginning with various 'experiments', which 'then in the second part of my program are explained. Only in this way is it possible to protect the public from succumbing to the swindle of "clairvoyants" in the future'.[213] In brazen fashion, Neumann then volunteered to report true 'swindlers' who were passing themselves off as magicians in order to perpetuate occultism – which was obviously what Neumann was doing.[214]

In order to maintain the ruse that he was interested in promoting 'enlightenment', Neumann wrote to the RMVP in late August requesting permission to schedule a performance in Hahnenklee. Nestled in the Harz mountains, a centre of occult and pagan religious activity, 'a true Earth-Ray psychosis' dominated Hahnenklee, 'apparently caused by the local Natural Healer Saint Elm'. All the more 'necessary', Neumann argued, 'to carry out an experimental lecture there'. 'Such enlightening experiments are certainly very urgent', he added, 'though very thankless to carry out before a believing public', because such people were hard to convince.[215]

As 'I already explained to you over the telephone', Neumann continued, such delicate experiments could 'only be carried out in the form of entertaining; one may not reveal the purpose of enlightenment in the first part of the performance.' Unfortunately, since Neumann's rival St Elm had recently been detained – and apparently released – by the Gestapo, Neumann worried that 'the Gestapo likely would be apprised of [his] performance by his [St Elm's] followers', who would portray it as pure occult entertainment. For this reason Neumann wanted to confirm that no 'Gestapo officials would be observing the performance' without his knowledge. Under the circumstances of the Hess

Action, Neumann's cynical attempt to deceive the RMVP and avoid scrutiny by the Gestapo is truly astounding. If nothing else, it clearly affirms his intention to take advantage of the superstitious proclivities of Hahnenklee's 'believing crowd' in order to make a few extra marks.[216]

And yet, incredibly, Reich officials decided to give Neumann, a known commercial occultist, whose performances *should* have been banned as early as 1934, a chance to prove otherwise. Instead of arresting Neumann, the RMVP offered to organize, in conjunction with the KdF, a 'trial performance' in which 'Sylvéro' might demonstrate his tricks before a small group of experts. Unbeknownst to Neumann, whose cynicism they must have recognized, the RMVP invited representatives of Heydrich's Security Service (SD).[217]

The response of the SD and RMVP to Sylvéro's performance was dubious at best. Sylvéro had indeed proceeded along the lines developed by Stadthagen and Pelz, devoting the first part of the performance to occult and paranormal experiments and the second part to explaining them. According to one RMVP expert, however, Sylvéro's truly 'mystifying' performance, which was in every respect 'occultist', could have nothing but a negative impact on public enlightenment. 'I personally agree with both comrades from the SD that Sylvéro's artistic pieces leave behind a much deeper impression than the accompanying language of popular enlightenment. I hold the view that these presentations must fundamentally be forbidden.'[218]

Remarkably, it was only in the aftermath of this trial performance and critical report that the RMVP exercised due diligence in unearthing a number of reports on Neumann's occult activities from the 1930s, which clearly indicated 'that "Sylvéro" only wants to exploit the situation [of anti-occultism] as a businessman, though earlier he did just the opposite'. On 30 September 1941 the German Popular Education Division (DVBW) of the KdF agreed – reluctantly – to stop employing 'Sylvéro'.[219]

Despite Neumann's eight-year record of breaking the law against commercial occultism and blatantly deceiving Nazi authorities, despite the disingenuous nature of his 'anti-occultist' demonstration, and despite even the Hess Action – the KdF continued to lobby on Neumann's behalf! According to the KdF's sympathetic report of his test performance, Neumann had been hindered by the 'critical environment and rather cold atmosphere' during the performance, which caused him to be shy and nervous.[220] The Munich representative of the KdF concurred, writing on 16 October that 'During the whole show I could not dispel the feeling that this was the case of a man who, through the force of circumstances, must follow a particular line with which he is absolutely uncomfortable and which does not appear especially honest.'[221] In short, the KdF recognized that Neumann was a lifelong occultist *pretending* to debunk occultism.

Notwithstanding Neumann's obvious discomfort and dishonesty, the KdF representative indicated that he and his colleagues believed Neumann's performance was suitable to fill the need for public 'enlightenment'.[222] Clearly the KdF's sponsorship of Neumann had little to do with promoting enlightenment in the context of the Hess Action and everything to do with providing state-sponsored, occult-based entertainment along the lines of the Reich Magicians' Association.

Neumann, for his part, had no intention of accepting the RMVP report. If 'my lectures had a more entertaining character', Neumann explained to Walter Tiessler, the RMVP's liaison to Bormann's Party Chancellery, it was because 'the audience was constituted primarily from working-class circles'. Repeating his justification from a few weeks earlier, Neumann argued that such individuals had to be approached in a different fashion than the educated bourgeosie.[223]

Whoever in the RMVP suggested that Neumann's performance was openly dishonest, meanwhile, had made 'slanderous statements'. My 'right to defend myself cannot be abrogated', Naumann insisted, 'and those sources, which have so casually made such statements, must be called to account'.[224] One might expect a known occultist who accused Goebbels' RMVP (and unwittingly Heydrich's SD) of slander in the wake of the Hess Action to end up in a concentration camp, or worse. Instead, Tiessler proved sympathetic and reopened Neumann's case, appealing to Rosenberg directly.[225]

The response Tiessler received from Pfriemer in the Amt Rosenberg reiterated the feeling that Neumann's performance lacked 'inner honesty', merely mimicking the famous occult debunker, Wilhelm Gubisch. This dishonesty was unsurprising, Pfriemer observed, since Neumann earned his living for more than a decade 'from all possible telepathic and hypnotic experiments'.[226] It was completely obvious that he lacked the ability to 'explain the intellectual context' of his 'experiments'. In this regard, Pfriemer pointed out that his office had already sent a letter to the DAF/DVBW in June 1939, remarking on Sylvéro's occult-oriented activities.[227] 'We certainly do not support [the idea] that the past continues to follow an individual who today operates appropriately and is open about the clarity of his purposes and activities,' Pfriemer concluded. 'It is however precisely in the sphere of anti-occult enlightenment that it is necessary to have clean hands; whomever operated earlier in the occult camp, making people stupider, cannot expect today that we believe his anti-occultist point of view.'[228]

This decision was not unreasonable. Neumann had broken the law against commercial occultism repeatedly. He had lied about his intentions and the support of Hitler's Reich Chancellery, and he had stolen other performers' identities. Even in the liberal Weimar Republic, such obvious fraudulence for profit might have led to his arrest and trial. All Tiessler could muster in response to Neumann's repeated prevarications and complaints was the apologetic statement that 'the permission of anti-occult presentations and performances is supposed to remain restricted'. That is, Neumann was not prevented from performing due to his occultist past, but because 'anti-occultist' demonstrations were *still* being restricted, per the earlier interventions of the Magic Circle![229]

Neumann refused to let the matter rest. On 17 February 1942 he wrote to Tiessler angrily, 'I have neither time nor desire to carry on a war of paper and hope that my situation can finally be resolved through a conversation in your office at the earliest opportunity ... I can unfortunately not dispel the impression that there is somehow a regrettable lack of social empathy regarding my situation.'[230] At a time when the Holocaust was in full swing, it is darkly comical to see a known 'sectarian' taking Reich authorities to task for their lack of 'social empathy'.[231]

Nevertheless, some kind of agreement favourable to Neumann must have been reached. For Neumann's next letter to Tiessler, from 29 April, was far more amicable. It confirmed the particulars of their discussion and agreed to revisit whatever deal they had worked out six months hence.[232] While the paper trail ends thereafter, it seems as if Neumann received restricted permission to perform, conditional upon reporting to Tiessler. Indeed, other cases from the twelve months following the Hess Action indicate that most occult practitioners were subsequently required to clear their 'performances', whether for commercial ('entertainment') or scientific ('enlightenment') purposes, through Tiessler and the RMVP.[233] Despite bending over backwards to accommodate Neumann and other occultists, Tiessler was no moderate. This is the same RMVP official, after all, who insisted, in contrast to his chief Goebbels, that the Catholic bishop Count Galen should be executed for alerting his parishioners to the Nazi euthanasia program.[234] But when it came to occultism, Tiessler was clearly willing to exercise remarkable patience.

Even Rosenberg's office, Bormann's Chancellery, and the SD, which had worked assiduously to combat occultism before June 1941, remained constrained by Nazi affinities for border science and a nuanced attitude toward occultism. Such was the case in respect to Rosenberg's expert in the Office of Defence against Astrology and World Ice Theory (*Abwehrstelle gegen Astrologie und Welteislehre*), Kurd Kisshauer.[235] As Rosenberg's attack dog in occult and religious matters, Kisshauer believed that nearly every other Nazi office, from Goebbels' RMVP to Himmler's Gestapo, was infested with occultists.[236]

Kisshauer nonetheless decided to prevent the publication of an anti-occultist novel on the evils of commercial astrology, *Son of the Stars (Sohn der Sterne)*, because the book lacked 'astrological rigour'. While the plot was effective in attacking popular occultism – indicating the manipulative 'schemes of two dishonest horoscope readers' – the representation of astrology was too 'unscientific'. Kisshauer simply could not bring himself to approve a publication that failed to recognize the difference between exploitative popular and respectable scientific astrology. He further demanded the author of *Son of the Stars* delete a section mocking Hanns Hörbiger's World Ice Theory, including a passage that belittled Hörbiger's greatest living collaborator, 'Phillip Fauth, who had been honoured with a professor's title owing to his services by the Führer'.[237] Here we have the one official in the Third Reich *literally* charged with 'defending against astrology and World Ice Theory' making a systematic effort to prevent the unfair misrepresentation of the former and forbidding any criticism whatsoever of the latter.[238]

How does one explain this remarkable tolerance of occultism and border science only a few months after the Hess Action? When it comes to 'scientific occultism', we have already seen that many Nazis retained an open mind. Even the SS and Gestapo refused to prevent 'scientific' attempts to study and wield esoteric forces. But what about the persistence of popular occultism after the Hess Action, exemplified by Neumann or the Magic Circle, the kind of commercial exploitation of superstition that even the liberal Weimar Republic attempted to eliminate through policing or legal action?

The answer might be found in a 1941 report to Tiessler on behalf of Rudolf Irkowsky, an RMVP official active in the Austrian countryside near Hitler's home town of Linz. Irkowsky began by describing an action against 'superstition' initiated by the local Nazi subsidiary of Rosenberg's Party Education Office. The goal of the action, emblematic of competing efforts by Heydrich and Rosenberg, was to produce a pamphlet devoted to 'the enlightenment of political leaders in regard to all forms of charlatanry, superstition, and occultism'. Except Irkowsky recommended *against* distributing the pamphlet. In line with his superior Goebbels, he noted 'that themes, which do not directly contribute to victory, should not be dealt with in public, especially in the sphere of charlatanry, which is a very delicate theme'.[239]

Tiessler agreed that morale outweighed public education.[240] The Party Education Office should have run such controversial anti-occultist pamphlets by the RMVP, Tiessler wrote to Rosenberg in frustration. Goebbels' office remained 'extremely sceptical as to dealing with the question of superstition' through public education.[241] Following up a few days later, Irkowsky added that 'public education [*Volksaufklärung*] of the population in regard to this question [was] very impractical because here undoubtedly ... material for conflict would be introduced'.[242] Germans loved their superstitions. On that both Irkowsky and Rosenberg agreed. Where the RMVP departed from the Amt Rosenberg was in trying to attack those beliefs in the midst of total war.

Superstition was not just a rural phenomenon. In 1943 some estimates recorded more than three thousand tarot readers in Berlin alone.[243] By the middle years of the war, Nazi anti-occultists seemingly acknowledged that they 'could never be free from [occultism inside and outside the party] in spite of all measures against it.'[244] Indeed, although the Hess Action is viewed by some historians 'as the forceful end of collective activity in various areas of "esoteric sciences" in Germany', it did not push occultism underground. To the contrary, occultists and border scientists were enlisted soon after by Nazi officials – a phenomenon we will take up in subsequent chapters.[245]

***

Most historians agree that there was widespread animosity toward the occult in Germany before 1933. But some believe this hostility only became institution-alized in the Third Reich.[246] This chapter suggests a more complex picture. Corinna Treitel says rightly of the liberal Weimar Republic that 'the state proved permissive toward those who absorbed occult phenomena into the sphere of scientific investigation, but relentless toward others' who 'sought to profit by selling their occult prophecies'. This approach was equally true in the Third Reich,[247] except the regime waited *eight* years, until the Hess Action, to carry out anything resembling 'relentless' persecution. Moreover, the Hess Action, as we have seen, was remarkably short-lived and uneven in its results.[248]

We can explain this inconsistency in policing the occult through two inter-related patterns. First, virtually all Nazi leaders appeared to recognize the distinction, shared by most border scientists, between popular and scientific occultism. That is one reason so little was done to eradicate occultism during the entire twelve years of the Third Reich. The line between popular (commer-cial) and scientific occultism was simply too porous and open to interpretation. Despite the anti-occultist crackdown in the spring of 1937 and the Hess Action of June 1941, Nazi leaders made extraordinary efforts to better understand, differentiate, and in some cases sponsor scientific occultism.[249]

Second, virtually all Nazis acknowledged, for good or ill, the widespread popularity of occult practices, popular superstition, and border scientific thinking. That is another reason why neither Hitler nor the Propaganda Ministry nor even the Gestapo or SD would endorse a blanket campaign against occultism during the first eight years of the Third Reich. To the contrary, the anti-occultist movement remained confined to a group of relatively obscure debunkers around Mathilde Ludendorff – debunkers who were motivated by their own, rival esoteric doctrines. The widespread popularity of esoteric thinking across the party and civil society, including those charged with combating the occult, explains why its policing was so uneven and rife with exceptions.[250]

Hitler and Goebbels' desire to assuage professional 'magicians' at the expense of public 'enlightenment' was emblematic of a general tendency to tolerate even popular occultism – a trend noted ruefully by Bormann and Rosenberg. From early 1940 on, professional debunkers faced increasingly restrictive guidelines on their anti-occultist activity. Eventually bans were established, seemingly, by Hitler himself. Even the Hess Action, upon closer inspection, did little to eliminate popular (much less 'scientific') occultism.[251] The rhetorically 'uncompromising anti-esoteric stance' taken by many Nazis masked the extraordinary 'receptiveness toward the occult' among others. In fact 'several of the more zealous Nazi opponents of occultism came from occult backgrounds themselves'.[252]

Ultimately, there was never a strict tension between *völksich*-esoteric Nazis like Himmler, Hess or Walther Darré and putatively 'anti-occult' Nazis like Hitler, Rosenberg, or Bormann. Rather there was simply a running debate – typical of debates *within* occult circles – regarding the need to draw distinctions between 'scientific' occultism and charlatanry. This mostly epistemological debate within the Nazi Party combined with a general consensus that popular occultism and sectarianism more generally were politically dangerous in their ability to manipulate public opinion. This understandable fear of sectarianism in a state with totalitarian pretensions should not be confused with an ideological antipathy to occult or border scientific thinking. Occultism and border science, as we shall see in the next five chapters, found a surprisingly receptive audience in the Third Reich.

THE STARS COME DOWN TO FROZEN EARTH
Border Science in the Third Reich

'National Socialism is a cool and highly reasoned approach to reality based on the greatest of scientific knowledge and its spiritual expression ... This philosophy does not advocate mystic cults, but rather aims to cultivate and lead a nation determined by its blood.'

Adolf Hitler (1938)[1]

'The power of occultism, as of Fascism ... lies in the fact that in the lesser panaceas, as in superimposed pictures, consciousness famished for truth imagines it is grasping a dimly present knowledge ... Facts which differ from what is the case only by not being facts are trumped up as a fourth dimension ... With their blunt, drastic answers to every question, the astrologists and spiritualists do not so much solve problems as remove them by crude premises from all possibility of solution.'

Theodor Adorno, *Theses Against Occultism* (2005)[2]

'They [the SS leadership] all believed in World Ice Theory. That is naturally entirely unscientific. But the men read no other books. It is such a fantastic story, that one can hardly believe it. They all tended to the occult perspective.'

SS zoologist and leader of the Tibet Expedition, Ernst Schäfer[3]

In 1947 the German science writer Willy Ley published an article in the popular journal, *Astounding Science Fiction*. Entitled 'Pseudoscience in Naziland', the eight-page spread was one of the first published accounts of Nazi border science. According to Ley, the Third Reich frequently eschewed mainstream science in favour of 'magic', reflecting the 'willingness of a noticeable proportion of the Germans to rate rhetoric above research and intuition above knowledge.'[4]

In seeking a magical alternative to the materialism of Jews and Marxists, Ley continued, the Nazis appropriated border sciences that 'originated in Germany and, while not completely unknown elsewhere, had a special appeal to Germans'.[5] These doctrines flourished in the Weimar Republic, to be sure. But their broader influence was 'hemmed in by the authority of the scientists'. After Hitler became Führer, it was 'the other way round'. All flavours of esoteric racial theory and faith-based science found official sponsorship.[6] Small wonder, Ley concluded, that border scientists 'experienced a heyday under such a regime'.[7]

In his post-war essays, *Theses Against Occultism* and *The Stars Down to Earth*, Theodor Adorno agreed. The power of occultism was rooted, like fascism, in its appeal to 'semi-erudite' individuals 'driven by the narcissistic wish to prove superior to the plain people', though incapable of carrying through the 'complicated and detached intellectual operations' necessary to reach an understanding of the natural world. Alongside racism and anti-Semitism, the occult sciences therefore provided a sociopolitical and scientific 'short-cut' by reducing complex problems to 'a handy formula'. To those who felt 'excluded from educational privileges' the occult offered the 'pleasant gratification' that they belonged 'to the minority of those who are "in the know"'.[8]

The Third Reich epitomized such border scientific thinking. In order to reframe scientific inquiry, improve medical practices, increase economic production or shape racial and settlement policy, Nazi leaders sponsored everything from astrology, parapsychology, and radiesthesia to biodynamic agriculture and World Ice Theory (*Welteislehre*, or WEL). If Nazi leaders rejected rival views as unscientific, that just indicates the extent to which a 'cult of science had taken the place of religion' in occult circles. For in the border scientific world of 'deception and self-deception', observed Konrad Heiden, everyone claimed to work 'along strictly scientific lines'.[9] The Third Reich was no different.

Astrology and Parapsychology in the Third Reich[10]

Many critical intellectuals saw the waning years of the Weimar Republic as an exceptional time, a period when 'the materialization of the extraordinary found wide acceptance'.[11] Fuelled by constant 'talk of intuition, of presentiment, of phantasmagoria', a generation of esotericists claimed to have made advances 'into certain fields of the spirit' that would soon be accepted by mainstream scientists.[12] As the thirty-year-old astrologer Karl Krafft wrote to his friend Hans Bender, then a doctoral student at the University of Bonn, perhaps the time was coming when 'real, that is, unfalsified astrological . . . knowledge can be made accessible to a broader public'.[13] Bender was more sceptical. Before astrology or parapsychology could thrive, it was urgent that they be recognized as real science, something the liberal Weimar Republic was unwilling to do.[14]

Four years later, Bender was far more enthusiastic about the potential of border science.[15] Despite the continuing difficulty of being recognized as 'pioneers' by mainstream science, some 'border areas' of the sciences had gained recognition in the Third Reich. These included scientific astrology, the study of '[cosmic] rays [and] other parapsychological phenomena like apparitions, telepathy, and clairvoyance'.[16] In order for this promising trend to continue, Bender recommended that occultists dispense with phrases like 'parascientific' and 'paranormal' in favour of 'border areas' or border science.[17] It was better to couch one's experiments in an 'epistemology of science', Bender insisted, than to traffic openly in 'spiritualism, esoteric teachings and esoteric lodge activities' that could not be proven.[18]

The parapsychologist Walther Kröner agreed. Blinded by their 'materialist-induced confusion and ignorance regarding all things magical', mainstream German scientists continued to dismiss individuals who studied 'magic and occult occurrences' as 'occultists, parapsychologists, or metabiologists'.[19] But border scientific research was poised to 'step out of isolation' in the Third Reich and become the leading 'epistemology' of 'a new scientific and cultural epoch'. To receive the attention they deserved, all border scientists had to do was dispense with the term occultism.[20]

In making this argument Bender and Kröner tapped into a broader Nazi *Zeitgeist*. How else could one explain the persistence of astrology in the Third Reich? The answer, wrote one sceptic, was that Nazism had erased astrology's 'oriental origins' and 'anti-Semitic fatalism' by proclaiming that occultism was now an 'ancient-Germanic–holy body of knowledge'. With 'great effort and speed' the Third Reich proceeded after 1933 to 'paint the old astrological fairy tales as Germanic or National Socialist', giving astrology a scientific name, such as 'cosmology or cosmobiology'.[21] Thereby a range of border sciences 'long-combatted' – none more prominent than astrology and parapsychology – became 'politically relevant'.[22]

The Persistence of 'Scientific Astrology' in the Third Reich

Nazi preoccupations with astrology were evident from the earliest days of the party. There was no shortage of Nazi-affiliated astrologers in the Weimar Republic, from Wilhelm Gutberlet and Rudolf von Sebottendorff to Karl Heimsoth and Theodor Becher.[23] The astrological proclivities of Hess, Himmler, and Röhm are also well known.[24] While Hitler was more sceptical, he made a number of comments about the world and its relationship to cosmic forces that incorporated 'a biological mysticism' akin to cosmobiology.[25] Germany's two largest astrological organizations endorsed the NSDAP after all; the regime also approved a *Working Community of German Astrologers* (ADA), composed largely of Nazis.[26]

The Third Reich *was* concerned – as we saw in Chapter Four – about the proliferation of commercial astrology and the ease with which this could be used to manipulate the public.[27] But pro-Nazi astrologers and Nazis sympathetic to astrology worked to make the discipline acceptable by linking it with Germanic religious and scientific traditions. The *völkisch* theologian and folklorist, Otto Sigfrid Reuter, for example, argued that the ancient Nordic peoples were highly skilled in reading the stars, which is one reason why both Rosenberg, who ostensibly opposed astrology, and Himmler, who embraced it, cited Reuter's work.[28]

In addition to emphasizing the Germanic origins of astrology, many Nazis insisted on its legitimacy as a modern border science.[29] Scientific 'cosmobiologists' claimed astrology could be used to study the science of heredity, linking cosmic forces to racial (characterological) and biological processes. Astrologers who practised cosmobiology and characterology, such as the SA doctor Heimsoth, even developed complex mathematical equations to legitimize their findings.[30] As the Nazi occultist H. H. Kritzinger put it, 'In a study of cosmobiological contexts' many 'scientifically trained' individuals have accepted the relationship 'between the signs of the Zodiac, human fate and character'.[31] For the 'planets and their zodiac symbols', Kritzinger observed, 'are nothing other than the genius or demon. Whoever gets in touch with it puts magic in motion.'[32]

What distinguished cosmobiology from street-corner astrology was of course largely arbitrary, contingent on framing one's work as more rigorous than run-of-the-mill tarot-card readers. Dismissing popular and commercial astrology without denigrating the field entirely was a careful balancing act, however. In reviewing the astronomer Robert Henseling's *Umstrittenes Weltbild*, which attempted 'to make astrology appear laughable in the face of natural scientific observations', Bender urged Krafft to dismiss the astronomer's critique in such a way 'as to reduce the manoeuvre of Herr Henseling to nothing' without 'overburdening' a 'public that was sceptical if not antipathetic toward astrology'.[33]

In practising cosmobiology, it also helped to have an academic degree in a mainstream scientific field. Kritzinger had degrees in astronomy and engineering, for example, which lent his 'experiments' in dowsing, astrology, and cosmic 'death rays' the imprimatur of 'science'.[34] The parapsychologist and religious mystic Gerda Walther, who earned her PhD with the renowned philosopher Edmund Husserl, was permitted to continue her 'experiments' throughout the 1930s and was eventually employed by the Third Reich during the war. That Walther claimed to have spoken with the ghost of the SA Chief Ernst Röhm on multiple occasions seems not to have undermined her scientific credibility.[35]

When it came to practising astrology, one's Nazi credentials might also compensate for the lack of academic pedigree. Take the defrocked pastor and prominent Nazi astrologer, Alexander Centgraf (a.k.a Alexander Centurio). After installing a stained-glass window commemorating Hitler's Beer Hall Putsch in his church *before* the Nazi seizure of power, Centgraf joined the SA in 1933.[36] Fired by the local diocese in 1935 for his 'immoral' attitude, Centgraf discovered a new career in another faith-based field: scientific astrology. As we shall see in Chapter Seven, Centgraf's work was later utilized by Goebbels to produce propaganda pamphlets based on the quatrains of Nostradamus.[37]

Arguably the Third Reich's two most influential astrologers, Karl Krafft and Wilhelm Wulff, had no scientific credentials whatsoever. Krafft was a Swiss-German occultist who ingratiated himself with the regime through a series of pro-Nazi horoscopes and political predictions.[38] For years Krafft was allowed to publish his 'research' in major German newspapers and send unsolicited reports to the Reich Chancellery and SS.[39] But it was his supposed prediction of the assassination attempt on Hitler by Georg Elser in November 1939 that brought Krafft to Goebbels' attention, leading to Krafft's wartime work for the Propaganda Ministry (see Chapter Seven).[40]

Himmler's personal astrologer, Wilhelm Wulff, began his career, like Hitler, as a failed artist. His brief foray into art did, however, bring Wulff into contact with Leonardo da Vinci's extensive ruminations on the occult, which proved extremely helpful in catering to the post-war market in astrological speculation.[41] Despite charging 50 to 300 marks per horoscope – a clear infringement on the laws against commercial occultism – Wulff was merely put under surveillance by the Gestapo before 1941. Temporarily detained after the Hess Action, he was soon released into Himmler's trusted employ.[42] The only difference between Krafft or Wulff and the 'charlatans' that the Third Reich intermittently prosecuted is that the former managed to convince the authorities, namely Goebbels and Himmler, of their political reliability.[43]

Even after the 1937 police action, various Reich offices continued to facilitate the efforts of those who produced 'positive' astrological work.[44] A July 1938 study by Heydrich's SD concluded it was possible that the stars and planets influenced people in predictable ways.[45] Hence, when 'commercial' astrology was interdicted 1938, Heydrich made certain that 'astrology as a research field, as the indication of the effect of the stars on the soul and nerves should, on consultation with the Reichsführer, not be prevented'.[46] This support for scientific astrology was confirmed in January 1939, when Himmler urged Heydrich to negotiate 'the question of astrology' in a way that we 'allow specific research communities in this area'.[47]

The same goes for Hörmann's Reich Office for Public Health (RVG). Although he helped initiate the Spring 1937 campaign against commercial occultism, Hörmann repeatedly expressed a desire to 'clarify this politically really important question through experiments and precise investigations, so that one can exclude at least the obvious swindlers through legal means'.[48] As part of these 'investigations', Hörmann sent two experts to report on a major astrological congress in late 1938.

The more critical reviewer, Foltz, was sceptical as to the scientific potential of astrology. He nonetheless reported positively on the keynote address of a Nazi astrologer who proclaimed that the Third Reich had 'eliminated Jewish ideas from astrology' and made 'a sharp distinction between [scientific] and flea-market astrologers. The party does not oppose us but wants regulation and subordination.'[49] Foltz cited positively another astrologer for working to eliminate (philo)Semitism, sectarianism, and any attempts to undermine 'popular morale'.[50] Foltz even applauded a talk on the role of astrology in uniting 'science and faith' in the interest of combating materialism.[51]

Hörmann's second peer reviewer, Kiendl, was more positive. The conference gave the impression, Kiendl reported, that astrology remained popular within the Nazi Party and across the population at large.[52] Kiendl acknowledged that mainstream scientists continued to view astrology as 'unworthy of discussion'. And yet he blamed this scepticism on the lack of an effective 'censoring' mechanism before the spring of 1937, when Hörmann and Heydrich finally began policing commercial occultism. The state's traditional failure to differentiate between popular and scientific astrology did not mean that one could 'summarily dismiss everything that belongs to occultism'.[53] In spite of decades of scrutiny, astrology had never been proven wrong, Kiendl concluded. He recommended that Hörmann supplement 'one or the other astro-medical test experiments' with the 'original and useful method' pursued by the 'Expert for Cosmobiology' in Goebbels' Reich Literature Chamber (RSK), Dr Werner Kittler, who 'creates working groups of natural scientists and astrologers'.[54]

As 'Expert in the Cosmobiology Division of the Reich Literature Chamber', Kittler had assembled an extensive 'working group on cosmobiological research' within Goebbels' RSK.[55] In recruiting his team of astrologers, dowsers, and natural healers, Kittler explained that 'currently an ongoing effort and reconcepualization of all publications in the sphere of cosmobiology is being undertaken with the goal of producing a pragmatic foundation for corresponding scientific research'.[56] Kittler tracked down nearly every 'specialist' that he could find in the 'sphere of astro – or better yet cosmological-meteorological research'.[57] These recruits included the famous Weimar cosmobiologist Reinhold Ebertin; the amateur astrologer Thomas Ring, who later worked at the Nazi-sponsored Paracelsus Institute; and the above-mentioned Kritzinger, who contributed to astrological propaganda during the war.[58]

Most of those who answered the call were obvious charlatans. Take the self-important R. Herlbauer-Virusgo, who insisted that his soon-to-be patented cosmobiological system ('Dulcanoster') constituted a robust response to Rudolf

Hess's charge at the 1933 Reich Homoeopathic Conference to find a 'rigorous' application of 'astromedicine'.[59] Rather than laugh him off as certifiable, Kittler invited Herlbauer to join the subgroup on 'astro-medicine' within the RSK's larger research effort.[60]

Alfred Rosenberg's office was furious. But his anger became all the more palpable when Kittler was transferred, in early 1939, from Goebbels' RSK to Bouhler's PPK. Now ensconced in Hitler's Chancellery, Kittler had even greater authority to foment occultism through official channels.[61] When Rosenberg's associate Hugo Koch attempted to ban astrological literature in 1940, for example, citing the exigencies of war, Kittler made Koch meet with his colleague in the PPK, Karl Heinz Hederich. During the meeting Hederich insisted that 'actual astrology needed to be taken seriously. A complete ban could not be approved without party decisions at the highest level and it would be a *risk for [Koch's] office as well as for [him] personally if [he] continued along this party line* [my emphasis].'[62] Hederich made it clear that Rosenberg's office had no authority over the PPK and emphasized 'that in the sphere [of astrology] currently under discussion there are very serious efforts underway that deserve attention and whose ban cannot come into question'.[63] In fact, in early 1941 Heydrich's SD overturned a ban on a number of astrological tracts, reporting that they were ordered to do so by the PPK.[64]

This positive approach toward astrology – which pervaded Himmler's SS, Hörmann's RVG, Goebbels' RSK, and even Hitler's Chancellery – was far too embedded in the mental world of the Third Reich to be easily eradicated in the wake of the Hess Action. In late May 1941, for example, an RMVP official, Rudolf Erckmann, composed a report on the persistence of astrology in the Third Reich. According to Erckmann, prominent Nazis, not least of which Hess and Hederich, believed that 'astrology based on the fundamental doctrines related to a precise calculation of the stellar constellations was consonant with the National Socialist worldview'. The assumption that holding 'these views [was] consistent with the NSDAP was prevalent throughout leading circles of the party'. If the party 'rejected the cheap street fortune-telling [*Jahrmarkt-wahrsagerei*] as impossible', it continued to endorse 'so-called exact astrology'.[65]

Not only was astrology viewed as 'scientifically justified and completely accurate', Erckmann continued, but it was deemed essential to anticipating 'the destiny of the individual', the 'Reich', and the 'National Socialist movement'. According to many Nazi leaders, 'cosmic space radiation exercised certain effects [on events] fixed by destiny – such as the moment of conception of a child or the emergence of a political idea – which should be recognized on a scholarly basis and taken into account in the interpretation of the future'.[66] No wonder that Himmler, Goebbels, and the German Navy came to employ 'scientific astrology' during the war (see Chapter Seven).

The Institutionalization of Parapsychology

Based on his limited conversations with Hitler in the early 1930s, Hermann Rauschning recalls that the Nazi Führer must have been familiar with a 'savant of Munich' who had 'written some curious stuff about the prehistoric world, about myths and visions of early man, about forms of perception and supernatural powers. There was the eye of Cyclops or median eye, the organ of magic perception of the Infinite, now reduced to a rudimentary pineal gland.' 'Speculations of this sort fascinated Hitler,' Rauschning continued, 'and he would sometimes be entirely wrapped up in them. He saw his own remarkable career as a confirmation of hidden powers.'[67] To obtain 'magical insight' was 'apparently Hitler's idea of the goal of human progress. He felt that he already had the rudiments of this gift. He attributed to it his successes and his future eminence.'[68]

Rauschning's account, as indicated earlier, must always be taken with a grain of salt. In this case, however, his observations appear to be corroborated.[69] The Munich occultist to whom Rauschning alludes was probably the parapsychologist Ernst Schertel, whose book on *Magic* Hitler had read and annotated so carefully.[70] Schertel had observed, in passages highlighted by Hitler, that modern science labelled those with 'magical insight' as hysterics – a label often applied by contemporaries to the Führer.[71] It would be 'senseless to counterpoise the empirical perceptions as "real" opposite the "fictive" conceptions of the demonic,' Schertel explained, 'for the empirical world is also "fictive", resting on an imaginative synthetic foundation'. What materialists deemed 'empirical "reality"', Schertel suggested, was 'in its roots "demonic" – or "magic" in nature'.[72]

Schertel claimed, in a passage underlined by Hitler, that the human soul was the 'sum of all world energies', constituting an 'accumulation of potential and kinetic world energies' beginning with 'the first stardust'.[73] The future Führer took great interest in Schertel's ruminations on how humanity became imprisoned by the sensory world, making it hard to draw upon magical powers.[74] Nevertheless, by acquiring insight into this 'jugglery of fantasy, which we call the "objective world"', Schertel suggested, a trained magician might gain the ability to 'intervene in this structure, that is to say change the world according to our will'. That was 'magic', per Schertel, namely the ability 'to create reality where no reality exists'.[75] The magician or parapsychologist's 'special capabilities', such as 'clairvoyance, release of astral bodies, materialization power, psycho-kinesis, etc'. – to say nothing of autosuggestion, hypnosis, or magnetism – arose from focusing these 'magical-demonical forces on one idea' on 'a desirable goal'.[76]

How many Nazi leaders shared Hitler's apparent fascination with parapsychology? Part of the answer to this question can be found in official policy. Hess indicated a profound interest in parapsychology, as did Himmler, whose occult library included works by the renowned parapsychologist Baron du

Prel.[77] The famous SS zoologist and Tibet explorer Ernst Schäfer admitted that he had 'experienced truly strange things' in the context of Tibetan occultism, similar to phenomena recorded by parapsychologists.[78] Indeed, the Third Reich's curiosity regarding border science crystallized around the 'National Socialist desire to understand seemingly irrational phenomena in the framework of ideas such as parapsychology'.[79] So long as it comported with 'Nordic-Germanic feeling', research on 'mind-reading and telepathy, clairvoyance, second sight, mediumism and trance states, levitation, spook-phenomena', then parapsychology was accepted as legitimate by the Third Reich.[80]

Of all the names associated with German parapsychology, Hans Bender is the best known. Bender's fame is largely due to his role as a 1960s media maven and popularizer of the occult through entertaining duels with debunkers on West German television. But the future 'spook professor' (*Spukprofessor*) – a punch line in the Federal Republic – was taken far more seriously in the Third Reich, a time when parapsychology was still deemed a legitimate field of (border) scientific study.[81]

Bender finished his dissertation on ESP in 1933, becoming an assistant professor at the University of Bonn, where he worked to establish parapsychology as a legitimate science.[82] Bender was also a Nazi, joining the SA in 1933 and the NSDAP in 1937.[83] As mentioned in Chapter Four, Bender's work on clairvoyance attracted considerable media attention in the mid-1930s. He later declared himself 'surprised and astonished to see that his results had somehow started to live a life of their own in the public', and he was grateful that the Nazi regime appeared to support his work.[84] It didn't hurt that, like Steiner and Hörbiger, Bender was extraordinarily good at public relations. While he worked hard to gain the acceptance of mainstream colleagues, he understood the importance of politics and the mass media in securing the legitimacy of parapsychology through appeals to a lay public.[85]

By the late 1930s the success of this strategy became clear. Parapsychology had been legitimized and Bender had become its most prominent figure. Even after the 1937 crackdown, high-ranking state ministries and party officials supported him, and continued to do so after the Hess Action.[86] As Bender recalled, the Hess Action was not the end of occultism in the Third Reich. It represented rather the culmination of a process of vetting and coordination, begun in 1937, which entrusted trained border scientists with occult and parapsychological research while preventing its misuse by amateurs.[87]

Bender was the right person in the right place at the right time. In 1941, with the Hess Action in full swing, Bender published his second academic book, *Experimental Visions: A Contribution to the Problem of Sensory Deception, Consciousness of Reality and the Structures of Personality*, which got him an appointment as Full Professor and Director of the Institute of Psychology at the newly founded Reich University of Strasbourg.[88] According to his Dean, Ernst Anrich, an esoterically inclined Nazi historian and member of the SS, the purpose of the new university was to promote holistic, organicist, and *völkisch* science in ways that comported with Nazi ideology. As Anrich put it in a 1942 address to the faculty, 'There are questions in which the forces of the soul and the forces of science – which are always narrowly related – engage each other in the most powerful ways.'[89]

In addition to Anrich, Bender had another loyal sponsor, the Alsatian nationalist leader and esotericist, Friedrich Spieser.[90] An SS Stürmbannführer with personal connections to Himmler, Spieser had an intense interest in alternative medicine, astrology, and radiesthesia.[91] Spieser was therefore eager to fund Bender's research, which sought to move questions from 'the sphere of myth and superstition into the realm of scientific testability'.[92]

A decade earlier, in the waning months of the Republic, we saw how pessimistic Bender had become about the professionalization and institutionalization of border science. Now a full professor at an exclusively Nazi university, supported by deans and donors bent on sponsoring scientific occultism, Bender could finally realize his dream of creating 'a research institute for psychological border sciences'.[93]

Already in the mid-1930s Hess had suggested creating a Central Institute for Occultism to sponsor certain border scientific doctrines. Himmler's SS Institute of Ancestral Research (Ahnenerbe), discussed in more detail below, viewed border science as one of its chief areas of investigation as well.[94] It was Bender, however, who managed to open the first independent institute devoted entirely to research on parapsychology, astrology, and other occult sciences. Spieser offered a 'significant endowment' in 1942 to get this so-called 'Paracelsus Institute' – named after the Early Modern German (border) scientist – off the ground.[95]

Bender also contacted the SS's Reich Security Main Office (RSHA) to solicit funding for the institute, which he stated openly would focus on 'the investigation of "occult teachings"'.[96] In fact, at the moment that Bender contacted the SS, Himmler was thinking about creating his own 'library of occult esoteric sciences (theosophy, cccultism, etc.)' that would draw on the extensive border scientific materials they had confiscated during the Hess Action.[97] The SS responded positively to Bender's request, urging his institute to conduct research into astrology and transferring a number of 'confiscated collections of books to produce a first-class Astrological Library', which Anrich negotiated with the RSHA on Bender's behalf.[98]

And so the stars aligned perfectly for Bender, who was given the green light to open his Strasbourg-affiliated '[Paracelsus] Institute for Border Science' in October 1942.[99] In addition to Spieser and Anrich, the governing board included the chief of Hitler's presidential chancellery, Otto Meissner, the SS mayor of Strasbourg, Robert Ernst, and other prominent Nazi officials and intellectuals.[100] As steward of Hitler's discretionary fund, Meissner contributed an additional 20,000 reichsmark a year to the Reich University, which Anrich 'succeeded with ease to convince Meissner to allow' to 'flow into the [Paracelsus] Institute'. Although 'certainly without knowing it, Hitler therefore 'co-financed this astrological research in Strasbourg'.[101]

Indicating the importance that the Reich University of Strasbourg attributed to Bender's institute, Anrich relieved Bender of his primary teaching duties so that he could focus on his border scientific research.[102] Bender was also permitted to hire his friend and colleague, the amateur astrologer Thomas Ring, as his assistant and eventual director.[103] Unsurprisingly, Ring's dubious scientific background as a 'sketch artist, painter, [and] poet' did nothing to undermine Bender's faith in his assistant's ability to gauge the scientific validity of 'the stars on human character and reading the future'.[104]

As director of a massive research apparatus supported by Himmler and (indirectly) Hitler, Bender had the 'opportunity to test different institutional structures in both academic and non-academic contexts'. This authority aided Bender in establishing a network of occultists, Nazi politicians, and military elites who wished to pursue investigations into parapsychology, astrology, cosmobiology, pendulum dowsing, and alternative medicine, including magnetopathy and various forms of radiesthesia.[105] Bender's network included, for example, members of the SS; scientists at the Göring Institute in Berlin (run by Hermann Göring's cousin, the psychologist Matthias Göring); and the Luftwaffe, which was interested in the psychological impact of flying under extreme conditions.[106]

Bender recognized the doubtful nature of some of these projects, ranging from the otherwise harmless 'iron-fork' divining technique promoted by Spieser to the SS doctor Otto Bickenbach's human experiments with phosgene gas at the nearby Natzweiler-Struthof concentration camp.[107] But he continued to tolerate such endeavours in order to maintain Hitler and Himmler's sponsorship. That is, Bender knowingly countenanced border scientific work that he found, at best, scientifically worthless and at worst murderous in order to preserve the funding and independence of his institute.

Why would Bender – or his old colleague Krafft – complain? A decade earlier Krafft could hardly have imagined that he and his fellow astrologers would be recruited by the regime to lead a counter-propaganda campaign against the Allies or provide military intelligence to the Navy and the SS.[108] Nor could Bender, for all his charisma and parapsychological gifts, have predicted that he would become one of the most important border scientists in the Third Reich, head of a Reich institute sponsored by Hitler and Himmler.[109] And as we shall see in subsequent chapters, Bender, Krafft, and other border scientists received their greatest offical support from the Third Reich during the Second World War.

Radiesthesia, Anthroposophy, and Biodynamic Agriculture

In 1931, Krafft wrote to Bender on the topic of anthroposophy. If 'I hold [Rudolf Steiner] for one of the most talented, decisive, and astute (intuitive) thinkers,' Krafft averred, one has to admit that his followers were far too given to 'personal polemics and sublime spitefulness'. Due to the 'magic power of "the Master's" suggestion', they were unable to evaluate Steiner's doctrine objectively.[110] A few years later, Bender wrote to Krafft in a similar vein: 'It appears to me as if the anthroposophists too often favour the holistic view over the building blocks and disdain the empirical aspects of the world of the senses ... that is not how one pursues science'.[111] Unlike true border sciences such as astrology and parapsychology, Bender and Krafft suggested, anthroposophy was too intuitive, faith-based, and sectarian in its approach.[112]

If rival occultists dismissed anthroposophy as insufficiently scientific, however, many Nazi leaders embraced Steiner's esoteric doctrines as the natural corollary of their holistic, syncretist view of biology and spirituality.[113] Anthroposophy incorporated the border scientific disciplines of parapsychology and astrology, after all, while offering biodynamic and naturopathic theories popular in the Austro-German life reform (*Lebensreform*) movement before the First World War.[114] Many Germans who were 'committed to both National Socialism and Lebensreform' dedicated themselves 'to recreating a life in harmony with the laws of nature and biology and made their organicism an important element in their movement's worldview'.[115]

Among the millions of Germans who turned to occult health practices were 'top Nazi leaders, whose reasons for dabbling in the occult affords us a well-placed window on the affinities between occultism and Nazism'.[116] For the '"natural" or "organic" strain in Nazism,' writes Corinna Treitel, 'was neither discontinuous with the German past nor tangential to the regime's ideology'. It tapped into 'a deep current of ambivalence' that both Germans and Nazis 'held about the recent triumph of biomedicine and the construction of the modern health bureaucracy'.[117] Whatever measures the Nazis took to police less scientific occult fields, most border scientists had confidence that the regime would apply the 'wisdom of the Brahmins' in sponsoring natural healing, biodynamic agriculture, and other esoteric practices that might improve the health and well-being of the German people.[118]

Radiesthesia and Natural Healing

Modern debates about the organicist relationship between mind and spirit, body and soul, have roots in the late nineteenth-century occult revival. With the rise of anthroposophy before the First World War, not to mention broader trends in holist and vitalist thinking, such doctrines found further border scientific justification.[119] By the 1920s, Germans had become widely enamoured of holistic approaches to medicine and soil cultivation that restored some level of enchantment to nature.

To be sure, 'organic' approaches to health and agriculture spread across much of Europe in the first half of the twentieth century, influencing a number of progressive, reform-minded individuals. In German-speaking central Europe, however, the *völkisch*-esoteric elements inherent within these doctrines were particularly strong.[120] Nourished by an ' "irrational" German "hunger for Wholeness', Anne Harrington observes, radiesthesia, natural healing, and related border scientific practices therefore abdicated the 'right to be called "real" science' and became instead 'a dangerous reflection of (largely rightist) politics'.[121]

A *völkisch*-esoteric, organicist view of race and biology was prevalent even among 'mainstream' German scientists.[122] The biologist Jakob Johann von Uexkull advocated a holistic form of biology that would purify Germany racially and spiritually from Jewish democracy and the 'gorilla-Machine' of materialism.[123] The vitalist biologist Hans Driesch likewise attempted to bring together Western biology and Eastern spirituality in advocating alternative medical practices and natural healing. In the 1920s, as he became progressively immersed in parapsychological speculations, Driesch's ideas became increasingly detached from mainstream biology. By the 1930s many *völkisch*-esotericists and Nazis consumed his occult-inspired, holistic views with great interest.[124]

The above-mentioned Walter Kröner, Driesch's colleague and writing partner, exemplifies the Third Reich's border scientific approach to race and biology. In the 1920s, as chairman of the Potsdam chapter of the DGWO, Kröner worked closely with Leopold Thoma in promoting the use of occult doctrines in policing and medicine.[125] After Hitler's seizure of power in 1933, Kröner produced two of his most important works, *The Rebirth of the Magical* (*Die Wiedergeburt des Magischen*, 1938), with an introduction by Driesch, and *The Decline of Materialism and the Foundation of the Biomagical Conception of the World* (*Der Untergang des Materialismus und die Grundlegung des biomagischen Weltbildes*, 1939).[126]

According to Kröner, the mechanistic approach that defined mainstream science before 1933 was rightly being questioned in the Third Reich:

> For it is precisely in our day [1938] that this mystical feeling, this inner certainty of the Divine foundation and background forces of being begins. Blood ties awaken, the floor, the stones begin talking again ... The myth in the blood is heard anew, and an ideal sent from the deepest, buried magical roots, according to a world organized by cosmic principles, to conquer the artificial mechanistic cultural spheres of our world and to organize it anew in organic fashion ... We can already see from these few hints how we can bring a holistic, organic formula from the basic attitude of the modern

parapsychologists, the magical image of the world that provides us a holistic, biological formula for occult phenomena and opens unimagined possibilities and perspectives regarding future research on life and metaphysics.[127]

Here Kröner brings together parapsychology, spiritualism, and *völkisch*-esoteric obessions with blood in a syncretic cocktail reminiscent of Rudolf Steiner's anthroposophy or Walther Darré's theories of blood and soil.[128]

The border scientific discipline that best represented the practical application of Kröner's 'holistic, biological formula' was probably radiesthesia. As we saw in Chapter One, Germany was a centre of research into radiesthesia. By the 1920s hundreds of scientific radiesthesiologists across Germany insisted they could find arable land, uncover scarce resources, or locate dangerous radiation by employing a specially shaped rod, fork, or pendulum.[129] While Siegfried Reuter explored ways of finding precious metals, H. H. Kritzinger, Ludwig Straniak, and Gustav von Pohl studied cancer-causing radiation along geological or pathogenic fault lines.[130] Other radiesthesiologists, such as Graf von Klinckowstroem and Rudolf von Malzahn, developed the interdisciplinary subfield of 'environmental health', which linked disease to particular weather conditions or cancer-causing 'earth rays' that could only be discovered with the use of divining rods.[131]

Radiesthesia and the related field of geomancy had received little attention from either the Weimar government or mainstream science before 1933. The onset of the Third Reich changed the picture considerably, however, as radiesthesiologists and geomants emerged from the shadows. Some, like the ariosophist Gunther Kirchoff, went to work building a magical geomantic 'triangle' for the SS in order to harness specific 'streams of energy' emanating from Earth's magnetic core.[132]

Others, like Kritzinger, promoted radiesthesia as a mainstream science. Before 1933, he observed, most mainstream geologists, biologists, and physicists had rejected unseen radiation and divining as occultism. But now, with the rise of the Third Reich, many German industrial firms and organic farms had begun to employ these border scientific disciplines with regularity.[133] They acknowledged that electromagnetic forces underground interacted with cosmic forces from the stars in explaining seemingly inexplicable biological phenomena.[134] A proper understanding of 'Earth rays', 'inflammation stripes', and divining rods, Kritzinger explained, could prevent cancer, improve agricultural production, and surmount the 'dark powers of the deep'.[135]

In a later book, *Death Rays*, Kritzinger elaborated on how weather affected people through rays emanating from the sun, stars, and planets. Such rays could only be located with divining rods.[136] Here Kritzinger explicitly acknowledged anthroposophy's important contribution to the field of radiesthesia, namely its emphasis on the relationship between the health of the soil and hidden forces above and below the ground (what Steiner called biodynamic agriculture).[137]

Although respectful of Steiner, Kritzinger viewed Ludwig Straniak, his future colleague in the wartime 'Pendulum Institute' (see Chapter Seven), as 'the most serious researcher' in the scientific field of dowsing.[138] Well-versed in all aspects of radiesthesia, Straniak's particular talent was the sidereal pendulum. Sidereal pendulum dowsing was a subset of divining, in which a Y- or L-shaped stick might be employed to locate earth rays or ley lines under the Earth. A brass pendulum could also be used to locate objects on a map or provide answers to 'yes' or 'no' questions.

Unlike Gutberlet – the early Nazi who claimed to be able to unmask Jews with his divining skills – Straniak was a 'scientific' practitioner. He wrote academic tracts on exploiting the so-called 'eighth force of nature', for example, a force, he claimed, that was hidden in the atmosphere and pushed the pendulum (or acted on the divining rod) to produce physical results.[139] Operating independently in the Third Reich, Straniak helped found the Society for Scientific Pendulum Research (GfWPF) and pursued various 'scientific' studies in occultism, pendulum dowsing, and radiesthesia.[140] Even after the GfWPF was 'coordinated' by the regime in 1938, the SS and other Reich organizations continued commissioning studies and peer reviews in order to differentiate scientific dowsing from charlatanry.[141]

We should hardly be surprised that dowsers deemed sufficiently scientific, like Straniak, would join Wulff, Krafft, Kritzinger and other border scientists in working for the Third Reich.[142] Many Nazi leaders, as we have seen, were fascinated by such practices. In 1934, Hitler himself hired Germany's most famous dowser, the above-mentioned von Pohl, to police the Reich Chancellery for harmful death rays.[143] Hitler also agreed to a personal interview with the Austrian border scientist Viktor Schauberger, who claimed to have located invisible 'free energies' in nature that might be harnessed to remarkable effect (see Chapter Nine).[144]

Himmler was obsessed with natural healing and rejected many aspects of modern medicine. Among various alternative medical practices, he studied herbalism, homoeopathy, mesmerism, and naturopathy.[145] He also followed the advice of ariosophic thinkers such as Emil Rüdiger and Karl Maria Willigut, who believed that practising yoga could release cosmic energies, tied to astral bodies such as the 'black sun'.[146] Through his Ahnenerbe and Schäfer's Tibet institute, Himmler sponsored geomantic research as well. Led by border scientists such as Wilhelm Teudt, Frenzolf Schmid, Günther Kirchoff, and Karl Wienert, the SS conducted extensive research into subterranean geomantic energies and ley lines. Some projects included 'Atlantian-Germanic Circles', 'triangles of Spirit', and the 'Aryan pentagram'.[147]

Himmler also instructed the Ahnenerbe to study the ancient Germans' 'extraordinary understanding of electricity', ostensibly inherited from the

Norse gods.[148] He even funded an expedition by Yrjö von Grönhagen – a Finnish film enthusiast with no medical or anthropological training – to investigate lost Aryan magical rites and healing rituals still performed in Karelia.[149] When Grönhagen returned, he was asked to share his research on 'traditional Aryan methods of body cleansing' with SS medical staff.[150]

Rudolf Hess's personal interest in vegetarianism, homoeopathy, and natural healing are well known.[151] The Deputy Führer also believed in geomantic energy, naturopathy, and magnetopathy (which ostensibly protected one from harmful radiation).[152] He employed a dowser and personal astrologer and structured much of his dietary and personal life around anthroposophical practices.[153] Most conspicuously, Hess encouraged official research into the 'New German Art of Healing', a form of alternative medicine that drew liberally on anthroposophy, radiesthesia, and holism.[154] His investment in the New German Art of Healing included promoting Steiner's theories opposing vaccination, since vaccinations ostensibly failed to address the spiritual sources of health and illness.[155] In 1934 the Deputy Führer opened the Rudolf Hess Hospital in Dresden, a centre for alternative medical practices.[156]

An interest in natural healing, life reform, and radiesthesia, influenced by anthroposophy, extended well beyond Hitler, Himmler, and Hess. Proponents included Julius Streicher, Gauleiter of Nuremberg and editor of *Der Stürmer*; Walther Darré, head of the Race and Settlement Office (RuSHA) and Reich Food Estate; Robert Ley, head of the Nazi Labour Front and the NSDAP party organization; and Heydrich's deputy, Otto Ohlendorf. But it was biodynamic agriculture, more than any other anthroposophic or occult doctrine, that received the greatest official sponsorship by the Third Reich.

Anthroposophy and Biodynamic Agriculture

On 27 May 1941 Hans Merkel, a Nazi official in the Reich Food Estate, wrote to his former superior Walther Darré a long, candid letter.[157] Merkel confessed that he had become an unqualified supporter of 'biological-dynamic agricultural methods' for 'agrarian political as well as ideological reasons'.[158] The 'ideas of blood and soil must be the preeminent foundational ideas for a new peasantry,' Merkel began. That the peasantry must be firmly rooted in blood and soil to be productive was widely accepted for most of history. But this conviction, Merkel continued, had been destroyed in the wake of capitalism and industrialization. These processes spurred the rise of individualism and destruction of the communal and organic bonds that tied the farmer to his family, land, and community. Over the course of the nineteenth century the 'Ur-wisdom' of the German peasant was replaced by the 'soulless ways of thinking of the West'.[159]

When the Third Reich took over, Merkel argued, the government faced a situation where the 'farm had become a factory' through the intensification and mechanization of agriculture. Continuing this process meant 'necessarily destroying the idea of the peasantry'.[160] Although some experts tried to dismiss it as 'dreaming, mysticism or romanticism', biodynamic agriculture (BDW) was a remarkably promising answer to these problems. In reading the works of Rudolf Steiner, 'with whose life work I have engaged deeply,' Merkel concluded, it was clear that one 'could trust the fundamental principles of biological-dynamic agricultural methods'.[161]

Merkel was not alone in his fascination with anthroposophy or, indeed, biodynamic agriculture.[162] His correspondence partner, Darré, agreed that 'we need a better knowledge of man; health through natural living; harmony between blood, soil and cosmos; life reform as a national aim'.[163] So did Ohlendorf, a high-ranking official in Heydrich's intelligence service (SD), specialist in the Reich Economic Ministry, and chief of the SS special task force (*Einsatzgruppe* D) that murdered tens of thousands of Jews on the Eastern Front. Ohlendorf was also, like Darré, a dedicated proponent of anthroposophy.[164]

In his post-war testimony Ohlendorf proudly acknowledged his familiarity with anthroposophic doctrines and institutions. He found 'in many branches of [anthroposophic] research valuable suggestions and results that promised to lead out of the impasse in which [the natural sciences] were invested'. The spiritual aspects of anthroposophy were useful, Ohlendorf suggested, since 'National Socialism had in the short time of its existence [developed] no spiritual education'. Hence it seemed especially 'imperative for the overall intellectual development of National Socialism'. Ohlendorf reasoned, 'not to disturb [anthroposophic] research and their institutions, but to leave them in peace, to develop without violent influence from the outside, regardless of the direction of the research'.[165]

The Nazi medical expert Hanns Rascher, father of the notorious SS doctor Sigmund Rascher, was also an anthroposophist. So was Georg Halbe, a ranking official in Darré's RuSHA; Franz Lippert, an SS officer and later overseer of the SS biodynamic plantation at Dachau; and Alwin Seifert, a leading Nazi environmentalist (Reich Advocate for the Countryside). While not a practising anthroposophist, Ohlendorf's colleague Oswald Pohl, the SS economic expert and head of the concentration-camp system, was a consistent supporter of biodynamic agriculture.[166] In fact, by the outbreak of the Second World War its supporters included the Nazi Minister of Church Affairs, Hans Kerrl; Hederich in the PPK; and Alfred Baümler, the head of the science division in the ostensibly anti-occultist Amt Rosenberg. Even the Third Reich's Minister of the Interior, Wilhelm Frick, embraced aspects of anthroposophy.[167]

It may appear remarkable that so many Nazi leaders would endorse a central element of Rudolf Steiner's occult doctrine of anthroposophy – a doctrine that even fellow border scientists such as Bender and Krafft found insufficiently rigorous. Although it makes perfect sense when we take into account the dizzying array of border scientific practices that anthroposophy incorporated, promising to heal the body, restore the mind and spirit, and renew the soil and environment in holistic fashion.[168] By drawing on the 'same currents of Lebensreform as the occult movement', Anthroposophy – and its most successful outgrowth, biodynamic agriculture – epitomized the 'deep antagonism toward conventional medicine and the strong conviction that modern life had damaged their souls and bodies'. That widespread antagonism, according to Treitel, 'led many Germans of all political persuasions, including fascism, to embrace nature cures, folk remedies, vegetarianism, fresh-air exercise, occult medicine, and other, similar practices'.[169]

Developed by Steiner toward the end of his career, biodynamic agriculture was based 'on a holistic view of the farm or garden as an integrated organism comprising soil, plants, animals, and various cosmic forces, with sowing and harvesting conducted according to astrological principles'. Biodynamic growers rejected monoculture, artificial fertilizers, and pesticides, 'relying instead on manure, compost, and a variety of homoeopathic preparations meant to channel the etheric and astral energies of the Earth and other celestial bodies'.[170]

Proponents of biodynamic agriculture viewed the Earth 'as an organism with magnetic properties of sympathy and attraction' that might 'be damaged by the use of artificial fertilizers'.[171] Advocates of modern science – not to mention the chemical fertilizer industry – rejected this 'spiritually aware peasant wisdom' as both economically and ideologically deficient. But that did little to deter many Nazis, for reasons articulated by Merkel above, from embracing the idea of a more organic approach to agriculture that drew on cosmobiological forces.[172]

The key figure in promoting biodynamic agriculture in the Third Reich was Erhard Bartsch, a protégé of Steiner and expert in the field. In July 1933, barely six months after the Nazi seizure of power, Bartsch formed the Reich League for Biodynamic Agriculture. The League combined romantic, *völkisch*-esoteric blood-and-soil rhetoric with arguments about the practical economic advantages of biodynamic methods.

Many Nazis were already predisposed toward biodynamic agriculture – or at least natural, holistic approaches – due to their border scientific proclivities. Bartsch's clever and concerted propaganda efforts nonetheless helped biodynamic agriculture spread to unlikely circles, from the Ministry of the Interior to the Wehrmacht.[173] Bartsch managed to enlist the support of numerous individuals in the SS and Nazi economic sphere. These included Seifert, the aforementioned 'Reich Advocate for the Countryside', as well as high-ranking SS and Nazi functionaries such as Merkel, Halbe, and Gunther

Pancke in the RuSHA. The RuSHA desired independence from foreign-made fertilizer and other scarce industrial chemicals as part of the move toward economic autarchy under Hermann Göring's Four Year Plan.[174]

Here it is important to emphasize the nexus of border science and environmentalism in Nazi thinking. Rudolf Hess, in his passion for natural methods drawn from the occult, would chastise 'industries interested in artificial fertilizer, preoccupied with the height of their dividends' for 'carrying out a kind of witch trial against all people who would experiment [with biodynamic agriculture]'.[175] Ohlendorf also couched his support for biodynamic agriculture in progressive-sounding, anti-corporate, environmentalist language. The duty of the party was to work against bureaucrats in various ministries who were interested in pursuing monopoly claims, backed by IG Farben and other chemical industries. Ohlendorf even got the Gestapo to loosen rules against anthroposophy in 1936, working with Bartsch in sponsoring research into biodynamic agriculture.[176] Meanwhile Kittler in the PPK argued that 'cosmobiological knowledge' was a 'valuable core in conjunction with experiences of modern agricultural tillage'.[177] By 1936 biodynamic agriculture had become so widely accepted among esoterically inclined Nazis that Berlin's athletic fields for the Summer Olympics were treated biodynamically, which garnered much praise.[178]

Perhaps biodynamic agriculture's most consistent supporter, after Hess and Ohlendorf, was Darré, the Reich Minister of Food and Agriculture. While economic considerations had something to do with his emerging interest in biodynamic agriculture – namely the drive toward economic autarchy in agriculture – Darré's blood-and-soil *völkisch*-esotericism played an important role.[179] Darré's correspondence is littered with excerpts from Steiner's writings, belying Darré's claims that his interest in anthroposophy was purely pragmatic.[180] Moreover, the Reich Minister's justifications for biodynamic agriculture – wanting to restore man's organic relationship to God, 'who works and lives in everything that's essential in this world' – blurred the same lines between science and the supernatural as Steiner's original doctrine.[181] If mainstream biologists could argue that plants grow through 'invisible' rays generated by the sun, Darré wondered, then why couldn't they accept the cosmic forces behind biodynamic agriculture?[182]

Darré fell out of favour with Himmler over various matters in the late 1930s and eventually lost his position as head of the RuSHA and Reich Food Estate.[183] Fortunately, Bartsch had many other Nazi allies willing to carry the torch. In 1937, Ohlendorf volunteered to act as the point person for biodynamic agriculture, making efforts to facilitate Bartsch's research.[184] By the outbreak of the Second World War, additional high-ranking party members, including Rosenberg, Ley, and Frick, had visited the biodynamic agriculture headquarters and expressed support for Bartsch's organization.[185] Oswald Pohl and Pancke,

Darré's successor as head of the RuSHA, went so far as to urge Heydrich to allow Bartsch into the SS.[186]

Bartsch's eventual fall from grace, even as biodynamic agriculture became widely accepted, examplies the larger pattern we have seen in Nazi approaches to border science. For Bartsch was a charismatic, uncompromising sectarian. According to one of his chief sponsors, Ohlendorf, Bartsch's application to join the party was not rejected because of his commitment to biodynamic agriculture or any other border scientific doctrines. Bartsch's mistake was insisting that anthroposophic methods 'could be used only by people who were inwardly convinced of the intellectual foundations of these fundamental beliefs', namely loyal followers of Steiner. Bartsch worked to exploit the sympathies of Nazi leaders 'not only to enforce biodynamic agriculture', Ohlendorf observed, but to impose the 'anthroposophical worldview' on everyone in the Third Reich. He even tried to convert Hitler.[187] 'Any attempt to explain to him the absurdity of this [idea],' Ohlendorf recalled, was 'in vain'.[188]

This explains why the Gestapo finally arrested Bartsch in the wake of the June 1941 Hess Action. He was an unrepentant sectarian.[189] Heydrich nonetheless assured Darré that the SD and Gestapo would continue to permit German farmers to experiment with biodynamic agriculture. The only caveat, Heydrich assured Darré, was that its practitioners should not become *ideologically* committed to Steiner's anthroposophy as an individual sect.[190]

Fortunately for the proponents of biodynamic agriculture, by the time of Bartsch's arrest it had found a new and far more powerful sponsor: the Reichsführer SS.[191] Like Hess, Ohlendorf, and Darré before him, Himmler's interest in biodynamic agriculture stemmed from a combination of *völkisch*-esoteric predispositions and a practical desire to improve the quality and productivity of German agriculture. 'In regard to biological-dynamic fertilization,' he declared, 'I can only say: as a farmer I am generally sympathetic.'[192] Before September 1939, Himmler had scant opportunity or incentive to experiment with biodynamic agriculture, focused as he was on policing the Third Reich. With the wartime drive to resettle German peasants and reclaim eastern European living space, however, Himmler suddenly found biodynamic agricultural practices, as we shall see in Chapter Eight, far more attractive.[193]

World Ice Theory

'I tend to support World Ice Theory,' Hitler declared in 1942. Hörbiger's theory was convincing, the Führer suggested, in proving that icy moons had crashed into Earth, creating geophysical forces that caused a flood from which only 'a few humans had survived'. Certainly, World Ice Theory could only be gleaned by looking at 'intuitive context', though perhaps, Hitler added, such methods would show the way for so-called 'exact science'.[194] 'Legend cannot be extracted from the void,' he reasoned, for 'mythology is a reflection of things that have existed and of which humanity has retained a vague memory.'[195] 'In all the human traditions,' Hitler continued, 'one finds mention of a huge cosmic disaster ... In the Nordic legend we read of a struggle between giants and gods. In my view, the thing is explicable only [based on] the hypothesis of a disaster that completely destroyed a humanity which already possessed a high degree of civilization.'[196]

Hitler was not alone in these bizarre ruminations. There was no border science in the Third Reich that was more widely or uncritically embraced than 'Glacial Cosmogony', also known as World Ice Theory. Both astrology and biodynamic agriculture were closely associated with Austro-German occult doctrines such as ariosophy and anthroposophy. But they still derived from occult traditions that carried with them *potentially* 'Jewish' or 'oriental' elements that needed to be filtered out or refashioned before being appropriated by the Third Reich. World Ice Theory, on the other hand, was authentically 'German', providing an alternative system of understanding the physical and metaphysical world that helped buttress Nazi views on race and space, science and religion.[197]

World Ice Theory also stood at the centre of Nazi attempts to reframe science and reestablish the 'interdependence of all spheres of research and knowledge' as it had 'ostensibly been in the Middle Ages'. The Nazis, per Michael Kater, characterized 'the traditional distinction between humanistic and natural science' as 'specialist fetishization', which unnecessarily separated off 'individual scientists into their special fields'. In the Third Reich, according to many Nazi leaders, humanistic, social scientific, and natural scientific fields would be merged, producing 'the unity of soul and body, intellect and blood, God and world as precondition of a new indo-Germanic worldview'.[198] With its inane claims to constituting a grand unified, interdisciplinary theory of the universe, while simultaneously incorporating *völkisch* conceptions of race, space, and Nordic mythology, World Ice Theory was the perfect exemplar of Nazi border science.[199]

In the following section we begin by looking at its influence on prominent Nazi leaders and its growing role within Himmler's Institute for Ancestral Research. We then turn to the attempts of the Ahnenerbe to institutionalize World Ice Theory as an official scientific doctrine in the mid- to late 1930s. While not entirely successful, the immense effort expended by Nazi leaders to prop up World Ice Theory exemplifies the centrality of border scientific thinking in the Third Reich.

World Ice Theory and Himmler's Institute for Ancestral Research

Of the many esoteric theories that did not meet the empirical or methodological standards of mainstream science none had greater resonance among *völkisch* thinkers in Germany and Austria than World Ice Theory.[200] Part of this was due to the fact that Hanns Hörbiger was a brilliant self-promoter who managed to make his fantastical ideas appear scientific to the dilettantes that defined the occult public. But World Ice Theory also had the ideological advantage over other border sciences in that it was almost perfectly compatible with a Nazi cosmology.[201]

World Ice Theory, according to the Nazi intellectual Edgar Dacqué, represented a 'racial spirit of the times and science' rolled into one. It was an 'aggressive response and revolutionary departure from the system of foreign scientific powers', including the 'self-satisfied-bourgeois' astronomy and physics of the West.[202] Both Nordic mythology and *völkisch*-esoteric doctrines such as ariosophy had posited a series of Ur-cataclysms and ice ages, which caused biological mutations in Earth's inhabitants, producing Atlantean supermen and monstrous humanoids. Weaned on Wagner, Houston Stewart Chamberlain, and Lanz von Liebenfels, many *völkisch* thinkers consequently recognized in World Ice Theory the ancient Aryans (Atlanteans) whose civilization had been destroyed by their former 'Tschandal' slaves.[203] Supporters of World Ice Theory were likewise keen to point out parallels between the Austrians Hörbiger and Hitler, including their mutual success, as so-called amateurs, in conquering the fields of science and politics respectively.[204]

As suggested above, World Ice Theory was the only 'border science' that Hitler embraced wholly and with conviction.[205] There is much discussion of 'pre-moon humanity' in Greek sources, Hitler opined to Himmler, which in the Führer's opinion had to do with the 'World Empire of Atlantis, which fell victim to the catastrophe of the moons falling to Earth'.[206] He read the fanciful books authored by the proponents of World Ice Theory and appeared to believe its predictive qualities when it came to geological and meteorological phenomena.[207] Hitler even talked of erecting a great observatory in his home town of Linz, Austria, representing 'the three great cosmological conceptions of history – those of Ptolemy, Copernicus and Hörbiger'.[208] In regard to religion, Hitler is supposed to have suggested that World Ice Theory might eventually replace Christianity.[209]

Hitler had lots of company. Hess was an ardent supporter, sponsoring the above-mentioned Dacqué for a Chair at the University of Munich and later Divisional Head in the Reich Ministry for Science, Education, and Popular Education.[210] Also enthusiastic were both heads of Himmler's Ahnenerbe, Hermann Wirth and Walther Wüst, as well as the Chief of the Third Reich's press corps, Albert Herrmann, who published a book inspired by World Ice Theory in which he argued that the original Atlantis was in Tunisia.[211] Robert Ley, who always seemed to find time for esoteric pursuits, is reported to have said that 'Our Nordic ancestors grew strong in ice and snow: belief in the World

Ice is consequently the natural heritage of Nordic Man.'[212] Equally illustrative of the widespread acceptance among leading Nazis of World Ice Theory is the fact that Hitler's normally more sober and pragmatic second-in-command, Hermann Göring, and the head of the German Youth movement, Baldur von Schirach, were supportive.[213] Even Heydrich's SD and the Amt Rosenberg – two organizations explicitly tasked with eradicating sectarianism – proved remarkably sanguine about the related teachings of World Ice Theory.[214]

If many Nazis were excited about the possibilities of World Ice Theory, however, Himmler was arguably its strongest supporter. For Himmler, World Ice Theory stood at the esoteric nexus of Nazi border scientific and religious thinking.[215] The 'Aryans did not evolve from apes like the rest of humanity,' Himmler argued, 'but are gods come directly from Heaven to Earth' who emerged from 'living kernels' that were conserved in the 'eternal ice of the cosmos.'[216] These ancient superhumans once possessed 'paranormal powers and extraordinary weapons' akin to Thor's 'thunder hammer'. The Thunder God's powers 'didn't have to do with natural thunder and lightning' but 'pertained to an earlier, highly developed tool of our ancestors that was obviously only in the possession of a few, namely the "Asen" who were gods and were privy to an unheard of knowledge of electricity'.[217] World Ice Theory also confirmed Himmler's theory that the Chinese and Japanese were 'once colonial races with a central state originating from peoples who centuries or millennia earlier had had an Atlantean ruling class'.[218]

For these reasons Himmler made an enormous effort to sponsor World Ice Theory as a state science. The most famous example is Himmler's (and Hitler's) unqualified support for Hörbiger's elderly co-author Philip Fauth, an amateur scientist whose theories were perched on that 'narrow intersection between the pure scientific and the speculative and fantastical'.[219] Appointed as Ahnenerbe astronomer and named full professor by Himmler in 1939, at the age of seventy-three, Fauth also received an honorary doctorate from Hitler himself.[220]

Another prominent supporter of World Ice Theory who experienced a career renaissance in the Third Reich was the rabidly anti-Semitic writer and SA leader, Rudolf von Elmayer-Vestenbrugg (or Elmar Brugg). Like Himmler, Elmayer insisted that World Ice Theory provided the only 'scientific basis for a true Nordic worldview'.[221] In his most influential book, *The Enigma of Universal Phenomena* (1937), Elmayer argued that World Ice Theory would replace Darwin's now 'defunct' theory of evolution and that the Aryan race had been incubated in the arctic world before founding the civilization of Atlantis.[222] No wonder that Elmayer, despite his utter lack of scientific credentials, would later be tapped by Himmler to head the World Ice Theory division within the Ahnenerbe.

Perhaps the most important sponsor of World Ice Theory in the Third Reich was SS *Obersturmführer* Hans Robert Scultetus.[223] Although technically trained as a meteorologist, Scultetus was equally interested in astrology and other paranormal phenomena, seeking funding for a research expedition to Abyssinia (Ethiopia) to conduct experiments on 'Zodiacal lights' and 'heavenly apparitions'.[224] As head of the Ahnenerbe's Institute for Meteorology, Scultetus became the most influential proponent of World Ice Theory in Himmler's inner circle.[225]

Himmler's World Ice Theory brain trust also included Edmund Kiss, a novelist and explorer who combined science and fiction in propagating this border science.[226] An amateur archaeologist, Kiss had participated in an expedition to the Andes in which he claimed to have found sculptures with Aryan features and a calendar that recorded a time when Earth was circled by another moon (which ostensibly fell to Earth and destroyed the Andean capital, according to World Ice Theory).[227] Kiss further popularized World Ice Theory with fanciful novels that drew a connection between it, ariosophy, and Hollow Earth Theory, a doctrine that speculated about a subterranean civilization under the Himalayas.[228]

In late 1935, Himmler brought these World Ice Theory theorists together, along with a couple of Hörbiger's sons, in the Ahnenerbe.[229] The idea for an interdisciplinary institute that combined many strands of *völkisch* border science had been percolating in Himmler's mind before 1933. Already in 1928 he had founded an Ahnenerbe office aimed at researching Aryan geneaology.[230] In the giddy months after the Nazi seizure of power in January 1933 the Reichsführer added an archaeological division within his personal staff as well as ad hoc research posts linked to the Race and Settlement Office (RuSHA).[231] Although it was not until July 1935 that Himmler, Darré, and the *völkisch*-esotericist Hermann Wirth created an independent research institute within the SS, the Ahnenerbe, focused on exploring 'the space, spirit and deed of the Indo-Germans'. Its goal was to popularize 'relevant research findings among the German people' in order to encourage all Germans to participate in these endeavours.[232]

The border scientific premises of the Ahnenerbe were evident from the beginning. Alongside the 'pseudo-prophet' Wirth, both the Nazi race theorist H. K. Günther and the three most important progenitors of the Ahnenerbe – Himmler, Darré, and Wolfram Sievers – were members of the *völkisch*-esotericist Artamanen movement during the Weimar Republic. All three were likewise influenced by ariosophic mystics such as Karl Maria Wiligut and Friedrich Hielscher.[233] The controversial Wirth was made head of the Ahnenerbe in great part *because* he was persecuted by 'official science', which burnished his border scientific credentials.[234] Wirth's research on the forged Ura Linda chronicles turned out to be bogus and led to his dismissal from the Ahnenerbe in 1938. But Wirth's successor, the ostensibly more respectable Indologist Walter Wüst, made few changes in academic approach.[235] Under Wüst the Ahnenerbe continued to invest in research projects 'impulsively and without solid goals'. The institute's 'proclivity for fantasy' and disdain for scientific boundaries, Kater argues, was 'always stronger than the push for objectivity and discipline. The unreal always won the upper hand at the cost of the real.'[236]

Despite this explicitly border scientific approach, the Ahnenerbe grew rapidly. By the end of the 1930s, Himmler had developed connections to mainstream academic organizations and research institutes as well as the army, navy, and air force. The Ahnenerbe also expanded its interdisciplinary reach from the humanities (primarily folklore research) in the mid-1930s to the natural and social sciences a few years later.[237]

The Ahnenerbe proudly embraced interdisciplinarity and eschewed the 'specialist-fetishization' (*Spezialistentums*) of mainstream natural science. Himmler and his colleagues insisted, for example, on the 'interdependence of all research and scientific fields' – the way that knowledge had ostensibly been pursued in the Middle Ages. For the 'organicist-thinking Himmler', who 'opposed the siloing off of individual scientists within their special spheres', this border scientific emphasis on interdisciplinarity meant the concerted integration of the Natural Sciences into the Ahnenerbe's Human and Social Science divisions.[238] The Ahnenerbe, Himmler wrote to Heydrich excitedly, might bring the Indologist Wüst and renowned physicist Werner Heisenberg into 'cooperation with our people from World Ice Theory' in an Indo-Aryan *Academia Universalis*.[239]

Of course, this uncritical interdisciplinarity within the Ahnenerbe led to the unsystematic elision of individual academic fields and border scientific perversion of academic inquiry.[240] Whereas amateurish hacks such as Wirth and Wiligut reached the highest levels of authority, Nobel Prize-winning physicists like Max Planck and Albert Einstein were dismissed as 'mystics' and charlatans.[241]

To be sure, the dilettantish Himmler, like most border scientists, desperately sought approval and support from mainstream scientists. Since most 'serious natural scientists wanted to have nothing to do with these kinds of propositions', however, Himmler was ready to hand over the keys to 'fantasists' such as Elmayer, Kiss, and Scultetus, 'dubious scientists' whose research was 'reminiscent of the occult-enshrouded craft of medieval alchemists'.[242] Perched at the centre of the Ahnenerbe's efforts to legitimize these many border sciences was World Ice Theory.[243]

World Ice Theory and the Apotheosis of Nazi Border Science

Even after the Nazi seizure of power, the proponents of World Ice Theory continued to face the virtually unanimous opposition of mainstream scientists and sceptics.[244] Of all the 'superstitious secret sciences' prevalent in the Third

Reich, wrote the anti-occultist Otto Urbach in 1938, the worst was World Ice Theory. 'What so very much compromised World Ice Theory, which has found no resonance in circles of astronomers,' Urbach noted, was the fact that it was a 'concealed religion, a spiritual sect'.[245] The great German physicist, Heisenberg, referred to World Ice Theory as 'nonsense', while even the pro-Nazi physicist Philip Lenard deemed it 'pure fantasy'.[246] As Scultetus wrote to SS-Hauptsturmführer Bruno Galke, a member of Himmler's personal staff, the 'widespread opposition to World Ice Theory' in the greater scientific community was proving to be a challenge in lending it official status.[247]

Himmler was enormously frustrated. According to the Reichsführer, if scientists believed in 'free research in every form' why shouldn't that include 'the free research of the World Ice Theory. I seek to support this free research in the heartiest fashion and find myself here in the best circles, since the Führer and Chancellor of the German Reich, Adolf Hitler, has for many years been a convinced proponent of this theory that has been mocked by those who consort with the closed guild of science.' He then added, 'There are so many things that we do not know, the research of which – even by lay people – we must accept.'[248] In contrast to the arrogance and close-mindedness of 'calcified scientific fat cats', Himmler suggested, the Ahnenerbe was committed to intellectual freedom, tolerance, and openness to unconventional ideas.[249]

Himmler's assertions regarding the closed-mindedness of the academic establishment was typical of many border scientists. Except even Ludwig Straniak and Hans Bender were willing to acknowledge the dangers of *purely* faith-based reasoning, as indicated by Bender's criticism of anthroposophy, and many scientific occultists still hoped to convince mainstream scientists of their results. Hitler, Hess, Himmler, and Rosenberg, on the other hand, tended to invoke their support for 'free research' and 'interdisciplinarity' only when it suited their ideological agenda. For them, the idea of gaining the imprimatur of 'Jewish' materialists such as Einstein or arrogant 'fat cats' like Planck was both asinine and unnecessary. If a German scientist wasn't a Nazi first and foremost – or at least politically quiescent, like Heisenberg – Himmler and company had little patience for their 'free research'.[250]

Nazi hypocrisy regarding free research became readily apparent in July 1936 when Scultetus, encouraged by Himmler, issued the so-called Pyrmonter Protocol. In designating Hörbiger's theories as 'the intellectual gift of a genius', the signatories of the protocol agreed to the precondition that 'all people working on World Ice Theory' could do so only 'under the leadership of a spiritual leader, whose sole responsibility was to the Reichsführer-SS'.[251] Signed by Scultetus, Kiss, Fauth, and Hörbiger's son Alfred, among others, the protocol stated that scientists deviating from 'Meister Hoerbiger's' theories in their 'fundamental form' would cease to receive funding and could be subject to disciplinary procedures.[252]

This blatant attempt to prevent any dissent from Hörbiger's original principles was obviously contradictory given Himmler's repeated criticism of mainstream science's refusal to allow alternative viewpoints. But it comported with the Third Reich's subjective approach to border science: accusing ideologically independent or commercial occultists of 'sectarianism' while protecting and even sponsoring esoteric doctrines favoured by Nazi leaders.[253] All that an occult or border scientific doctrine needed was to be deemed sufficiently 'Aryan' and/or 'scientific' by the right Nazi leader. Thus Himmler passed over Hörbiger's eldest son as 'spiritual leader' of the new Institute for Meteorology in favour of the more devoted Nazi, Scultetus.[254]

One of the first proponents of World Ice Theory to run afoul of the Pyrmonter Protocol was Georg Hinzpeter, president of the Society for the Sponsorship of World Ice Theory (*Gesellschaft zur Foerderung der Welteislehre* or GFW).[255] Hinzpeter's research on various astronomical and meteorological questions – in particular his critique of Hörbiger's icy basis of the Milky Way – clearly represented a deviation from a fundamentalist understanding of Hörbiger's original findings.[256] When it became clear that Hinzpeter's research was causing friction between the GFW and the Austrian Hörbiger Institute, run by Hörbiger's son, Scultetus stepped in.[257]

In December 1936 Scultetus began lobbying to get rid of Hinzpeter as president of the GFW and editor of the GFW-sponsored *Journal of World Ice Theory* in favour of the above-mentioned Elmayer-Vestenbrugg.[258] In making his case, Scultetus cited the draft of Elmayer's recent article entitled 'Hanns Hoerbiger, the Copernicus of the 20th Century'.[259] Scultetus envisioned Elmayer working directly with World Ice Theory's co-founder Fauth to promote this border science to the German public.[260]

Unfortunately, Elmayer proved to be a problematic replacement. After Elmayer's article appeared in the popular periodical, the *Illustrated Observer* (*Illustrierte Beobachter*), the publisher received a flurry of angry letters from professional scientists. A Rostock physicist observed that Elmayer approached World Ice Theory with a 'nearly religious fervour', which did 'no service either to the man on the street nor the state'.[261] The Wehrmacht engineer Peter Lautner stated bluntly that the article 'damages the reputation of German science', which has 'no time for fruitless debates with religious theories'. How could 'fairy tales' be lent 'the name of science' at a moment when young men were coming to the Wehrmacht with minimal 'knowledge of mathematics and physics'? Lautner sent his letter to the Ministry for Science, Art and Public Education, urging Reich authorities to 'put the tellers of fairy tales in their place'.[262]

The head of the Berlin astronomical observatory could not believe the 'plethora of factual inaccuracies and arbitrary claims' made by proponents of World Ice Theory. What impression must a reader get, when confronted with a bizarre theory that surpasses 'everything we know up to this point' and is 'destined to put our entire worldview and mastery of nature on new foundations?' Moreover, what would readers think when told that mainstream 'science – German science in particular – has refused to recognize' this theory, 'partly out of incompetence and partly out of ill-will?' Readers might well come to the conclusion that government posts 'trusted with the propagation of science, are filled partly with idiots, partly with narrow-minded bureaucrats, who stand in the way of progress'. They might even 'take a critical view toward those individuals who appointed' such representatives – namely the Nazi Party.[263]

Faced with such mordant criticisms one might have expected Himmler and Scultetus to attack the Reich's chief astronomer or back down in their support of Elmayer. They did neither. Instead they came to Elmayer's defence – at least for a time – and offered to bring in Goebbels' Propaganda Ministry to lead the campaign against Hinzpeter.[264] Scultetus then instructed Hinzpeter that his work was no longer going to be supported by the regime because it deviated from Hörbiger's original theory.[265]

Conceding his amateur scientific training – which had never stopped Hörbiger or Fauth – Hinzpeter explained in response that World Ice Theory must consider alternative data and conclusions if it wanted to be taken seriously. 'If I may make a comparison,' he wrote, 'no one would call into question the extraordinary service of Daimler or Benz' in creating the earliest motorcars. One would nevertheless prefer a newer 'model with a more modern style' to a model built thirty years earlier. For the same reason, Hinzpeter reasoned, 'no one would think of diminishing the great service of Hanns Hörbiger, but would focus on maintaining the living development of World Ice Theory'. Although expressing gratitude for Himmler's financial support and interest in his work, Hinzpeter agreed that he would not be able to continue working for the Ahnenerbe under the restrictive parameters of the Pyrmonter Protocol.[266]

Scultetus and others were not willing to let the matter drop with Hinzpeter's exit from the Ahnenerbe.[267] A few days after Hinzpeter's departure, Hörbiger's son wrote an open letter to the GFW admonishing Hinzpeter to stop writing in Hörbiger's name. According to Hörbiger, the goal of the Hörbiger Institute was to sponsor World Ice Theory in the fundamentalist form his father desired. That was along the lines of Hitler's 'führer principle' (*Führerprinzip*), as embodied in the Pyrmonter Protocol. If supporters of World Ice Theory were free to conduct their own experiments in the context of the GFW, Hörbiger conceded, dissenters needed publicly to acknowledge that they did not represent the Hörbiger Institute or its Proceedings (*Mitteilungen*). Hörbiger then announced his departure from the GFW, whose research, as represented by Hinzpeter, no longer comported with the fundamental vision of his father.

The younger Hörbiger recognized the irreconcilable contradiction between perpetuating a fundamentalist vision of World Ice Theory and allowing free research. Which is why he agreed, initially, 'not to interfere with the sovereignty of the GFW'.[268] But when Hinzpeter announced his desire to submit a defence of his views to the Prussian Academy of Science, Hörbiger quickly changed his mind, asking Himmler and Wüst to intervene.[269]

Acting as an anonymous reviewer for the Ahnenerbe, the fantasy novelist Edmund Kiss noted Hinzpeter's vast knowledge and good intentions. The fiction writer likewise admitted that 'he lacked, like the authors of the paper, a thorough scientific education [gründliche Fachausbildung]'. Kiss nonetheless concluded that Hinzpeter's paper, which enumerated many areas where Hörbiger's claims failed to hold up to scrutiny, was incompatible with the Pyrmonter Protocol. It would therefore not serve to improve 'the image of World Ice Theory' were his research sent to the Prussian Academy of Sciences. Only by close adherence to the Protocol, Kiss concluded, could World Ice Theory achieve wider recognition in the scientific community.[270]

Just as the Ahnenerbe was emerging from the Hinzpeter affair, a new controversy arose, this time involving Hörbiger's co-author, the amateur astronomer-cum–SS officer (Obersturmführer) Fauth. The controversy stemmed from a January 1938 article, 'Science and World Ice Theory'. published by the geologist Karl Hummel in the well-respected Journal of the German Geological Society.

Hummel began cautiously: 'If unscientific thoughts on scientific issues can gain a foothold in many parts of the population, it is on the one hand a sign of the positive fact that widespread interest in these scientific issues are present in the people'. But misguided ideas about science represented 'on the other hand a reproach to the relevant representatives of science, who have failed to meet the scientific needs of the people due to their better judgement'.[271] The marginalization of mainstream science, Hummel continued, was partly a result of Weimar's 'Marxist' culture in which 'all traditional authorities,' including mainstream science, were called into question.[272] Still, those Germans most likely to embrace World Ice Theory and other esoteric ideas, Hummel conceded, were those most likely also to support Nazism.[273] Nazi voters came from the same 'bourgeois groups' that failed to recognize 'the importance and indispensability of science (and in particular the natural sciences) for the life of the people'. This unscientific culture, Hummel concluded, 'is not yet fully overcome today'.[274]

Fauth was furious and the Nazi authorities were deeply troubled. Scultetus immediately forwarded Hummel's article to Wüst, the head of the Ahnenerbe, along with an angry response from Fauth. In typical border scientific fashion, Fauth took Hummel to task by invoking the same call for interdisciplinarity and 'free research' expressed by Himmler above. World Ice Theorists would never make absolutist assertions such as 'We know, we have concluded, we have calculated, we have proven,' Fauth explained, because they were open to alternative points of view – a completely disingenuous response from someone who had just excoriated Hinzpeter for deviating from the Pyrmonter Protocol.[275]

Although he undoubtedly recognized that Hitler and Himmler supported Fauth, Hummel was not about to back down. A debate with Fauth was impossible, Hummel responded, 'because one can refute a rational [argument], but never a faith-based [*glaubensmaessige*] conviction through objective counter-arguments'. 'You demand the right to reject every scientific "claim to authority",' Hummel observed. And 'in this principle you are united with me and most scientists worth taking seriously'. Instead of accepting the terms of critical scientific inquiry, however, 'you have merely taken from the discussion that science is in disagreement over some questions'. Indeed, there was a vast difference between 'recognizing the disagreement over this or that question' and 'the conclusion you draw that any hypothesis you like, no matter how questionable, any air-headed collection of thoughts that completely contradicts empirical observations, may claim equal academic value'.[276]

In conclusion, Hummel advised Fauth not to be surprised that 'the theories of World Ice Theory are [not even] used by scientists in otherwise hopeless cases' since 'there is simply too much evidence against the principles of World Ice Theory'.[277] It is hard to say what is more remarkable about Hummel's article and the ensuing exchange with Fauth: the fact that Hummel so openly exposed the Third Reich's faith-based approach to science or the fact that Hitler, Himmler, and others continued to defend World Ice Theory regardless.[278]

Fauth and his Nazi allies would in any case have the last laugh. In the wake of the Hinzpeter Affair and Hummel controversy, the Ahnenerbe decided that it was time to enforce the Pyrmonter Protocol more rigorously— 'free research' be damned.[279] In summer 1939, on the third anniversary of the Protocol, the Ahnenerbe sponsored a conference focused on using World Ice Theory to predict long-term meteorological events in support of the Luftwaffe. Himmler invited only World Ice Theory proponents favorable to the Ahnenerbe's point of view.[280]

When it came to a discussion of how to proceed regarding the Pyrmonter Protocol, Scultetus insisted that the regime issue a more binding agreement. He followed up with a letter to Sievers, Wüst, and Himmler, suggesting that Hinzpeter's GFW and other dissenters should now 'disappear, so that the complete efforts of the Ahnenerbe could no longer be called into question'. As soon as all independent organizations were 'dissolved', Scultetus argued, the Reichsführer SS could exercise complete 'protective control [*Schirmherrschaft*] over World Ice Theory'.[281] The ensuing agreement instructed all recipients that the 'promotion [of World Ice Theory] through lay publications be kept at a minimum and that no signees of the Pyrmonter Protocol may compose new works of that kind' in order to guarantee that 'the reputation of World Ice Theory was no longer endangered by dilettantish treatment by other circles.'[282] Completely discredited within the mainstream scientific community, World Ice Theory had found another way to flourish: through monopoly support by the Third Reich.[283]

***

According to some accounts, border science 'ceased its highly public presence as part of Germany's reformist milieu of cultural experimentation' after 1937, when 'the Nazi regime suppressed occultism as one of its many ideological enemies.'[284] The evidence we have seen in this chapter paints a rather different picture.[285] First, in terms of astrology and parapsychology, biodynamic agriculture, and World Ice Theory, the regime's approach was often highly public. Goebbels hired astrologers to produce propaganda. Bender's parapsychological experiments were reported in major newspapers and sponsored by a Reich-financed university institute with connections to Hitler and Himmler. High-profile support for border science is equally evident in the regime employing biodynamic agriculture to prepare the athletics grounds for the 1936 Olympics or in Hitler and Himmler promoting World Ice Theory as official science despite the opposition of the entire academic establishment.

Second, the Third Reich was clearly drawn to border science because of their interest in the 'reformist milieu of cultural experimentation.'[286] The regime may have attempted to marginalize certain occult doctrines insofar as they represented a sectarian belief system or were sponsored by a rival charismatic Führer, such as Steiner or Sebottendorff. But that did not prevent Nazi leaders from seeking to coopt border scientific ideas and practices for their own 'interdisciplinary' purposes.[287] In regard to astrology and parapsychology, the Third Reich's epistemological commitment to border scientific experimentation was always stronger than the regime's general antipathy to 'sectarianism'.

The same pattern held for the remarkably influential doctrine of anthroposophy. As a rival *Weltanschauung* with its own *Führer* (Steiner) and sectarian tendencies, many Nazis deemed anthroposophy to be 'un-German'. When it came to anthroposophy's border scientific approach to 'higher knowledge', however, whether in terms of radiesthesia, natural healing or biodynamic agriculture, a remarkable number of Nazis expressed enthusiasm and support. In terms of World Ice Theory, the regime's commitment was all the more powerful, illustrating better than any other doctrine the Third Reich's considerable investment in border scientific thinking. During the Second World War this border scientific approach to decision-making and policy, as we shall see, helped facilitate projects both fantastical and monstrous.[288]

LUCIFER'S COURT
Ario-Germanic Paganism, Indo-Aryan Spirituality, and the Nazi Search for
Alternative Religions

'We're struggling towards a final form of belief ... But it's not right to root
children up from their familiar world and make them face the problems of
faith before they've fully grown ... Faith has to grow on its own accord; you
can only clear the way for it, not dictate it.'

Heinrich Himmler, as reported by Felix Kersten[1]

'Just as in Islam, there is no kind of terrorism in the Japanese State religion, but,
to the contrary, a promise of happiness. This terrorism in religion is the
product, to put it briefly, of a Jewish dogma, which Christianity has universal-
ized and whose effect is to sow trouble and confusion in men's minds.'[2]

Adolf Hitler (1942)

'My ancestors were witches and I am a heretic.'[3]

Otto Rahn, SS Obersturmführer (1937)

In the spring of 1943 the Third Reich's Plenipotentiary in Denmark, SS
Obergruppenführer Dr Werner Best, requested two copies of a strange-
sounding book called *Lucifer's Court*. The book was written by the Third Reich's
'real Indiana Jones', the philologist and explorer Otto Rahn.[4] Plucked from
obscurity by Heinrich Himmler's chief esotericist, Karl Maria Wiligut, Rahn
was tasked with conducting research into the Holy Grail and the lost civilization of the Thule. Rahn's widely popular first book, *Quest for the Grail* (1933),
had outlined a theory that medieval heretics known as the Cathars were the
true protectors of pagan Aryan religion.

Rahn's second book, *Lucifer's Court* (1937), written under the auspices of
Himmler's Ahnenerbe, went further. In it Rahn speculated that the Grail lay at

the centre of a Cathar cult of Luciferians – literally Devil worshippers – who practised an Ur-Aryan religion drawn from Tibet and northern India, via Persia, in pre-modern times. Accused of heresy and witchcraft, these last representatives of the Indo-Aryan civilization of Thule (Atlantis) had been eradicated by the Catholic Church, their teachings preserved by the Knights Templar and Tibetan monks. During the second half of the nineteenth century this Luciferian tradition was resuscitated by the theosophs, ariosophs, and other *völkisch*-esoteric groups, paving the way for a renaissance in Ario-Germanic religion. Although *Lucifer's Court* was out of print, Himmler's adjutant Rudolf Brandt made sure to obtain two copies and have them sent to Best in Denmark immediately.[5]

The idea of Nazism as a neo-pagan movement with Indo-Aryan, even 'Luciferian', antecedents, is nothing new. In the immediate post-war period many historians maintained that Nazism was profoundly anti-Christian and 'preached an alternative, paganist religion founded on mythical gods of the Germanic Middle Ages, on Thor and Wodan and their ilk'.[6] A number of scholars, however, have since questioned Nazism's paganist, *völkisch*-esoteric roots. A few have highlighted the movement's Christian elements.[7] Others have argued that Nazism was not in itself religious but appropriated mystical symbols and ritual forms to create a secular 'political religion' based on a shared faith in racial community.[8]

The reality is that the Third Reich embraced a range of pagan, esoteric, and Indo-Aryan religious doctrines that buttressed its racial, political, and ideological goals.[9] That is why Nazism, according to the British theologian Christopher Dawson, posed a different threat to Christianity than secular liberalism or atheist Marxism. The danger is 'not that the Nazi movement is anti-religious', Dawson observed, but that it has 'a religion of its own which is not that of Christian orthodoxy'. Nazi religiosity was a 'fluid and incoherent thing which expresses itself in several different forms'. There was the 'neo-paganism of the extreme pan-German element', the 'Aryanized and nationalized Christianity of the German Christians' and 'the racial and nationalistic idealism which is characteristic of the movement as a whole'. All these strains, Dawson worried, could 'develop a mythology and ethic' that may 'take the place of Christian theology and Christian ethics'.[10]

This eclectic appropriation of Ario-Germanic paganism and Indo-Aryan religions cannot be dismissed as the pet project of Heinrich Himmler or Rudolf Hess. Nor can it be written off as the province of a few *völkisch* prophets on the fringes of the Third Reich.[11] Nazi attitudes toward religion, as we have seen, had profound roots in the fin-de-siècle esoteric, New Age, and *völkisch*-religious revival. Part of a shared supernatural imaginary, these various religious strains were to some extent embraced and exploited by the Third Reich in the process of building spiritual consensus across a diverse Nazi Party and an even more eclectic German population.

Nazi Anti-Christianity and the Search for Alternative Religion

On 22 December 1920 the Nazi Party sponsored a Winter Solstice festival. The festival was important, the *Völkischer Beobachter* reported, in restoring *völkisch*-spiritual unity in the wake of the war and left-wing revolutions of 1918–19. 'All this the Edda and the teachings of the Armanen had already prophesied in ancient times,' declared one speaker, promising that 'One day more happy times will come for the Aryan race.'[12] According to Anton Drexler, co-founder of the NSDAP, a 'visible sign of the return to German thought is the resurgence of the wonderful old custom of the festival of solstice'. Another speaker talked of Baldur, the sun-god, pagan gods and heroes, and the history of the great Nordic mythological hero, Siegfried ('his birth in us – that is our solstice prayer').[13]

The Nazis did not invent the tradition of a pagan 'German Christmas'. As the *VB* observed, the organizers were indebted to similar solstice festivals celebrated a decade or so earlier by the ariosophists Guido von List and Lanz von Liebenfels. But the NSDAP made good use of these *völkisch*-esotericist traditions in their attempts to sponsor a more authentic Germanic religiosity – an alternative to both mainstream Christianity and liberal or Marxist secularism.[14]

The first part of this chapter argues, with Wolfgang Kaufmann, that virtually 'all leading ideologues' in the Nazi movement 'rejected Christianity'.[15] If some disagreed as to how far Christianity had to be mollified in the short term, most shared the firm conviction that it had either to be replaced or profoundly 'Germanized' (Aryanized).[16] We will explain below some of the reasons why the Nazis rejected Christianity, at least in its traditional form, focusing on their view that the medieval and Early Modern witch trials were an attempt by the Catholic Church to eliminate German culture, race, and religion. I then explore, briefly, the spiritual and ideological elements that many Nazis sought in (re)constructing a religious alternative to Christianity.

The SS Witch Division and Nazi Anti-Christianity

For nearly a decade between 1935 and 1944 Heinrich Himmler charged a 'Special Task Force on Witches' (*Hexen-Sonderauftrages*) with collecting, purchasing, and/or stealing archival material throughout central Europe. The fourteen members of the witch division, working within the framework of Heydrich's SD, assembled nearly thirty thousand documents out of various local and regional archives, from the Rhineland to Bohemia. They left behind a massive card catalogue and library documenting hundreds of accounts of witchcraft and the occult.[17]

Himmler would claim the project was primarily about investigating 'superstition in rural areas' and other aspects of Germanic religion and folklore typical of the Ahnenerbe's *völkisch*-esoteric research efforts.[18] But the *Sonderauftrag* had a parallel goal of 'great wartime importance' (*kriegswichtig*) that went beyond folklore research.[19] This second task, linked to the SD's role in 'opposition research' (*Gegnerforschung*), explains why the Witch Division was entrusted not to the academics of the Ahnenerbe but to Heydrich's SD. For the goal of *Gegnerforschung* was to conduct research on oppositional groups, including Jews, Communists, and Masons, assumed to be a racial and/or ideo-logical threat to the Third Reich.[20]

In this context of 'opposition research', Himmler asked the Witch Division to solve the riddle of how the 'dominant Aryan-Germanic religion of Nature could be defeated by the decadent Jewish-Christian religion?'[21] Himmler and the SD believed that researching Judeo-Christian attempts to wipe out German religion in the Middle Ages would provide insights into combating Jewish and Christian attempts to undermine the Third Reich.[22]

The SS witch researchers came to the conclusion that witches were the 'guar-antors of German faith' and 'natural healers' from the oldest Germanic sagas. By accusing so-called witches of consorting with the Devil, the Church could crim-inalize the practice of German religion (culture) and justify the murder of its spiritual leaders.[23] To Himmler and his SS colleagues, the Early Modern witch-craft trials therefore represented a 'capital crime against the German people', instigated by the Jews and presided over by the Catholic Church.[24]

The idea that the Catholic Church had employed witchcraft accusations to eradicate Ario-Germanic culture and religion had roots in the late nineteenth-century *völkisch*-religious revival.[25] This folkloric fascination with witchcraft and witch trials continued through the interwar period and into the Third Reich. In his 1936 book *Earth Mother and Witches*, for example, the Bavarian historian Anton Mayer argued that Indo-European magic and witchcraft were based on an ancient Germanic belief in the Earth mother as the protector of nature and possessor of 'demonic' powers derived from nature, akin to those described by Ernst Schertel.[26] Christianity eroded these healthy beliefs in pagan magic and women-centred religiosity, Mayer continued. Soon the ability of Earth mothers to commune with nature and wield magical power was demonized as 'witchcraft', as reflected in early Christian texts such as *Beowulf* and the King Arthur legends.[27] This prevailing association of Germanic paganism with Devil worship, Mayer argues, was 'the new framework for the anti-feminine witchcraft persecutions.'[28]

Another historian, Gustav Lassen, located the roots of witchcraft in fertility cults imported from the Indo-European (Indo-Aryan) past. In their attempts to destroy the woman-centred, magical basis of German beliefs, such as Walpurgisnacht, 'witch hunts' were obviously 'anti-feminine'.[29] Despite her virulent anti-occultism (which presumably included hostility to witchcraft), the Nazi fellow traveller Mathilde Ludendorff agreed. In her book *Christian Terror Against Women* she argued that the Catholic Church had employed witchcraft accusations to eradicate an authentic, pagan Germanic culture and religion.[30]

These proto-feminist accounts of German paganism enjoyed wide currency across the Nazi ranks. Himmler went so far as to argue that the 'so-called witches were relics of a pre-Christian Celtic-Germanic community of faith against which the Catholic Church practised genocide'.[31] This delusion 'cost the hereditary blood of hundreds of thousands of victims', Himmler reasoned, in Catholic and Protestant areas alike. The sacrifices of the 'witches and wizards of the early modern period', forgotten casualties of 'the ideological struggle of the Germanic tribes', should be 'written on the blood flag of the movement'.[32] On another occasion Himmler claimed the Catholic Church was a 'homosexual association' that had 'terrorized humanity for 1800 years'.[33]

Although less enthusiastic about occultism (witchcraft) than Himmler, Alfred Rosenberg was remarkably supportive of this argument. According to him, the Church's 'Christianization' campaign aimed at wiping out paganism was in fact directed at the biological 'roots of healthy racial stock', resulting in the murder of thousands of innocent German women and men.[34] More fantastically, Walther Darré estimated the number of 'fighters for justice, champions of the faith, heretics, and witches who had been murdered, tortured to death, and burnt' to be nine million![35]

Himmler, Rosenberg, and Darré's detestation of Christianity is well known.[36] Their broader antipathies to Christianity, however, exemplified by the SD's witch research, were shared by many Nazis.[37] Bormann's letters reveal a deep-seated hatred of Christianity, interest in paganism, and desire to arrest and murder Church leaders.[38] The Nazi head of the Labour Front, Robert Ley, claimed 'the rejection of Christianity' would lead to a 'stronger commitment to the ideology of National Socialism' and a 'sharper rejection of Jewish influence in society'.[39] Baldur von Schirach, the Hitler Youth leader, held a visceral theological and institutional disdain for the Christian churches as well.[40] Goebbels, though raised a devout Catholic and extraordinarily sensitive to public opinion, expressed similar antipathies toward both the Catholic and Protestant churches.[41] The more cynical and pragmatic Göring shared these anti-Christian views.[42]

For his part Hitler paid little attention to Heydrich's 'opposition research' on witches. Nevertheless, he clearly accepted the SD's conclusions. The Führer railed repeatedly against the Christian churches' cynical exploitation of ordinary Germans' desire for spiritual fulfilment.[43] The 'Indo-European peoples' aristocratic view of the world,' Hitler asserted, was 'torn apart by the intrusion of the Old Testament, brought in by the Jewish desert spirit.' That spirit, he insisted, continues to 'chain and undermine the Christian churches'.[44]

Christianity itself was 'universally destructive', Hitler argued, metaphysically akin to 'naked Bolshevism'.[45] By introducing 'that mad conception of life that continues into the alleged Beyond' and 'regard[s] life [as] negligible here below', Hitler opined, Christianity had 'crippled humanity's natural search for meaning'.[46] He believed that 'Priests of both confessions [Protestants as well as Catholics] represented the greatest public danger' and looked forward to a time when he could settle accounts with these priests without worrying about 'juridical niceties'.[47] No wonder that many contemporaries perceived Hitler to be 'an outspoken enemy of Christianity'.[48]

Given these attitudes, which ranged from generally critical to openly hostile, why did the Third Reich not move more aggressively against the churches? One reason had to do with the Nazis' paranoid, supernaturally derived, conspiracy-laden fear of (Judeo-)Christianity, which paralleled and intertwined with their fantastical theories regarding the power of Jews and Freemasons. And yet one could not eliminate millions of otherwise 'Aryan' Christians the way one might imprison, expel, or murder a relatively small cohort of Masons or racially 'alien' Jews. That is why the Nazi leadership planned to move against the Christian churches only after a victorious war.[49]

According to Himmler, the 'two great world powers, the Catholic Church and the Jews', were 'striving for world leadership ... united in their struggle against the Germanic people. We've already removed one of these powers [the Jews], at least from Germany; the time will come to settle accounts with the other after the war ... Then we'll unfrock these priests – neither their God nor their Virgin Mary will be able to do a thing for them then.'[50] Despite their long-term desire to eliminate Christianity, Rosenberg, Heydrich, and Bormann took a similar approach.[51]

According to Hitler's secretary Christa Schroeder, the Führer too expressed a desire to move against the churches after the war, when this act would have 'symbolic meaning before the world – the end of one historical epoch and beginning of a new era'.[52] Because National Socialism was an alternative 'form of conversion, a new faith', Hitler explained, we 'don't need to raise the issue [of eradicating Christianity] ... it will come of itself'.[53] Until then, he reasoned, one must let the churches 'die a natural death'. A more aggressive course was dangerous politically.[54]

This leads to the second reason why the Nazis did not move more aggressively against the churches: pragmatism. Hitler often closed 'his speeches by invoking divine providence', Schroeder observed, in her view a cynical attempt to 'win the sympathies of the Christian-inclined population'.[55] In spite of the decline in traditional religion, for all the excitement about new, *völkisch*-esoteric ideas, Germany was still a Christian country. Nazism's conscious (and subconscious) appropriation of Christian tropes was therefore, with rare exceptions, practical, part of their concerted efforts to attract voters before 1933 and manage public opinion, coordinating and competing with the Christian churches, thereafter.[56]

The early Nazi Party, we must remember, emerged in a Bavarian Catholic milieu which, while perhaps more *völkisch* and particularist than the rest of Catholic Germany, was still Christian.[57] For these reasons, the Nazis invoked the concept of 'positive Christianity' in their 1920 party platform and employed vaguely Christian tropes in their propaganda.[58] They made biblical allusions and talked frequently of God and the Devil, good and evil, providence and fate.[59] They incorporated Christian ideas of millennialism, messianism, and apocalypticism as well, parroting certain heretical (Gnostic) traditions.[60]

This opportunistic invocation of Christianity should not distract us from the fact that the NSDAP celebrated the solstice and chose the pagan 'sun-wheel' of the swastika as its symbol.[61] After the seizure of power, the NSDAP's half-hearted attempts to attract Christian voters shifted, logically, toward a desire to work out a modus vivendi with the churches, based on a mutual hatred of Communism, virulent nationalism, and latent anti-Semitism.[62] Whatever the short- or medium-term necessity of mollifying the churches, however, most Nazis were unprepared to tolerate any religion 'which transcended the Third Reich', least of all Christianity.[63] It might take time, Darré acknowledged, but the 'age of the fish, which is the symbol of Christ, is coming to the end'.[64]

The Nazi Search for Alternatives

A number of contemporaries perceived Hitler as irreligious in temperament, hostile to any form of transcendental belief.[65] Some of his most intimate associates, however, believed that he 'was in his heart fundamentally a religious man – or at least someone who was seeking religious clarity'.[66] Hitler was certainly convinced of the human necessity of faith and belief. People needed superstition, he remarked, 'since the notion of divinity gives most men the opportunity to concretize the feeling they have supernatural realities. Why should we destroy this wonderful power they have incarnating the feeling for the divine that is within them?'[67] Religion and superstition were necessary, Hitler added, in order for people to explain 'unexpected events which they cannot possibly foresee and with which they cannot cope'.[68]

Whereas Hitler acknowledged the need for a Nazi-friendly religiosity, Himmler and Rosenberg actively contemplated what this new Germanic 'substitute religion' might look like.[69] Himmler's 'hostility towards Christianity', Felix Kersten reported in his *Memoirs*, 'led him to take a systematic interest in other religions'.[70] With this exploration of alternative religions in mind, Himmler planned to set up observatories across Germany 'to give the broadest range of people the opportunity of taking an interest in astronomy and by this means to discover a partial substitute for the Christianity we plan to transcend'.[71] Rosenberg agreed. National Socialism could never leave 'the important realm of spiritual leadership ... of the whole human being' to the churches.[72] 'For it has not been lost on the churches,' Rosenberg noted, 'that with control over the soul' one gains 'the power to shape imagination, thought, and action.'[73]

That is, Hitler, Rosenberg, Himmler and Goebbels spoke often about the need to create an alternative religiosity by emulating the tactics of the churches.[74] *Theologically*, however, Catholicism and Protestantism could never provide a model for the Third Reich because Christianity represented the desacralization of nature and the blood. To assert its 'authority over the earth', Christianity had to 'despiritualize nature, removing divinity from it through the establishment of a transcendental God'. National Socialism, in contrast, privileged the sanctity of nature – of blood, soil, and race.[75]

By eschewing a transcendental conception of divinity, the Nazis did not reject mysticism outright, but the 'literal belief in some sort of deity *above* nature ... characteristic of Judaeo-Christian thought'. The Nazis were, according to Robert Pois, 'strong believers in a religion of nature' that was '*heavily* mystical in content'.[76] Or as the British folklorist and anthropologist Lewis Spence put it, while the 'great and genuine mystic' approached the 'halfway house betwixt earth and heaven' as 'a place of divine rapture', Hitler and his acolytes viewed 'the bridge betwixt the plains of the material and the terrestrial' as 'merely a series of pontoons for the march of his personal ambitions and hopes'. Instead of constituting 'a heavenly isthmus' approaching paradise, the divine was for the Nazis 'the bridge Bifrost of Teutonic mythology', connecting German religiosity to everyday social and political life.[77]

This brings us to the first element in the Nazi search for alternative religions: a pre- (or post-) Christian spirituality grounded in Germanic traditions of nature, blood and folk beliefs.[78] Underneath the superficial edifice of German Christianity, Hitler argued, 'hides an authentic faith that is rooted in nature and the blood'.[79] Christianity 'wants you to prepare for the beyond,' Rosenberg added, which 'is fundamentally false and short-sighted'.[80] Ley made similar points, emphasizing the importance of seeking an alternative to Christianity that focused on 'life energy, courage, joy of life', spiritual experiences that 'make life worth living for this world, no empty promises on a beyond'.[81]

In other words, the problem with Christianity – besides its Jewish provenance – was its focus on the 'hereafter (*Jenseit*) rather than on this world (*Diesseit*)'.[82] Hence the Nazis sought to replace the transcendent or 'transworldly' (*überweltliche*) religion of Judeo-Christianity with 'inner-worldly' (*innerweltliche*) religious feeling 'that find[s] the divine in the sub-contents of the world', in the purity of blood and soil, Nordic mythology, and the rituals of *völkisch* community.[83]

A second aspect of Nazi religiosity was a relativistic view of good and evil, an 'ethnotheism', in the words of Samuel Koehne, that favoured the apotheosis of one's own race over universal morality.[84] The unfortunate consequence of displacing older magical traditions with monotheistic religions, Hitler underscored in his copy of Schertel's book *Magic*, was 'the establishment of an absolute morality, which was seen as applicable for all people'. The more spiritually authentic pre-Christian epoch

> knows no morality in this universal sense. Its rule of life is given by the folkish 'custom' and by the will of the tribal god, whose governing was utterly autocratic, and was giving orders at his discretion. These as well as the customs of the people can potentially be very violent and 'immoral', they can demand blood and destruction and have nothing to do with 'humaneness', 'brotherly love', or an abstract 'good' of some sort. The pertaining rule of life always stays limited to the individual nation and this nation conceives it as completely natural that other people again have other guidelines for their way of life.[85]

In other words, ethnoracial 'egoism can be good, and [universal] altruism can be bad'.[86] Indeed, if we rely on Hitler's citations in Schertel, it is clear the future Führer envisioned 'a new basic attitude toward existence', a 'completely irrational, supra-moral, and supra-personal transformation'[87]

Hitler was hardly alone in this respect. Many Nazis repudiated the Christian idea of good and evil, in which Satan is the 'rebel against divine authority', as an Old Testament 'Jewish' invention.[88] Instead they promoted a 'religious relativism', insisting, per Rosenberg, that 'what we denote as good, others see as evil, what we call God, appears to others as the Devil'.[89]

The Third Reich might not initially attract all Christians to this moral and spiritual revolution. It would take time to cobble together the everyday rituals and liturgy – the marches and solstice festivals, the birth, marriage, and death rites – to dechristianize Germany and institutionalize a new morality.[90] Nevertheless, 'for those millions who were unbound and searching for 'new world view commitments''', notes the historian Irving Hexham, Nazism 'offered a new faith based on a new mythology that would create a new type of human being'.[91]

Intrinsic to the idea of a *völkisch* revolution in morality was a third element of Nazi religiosity: the need for a 'this-worldly' prophet, a 'sacred king incapable of wrongdoing', who could stand opposed to the Christian God.[92] In attempting to build a new faith in the collective will and morality of the racial community, the Nazi movement transformed Hitler 'into a holy medium for the salvific dictates of what became, by the early 1930s, an unimpeachable "Volkswille" [popular will]'.[93] First the Nazis and later many Germans began to view Hitler as a Messiah at the centre of a moral and spiritual revolution.[94] The Führer himself believed in a 'providential God who had chosen him to lead the German nation in accordance with the ancient Germanic principle of the leader and his followers'.[95]

A fourth aspect of Nazi religiosity was the cult of death and rebirth. Relying on a 'widely available and intimately familiar set of symbols and concepts', observes Monica Black, this death cult privileged 'earthly immortality – Germanic faith and its incorporation in the racial tribe'.[96] According to Bormann, there was 'no such thing as death' since 'every human being lives on for ever' as part of the organic ethnoracial community. 'Christians ought never to have represented the phenomenon they call *Death* as a fearsome, ghostlike, bone-rattling creature armed with a scythe,' Bormann wrote to a friend, but 'as the kindly gate-keeper to a better hereafter'. 'A man's physical extinction denotes neither death nor parting,' he continued. It 'lives in the other's consciousness after the separation more intensely than ever before'.[97]

This cult of death and rebirth resonated particularly strongly in a martial context. Hitler referred to those who had fallen during the time of struggle as 'my apostles' who, like the German Empire, had 'risen from the dead'.[98] In perishing for the fatherland, Ley explained, dead soldiers 'found the road to eternity'.[99] 'Grieve no more!' exclaimed a Nazi poet. 'For they [the soldiers] have left their graves/And returned, in freedom/To the ranks/They march through the streets, and lanes, like life-giving suns.'[100] In this mystical vision of soldierly comradeship the Nazis 'guaranteed intense social life, security, and emotional warmth in the midst of the cold bleakness of mass death'.[101]

Fifth and finally, as suggested above, the Nazis embraced a religion of nature, a 'this worldly' blood and soil mysticism grounded in *völkisch* paganism and Eastern religions.[102] In his copy of Schertel's *Magic*, Hitler repeatedly underscored passages on the latent energies pervading all living things. These passages included the claim that man's spiritual relationship to nature 'was fostered in ancient times through gods and concrete ceremonies', producing a 'whole cult with its temples and underground vaults, his idols, his sacred groves, gardens, lakes and mountains, his whole magic pomp and solemn ritual'.[103] Himmler and Darré also sought to resurrect an Ur-Germanic faith community of blood, soil, and nature that dispensed with the accoutrements of Christianity. A 'cult of mother earth', Darré explained, is in reality far more authentic than a 'divinely ordained' faith. This 'Ur-faith viewed the apparition of the mother in the earth, the effect of the father in the son, and the forces bringing both together in the moon'.[104]

'Anyone who feels himself to be a creature of this life,' Bormann explained, 'in other words, by the will of All-Highest, of Omnipotence, of Nature', anyone who 'feels himself to be merely one of the countless meshes of the web we call a people – cannot be frightened by the hardships of this existence. He will really fare as in the old hymn: "No harm can ever touch me" . . . We are woven into the eternal pattern of all life, that is, the cycle of Nature, and it cannot be otherwise.'[105]

Whether Hitler or Darré, Himmler or Bormann, Ley or Rosenberg, we find Nazi leaders portraying the soul in terms of a Buddhist-like 'consubstantiality, a state in which the individual considers himself part of an overreaching, godly essence that is seeking to unfold itself'.[106] In negating the distinction between humanity and nature, the Nazis managed to refashion 'an ancient repertoire of symbols, building on the centuries-old Christian ideal of transcendent death, romantic notions of an organic and harmonious union between humans and nature, and the powerful symbolic legacy of sacred blood'.[107]

After 1945 some disillusioned Nazis would claim that Hitler and Bormann, in contrast to Himmler and Darré, betrayed Nazism by eschewing its authentic 'spiritual-*völkisch*' foundation and favouring a 'materialist-racist' approach to the world.[108] Hitler and Bormann were certainly less preoccupied by 'spiritual-*völkisch*' concerns – at least publicly – than Himmler or Rosenberg. As we have seen, however, they all agreed more broadly on the need to find an authentic Ario-Germanic substitute for Christianity, 'a new syncretism that would bridge Germany's confessional divide'.[109]

When the Nazis took power in 1933 the contours of this *völkisch*, Ario-Germanic syncretism remained unclear. Central elements would nonetheless include a non-transcendental religion similar to occultism in its 'this-worldly' mysticism; a moral revolution based on power, race, and loyalty to the Führer; and a metaphysical emphasis on death and rebirth within the context of blood, soil, and race.[110] If traditional Christianity was largely incompatible with this vision, there were plenty of alternative spiritual traditions within the German supernatural imaginary on which to draw.

Luciferianism, Irminism, and *Völkisch*-Esoteric Alternatives

In his 1940 book, *Occult Causes of the Present War*, Lewis Spence put forward a provocative argument – Nazism was 'satanic' in its religious and ideological roots.[111] In Germany, Spence observed, witchcraft 'possessed some of the attributes of a fertility cult, that of the great earth mother', and had 'stronger associations with the old religion of the soil than elsewhere'. In the Middle Ages this folk religion merged with 'the first traces of the Eastern heresy of Luciferianism in Germany in the indictment and execution of a certain Cathari at Goslar in 1051'. From that time, Spence averred, 'heresy hunts and burning became a feature of life in the German cities. The countryside seems to have teemed with Satanists, and kings, governors, and bishops vied with each other' in the extirpation of 'these folk worshippers of Lucifer'.[112]

These Satanists ostensibly carried on their Luciferian traditions in secret in the Early Modern Period through an array of underground societies and pagan religious cults culminating in the late nineteenth-century occult revival.[113] Now, under the guise of preserving 'positive Christianity', the Nazis had resurrected the 'German fertility goddess Holle, patroness of witches' in order to 'attract Germans to a new paganism'.[114] 'Replacement of the Cross by the swastika, the abrogation of the Sacrament in favor of a rite resembling that of the mysteries of Demeter, the persecution of the Christian Churches,' Spence observed, 'all this affords the clearest proof of Germany's relapse' into paganism and the Third Reich's desire for the 'destruction and extirpation of the Christian faith'.[115]

For all its bias and sensationalism, Spence's argument is in many respects accurate. We have already discussed the efflorescence of neo-pagan movements in the decades before the First World War, which 'sought to restore supposedly Germanic cultural practices of the distant past'.[116] Influenced by these *völkisch*-esoteric traditions and inspired by the research of border scientific intellectuals, many Nazis appropriated elements of Luciferianism and the related tradition of 'Irminism' drawn from the Armanism of List and Lanz von Liebenfels.[117] With the support of Himmler, Rosenberg, and other prominent leaders, these 'theologians of the new German faith' led expeditions in search of the Holy Grail, conducted excavations at pagan holy sites, and worked out strange theories about ley lines and the 'black sun', seeking to create a 'system of folk belief and natural theology, as well as a moral code'.[118]

In attempting to resurrect 'putatively ancient practices' these Nazi leaders were not doing anything new. These efforts had been ongoing since at least the middle of the nineteenth century. After 1933, however, Ario-Germanic religious groups benefited from the backing of some powerful Nazi institutions and individuals in pursuit of their goals.[119] If none of these practices became official doctrine, the depth and breadth of interest in Luciferianism, Irminism, and Indo/Ario-Germanic religious practices adds an important dimension to our understanding of Nazi religiosity.

Otto Rahn, Luciferianism, and the Holy Grail

A fascination with the Holy Grail is not unique to Nazism. From Christian apocrypha to the medieval Arthurian mythos; from the Knights Templar to the Freemasons, the belief in the existence of the Grail, the chalice used by Christ at the last supper, has persisted in European culture. The Grail has taken many forms. It can be seen as the literal cup of Christ or a pagan Celtic kettle used for resuscitating the dead. It has also been interpreted by some as a metaphor for 'Lucifer's Crown' or the actual wife of Christ. All the while its mystical resonance has grown, finding new life among the late nineteenth–century pagans, *völkisch-*esotericists, and German Christians that we surveyed in Chapter One.[120]

Among the locations where the Holy Grail is supposed to have been hidden, Montségur ('secure mountain' in Occitan) in the French Pyrenees is one of the most prominent. This region was home to the famous Cathar or Albigensian heresy, which was eradicated by the Catholic Church in the thirteenth century. Although nominally Christian, the Cathars propagated a Gnostic theology that insisted on the intrinsic connection between spiritual and material, good and evil, God and the Devil, which connected all living things. For these reasons they were deemed heretics – even 'Luciferians' – by the Church and tried before the Inquisition.[121]

Before the Cathars' demise, some Grail experts speculated, they ostensibly managed to smuggle a number of holy relics, including the Holy Grail, down the back side of the mountain. By the early twentieth century, many *völkisch-*esoteric thinkers had embraced and elaborated upon aspects of this mythos, including the link between the Cathars, Luciferianism, and the Grail.[122] It was the above-mentioned philologist Otto Rahn, however, who brought this Luciferian interpretation of the Grail to the attention of the Third Reich.

Rahn was born in 1904 in the Austrian Tyrol. He studied German medieval literature and archaeology after the First World War, eventually developing a fascination for the Cathars. In 1928 he travelled to Paris to advance his studies of the Albigensian crusade, soon meeting the esotericist Maurice Magre, who advanced the theory of a connection between Tibetan Buddhism and Cathar religion, centring on the Grail. Through Magre, Rahn met his future sponsor in Grail Studies, Countess Miryane Pujol-Marat. Pujol-Marat was herself a member of the French theosophic group known as The Polar Society, which advocated Magre's fanciful theories about the Grail, its link to the Ur-Aryan civilization of Atlantis, and World Ice Theory.[123] With the support of Pujol-Marat and the Polar Society, Rahn began investigating Cathar sites in Languedoc, where he met the anthroposophist Déodat Roche and Cathar scholar Antonin Gadal. Gadal introduced Rahn to the idea that the Grail was hidden in the caves around Montségur, where the two searched for signs of the 'Cathar-Grail-Shambala' tradition, the last remnants of the Aryan civilization of the Thule.[124]

Assembling all these border scientific theories in a single book, Rahn's 1933 monograph, *Crusade for the Grail*, argued that the Albigensian heresy, Buddhist religion, and the Holy Grail were interconnected by an Indo-European Gnostic tradition. He postulated that Albigensianism ('Luciferianism') was brought to the Germans via the Celts and Iberians who had earlier appropriated the religious traditions of northwest India and ancient Persia. The Grail, according to Rahn, came from the Indian mani, a magical jewel or divine relic that fell from the sky and bequeathed power to its possessor.[125]

Rahn's work soon came to the attention of Himmler through his religious expert, Karl Maria Wiligut. Wiligut offered Rahn research support and work as a consultant in Darré's Race and Settlement Office (RuSHA).[126] Officially sponsored by the Ahnenerbe, Rahn was tasked with continuing his research on the Holy Grail and related attempts to recover an Ur-Germanic, Indo-Aryan religion – efforts that would eventually produce his second book, Lucifer's Court (1937).[127]

Lucifer's Court indicates that Rahn's interpretation had evolved in a more explicitly 'Luciferian' direction.[128] While Satan had still been nominally representative of evil in Rahn's earlier work, Lucifer was now the (Aryan) purveyor of light. Here the Cathars become Luciferians ('light bearers'), who protected the Grail according to the old Indo-Aryan tradition of the Thule (Shambala) and were burned by the Dominicans as a result.[129] More concretely, per Lewis Spence, Rahn's book linked Nazi Ario-Germanic religion explicitly to the paganism and witchcraft practised across Germany in the Middle Ages, at places such as Brocken in the Harz mountains, the site of the Walpurgisnacht scene in Goethe's Faust.[130]

Although dubious by any academic standard, Rahn's ideas resonated with Nazi politicians and intellectuals.[131] According to Wiligut, Rahn's research confirmed Ario-Germanic, 'Irminist' theories – drawn from List and Liebenfels, among others – that Jesus Christ was an Indo-European Aryan akin to Baldur of Norse mythology.[132] The SS ariosophs Gunter Kirchoff and Frenzolf Schmid welcomed Rahn's work for affirming their mystical theories regarding the 'geomantic' centre of Irminist religion.[133]

The SS researcher Rudolf Mund and other members of the SD witch division eagerly embraced Rahn's ideas as well. They found them particularly useful in validating their theory that the medieval Church attempted to eliminate the Aryans (Luciferians) who survived the collapse of Atlantis.[134] Rahn's theories likewise reinforced Himmler's spiritual predilections, from appropriating the Grail mythos for his SS to justifying the importance of Tibetan Buddhism and World Ice Theory in the history and religion of the Indo-Aryan peoples.[135] Even Rosenberg, though critical of many SS projects, embraced Rahn's idea that the Cathars were martyrs to the Judeo-Catholic Church and ancestors of the Nazis.[136]

So ecstatic was Himmler about Rahn's arguments in Lucifer's Court that he ordered one hundred copies of the book for the SS. Ten would be bound in pig leather and ten more in luxurious Pergament. He even gave one to Hitler for his birthday.[137] Himmler subsequently encouraged Rahn to give lectures within the SS regarding Lucifer's role as the bringer of enlightenment and enemy of the Jewish God.[138] He also financed a number of expeditions to Iceland and paleolithic sites across Europe to help prove the connections between Rahn's Luciferian thesis and the Thule (Atlantean) civilization.[139] Although rumours circulated about Rahn's sexual preferences and political unreliability, he was promoted to Oberscharführer in 1937 and continued to work closely with Himmler, Wiligut, and other SS researchers.[140]

Rahn did gradually fall out of favour with the Nazis due to persistent reports of alchoholism and homosexuality, eventually committing suicide in 1939.[141] Nevertheless, shortly after his death Rahn was rehabilitated by Himmler.[142] *Lucifer's Court* was also still widely read. As late as November 1943 the SD Director and SS Brigadeführer Erich Naumann – Arthur Nebe's successor as commander of the infamous Einsatzgruppe B – approved printing another 10,000 copies of the book.[143] Indeed, despite subsequent paper shortages, the D-Day landing, and a bomb attack destroying the publishing house that owned the rights to the book, Naumann was still willing to approve a print run of 5,000 new copies in June 1944. According to his staff, Himmler 'intended the greatest portion of the books for the units stationed in France'.[144]

Just as importantly, the SS continued to sponsor Grail research. Rahn's Italian fascist counterpart, for example, Baron Julius Evola, was an unabashed paganist and esotericist who began collaborating directly with Walther Wüst from 1937. Over the next two years Evola gave a series of speeches in the Third Reich, which were distilled into a well-received book titled *Grail Mystery and Conceptions of Empire*.[145] Evola's idea for a bilingual (German-Italian) fascist journal focusing on esoteric research received support not only from Himmler but the normally more sober Göring. Because his esoteric research intersected with that of the SD Witch Division, Evola also began a scholarly collaboration with SS-Brigadeführer Franz Alfred Six, head of the RSHA's Amt VII for 'opposition research', including witches.[146] Finally, in the spring of 1939 the 'research offices of the SD' agreed to open its archives on 'lodges and sects' to Evola because of the Grail researcher's desire to write an ambitious history of mythology and occult societies, urging him to make 'the earliest results of his research available' to the SD.[147]

Rahn's mentor, Karl Maria Wiligut, provides another important link to Ario-Germanic religiosity in the Third Reich.[148] Born in Vienna in 1866, Wiligut embarked on a military career as a young man. After joining a Masonic lodge in 1889, he became immersed in the ariosophic circles of List and Liebenfels, publishing an epic retelling of the Siegfried story in 1903 and an Irminist handbook in 1908. After serving on the Eastern Front during the First World War, he edited a *völkisch*-esoteric journal, *The Iron Broom*, aimed at exposing conspiracies of the Jews, Masons, and Catholic Church.[149] Due to a number of personal and psychological crises, Wiligut's wife had him committed to a Salzburg asylum in 1924, the same year as Hitler's imprisonment in Landsberg.[150]

Released in 1927, Wiligut renewed his contacts with the Edda Society and Lanz's Ordo Novi Templar. Eventually he moved to Munich, where he taught classes on ariosophic topics. Having both participated in the founding of the German Faith Movement in June 1933 and impressed Himmler during an initial meeting in September, Wiligut received an invitation to join the SS. He rose quickly through the ranks, being appointed head of the Department for Pre-History in Darré's RuSHA, joining Himmler's personal staff and taking a central role in sponsoring border scientific research within the Ahnenerbe.[151]

In this capacity Wiligut, who called himself 'Weisthor' (Wise-Thor), had a hand in almost every aspect of SS attempts to construct an Ario-Germanic religion. Clearly inspired by ariosophy and World Ice Theory, Wiligut's Irminism 'blended the Teutonic archaism of List with the Ario-Christianity of Lanz, albeit in a novel form'.[152] Like List, Wiligut believed he had spiritual powers derived from his God-like ancestors who were themselves descendants of the Aesir and Vanir of Norse mythology, including Thor, Wotan, and the ancient Germanic hero, Arminius.[153] Wiligut's 'spirits' instructed him that there were 'nine commandments of God', which originated from the 'occult transmission of our Asa-Una clan Uilligotis'. He even claimed to be a medium who could contact his ancestors and gain occult knowledge through mystical means (which Himmler facilitated by providing Wiligut with ample drugs and alcohol).[154]

Wiligut argued that his religion was part of a superior Aryan civilization, which arose millennia before recorded history, 'a time when giants, dwarves and mythical beasts moved about beneath a sky filled with three suns'.[155] Wiligut and his supporters further claimed that the Irminist gods, the Asen, were divided into four classes – Odinist, Baldurist, Thorist, and Lokiist – all of whom could 'control the thoughts' of human beings. The white super race ('light children'), which descended from the Asen, had stood above the lower racial forms – Neanderthals, blacks, and Jews – for thousands of years.[156] Unfortunately, race-mixing and 'demonism' had produced a fatal war between Irminists and Wotanists, who differed over the divinity of a Germanic god named 'Krist' (the German Christ). As a result of this internecine conflict, the Irminic civilization collapsed. All that was left were ancient relics, such as the (putative) Irminist temple at the *Externsteine* (see below).[157]

Neither Wiligut nor his Irminist associates had any idea 'how to evaluate evidence'. Their 'dating was absurd' and their 'library contained many occult works by List, Koerner, and Gorsleben but almost nothing relating to scholarly prehistorical research'.[158] In fact, Wiligut and his Irminist and ariosophic colleagues – Emil Rüdiger, Wilhelm Teudt, and Günther Kirchoff, among others – posited the idea of a 'black sun', the core of a geomantic energy grid that could be tapped through yoga and whose centre lay somewhere in the Black Forest.[159]

Wiligut's bizarre theological claims and scholarly incompetence did nothing to dissuade Himmler, Wirth, or Wüst, who granted him immense authority. Wiligut designed the 'death's head ring' given to all new SS initiates. He determined how ritual objects should be used in SS birth, marriage, and burial ceremonies. He also directed massive archaeological projects in search of religious relics, like those at the Externsteine. One of the most mysterious aspects of Wiligut's research on resuscitating ancient Germanic rituals came in the form of the enigmatic Halgarita Charms, Irminist mantras intended to enhance ancestral memory and facilitate the re-emergence of Ario-Germanic faith.[160] In pursuing these research efforts both mainstream academics like Wolfgang Krause and esotericists such as Karl Theodor Weigel sought Wiligut and Wirth's sponsorship.[161]

This highly unscientific belief in runes stood at the core of Wirth's attempts to reconstruct an ancient Ario-Germanic religion. Before being named chief of the Ahnenerbe, Wirth made a career investigating the Ur-religion and Ur-Aryan civilization of Atlantis or Thule through dubious runic and symbological studies, which were rejected by mainstream academia though embraced by Himmler and other *völkisch*-esotericists.[162] Wirth saw the Ahnenerbe's primary goal as the 'renewal and strengthening of German spirituality', highlighting the holy origins of the swastika and defining National Socialism 'as a struggle for the German soul'.[163] Hence Wirth's 'wild Atlantean Runomania' and 'Arcto-Atlanticism' dovetailed perfectly with Wiligut's Irminism. Both were intent on proving the existence of a two-million-year-old Aryan civilization (Atlantis or Thule) destroyed by a cataclysm and preserved in ancient runes.[164]

Crucial in facilitating this process were Wiligut and Wirth's efforts to excavate and renovate ancient Germanic 'holy places'. These sites included, notably, the Wewelsburg castle near Buren in Westphalia, the burial site of Henry I in Quedlinburg, and the Externsteine near Detmold.[165]

Wiligut was the first to suggest that Himmler purchase and refurbish the Wewelsburg castle as the religious and ideological 'centre of the world'. As Himmler's *spiritus rector*, Wiligut presided over its conversion from a museum and education institute to an Irminist church, inspired by List, Rahn, and Kirchoff. In redesigning the castle, there were numerous allusions to the Holy Grail and other esoteric and 'geomantic' features, including a 'black sun' emblem in the crypt.[166]

Wiligut included a 'Grail Salon' as well, intended as a ritual space for ceremonies particular to Himmler's elite circle within the SS.[167] In this fashion Wiligut shaped the Wewelsburg into a centre for the 3,000-year-old Irminist faith, an 'Atlantean castle' replete with pagan wedding services for SS officers and solstice festivals for local Germans.[168]

Two dozen miles northeast of Wewelsburg, near Detmold, were the Externsteine, another religio-cultural centre for the SS. Many *völkisch* thinkers, including Wiligut, Wirth, and Himmler, believed it to be a pagan Germanic religious centre, the 'Irminsul', the sanctuary of the Saxon chief killed by Charlemagne.[169] In concert with Wirth, Wiligut led the SS excavations around the Externsteine in order to prove his theories, simultaneously preventing publications that contradicted the Externsteine's archaeological and religious importance.[170] In building the Externsteine into a 'Neo-Germanic holy place', Wiligut had no trouble finding support among border scientists with dubious reputations. These included Rosenberg's favourite archaeologist, Hans Reinerth, head of the Reich Association of German Prehistory (*Reichsbund für Deutsche Vorgeschichte*), as well as 'astro-archaeologists' such as Wilhelm Teudt.[171]

These faith-based excavations, expeditions, and preoccupations with runology continued long after Rahn, Wiligut, and Wirth had fallen out of favour.[172] Although Wiligut lost his official position in 1939 due to a variety of scandals, Himmler kept Wiligut's death's head ring in his personal vault and continued to consult him on military and spiritual matters.[173] Himmler's Rasputin may have retreated into the shadows. His Irminist religion, however, supplemented by Otto Rahn's Luciferian musings, survived in the Nazi search for an authentic Ario-Germanic religiosity.[174]

Ario-Germanic Religion in the Third Reich

In the early 1920s the *Völkischer Beobachter* published a series of articles by the *völkisch*-esotericists Johannes Dingfelder and Franz Schrönghamer-Heimdal, exploring the roots of Ario-Germanic religion in the Edda and Nibelungen. Dingfelder was an associate of Fritsch's ariosophic German Order and then the Thule Society, later helping Drexler and Hitler promote the DAP.[175] Just as Wiligut insisted he was a descendant of Thor, and Himmler believed he was the reincarnation of the Saxon King Henry the Fowler, Schrönghammer saw himself as a descendent of the Norse god Heimdal.[176]

Dingfelder and Schrönghammer likewise praised the Aryan 'racial soul' and deemed the cross as 'an ancient Aryan sacred symbol that derives its origin directly from the swastika'. And yet the two ariosophists did not abandon Christianity entirely. In hoping to resuscitate the 'church of Wotan or the

Armanen', they endorsed an amalgam of *völkisch* paganism and 'Aryan Christianity' along the lines of Lanz and Wiligut. They emphasized the 'degeneration and bestialization' of 'Tschandalen' while invoking the Irminist idea of an Aryan 'Jesus Christ', whom the Norse 'called Frauja' or 'Froh'.[177]

What does this vignette suggest? First, it reminds us of the ideological continuities between the pre-war *völkisch*-religious movement and NSDAP. It also shows, in the words of Samuel Koehne, that we 'cannot assume an inherent dichotomy within the Nazi Party between those adhering to paganism and those adhering to Aryan Christianity'. Nor can we assume that 'references to Jesus Christ, Christianity, or the Bible necessarily excluded paganism'. To the contrary, Dingfelder, Schrönghammer, and many Nazi co-religionists compared Jesus Christ to Baldur or some form of 'light-god'. They argued further that 'the Bible might be seen as a corrupted version of the Edda' and that the 'cross could be viewed as a sun-wheel'.[178]

Following the traditions of Aryanism, some pro-Nazi religious thinkers highlighted the 'eternal struggle between Ormuzd and Ahriman [divine Zoroastrianist spirits in pre-Islamic Persian], between light and darkness', which has 'once again ended in the victory of the sun, whose symbol is the ancient Aryan sign of salvation: the swastika'. Others, more immersed in the traditions of Nordic *Germanentum*, alluded to 'battles of Thor' with ice giants and recalled the 'spirits of the Wild Hunt' who 'ride through the storms at the head of a ghostly army during the Twelve Nights of Yuletide'. The fact remains that early Nazi discussions of the 1920s featured ariosophic (Irminist) concepts 'derived from Madame Blavatsky and popularized by Theodor Fritsch', supplemented by paganism, Germanic folklore, and Nordic mythology.[179]

This syncretic mélange of Ario-Germanic religiosity was never confined to obscure Nazi fellow travellers. Nor did it dissipate with the Nazi seizure of power.[180] From its earliest days the Nazi Party was 'immersed in the *völkisch* movement, including its pagan trends and traditions'. The religious ideas of Hitler, Himmler, and their colleagues were inspired by and 'intermingled with the ideas of Guido von List and Jörg Lanz von Liebenfels, Theodor Fritsch, and Artur Dinter'.[181]

The progenitor of Nazi blood-and-soil ideology, Walther Darré, eagerly embraced the Ario-Germanic emphasis on a 'religion of the blood', the Nordic-Germanic roots of Jesus and the Aryan race's origins in Atlantis.[182] Darré agreed with Wiligut that the Catholic Church had adopted the teachings of the Aryan Christ (Krist), but then distorted them from God's true racial mission, which lay in blood and soil.[183] In his daybook, Darré made religious observations about the signs of Thor's hammer and proclaimed his own 'heathenism' (*Heidentum*), extolling a pantheistic religion based on a combination of Indo-Aryan and Germanic pagan values.[184]

Alfred Rosenberg advocated many elements of Ario-Germanic religiosity.[185] Drawing on German pagan and ariosophic traditions, Rosenberg's goal was to awaken the 'old Nordic myths and values symbolized by Gods'.[186] His *Myth of the Twentieth Century* (1930) propagated the idea of a 'racial soul', which blended pagan Germanic ideas with the notion of a lost Indo-Aryan civilization of Thule or Atlantis.[187] Rosenberg advocated ancestor worship, a cult of the dead, and pagan Germanic rituals that we see in Himmler's own musings.[188] He believed that the Third Reich's research 'in the field of Nordic religious history' would 'form the yeast that will permeate the former Catholic and former Lutheran components of the German Church. Then the Nordic sagas and fairy tales will take the place of the Old Testament stories of pimps and cattle dealers'.[189] Through the Amt Rosenberg, he managed to sponsor hundreds of festivals, archaeological excavations, and publications extolling Germanic paganism.[190]

Although equally invested in the search for an Ario-Germanic religion, Himmler never tried to develop a particular religious catechism or specific articles of faith.[191] Like most Nazi leaders, the Reichsführer was too much of a dilettante. He preferred an array of 'symbols, insignias, myths and shrines, festivals and rituals', which might give 'sensuous expression to his fantasy world' and encourage the SS's 'elite character as keeper of the Holy Grail of Nazism'.[192]

With these goals in mind, Himmler sought 'to replace the Christian rites with rituals he deemed more Aryan'. Because he believed 'the sun played a central part for the primordial religion of the Nordic race', for example, 'he wanted to create an SS summer solstice festival to celebrate life and the winter solstice festival to remember the dead and honour ancestors'.[193] Himmler also sought to reinstitute the so-called 'Odal' law ostensibly practised by ancient Nordic peoples. Finally, he gave SS leaders swords of honour, yule lights, and death's-head rings designed by Wiligut, while SS women received runic brooches and life lights to honour motherhood.[194]

In the meantime, the Wewelsburg and Externsteine were chosen to (re)invent positive spaces that might substitute for Christian holy sites and churches.[195] Himmler created a 'Saxon's grove' (*Sachsenhain*) near Derven to commemorate the supposed execution of 4,500 Saxons by Charlemagne in 782, which he and Rosenberg jointly inaugurated in 1935.[196] Himmler even sent an Ahnenerbe expedition to Karelia in Finland ('the land of witches and sorcerors') to recover the Ur-Germanic religion drawn from the Edda.[197] Based on this expedition and the SD's witchcraft research, Himmler commissioned popular children's literature as well as more adult-oriented 'Witch novels in the form of a trilogy'.[198] Such efforts were at least moderately successful in expanding popular interest in Ario-Germanic religiosity.[199]

Beyond his pragmatic interest in sponsoring Ario-Germanic religiosity, Himmler seems to have believed in Germanic deities such as Wotan and

Thor.[200] He asked Wüst to 'research where in all of North-Germanic Aryan culture the concept of the lightning flash, the thunderbolt, Thor's hammer, or the hammer thrown or flying through the air appears . . . [and] where there are sculptures of a god holding an axe and appearing in a flash of lightning'. All such evidence, 'whether in pictures, sculptures, writing, or legend', Himmler suggested, could be used to distinguish 'between natural thunder and lightning . . . [and] earlier, highly developed weapons possessed by only a few, namely by the Aesir, the gods, and presuming an extraordinary knowledge of electricity'.[201]

Himmler continued to make rune studies virtually obligatory for SS officers. Evidence suggests he believed they held mystical power that might be used to place protective runes on uniforms and buildings.[202] Himmler's interest in the magical energies surrounding the Brocken mountains – the so-called 'Devil's Pulpit', where German paganists celebrated Walpurgisnacht – is also well known.[203]

While Hitler didn't share the passion of Darré, Rosenberg, or Himmler for Germanic prehistory, he was enthusiastic about many elements of Ario-Germanic religiosity. In Schertel's *Magic*, for example, Hitler underscored the passage: 'Satan is the beginning . . . Satan is in everything that lives and appears . . . Out of this, which is unreasonable (irrational), reason in the true sense is born. Without this preceding gloom, creation would have no reality; darkness is its necessary heritage.'[204] Hitler also highlighted Schertel's statement regarding Satan's 'creative/destructive role', without which the peaceful 'Seraph' could not exist.[205] These passages, which at first glance appear remarkable, make sense in the context of Luciferian traditions.

Hitler's interest in paganism and Gnosticism extended beyond Schertel. He approved Germanic solstice celebrations and invoked religious tropes drawn from Norse mythology.[206] He identified with Siegfried, idealized Wotan (Odin), and spoke of honouring dead warriors who were going to Valhalla (following his passion for Wagner).[207] Nordic myth, Hitler argued, could be used to bring German youth to nature, 'to show them the powerful workings of divine creation . . . keeping youth out of salons and "airless dives"'.[208]

In terms of Ario-Germanic paganism, Hitler accepted that the *Externsteine* were important to ancient Germanic tribes and showed interest in Wirth's 'Germanomaniacal Gnostic symbol research'.[209] Combining elements of ariosophy and World Ice Theory, Hitler moreover claimed that the 'Aryan, during the ice age, engaged in building his spiritual and bodily strength in the hard fight with nature, arising quite differently than other races who lived without struggle in the midst of a bountiful world'.[210] Following the Armanists/Irminists, Hitler likewise asserted that the historical Jesus was blond with blue eyes, probably a renegade from a lost Aryan tribe.[211]

According to Rauschning, Hitler claimed that 'man's solar period was coming to its end', as foretold in 'the imperishable prophecies of the old Nordic peoples'.

The 'world has continually to renew itself,' he added, 'the old order perishing with its gods.'[212] Rauschning's possibly embellished appraisal is corroborated by Hitler's claim in the early 1920s that the Aryans 'held one sign in common: the symbol of the sun. All of their cults were built on light, and you can find this symbol, the means of the generation of fire, the Quirl, the cross. You can find this cross as a swastika not only here [in Germany], but also exactly the same [symbol] carved into temple posts in India and Japan. It is the swastika of the community (Gemeinwesen) once founded by Aryan culture (Kultur).'[213]

To argue that many prominent leaders of the Third Reich sympathized with Ario-Germanic religiosity is not to deny the heterogeneity of these ideas or efforts. These disparate strains included, for example, the officially sponsored German Christians. Led by the Nazi Bishop Ludwig Müller, German Christians were a *völkisch* branch of Protestantism that had eliminated the Old Testament, excluded non-Aryans, and incorporated pagan Nordic elements.[214] The Third Reich also tolerated Mathilde Ludendorff's Society for the Knowledge of [a German] God, which rejected Christianity altogether.[215]

Competing with the German Christians and the Ludendorff movement was J. W. Hauer, Ernst Reventlow, and Herbert Grabert's German Faith Movement (*Deutsche Glaubensbewegung*).[216] Its supporters, who had strong roots in interwar *völkisch*-paganism, 'wanted to shape the cultural milieu of politics, religion, theology, Indo-Aryan metaphysics, literature and Darwinian science into a new genuinely German faith-based political community'.[217] Hess worked to ensure the movement's legality after 1933, while Heydrich and Himmler deigned to meet with Hauer to discuss potential collaboration. For a few years the ideas of Hauer and his cohort were intermittently – if tepidly – sponsored by the SS.[218]

None of these groups managed to gain official recognition.[219] But the predictable failure of any one Ario-German splinter movement to displace Christianity belies the popularity of broader concepts like the ' "Aryan-Nordic" or "German" blood races . . . [which were] sacralized and deified in the sense of a new religious belief' and arrayed against the 'old faith' of Christianity.[220] Many, perhaps most, Nazis embraced and propagated religious views that 'ranged from paganism to some kind of Aryan Christian belief', where the 'concept of an Aryan Jesus intermingled with the ideas of Guido von List and Jörg Lanz von Liebenfels, Theodor Fritsch, and Artur Dinter'.[221] Not surprisingly, these views incorporated Middle Eastern and East Asian religious doctrines that reflect longer-term trends in the Austro-German supernatural imaginary.

Indo-Aryan Spirituality and Eastern Religions

In 2007 an ancient Buddha statue bearing a swastika on its belly was sold at auction and later analysed by scientists at the University of Stuttgart. Carved from a 15,000-year-old meteorite, the statue depicts the god Vaisravana, the Buddhist King of the North, apparently brought back to Germany in the late 1930s as part of Ernst Schäfer's famous Nazi expedition to Tibet.[222] Taken on its own, this curious find might be viewed as any other 'oriental' relic stolen by Europeans in the age of imperialism. Except, unlike the Egyptian obelisks and mummies stored in the Louvre or British Museum, the statue carried much the same religious and spiritual meaning for the Nazis as it did for the Tibetans themselves.

The Nazi Tibet expedition – and the religio-esoteric reasons behind it – have garnered a now legendary reputation, a mix of myth and reality.[223] In terms of myth, there is no evidence of Nazism being sponsored by a shadowy, Tibet-inspired 'Vril Society', a favourite shibboleth of crypto-historians. Nor do we have any reason to believe Hitler was guided by a group of Tibetan sages, the 'Agarthii', connected to the Russian mystic George Gurdieff.[224]

There are nonetheless elements of truth in these mythologies.[225] From Hitler, Hess, and Himmler to Rosenberg and Darré, most Nazi leaders shared a profound interest in South and East Asian religion, spiritualism, and esotericism. When Rauschning claimed that every German has one foot in Atlantis and one in Tibet, he was referring precisely to this belief in the ethno-religious connections between the lost Ario-Germanic civilization of the Thule (Atlantis) and an Indo-Aryan civilization centred in northern India.[226] Many Nazis believed that Tibet 'was a refuge, in which important elements of an "Aryan-Nordic-Atlantean Ur-culture" had survived'. Others embraced 'Buddhist-lamaist elements of faith with supposedly "Ur-Aryan" or "Ur-Germanic" roots (such as the doctrines of reincarnation and karma)', which they integrated into 'a Nazi substitute religion'.[227]

In selectively appropriating these Indo-Aryan traditions, of course, the Nazis were following a longer *völkisch* religious tradition. They were seeking, in the words of one *völkisch*-esotericist, an alternative to the 'all powerful, all-knowing God of Christian theology, which neither the Indians nor Chinese, neither Buddhism nor Taoism recognize'.[228] For despite their talk of Nordic racial purity, the Nazis were equally preoccupied by Indo-Aryan religion and spirituality.

From Buddha to Hitler

Nazism's fascination with Buddhism, Hinduism, and Tibet has many roots. As we have seen, theories of a lost Thulean civilization drawn from Blavatsky, Lanz, and Hörbiger inspired the *völkisch*-esoteric belief that Tibet was the last refuge of the Aryans, who had fled Atlantis after a great flood.[229] A generation of *völkisch* thinkers were likewise influenced by H. K. Günther, whose

Indo-Aryan racial theories were cited with equal authority by Hitler and Himmler.[230] Günther put forward the thesis that Nordic tribes had at some point swept into East and South Asia, most likely after a natural catastrophe. The Nordic interlopers had then bred with Asian peoples, providing the ruling Brahmin caste of India, inspiring Buddhism, and forming the core of the ancient Japanese samurai.[231]

Most important in understanding the Indo-Aryan religious traditions that pervaded the Nazi supernatural imaginary is the work of Jakob Wilhelm Hauer and Walther Wüst. Before the Nazi seizure of power, Hauer had been an anthroposophist and prominent scholar of Indian religion who maintained ties to numerous South Asian intellectuals and religious leaders. In this capacity Hauer became one of Weimar Germany's greatest proponents of Indo-Aryan, neo-pagan religious thinking, connecting the blood-and-soil theories of National Socialism with an Ur-Aryan religion centred in northern India. After 1933, Hauer employed his position as head of the German Faith Movement and member of the SS to spread these ideas more widely.[232]

When it became clear that the Third Reich was not about to make Hauer's 'German Faith' the state religion, he stepped down as leader of the movement in 1936. Hauer's obsession with institutionalizing his own particular religious doctrine was typical of *völkisch*-esotericists criticized by Hitler and Goebbels, including Sebottendorff and Dinter. Once Hauer put his theories in the service of the Third Reich, however, his reputation soared.[233] In fact, after joining the NSDAP in 1937, Hauer received a prestigious professorship at the University of Tübingen, where he continued to work with Himmler and the SS.[234]

No longer saddled with running a religious movement, Hauer redoubled his efforts to outline the Indo-Aryan foundations of an NS-religion. 'Buddha did not belong to the native born of India, but to a royal race of Aryan-Indian racial origin,' Hauer argued, making the teachings of Buddha intrinsic to 'German faith'.[235] Piecing together ideas taken from the 'Vedas, Upanishads, Mahabharata (Bhagavadgita) and Pali-canon (the teachings of Buddha)', Hauer made accessible 'a gigantic arsenal of Indian gods and demons for NS-debates on religion ... [connecting] racist blood mysticism and Indian metaphysics'.[236]

Hauer further advocated the sacral techniques of the eastern Yogis as 'Aryan-Nordic' teachings. Yoga had been established by Indo-Germans in Europe and then travelled back east to the Asian subcontinent, Hauer argued – giving credit to theosophy and other occult philosophies for bringing these teachings back to Europe.[237] The SD acknowledged that Hauer's 'Indian philosophy and eastern ways of thinking ... [stood] very near to theosophy and anthroposophy'.[238] Yet his influence would only increase during the war, as he founded an 'Aryan Seminar' at Tübingen to promote his religious views.[239]

Walther Wüst, president of Heinrich Himmler's Ahnenerbe from 1937 to 1945 and rector of the University of Munich between 1941 and 1945, had significant influence over academic and public opinion as well.[240] Wüst saw the Germans as descendants of Atlantis, an ancient Indo-Germanic Empire whose religious teachings survived in South Asian Buddhism, preserved by the monks of Tibet.[241] In a 1936 lecture entitled 'The Führer's Book "Mein Kampf" as Mirror of an Indo-Germanic Worldview', Wüst argued that the 'Indo-Germanic worldview' stood at the centre of Hitler's ideology.[242] Wüst further compared Hitler to Buddha insofar as the Führer had inherited Buddha's holy mission to preserve the Indo-Aryan race and religion.[243]

Citing the myth of Atlantis and German fairy tales, Wüst argued that elements of this once transcendent Indo-Aryan civilization still flourished across Europe.[244] Moreover, thanks to anthroposophy (and other esoteric doctrines), Hinduism, Buddhism, Yoga, and other South Asian spiritual traditions had crept back into German cultural and religious life. From these surviving religio-racial traditions, Wüst suggested, one could (re)construct a religion that combined Nordic and Hindu-Buddhist traditions.[245]

The remarkable convergence between academic Indologists such as Hauer and Wüst, Nordicists like Günther and Wirth, and Irminists and Luciferians such as Wiligut and Rahn is indicative of the syncretic nature of Nazi religious thinking.[246] Rahn argued that the Cathars practised a variation on Tibetan-Buddhist religion originally invented in Nordic Atlantis and transferred to Tibet after the flood, only to return to the Germanic peoples via northern India and Persia. Günther, one of the strongest proponents of Nordic *Germanentum*, agreed.[247] So did the 'Atlantomaniacal' Wirth, who insisted on the commonalities in race and culture between Nordic 'Hyperboreans', who lived in the city state of Ultima Thule, and the Indo-Aryan peoples of the *Veda, Brahmana, and Mahābhārata*.[248] Wiligut too was fascinated by the idea of a shared Indo-Aryan religion. He studied Tibetan legends, practised yoga, and vividly described an out-of-body experience in which he passed a test by Tibetan priests.[249] Wiligut furthermore claimed, with no scientific evidence, that German runes derived from a common Indo-European language that appeared in Tibetan as well as Central Asian and Chinese script.[250]

One of the reasons that Wiligut recruited Gaston de Mengel, one of Rahn's colleagues from the esoteric Polar Society, was to instruct Ahnenerbe researchers on the links between pre-Christian Indian, Persian, and Chinese literature and the Edda, Vedas, and Kabbalah. Impressed, Wiligut urged Rahn to translate into German de Mengel's work on the legendary Tibetan city of Agartha and kingdom of Shambala.[251] Wiligut then forwarded Rahn's translations to SS-Obersturmführer and ariosophist, Frenzolf Schmid, who two decades earlier had published a novel expressing the idea of a shared

Indo-Aryan religion, *The Last Ramadan*.[252] Employing de Mengel's translations, Schmid sought to prove the existence of an 'Atlantean-Aryan' world
triangle or 'geomantic axis' that connected the Nordic countries with France,
South Asia, and Tibet.[253]

Such Indo-Aryan musings were rampant across the SS. Wiligut's Irminist
protégé, Günther Kirchhoff, argued that the geomantic points of Urga (the
Buddhist monastic city of Ulaanbataar) and Lhasa were the world's 'two important Lama-centres'.[254] Similarly, Friedrich Hielscher, an SS paganist close to the
Ahnenerbe's managing director, Wolfram Sievers, advocated a theocracy based
on Indian and Japanese traditions of ethno-religious purity. There was an
organic relationship, Hielscher argued, between 'state and sacrality, rule and
priestly caste'. Hielscher also invoked parallels that many Indian and German
religious scholars had noted between the Vedas and *Bhagavad Gita* on the one
hand and Nordic mythology on the other. Sievers and the World Ice Theorist
Edmund Kiss embraced these theories as well.[255]

Fuelled by these ideas Himmler himself became convinced that an 'advanced
civilization' had once existed 'in the mountains of Tibet', possibly 'the product
of an original, sophisticated race that had sought refuge there from a global
catastrophe'. The civilization in question must have been connected to the
legend of 'Atlantis'. After some kind of natural catastrophe 'the stranded ruling
class of Atlantis', Himmler reasoned, 'spread out from there to Europe and East
Asia'.[256] He further confided to Schäfer 'that the Nordic race did not evolve, but
came directly down from heaven to settle on the Atlantic continent', citing the
Japanese General Oshima's belief 'in a similar theory concerning the origin of
the noble castes in Japan' (which Oshima personally explained to Hitler as
well).[257]

Although the roots of many Nazi religious theories clearly lay in Tibet, the
opportunity for an official expedition only arose in 1938.[258] The impetus was
an invitation from the Tibetan government to participate in the Losar Year
celebrations. The invitation had little to do with Tibet's interest in abetting Nazi
theories on Indo-Aryan religion. With the Sino-Japanese War having broken
out in 1937, Tibet was profoundly interested in garnering Axis support against
China.[259] Himmler took advantage of Tibet's interest in a military alliance to
get Hitler's approval for an expedition that touched on diplomacy but focused
on border science and religion.[260]

The bookish, unassuming Rahn is sometimes viewed as the 'real Indiana
Jones' because of his search for the Holy Grail on behalf of the SS. And yet the
handsome, dashing scientist and adventurer Ernst Schäfer – whom Goebbels
referred to as 'an example of true German manhood' – comes closer to Steven
Spielberg's inspiration.[261] Not only had Schäfer participated in two previous
Tibet expeditions, but he completed a doctoral degree in zoology in 1937, at the

ripe young age of twenty-seven. Because Schäfer combined youthful energy, scientific respectability, and political-ideological reliability, Himmler felt he was the perfect individual to lead the expedition.[262]

The Reichsführer's expectations were ambitious. In addition to conducting geological research to confirm World Ice Theory, Schäfer was to collect archaeological and anthropological evidence that Tibet was the mystic refuge of the Aryans. For professional and interpersonal reasons Schäfer balked at the idea of including the World Ice Theorist Edmund Kiss on the expedition.[263] Still, Schäfer was no hard-nosed empiricist. He agree to get advice from Wiligut – and reported that Wiligut was reading his mind during their meeting, per the 'telemetry' of Tibetan lamas![264] Schäfer also included Bruno Beger, a student of H. K. Günther's, who later conducted border scientific experiments on human beings for the SS. The young geologist Karl Wienert, a discipline of the Nazi geophysicist Wilhelm Filchner, accompanied Schäfer as well, receiving a crash course in geomancy, ley lines, and occult theories about Tibet.[265]

Over the course of their travels Schäfer and his companions proved to be remarkably effective sponsors of Nazi ideology and religious preoccupations. Referring to the expedition as a 'meeting between western and eastern swastika', Schäfer observed that 'we opened during our two-month visit in the Tibetan capital the secret chambers of the Tibetan palaces and temples, not to mention the Tibetan racial soul (*Volksseele*)'.[266] When he arrived in Tibet, Schäfer made a point of celebrating the pagan 'Yule fest' during the winter solstice. On another occasion he offered pagan prayers to celebrate the martyrs of 9 November 1923.[267]

These actions cannot be dismissed as propaganda. After meeting the Tibetan leader Pinpoches, Schäfer suggested that he was a supernatural figure akin to Hitler. He then compared the Tibetan leader's swastika-adorned throne to the Norse 'thunderbolt'.[268] Schäfer further claimed that the lamas had access to a 'magical mystical world' and 'were privy to an esoteric Ur-knowledge', such as reading minds, that could be mastered by the SS.[269] For his part Beger sought to collect stories from the 'ancient Tibetan epic, the *Gesar*; pictures and drawings of the Tibetan gods; copies of the Tibetan astrological tables and calendars; and detailed information on the old holy places of the ancient shamanistic religion of Tibet, known as the Bon, which pre-dated Buddhism'.[270] Lastly, Schäfer and Beger studied the magical rites that Tibetans used to honour the dead, suggesting that the macabre place of death and rebirth, terror, and the death's head were similar to Germanic paganism.[271]

Upon returning to Germany, Schäfer's expedition provided a windfall for Nazi esotericists, orientalists, and rune occultists alike.[272] His 'research' likewise found its way into an updated addition of Schäfer's popular 1933 book, *Mountains, Buddhas, and Bears*, as well as a new volume on the 'New Year's celebration in Lhasa.'[273] Schäfer thanked Wüst for his support by giving the Ahnenerbe chief one of the only existing copies of the 'Encyclopedia on Lamaism from Kandschur'.[274]

In order to bring all this material together for the public, Schäfer produced a live action documentary entitled *Secret Tibet*, the culmination of a series of so-called 'Himalayan' films celebrating Tibetan religion and the 'triumph of the will' in Tibetan Buddhist philosophy.[275] Schäfer took the occasion of the movie's premiere to present personal gift from Pinpoches to 'his Majesty Herr Hitler', a piece of clothing from the last Dalai Lama.[276] Impressed by Schäfer's success, Himmler decided to open a Tibetan Institute for Central Asian Research – eventually renamed the Sven Hedin Institute, after Hitler's favourite Tibet explorer. He appointed Schäfer as the director.[277]

National Socialism and the Religions of the East

When it comes to promoting the 'Buddhist-Lamaist' ties between Nordic and Asian religions, the Nazi fascination with Tibet was merely the tip of the iceberg.[278] Hitler's interest in Eastern religions is evident from a variety of sources.[279] According to Dietrich Eckart, Hitler lamented the murder (by Jews) of '75000 Persians' and 'hundreds of thousands of non-Jews of noblest blood in Babylon, Kyrene, and Egypt'.[280] In his table talk Hitler pointed out that 'fasting and many teachings of natural healing are useful'. It was 'no accident that the Egyptian priesthood was simultaneously the medical profession,' Hitler observed, for 'if modern science does nothing more than to eliminate [ancient healing practices] then it causes damage'.[281] From his perspective, there was much that was attractive in Hinduism as well, from vegetarianism to a shared belief in racial purity.[282] Hitler underlined passages in Schertel that emphasized ritual prayer, yoga, reincarnation, meditation, homeopathic medicine, and other practices drawn from Buddhism and Hinduism.[283]

Hitler was not as invested in Tibetan Buddhism or Atlantean mythologies as Hess or Himmler. But he shared the quasi-mystical fascination of many other Nazis with Tibet, following European expeditions carefully.[284] Hitler's admiration for Japanese Shinto comes up repeatedly as well.[285] God reserved his 'mercies for the heroes of Japan', Hitler suggested during the war, because the 'religion of the Japanese is above all a cult of heroism, and its heroes are those who do not hesitate to sacrifice their lives for the glory and safety of their country'. 'The Japanese religion,' Hitler continued, 'rouses men to enthusiasm by the promise it holds of the rewards in the Hereafter, while the unfortunate Christian has no prospect before him but the torments of Hell'.[286]

Here we might recall Hitler's assertion above that, as in Shinto, 'there is no kind of terrorism' in Islam, only 'a promise of happiness'.[287] Hitler supported general propaganda efforts in drawing parallels between German and Islamic civilization, because the latter possessed a 'superior religion'.[288] In fact, contemporary observers as disparate as Lewis Spence and Carl Jung compared Hitler to a 'new Mohammed'.[289] National Socialist religion was 'nearest Mohammedanism', Jung argued, insofar as it was 'realistic, earthy, promising the maximum of rewards in this life, but with a Moslem-like Valhalla into which worthy Germans may enter and continue to enjoy themselves. Like Mohammedanism, it teaches the virtue of the sword.'[290]

As the Third Reich's foremost 'theologian', Alfred Rosenberg was perhaps less convinced than Hitler, Hess, Darré, or Himmler regarding Hinduism, Shintoism or for that matter Islam's central role in Ario-Germanic religious traditions. Rosenberg nevertheless sympathized with the idea of an Ur-religious commonality between Buddhism and Germanic religion as well as the Indo-Aryan premises of the 'Shambhala theory'.[291] He seems moreover to have accepted that an ancient race of Ario-Atlanteans had taken refuge in South Asia, where they created a dominant civilization based on a religion of castes and blood purity (Brahminism). Before this civilization disintegrated through interbreeding, Rosenberg argued, a branch of the Aryans immigrated to Iran where they developed a Persian variant of Indo-Aryan religion, which preached the eternal Gnostic struggle between light and darkness.[292] Hence Rosenberg's neo-Nordic religion incorporated the same Indo-Aryan elements as Rahn, Günther, Himmler, and others. More practically for Rosenberg, the Indian caste system and Asian concepts of self-sacrifice and spirituality provided a basis on which to justify National Socialist visions of racial and religious community.[293]

Interestingly Bormann – though enormously sceptical of Christianity – shared a fascination with Eastern religions. Bormann believed that Eastern-style mysticism surmounted the narrow materialism of birth and death in ways that Judeo-Christian theology did not.[294] Bormann's wife, Gerda, likewise reported to her husband how much she enjoyed a lecture she attended that divided humanity into three groups, 'virtuous, cultured peasants like the Germans and the Japanese, shifting nomads like the Russians, and "commercially minded parasites" like the British, Americans, and Jews'.[295]

The Bormanns discussed Islam in favourable terms as well. Mohammed 'really was a very clever man', Gerda wrote, 'what wonderful fellows those Mohammedans were in the scientific field – they put the whole Roman Church to shame with their astronomy and geometry'. 'For Mahomet, who let his faith be spread by fire and the sword,' she continued, 'the introduction of polygamy was an absolute necessity. How else could he always have raised enough soldiers? It is just another proof of the miserable pettiness of both the Christian churches that these points were always interpreted as symptoms of the utmost backwardness and barbarism'.[296]

In party circles many referred to Hess as 'The Yogi from Egypt', due not only to his exotic birthplace, but a fascination with Asian religions picked up through his mentor, the Japanologist Karl Haushofer.[297] Hess shared Haushofer's desire to strengthen Germany's ties to Asia through emulating Shinto's 'mystical unity with nature, ancestors and rulers, surrounded by a reverence for the divine and unconditional obedience' toward the Emperor, 'who was seen as a direct descendant of the sun king'.[298] Hess apparently read the Koran, which he recommended to Himmler, and was broadly immersed in ideas drawn from Hinduism and Buddhism via anthroposophy.[299] According to the SD, Hess promoted the Nazi esotericist Edgar Dacqué to a high-ranking position in the Ministry of Education due to his extensive knowledge of 'Indian philosophy and Eastern ideas' derived from 'theosophy and anthroposophy'.[300]

Darré was equally enamoured of East Asian religions.[301] Like Himmler, Darré was invested in Eastern ideas of reincarnation and ancestor worship, citing Confucius and Steiner on the importance of 'oriental wisdom'.[302] He observed with admiration the 'holy trinity' that undergirded Chinese religion: the 'peasantry, the cult of ancestor, and the duty to produce masculine progeny that at some point are supposed to serve at the gravesite of the ancestor'. This latter tradition preserved the 'long-lasting, *völkisch* life of the Chinese people in this world'.[303] In language typical of Buddhism, Darré also talked about humanity's goal of obtaining spiritual harmony with the 'divine world'.[304] In regard to Japanese Shinto, Darré speculated in his diary that the 'noble class of the Japanese [were of] Aryan origin'. 'The Shinto religion,' Darré continued, parroting Günther, Wüst, and Hauer, 'is likely the still authentic old heathen religion of the Germans. Remarkable similarities for example between the Japanese pagoda and a traditional Norwegian church'.[305]

Of course, Himmler was among the most ardent if eclectic consumers of Eastern religions. He frequently invoked 'the wisdom of Indian religious figures,'[306] citing the Hindu *Arthasastra* (*Manual of Politics*) and claiming that Hinduism was instructive in learning to balance pleasure (*kama*) with moral (*dharma*) and practical (*artha*) concerns.[307] The Reichsführer walked around with his own copy of the *Bhagavad Gita* as well, remarking on parallels between Hitler and Krishna in the Gita.[308] Following a decades' old tradition in German Indology, Himmler compared the heroic racial consciousness of the Aryan-Hindu and Kshatriya warrior caste in the Gita and *Mahābhārata* to the traditions of the Edda and *Nibelungenlied*. Just as Rome had eliminated the Cathars, who preserved the traditions of Indo-Aryan religion, Himmler believed that the *Kshatriya*'s 'degradation was an act of revenge of the Brahman priests, in order to eliminate the "warrior yogis" as dangerous rivals'.[309]

Hindu ideas of karma and reincarnation were also favourite themes, which Himmler, Rahn, and others saw represented in Cathar Luciferianism.[310] By emulating Eastern religious practices, Himmler thought 'he could penetrate directly to the world of the Germanic ancestors' and 'be reincarnated'.[311] 'The Indo-Germanic peoples', he explained, 'believe in rebirth. Life doesn't come to an end with one experience of it. The good and evil deeds which man does on this earth affect his next life in the form of his Karma, which is not an inexorable fate.' Indo-Germanic beliefs, Himmler continued, entail 'no surrender to divine grace, but the knowledge that what you have done on this earth will witness for you or against you, inescapably. But you have a chance to alter your fate by your own efforts in a new life.'[312]

Himmler's religious preoccupations included Buddhism as well. Although not a practising Buddhist, Himmler followed some of its tenets, including vegetarianism. He also admired his astrologer Wilhelm Wulff's more serious adherence to Buddhist principles.[313] For similar reasons Himmler lauded his homoeopathic massage therapist, Felix Kersten, as his 'magic Buddha', because he was trained in Chinese manual therapy.[314]

Inspired by Chinese Taoism, Buddhism, and Confucianism, Himmler meanwhile attempted to build a cult of ancestor worship within the SS, of 'earthly immortality', which he equated with the perpetuation of the Volk. 'I must say that this belief has as much in its favour as many other beliefs,' Himmler wrote. 'This belief can no more be proved by the methods of exact science than Christianity, the teachings of Zarathustra, Confucius, and so on. But it has a big plus: a nation that has this belief in reincarnation, and reveres its ancestors and thus itself, always has children, and such a nation has eternal life.'[315] For these reasons Himmler encouraged his Tibet specialists to research the lost civilization of Shambala and ordered Heydrich's successor as SD and Gestapo (RSHA) chief, Ernst Kaltenbrunner, to export Buddhism to occupied territories.[316]

Like Hitler, Darré, and others, Himmler's Indo-Aryan religious affinities included Japanese Shinto. He wanted the SS to inculcate the values of the Japanese samurai, contributing the foreword to Heinz Corazza's book, *The Samurai: Honourable and Loyal Imperial Knights*. In 'distant times the people in the Far East had the same code of honour as our fathers had long ago in a past all too soon destroyed,' Himmler wrote, concluding that it is 'frequently minorities of the highest calibre [such as the SS and samurai] who give a nation eternal life in earthly terms.'[317] In short, Himmler came to believe, as had Wüst, 'that the elites of Asia – the Brahman priests, the Mongolian chiefs, and the Japanese samurai – all descended from ancient European conquerors.'[318] Finally, Himmler saw Islam as a noble religion with admirable racial and martial virtues.[319] He ordered the SS to make a sincere effort to draw parallels between ancient Germanic texts such as the Edda and the Koran, which the Reichsführer read with interest, in order to propagate the idea of a common Indo-Aryan racial and spiritual heritage between Germans, Arabs, and Persians.[320] In a speech to a volunteer division of Islamic troops recruited to the Waffen-SS, Himmler declared that Germans 'were friends of Islam on the basis of convictions'. 'We Germans' and 'you Muslims,' Himmler added, 'share the feeling of thankfulness to destiny that almighty God – you say Allah, it is of course the same thing – sent the Führer to the tortured and suffering people of Europe'.[321]

By ignoring the obviously 'Semitic' roots of Arab religion and civilization, Himmler was on solid border scientific ground. After all, we began this section with the ariosophic speculations of Dingfelder and Schrönghamer-Heimdal, of List, Fritsch, and Dinter – even of Hitler himself – all of whom insisted that Jesus was in fact an Aryan, part of a proto-Aryan Canaanite or Aramaic people who preceded the Jews.[322]

In *German Orientalism in the Age of Empire*, the historian Suzanne Marchand suggests that German intellectuals were more sensitive to Asian and Middle Eastern cultures than their British and French counterparts. Through their study of the East, Marchand contends, German orientalists began to question the superiority of their own Eurocentric and Christian worldviews, leading to a form of 'multicultural thinking'.[323]

At the end of this chapter we should have little doubt that Marchand is right, except for the caveat that even the Nazis need to be included in that group. Nazi leaders were as invested in Indo-Aryan religions as their orientalist forebears. From the Vedas, *Bhagavadgita*, and Hindu tantrism to the teachings of Tibetan lamism, from Japanese Shinto to Zen-Buddhism and Bushhido, a remarkable array of Asian religious influences were appropriated by the Third Reich 'as expressive forms of 'Aryan-spirit'.[324] By letting themselves be 'inspired by Asiatic mythologies, philosophies and religious practices such as Vedism, yoga, Buddhism, and Zen', moreover, the Nazis helped create 'the ideological and religious foundation for a Greater Empire', a topic we will take up in Chapter Seven.[325]

***

According to Himmler's biographer, Peter Longerich, the main outline of the Reichsführer's religious and ideological picture was clear: 'the restoration of a de-Christianized, Germanic' spirituality through the 'myths of Atlantis and Tibet' and 'via Cosmic Ice Theory/astrology/astronomy'. Through this mélange of history and myth, Germanic paganism, reincarnation, and occultism, combined with esoteric theories of creation, 'a real substitute religion was created'.[326] Certainly Himmler was more invested in this particular conception of a 'substitute religion' than Hitler, Goebbels, or even Rosenberg. As the evidence in this chapter suggests, however, many, perhaps most Nazi leaders shared some or all the elements described by Longerich.

Nazi religious thinking included a fundamental anti-Christianity, which separated Nazism from other fascist movements. Whether Mussolini's Blackshirts, the *Action Française*, or Franco's Falange, most fascist movements, while focused on subordinating Christianity to the state, were ideologically ambivalent, even sympathetic, in their attitudes to the Church.[327] The same cannot be said of the Third Reich and certainly not Nazism as a movement. The Nazis' inherent hostility to Christianity as both an ideological *and* socio-political rival is what spurred their attempts to find a suitably Ario-Germanic alternative.

The Ario-Germanic alternative to Christianity was never meant to become a state religion. As Rosenberg put it, 'National Socialism is above all denominations and encompasses them all through [incorporating] them into the essence of Germanness.'[328] That is why Rosenberg, Hitler, and Himmler were careful not to become too prescriptive. So long as such religious and spiritual alternatives might 'guarantee the stability of German will formation and therefore political leadership', there was no need to meddle in everyday superstition and belief.[329] The introduction of numerous pagan and National Socialist holidays indicates less the desire to create a new religion than to revive and exploit existing Ario-Germanic and Indo-Aryan traditions within the Nazi supernatural imaginary.[330]

To be sure, the Third Reich never managed, in its twelve short years, to displace Christianity as Germany's preeminent belief system. The Nazis made substantial inroads, but the vast majority of Germans remained Protestant or Catholic in 1945, at least nominally.[331] Nor could the Nazis themselves agree on the precise admixture of liturgical or theological elements in their search for alternatives to Christianity, whether Irminism or Luciferianism, anthroposophy-inspired Hinduism or the Nazis' received views of Tibetan Buddhism.

Nevertheless, this religious eclecticism, characteristic both of Nazism and the *völkisch*-esoteric milieu on which it drew, masks a larger, more important consensus.[332] A surprising number of Nazis agreed after all as to the 'holy bond between Führer and his followers', to 'hero and ancestor worship, animistic communication with nature (animals, trees, water sources), archaic cult celebrations', and 'male warrior bands'. An almost equal number worked to establish 'an Indo-Aryan codex of symbols (Swastika, Irminsul)', which included the 'resacralization of holy places (geomancy), initiation rites and creating pilgrimage sites.'[333] If many of these religious and mythological traditions 'seemed to be going in different directions,' George Williamson observes, they all served 'the purpose of forging a national religiosity that the Nazi regime wanted.'[334]

PART III

THE SUPERNATURAL AND THE SECOND WORLD WAR
Folklore and Border Science in Foreign Policy, Propaganda, and Military Operations

'We consider folklore to be of assistance in our struggle for the preservation of our own nationality ... It should eliminate the outdated and harmful way of thinking according to sub-regions ... It should show ... how current German life and German character poured through ... to the east ... that these tribal groups are the blood of his blood. It will hammer home to the Silesians that their tribal brothers are at home in all three regions of Poland.'
SS folklorist, Alfred Karasek (1935)[1]

'Early to bed. Spent a long time reading. Nostradamus prophecies. Very interesting for those of us today. Hopefully the daring commentary is right. Then England will have nothing to laugh about ... I tell [Hitler] about the prophecies. Given the times we're in they are astounding ... The Führer is very interested.'[2]
Joseph Goebbels, diary entry (23 November 1939)

In March 1940, Hans Bender, now Germany's leading parapsychologist, wrote a pessimistic letter to Karl Krafft. Since 1937 they had both witnessed growing restrictions against occultism. This escalating repression, Bender feared, would be exacerbated by the outbreak of war.[3] 'About the prospects of border sciences in our generation,' Krafft reassured his colleague in reply, 'I'm not as pessimistic as you. 'Especially in government circles,' he insisted, 'they are seeking people' who 'have something to say' in terms of border scientific research.[4]

Krafft knew what he was talking about. By March 1940 he was working closely with Goebbels' propaganda ministry and the Reich intelligence services to produce propaganda and wage psychological warfare against the Allies. Many of Krafft's fellow experts in astrology and divining would soon be recruited as well. Bender's own border scientific research, as we saw in Chapter Five, began to receive official sponsorship only during the war. For just as the conflict released previously bottled-up economic energies, it also led to a greater Nazi willingness to experiment with and exploit border sciences in the interests of foreign policy, propaganda, and military science.[5]

On the one hand, the genesis and course of the Second World War has little to do with supernatural thinking. The war was a consequence of the Third Reich's aggressive efforts at revising the Versailles Treaty, obtaining resources, and garnering living space (*Lebensraum*) in eastern Europe.[6] When one looks closely at the ideological justifications and deployment of those goals, however, one finds many ways in which folklore and border science influenced Nazi foreign policy.[7]

As George Mosse reminds us, folklore and mythology helped to provide a 'dream of the Reich' that was yet to be achieved.[8] This supernaturally inspired dream gradually became a reality after 1933, as the Third Reich deliberately appropriated folklore and border science to justify military aggression and territorial expansion.[9] Elements of Indo-Aryan religion and mythology, drawn from the supernatural imaginary, also informed Nazi conceptions of geopolitics and efforts to cultivate alliances with Asian and Middle Eastern powers.[10]

Rather than rely on a practical evaluation of risks and rewards, Hitler frequently tapped into his own intuition in making foreign-policy decisions and appealed to the German people's collective unconscious in selling his aggressive policies.[11] Abetting Hitler's faith-based foreign policy, the Propaganda Ministry and Foreign Office employed professional astrologers and diviners to produce wartime propaganda aimed at both the Allies and the German public. Finally, the Third Reich utilized occultism and border science to gather military intelligence, search for enemy battleships, and train Nazi soldiers. The Second World War was neither caused nor directed primarily by occult designs. But many aspects of the war were influenced or determined by folklore, border science, and the broader Nazi supernatural imaginary.

Folklore, Border Science, and Geopolitics 1933–9

In 1930 the future SS folklorist, Alfred Karasek, published an article in the popular *völkisch* journal, *People and Race*, entitled 'On the Folklore of the Carpathian Germans'. He observed that folklore might serve as a kind of cultural genetics, indicating the ethnic origins and territorial claims of a particular nationality.[12] The folkloric tradition of 'wild hunters', who emerge at night to seek revenge on their oppressors (probably the inspiration for Washington Irving's headless Hessian horseman), occurred across German-speaking central Europe.[13] The tradition of wild hunters was nonetheless strongest, Karasek suggested, in unsecured regions where Germans had experienced centuries of violence from Slavic neighbours.[14] No matter the vicissitudes of history, he explained, a 'typical immutability in ethnocultural tradition' remained.[15]

For Germans in the interwar period folklore was not a mere collection of children's stories. As the left-wing philosopher Ernst Bloch observed in the early 1930s, the allegorical meaning of sagas had been set in motion by *völkisch* thinkers in order to 'infer petty bourgeois visions of great style and then to wield the folk tales, lacking real proof, in "natural scientific" fashion'. These tales became the ' "world-historical events" for the half-educated', fomenting 'apocalyptic opinions in the petty bourgeoisie – a philistine fantasy'. Magical thinking bloomed 'over town and country in mythical fashion' sowing 'utter confusion'.[16]

Born in the Sudetenland, Karasek may have been especially keen on deploying folk tales to justify the reincorporation of ethnic Germans into the Reich.[17] And yet he was typical of thousands of *völkisch* anthropologists, historians, and geopoliticians who, as Bloch suggests, utilized folklore and Indo-Aryan border science as a means to 'show the world the mission of the German folk', anticipating 'the path of destruction, even before folklorists became instruments for the scholarly legitimization' of the Nazi imperial project.[18] If virtually all social and human sciences were enlisted in this project, no academic discipline became as interwoven with Nazi dreams of empire as ethnology and folklore studies (*Volkskunde*).[19]

Folklore and Empire

The practical exploitation of folklore and border science in foreign policy was laid out in the last decades of the Wilhelmine Empire and early years of the Weimar Republic. The quasi-mystical belief in *Lebensraum*, as we saw in Chapter One, was drawn from Nazi geopoliticians such as Karl Haushofer, through his mentor Friedrich Ratzel.[20] In its border scientific premises and geopolitical malleability, *Lebensraum* justified virtually any German intervention into central and eastern Europe, simultaneously providing an important 'scientific' basis for the resurgence of anthropological interest in German folklore.[21] So too did late Wilhelmine movements such as anthroposophy and ariosophy, which offered an Indo-Aryan view of race and space that helped fuel post-war conceptions of empire.[22] After the First World War these border scientific traditions dovetailed perfectly with Hans Günther's Nordic racialism and the 'imperialistic deliberations of the new experts on the East'.[23]

In the interwar period a number of folklorists made the case that Weimar's borders were not the natural limit of German territory.[24] Instead, in their studies they focused on highlighting a 'network of localities' and German 'speech islands' (*Sprachinseln*) that lay outside the Reich. The unification of all these ethnic Germans and territories with the Reich carried 'eminent political importance'.[25] These studies were supplemented by the 'fighting folklorism' of paramilitary groups such as the Werewolves, *Schutz- und Trutz Bund*, and Artamanen, to which many Nazis belonged. Employing slogans such as a 'people without space' (*Volk ohne Raum*]) and 'warrior peasants' (*Wehrbauern*), these groups inspired a generation of Nazi imperialists, including Himmler, Darré, and Wolfram Sievers, managing director of the Ahnenerbe.[26]

After 1933, a number of Nazi leaders enlisted, encouraged, and rewarded anthropologists, geopoliticians, and historians who promoted these views of race and space.[27] Hermann Göring's Reich Forest Office, for example, charged its employees with studying 'all manner of "Ario-Germanic" traditions' that might facilitate eastern expansion and 'inner colonization'.[28] For similar reasons Hess promoted the Nazi esotericist Edgar Dacqué to a Chair at the University of Munich and to Divisional Head in the Reich Ministry for Science, Education, and Popular Education.[29] As a 'mythologist, folklore interpreter, and researcher', the normally sceptical SD reported, Dacqué had 'made remarkable contributions' transforming 'folklore and myths' into a 'historical source ... of equal value to paleontology and geology'. Dacqué's research was particularly convincing, the report continued, in revealing 'real memories ... magical insights into nature ... passed down over millions of years'.[30] That the scientific absurdity of such observations was lost on the most anti-sectarian organization in the Third Reich indicates the power of border scientific thinking in Nazi conceptions of race and space.

If Göring and Hess remained enthusiastic about the geopolitical uses of folklore and border science, it was Himmler and Rosenberg who sponsored these ideas most vigorously. The Third Reich's 'black' (SS) and 'brown' (NSDAP) folklore industries were led respectively by Himmler's Ahnenerbe and Rosenberg's Office of Folklore Research.[31] Like the Ahnenerbe, the Office of Folklore Research evolved from a pre-1933 Nazi organization, in this case the Militant League for German Culture (*Kampfbund für deutsche Kultur*). After 1933, Rosenberg established nine different folklore-oriented institutes, from the Bavarian Institute for Folklore to the Berlin Institute for German Folklore and Office for Folklore and Celebration Planning. All these offices intended to deploy folklore studies in domestic and foreign policy.[32] Rosenberg was assisted in his efforts by the archaeologist Hans Reinerth, head of the Reich Association for German Pre-History (*Reichsbundes für Deutsche Vorgeschichte* or RDVG).[33]

Himmler had started the SS Race and Settlement Office (RuSHA) in 1931, appointing Darré as head. Its pre-1933 mission, inspired by the Artamanen, was to help produce a yeoman Nordic peasantry that could reclaim and repopulate

German territory to the east. After 1935, now supported by the Ahnenerbe, the RuSHA's mission expanded to include ransacking 'the German past' in search of ancient lore that could be used to justify Europe's subjugation under their new 'Aryan lords'.[34] 'It is all the same to me whether this or some other one is the real truth about the prehistory of the Germanic tribes,' Himmler wrote. 'The only fact that is of importance, and for this these people are being paid, is to have the kinds of thoughts about history that will strengthen our people in their much needed national pride'.[35] In pursuing this border scientific mission, the Ahnenerbe received funding from respected academic agencies and private donors as well as Himmler's vast resources as head of the German police.[36]

The long-running ideological and organizational rivalry between Rosenberg and Himmler played out in the competition between Rosenberg's Office of Folklore Research and Himmler's Ahnenerbe. The Office of Folklore Research was arguably more focused on propagating the Nordic, *Germanentum* angle than the Indo-European *Ariertum* of Himmler and Walther Wüst.[37] Some members of Rosenberg's organization attacked Himmler's Ahnenerbe for its overly esoteric approach.[38] SS folklorists accused Rosenberg in turn of fraudulent academic work that undermined the 'holy mission' of folklore studies.[39]

Both Rosenberg and Himmler, however, were invested in the 'business of myth-making'.[40] Both dismissed academic history in favour of irrational myths that propagated pagan, *völkisch* ideology.[41] And both wanted to nurture the 'German folk soul in its totality' through an emphasis on homeland (*Heimat*), ancestral worship, blood, and soil.[42] Hence their most prominent researchers 'devoted themselves to distorting the truth . . . churning out carefully tailored evidence to support the racial ideas of Adolf Hitler'. Some 'twisted their findings consciously' whereas others 'warped them without thought, unaware that their political views drastically shaped their research'.[43] Whatever the justification, both Rosenberg and Himmler's institutes drew on folklore studies and settlement archaeology to justify claims to territory in eastern Europe that had little basis in scientific reality and no legal justification.[44]

Before 1939 these efforts focused on building a sense of racial community at home. Rosenberg and Himmler worked closely with the Hitler Youth leader Baldur von Schirach, the Labour leader Willy Ley, and the Minister of Agriculture and Settlement, Walther Darré, to promote the idea of *völkisch*-organic unity. By the spring of 1934 there were already ten thousand politically coordinated societies and four million people under the Reich Union for Folk-Nation and Homeland, which inculcated the idea of an organic 'racial soul' into the Hitler Youth, Union of German Girls, Reich Work Service, and even folk art.[45] Such groups also helped propagate the importance of living space, including the assumption that 'ancient Germanic settlements in eastern Europe validated German claims for sovereignty over Slav-populated regions'.[46]

In the late-1930s, as the Third Reich prepared for war, these efforts became both more deliberate and more aggressive.[47] In 1937, for example, Himmler unleashed a propaganda assault on Slavic archaeologists for ostensibly covering up and misrepresenting 'ancient German remains'.[48] In July 1939 the editor of the Ahnenerbe-sponsored journal *Germania*, Otto Plassmann, argued that the 'eastern policy' of the medieval Saxon King Henry I ('the Fowler') provided a historical model for 'the creation and reconquest of German racial living space' in eastern Europe.[49] Wüst, as president of the Ahnenerbe, made a similar case. Germany had a right to invade the Low Countries, Poland, France, and Yugoslavia based not on 'material interests' but the 'eternal laws recorded in the holy scriptures of the Aryans for thousands of years'.[50]

With the German invasion of Poland in 1939, many of these folklore-inspired ideas took on 'new and more urgent meaning'.[51] Himmler and Rosenberg gave their folklorists and historians 'archaeological shopping lists' meant to legitimize border scientific ideas of race and space through the 'organized looting of eastern European antiquarian collections'.[52] Leading border scientists such as Wüst, Reinerth, Günther, and Teudt were instrumental in this regard.[53] So too was a larger group of professional archaeologists, including respected scholars such as Heinrich Harmjanz and Eugen Fehrle.[54]

A professor of ethnology at the University of Frankfurt, Harmjanz came to lead the Folk Research and Anthropology division of the Ahnenerbe, which created highly aspirational maps justifying the widest stretch of German expansion.[55] Fehrle, a professor of ethnology and philology at Heidelberg University, employed Günther's border scientific racial theories to justify eastern expansion and the racial regeneration of the German peasantry.[56]

While Harmjanz and Fehrle established a broad ideological consensus regarding the geopolitical implications of folklore-inspired border science, other scholars pursued empirical research to justify expansion into particular regions. The so-called Nordmark (Scandinavia) was one such region.[57] Jürgen Hansen, a professor of folklore and ethnology at Kiel in Scheswig-Holstein, argued that the 'tribal homeland, the habitat of a tribe that settled here since time immemorial' was connected to the Nordic people 'by race and history'. Germans roots in the northern homeland (*Heimat*) were 'not just purely physical' but 'spiritual and emotional'.[58] Hansen further lauded Nordic folk belief 'in demons and magic' as examples of a pan-Germanic Ur-religion, which helped justify incorporating Scandinavia into the Reich.[59]

Himmler and Rosenberg pursued such theories with alacrity. Through Reinerth, Wirth, and Wüst – not to mention Rahn, Wiligut, and Fehrle – the Ahnenerbe and Office of Folklore Research sponsored multiple expeditions across Scandinavia.[60] They explored the once Danish (later British) Helgoland to determine whether the island was a remnant of Atlantis – undergirding

1. Madame Helena Blavatsky, founder of Theosophy.

2. Jörg Lanz von Liebenfels, co-founder of Ariosophy, in front of his 'Order Castle' of the New Templar.

3. The parapsychologist Albert von Schrenck-Notzing conducting an experiment.

4. Hanns Hörbiger, founder of World Ice Theory ('Glacial Cosmogony'), at his desk.

5. Emblem of the Thule Society, 1919.

`E / THEORIE / PRAXIS

Dedication from Dr. Ernst Schertel to
Adolf Hitler:

*"Adolf Hitler – with venerated
dedication from the author."*

6. Dedication from the parapsychologist
Ernst Schertel found in Hitler's copy of
Magic: History, Theory, Practice: 'Adolf
Hitler – with dedicated veneration from
the author.'

7. Hermann Löns at his desk (1912), shortly after publishing his most famous work *The Werewolf* (*Der Wehrwolf*).

8. Emblem of the German paramilitary Werewolf association.

9. Horror writer and Nazi propagandist Hanns Heinz Ewers, photographed by Hitler's official photographer, Heinrich Hoffmann (1933).

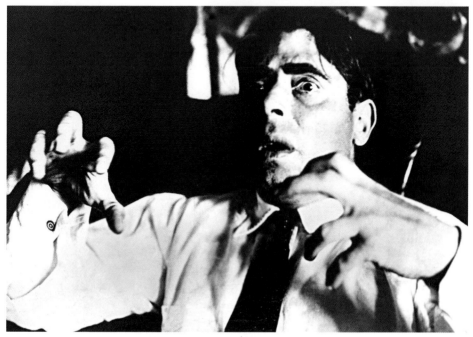

10. The magician and clairvoyant Erik Hanussen (aka Hermann Steinschneider) gesturing for the public.

11. Erik Hanussen's *The Other World* magazine.

12. Mathilde Ludendorff, leader of the Society for Knowledge of a German God (Ludendorff Movement), 1935.

13. Helmut Schreiber, head of the Magic Circle, with Adolf Hitler at the Obersalzberg, 1943.

14. The wreckage of Hess's plane after his flight to Scotland, May 1941.

15. The astrologer Karl Krafft a few years before he began working for Goebbels' Propaganda Ministry.

16. The Nazi-sponsored parapsychologist Hans Bender.

17. Wolfram Sievers, managing director of the SS Ahnenerbe.

18. The SS's leading esotericist, Karl Maria Wiligut, aka 'Wise Thor' (far left), accompanying SD Chief Reinhard Heydrich (slightly obscured), SS Chief Heinrich Himmler, Himmler's Chief-of-Staff Karl Wolff, Margarete Himmler, and Lina Heydrich to a medieval Baltic church, 1934.

19. SS 'Generals' Hall' with 'Black Sun' emblem, located in the Wewelsburg castle, Büren, Westphalia.

20. The SS zoologist Ernst Schäfer in Tibet.

21. Heinrich Himmler meeting the Grand Mufti of Jerusalem, Mohammad Amin al-Husayni, 1943.

22. Heinrich Himmler exploring ancient Germanic runes in Westphalia.

23. Hitler meeting the Indian Nationalist leader, Subhash Chandra Bose, 1942.

24. Benito Mussolini, shortly after being rescued by SS special forces leader Otto Skorzeny (pictured) in September 1943.

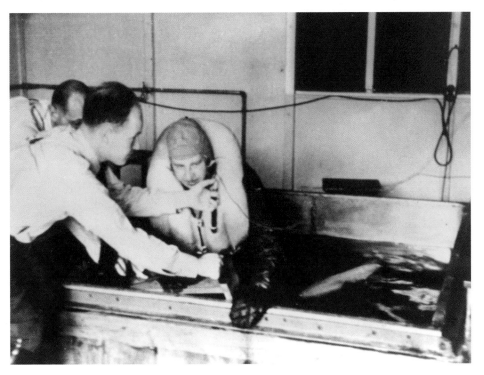

25. SS doctor Sigmund Rascher prepares a 'volunteer' from Dachau concentration camp for one of his 'freezing' experiments, 1942.

26. SS anthropologist Bruno Beger measures skulls in the Himalayan Kingdom of Sikkim.

27. Promotional poster for the vampire film *Nosferatu*, 1922.

28. Promotional poster for the Nazi film *The Eternal Jew*, 1940.

29. A reconstruction of the Nazi 'miracle weapon' known as 'The Bell'.

30. Adolf Hitler at his Werewolf headquarters in the Ukraine, August 1942, flanked by Minister of Armaments Albert Speer (left) and Head of the Party Chancellery Martin Bormann (right).

31. British soldiers surveying an executed member of the Nazi Werewolf.

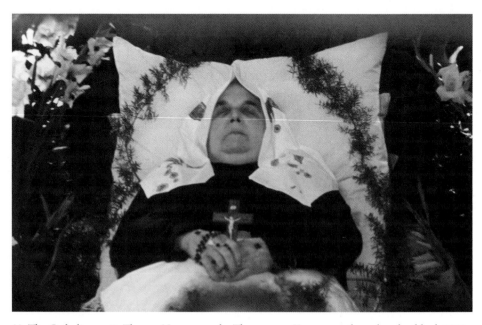

32. The Catholic mystic Therese Neumann, aka Therese von Konnersreuth, on her deathbed, 1962.

attempts to reclaim the strategic territory for the Third Reich.[61] The trips by the Finn Yrjö von Grönhagen between 1936 and 1938 to investigate magical rites in his homeland helped insinuate the extension of the German Empire to the north.[62] SS-sponsored research on Ario-Germanic paganism and esoterica likewise provided a bridge to the collaborationist movement in Norway, where in 1942 Vidkun Quisling became minister-president.[63] In 1942, Himmler set up the German Scientific Task Force (*Germanischer Wissenschaftseinsatz*) explicitly to 'strengthen ideological unity with Nordic nations', opening branch offices across Scandinavia and the Low Countries.[64]

Folklore studies and settlement archaeology proved instrumental in the project of expanding into the *Westmark* as well, namely Alsace, the Netherlands, and parts of France. Herman Wirth's occult-inspired interpretation of the fraudulent Ura Linda chronicle located the source of Ur-German religion in the Netherlands.[65] The SS esotericist and Dean of Humanities at the Reich University of Strasbourg, Ernst Anrich, assumed that his faculty's border scientific 'west-research' (*Westforschung*) would help justify the integration of Alsace, Lorraine, Luxembourg, and Holland into a Greater Germanic Empire.[66] Assien Bohmers' work on the putatively Nordic character of the Cro-Magnon cave drawings helped justify Nazi expansion into the region of southern France that Otto Rahn claimed was the home of an Ario-Germanic Cathar religion.[67]

Meanwhile, the contributions of these border scientists resonated beyond the SS.[68] Goebbels even recruited the Ahnenerbe historian Plassmann to work on his Holland Plan aimed at 'Germanizing' the Low Countries.[69]

Himmler, Rosenberg, and Göring also funded 'pre-history' trips to Italy and Greece. The SS-affiliated archaeologists Franz Altheim and Erika Trautmann, sponsored by Göring, collected various glyphs to legitimize their theory that the wars of the Roman Empire were defined by a struggle between 'Indo-Germanic peoples of the north' and 'the Semites of the Orient'.[70] The Silesian art historian Josef Strzygowski and the Nazi classicist Hans Schleif worked creatively to establish religio-cultural and racial links between the Greco-Roman and Nordic German Empire.[71] Not to be outdone, Rosenberg sent Reinerth to southern Europe to find proof of Aryan settlements preceding Greek and Roman civilization.[72]

Nazi scholars invoked mythical legend and the 'ecstatic cult' of folklore to justify incorporating much of the former Habsburg Empire (*Sudostmark*).[73] Altheim and Trautmann used their expeditions to develop ties with Romanian fascists and to pave the way for potential Nazi incursions into Greece and Turkey as well.[74] This project was assisted by the propaganda efforts of fascist mystics such as Julius Evola, whose 'Aryan doctrine of holy war' against Bolshevism, Jewry, and other subhuman races was aimed directly at fascists in Italy and Romania.[75] By the time the Nazis bailed out the Italians in Greece militarily in the spring of 1941, they had developed border scientific arguments for the extension of the German Empire into southeastern Europe.

What mainstream academics said of Altheim's research – that it was based on insufficient evidence and fuelled by a mystical faith in German racial superiority – applied doubly so to Nazi academics working in eastern Europe.[76] The Greifswald folklorist Lutz Mackensen connected the world of spirits and revenants to German border politics in the Polish *Wartheland*, whence Himmler planned to displace Slavs and settle Germans.[77] Harmjanz's prehistorical research between November 1939 and October 1940 further justified population exchanges between the Polish Wartheland and Baltic countries.[78]

The same could be said of much of Karasek's folklore 'research'. Taking the allegedly haunted Carpathian mountains as his case study, he observed that long-separated German splinter groups never relinquished their ethnoracial purity, which could be construed through comparison with the ethnically 'alien' folk tales of the Slavs. Recovering and preserving Germanic folklore would help reconstitute the German race and empire in eastern and central Europe.[79]

Following Karasek, Gustav Jungbauer's *Sudeten German Journal for Folklore Studies* (*Sudetendeutschen Zeitschrift für Volkskunde*) and *Contributions to Sudeten German Folklore Studies* (*Beiträge zur Sudetendeutschen Volkskunde*) promoted the idea that the German-speaking region of Czechoslovakia, the Sudetenland, belonged to the Reich.[80] The study of Sudeten German folklore, Jungbauer argued, served the mission of acquiring territory for a German 'people without space' (*Volk ohne Raum*).[81] Himmler and Rosenberg sponsored similar research as far afield as Bulgaria, Serbia, Croatia, southern Russia, and even the Caucasus.[82]

Promoting esoteric prehistory in the interests of imperial expansion and eastern colonization was never confined to academic folklorists. Behind the scenes we find Himmler, Rosenberg, and the General Governor of Poland, Hans Frank (a former Thulist), eagerly discussing the provenance of the obscure 'spearhead of Kovel' with the SS runologist Wolfgang Krause. Discovered in what is now northwestern Ukraine in the nineteenth century, the spearhead of Kovel was looted from its Polish owner by the Nazis in 1939. In the midst of the Spring Offensive of 1942 against the Soviet Union all four Nazis agreed that the spearhead provided evidence of Ur-Germanic settlements in Volhynia – the German *Wartheland* – and therefore justified German resettlement in and the expulsion of Jews and Slavs from the same region.[83]

The Third Reich's imperialist motives were also exceedingly public and overtly didactic. While Himmler, Frank, and Rosenberg carried out their border scientific discussion about the spearhead of Kovel, for example, Rosenberg's head archaeologist was invited to contribute an article summarizing these efforts to the Third Reich's flagship journal, the *Völkischer Beobachter* ('Research

Assignment for Professor Reinerth: Pre- and Early Historical Research in the Occupied Eastern Territory').[84] Karasek, for his part, was accused of espionage during his 'research' trips across eastern Europe and was eventually expelled from Poland.[85] With the outbreak of war, Reinerth, Karasek, and others had to literally force their way back into eastern European archives and onto archaeological sites.[86] The consequences of this 'research' in terms of race and space, as we shall see in Chapter Eight, were significant. But Nazi dreams of empire did not stop at the borders of eastern Europe. They extended into the Orient.

Indo-Aryanism and Geopolitics

According to the 'current state of our entire prehistorical knowledge,' wrote Walther Wüst, the Ahnenerbe president, 'the Indo-Germans were racial tribes' of 'Indo-Germanic language and primarily Nordic race' who 'forced themselves into power belts beyond the great mountain ranges – the Alps, Carpathians, Caucasus, Urals, Himalayas – and split off into individual ethnic groups'. Perhaps, he conceded, they did not possess 'what we today call an Empire'.[87] One could nonetheless perceive the 'elementary relation' between all Indo-Germans over time, which proved they were natural 'rulers of the World' (*Welthersscher*).[88] Citing Jakob Wilhelm Hauer, Wüst explained that this new Indo-Germanic Reich was not 'a kingdom, not a state' but 'a life-supporting and life-giving unit, a perfected spiritualization of a community of blood and culture . . . anchored in reality' and at the same time 'not of this world!'[89]

Wüst's imagined empire of 'old Aryans' extended from Iceland in the northwest to Persia and northern India in the southeast. It then ostensibly declined through racial miscegenation with 'Semites' and 'Africans', who 'undermined the state of the ruling race and its fundamental principles, blood and soil'.[90] Although divided for centuries, however, the Indo-Germanic people could one day reunite to restore the old 'Imperium'.[91] Albeit highly fanciful, Wüst's account of the 'Aryan cosmocracies of India and Persia' helped fuel the Nazi imperial project. If the ancient Indo-Aryans were natural colonizers whose racial and spiritual footprint extended beyond the European continent, so too should the Third Reich's.[92]

Drawing on this affinity with once great Indo-Aryan empires, *völkisch*-esoteric thinkers saw Germans as a 'colonized' people fighting the same struggle as India and Persia against France, Great Britain, and Soviet Russia. Many German orientalists, occultists, and eventually the Nazis viewed their Indo-Aryan brethren as important allies in opposing the liberal imperialist and Communist states.[93] 'Nationalist thinkers in Germany and India,' writes Kris Manjapra, viewed each other as 'visionary holistic representatives' of a 'new world order'.[94] Ernst Bloch likewise recognized this kinship between Nazis and

anti-colonialists in terms of their mutual 'pursuit of false utopias'. As opposition
to British and French colonialism 'brought "underdog" nationalist thinkers
together', Manjapra concludes, 'Germans and Indians generated potentials for
liberation, for solidarity building, for retaliation, for jingoism, and even for
genocide'.[95]

Hitler was clearly influenced by these Indo-Aryan conceptions of geopolitics. In the early 1920s, Karl Haushofer first introduced him to such ideas.[96] A
decade later Hitler attended lectures by Hans Günther during which he claimed
that the Aryans had launched their first assault into Asia more than two
millennia before Christ. Some made it to Japan and China, becoming nobles,
which is why the Chinese and Japanese aristocracy had Nordic traits such as 'a
decidedly long skull and an almost white skin, sometimes combined with
handsome European features'. The rest of the Aryans swept through the
Caucasus and pushed into India. There they made a caste system to protect
their bloodline and 'a wealthy young Nordic couple gave birth to a prince –
Buddha'.[97] These Indo-Aryan conceptions undergirded Hitler's alliance with
Japan and helps explain his talk of creating a world empire, including a railway
from the French coast all the way to Manchuria.[98]

Fantastical claims about the Nordic origins of Asian civilization made a
deep impression on Himmler as well, who was 'keen to unearth hard archaeological proof of these "gold-haired" conquerors'.[99] Himmler believed that
ancient emigrants from Atlantis founded a great civilization in central Asia,
with a capital called Obo, citing the Japanese nationalist Oshima's belief in a
similar theory.[100] According to Himmler, the 'elites of Asia – the Brahman
priests, the Mongolian chiefs, and the Japanese samurai ... descended from
ancient European conquerors'.[101] These border scientific conceptions of Indo-
Aryan civilization clearly influenced Himmler's desire to create a 'Germanic
world empire' united by 'Aryan Germanness'.[102]

A number of mid-level party functionaries and SS researchers drew similar
connections.[103] In an article entitled 'The Mystery of the Grail and the Idea of
Empire' the SS-sponsored Italian mystic Julius Evola invoked a combination of
Indo-Aryan border science and Grail occultism in making the case for Axis
domination of the globe.[104] Sievers, Himmler, and Wüst showed an interest in
Evola's arguments, including his suggestion that the Holy Grail represented a
'weapon' in a 'secret war' against Jewish 'agents of darkness'.[105] Wüst in particular found his 'metaphysical justification of imperialistic warfare' on Indo-
Aryan grounds exemplary.[106]

In fact, the SS contemplated a German-dominated global empire divided
into Indo-Aryan tribes.[107] Himmler sponsored Edmund Kiss's research on the
possibilities of Ur-Aryan colonization of South America and Africa for similar
reasons.[108] Meanwhile Otto Huth, a specialist in theology for the Ahnenerbe,

even argued that Canary Islanders were a pure line of the Nordic race who had preserved Aryan religious practices until forcibly converted by Judeified Spaniards. His dubious claims were based on mummified remains that showed Canary Islanders had blond – obviously bleached – hair. But the Ahnenerbe was slow to reject his findings.[109]

Even more fantastically, the SS researchers Frenzolf Schmid and Günther Kirchoff justified global empire based on the assumption that Germany and Austria sat at the centre of a vast geomantic network of 'reference points'. These reference points, they argued, which carried substantial underground energies, once united ancient Indo-Aryan civilizations. Were the SS not able to win the magical arms race, learning to harness these energies, then the Third Reich would cede the field to the Allied powers, led by Jews, Bolshevists, and Jesuits.[110]

The most powerful of these theories centred on India. From Hartmann and Hübbe-Schleiden to Steiner and Lanz von Liebenfels, from Lagarde and Chamberlain to Günther, Hauer, and Wüst, a fascination with India and the Orient defined *völkisch*-esoteric views on race and geopolitics.[111] Günther, Wüst, and Hauer all saw India as an 'Indo-Germanic colonial land' settled by Indo-Aryan people who supposedly 'originated in the Arctic as well as central Europe'.[112] India, according to Wüst, was a 'wonderland' above which streams 'the solar symbol of the swastika'.[113] Hauer's 1932 book, *India's Struggle for the Empire*, argued further that 'East and West' had as their 'spiritual centre of the storm … India and Germany'. Himmler too embraced this point of view, insisting 'We Germans must already out of feeling of justice have the highest sympathy for the emancipatory struggle of the Indians.'[114]

As international tensions mounted in the 1930s, India played an increasingly strategic role in Nazi diplomatic and military preparations.[115] The Nazis supported the Indian freedom fighter Subhas Chandra Bose, for example, who sponsored the idea of a 'synthesis between Socialism and Fascism'. When Bose was sent back to India on a U-boat in 1943 to work for the Indian freedom movement, he wrote to Himmler 'in the name of the national Indian freedom movement', expressing a 'sense of true association in common struggle for freedom and victory'. Himmler replied that he shared 'this wish in the same way for you and your freedom struggle, which you lead for the Indian people'.[116]

For Tibetans, meanwhile, the positive relationship with the Third Reich emerged out of a largely pragmatic search for a powerful European ally against China. On the German side this relationship was fuelled at least as much by Indo-Aryan esotericism.[117] The Third Reich portrayed Ernst Schäfer's Tibet expedition not as a typical European colonialist exploring an exotic country. It was rather an occasion for the Germans to restore ties with their racial and spiritual cousins, for whom 'the old Indo-Aryan symbol of the swastika' was 'the highest symbol of happiness'.[118] Germany's own consul-general in Calcutta cited this odd mix of science, religion, and politics in explaining to Himmler why Schäfer and his men were having trouble obtaining entry visas from the British.[119]

Sure enough, after war broke out Himmler charged Schäfer with a secret diplomatic and military mission to help build Germany's Far Eastern alliances – a so-called 'continental block' – via Germany's then ally Russia.[120] Himmler wanted Schäfer and a small platoon of armed SS troops to stir up unrest against the British in Tibet as well.[121] For his part Schäfer insisted that his documentary, *Secret Tibet*, would 'not be just any film . . . [It] would reflect precisely what I have considered my ideal goal for more than ten years . . . [acquiring the] central Asian living space that is so essential to us', based on the laws of nature and the Indo-Aryan racial struggle.[122]

This fascination with Tibet brings us to the Nazis' more general pan-Asianism. Himmler and his rune occultists were attracted to Tibet due to its 'position between the mongolian and European racial groups'. This meant that Tibet might play a 'meaningful role in a pan-Mongolian federation of states' under the aegis of Germany and Japan.[123] The ease of negotiations between the Third Reich and Tibet, Schäfer observed, was facilitated by the fact that 'we Germans were the first white nation that have reached out our hand to an Asian people, namely the Japanese'.[124]

Wüst explained that the Japanese were racial 'comrades in suffering' with whom one could develop an alliance against the 'Anglo-Saxon exploiter democracies' and 'Jewish world capitalism'.[125] Gerda and Martin Bormann discussed the Axis alliance with Japan in similar terms, in the context of mutual Indo-Aryan ancestry and racial superiority.[126] The SD's foreign office opened an East Asian Institute (as well as an 'Indian Working Community') to build such connections with Japan.[127] It should hardly come as a surprise that the Nuremberg Race Laws were modified in the late-1930s so as not to implicate East Asians.[128]

Of course, Hitler and Hess's mentor, Karl Haushofer, had argued that Germany and Japan had a mutual right to expand their living space at the expense of existing Western empires, and at the cost of war if necessary.[129] The Japanese were an 'elite race' according to Haushofer, who valued proper breeding and martial values.[130] The empire of Japan therefore constituted the perfect 'middle man between East and West'.[131] Haushofer also proclaimed that 'the greatest and most important geopolitical turning point of our time is building a powerful Europe as part of a continental bloc containing North- and East Asia'.[132] Haushofer's influence may explain why Hitler modified his lukewarm feelings toward the Japanese, as initially expressed in *Mein Kampf* (where he referred to the Japanese as 'culture bearers' instead of 'culture creators' like the Germans). By the time of the Second World War, Hitler deemed the Japanese a 'highly cultivated' Indo-Aryan race that had preserved its purity in a 'bloody struggle against Mongolian Asians'.[133]

According to many Nazis, the Japanese and Germans shared the same 'highly developed soldierly spirit of the front experience and comradeship' that culminated in an 'increasingly powerful movement of renewal' whose highest goal, to quote the Japanese General Oshima, was 'a world order of justice'.[134] The Japanese invasion of China in 1937 and attack on Pearl Harbor in December 1941 merely reinforced these border scientific justifications for an Axis empire in the East and West.[135] That this geopolitical alliance was never firmly forged lies in the fact that the tide turned quickly against both Axis powers in 1942, leading to mistrust and pessimism on both sides.[136]

The Third Reich drew on Indo-Aryan esotericism in pursuing German interests in the Middle East as well.[137] Wüst's esoteric research on ancient Persia helped sponsor religio-political and diplomatic ties with Iran.[138] At the same time Altheim and Trautmann's border scientific study of ancient racial conflicts between Aryans and Semites, *The Soldier Emperors (Die Soldatenkaiser)*, ostensibly affirmed the Aryan heritage of Germany's Arab allies.[139] During their research expedition to the Middle East, Altheim and Trautmann were ordered by Himmler to discuss an alliance with the Bedouin Sheikh Adjil el Yawar and the Iraqi nationalist leader Rashid Ali al-Gaylani.[140]

After 1939, this research informed appeals by Hitler, Himmler, and Goebbels to seek an Arab alliance against 'Anglo-Bolshevik Imperialism', 'American materialism', and Jewish hegemony in Palestine.[141] Hitler proposed a Berlin-based council of Arabs, while Goebbels and the German Foreign Office courted Arab celebrities such as Iraq's Rashid al-Khilani and Palestine's Grand Mufti. In fact, the Third Reich made thousands of Arabic broadcasts between 1940 and 1944, aimed at Egypt, Afghanistan, Saudi Arabia, Palestine, Syria, Turkey, India, Iran, Sudan, and Ceylon.[142]

Some historians claim the Nazis were playing fast and loose with the 'doctrine of the Aryan master race in order to appeal to Arabs and Muslims', cynically ignoring their racial doctrine.[143] The reality is that pre-existing Indo-Aryan racial theories pervading the Nazi supernatural imaginary made such geopolitical arguments and diplomatic alliances plausible. Based on Schäfer and Beger's extensive research on race and space in central Asia, the Sven Hedin Institute and Ahenenerbe supported an alliance with the peoples of Turkestan, mostly Islamic in confession, while the RSHA founded a Turkestan institute in Dresden to promote such measures.[144]

Appealing to Islamic fundamentalism, nationalism, communitarianism, and anti-Semitism, Nazi officials encouraged Arabs and Persians in their paranoid, conspiracy-driven thinking against Jews and the British.[145] The Third Reich even distributed pamphlets portraying Hitler as a prophet fighting against Jewish demons, with Koranic verses representing war as an apocalyptic conflict against infidels. In this fashion the Third Reich created a 'political and ideological fusion between National Socialist ideology, radical Arab nationalism, and equally radical and militant Islam'.[146] Remarkably, this propaganda was taken seriously – and had a significant effect – on both sides.[147] The Iraq Baath Party, the Arab Committee, and the Grand Mufti of Jerusalem all showed wartime interest in Nazi diplomatic and military overtures.[148]

This largely border scientific Indo-Aryanism facilitated a highly malleable conception of geopolitics that made 'no attempt to differentiate between wish and reality, but merely indicated every one of [the Third Reich's] favourite stretches of land'. These included Italy, Dalmatia, Sweden, Norway, Holland, Belgium, France, England, the Balkans, the Near East, and Greece. For Asia, Africa, and overseas they favoured Columbia, Bolivia, Peru, the Canary Islands, Libya, Persia, and Tibet – 'altogether 122 domestic and foreign places appear as prospective sites for the research community', and by extension the Indo-Aryan confederation or German Empire.[149] The Nazis may not have been *primarily* interested in global empire, ceding much of East and South Asia to their Japanese allies.[150] And yet, insofar as Nazi folklore and esotericism helped sponsor a war for Axis 'living space', the Third Reich proved surprisingly optimistic about the prospects of resuscitating an Indo-Aryan Empire from the English Channel to the East China Sea.[151]

Foreign Policy, Wartime Propaganda, and the German Public

In a series of interviews with Western journalists in the immediate pre-war years, Carl Jung was asked to 'diagnose the dictators': Mussolini, Stalin, and Hitler. Jung suggested that Mussolini and Stalin were cynical strongmen who fit their country's respective national traditions. But Hitler was different. In conducting foreign policy no European leader relied as much on his own intuition fuelled by the collective unconscious of his audience. Hitler, Jung argued, would have been helpless in a room negotiating with an imposing physical presence such as Mussolini or a Machiavellian pragmatist like Stalin. For Hitler possessed 'little or no physical power' of his own. Only when surrounded by the 'power which the people projected into him' as 'seer' or 'medicine man' did Hitler become omnipotent. Indeed, Hitler's 'actual power' surpassed that of Stalin and Mussolini because the 'people agreed that he possessed magic – that is, supernatural ability'.[152]

Hitler's foreign policy could not have been sustained without a receptive public, including millions of Germans who viewed foreign policy in cosmic and metaphysical terms.[153] During the First World War, many *völkisch* esotericists had publicly welcomed the war as a prerequisite for 'the rebirth of our

German people'. War was 'cosmically necessary', a conflict 'anchored in the karma of the nations' which 'must happen for the salvation of all humankind'. According to Rudolf Steiner, war was the 'earthly manifestation of processes playing out among "the beings of the spirit world"', a 'world of demons and spirits which works through humankind when nations battle one another'.[154]

Many *völkisch* thinkers viewed war in similarly mystical terms. Since the goals of Germany's foreign policy could not be fulfilled immediately, they were transferred to the realm of 'dreams, hallucination, and fantasy'.[155] These fantasy worlds had their antecedents in *völkisch*-nationalism, esotericism, and the 'science fiction and war prophecies of the Wilhelmine era', but they manifested themselves with particular power in the 1930s, through the foreign policy of Hitler and the Nazi Party.[156]

In this section we will be looking at Nazi foreign policy, propaganda, and public opinion through the lens of the supernatural imaginary. First, we consider the esoteric elements in Hitler's approach to foreign policy, including his reliance on intuition and his ability to transcend Germany's precarious geopolitical reality by appealing to the collective unconscious.[157] Similarly, there is Joseph Goebbels' use of astrology in order to manipulate public opinion, producing both domestic and foreign wartime propaganda. Goebbels began employing astrologers, with Hitler's approval, only weeks after the outbreak of war, and he continued doing so – with little evidence of their efficacy. These case studies are not meant to suggest that German foreign policy can only be understood through a supernatural lens. But they do add an interesting and oft-neglected angle to our knowledge of Nazi foreign policy and wartime propaganda.

Prophecy, Fantasy, and Hitler's Foreign Policy

Hitler and Goebbels did not have to work hard to generate feelings of popular resentment or revenge. The devastating losses of the First World War and unpopular demands of the Versailles Treaty did the work for them. Geopolitical fantasies of imperial rebirth and military revenge 'reflected a need to overcome feelings of humiliation and a sense that all prospects for individual and collective fulfilment had vanished'. Eager for 'some form of immediate relief from a depressing reality', *völkisch* nationalists 'forecast imminent wars that always end with a triumphant Germany'.[158] Military defeat, economic crisis, and the occupation of German territory by French North African troops were thus 'transposed to a conceptual realm framed by notions of heaven-inspired retribution and miracles, of collective crucifixion and resurrection'.[159]

Frantz Fanon's description of the interwar resentments of North Africans against French colonialism applies to Germans in the Weimar Republic, equally frustrated as they were by French occupation.[160] For colonized people, Fanon observed, an 'atmosphere of myth and magic' integrated individuals in 'the traditions and the history' of their nation. In colonized countries, 'the occult sphere is a sphere belonging to the community which is entirely under magical jurisdiction ... supernatural, magical powers reveal themselves as essentially personal'.[161] The 'settler's powers' – the French, British, Jews, and Communists in the Nazi supernatural imaginary – became 'infinitely shrunken, stamped with their alien origin ... [a] frightening enemy created by myths'. Before 1933, devoid of weapons and opportunity, the fight against this enemy would be waged 'on the phantasmic plane', that is, within the supernatural imaginary.[162]

Much like Algerian nationalists subjected to French rule, völkisch-nationalists perceived the interwar period as 'a state of flux ultimately determined by the supernatural'. 'Unsuccessful in war and unable to adjust to a troubled peace,' Peter Fisher argues, nationalist thinkers 'dismissed what was for them an overly complex, difficult, and demoralizing reality and indulged in elaborating fantasies of a victorious war of revenge'.[163] The hard work of multilateral diplomacy and economic recovery was displaced by concerns and anxieties about 'a deadly struggle between enemy nations, races, or parties'.[164]

At the same time Germany's 'anxiety-ridden public' became 'susceptible to the messages and psychological manipulation' of nationalist literature. They read works such as Hans Martin's *Attention! East Mark Radio! Polish Troops Crossed the East Prussian Border Last Night* (1932), a war prophecy that falls into the subgenre of 'defense alarmism' (as opposed to 'revenge and renewal'). The book sold thousands of copies in East Prussia and caused feverish gatherings of locals who actually believed the Poles were attacking, creating 'psychosis through a book'.[165] The German public also read *The Psychological Field General: A Search for the Leader of the German Future* (1922) by the Nazi army officer Kurt Hesse, which argued that Germany needed to find a leader who might tap into the Reich's 'still not fully exploited reservoir of spiritual and military strength'.[166]

In the Weimar Republic liberal, Catholic, and Socialist leaders did their best to combat such fantasies by injecting a healthy dose of pragmatism into public discourse and foreign policy. But it has 'always happened in the struggle for freedom,' Fanon observes, that people who are 'lost in an imaginary maze, a prey to unspeakable terrors yet happy to lose themselves in a dreamlike torment', might become 'unhinged ... [and] in blood and tears' seek out 'real and immediate action'. For many years such imaginary sentiments fed Germany's '*moudjahidines*' (in Fanon's words) – millions of *völkisch* nationalists and paramilitary, who fantasized about eliminating the Socialists, Communists, and Jews, and dreamed of restoring a Greater German Empire.[167]

The Nazi seizure of power let this foreign-policy genie, previously confined to the realm of fantasy, out of the bottle. Hitler promised nationalist 'moudjahidines' across German-speaking Europe that he would restore a Reich 'believed to be invincible' that had been 'crushed and broken, bereaved of the fruits of her previous victories, of her colonies, of her honour' by a shameful peace.[168] The Nazis' fantastical vision of Germany's internal and external situation – of being surrounded and infiltrated by a secret cabal of Jews, Masons, and Communists – found a receptive audience.[169] As we have seen, millions of Germans and Nazis were convinced that the 'course of world history was the sinister result of the ministrations of ancient secret societies, such as those of the Masons, the Jews, and the Jesuits'.[170] The Führer could turn these supernaturally infused, conspiracy-driven resentments into political, geopolitical, and institutional reality.[171]

Hitler could also exploit the popular desire, at least on the *völkisch* right, for a strong Führer. Interwar Germany was awash with hopes for a 'national savior'. Popular literature and the press extolled the virtues of generals, charismatic dictators, and 'fictive superhumans' who could 'foreshadow the materialization of a powerful and real savior'.[172] 'Since their defeat in the World War,' Jung observed, the Germans 'have awaited a Messiah, a Savior ... characteristic of people with an inferiority complex'.[173] Citing fate and destiny, good and evil, German nationalists looked to the coming of a 'magical priest' (*Zauberpriester*) who might act as a translator of powerful forces the ordinary person could not understand.[174] Although no friend of the occult, Alfred Rosenberg declared point blank that the Weimar renaissance in astrology and clairvoyance had paved the way for 'would-be prophets' such as Hitler.[175]

No wonder that the *völkisch* prophets of the 1920s, Hitler included, portrayed themselves as messiahs, 'miracle makers' sent to rescue the Germans from the disaster of 1918.[176] None were more effective than Hitler, viewed by his followers as an Old Testament prophet whose mission it was to unite the German people and lead them to the Promised Land.[177] In his role as Führer he could, for example, 'assist or obstruct the way to a happy life after death, put a ban upon an individual, a community or a whole nation, and by excommunication cause people great discomfort or pain'.[178] 'It is as if he possesses nervous tentacles stretching out in every direction,' Jung averred. Like the 'medicine man, the mystic, the seer', Hitler appeared 'sensitive to all his nation is feeling'. By telling Germans 'simply what they want to hear', he became 'the mirror of that inferiority complex' characterizing German foreign policy in the interwar period.[179]

Nazi propaganda proved effective at integrating the 'popular will with that of an anticipated Führer', creating the image of 'a single prophet' who would both serve and preserve Germany against all odds.[180] 'Once I heard Hitler talk about the coming German war of revenge and liberation,' Heiden recalls, and 'I could only think, "When will he stop spouting this nonsense?"' Yet the

First World War's greatest hero 'General Ludendorff's voice trembled with emotion when he rose and modestly, almost respectfully, thanked the speaker' for his 'wonderful' words.[181] Similarly, the DGWO leader Fritz Quade proclaimed in 1933 that Hitler's superhuman ability to see into the 'beyond' (*Jenseits*) would give him insights into foreign policy that other politicians didn't have.[182]

Hitler's ability to convince Germans of the infallibility of his foreign policy would have been dangerous under any circumstances. It was all the more dangerous, however, because he appeared to believe it. In conducting foreign policy, Jung suggested, Hitler was 'a man acting under compulsion', like a patient who cannot disobey his inner voice.[183] He 'listens intently to a stream of suggestions in a whispered voice from a mysterious source and then acts upon them.'[184] Hitler could not honour a treaty or promise made to a foreign power, Jung observed, because there 'is no person there to give the promise! He is the megaphone which voices the mood or the psychology of the eighty million German people.'[185] Because Hitler's 'magical solutions also seemed to be successful,' writes the historian Raymond Sickinger, they 'confirmed to him the genuineness of his approach. As a result, Hitler learned not to question his way of thinking, but rather to blame those who were unfaithful to following it precisely.'[186]

Until 1939 this magical mode of conducting foreign policy, based on faith and intuition, appeared successful. It facilitated the Third Reich's three greatest foreign-policy victories, 'each of which involved the acute danger of war: when he marched into the Rhineland in March, 1936, and into Austria in March, 1938, and when he mobilized and forced the Allies to abandon Czechoslovakia.'[187] That does not mean that Germans accepted Hitler's faith-based approach to foreign policy uncritically. His decision to remilitarize the Rhineland was initially received with scepticism and even unofficial resistance by many military leaders, who 'feared that the army was not ready for any retaliation from the French and British'. But Hitler, believing 'that his instincts were superior', went forward, which convinced him that his insight into the future outcome of present actions was sound: 'You can serve God only as a hero ... I go the way that Providence dictates with the assurance of a sleepwalker.'[188]

In the lead-up to the Munich Crisis of 1938, many of Hitler's most influential military advisers warned him against annexing the Sudetenland, which they believed the Allies would resist. But Hitler, according to Jung, 'was able to judge his opponents better than anyone else'. Although it appeared inevitable that his actions would lead to war, Hitler somehow 'knew his opponents would give in without fighting', as he seemed to believe when Neville Chamberlain came to Berchtesgaden.[189] Confident in 'providence' and intuition, Hitler took risks that few other statesmen would take in a modern industrial country, supported by millions of Germans who recognized those risks but retained faith in the Führer's judgement.[190]

In the case of Czechoslovakia, Hitler's 'voice was correct'.[191] By March 1939, in fact, he had obtained many of the foreign-policy objectives he had proposed as early as the 1920s. But what would happen should his voice prove incorrect? Hitler was not content to stop with these immense and mostly bloodless gains. His repeated success 'reinforced Hitler's belief in himself – that he had a special "intuition" and could predict the future'. 'I am convinced,' he declared, that the 'greatest successes in history' were based not on logic 'but on inspirations of the moment'. It was 'intuition', Hitler continued, that played the greatest part in 'politics, statecraft, and military strategy'.[192]

On 24 August 1939, a day after signing the Non-Aggression Pact with the Soviet Union, Hitler met with his inner circle at the Eagle's Nest above Berchtesgaden. Watching a display of northern lights, he ostensibly 'saw an omen in the predominantly red light cast on him and his friends'. Hitler told his aide that 'the omen clearly meant that without force, Germany would not make it this time'.[193] This omen confirmed Hitler in his decision, according to some witnesses, to go forward with the invasion of Poland a week later. He would not look back, taking a 'magical' approach to wartime operations for the duration of the war. Nor would Hitler allow retreat. For retreat could only be the outcome of a nuanced calculation of real world military situations and might 'indicate that his insights and his magic formula for Germany were not infallible. Any deviation from his plans, like the deviation from a precise set of magic rituals, would spell disaster'.[194]

Astrological Propaganda and Psychological Warfare

Before September 1939 the Third Reich had been ambivalent about sponsoring astrology in an official capacity. With the outbreak of war, any lingering reservations about enlisting border science for the benefit of the regime dissipated. Only four days into the war, Rosenberg's attack dog in occult matters, Kurd Kisshauer, produced a policy paper entitled 'Astrology as a Means to Influence Public Opinion'. The report indicated that the British had used fake horoscopes to good effect in Germany. If the Germans were susceptible to occult thinking, why not employ similar astrological propaganda against the Allies?[195]

On 30 October 1939, Goebbels reported on a ministerial conference during which he announced that he was examining astrological writing 'to determine himself whether there were any inherent dangers'.[196] Two weeks later he brought Karl Krafft's letter of 2 November to a lunch meeting with the Führer; the letter had predicted Johann Georg Elser's assassination attempt on Hitler on 8 November at the Bürgerbräukeller in Munich. Hitler was fascinated and

asked Goebbels to explain the details. Himmler, at the time soliciting astrological materials for his own occult library, took great interest as well, agreeing
that the letter and its 'prediction' were genuine. Goebbels was clearly encouraged by Hitler and Himmler's response.[197] As he reported in his diary two days
later, 'I broached the idea of Nostradamus [to his colleague in the Propaganda
Ministry, Herwarth von Bittenfeld] for the first time. The whole world is full
of mystical superstition. Why shouldn't we exploit that in order to undermine
the enemy front?'[198]

Now committed to sponsoring astrological propaganda, Goebbels passed a
ban on German civilians employing astrological predictions. The mephisto-
telean Minister of Propaganda wanted to make sure that *he* controlled the
message.[199] But that did not mean he rejected scientific astrology out of hand.
In December 1939 he remarked that the brochures produced by the RMVP
'should have propagandistic not scientific character', suggesting that he believed
'scientific' astrology was indeed possible.[200]

In building his team of crack astrologers, Goebbels first paid a visit to Hans-
Hermann Kritzinger, who said he was too busy to get involved, but recommended Krafft.[201] Krafft was already dabbling in high-level diplomacy, notably
in advising the Romanian ambassador to Britain, Virgil Tilea. The ambassador
gained trust in Krafft's clairvoyant abilities when the astrologer did his horoscope and seemed to read it effectively.[202] After Tilea leaked German demands
on Romania to the British in 1939, Krafft took it upon himself to convince the
diplomat to adopt German policies in the east, including the concept of
Lebensraum.[203] By early 1940 these dilettantish political interventions – including
Krafft's prediction of the Elser assassination attempt – had raised the hackles of
Heydrich's RSHA.[204] But Krafft's predictive abilities impressed Goebbels enough
to invite him to join the RMVP's 'expert committee' of astrologers.[205]

Goebbels was so anxious to try out his new propaganda strategy that he
began producing Nostradamus prophecies even before hiring Krafft. In late-
November 1939, Goebbels charged two officials in the Propaganda Ministry,
Bittenfeld and Leopold Gutterer, to draft a propaganda pamphlet deriving pro-
German prophecies from Nostradamus' *Centuries*.[206] Hardly experts in
astrology, Bittenfeld and Gutterer decided to employ Nostradamus' thirty-
second 'Century' ('The great empire, dismembered early/Will grow from the
inside out/From a small country./In his lap the sceptre shall rest') to justify
Hitler's systematic revision of the Versailles Treaty. Useful for the pending invasion of France was the thirty-third 'Century', in which Nostradamus observed
that 'Brabant, Flanders, Ghent, Bruges and Boulogne/Are temporarily united
with greater Germany.'[207]

According to Goebbels, the brochure's talking points would include the reconstruction of Europe, temporary occupation of France, and coming thousand-year

Reich. The material about the 'great Prince of Armenia', however, would be 'put on ice until the Lord Stalin from Georgia declares war on us – or we on him'. 'Caution! Show nobody Nostradamus', Goebbels concluded, reminding everyone of the dangers of publishing astrological predictions without RMVP approval.[208] After producing an 'outstanding' cluster of brochures predicting German victory, Herwarth and Gutterer were instructed to develop horoscopes of leading men of the Western powers, along with astrological crossword puzzles, to be spread within France and the Low Countries.[209]

By late February 1940, bolstered by the arrival of Krafft and another 'scientific' astrologer, Georg Lucht, the 'Nostradamus' division began preparing for the invasion of Denmark, Norway, the Low Countries, and France.[210] According to Goebbels, Krafft and Lucht produced a 'glowing brochure' to be distributed in Sweden and neutral countries.[211] In late April, Goebbels ordered brochures to be distributed to Denmark, Holland, and Switzerland.[212]

Two weeks later, with the invasion of the Low Countries and France, Goebbels' astrological propaganda efforts shifted south and west.[213] Between 24 April and 27 May he enthused multiple times about his Nostradamus pamphlets, citing radio reports claiming, with only anecdotal evidence, that they were having a significant effect: 'Our panic propaganda in France is very successful. Over there Nostradamus-followers represent a fifth column. We're increasing our efforts in that respect. Most of the day is spent on this project.'[214] On 26 and 27 May, as it became clear the tide was turning in Germany's favour, Goebbels suggested ratcheting down the prophecies in order not to 'undermine their diplomatic efforts' – as if the military situation had actually been influenced by his Nostradamus pamphlets![215]

Because of their great 'success', Krafft and his colleagues were made full partners of the regime.[216] Krafft spent much of the spring of 1940 attending lavish parties and high-society events where he met – and impressed – leading Nazis. These occult-friendly Nazi notables included Hans Frank, Robert Ley, and Hitler's favourite sculptor, Arno Breker.[217] Under the circumstances we can understand why Krafft had written to Bender so enthusiastically in March 1940 'about the prospects of the border sciences in our generation'.

Nevertheless, privately, Krafft and Lucht were beginning to have serious qualms about Goebbels' unscientific misreading and manipulation of the prophecies. Lucht simply quit on 2 April 1940. Goebbels subsequently brought in the more politically reliable Kritzinger to work with Krafft. But Krafft and Kritzinger could not agree on a reading of the Nostradamus quatrains that suited Goebbels' purposes.[218] As a scientific astrologer, Krafft simply wasn't interested in following the party line. He was openly insubordinate as well, refusing to acknowledge any wrongdoing in the Tilea Affair even after Krafft's incriminating letters and Tilea's pro-British attitude came to light. Finding the conditions under which he was working intolerable, Krafft resigned from the RMVP and returned to 'private practice'.[219]

Despite Krafft resigning from the RMVP, the astrologer's publications continued to receive approval. In fact, Goebbels employed Krafft's pamphlets and books intermittently through October 1940, when Hitler shifted his attention to the Soviet Union.[220] That Krafft was determined to lecture on foreign policy and make public remarks about 'impending military operations in the east' did nothing to endear him to the Gestapo. And yet for nearly a year after his resignation he managed to ignore the regime, repeatedly breaking the RMVP's law against making unofficial astrological predictions. Only in June 1941, with the Hess Action, did Krafft pay the price for his lack of party discipline.[221]

Krafft's fall from favour and subsequent arrest did nothing to discourage Goebbels.[222] With Krafft gone and France subdued, Goebbels simply shifted his propaganda emphasis to support the invasion of Britain and Hitler's percolating war aims in eastern Europe.[223] On 22 July, as the Battle of Britain commenced, Goebbels reported on a detailed debate regarding the best way to promulgate Nostradamus propaganda in English circles. He settled on the covert radio stations run by the RMVP's Adolf Raskin because they could reach the greatest number of people. The carefully orchestrated astrological propaganda worked 'in stages, first illustrating what Nostradamus prophesied correctly for earlier times, and then gradually introducing prophesizing that would show the destruction of London in the year 1940'.[224]

Although Britain showed no signs of surrender, Goebbels insisted that his brochures were having the desired effect. Remarkably, the German Foreign Office and Heydrich's SD agreed.[225] Walter Schellenberg, who would succeed Heydrich as head of the SD in 1942, claimed that the prophecies were particularly helpful in countering British intelligence's distribution of fake horoscopes and counterfeit copies of the astrological journal *Zenit* across Germany.[226]

The difference, of course, is that the British put no credence on the impact of astrology on domestic opinion.[227] Goebbels, Schellenberg, and Raskin, on the other hand, truly believed that astrology was a concrete factor in influencing opinion at home and abroad.[228] In line with this thinking, Goebbels even loosened the restrictions on promulgating astrological works *within* Germany in the summer of 1940. The only caveat was that they toe the party line.[229]

By September 1940 it had become clear that Göring's Luftwaffe was not going to be able to defeat the RAF. Yet Goebbels, seemingly oblivious, held out hope that his Nostradamus project would somehow turn the tide: 'Lord Haw-Haw [the pro-Nazi British radio broadcaster, William Joyce] is supposed to indicate the prophecies of Nostradamus today, which should now come to be fulfilled.'[230] With Lucht and Krafft having quit the RMVP and Kritzinger occupied by his ballistics work, Goebbels decided to rely on the more politically compliant (if hardly 'scientific') astrologer, Alexander Centgraf.[231] The rabid Nazi's prophecies, in contrast to Krafft and Lucht's, fell perfectly in line with Goebbels' new propaganda efforts, which focused on Hitler's plan to attack the 'Jewish-Bolshevik Soviet Union'.[232]

With the Eastern campaign on his mind, Goebbels charged the RMVP to begin working on the famous Nostradamus passage regarding the 'great Prince of Armenia'. Due to changing circumstances, Goebbels now wanted the prophecy to refer to Hitler and not to Stalin. Instead of the 'Armenian' Stalin attacking Germany, as Goebbels anticipated a year earlier, it would be Hitler who planned to break the mutual Non-Aggression Pact by carrying out a surprise attack on the Soviet Union.[233] The 'great Prince of Armenia [Stalin]' was therefore changed in official propaganda to the 'great Prince from Arminius [Hitler]', a reference to the Germanic chieftain Arminius, who led the Germanic tribes in their victorious onslaught on Rome.[234]

Goebbels and his colleagues produced many hundreds of books, pamphlets, and radio programmes, in multiple languages, between November 1939 and 1943. While utterly ineffective, these efforts show how important Goebbels, Schellenberg, and a few members of the Foreign Office thought astrology might be for the purposes of propaganda and psychological warfare.[235] In the spring of 1942, as the tide turned in North Africa, Goebbels was still hanging his hopes on a new slate of 'occult propaganda' aimed at the Allies. Because 'the Americans and English fall so easily for that kind of propaganda,' Goebbels explained, we're 'employing in every way possible the crown jewels of occult soothsaying. Nostradamus must be believed in again.'[236]

This raises the question as to why the Allies 'confined themselves to using almost exclusively classical methods of psychological warfare', with 'propaganda activities in the "occult" sphere worth only tangential attention'.[237] The answer, perhaps, is that the British simply did not believe the mass of the population could possibly be susceptible to Nostradamus quatrains.[238] The Germans, on the other hand, were 'well-informed in occult matters'. Which is why, Schellenberg recalled, they remained susceptible to 'occult propaganda'.[239]

Waging War with Border Science

On 12 September 1943 the SS captain Otto Skorzeny conducted a daring raid on the Campo Imperatore hotel in Italy's Gran Sasso mountains. His mission was to liberate Il Duce, Benito Mussolini, whom the Italian people had deposed and arrested in the wake of the Allied landings in Sicily during July and August. For weeks the Italians had been moving Mussolini from one obscure site to another in order to prevent just this kind of rescue operation. But somehow Skorzeny found the dictator's location. In a matter of hours his airborne troops swooped in on their DFS 230 gliders and defeated Mussolini's captors without firing a shot.

Whisked off to Vienna, Mussolini was named leader of the new Italian Social Republic, a German-dominated rump state desperate to hold off the Allied advance. In the midst of Germany's last offensive in the east, Operation Citadel, which had been halted by Soviet forces only weeks earlier at the battle of Kursk, the Mussolini Raid, codenamed Operation Oak, constituted one of the Third Reich's last public-relations victories.[240]

Nevertheless, the most remarkable aspect of the raid was not Operation Oak. It was Operation Mars, the intelligence operation that ostensibly located Mussolini. Evidence suggests that the information on Mussolini's whereabouts was pieced together by conventional intelligence operations aimed at breaking Allied radio codes. But Himmler and Schellenberg insisted they had garnered this information from an expert team of occultists assembled in a villa under SS administration.

Operation Mars was hardly the only time that astrologers, clairvoyants, or diviners would be recruited to help the regime. For four years after the Hess Action, the SS employed border scientists in military technology and research, seeking ways to improve morale, extract intelligence, and exert mind control.[241] Even the German Navy joined in, assembling a group of diviners and astrologers to locate Allied battleships.[242] In this final section, we will examine these two quintessential case studies of border science in military intelligence, concluding with some of the less systematic though equally interesting military applications of border science initiated by the war.

The Navy Pendulum Institute and Operation Mars

After World Ice Theory, no area of border science was deemed more valuable in the Third Reich than radiesthesia.[243] We will recall that many Nazi leaders, most notably Himmler and Hess, believed in the existence of cosmic forces or earth rays (radiation) that could be detected and harnessed with the proper training. Hitler had ordered one of Germany's most famous diviners to check the Reich Chancellery for malignant forms of the latter. Goebbels also hired dowsers like Kritzinger to assist with Nostradamus propaganda. Perhaps the strangest and most telling experiment in radiesthesia was initiated not by the Nazi Party, however, but by the German Navy.[244] By the summer of 1942 the British had begun to turn the tide in the battle of the Atlantic, sinking a much higher percentage of German U-boats. Their success had nothing to do with dowsing. To locate enemy submarines the British employed quite natural scientific methods, namely Radar (ASDIC) and Sonar. They were aided in these efforts by sophisticated code-breaking and the extensive use of American convoys.[245]

Among the German Navy officials who were puzzled about this sudden shift in the battle of the Atlantic was the U-boat captain Hans Roeder, a science expert in the Navy Patent Office. An amateur pendulum dowser himself, Roeder was convinced the British were employing such means to locate German ships. As a countermeasure, Roeder suggested that the navy begin employing border scientific methods.[246] Were Roeder operating in the Royal Navy, his suggestion to set up an officially sponsored Pendulum Institute would likely have been dismissed as outrageous. And yet Roeder was operating in the Third Reich, where many ranking party officials and military men were open to border scientific doctrines.[247]

According to the emigré rocket scientist Willy Ley, some German naval officers already accepted the bizarre 'hollow Earth theory', which posited that one could locate the British fleet through infrared rays 'because the curvature of the Earth would not obstruct observation'. A group of navy-affiliated scientists under the leadership of Dr Heinz Fischer, Ley reported, 'was sent out from Berlin to the Isle of Rügen to photograph the British fleet with infrared equipment at an upward angle of some forty-five degrees'.[248] Navy officers also conducted test experiments with Ludwig Straniak prior to the war.[249]

Given the context it comes as no surprise that, in September 1942, Roeder received approval from the Navy Intelligence Service (*Marine Nachrichten Dienst* or MND) for his Pendulum Institute. Its purpose was 'to pinpoint the position of enemy convoys at sea by means of pendulums and other supernatural devices, so that the German submarine flotillas could be certain of sinking them'.[250] As Rear Admiral Gerhard Wagner, Chief of the Navy's Operational Department, admitted, Roeder, 'the pendulum user, was well known to all of us. From the point of view of those days his work was not that unusual. After all, one was constantly thinking about new techniques, and if someone came and claimed to be able to achieve something by way of a certain method, it was a matter of course that he was given the opportunity'.[251]

Now that he had gained official approval and financing, Roeder set out convening a 'strange band' of psychics, pendulum users, Tattwa researchers, astrologers, astronomers, ballisticians, and mathematicians.[252] These individuals included the Luftwaffe astronomer/astrologer Wilhelm Hartmann, Wilhelm Wulff, and Straniak – the first dowser to claim he could teach lay people how to employ a pendulum to locate large metal objects hundreds of miles away.[253] Roeder also tapped the prominent astrologers Kritzinger and Krafft, the latter recruited directly from prison, where he had languished for a time since the Hess Aktion. Gerda Walther, a parapsychologist who weaved in and out of Heydrich's crosshairs over the years, was invited to join the group as well.[254] That the group included Fritz Quade and Konrad Schuppe from the German Society for Scientific Occultism (DGWO) further confirms the regime's desire to coordinate and exploit border scientific thinking. For while the DGWO's last remnants of independence had dissipated in the wake of the Hess Affair, its members' expertise in earth rays and divining rods became all the more interesting to the regime.[255]

The activities and location of the Pendulum Institute in Berlin were supposed to be secret. Within weeks of the department opening, however, it became widely known that the regime had enlisted the help of occultists in the war effort.[256] The primary method employed at the headquarters was radi-esthesia, meaning that a 'large map of the Atlantic was spread out horizontally, with a one-inch toy battleship as test object'. Then a 'pendulum, consisting of a cube of metal about one cubic centimetre and a short string, was swung above the battleship. If the pendulum reacted, it proved the presence of a true battle-ship at that location.'[257]

The institute employed a wide range of 'occult groups and individuals with different tasks and using different techniques'. Serious border scientists such as Roeder and Straniak insisted on the physical laws behind the pendulum, whereas less rigorous occultists such as Gerda Walther cited paranormal phenomena in explaining their results. Day after day dowsers were forced by the SS to stand 'with their arms stretched out across the nautical charts' just in case the pendulum made the slightest movement. In order to increase their likelihood of making predictions a number of clairvoyants, according to Wulff, were 'constantly in a trance'. Despite the chaotic nature of the proceedings, most participants attested to the regime's seriousness, including multiple tests to ensure their 'scientific' talents.[258]

According to a number of navy officers, the institute produced no mean-ingful results.[259] Nevertheless, the Pendulum Institute indicates that the Third Reich, fuelled by wartime necessity, had moved into a new, more open phase of border scientific experimentation. Certainly not all naval officers were 'driven by an esoteric belief in miracles'. It is noteworthy, however, that the 'Sideric Pendulum was deemed a possible practical-technological tool of warfare' in the first place. For well after the navy gave up on the Pendulum Institute, the SS and Nazi leadership made increasing efforts to master the technological 'founda-tions and possibilities' of radiesthesia.[260]

The search for Benito Mussolini is emblematic of these continuing efforts.[261] The inspiration for Operation Mars most likely grew out of the Pendulum Institute, which brought the SS into closer contact with a number of prominent border scientists, including Wilhelm Wulff. Himmler's masseur and confidant Felix Kersten claims to have facilitated Wulff's rise by soliciting a horoscope of Hitler, which was forwarded to Arthur Nebe and the Kripo police. It is more likely that Wulff's yeoman work for the Pendulum Institute brought him to the attention of Nebe, Schellenberg, and eventually Himmler.[262] Whatever the reason, on 28 July 1943 Himmler ordered the Gestapo to bring Wulff to Berlin. There he met Nebe, who instructed him as to the particulars of his mission: Mussolini had been kidnapped and Himmler wanted Wulff to locate il Duce by astrological means.[263]

Wulff was the first of many occultists contacted. A few days after Wulff's interview with Nebe, the seer Curt Münch reported being taken from Sachsenhausen to Berlin where he was asked to locate Mussolini.[264] Over the next few days nearly forty more representatives of the occult sciences were assembled in a comfortable villa in Wannsee, probably Nebe's International Criminal Police Headquarters. Upon arrival they demanded – and were proffered – copious amounts of food, alcohol, and cigarettes. Schellenberg would in fact complain that these 'séances cost us much money, as these "scientists" need of good food, drink and tobacco was quite enormous'.[265] Schellenberg's RSHA colleague, Wilhelm Höttl, was more sympathetic to their 'seemingly epicurean requests'. No wonder that the 'poor devils', having lived 'on the starvation rations of the concentration camps for years, exploited the opportunity to enjoy honeypots, cigarettes and alcohol'.[266]

All this food and drink did nothing to dull the preternatural senses of Wulff's border scientific colleagues. Wulff argued that his own calculations, which took most of August and early September to complete, were instrumental in locating Mussolini. So too did Münch, who claimed that the SS produced an ersatz pendulum and a map of Italy, on which Münch identified a 'dead spot' in the Abruzzo mountains.[267]

Most documentation indicates that it was the conventional intelligence of the SD and SS, assisted by the captain of a German seaplane squadron, that pieced together Mussolini's location.[268] Years later Höttl himself admitted that it was conventional intelligence that located il Duce. The whole operation, he suggested, had been organized to placate Himmler, whose belief in the occult sciences were well known.[269]

It is nonetheless interesting to note that Höttl's earliest memoir of the experience – written before the negative post-war connotation associated with the Nazi occult – claimed that the astrologers and dowsers had indeed been successful.[270] Equally significant is Schellenberg's account, which asserted that the astrologers and diviners somehow located Mussolini despite having 'no contact to the outside world'.[271] Skorzeny himself reported after the war that the SS had relied on 'seers and astrologers to glean Mussolini's whereabouts'.[272]

Such accounts indicate that many Nazis – and not only Himmler – took Operation Mars seriously. So does the fact that Himmler, Nebe, and Schellenberg extracted more than forty occultists from all over Germany, including the concentration camps, and moved them to a luxurious villa in Wannsee.[273] Himmler even followed through on his promise to grant occultists 'their freedom as well as one hundred thousand Reichsmarks' if were they successful.[274] When Münch submitted his petition for release from Sachsenhausen, the camp commander, no doubt nonplussed by the request, countered with the option of a cushier position as camp elder. The astrologer nevertheless insisted on his full release, citing his work on behalf of 'the liberation of Mussolini'. After the commander contacted the SS leadership, Münch was freed.[275] Wulff received amnesty as well. But the astrologer followed up with a request that the SS return the books and other occult materials the Gestapo had confiscated in the Hess Action more than two years before. In late 1943 Nebe ordered the return of Wulff's entire library. A few months later Wulff became Himmler's personal astrologer.[276]

The Military Applications of Border Science

Well before the Nazis took power, there was interest in miracle technologies and a faith-based conviction in the superiority of the German Army. *Völkisch*-esotericists and nationalist army officers, fantasy writers, and right-wing politicians shared a quasi-religious belief in the German military's efficacy and invincibility.[277] Invoking the mythical struggle between Thor and the Nibelungen, Germans and Jews, Aryan civilization and Bolshevism, a mélange of militarism and apocalyptic mysticism was adopted by *völkisch* nationalists in the interwar period. To help civilians 'share the soldier's quasi-religious experiences of transcendence and eternity',[278] erstwhile combatants furthermore interpreted 'battlefield bloodshed as a form of holy communion that had transformed them into the apostles of "the nation"'.[279]

Without an abiding faith in Ur-Germanic religion and folklore, argued the SS folklorist Richard Wolfram, 'what could be given as a *Weltanschaaung* to the soldiers in the trenches'.[280] Many Nazis had appropriated the Artamanen concept of 'warrior peasants', for example, who would occupy the East through violence.[281] The SS took the Artamenen model of a black-clad knightly elite fighting in the name of 'death and the devil' as inspiration.[282] The SS death's head, skull, and crossbones were inspired by the wild hunters who garnered so much attention from Nazi folklorists.[283] The Nazis insisted on the 'regenerative and creative powers of an expressly masculine and unflinchingly heroic death', apotheosizing the Norse berserker as a hero and those who died, including women, as warriors in Valhalla.[284] As a subordinate in the Amt Rosenberg wrote in a dissertation on the German werewolf, Odin's berserker warriors frequently turned into wild dogs or wolves to devour their prey.[285] This idea of Odin's berserkers was supplemented by Hermann Löns' concept of partisan werewolves, warrior peasants who emerged to defend their Heimat with ferocity in times of war.[286]

Ario-Germanic fantasies of wild hunters, werewolves, and berserker heroes were supplemented by Indo-Aryan martial traditions. Prominent among these was the idea of the Kshatriya warrior caste, drawn from the Hindu Vedas. From the late nineteenth century, German Indologists had insisted on the ethnocultural parallels between ancient German warrior castes and the Vedic Kshatriya, analysing the epic Hindu Gita and Nordic Edda for similarities.[287] Nazi Indologists such as Hauer and Wüst took up these arguments in the Third Reich. In his 1939 book *The Aryan Warrior God*, Hauer portrayed the Vedic god Indra as a model for Nazi soldiers, embodying 'discipline, control of feelings, readiness to sacrifice, obedience'. Hauer even represented Indra with red hair and 'a lightning sling in his hand' in order to claim that this 'divine archetype of the ur-Aryan religion [had] many common characteristics with the Germanic gods Thor and Odin/Wotan'.[288]

Elsewhere Hauer construed the yogi as a warrior ('warrior yogi') and Buddha as a 'passive hero' who operated through the 'Aryan discipline of the spirit'.[289] Wüst likewise emphasized the 'solar', 'cosmic', and 'microcosmic' powers of the Buddhist Chakravartin, or 'sacral world ruler', whom Hitler represented as 'warrior master'.[290] The SS-affiliated religious theorist Friedrich Hielscher agreed that Buddha was not a pacifist but a 'wise warrior'. 'If militarism and wisdom are contradictions, if warriors stand below the wise,' Hielscher reasoned, 'then reality cannot perfect itself, for it is militarist'.[291]

Picking up on this idea of the 'warrior yogi', the Reichsführer promoted Ernst Schäfer's film *Secret Tibet* as a way of encouraging martial values and rituals across the SS and the Wehrmacht. Schäfer interpreted the Tibetan Buddhist lamas, 'magic, incantation, and meditation', as well as 'ritual dances for the invocation of the war gods', as a model of education for the German troops.[292] Himmler gave a propaganda speech in which he cited the 'military tradition of the lamas' in order to inspire German morale and willingness to sacrifice.[293] To spread Indo-Aryan martial values within the SS Himmler further advocated regular meditation sessions according to 'Indian religious leaders'.[294] He also rationalized the Night of the Long Knives and other terrible SS crimes by citing 'the sacralization of terror' embodied in the Kshatriya code and *Bhagavad Gita*.[295]

Such fantasies about resuscitating an Indo-Aryan martial spirit extended to Persia and the Middle East. Citing the Iranian doctrine of Mithra, the fascist mystic Julius Evola supplemented the SS's bizarre theories on the Kshatriya warrior caste and Buddha as a warrior yogi with the idea of 'the warrior without sleep' who leads his allies against the 'satanic enemies of the Aryans'. Evola envisioned a small elite of Indo-Aryan heroes, similar to the SS, who could wage a

'Holy War' against lesser races. This heroic fighting spirit might be achieved through 'objective spiritual techniques' that tapped into one's 'divine potency'.[296] To a volunteer division of Muslims within the Waffen-SS, Himmler likewise praised Islam as 'a religion that is both practical and appealing to soldiers', for it 'promises them heaven if they have fought and fallen in battle'.[297] In Himmler's reading of Islamic 'traditions and myths' Hitler was 'an avenging prophet' who would help liberate the Arabs from the imperialist British and Jews.[298]

Meanwhile Hitler and Himmler extolled the Japanese as a warrior race, with Himmler speculating that the SS 'should become the German samurai'.[299] Excerpts from the Reichsführer's glowing foreword to Heinz Corazza's book *The Samurai: Honourable and Loyal Imperial Knights* (1937) were published in the SS paper, *Die Schwarze Korps*.[300] Wüst also compared the martial traditions of the samurai to the Teutonic knights, which needed to be resuscitated.[301] Wartime publications made similar arguments about the Japanese people's 'courageous willingness to sacrifice one's life' embedded in the 'deeper' religious feeling of 'Zen education'.[302] As one SD report put it, the situation in Japan, in which 'life, politics, and military engagement' are based on 'a non-Christian religious-ideological foundation', provided a model for the German people.[303] Unfortunately, the SD worried that constant celebration of Japanese racial and warrior virtues in the press and propaganda was leading to a German 'inferiority complex'.[304]

These Indo-Aryan fantasies had military consequences. The SS put together an Indian legion of putatively Aryan soldiers drawn from the subcontinent.[305] Himmler wanted to create an SS division of Bosnian Muslims as well, seeking to enlist additional Muslim soldiers from across Europe and the Middle East.[306] As many as 100,000 'Turkestaner' were recruited for a 'Turkestan Legion' under the 'flag of Islam'.[307] Bruno Beger also convinced Himmler to create a cavalry division of Mongolian Kalmyen because they were putatively Indo-Aryans who worshipped the Dalai Lama.[308]

Ariosophists such as Guido von List, Lanz von Liebenfels, and Rudolf Gorsleben had believed that the ancient Aryans possessed superhuman mental and physical abilities, which might be recovered by studying ancient texts and experimenting with their rituals.[309] No surprise that the SS researchers Günther Kirchoff and Karl Wiligut, both schooled in ariosophic traditions, insisted that they might harness 'streams of power' located in the Ur-Aryan 'Arcto-Atlanticist' region between Greenland and the North Pole.[310] Himmler instructed Wulff to experiment with 'human wave' methods drawn from Indo-Aryan esotericism as well.[311]

As the Ahnenerbe's focus shifted toward 'military science' in the late 1930s, SS border scientists began to explore new technologies.[312] Himmler instructed Wüst, for example, to 'research where in all of North-Germanic Aryan culture the concept of the lightning flash, the thunderbolt, Thor's hammer, or the hammer thrown or flying through the air appears. Also, where there are sculptures of a god holding an axe and appearing in a flash of lightning.'[313] The Reichsführer requested all such evidence, 'whether in pictures, sculpture, writing or legend', because he was convinced that it represented not 'natural thunder and lightning [but] an earlier, highly developed weapon' possessed by the 'Aesir, the gods, and presuming an extraordinary understanding of electricity'.[314]

Himmler further recommended sending the border scientist, Ludwig Ferdinand Clauss, to collaborate with Beger in conducting 'phenomenological' research on the 'racial soul of Central Asians'.[315] Of particular interest to Beger and Clauss was the difference 'in the actions of races in battle', including the SS-sponsored Bosnian Muslim divisions, and what practical consequences that might have in the struggle against an opponent of foreign race.[316] For similar reasons the esotericist Dr Kurt Wessely was tasked with examining 'so-called military borders' and motivating partisan forces.[317]

The natural outgrowth of the Ahnenerbe's growing investment in military science was the Institute for Military Scientific Practical Research (*Institut für Wehrwissenschaftliche Zweckforschung* or IWZ).[318] Directed by Wolfram Sievers, head of the Ahnenerbe, the IWZ was founded in the summer of 1942 and funded by Oswald Pohl, head of the concentration-camp system. It brought together many 'scientific' institutes and some branches of the military for the express purpose of conducting practical research helpful to the war effort.[319] Wüst himself worked with the Military Humanities Unit (*Kriegseinsatz der Geisteswissenschaften*), a complement to the IWZ, to apply humanities research in ideological warfare.[320] After Operation Mars, Wulff found himself employed by the IWZ-affiliated Institute for Occult Warfare, where Hartmann, Straniak, Gutberlet, and others worked on military applications of border science.[321]

In concert with Franz Alfred Six's Ideological Research Division, Wulff and his colleagues explored brainwashing techniques and psychic warfare.[322] Another project sought to determine whether there was an astrological way to calculate the weather (a question that the SS had World Ice Theorists explore as well).[323] The IWZ also sponsored projects seeking practical military applications of the dowsing rod.[324] Finally, there were divisions within the Ahnenerbe, with links to the IWZ, that dealt with 'military geology' and human experiments (see Chapter Eight).[325]

The Nazi proclivity for border scientific experimentation in military matters did not begin or end with the IWZ.[326] In the summer of 1940 Hans Bender began collaborating with Hermann Göring's cousin, the prominent psychologist Matthias Göring, in employing (para)psychological techniques in military training.[327] Bender also worked with the regime on experiments testing the validity of graphology. As Bender enthused in early August 1940, 'it was exciting that these experiments were carried out and will continue to be carried out with the help of a Reich administrative office'.[328]

Eventually, Bender came into contact with members of the Officer Corps and navy officials associated with the Pendulum Institute. According to him, the experiments had failed because they employed 'people who had not been properly vetted'.[329] In order to avoid these problems in future pendulum experiments, Bender's SS sponsor Friedrich Spieser suggested that it 'might be practical to ask the SS for the instruments that were commandeered by the SS [including] a great collection of divining rods in various form named after elements; hence apparatuses whose economic utility it seems worth investigating'.[330] With these experiments in mind, Spieser urged Bender to travel to Berlin as soon as possible, together with Ernst Anrich, Dean of the Humanities at the University of Strasbourg. There, Spieser suggested, Bender might brief 'the responsible SS-men in the main office (Spengler, Brandt usw.) in confidence about our experiments, and do everything possible to obtain what we need for free research'.[331] Not only did Bender receive SS support as a result, but his institute subsequently developed close ties to notorious Nazi doctors with border scientific proclivities, including Sigmund Rascher and the Reich University's president, August Hirt.[332]

Before concluding, it is important to touch on Hitler's own investment in supernaturally inspired military science. The concept of the Thule, the icy homeland of Nordic Atlanteans, persisted in Hitler's supernatural imaginary. In August 1942 he personally christened a new tank regiment, the 'Thule', within the SS-Death's Head Division and asked that a 'celebratory naming ceremony' should follow.[333] Himmler ordered the division to be given 6,000 new SS volunteers in preparation for brutal fighting on the Eastern Front over the winter of 1942–3.[334] Hitler's strategic choice of military headquarters, 'The Wolf's Lair', may have been based on the 'sacred geography' promoted by Josef Heinsch, Wilhelm Teudt, and other Nazi geomancers.[335]

Finally, we cannot ignore the possibility that World Ice Theory influenced major military decisions and operations.[336] Hitler seemingly believed that Operation Barbarossa had a better chance of success because World Ice Theorists in Himmler's meteorological institute had predicted a mild winter. Based on *Welteislehre*, Hitler and Himmler also conjectured that Nordic soldiers were better prepared than Slavs for fighting in cold weather and consequently did not equip them properly for war on the Eastern Front, resulting, for example, in the terrible loss of life at Stalingrad.[337]

Indeed, 'Hitler's grotesquely justified commitment to World Ice Theory', writes Christina Wessely, indicates the border science's 'unbroken potential to combine random, everyday experiences with supercharged, prognistication-prone intuition and label it scientific method'.[338] Dangerous as these border scientific methods might have been in influencing Nazi foreign policy and military science, they proved all the more monstrous when it came to questions of race, space, and eugenics.

***

As the stakes rose during the Second World War, so too did the Third Reich's investment in border science. The Nazi obsession with folklore and border scientific conceptions of geopolitics constituted an important prelude to wartime expansion, directed toward the 'extremely important midpoints of the Aryan-Nordic belt of cultures that span the entire earth'.[339] Hitler himself took a magical approach to wartime operations. In attracting popular support and making decisions, he relied at least as much on intuition and faith as he did on a practical assessment of the military circumstances, secure in his belief that 'he merely had to will what he wanted to happen and it would happen'.[340]

The centrality of border science in propaganda and intelligence gathering is equally remarkable. From Krafft and Kritzinger's work for Goebbels to Wulff's efforts in the Navy Pendulum Insitute, border scientists were extremely active during the war. Due to his occult talents, Wulff went from being imprisoned in the summer of 1941 to becoming personal advisor to the second most powerful Nazi in the Third Reich.[341] That Himmler and Schellenberg wined and dined three dozen occultists gathered in the Berlin suburb of Wannsee, only streets away from the villa in which their colleagues Heydrich and Adolf Eichmann planned the Holocaust, is further evidence that the trajectory of occultism and border science in the Third Reich was in many ways the opposite of that experienced by Jews, gypsies, or the disabled.[342]

Some scholars have viewed this 'zig-zag' course in the Third Reich's attitude toward 'occult-scientific practices, doctrines and research projects' as a blatant contradiction, defined by 'ambiguities and duplicities'. The wartime investment in border science, however, was hardly contradictory. Nor was it simply a matter of the Nazis being flexible, as one scholar puts it, in 'balancing their practical military objectives with their putatively anti-occultist ideological convictions'.[343]

To the contrary, the Third Reich's wartime exploitation of folklore and border scientific doctrines epitomizes a pattern we have seen from the early days of the movement: criticizing sectarian tendencies deemed ideologically untenable while selectively embracing border scientific doctrines with long traditions in *völkisch*-esoteric circles – especially when these doctrines proved politically or ideologically advantageous.[344] In short, so long as 'their politics or practices did not all too blatantly contradict official National Socialist ideology', occultists could find opportunities to collaborate with the Third Reich.[345] As we shall see in the last two chapters, these border scientific practices would continue, helping to define both Nazi racial policies and the desperate pursuit of miracle weapons and technologies during the final years of the war.[346]

MONSTROUS SCIENCE
Racial Resettlement, Human Experiments, and the Holocaust

'Occultists rightly feel drawn towards childishly monstrous scientific fantasies.'

Theodor Adorno, 'Theses Against Occultism', *Minima Moralia* (1951)[1]

'Since [the Jew] himself never cultivates the soil but regards it only as a property to be exploited ... His blood-sucking tyranny becomes so great that excesses against him occur ... The end is not only the end of the freedom of the peoples oppressed by the Jew, but also the end of this parasite upon the nations. After the death of his victim, the vampire sooner or later dies too.'

Adolf Hitler, *Mein Kampf* (1925)[2]

The biologist Hanns Rascher was fascinated by the scientific applications of occultism. After studying theosophy and anthroposophy before the First World War, he developed an expertise in occult physiology, natural healing methods, and holistic medicine. While studying homoeopathy after the war, Rascher met the Thule Society's co-founder, Rudolf von Sebottendorff, with whom he discussed ways of promoting border scientific ideas among the German public. In 1931, Rascher joined the NSDAP and subsequently worked to sponsor Rudolf Steiner's teachings, including natural healing and biodynamic agriculture, in the Third Reich.[3]

An interest in holism, natural healing, and alternative spirituality spanned the Weimar political spectrum, yet Rascher's border scientific theories were far from innocuous. As we shall see, they helped to inspire the racial hygienic practices of a 'regime that murdered millions'.[4] There is a more direct link between Hanns Rascher and the victims of Nazism, however: his son, the SS doctor

Sigmund Rascher. Rascher the younger became one of Himmler's most noto-rious acolytes, conducting appalling human experiments at Dachau – the same place that concentration-camp prisoners experimented with his father's teach-ings to improve German peasant farming in the East.

The Raschers epitomize the border scientific nexus between supernatural thinking and Nazi racial science, which together produced some of the worst crimes of the twentieth century. This is not to deny Nazi Germany's recourse to eminently modern, technocratic means to eliminate 'life unworthy of life' or commit mass murder.[5] Nor is our emphasis on supernatural thinking incompatible with arguments that highlight the inherent irrationality of modernity. Nazi eugenical thinking was certainly part of a broader, European project to reshape the world through applied biology, capitalism, and coloni-alism.

Nevertheless, a general European penchant for biopolitical rhetoric and imperialism cannot explain the extreme nature and unprecedented scope of Nazi racial policies.[6] We still need to understand how 'vicious little social programs of dubious scientific value' in Britain or the United States 'became elevated to the level of literally *cosmic* importance in Nazi Germany'.[7] To understand the divergence of Nazi policies from the already fraught European norm, the 'cranky theories, superstitions and occult flummery of the SS need to be taken seriously'.[8] The Third Reich's crimes took on monumental dimensions because the Nazis drew both on border scientific theories peculiar to the Austro-German supernatural imaginary *as well as* a broader European mix of eugenics, racism, and colonialism.[9] This chapter examines the role of supernatural thinking in facilitating the Third Reich's monstrous project of racial resettlement, human experimentation, and Jewish genocide.

Border Science, War, and Racial Resettlement

In the introduction to his 1943 book *Indogermanisches Bekenntnis (Indo-Germanic Confessions)*, Walter Wüst touched on the importance of the ancient Germanic site of Detmold, a place of religio-racial transcendence, but also a 'shocking example' of Germany being divided and subjugated for centuries by 'the hatred of the alien race'.[10] Just as the Judeified Vatican had once attempted to extirpate the 'Germanic-Nordic' community represented by Detmold, the Second World War constituted another 'exterminatory attack of racially alien hate against the foundation' of Germanness.[11] In reviving the medieval tradi-tion of Teutonic knights flooding east, the Third Reich could reclaim the 'fundamental building blocks' of German race 'anchored in culture and history' and secure a return of its 'heroic blood'.[12]

Through the lens of the supernatural imaginary, Wüst and his Nazi colleagues funnelled a 'gooey fusion of religion, worldview, art, architecture, music, sculpture, poetics, sagas, ethnology, Indology, orientalism, and just about every other humanistic discipline' into their justifications for racial expansion and resettlement.[13] Before the war, folklore and mythology were used by Wüst and others for the mythical demonization of foreign and domestic enemies.[14] After 1939 these theoretical conceptions of race war, mass violence, and ethnic cleansing became reality.[15] As the war unfolded, millions of German soldiers 'were reconceived as instruments of colonization, through which foreign lands would be remade as homeland, or Heimat'. This 'reconfiguration of space had as its direct counterpart the simultaneous destruction of Jews, Poles, and other racial outsiders'.[16]

Because the Second World War was, in the Nazi mind, a colonial war, at least on the Eastern Front, the Nazis could legitimize techniques, as George Steinmetz reminds us, that would be disdained in 'civilized' warfare.[17] In comparison to European colonial policies in Africa or Asia, Nazi empire-building in eastern Europe was both more focused on biopolitical engineering inspired by border scientific racial theories and more explicitly motivated by fantasies of recovering a lost Indo-Aryan utopia.[18] If the Nazi imperial project incorporated European-wide colonial practices, these were informed and radicalized by supernatural conceptions of race and space drawn from folklore, border science, and *völkisch* esotericism.[19]

Blood, Soil, and Resettlement Fantasies before 1939

Friedrich Ratzel, Gustaf Kossina, and Alfred Ploetz; Hans Günther, Fritz Lenz, and Jakob Wilhelm Hauer – these early twentieth-century doyens of race and space produced an entire body of blood-and-soil theories that were assimilated by the *völkisch* right during the interwar period.[20] By the 1930s the focus of these individuals on racial hygiene and the Germanic past fed straight into the conceptualization of blood, soil, and living space propounded by Darré, Himmler, and other Nazi leaders; this included the 'idea that ancient Germanic settlements in eastern Europe validated German claims for sovereignty over Slav-populated regions'.[21]

In a 1937 speech to the SS entitled 'The SS as Anti-Bolshevistic Battle Organization', Himmler laid out his case. Based on ancient wisdom and teachings, he began, the 'German people were convinced by the divine order of this entire earth, the entire plant and animal world ... [that] blood is regarded as an obligation as a sacred legacy'. A 'race and a people have eternal life'.[22] The 'whence and whereto of our existence cannot stop with Germanic sources', Himmler argued elsewhere, 'but must reach backward in time to the original connection of all peoples of Nordic blood within the broad Indo-Germanic culture'.[23]

The research methods articulated here correspond to Himmler's 'peculiar view of Germanic history ... [which] was not to be differentiated on the basis of myth or reality'.[24] His ideology, observes Peter Longerich, was a 'construct of the imagination dependent on a capriciously applied concept of race, and the hated enemies ... [in the East] described so imprecisely ... they were practically interchangeable and could be blamed for anything'.[25] No wonder that scholars have identified parallels between the SS preoccupation with witches and Nazi attitudes toward policing race and space in the East.[26]

Esoteric racial theories served to confirm that the Third Reich was entitled to (re)construct an 'Indo-Aryan' Empire in eastern Europe and subjugate or eliminate its peoples.[27] After resettling ethnic Germans, Himmler was determined to recover any remaining 'superhuman' blood from mixed-race peoples. The rest of the population would be left to 'vegetate in a primitive way of life'.[28] To be sure, völkisch folklorists, archaeologists, and historians employed such arguments to justify reintegrating ethnic German populations in the Ostmark (Austria) and Bohemia as well as in Alsace and the Low Countries.[29] Still, the primary focus was always on the East, where peasant farmers would settle after a cull of the local Slavic and Jewish populations.[30]

The SS Race and Settlement Main Office (RuSHA), first led by Darré, became the centrepiece of this racial and imperial mission.[31] As members of the Artamanen in the 1920s, Himmler and Darré had developed a template for 'settler schools' based on blood-and-soil mythology.[32] After 1933, they built a model SS colony east of Berlin, where inhabitants were encouraged to hold pagan winter and summer solstice celebrations modelled on the Artamanen. The Ahnenerbe also wanted to bring back ancient Germanic building styles and language – even prehistoric breeds of animals (!). In turn periodicals such as the Völkischer Beobachter and Germania publicized this border scientific 'research' to the German public.[33] Once resettled, these so-called 'armed farmers' (Wehrbauern) would live in medieval-style houses, heal the sick with natural remedies, and recreate an ancient Germanic pagan culture and religion.[34]

The utopian promotion of German settlement, however, was merely the positive foil to the 'almost overwhelming negativity of National Socialist thought ... demonizing and extermination'.[35] Hence the SS planned to establish 'outposts' or armed peasants, 'border fighters' in the spirit of the Artamanen, who would lead the 'border struggle against other races' in order to create new living space.[36] These peasants could only continue their farming in a more 'German' setting by subordinating or eliminating Poles and Jews.[37]

Some blood-and-soil activists, such as Darré, were more focused on restructuring society through 'an organic link between soil and the Volk' than preoccupied by imperial expansion. But Himmler was very much a *völkisch* imperialist, agreeing with Hitler that their goal was a racially pure empire devoid of 'alien and treacherous elements'.[38] Himmler and the young anthropologist Bruno Beger were convinced that an admixture of Mongol and Slavic blood was what made the Bolsheviks so dangerous.[39]

Wüst too characterized the history of the Germanic race and religion as one of warding off 'genocidal efforts' by foreigners, which would in his mind be the 'basis of the next war'.[40] According to Wüst, Indo-Germans had the historical duty to 'eliminate everything ill and alien to the *völkisch* community with deadly hatred'.[41] Echoing the Italian fascist mystic Julius Evola,[42] Wüst (and Hauer) invoked an 'arsenal of Indian Gods and Demons' in order to propagate an imperialist ideology fuelled by 'racist blood mysticism'.[43] The coming battle would be a continuation of the millennia-long struggle between the Aryan light races and monstrous 'lower racial forms' such as Neanderthals, Africans, and Jews, who propagated 'fanatical persecution' (*Verfolgungswahn*) and the 'unleashing of demonism'.[44] Propelled by these 'historical legends', the Nazi imagination gave birth to 'wolves, murderers, and all kinds of monsters' that peopled the wild Bolshevik East.[45]

Folklore and border science even suggested the methods and rationale for eliminating the racial other. 'It is the burden of a great man,' Himmler argued, 'that he must step over corpses in order to create new life . . . the space must be free of weeds, or nothing can grow on it.' 'A ruling people,' he added, 'must be in the situation to eliminate from the community a human being who is harmful for the community without Christian mercy.'[46] We will recall that Himmler cited the salvific nature of the Kshatriya warrior caste's willingness to sacrifice others for a greater purpose.[47] In order to protect Germany's racial core and promote its increased purity, Himmler argued, the SD and Gestapo need not worry about being loved by the Germans, nor even being feared by them. Their only purpose was to embody 'a merciless executioner's sword' against Jewish-Bolshevism in order to give the German people 'eternal life'.[48] For Himmler, validating racial resettlement and murder 'with fairy tales' and glorifying 'gruesome death as honourable' conformed with the 'elite consciousness of the SS'.[49]

The purpose of the SS for Himmler had always been to carry out this mission, to prove the superiority of 'Aryan humanity' and the 'intellectual world domination of Aryan Germanness' as a precondition for racial resettlement and ethnic cleansing in the East.[50] In these settlement fantasies the character Hagen from the Nibelungen mythology became a hero who may have 'operated from inhuman motives, but as executioner of the law of honour and loyalty' he took a 'heinous deed on himself'.[51] Both Himmler and Rosenberg invoked the ravages that the Teutonic Knights had visited on local Slavic and Jewish populations. In their religio-racial mission to settle the eastern territories, the Nazis would once again ride eastwards as dark knights confident in their 'invinci-bility'.[52] The Führer too was certain that might and divine right justified the 'ice-cold decisions' that would 'probably be condemned by the human rights currently in practice'.[53]

The Ahnenerbe and Amt Rosenberg consequently recruited border scien-tists that 'subordinated their research methods, topics, disciplines, and affilia-tions' to battle against the racial enemy.[54] Joseph Otto Plassmann, editor of *Germania*, employed his role as chief Ahnenerbe historian to advocate a range of policies justifying race and conquest, advocating a war of 'struggle, death, and blood' against 'Jewish instrument peddlers'.[55]

Meanwhile the political scientist Franz Six and historian Günther Franz parlayed their witchcraft investigations into opposition research on Jews, Communists, and Freemasons.[56] Through these efforts virtually all scientific disciplines – biology and anthropology, history and political science, even 'Indo-Germanic-Aryan language studies' – become camouflage for racial reset-tlement and mass murder.[57]

Racial Resettlement after 1939

This mostly theoretical relationship between border science and racial empire became real in September 1939.[58] The German invasion of Poland 'formed a turning point in mentalities of death,' observes Monica Black, as many existing racist and imperialist ideas 'took on new and more urgent meaning'.[59] The 'aggressive war of conquest was transfigured; Germans set forth to win new land for light and life in the land of the demons [*Utgard*], the dark Empire of Bolshevism and world Jewry'.[60] Nearly every Nazi leader, from Rosenberg and Darré to Göring and Hans Frank, joined in this border scientific project to remake race and space in the East. And yet Himmler and the SS's central role in policing and resettlement, not to mention racial border science, gave them pride of place.[61]

As early as October 1939 Himmler's subordinate, the classical archaeologist Hans Schleif, became trustee for all SS-Ahnenerbe activities in Poland. In this capacity he worked with Göring's Main Trustee Office (*Haupttreuhandstelle Ost* or HTO) to obtain control over Polish and Jewish property. In November, Himmler, as Reich Commisar for Securing German Nationality (*Reichskommissar für die Festigung deutschen Volkstums* or RKF), began to take a personal role in the process. In December he instructed the Ahnenerbe to plunder private houses as well as Polish and Jewish museums and archives in search of histor-ical and prehistoric sources that were important for 'cultural historical purposes', and to reconstruct the Germans' role in the 'historical, cultural, and economic build-up of the country'.[62]

Folklore and border science now merged seamlessly with Nazi policies of race and resettlement.[63] The Nazi professor of Nordic religion and folklore, Bernhard Kummer, for example, gave a series of lectures in 1940 that made use of an old German folk song used by the Artamanen to sponsor eastern colonization.[64] Beger was charged with studying the 'life of the soul of the Central Asian race' in order to differentiate 'the borders of Germanic essence . . . thereby to purify' the Aryans of Central Asian elements.[65] And Himmler named the folklorist and historian, Heinrich Harmjanz, General Trustee in 'recording and processing the entire material heritage of all resettled ethnic Germans . . . [and] all prehistoric and early historic and ethnographic issues in the new East'.[66]

In a September 1942 speech to the SS, Himmler explained that the great Central Asian leaders such as Atilla, Genghis Khan, Tamerlane, and Stalin were produced by mixing lost traces of Nordic blood with Turkic and Asiatic blood. This racial mixture made Central Asian peoples both exceedingly powerful and dangerous. In order to reclaim the 'good blood' and prevent Europe being overrun by Asiatics, Himmler concluded, these mixed-race 'subhumans' needed to be destroyed.[67] Every individual had to go through racial assessment to prevent new 'mongrel types from emerging in the territories that are to be newly settled'.[68]

One of the focal points for this border scientific policy of racial resettlement was the Polish Wartheland (Wolhynia), home of the prized spearhead of Kovel (discussed in Chapter Seven). As part of the process of building a model colony in German-occupied Poland, the Nazi classicist Hans Schleif had wagons of Germanic artefacts confiscated from Jews and Poles and shipped to Wolhynia.[69] Wolfgang Krause, head of the Ahnenerbe's 'Rune' division, simultaneously carried out excavations of prehistoric sites in the region. Such archaeological efforts would help justify German resettlement as well as the relocation – and eventual mass murder – of Poles and Jews.[70]

Shortly after the invasion of Poland, none other than the *völkisch* folklorist Alfred Karasek was appointed chief of the 'Resettlement Kommando Wolhynien'. The Kommando worked with the Wehrmacht and *Volksdeutsche Mittelstelle* in overseeing the resettlement of 34,000 ethnic Germans (*Volksdeutschen*) to the Wartheland. In August 1941, as the SS Einsatzgruppen ramped up their murder of eastern European Jews, Karasek was assigned to the SS Death's Head unit *Oranienburg* in the Ukraine. There he organized the resettlement of another 27,000 Bessarabian Germans. Shortly afterwards Karasek was named 'Special Leader Z' of the *Sonderkommando Künsberg* under Army Group Middle, becoming more directly engaged in the process of resettlement. Karasek next took a position in the Crimea as SS Sonderführer with a rank of Untersturmführer in the Waffen-SS. In 1942 he was appointed 'Expert for Landeskunde' with Einsatzgruppen B at Stalingrad. While presiding over the fate of tens of thousands of ethnic Germans (and by extension Jews and Poles), Karasek still found the time to plunder archives, libraries, and museums across the Ukraine – until finally forced to retreat from Stalingrad with the rest of Einsatzgruppen B in October 1942.[71]

Lutz Mackensen, Professor of German Studies at the new Reich University of the region, employed folk tales of the living dead, revenants, and spirits as evidence for the Germanic nature of the Wartheland.[72] Germans on the borders of the Reich were preoccupied by the idea of the 'wild hunt', Mackensen contended, because they recalled a time when Germans were surrounded by alien Slavs against whom these 'wild riders', residing in the surrounding mountains, might defend them.[73] For Mackensen the German invasion – and resettlement of Poles, Jews, and Germans – represented both a physical and spiritual homecoming, like dead spirits returning from their mountain hiding places to admonish Germans not to forget their heritage.[74] Mackensen was an expert in folklore and supernatural speculation, not biology or genetics. But he was nonetheless charged by the SD with evaluating refugees arriving from the Baltic, Bessarabia, and Bukovina to determine whether they might provide a 'new settler racial branch' for 'borderland peasantry'.[75]

This pattern of folklorists and border scientists taking active roles in the process of plunder, colonization, and racial resettlement occurred throughout Europe.[76] In direct contradiction of the Hague conventions, Sievers and the Waffen-SS archaeologist, Herbert Jankuhn, worked with the SD Sonderkommando to have dozens of crates of historical, ethnological, and religious materials confiscated from the Caucasus, Baltic countries, and southern Russia. Jankuhn used the materials to back up his own thesis about the historically Germanic nature of these territories.[77] In southeastern Europe the repression and elimination of racial inferiors went hand in hand with a battle to plunder putatively Germanic artefacts and conduct border scientific research on people and settlements.[78] In northern Europe the SS and Ahnenerbe carried out these efforts under the imprimatur of the Germanic Scientific Unit (*Germanische Wissenschaftseinsatz* or GWE), tasked with developing a Greater Space policy (*Grossraumpolitik*) in Scandinavia and the Low Countries.[79]

Through the GWE, Himmler formalized the cooperation between the Military and Waffen-SS service and the Ahnenerbe, attaching SS border scientists and folklore experts to commandos in the field.[80] In February 1942, for example, the SS-Oberscharführer, RMVP propagandist, and esotericist Dr Kurt Wessely was charged with studying 'so-called military borders' to determine the extent of 'central European German living space'.[81] Beger, inspired by his studies of Tibetan skeletons, accompanied the Wehrmacht in order to assess which 'Nordic types' among the Soviet population to Germanize and which to send to Siberia.[82] Odilo Globocnik, the SS leader in charge of the Final Solution ('Operation Reinhard') across much of eastern Europe, employed the supernatural code name 'Werewolf' for his own racial resettlement operations aimed at reintroducing 'the *Volksdeutsche* and people of German racial origin'.[83] Finally, Rudolf Levin and Günther Franz of the infamous Witch Division cited the lessons of their 'opposition research' on Jews and the Catholic Church in justifying clearing and purifying a Greater Germanic Space.[84]

The faith-based science of race and space facilitated the recruitment of putative Indo-Aryans, such as Balts, Indians, and even Arabs, into mobile killing units and the Waffen-SS. In this way Nazi border science buttressed the cynical necessities of SS-commandos in the field, who needed non-Germans for military, administrative, and ethnic-cleansing purposes.[85] Folklore researchers and border scientists who couldn't take direct part in the process of racial resettlement or military operations due to age or injury joined the War Division of the Humanities, Indo-Germanic Culture and Intellectual History. The division organized local folk music and festivals in order to encourage the development of ethnic German racial identity once the Jews and Slavs had been 'evacuated'.[86] Obviously, in the words of Michael Kater, these efforts had less to do with authentic scientific research than the implementation of 'practical measures in the sphere of ethnic policy'.[87]

The border scientific foundations of racial resettlement and eastern colonization are also evident in the implementation of biodynamical agricultural methods (*Biodynamische Wirtschaftsweise* or BDW) after September 1939. From the outbreak of the war, Himmler enlisted biodynamic growers to collaborate with the SS on 'various projects, including plans for agricultural settlement and colonization in the occupied East'.[88] A few weeks after the invasion of Poland, Himmler charged the SS economics czar Oswald Pohl and Günther Pancke, Darré's replacement as head of the RuSHA, with thinking about reshaping the East 'along organic lines'. Slavic populations would be removed in favour of 'ethnic German farmers' who would build an 'agrarian empire' fuelled by biodynamic plantations.[89] Hess, Darré, Rosenberg, and Ley visited Erhard Bartsch's biodynamic farm in Marienhöhe, indicating widespread enthusiasm for Pohl and Pancke's project.[90]

Encouraged by these experiments, Himmler, Hess, Darré, Pancke, and Pohl called independently for greater state investment in BDW to help foster settlements of German 'soldier-farmers' in the East.[91] In October 1939, only weeks into the invasion or Poland, the SS 'requisitioned a large estate in the occupied province of Posen to turn it into an agricultural training facility based on biodynamic principles, with the active cooperation of the Reich League for Biodynamic Agriculture'.[92] Sponsored by the German Research

Facility for Food and Nutrition (*Deutsche Versuchsanstalt für Ernährung und Verpflegung* or DVA), Pancke, Pohl, and Hans Merkel established additional biodynamic plantations across the eastern territories as well as Dachau, Ravensbrück, and Auschwitz concentration camps. Many were staffed by anthroposophists.[93]

To be sure, Heydrich and Bormann initially protested over the use of known occultists at the core of the SS racial, imperial, and economic system: the concentration camps. But Pohl, who was in charge of the camps, and Heinrich Vogel, the head of the DVA's agricultural section, prevailed. In July 1941, Heydrich acquiesced to the policy of permitting former members of the Reich League for Biodynamic Agriculture to sponsor their teachings across the concentration-camp system and eastern territories.[94]

The anthroposophist Franz Löffler, whose Berlin Natural Healing Institute cultivated sixty acres employing BDW methods, regularly supplied products to high-ranking party personalities.[95] Dachau's operations were likewise overseen by the prominent SS anthroposophist Franz Lippert. A head gardener at Steiner's Weleda since the mid-1920s, Lippert employed former anthroposophists and BDW proponents with impunity. He also worked closely with Rudi Peuckert, Commissar for the Peasantry and Eastern Territories, and the SS officer Carl Grund, charged with developing biodynamic plantations in the East. Himmler even entrusted Lippert with the important task of training settlers as 'part of SS plans to use biodynamic cultivation in the environmental and ethnic reordering of the East'.[96]

When the number of workers available for conventional military production became scarce, Peuckert relied on his connections to the General Plenipotentiary for Labour Deployment, Fritz Sauckel, to ensure that BDW plantations received sufficient slave labour.[97] In addition to Merkel, who pushed BDW from his position in the RuSHA, Darré's protegé Georg Halbe was appointed to the Ministry of the Occupied Eastern Territories, where he cited BDW as an important component of German resettlement and occupation policies.[98]

In 1943, more than two years after the Hess Action, Himmler continued to employ (former) members of the Reich League for Biodynamic Agriculture in helping the SS and Wehrmacht settle the East.[99] These border scientific and slave labour-fuelled efforts at agricultural cultivation and racial resettlement, including experiments with ostensibly superior grain from Tibet, continued until January 1945, ending only with the liberation of the camps.[100] Indeed, the concentration-camp system represents the border scientific nexus between SS race and resettlement policy, human experiments, and genocide. It was the camp system, after all, where the work of the Nazi anthroposophist Hanns Rascher merged with that of his son Sigmund Rascher, the Nazi doctor whose 'experiments' we will explore below.[101]

Border Science, Eugenics, and Human Experiments

In 1938, shortly before the Third Reich's first attempts to eliminate 'life unworthy of life', Hitler opined that Nazism was a 'a cool and highly reasoned approach to reality based on the greatest of scientific knowledge and its spiritual expression'. 'The National Socialist Movement is not a cult movement,' he continued. 'It is a *völkisch* and political philosophy which grew out of considerations of an exclusively racist nature. This philosophy does not advocate mystic cults, but rather aims to cultivate and lead a nation determined by its blood.'[102] More than anything else, Hitler wanted Germans – and his party colleagues – to accept that Nazism was politically applied biology.[103]

Nevertheless, the Führer's insistence on Nazism's abhorrence of mystic cults, as with his earlier criticisms of wandering scholars clothed in bearskins, betrays an underlying awareness of the supernatural thinking behind Nazi racial science. Hitler himself, according to some eyewitnesses, thought about race in terms well removed from mainstream biology. According to Rauschning, Hitler believed the world 'was in the throes of a vast metamorphosis'. With man's 'solar period' coming to its end, Hitler ostensibly added, a 'new variety of man is beginning to separate out'. 'Just as the Nordic peoples took the sun's passing of the solstices as a figure of the rhythm of life, which proceeds not in a straight line of eternal progress but in a spiral ... [so too] must man now, apparently, turn back in order to attain a higher [evolutionary] stage.'[104]

Rauschning's impressions of Hitler, embellished as they may be, say much about the way contemporaries interpreted National Socialism's 'highly reasoned approach to reality'. As the Nazi academic Ernst Anrich observed, there were two strains at work in the Third Reich, one 'materialist racist' and another 'spiritual-racialist (*völkisch*)' in character.[105] While some contemporaries believed these two strains were incompatible, for most Nazis they were mutually reinforcing elements in their *völkisch*-organicist conception of race.[106] Nazi experiments on human beings, though inspired by eugenical thinking popular across Europe, were given additional impetus by border scientific theories grounded in *völkisch* esotericism and Indo-Aryan fantasies. In this section we will look at the interplay between natural science and border science in Nazi conceptions of eugenics, examining the ways in which the two elements interacted, producing a monstrous approach to human experimentation that was anything but 'highly reasoned'.

Nazi Eugenics before 1939

Throughout the interwar period the idea of being able to improve the individual and the nation through eugenics existed, in varying degrees, across Europe.[107] German doctors and biologists were preoccupied by many of the same questions that interested other Western medical professionals. Can one transplant skin and organs? What happens to human beings in extreme cold and heat? How do we prevent and battle cancer?[108] In attempting to understand the criminal actions of Nazi doctors we cannot ignore the degree to which American scientists at Tuskegee in Alabama or Edgewood in Maryland conducted inhumane, even murderous human experiments. Nazi experiments and medical practices, however, were not merely an exaggerated version of the Western norm.[109] Nazi doctors took their monstrous science far beyond the experiments that occurred in the United States, Great Britain, and Scandinavia due, at least in part, to border scientific ideas and premises.

Before the First World War, as we will recall, anthroposophy and ariosophy emphasized different stages of spiritual and biological development, arguing that an Ur-Aryan (Atlantean) racial purity might be recovered through proper breeding.[110] Such 'non-academic groups' were clearly 'outside science', yet felt justified in producing 'research' on race – a practice rarely glimpsed in Anglo-American contexts.[111] J. W. Hauer argued, for example, that the 'laws of heredity would be deeper understood in half mystical form than in the primarily [materialist] theories of the West'. In concert with the 'cosmic-ethical laws of karma', German racial science emphasized both 'blood and spirit'.[112] Statements such as Hauer's are what caused the German-Jewish biologist Hugo Iltis to dismiss Austro-German racial science as a *völkisch* religion in which the greatest emphasis was placed on 'fantasies of racial faith'.[113]

At the same time German racial science diverged from mainstream British or American biology and anthropology in applying totalizing, organicist, polit-ical-ideological arguments that increasingly ran counter to a more nuanced understanding of genetic markers and the complex interplay between biology (nature) and environment (nurture).[114] No wonder that Nazi racial theorists could justify eliminating Jews who looked 'German', but could simultaneously work to preserve 'racially pure' gypsies or ally with putatively Indo-Aryan Indians and Japanese.[115] For insofar as 'German holistic science was nourished by an "irrational" German hunger for Wholeness,' Anne Harrington reminds us, it abdicated the 'right to be called "real" science at all and became merely a dangerous reflection of (largely rightist) politics'.[116]

In contrast to American studies of racial intelligence, German racial psychology favoured broader, more holistic characterological analyses, which invoked *völkisch*-esoteric and religious doctrines to justify eugenical interven-tions.[117] As the Nazi-era occultist Walther Kröner put it in his 1939 book, *Decline of Materialism*, 'the biomagical perspective' privileges a 'cultural age once again bound together back by soil, blood and community'.[118] One could no longer rely on 'empirical and rational recognition of nature,' he continued, for 'the voice of the blood' needed to combine nature and 'vitalistic metaphysics'.[119]

As with other holist and *völkisch*-esoteric thinkers, Nazi race theorists did not view society as a collection of parts. The *Volksgemeinschaft* was seen rather as a collective racial-organicist entity where the individual was subsumed by the whole.[120] According to Ernst Lehmann, founder and editor of the official journal of Nazi biology teachers, 'only through a reintegration of man in the Wholeness of Nature can our Volk be restored to strength'. That, he argued, 'is the deepest purpose and true essence of National Socialistic thinking'.[121]

The flipside of this border scientific obsession with wholeness was the singling out of the congenitally weak and disabled. Such elements were 'ballast' and 'parasites' within the 'organismic body of the nation', people who 'were to be sanitized out of the German social body' through mass sterilization and euthanasia.[122] The goal of 'National Socialist science', according to Walter Wüst, was to free 'itself from any foreign racial ballast, which only hinders it from reaching its highest goals: the new creation of a Nordic ruling class.'[123]

In fact, many Nazi leaders and SS scientists dismissed the idea that humans evolved from apes as 'scientifically totally false' and 'quite insulting to humans'.[124] They believed rather that Aryans descended from an ancient ruling class of God-men who had taken root in Tibet, which added clearly supernatural, faith-based contours to their racial hygienic project.[125] As Wüst wrote in 1943, 'völkisch reality' was not a product of material science, but 'climbs out of a unity of space, blood and spirit', representing 'the precondition of creating a higher humanity'.[126] Himmler and Darré's approach to racial breeding and eugenics was buttressed by a 'pantheistic religious feeling' and 'naturalistic holism' as well.[127]

Certainly for Himmler the Nordic race 'did not evolve, but came directly down from heaven to settle on the Atlantic continent'.[128] Obsessed with magic and horoscopes, Himmler 'sought the origins of Germanic humanity, in rejecting Darwin's evolutionary theory, by relying on the content of a saga, which for [them] naturally was fact, not a fairy tale'.[129] In lieu of evolutionary biology Himmler propagated the arguments of Wiligut, Frenzolf Schmid, and other SS border scientists that the Edda and Halgarita offered a lesson in racial hygiene which might return humanity to its Atlantean purity.[130] Such Indo-Aryan epics indicated that only a superior caste or breed should be allowed to reproduce.[131]

Hitler ostensibly articulated similar views to Rauschning. 'The old type of man will have but a stunted existence', Hitler is supposed to have said. 'All creative energy will be concentrated in the new one. The two types will rapidly diverge from one another. One will sink to a sub-human race and the other rise far above the man of today. I might call the two varieties the god-man and the mass-animal'. National Socialism is 'more even than a religion, Hitler concluded, 'it is the will to create mankind anew'.[132] 'We certainly can't breed the superman', Rauschning recalls saying to Hitler. All a politician might achieve was a form of 'unnatural' selection: 'That, after all, was all that we farmers did, I told him. If a variety turned up, we kept it alive, deliberately selected it for propagation, and so hurried on the natural process. In scientific language, we sought for the homozygous plus-variation and cultivated it.'[133] However, Hitler, according to Rauschning, dismissed his careful response, insisting that 'the breeder' could 'assist nature' in more aggressive fashion (how, he did not explain).[134]

That Himmler, Hitler, and other Nazis had inculcated border scientific theories of human evolution and genetics helps explain their willingness to suspend disbelief when it came to matters of eugenics.[135] Combined with vulgar Darwinism ('politically applied biology'), these border scientific racial theories helped produce a radical approach to eugenics and human experimentation. At times, of course, such border scientific reasoning might produce seemingly 'progressive' results. Based on their understanding of 'earth goddesses' in Germanic religion and 'fighting valkyrie' in Nordic mythology, Himmler, Wirth, and other *völkisch*-esotericists justified relatively (if selectively) liberal attitudes toward gender and sexuality.[136]

And yet this kind of border scientific reasoning, which had little to do with either modern science or feminism, could just as easily yield horrific results. Himmler theorized, for example, that bogeymen in northern peat bogs were 'homosexuals who were put to death for their transgressions against ancient German laws'. The Reichsführer cited such theories in justifying grisly castration experiments against homosexuals and other sexual 'deviants'.[137] The dangers of Himmler's 'pseudoscientific research becomes evident through the principal of *Lebensborn*' or 'fount of life' breeding programme as well. The idea was to endorse as many births by pure racial couples as possible and, failing that, the adopting or 'kidnapping' of racially recoverable children from other countries, including eastern territories. Inspired by racial border science, Himmler believed his scientists could 'extract' the Jewish and Slavic blood from the population and produce 'racially unobjectionable Germanic people'. The one-time chicken farmer instructed his colleagues to base the programme, not on modern genetics, but on pagan Germanic laws of marriage and heredity, hoping to produce Germans with 'Greek noses' and other 'specific racial characteristics'.[138]

This border scientific approach to racial hygiene pervaded the Nazi medical establishment. Encouraged by Himmler, Hess, and Rosenberg, academic journals and well-respected universities began to sponsor racial border science through independent institutes and research programmes.[139] The Third Reich also found eager proponents of racial border science, such as the infamous Sigmund Rascher, who had been immersed in his father's anthroposophic traditions as a child and young adult. The Strasbourg anatomy professor August Hirt was no less immune to border scientific speculations. Hirt collaborated

with Günther Franz, one of the central figures in the Witch Division, to determine the racial origins of victims of witchcraft by examining their skeletal
remains. Their bizarre conclusion was that Lutherans were 'Nordic-Germanic'
whereas Catholics were 'Mediterranean-Jewish'.[140]

Ernst Schäfer's Hedin Institute for Central Asia became another site of
racial border science. Schäfer's right-hand man, Bruno Beger, would cite his
occult and magical experiences in Tibet in confirming the biological superiority and powers of the Tibetan (Indo-Aryan) race.[141] The Asia institute even
modelled its 'total research' in the Caucasus on the 'holistic' (border scientific)
Tibetan model: merging the humanities, social and natural sciences willy-nilly
in an attempt to prove Nazi racial theories.[142] Such 'racial hygienic principles',
derived from border scientific premises, were later applied in the extermination of Jews and other undesirables.[143]

When a German scientist refused to accept these fantastical theories, he or
she was systematically marginalized. Hence the SS wrote an unfavourable
report on the well-respected biologist and natural philosopher, Eduard May.
May was hired to work as leader of the entomological division of the Institute
for Military Scientific Practical Research (*Institut für Wehrwissenschaftliche
Zweckforschung* or IWZ) in Dachau. At issue was May's 'positivistic' approach
to science and rejection of relativism. 'The observations of May suffer from his
determination of absolute, transcendent, eternal notion of truth,' wrote the SS
peer reviewer, a product of the 'Jewish' Vienna School that stubbornly refused
to endorse scientific conclusions without empirical evidence.[144]

That SS peer reviewers considered May's empirical approach problematic
in making 'remarks on the race problem' exemplifies the faith-based, border
scientific reasoning underlying Nazi eugenics. It also explains why May
was never asked to take a direct role in human experiments at Dachau or
Auschwitz (he would be acquitted of war crimes at Nuremberg in 1945).[145] May
was still put to work developing means of exterminating pests in the camps.
However, the Auschwitz commandant and former member of the Artamanen,
Rudolf Hoess, preferred that May focus on 'natural' as opposed to chemical
remedies – another outgrowth of the Nazi penchant for esoterically inspired
alternative medicine.[146]

If May was marginalized, the SS still found plenty of doctors willing to
experiment with eugenics while employing less 'positivistic' means. These
included the aforementioned Sigmund Rascher, who was given free reign at
Dachau.[147] They also included Hirt and Beger, who pursued their medical
experiments in affiliation with the wholly Nazified Reich University of
Strasbourg.[148] This university was headed by Hirt. Its humanities faculty was
chaired by the SS-mysticist Anrich. And its Psychological Institute was spearheaded by the parapsychologist Hans Bender, who was conducting his own

border scientific experiments on behalf of the Luftwaffe.[149] Bender's institute would employ Otto Bickenbach, who was arrested after the war for conducting terrible human experiments with phosgene gas at the nearby concentration camp, Natzweiler-Struthof.[150] Even Bender, though a proponent of occultism, recognized the empirical dubiousness of many projects sponsored by the Reich University – experiments his institute reluctantly countenanced in order to maintain funding and independence. Bender's border scientific colleagues – Bickenbach, Hirt, Rascher, and Beger – had no such qualms.[151]

Border Science and Human Experiments

Once unleashed in the colonial East, Nazi dreams of empire and ethnic cleansing were brought back, in the words of George Steinmetz, into 'contexts in metropolitan life in which the defense mechanisms that normally limit the expression of wishful fantasies are attenuated and a dreamlike sense of omnipotence is encouraged'.[152] Nothing illustrates better the monstrous consequences of these wishful fantasies or dreamlike sense of omnipotence than the Third Reich's systematic experimentation on 'life unworthy of life'.

While Matthias Göring corresponded with Bender regarding relatively innocuous studies of soldiers' psychology, his cousin Hermann Göring was becoming increasingly concerned about the Luftwaffe's ability to defend itself against high-altitude bombers. Altitude experiments were already being conducted with apes. But in late 1941 Sigmund Rascher suggested the Luftwaffe take advantage of the burgeoning supply of human subjects in the concentration camps to conduct human experiments.[153]

For some time the SS had sponsored Rascher's research on administering 'plant extracts' to human cancer patients culled from Dachau. Impressed by his proposal for high-altitude experiments, Sievers and Wüst went to work securing his release from the Luftwaffe so he could work with the SS full-time.[154] By 1942 Rascher had moved to the Munich Institute for Aviation Medicine under Dr Georg August Weltz.[155] In order to acquire more test subjects, Rascher decided to start labelling healthy inmates as 'terminal'. Then, to further impress Himmler regarding the 'value' of these experiments, he decided to film them.[156]

Over the course of two weeks in 1942, Rascher forced nearly two hundred Jews, Russians, Poles, and German prisoners to participate, murdering close to half of them in the process.[157] Undeterred by the grisly results and doubtful scientific value of Rascher's experiments, Himmler approved the construction of a pressure chamber to continue his work.[158] In fact, Rascher eagerly pursued Himmler's query whether it was possible to kill test subjects and then 'bring these kind of human beings back to life'.[159] To be sure, some Luftwaffe officials had reservations. Even Schäfer, who observed Rascher's experiments in Dachau, was struck by their gruesome nature and put off by Himmler's perverse desire to film them. No one felt strongly enough, however, to discontinue the experiments.[160]

In the summer of 1942, inspired by Rascher and Ruff's 'successful' collaboration, Himmler founded the above-mentioned IWZ.[161] With Hitler's approval, the IWZ was set up directly under the umbrella of the Ahnenerbe and funded by Oswald Pohl, head of the concentration-camp system.[162] The reasons for creating an independent 'military medicinal research' facility with no direct oversight from the armed forces had something to do with the fact that the research was on the fringes ('borders') of medical science. But a typical SS desire for secrecy and control was equally important.[163] As Thomas Kühne reminds us, the Nazis' use of secrecy and symbolic language contributed to the Third Reich's ability to break taboos and foster moral transgression on a scale that was most likely impossible in a primarily scientific context.[164] Whoever worked in the concentration camps, including infamous Nazi doctors such as Josef Mengele, could already do what they wanted outside the law (so long as it was approved by Himmler).[165] The IWZ guaranteed Nazi doctors a similar degree of independence and authority beyond the camp structure.

Over time the IWZ, like the Ahnenerbe before it, expanded to incorporate natural scientific fields and projects beyond 'practical' research. Encouraged by Sigmund Rascher's unconventional cancer studies, for example, Himmler instructed the IWZ to work on *Volksmedizin* – holistic and homoeopathic methods inspired by anthroposphy and life reform, which pulled in Hirt and May as well. A mathematical divison was set up in Sachsenhausen concentration camp in 1944 and a botany institute was set up in early 1945.[166] Indeed, the IWZ employed many border scientific personnel already affiliated with the Ahnenerbe or Schäfer's Hedin Institute.[167]

Despite its obviously border scientific premises, Göring's Luftwaffe was eager to work with the IWZ. In the summer of 1942 the air force participated in joint experiments – seemingly inspired by Himmler's desire to bring the dead back to life – on the effects of artificial heat in resuscitating human beings who had succumbed to extreme cold. Rascher would drop a live human subject in freezing water and then attempt to revive the victim through the application of artifical heat, which, he dutifully reported, didn't work. Undaunted, Himmler advised Rascher that he should continue the experiments by applying natural 'animal warmth' instead, since the Reichsführer 'could imagine that a fisherman's wife simply would have to take her half-frozen husband into bed and thereby warm him up. Everyone knew that animal warmth worked differently than artificial warmth. Rascher must know that also. Experiments in this direction must be made without question.'[168]

Emboldened by Himmler's folk wisdom, Rascher tried a number of unconventional methods to resuscitate the dead and dying. He even ordered female
prisoners ('fishermens' wives') to help 'warm' frozen subjects in natural 'animal'
fashion, creating scenes more reminiscent of a Roman orgy than a scientific
experiment – scenes that Himmler attended with enthusiasm. Well aware of
the absurd turn in these experiments, the Luftwaffe did nothing to intervene. In
the end more than a quarter of the nearly three hundred 'volunteers' perished
in the proceedings.[169]

Rascher fell out of favour with Himmler in the spring of 1944, when it
emerged that his wife – with Rascher's knowledge – was kidnapping children
off the street and claiming they were her own.[170] Still, there were plenty of SS
border scientists to pick up the slack. Chief among them was August Hirt. In
July 1942 Hirt got Himmler to set up a division of the Ahnenerbe named 'Amt
Hirt' (or 'Amt H') in order to facilitate his grisly experiments.[171] In the spring of
1943, frustrated by the inconclusive test of the effects of mustard gas on
animals, Hirt obtained Sievers' approval to begin experimenting with phosgene
gas on human subjects in cooperation with another Strasbourg professor, the
aforementioned Otto Bickenbach.[172]

In 1942 Hirt invited Bruno Beger to Strasbourg as well. Beger's mission was
to collect and examine human skulls. As we will recall, Beger began his career
developing criteria for sterilization, castration, and abortion for the RuSHA.[173]
After accompanying Schäfer to Tibet, Beger had risen quickly in the SS ranks,
impressing Himmler, who invited him to join Schäfer's Institute. Beger was
encouraged by Himmler to pursue a PhD under the *völkisch*-esoteric psychologist, Ludwig Ferdinand Clauss, whose work on the 'racial soul' the Reichsführer
admired. In 1943 Sievers made the newly minted Dr Beger the SS's 'designated
anthropologist' and 'racial expert of the Ahnenerbe'.[174]

Beger's macabre fascination with collecting human skeletons became
apparent during the Tibet expedition, where he gathered skulls in order to
prove that Germans and Tibetans descended from the same Ur-Aryan super-
race.[175] Now, with the Holocaust underway, Beger suggested to Sievers that he
begin collecting and studying Jewish skulls. Beger admitted that there were still
'too few skulls available' to produce 'conclusive results'. But the 'war in the East
offers us the occasion to rectify this lack [of skulls]. In the Jewish Bolshevik
commissars, who embody a despicable though characteristic race of subhumans, the possibility of obtaining this scientific documentation in regard to
skulls is within reach.'[176]

In carrying out his grotesque research, Beger determined to collaborate
with his 'dear comrade' August Hirt, whose Reich University of Strasbourg was
already a centre of border scientific research and human experimentation.[177]
Indeed, Hirt and Beger wrote up a joint research proposal arguing that 'the new

Strasbourg Reich University would be the most appropriate place for the collection of and research upon these skulls thus acquired'.[178] To obtain his first batch
of skulls, Beger asked SS special task forces to take measurements of Jewish
prisoners in the camps and, were they found suitable, to then execute them
without damaging their bones.[179]

Shortly after Beger and Hirt began their research on skeletons at Strasbourg,
Wüst offered them a chance to investigate the origins of lost Jewish tribes in
Central Asia. Wüst and Himmler apparently wanted to determine whether
Central Asian Jews were in reality ethnic Slavs or Indo-Aryans who might be
employed as slave labour. While the more ideologically driven folklorists affiliated with the Ahnenerbe argued that they were racial Jews, the local SD chief
claimed that 'mountain Jews' in the Caucasus were merely 'converts' who could
be enlisted for labour. In the Crimea as well there was little consensus. Some
skilled Jews were deemed suited for labour whereas others were classified as
'unconditionally racially Jewish' and murdered.[180]

The impetus for this Central Asian Institute-sponsored 'Caucasus
commando' may have had to do with the practical matter of resolving wartime
labour shortages. Nevertheless, the subsequent attention received by Central
Asian Jews – and Central Asians in general – recalls the broader supernatural
premises of Nazi racial science, part of Himmler's larger goal of making 'Tibet
and the entire research [complex] on Asia' a military priority.[181] Certainly the
equipment Schäfer ordered to accompany Beger's trip to the Caucusus,
including dozens of scalpels and 'skinning machines', does not accord with the
stated goal of measuring the 'skulls of living persons' and preserving as much
labour as possible.[182] Beger's insistence on studying the Central Asian Jews
'parapsychologically' (whatever that meant) as well as 'racial psychologically'
attests to the Schäfer-Commando's border scientific premises.[183]

By the autumn of 1942, Sievers, Hirt, and Beger had in any case agreed that
the death camps were a better source than Central Asia for unambiguously
Jewish skeletons. Since most Jewish skeletons were sent directly to the crema-
toria, Beger got approval from Adolf Eichmann to visit Auschwitz and select
his own subjects. In June 1943 Beger arrived at the camp and requested
from Eichmann '115 [individuals], including 79 male Jews, 2 Poles, 4 Central
Asians, and 30 Jewesses'. These individuals were then transferred to
Natzweiler-Struthof concentration camp, 30 miles from Strasbourg, where the
SS-Hauptsturmführer Josef Kramer murdered the inmates in a makeshift gas
chamber employing chemicals prepared by the university's own president, Hirt.
Hirt and Beger then received the 'fresh' skeletons for further examination.[184]

Even the seemingly innocuous partnership between anthroposophy,
Nazism, and natural healing came at a deadly price. In return for their continued
existence, the SS pressured anthroposophic institutes that practised BDW to

participate in a T4 euthanasia programme by which Nazi physicians murdered at least 70,000 elderly and disabled Germans deemed 'life unworthy of life'.[185] The desire to experiment with natural healing methods also led the SS to infect concentration-camp inmates with cancer, typhus, and malaria.[186] As Michael Kater observes, Himmler and other Nazis' 'fanaticism for herbal and natural healing' aligned with a general rejection of 'traditional medicinal research methods that were constrained by ethical guidelines'. Only by discarding 'outdated' methods, as defined by mainstream biology or Christian morality, could Himmler discover the 'sorcerer's stone ... [lying] outside the borders of any medical ethics'.[187]

Near the end of the war Felix Kersten, Himmler's masseur, asked his boss directly how he could abhor killing and experimentation on animals while enlisting human beings in bizarre experiments and slaughtering them in gas chambers.[188] Himmler replied that Jews and Slavs, unlike animals, were biologically inferior and physically dangerous, while science would benefit from the results of SS research (how research conducted on subhumans would naturally translate to Aryans was never explained). Anyone who objected 'to these human experiments', Himmler added, was a traitor who would prefer to 'let brave German soldiers die'.[189]

Nazi eugenics and human experiments were not the product of border science alone. In the context of total war, shibboleths about the well-being of the troops and the importance of Hitler's will helped Nazi doctors surmount ethical barriers.[190] Wartime politics and military necessity only go so far, however, in explaining the Third Reich's turn toward monstrous science.[191] As the German physiologist Viktor von Weizsäcker noted after the war, human experiments may have been conducted 'under the mask of science'. But they were in reality 'nonsensical and harmful'.[192] Immersed in border scientific theories, the Nazis possessed a totalizing vision of racial science and eugenics that went far beyond any reasonable application of evolutionary biology or human genetics extant in the 1930s and 1940s.[193] Their experiments were therefore more 'flexible, brutal, [and] pseudo-scientific' than their Anglo-American equivalents, driven by 'SS racial ideology' more than any empirical problem to be solved.[194]

This proclivity for border scientific racial theory and practice, moreover, cannot be written off to a few deviants or sociopaths, hand-picked by Himmler. Whereas Rascher's esoteric background was clear, Hirt was a respected academic. Nevertheless, both engaged equally in 'scientifically camouflaged murder'.[195] Both were motivated by border scientific racial theories and a macabre fascination with eliminating 'life unworthy of life'.[196] And these unconventional attitudes toward life and death extended beyond the laboratory. When receiving her good friend Gerda Bormann, Himmler's mistress Hedwig

Potthast showed her a chair made of human pelvic bone and a personal copy of *Mein Kampf*, ostensibly bound in human skin – gifts from the Reichsführer himself. There is no evidence that Gerda Bormann felt any discomfort at Potthast's enthusiasm.[197]

Demonization and Genocide

On 14 January 1942, as Reinhard Heydrich prepared the infamous Wannsee Conference convened six days later to plan the Holocaust, the Nazi screen-writer Hans Fischer-Gerhold sent a manuscript to Rosenberg's Party Education Office a few miles away in Berlin-Charlottenburg. Entitled 'Superstition in Film', the manuscript described the need to protect the German public from manipulation by supernatural elements pervading Weimar horror films. These included *The Golem* (1915), a film about Rabbi Löw of Prague, who drew on kabbalistic magic to take revenge on his Gentile enemies. To be sure, the film had a positive ending, according to Fischer-Gerhold, because the 'Golem is deprived of its life force ("entseelt") by a blond, Aryan child'. 'As always,' he explained, 'the Jew is conscious of the fact that for him the greatest danger is the Germanic, Nordic man.' He then moved on to the 'fetishistic' appearance of the undead in other films, *Nosferatu* (1922) in particular. The 'vampire of Slavic origin,' Fischer-Gerhold observed, returns from the grave to suck the blood of the innocent Aryan. The lesson of both films was clear: only one individual could survive, 'either the [superhuman] German or the [monstrous] Jew'.[198]

The juxtaposition of the Wannsee Conference and Fischer-Gerhold's study of 'superstition in film' may seem incongruous. The Holocaust – or what the Third Reich referred to as the 'Final Solution' to the 'Jewish Question' – was a massive, highly technical process of industrial mass murder. Scholars inter-ested in understanding how, when, and why the 'Final Solution' occurred have therefore tended to focus, understandably, on political, military, and economic circumstances. Many have examined the relationship between anti-Jewish policies developed by higher Nazi authorities in Berlin and the way in which those policies were interpreted and carried out by SS task forces in the field.[199] Others have emphasized the Darwinistic rationale behind the 'Final Solution', conceived in a wartime environment of escalating brutality and scarce resources.[200] Recent research has also linked the Holocaust to European impe-rialism and ethnic cleansing in Africa, Asia, and the New World, viewing the 'Final Solution' as the extension of a broader colonial project.[201]

But alongside this emphasis on technical processes, wartime circumstances, and colonial legacies is the closely related question of why the Jews needed to be eliminated in the first place – a question embedded in Fischer-Gerhold's analysis of German film. The Nazis first needed to imagine a 'world without

Jews', according to Alon Confino, before they could implement genocide.[202] What was it in the central European imagination that made a world without Jews so indispensable?

One theory suggests that Nazi anti-Semitism was a byproduct of racist and social Darwinist theories extant across Europe from the late nineteenth century.[203] From this perspective the Jews were merely the most dangerous biological threat to the German body politic. Whereas Slavs and gypsies, the mentally disabled and homosexuals, might be gradually sterilized, starved, or selectively murdered, the Jews, as a particularly virulent biopolitical threat, had to be eliminated wholesale. Insofar as Nazi anti-Semitism was biopolitical in origin, the Holocaust becomes the most egregious example of a wide-ranging eugenical project endemic to the West.[204]

Nevertheless, there is also a group of scholars who emphasize the 'magical background of modern anti-Semitism' – what Saul Friedländer has called 'redemptive anti-Semitism' and Confino refers to as the 'Christian imaginary tradition about the Jews'.[205] As Jonathan Steinberg observes, the highly modern, technical methods employed in eliminating the Jews should not distract us from the 'power of racial dogmas and the almost mystical crusade' that under-girded Nazi anti-Semitism.[206] Without the supernatural figuring of the monstrous Jew, the highly technical process of genocide could never have been applied as widely or vociferously as it was.[207]

In pursuing this argument, I do not want to discount the important role of biopolitical thinking, wartime radicalization, or the invasion of the Soviet Union in catalyzing the 'Final Solution'. Rather, I want to suggest that the Holocaust was only possible in its scope and severity because of the elision of these biopolitical and circumstantial factors with *völkisch*-esoteric, fantastical, even magical conceptions of Jewish monstrosity.[208] Without the decades-long process of demonizing the Jews not only in traditionally Christian terms but also pagan and occultist ones, the radical conception and solution to the 'Jewish Question' would most likely not have occurred.[209] This conception of the Jews as simultaneously a biological threat to the racial body politic and vampiric monsters operating outside the bounds of humanity, invited, in turn, all the more radical and totalizing solutions to the 'Jewish Question' – culminating in the Holocaust.[210]

Jewish 'Vampirism' and Demonization, 1919–39

The ghoulish visage, impossibly long, sharp nails, sunken eyes, and serrated teeth – Max Schreck's horrifying portrayal of the vampire Count Orlok is forever burned into the twentieth-century imagination.[211] Artistically, *Nosferatu: A Symphony of Terror* remains an impressive example of Weimar-era

Expressionism. But the film also constituted, for *völkisch* thinkers, a rumination on the eastern European Jew: a nearly omnipotent supernatural interloper with cartoonish Semitic features, immense wealth, and strange powers of psychosexual manipulation.[212] Associated with vermin, plague, and death invading from the Slavic East, Count Orlok presides over an international syndicate of cretinous servants ready to do his bidding.[213] His arrival leads to a quick-spreading infection of Ario-Christian blood, stolen from women and children at night, recalling both the medieval blood libel and modern biological idea of disease. This idea of 'a deformed, toxic, blood-sucking Jew', embodied in central Europe's 'folkloric traditions, not to mention the vampire of literature and screen', was a fundamental feature of interwar anti-Semitism.[214]

It comes as no surprise that such vampiric traits and metaphors were widely reproduced in Nazi depictions of Jews. In *Mein Kampf*, Hitler makes multiple references to Jews as 'vampires', 'bloodsuckers', and 'spongers': wherever the Jew appears, 'the host people die out after a short period'.[215] He added that the Jew 'never cultivates the soil, but regards it only as a property to be exploited'. Through the 'most miserable extortions on the part of his new master, the aversion against him [among the peasants] gradually increases to open hatred. His blood-sucking tyranny becomes so great that excesses against him occur'.[216] Here Hitler conjures up the image of angry Aryan townspeople trapping the Jewish vampire in his crypt and plunging a stake through his heart.

The metaphor does not end there. After the 'death of his victim, the vampire sooner or later dies too', Hitler explained. The Jews would always search for new, healthy societies on which they could feed for long periods of time.[217] 'To put any one of these [Jewish vampires] out of the way was completely irrelevant', Hitler added, for the 'chief result was that a few other bloodsuckers, just as big and just as threadbare, came into a job much sooner'.[218] Like an undead vampire, the Jew needed 'the smell of decay, the stench of cadavers, weakness, lack of resistance, submission of the personal self, illness, degeneracy! And wherever it takes root, it continues the process of decomposition!' Only 'under those conditions', Hitler concluded, could a Jew 'lead its parasitic existence'.[219]

Dozens of *völkisch* anti-Semites and early Nazis spoke of the Jews' parasitic exploitation of German society and poisonous corruption of Aryan blood.[220] For the Artamanen, to which Himmler, Darré, and the Auschwitz commandant Rudolf Hoess belonged in the 1920s, the vampire merged with the idea of the 'Jew as the symbol of the corrupt city', who destroys 'the good elements of rural life', an evil parasite who infects 'good German values'.[221] Influenced by esotericists such as Sebottendorff and Evola, Nazi leaders further argued that Communist and Masonic symbols derived from Jewish mysticism and were proof of the Jews' millennia-old plans for world domination.[222] The fight taken by 'Jewish Bolshevism' to the German people, Himmler instructed the SS in

1937, was the 'fight of pestilent bacteria against a healthy body', but also a cabal of Jewish-led Masons who had spearheaded the murder of Aryan men and women in the French and Bolshevik Revolutions.[223]

We have to acknowledge that such bizarre claims were not just metaphorical. 'Since pure light blood was at a premium', Karl Maria Wiligut argued, 'the epoch of ritual murder emerged, by which dark vampiric creatures [the Jews] consumed the blood of sacrificed light creatures [the Aryans].'[224] Martin and Gerda Bormann referred to the Jews as 'commercially minded parasites'.[225] Rosenberg repeatedly referred to 'the Jew' as a 'bacillus', a 'parasite', and other quasi-biological, quasi-vampiric metaphors.[226] The notorious anti-Semite Julius Streicher spread the idea that Jewish blood, breath, and fluids, like that of vampires, were noxious and could infect a female body.[227] According to Streicher, the Jew was a 'poisonous mushroom' (Giftpilz) that needed soil to grow, just as vampires carried coffins filled with fetid soil.[228] Not to be outdone, Rosenberg's associate Gregor Schwartz-Bostunitsch, combined these tropes in a massive tome entitled Jew and Woman: Theory and Practice of Jewish Vampirism, Exploitation and Infection of Upright Peoples (1939).[229]

While the metaphor of the parasitic vampire took pride of place, Jews were linked to other supernatural monsters drawn from both Christian and occult cosmology.[230] Many Nazis resurrected the image of the 'wandering Jew', akin to the undead vampire, whose 'gruesomely spectral figure of Ahasuerus' played on the 'deepest emotions' of Germans by 'cheating death for ever'.[231] Jews were furthermore associated with Cain, the 'original monster' and 'embodiment of evil walking the earth, cursed by God and marked as such for all eternity'.[232]

No wonder that Hitler portrayed the Jews as children of the Devil and made extensive use of symbolism from the Book of Revelation.[233] The Führer argued that to forestall the 'Jewish apocalypse was our duty, our God-given mission – yes, it is the substance of Divine Creation altogether'.[234] He ostensibly told Dietrich Eckart that the Jew's very 'nature' compelled him toward the goal of 'world annihilation, even though he dimly realizes that he must therefore destroy himself'. To 'annihilate us with all his might, but at the same time to suspect that this must lead irrevocably to his own destruction. Therein lies, if you will, the tragedy of Lucifer.'[235] Hitler indicated that the Jews had murdered 75,000 Persians and 'hundreds of thousands of non-Jews of noblest blood in Babylon, Kyrene, and Egypt' – suggesting, as researchers in the Witch Division did, that the best defence was a good offence: murdering the Jews first.[236]

Similar to other völkisch thinkers, Hitler believed that 'the Jew' lacked ' inner spiritual experience', which is why the Jews killed off the original tribes of Palestine who had produced the Aryan Jesus. Christianity, according to Hitler, had been appropriated by Jews to destroy the 'cult of light' promoted by pre-Christian peoples (the same light/dark metaphor invoked by Wiligut above).[237]

Through Saint Paul, the Jews had perverted the teaching of Christ, which was originally, according to Hitler, 'a local movement of Aryan opposition to Jewry'. Once corrupted by Paul, Christianity became 'a supra-temporal religion, which postulates the equality of all men amongst themselves' and 'caused the death of the Roman Empire'.[238]

Hitler was not alone in citing biblical evidence of the Jews' malevolent plans, abetted by Christian institutions and cosmology. According to Himmler, 'the Jew-Pope' of today advanced Jewish interests through control of culture and the media, ensuring that 'their Old Testament spirit rotted everything'.[239] To justify his conspiracy theories Himmler cited the biblical accounts of Jewish participation in nefarious plots against righteous men, the genocidal implications of the Purim feast day, the temptations of biblical Jewish women, and the role of Jews in virtually every war throughout history.[240] Rosenberg and Schwartz-Bostunitsch referred to Jews as 'desert Demons', intent on committing ritual murder, creating a 'Moloch Cult' and 'burning Children'.[241] Schwartz-Bostunitsch further reminded his readers how Jacob slaughtered an entire village of Aryans who refused to abide by Jewish sexual law.[242]

All these bizarre theories recall the connection in the Nazi supernatural imaginary between the Jews and the Catholic Church's campaign to wipe out German pagan religion and culture.[243] The SD's researchers at the Witch Division in Amt VII of the SS, who worked closely with border scientists at the Reich University of Strasbourg, played an important role in developing this narrative.[244] Having begun with a study on Church persecution of witches, the SD researchers expanded their purview 'under [Franz] Six to focus first on the thematic complex of Freemasonry . . . [and later] due to Günther Franz's coordination, on Jewry, to which all other themes were subordinate'.[245] Franz and Six produced a report confirming Jewish racial difference based on skeletal analysis, according to Beger, and blamed the Jews point-blank for the Catholic Church's extermination of German women as witches.[246] Franz also turned the attention of Amt VII to researching 'historical attempts' at 'solving the Jewish Question' in other times and countries.[247] That Six was simultaneously working with the fascist mystic Evola on an 'anti-Freemason book' and propagating Indo-Aryan theories of Asian racial superiority indicates the entirely border scientific nature of Amt VII's 'research' on the 'Jewish Question'.[248] In representing the witch craze as an attempt by the Jews to destroy the German race – a kind of negative eugenics – Franz and Six nonetheless helped set the stage for the 'Final Solution'.[249]

The Nazi astrologer, Alexander Centgraf, picked up on this theme, accusing the Jews of 'demonic sexuality' aimed at annihilating the Aryan race. Citing Jewish sexual theorists such as Freud, Otto Weininger, and Magnus Hirschfeld, Centgraf argued that Jews had intentionally corrupted German women in order to undermine their social and biological role in securing German racial domination (much as the Jewish-dominated Catholic Church had murdered them outright five hundred years earlier).[250] The Jews' sexual corruption of German women and endorsement of homosexuality, Centgraf argued, was the 'byproduct of an Asiatic mind or a son of the desert, raised by the demons of the Gehenna'. The 'ideas of the Jew spring' from Dante's 'innermost hell', Centgraf continued. 'The poison of his demonic ejaculations of ideas [*dämonischen Gedankenejakulationen*] has paved the way for the spiritual disintegration of the Western peoples', he affirmed. 'Bolshevism may justly call him its apostle and harbinger'.[251]

Here the crypto-Christian, *völkisch*-esoteric, and biopolitical images of the Jew merged in the Nazi supernatural imaginary. Together these elements reflected, according to Anne Harrington, an 'explicit tendency to superimpose the terms of the holistic struggle against mechanism onto the idea of a racial struggle between Germans and Jews'. This border scientific conceit was 'subsequently adopted by Rosenberg and Hitler himself'.[252] According to Rauschning, the Führer believed that the 'Jew is the anti-man, the creature of another god ... [He] must have come from another root of the human race ... [as] widely separated as man and beast'. The Jew was 'a creature outside nature and alien to nature'.[253] In this border scientific cosmology the Third Reich was merely continuing a millennia-old battle between the Aryan 'light races' and 'lower racial forms', especially the Jews, who were defined by 'the loss of inner light and fine material'.[254] The Jews became, quite simply, the 'evil enemy of all light ... all mankind'.[255]

Michael Burleigh observed that the power 'ascribed to the Jews in this pseudo-cosmology differentiated anti-Semitism from other forms of racism', insofar as 'eugenic "burdens" and gypsy "nuisances" were not existentially menacing in the same comprehensive way'.[256] Decades' old laws against itinerant gypsies – even Heydrich's decree against 'gypsy fortune-telling' – never caused a sea change in policy toward the Roma or Sinti as a race.[257] Nor were the majority of gypsies murdered in the death camps.[258] To the contrary, inspired by Robert Ritter, the Nazi doctor in charge of gypsy policy in the Reich Institute for Criminal Biology, Himmler ordered Arthur Nebe and the Kripo to 'establish a closer and very positive contact with the gypsies ... [in order] to study the gypsy language and, beyond that, learn about gypsy customs'.[259] The reason was that Himmler, Ritter, and other Nazis 'believed the pseudoscientific tale of the Aryan origin of the gypsies and therefore wanted those considered "racially pure" preserved as a potentially valuable addition to the stock of Aryan blood'.[260] The Nazis simply did not see the gypsies as 'the kind of supernatural threat that the Jews allegedly posed'.[261]

The Third Reich played similarly fast and loose with racial theory when it came to other 'oriental' peoples. According to some Nazi border scientists, as we have seen, the Mongols were an Aryan-infused 'leader race' led by the 'light-skinned' Ghengis Khan with his 'green or gray-blue eyes and reddish-brown hair'.[262] Tibetans too were deemed far superior to Jews, despite their 'oriental' background.[263] None of these assertions regarding gypsies, Asians, or Jews were based on empirical study of genetic or anthropological evidence by the scientific standards of the interwar period. They were founded upon 'wild and hallucinatory accounts of the nature of Jews, their virtually limitless power, and their responsibility for nearly every harm that has befallen the world', theories 'so divorced from reality that anyone reading it would be hard pressed to conclude that it was anything but the product ... [of] an insane asylum'.[264] The Jews were a priori the epitome of evil based not on the science of eugenics or sociobiology – however flawed those disciplines were – but on a combination of 'religious anti-Semitism and Nordic myth'.[265]

The Nazis were immersed in a shared supernatural imaginary in which certain 'cosmological and ontological beliefs' about the Jews were virtually universal, a belief 'in the supernatural, that all foreigners are not human, that an individual's race determines his moral and intellectual qualities', and 'that Jews are evil'.[266] This mélange of folklore, mythology, and racial hygiene idealized the 'violent application of a prophylactic principle' within the 'German racial body'. In the crucible of war this border scientific, 'prophylactic principle' gave way to the Holocaust.[267]

From Demonization to Extermination, 1939–45

In the summer of 1943 the Regional Education Office of the NSDAP published a pamphlet with the evocative title 'The Jewish Vampire Brings Chaos to the World' ('Der jüdische Vampyr chaotisiert die Welt'). Part of a propaganda series on 'The Jew as World Parasite' sponsored by the Amt Rosenberg, the pamphlet argued that the Second World War was defined by an existential, millennia-old conflict between Aryans and Jews. The Jews were once again trying to destroy 'Germanically defined Europe ... [the] last decisive bastion in their quest for world domination'. The only way to avoid defeat, the pamphlet continued, was to recognize 'the parasitic nature of Jewry' as the main enemy. The stakes of the war were clear: 'a world infected by Jewry or a world free of Jewry'.[268]

Indicating the important relationship between anti-Semitic imagination and extermination, the author acknowledged that every civilization has a mythology that creates its power. 'Such a monstrous power reveals not only a pure creative dreamscape,' the author continued, but also 'the destructive Jewish dream of world domination. He has propagated political and economic black magic for three millennia ... If anywhere the power of the Nordic spiritual wings begin to become lame, so is the heavy essence of Ahasuerus [here again conflating the Jewish vampire with the wandering Jew] sucking on the weakening muscles ... Wherever a wound is ripped open on the body of a nation, the Jewish demon always feeds in the sick place ... [like a] powerful parasite from dreams.'[269]

Based on a quintessentially Nazi combination of supernatural reasoning and biopolitical window-dressing, the author insisted that Jews acted as they did because they 'have no organic form of soul and therefore no racial form'. Race researchers had proved this point, the Nazi propagandist insisted, based on 'rigorous scientific proof'. The biological laws of 'Jewish parasites' indicated that 'diverse forms of Jewry could only exist ... [through] parasitic feeding on the Nordic race'.[270] From the 'demon [Jew] springs the undaunted predator gnawing on all expressions of the Nordic soul'.[271] The 'evil demon of the Jews' ensured that nothing productive could take shape. Jews were 'spongers' (*Schmarotzen*), not in a metaphorical sense but in terms of the 'laws of life (biology)'. Just as 'parasitical apparitions' bored 'ever deeper' into their plant or animal victim, 'sucking out the last elements of life, so is it precisely the same when the Jew forces himself into society through open wounds, feeding on its racial and creative powers – until its disintegration'.[272] Having taken over the Soviet Union through Bolshevism, the Jews now threatened to bring the same infernal disease to Germany.[273] Only the Third Reich could 'provide an 'armoury in the bitterly hard struggle against the chaos-causing spirit of the Jewish vampire'.[274]

'The Jewish Vampire Brings Chaos to the World' employed all the anti-Semitic tropes circulating through the Nazi supernatural imaginary – the Jew as demon, vampire, parasite, apparition, Bolshevik, and secret occult wire-puller, sucking the life force out of Nordic-Aryan-Germanic civilization.[275] This was not mere propaganda. Nazi leaders genuinely viewed the Jews as omnipotent, supernatural monsters responsible for the devastation of the Second World War (and every other crime throughout history).[276] It was 'incredible that a handful of Jews should be able to turn the whole globe topsy-turvy!' Gerda Bormann wrote in private correspondence with her husband Martin. 'Because – as Goebbels says – we aren't fighting the three Great Powers, but a single power that is behind them, something that is much worse, and this is the reason why I can't at present imagine how we shall get peace ever, even if we win the war.'[277]

The Third Reich's brain trust truly *believed* these supernatural tropes. Such supernatural reasoning took on an increasingly violent and totalizing character in the summer and autumn of 1941, at the moment the decision for exterminating all European Jewry was made, in conjunction with the existential battle against Judeo-Bolshevism in the East.[278] In December 1941, shortly after approving Heydrich's initial plan for the 'Final Solution', Hitler remarked: 'Now, he who destroys life is himself risking death. That's the secret of what is happening to the Jews. This destructive role of the Jew has in a way providential explanation.' Nature, as Hitler had argued in *Mein Kampf* fifteen years earlier, 'wanted the Jew to be the ferment that causes peoples to decay, thus providing these peoples with an opportunity for a healthy reaction.' 'In the long run,' he concluded, 'nature eliminates the noxious elements.'[279] Here, plainly articulated, was the flipside of Hitler's border scientific glorification of Ario-Germanic racial purity: the 'demonizing and extermination of Jewishness'.[280]

In February 1942, Hitler employed another quasi-biological, quasi-supernatural metaphor to explain Jewish extermination: 'The discovery of the Jewish virus is one of the greatest revolutions that have taken place in the world. The battle in which we are engaged today is the same sort of battle waged, during the last century, by Pasteur and Koch. How many diseases have their origin in the Jewish virus!'[281] Auschwitz, in this sense, was the border scientific byproduct of the Nazis' faith-based vision of racial purification and Aryan utopia.[282] 'Hitler seems to have envisaged something akin to a nuclear winter in the event that "the Jew" triumphed,' Michael Burleigh reasons. The Jew's crown would represent 'the funeral wreath of humanity', the Führer warned, dooming the human race to near extinction, as it had done thousands of years before.' 'To forestall this dread outcome,' Hitler believed, 'only some massive act of purifying violence seemed commensurate'.[283]

How and to what extent would this act of purifying violence be carried out? Although the Jews were included in broader eugenical conversations, they were not initially subject to mass sterilization or euthanasia after September 1939. Nor were the Jews targeted, qua Jews, in the first wave of Hitler's Commissar Orders, which instructed the SS and Wehrmacht to eliminate Bolshevik partisans and party officials with extreme prejudice. The decision to include 'Jews in party and state employment' among the victims occurred relatively late in the process, ten days after the invasion of the Soviet Union on 22 June 1941.[284] Once the floodgates to murder had been opened, however, the decision to exterminate *all* European Jews, regardless of circumstance, appeared almost inexorable, drawing on an imaginary conception of the Jews as vampiric, near omnipotent monsters whose sole purpose was to destroy Aryan civilization.

This totalizing vision of Jewish monstrosity drew on Christianity and a vulgar form of Darwinism, to be sure, but also on folklore studies, occultism, and border science.[285] As Michael Kater reminds us, the SS Einsatzgruppen relied on the 'most German of all sagas: the Song of the Nibelungen' in justifying their inhuman actions against the Russian Jews.[286] And while German folklorists were not 'directly guilty of exterminating Jewish life,' writes Christoph Daxelmuller, the 'almost unbelievable pleasure taken by German-language *Volkskunde* in grotesquely caricaturing Jews as child and ritual murderers,

stinking subhumans, and sexual psychopaths' played an important role in justifying murder on the Eastern Front.[287]

So did the efforts of Himmler's SS Witch Division. Working with border
scientific researchers at Strasbourg, Franz Six, and Rudolf Levin helped develop
the ideological foundations for the 'Final Solution'.[288] Behind the 'martyred and
torn-apart bodies of our mothers and girls burned to ashes in the witch trials,'
Himmler averred, we can only suspect that 'our eternal enemy, the Jew, has
played his bloody hand under some mantle or through one of his organizations'.[289]

Drawing on this 'evidence' of Jewish wire-pullers behind the Church's extermination of 'witches' (German women), Six and others argued that Nazi
authorities did not have to rely on concrete evidence of criminal intent to
justify the elimination of the Reich's racial enemies.[290] Just as the Inquisition
believed that 'witches must be exterminated in order to destroy the devil and
interrupt the absurd genetics by which witches could only bear witch daugh-
ters', so the Third Reich believed that the 'Nordic master race' might achieve
world domination only by 'exterminating' the Jewish 'enemy race' that infected
the healthy population with 'racial tuberculosis'.[291]

Hence Nazi justifications for the 'Final Solution' were based on fantastical
conceptions of the Jews out of all relation to historical, biological, or anthropological reality.[292] There is no better proof of the scientific absurdity of Nazi
racial thinking than the Third Reich's efforts to cultivate a closer diplomatic
and military relationship with East Asian, Indian, and Middle Eastern ('Semitic')
peoples at the precise moment that they were expending enormous resources,
completely unnecessarily, to murder every possible Jew in Europe.[293] To resolve
this blatant contradiction, Nazi race theorists merely engaged in what Raymond
Williams called 'the labour of selective tradition'. They argued, without any
evidence, that Arabs, Persians, and northern Indians were part of a common
Indo-Aryan master race, whereas the Jews – who most biologists understood as
a mix of Semitic and European peoples – were deemed to be completely alien.[294]

Although tens of thousands of 'mixed race' Roma and Sinti perished at
Auschwitz, we must recall that Himmler, with Hitler's approval, ordered that
'pure' gypsies be allowed to survive. In the Nazis' border scientific cosmology,
after all, the gypsies were the likely descendants of the original Aryans from
northwest India.[295] 'Aryan' gypsies even received favourable treatment at
Auschwitz – from Rudolf Hoess no less, a former Artamanen – and were
considered for an 'Indian legion' of Aryan soldiers.[296] And yet every European
Jew, regardless of ethnic background, was to be tracked down and murdered.

To be sure, as noted earlier, many eugenicists in Britain and the United States
defined Jews and other peoples as racially other, often in arbitrary ways. Some
Anglo-American scientists promoted reprehensible policies of sterilization

and segregation as well. But the premise of the Nazi 'Final Solution' went far beyond the 'science' of eugenics, defining the Jews simultaneously as vampiric monsters and a pervasive biological disease outside the bounds of humanity. 'Vagueness about the desired dystopia, where the farmer prised the clods apart, the soldier stood sentinel, and mothers produced healthy "Aryan" babies seriatim,' writes Michael Burleigh, 'contrasted with the "thick description" lavished on the Jews, whose eradication was integral to Hitler's reading of the cycle from perdition to redemption.' The 'power ascribed to the Jews in this pseudo-cosmology differentiated anti-Semitism from other forms of "racism".'[297] The 'Final Solution' may have been facilitated by a broader European biopolitical and colonial project gone awry. It may have been catalyzed by total war against Judeo-Bolshevism on the Eastern Front. But regardless of the multiple factors that made the Holocaust possible, Jewish 'persecution and extermination', in the words of Alon Confino, was always 'built on fantasy'.[298]

***

In *A World Without Jews*, Confino emphasizes the 'patterns of meaning and purpose in a world of fantasies' about Jews that peopled the Nazi imagination.[299] This alternatively biopolitical and mythical figuring of one's friends and enemies – whether Aryan or Jew – was emblematic of the broader interplay between science and the supernatural in the Third Reich.[300] Not all Nazi science was pseudo- or border scientific, of course. Nevertheless, it is clear that frequent recourse to supernatural thinking made possible the wholly monstrous, *unscientific* approach that undergirded Nazi policies of racial resettlement, eugenics, and genocide.[301]

'German holistic science,' Anne Harrington suggests, 'worked as a multilevel discourse in part because its scientists found ways to craft their most certain truths out of words and images rich with cultural resonances.'[302] In other words, the Nazi invocation of the racial other – be they Jews, Slavs, or gypsies – was culturally contingent and highly malleable, part of a dream world in which 'illusory abstraction was made real through massive violence'. Once 'divorced from any restraining moral or spiritual frame of reference', such border scientific insights into race and space had lethal results.[303]

Before the war, Hitler, Himmler, and other Nazi ideologues had relatively few opportunities to realize their racial and eugenical fantasies. But what remained only a pipedream before September 1939 became a reality during the ensuing conflict.[304] Certainly the Nazi resettlement project was based on broader European colonial premises and practical military-economic necessities. The ideology that guided these policies, however, was fuelled by supernatural conceptions of race and space.[305]

Similarly, not all aspects of Nazi eugenics were motivated by border science. Even the Ahnenerbe produced *some* potentially valuable research.[306] It is, moreover, extremely difficult to differentiate consistently between border science or so-called 'pseudoscience, which supported the extermination policies of National Socialism', and ostensibly 'uncorrupted, innocent racial biology'.[307]

Although biopolitical, even eugenical thinking was popular across Europe, however, Nazi attempts to sterilize and murder millions went beyond any prevailing understanding of eugenics in natural scientific circles within the United States, Britain, or Sweden.[308] Were the 'Jewish Question' truly scientific in nature, it would have been both highly impractical and improbable for the Nazis to seek an alliance with Arab (Semitic) peoples, much less South or East Asians, while expending so many resources attempting to murder every Jew in Europe.

The Holocaust was part of a longer-term pattern of European colonial violence against the racial other, exacerbated by total war, economic scarcity, and virulent anti-Bolshevism. The Third Reich's specifically genocidal plans toward the Jews were nonetheless more radical than those of other European colonizers toward the ethnic other, because the Nazis drew on and distorted not merely Darwin, Rudyard Kipling, or the Bible, but a supernatural imaginary they shared with Lanz von Liebenfels and Theodor Fritsch.[309] If the process of genocide was conducted in a highly technocratic fashion, its foundations lay in a conception of the Jews as supernatural monsters.[310] Only by associating Jews with vampiric, parasitic, almost superhuman opponents locked in a centuries-old conspiracy to destroy the Aryan race could the Nazis lay the conceptual groundwork for murdering so many innocent civilians in so monstrous a fashion.[311]

NAZI TWILIGHT
Miracle Weapons, Supernatural Partisans, and the Collapse of the Third Reich

'You know that I think in real terms and that I would not like us to fall into the psychosis that ascribes too much meaning to the new [miracle] weapons. I am also not of the opinion that they should now play such a prominent role in the propaganda.'

Albert Speer (August 1944)[1]

'Bring me Germans; I want to drink blood, Swabian blood! I've killed 170 already and I still want more blood.'

German refugee, Elisabeth Kowitzki, reporting an attack she witnessed
by a 'blood-drinking' Slavic partisan (spring 1945)[2]

'If we are destined, like the old Nibelungs, to descend into King Attila's hall, then we'll go proudly and with our heads held high.'

Martin Bormann (April 1945)[3]

Richard Wagner, Hitler's favourite composer, called the final opera of his *Ring* cycle *Götterdämmerung* ('Twilight of the Gods').[4] Emblematic of the folklore revival that Wagner helped inspire, the title derived from the Old Norse 'Ragnarok', connoting the 'fate of the Gods', culminating in a final, cataclysmic battle with their enemies. Drawn from the thirteenth-century poetry and prose Edda, Ragnarok foretold a series of attacks by the Giants from Jotunheim, the Fire Demons of Muspellheim, and the Midgard Serpent. In this terrible melee Odin, Thor, Baldur and other gods are killed, the earth and sky are destroyed, and the sun turns black. Nevertheless, as foretold by prophecy, two of Thor's sons survive, Baldur returns from Hel, and the earth and humanity are reborn.[5]

Götterdämmerung is different in many respects from the Edda's *Ragnarok*, since Wagner's tetralogy was based primarily on the medieval *Nibelungenlied*, with the dwarves (*Nibelungen*) Hagen and Alberich standing in for the Edda's Giants and Fire Demons. But both accounts culminate in a final battle against implacable supernatural enemies. And both end the same way: with the Nordic gods and heroes consumed by fire in a message of redemption.[6] This idea of existential conflagration, a series of battles that would strain Germany to its core, producing either final victory (*Endsieg*) or total defeat, became especially prominent during the last years of the Second World War.[7]

Twilight imagery reinforced a wartime renaissance in supernatural thinking, an 'unshakeable faith in the power of miraculous discoveries in the context of war'.[8] Such miraculous thinking extended to armaments, producing a desperate search for hyper-destructive, increasingly fantastical miracle weapons.[9] Twilight-inspired thinking was equally apparent in Operation Werewolf, a Special Forces unit designed to carry out vicious guerrilla attacks on Allied occupiers and collaborators.[10] At the same time, and even more remarkably, ethnic Germans fleeing the Russians accused Slavic partisans of vampirism.[11]

During the final months of the war, when defeat appeared inevitable, many Nazis and millions of ordinary Germans wanted to believe that death was not permanent, that fantasy was reality, that a 'magical priest' might rescue them from annihilation.[12] In this way the regime's fanciful invocation of miracle weapons, of partisan werewolves and vampires, of ritual self-immolation, functioned as a form of therapy for Germans suffering through material and psychological distress.[13] If twilight imagery helped Germans reconcile themselves to everyday violence, criminality, and loss, however, it also augured the disintegration of the Third Reich and Germany's post-war rebirth.[14]

Miracle Weapons and Border Science in the Pursuit of Final Victory

In September 1945, Hitler's Armaments Minister Albert Speer assembled a selection of documents recording the history of 'miracle weapons' in the Third Reich. He began by excerpting a speech given by the Hitler Youth leader Baldur von Schirach on 6 October 1943, 'We have a collective secret of which the whole German people are already aware.' 'Details are certainly not known,' Schirach admitted. And it was 'too early to speak with certainty about the debut of these new weapons'. But sooner or later, the miracle weapons would arrive.[15] Speer believed that such faith-based assertions needed to be curtailed and spent the next eighteen months ratcheting down expectations regarding the potential of miracle weapons – but to no avail.[16]

Certainly all industrial states, especially fascist states, dreamt of new military technologies in the interwar period and over the course of the Second

World War. Nazi Germany, however, offered an ideal environment for pursuing so-called miracle weapons to the exclusion of more mainstream armaments production.[17] For the Third Reich combined a fetishization of new technologies with widespread border scientific reasoning – what George Mosse calls 'magic realism' and Alexander Geppert and Till Kössler call 'miraculous thinking'.[18] Such thinking, they argue, is intrinsic to understanding the Nazi pursuit of 'miracle weapons' at the end of the war.[19]

An obsession with new, destructive miracle technologies was a fundamental component of Nazi ideology and practice during the last phase of the war. It was a direct outgrowth of interwar, science fiction fantasies about developing weapons that might transcend Germany's strategic disadvantages in terms of geography, resources, or manpower.[20] A belief that final victory might be achieved through miracle technologies was moreover a logical corollary to many Nazis' fascination with ancient, possibly extraterrestrial superhumans, who possessed the ability to produce sophisticated weapons, exercise mind control, or wield lightning.

This first section looks at Nazi efforts to develop miracle weapons and border scientific technologies in the last years of the war. In proceeding, I do not want to suggest that all armaments efforts were defined by border scientific thinking. Nor do I dismiss the Third Reich's impressive wartime advances in military technology, from jet engines to guided missiles.

Instead, following Speer's admonitions above, I wish to emphasize the degree to which Germany's extraordinary military-industrial complex was repeatedly challenged, even undermined, materially and strategically by a Nazi belief in border scientific ideas and technologies. In their faith-based conviction that miraculous new (or lost ancient) technologies would somehow emerge from the ether to rescue Germany from *Götterdämmerung*, the Nazis' search for miracle weapons was only partially the result of wartime necessity, perched instead at the nexus of science and the supernatural that defined so much thinking in the Third Reich.[21]

Nuclear and Rocket Technology

Until Speer took charge of weapons production in February 1942, Hitler had no coherent armaments policy. He changed priorities rapidly based on a combination of shifting realities on the ground and his own arbitrary preferences for offensive over defensive weapons.[22] One area where Speer, Hitler, and many other leaders agreed was the German need for superior quality weapons – since the Allies, at least from 1942 on, would always win the munitions battle in terms of sheer quantity.[23] The decision to favour quality over quantity is part of what led to Speer's emphasis on efficiency and organization as well as Hitler and Himmler's interest in miracle technologies. Nevertheless, the headlong investment in miracle weapons derived from a Nazi fascination with border scientific thinking as well.

Abetting this border scientific trend was the SS. As the military situation deteriorated, the SS insinuated itself directly into armaments production. Himmler's interest in military technology, epitomized by the IWZ, brought dozens of concentration camps, hundreds of SS scientists, and thousands of slave labourers into the equation.[24] Himmler agreed with Hitler that the emphasis on 'qualitative superiority' meant focusing on single weapons. Also like Hitler, Himmler was a dilettante who eschewed highly complex projects in favour of ideas that were easily accessible or personally familiar. For this reason he paid little attention to nuclear technology, preferring to invest, like his Führer, in fighter production, rockets, and other weapons reminiscent of early twentieth-century science fiction (and less dependent on the revolutionary 'Jewish science' of atomic physics).[25]

Before we turn to Hitler and Himmler's extraordinary preoccupation with rocket technology, we should spend a moment on the Third Reich's nuclear research programme. The conventional wisdom holds that when the war ended the Third Reich was still years away from developing the technology for an atomic bomb.[26] Still, some circumstantial evidence suggests that small groups of scientists conducted research into weaponizing uranium at Auschwitz, Prague, and Nuremberg.[27]

Additional evidence, also fragmentary, indicates that the Germans may have been further along in enriching uranium than previously thought. Some reports indicate that a few scientists were working to develop a uranium-based 'dirty-bomb', possibly conducting tests in late 1944 and early 1945 in Ohrdruf, Thuringia, or the island of Rügen.[28] Recent excavations under the Mauthausen-Gusen labour camp, initially built for aircraft construction, indicate a high level of radioactivity, adding fuel to rumours of a secret atomic weapons laboratory sponsored by Himmler.[29]

Calling into question these reports – and Hitler and Himmler's seriousness about nuclear weapons – is a better-documented 1942 presentation on uranium–235 organized by the Reich Research Council and led by Werner Heisenberg. Apparently, Himmler missed the meeting because his secretary didn't consider it a priority. Hitler showed a similar disinterest.[30] The destruction of the Norwegian hard-water facility in February 1943 and sinking of the heavy-water transport ship *Hydro* a year later reinforced Hitler and Himmler's desire to focus on the rocket programme and other experimental aircraft.[31]

It is possible that nuclear technology was discussed in respect to other kinds of weapons. On 10 October 1942 the German Army High Command apparently commissioned an investigation into the possibility of atomic disintegration, chain reactions, and anti-gravity machines: 'flying saucers'.[32] Ostensibly developed by rocket experts, including Walter Dornberger and Rudolf Schriever, these flying saucers may have possessed powers of electrical and electromagnetic disruption (a goal of so-called death rays pursued by the SS, as we shall see below).[33] Ensuing test projects, named *Kugelblitz* and *Feuerball*, are potentially responsible for the so-called 'Foo Fighters', whose appearance in 1943 was reported by the Allied air forces. Witnesses reported small round flying objects that flew into the paths of Allied bombers to create confusion and cause electrical failures.[34] The archival documents do reflect an overwhelming German preoccupation with disrupting enemy bombing sorties, including all kinds of experiments, from the practical to the outrageous, aimed at stopping them.[35]

In the meantime, German rocket research was both extremely advanced and rife with border scientific speculation. Before 1933, German rocket enthusiasts, including Willy Ley, Johannes Winkler, and Max Valier, had started the Society for Spaceship Travel (*Verein für Raumschiffahrt*) – a Society, it should be noted, that included novelists and dramatists like Thomas Mann and George Bernard Shaw and science-fiction writers such as H. G. Wells. Wernher von Braun, who would become Germany's most influential rocket scientist, joined the Society in 1930.[36]

More remarkable are the views of von Braun's mentor, the early pioneer of the German rocket programme, Hermann Oberth. Like the head of the interwar Artamanen movement, the esoterically inclined Oberth was born in, of all places, Transylvania. Affiliated closely with Rudolf Hess, Oberth was fascinated by parapsychology and 'Thulean occultism'. In a series of post-war articles and interviews Oberth likewise insisted on the existence of UFOs and alien technologies that the United States had supposedly appropriated but refused to share with the public.[37]

In 1932 the German Army began supporting rocket research, employing Oberth, von Braun, Dornberger, and others. By the mid-1930s the Wehrmacht had settled on Peenemünde, an island in the Baltic, as the main development site. Over the next few years, led by Dornberger and von Braun, the German rocket industry achieved great success, improving upon techniques introduced by the American Robbert Goddard. By the summer of 1942 the army researchers had developed the A5 'Retaliation' rocket (*Vergeltungswaffe* or V–1) and plans for the first ballistic missile, the A4 (V–2).[38]

With the deterioriation of the military situation, the SS began to play an increasing role in aviation research. The SS first insinuated itself into aircraft production. Then, beginning in the summer of 1943, this expanded to rockets and other 'secret weapons'. Von Braun, who by this time had an SS rank, nonetheless continued to work for the army and air force. With the 20 July 1944 assassination attempt on Hitler, however, which he blamed on disgruntled army officers, Himmler was given control over the rocket programme. This marginalized the role of experts like von Braun in favour of ideologues such as the SS-Obergruppenführer Dr Hans Kammler.[39]

Kammler was a General Lieutenant in the Waffen-SS and Luftwaffe engineer. Prior to taking over the SS weapons programme, his claim to fame had been expanding the size and efficiency of Auschwitz's cremation facilities under the SS Concentration Camp Chief (and BDW advocate) Oswald Pohl.[40] Through his work at Auschwitz, Kammler gained a reputation for ruthless efficiency and creative thinking, soon being assigned to direct the Ahnenerbe's 'special projects unit' (see below). By the summer of 1944 Kammler, assisted by Himmler's aggressive sponsorship and Hitler's distrust of traditional military elites, officially replaced the rocket scientist Dornberger as head of the programme. The former architect of Auschwitz then enlisted thousands of concentration-camp prisoners, with Speer's approval, in order to build underground research facilities near the Harz mountains in Thuringia.[41]

In March 1945, Kammler was promoted to General Plenipotentiary for Jet Aircraft, becoming independent even of Speer.[42] In April 1945, 450 key scientists joined Kammler, including Dornberger and von Braun, whose efforts were now supplemented by thousands of slave labourers.[43]

Having commandeered the rocket programme from Dornberger and other professional rocket scientists, Kammler produced little of value in terms of miracle technologies. Still, he and his colleagues were responsible for hundreds of executions and thousands more deaths due to their abuse of concentration-camp labour and border scientific experiments.[44]

While Kammler and the SS promised increasingly exaggerated results, Speer became all the more cautious.[45] In early August 1944, as the long awaited V-2 rocket awaited its initial sortie, he warned that 'we cannot depend on the effect of these new weapons as a completely certain matter'.[46] Four weeks later he admonished Goebbels to ratchet down the Propaganda Ministry's campaign on behalf of the V-1 and especially the new V-2, which was unrealistic and gave false hope to the German people.[47]

There were important developments, Speer acknowledged, but 'it is necessary in this circle to make clear that these new weapons cannot promise a universal panacea'. 'Revenge weapons [V-1] ... [might] present [the enemy] with some discernible surprise,' he observed. And yet 'those new weapons, which we really need [such as the V-2] ... will not yet have a decisive impact for a few months'.[48] Goebbels shouldn't promise 'miraculous results' from the V-2, Speer argued, because one cannot 'expect in the next months a new weapon that will have a decisive impact on the outcome of the war'.[49]

The problem was the regime's consistently false expectations regarding military technologies out of all proportion with reality. 'What surprised us in particular in regard to the V–1 is its psychological effect [on the British]; Speer explained, which was not exceedingly severe. As for the psychological effect of the V–2, he continued, that too 'is something we cannot say . . . I can only say that . . . our new weapon . . . will require considerable time before it has any effect.'[50] Speer's admonitions were borne out by reports from the British and Americans, received a few weeks later, observing that the 'military value of the V–2' – and the likelihood of the V–3 ever reaching New York – were so 'negligible' that they must have been meant by the Germans as a mere 'diversionary' tactic.[51]

With the exception of Speer, however, nearly every leading Nazi seemingly believed that miracle weapons could turn the tide of war. On 15 September 1944, shortly after the V–2 was deployed, Speer therefore warned a group of political and military leaders, including Bormann, Himmler, and the generals Sepp Dietrich, Heinz Guderian, Gerd von Rundstedt, and Wilhelm Keitel:

> The faith in the soon-to-come deployment of new militarily decisive weapons is spread generally across the troops. They expect this deployment in the next few days. This opinion is also shared seriously among high-ranking officers. It is questionable whether it is the right thing to do, in such a difficult moment, to create disappointment that cannot but have an unfavourable effect on our military morale by encouraging hopes that cannot be fulfilled in so short a time. [Insofar] as the population waits daily . . . for the miracle of new weapons and doubt is thereby fostered as to whether we recognize that it is already 'a few minutes before midnight' and continuing to withhold these new, 'stockpiled' weapons can no longer be explained, it raises the question as to whether this propaganda makes sense.[52]

In November 1944, Speer again wrote to Goebbels, this time privately, urging him to discontinue the practice of propagating exaggerated reports of positive military developments, which gave people 'hopes that could not be fulfilled in the foreseeable future.'[53] Goebbels nonetheless doubled down on his faith-based propaganda.[54]

In December, Speer followed up with a detailed briefing to a group of military and political experts: 'You have got today a small insight into the various new developments which have been completed recently. You have certainly seen that we do not have and never will have a miracle weapon!' From a 'technical perspective it has always been clear, for anyone who wants to know it, that miracles [*Wunder*] in the technical sphere, as expected by lay people, are simply not possible'. For this reason, Speer reiterated, it made no sense to continue talking about miracle weapons, whether privately or publicly. What German leaders (and implicitly Hitler) should be doing instead, he suggested, was to repeat the words that 'Churchill once said after Dunkirk, when he promised the people "blood, sweat and tears"'.[55]

Speer, the Nazi official with the greatest knowledge of the Third Reich's technical capabilities, could not have been clearer or more consistent in his sobering assessment. And yet he was repeatedly frustrated by Nazi Party leaders' fantastical obsessions with obtaining and deploying miracle weapons that had little or no basis in military reality.[56] Goebbels not only ignored Speer's admonitions, but 'intentionally spread false rumors to divert attention from the increasingly doom-laden course of the war', including sending 'type-written prophecies, anonymously, through the mail suggesting that victory was imminent'.[57]

The cumulative effect of these false rumours is best represented by a conversation that Speer had with the Gauleiter of Lower Franconia, Otto Hellmuth, at the end of March 1945. Even as Allied tanks pressed their way into Würzburg, with the war nearly over, Hellmuth declared: 'It would all be nonsensical, if there wasn't a chance to change the situation at the last minute. Comrade Speer, when will the new weapon that we're all waiting for be deployed?' Speer responded, as he had for the previous eighteen months: 'they [the miracle weapons] are not coming, since the propaganda has not been correct; they have never been produced.'[58]

Despite Speer's repeated protestations, the 'highest party circles' insisted on believing 'in the air magic being put together by "Uncle Heinrich"'.[59] Even Bormann, normally sceptical of Himmler's pet projects, wrote to his wife Gerda in April 1945 that Kammler's long-promised secret weapons might come to fruition in time to salvage victory from the jaws of defeat.[60] Ironically, Kammler may have been the only Nazi leader, besides Speer, to acknowledge the truth. On 17 April 1945, one day after refusing a requisition by Himmler, Kammler mysteriously disappeared – and with him the last hopes that the Third Reich might be saved by a miracle.[61]

Death Rays and Anti-Gravity

Frustrated by Speer's resistance to dilettantish 'experiments' in military technology, Himmler instructed Kammler to set up his own 'secret projects office' within the context of the Ahnenerbe.[62] In March 1942, Himmler had already instructed the Director of the Skoda Works in the Reich Protectorate of Bohemia and Moravia, William Voss, to evaluate and duplicate captured Allied weapons. Since the Ahnenerbe's 'special projects office' was also charged with developing 'second generation' weapons, Kammler set up shop at the Skoda Works. There, Kammler directed projects on advanced weapons systems including, according to some accounts, anti-gravity devices, guided weapons, and anti-aircraft lasers ('death rays').[63]

As Kammler's projects ramped up during the final two years of the war, Himmler pursued his own border scientific agenda. Years earlier, the Luftwaffe officer Schröder-Stranz had attempted, without success, to get the Luftwaffe to sponsor his 'ray device' (*Strahlengeräte*) that might putatively shoot rival planes out of the sky. But Schröder-Stranz found an eager audience in the Ahnenerbe, as Himmler turned 'once again to a charlatan' in order to pursue his border scientific fantasies.[64]

Unfortunately, Speer had managed to convince Hitler in May 1944 not to invest money in *new* weapons projects. Thus Himmler and Schröder-Stranz argued that the ray device 'apparatus' was not a weapon. It was a device that could produce healthy 'rays' that had practical health purposes as well as 'death rays' that might be employed in combat. When the device inevitably proved ineffective as a weapon, Schröder-Stranz suggested it could be adapted for use as a 'detection device' (*Mutungsgerät*) to find oil reserves, something that excited Himmler due to the Reich's critical lack of natural resources.[65]

The timing of Schröder-Stranz's transfer from the Luftwaffe to the SS was perfect. Oswald Pohl, director of the SS concentration-camp system, economic specialist, and border science enthusiast, was convinced he could locate oil within the borders of the German Reich. Hence Pohl, despite the skepticism of professional radiologists, afforded Schröder-Stranz space at Dachau – alongside BDW researchers – to prepare a team of 'technicians' who might work on adapting his 'ray device'. Only seven months later, in February 1945, did Himmler finally pull the plug on this explicitly occult-based search for fossil fuels – not because of its border scientific premises but because the catastrophic situation at the front made further experiments impractical.[66]

While Schröder-Stranz worked on adapting his ray device for use in the search for oil, Himmler enlisted border scientists in a last-ditch effort to locate gold reserves. Himmler focused the project on the Rhine and Inn rivers, where Hitler, most likely inspired by Wagner's *Rheingold* and the local lore of his youth in Braunau-am-Inn, insisted there were considerable untapped resources. For his part, Himmler recommended the Isar in his own home town of Munich.[67] Since mainstream geologists tended to disagree with Hitler and Himmler's assumptions – finding no substantive evidence of gold in either river valley – Himmler enlisted the help of the SS border scientist Karl Wienert, a veteran of the Tibet expedition. Undaunted by the scientific literature, Himmler encouraged Wienert to focus his efforts on the areas around his home town and Hitler's, citing circumstantial evidence of 'panning for gold in the Rhine and Isar' from the eighteenth century.[68]

Of course, Wienert's efforts proved unsuccessful, which is why in the spring of 1944 Himmler decided to bring in another famous border scientist, the dowser Josef Wimmer. Wimmer had built his reputation by dowsing for the

Bavarian government in the 1930s. During the war Himmler charged Wimmer with various esoteric tasks, such as using his divining rod to look for bombs in the synagogues of Krakow. He also enlisted Wimmer to train teams of 'water seekers' in the homoeopathic (BDW) gardens at Dachau (by this time a veritable mecca of border scientific activity).[69] So impressed were Himmler and Wüst by Wimmer's work there that he was appointed head of the Ahnenerbe's Division for Applied Geology and afforded a level of independence previously granted only to the esoteric *Welteislehre*-infused SS Meteorological Institute under Scultetus.[70]

In the summer of 1942, Hitler himself designated Wimmer as special Reich geologist for his brilliance in teaching divining techniques to others.[71] Six months later, Himmler decided that every Waffen-SS geological troop unit needed at least one diviner; one Waffen-SS division in Belgrade had three. In August 1943, again seemingly inspired by the mythical 'Rhine gold', Himmler instructed Wimmer's dowsing teams to look for 'fabulous treasure' in the Hohenhöwen mountains near the Rhine in southern Germany. When Wimmer and his dowsers found no treasure, Himmler decided to team up Wimmer with Wienert, hoping that the two border scientists might achieve together what they could not alone. When that dream proved ephemeral, Himmler turned their attention from the Rhinegold to lodestone deposits.[72]

Alongside the desperate search for natural resources, Himmler continued to pursue border scientific weapons inspired by Germanic mythology. In October 1944, for example, the firm Elemag-Hildesheim proposed a weapon, loosely inspired by some of Tesla's experiments, that would use the insulating material in the atmosphere as a means to weaponize electricity.[73] Himmler's enthusiasm for this proposal was not based, however, on any familiarity with Tesla's experiments. It was grounded in his long-held occult-inspired belief that there were untapped electromagnetic forces in the universe, akin to Thor's hammer, which might be harnessed with appropriate technologies. These 'paranormal powers and extraordinary weapons', Himmler believed, 'didn't have to do with natural thunder and lightning'. They 'pertained to an earlier, highly developed tool of our ancestors that was obviously only in the possession of a few, namely the "Asen", who were gods and were privy to an unheard-of knowledge of electricity'.[74] Although he had relegated the more promising pursuit of atomic power to second-rate status, Himmler instructed the Reich Research Council to review Elemag's proposal, leading to the disappointing conclusion that the weapon was impossible to achieve with current technology (or without the Thunder God's ability to tap into the cosmic forces of the universe).[75]

Efforts to weaponize mystical electromagnetic and bioelectrical energies were reinforced by a more general belief in *Welteislehre* and radiesthesia, which posited the existence of untapped geological and physical forces hidden just below the Earth, in space, or in blocks of ice. Inspired by this esoteric belief in high-energy fields and ley lines, the Third Reich set up 'transmitters' at ancient mystical sites such as the Brocken and Feldberg. Some Nazi scientists apparently believed they could issue electrical impulses and possibly Very Low Frequency (VLF) soundwaves, which could interfere with human brain function. Wimmer's divining experiments and Schröder-Stranz's 'ray machine' might have inspired these attempts at harnessing bioeletrical energy for use in psychic warfare.[76]

Meanwhile, Kammler was busy sponsoring large-scale efforts to weaponize border scientific energies. The most legendary of these efforts is the 'anti-gravity' device known as 'the bell' (Die Glocke). One of many secret weapons experiments supposedly carried out in the East, 'the bell' was first reported by the Polish journalist Igor Witkowski, based on classified information ostensibly culled by Polish intelligence before the execution of the SS officer, Jakob Sporrenberg.[77] According to Sporrenberg, through Witkowski, a number of German scientists and test subjects died in late 1944 and early 1945 working on some kind of nuclear-powered, anti-gravitational device or 'bell' ('flying saucer') in Lower Silesia, at a facility known as 'The Giant' near the Wenceslaus mine at the Czech border.[78]

Sporrenberg claimed the bell was a device about twelve to fifteen feet high with two counter-rotating cylinders filled with a liquid, code-named Xerum 525. The fluid was obviously dangerous, looking similar to mercury and kept in lead containers. Other rare light metals such as thorium and beryllium peroxide were used in the experiments, according to one witness, in order to spur anti-gravity propulsion within the bell. Sporrenberg suggested the device used 'vortex compression' and 'magnetic field separation', techniques associated with anti-gravity pioneers such as Viktor Schauberger. Other details reported by crypto-historians, including the use of concave mirrors in order to 'see the past', are impossible to verify.[79]

What can be verified is that the Nazis, including Hitler, were interested in anti-gravity and 'free energy' devices, including the work of the enigmatic Schauberger. When the Nazis took power, Schauberger was best known in central Europe as an esoterically inclined biophysicist who studied the natural action of water, forests, and the earth, arguing that they contained powerful untapped energies. Like his Austrian contemporary Hanns Hörbiger, Schauberger's syncretic, border scientific approach, which included an interest in biodynamic agriculture and radiesthesia, was deeply attractive to many Nazis.[80]

In July 1934 the Nazi industrialist and head of the Third Reich's Economic Chamber (Reichswirtschaftskammer), Albert Pietzsch, organized a meeting between Hitler and Schauberger to discuss practical economic and military applications of Schauberger's border scientific ideas.[81] Reports on the meeting, which are available in the German federal archives, vary. Sceptical of Schauberger's reputation for self-promotion, Hitler requested a copy of the minutes and an assurance that the meeting would not be used 'as an advertisement for his ideas and activities'.[82] After the meeting Hitler and his head of the Reich Chancellery, Hans Lammers, expressed frustration at Schauberger's haughty attitude and coyness about sharing any technical specifics on purifying water, free energy, or other 'secret innovations' – which the biophysicist had promised to do prior to the meeting. Nor was Hitler satisfied with Schauberger's explanation of his relationship with Mussolini, with whom Schauberger had also been in contact.[83]

Suspecting that he had alienated the Führer, Schauberger followed up with a letter to Hitler (and another to Himmler), giving some specifics and now indicating his desire, as an Austro-German, to offer his secrets exclusively to the Third Reich (as opposed to playing Hitler and Mussolini off against each other).[84] By this point, however, Lammers was convinced that Schauberger was a fraud, who had had every opportunity to explain his inventions and failed. Schauberger reinforced the conventional wisdom, Lammers opined, that 'autodidacts' rarely contribute 'groundbreaking inventions' (ironic given the regime's official sponsorship of Hitler, Hörbiger, and other 'self-trained' border scientists).[85] Most revealing in Lammers' report was his concern that Hitler, despite the awkward meeting and dubious nature of Schauberger's work, would nonetheless be swindled, much as the Austrian Emperor Franz Josef had been duped by alchemists promising to turn lead into gold.[86]

Lammers was not wrong. Only a year after meeting Hitler, the esoterically inclined Julius Streicher organized a meeting between Schauberger and some managers at Siemens. The company hired Schauberger on Streicher's recommendation, but let him go in 1937 when his research and development efforts proved pointless.[87] Undaunted by these failures, Hitler permitted the armaments manufacturer Heinkel, in the context of the Four Year Plan, to enlist Schauberger to work on a 'Repulsator' ('repulsine') engine that could harness 'free energy' and possibly produce 'levitational flight'. In 1940, Rudolf Schriever, working for Heinkel, began applying Schauberger's unconventional ideas to a new kind of 'flying saucer' or 'flying top'.[88]

In May 1941, with Germany's invasion of the Soviet Union just one month away, Schauberger was pressured to assist the armed forces in secret experiments to harness invisible energies and anti-gravity devices. Against his will, the SS brought Schauberger to Mauthausen concentration camp, where he was ordered to handpick a group of engineers from among the prisoners.[89] With his new 'team', Schauberger developed multiple projects, nearly identical to those that brought him to Hitler's attention seven years earlier. These included a water purifier, a high-voltage generator to biosynthesize hydrogen fuel made from water, 'atom-smashing' devices, and most famously his rumoured flying saucer or 'Repulsine'.[90]

The Repulsine had a dual purpose, both as an energy generator and a power plant for an aerospace vehicle of saucer-like appearance. Based on second-hand accounts, the craft had 'a diameter of 1.5 meters, weighed 135 kilograms and was started by a small electric motor with takeoff energy supplied by the so-called trout turbine'. When it was tested in the spring of 1945, a scientist who worked with Schauberger reported that 'the flying saucer rose unexpectedly to the ceiling', trailing 'a blue-green and then a silver-colored glow'.[91] A few days after these tests, according to some accounts, a group of Americans arrived and took Schauberger into protective custody, seizing all his research materials under the classified rubric of 'atomic energy research'.[92]

The details of Schauberger's wartime work remain murky. Nevertheless, the combination of authentic primary documents and eyewitness accounts appear to confirm that Schauberger's experiments, which culminated in the Repulsine, brought together nearly all the border scientific ideas and miracle technologies discussed above: harnessing invisible earth rays and death rays; weaponizing electromagnetic forces and bioeletrical impulses; developing atomic energy; and producing new rocket technologies. These experiments seem to have led – admittedly against Schauberger's will – to the deaths of hundreds of concen-tration-camp inmates, scientists, and test subjects through dangerous work conditions, radiation poisoning, or outright murder by the SS.[93] There is, more-over, no evidence that Schauberger's experiments, involving hundreds of scien-tists and thousands of Reichsmarks, resulted in a single operational weapon or aircraft. Nor have the many reports of American exploitation of the border scientific research undertaken by Schauberger, Kammler, and other Nazi scien-tists, obtained via Operation Paperclip, been verified.[94]

With the notable exception of Speer's well-meaning attempts to focus the regime on practical applications of military technology, mainstream science faced a standoff with border science for the duration of the war.[95] Hitler and Himmler's interventions in the war economy were often 'simply nonsensical', whether concerning Wienert and Wimmer's dowsing experiments, Schauberger's 'free energy' devices, or Schröder-Stranz's death rays.[96] Even during the most desperate moments of the war, Nazi science was as preoccu-pied with faith-based fantasies of 'absolute conceptual boundlessness' as it was with practical military technologies. Himmler and others might have accepted natural science 'when it came to making mineral water', Michael Kater observes. When it came to larger, more important projects, however, such as ' "miracle weapons", free reign was given to [their] own speculations or intellectually dubious dreams and thereby ran into methodological labyrinths'.[97] One can only speculate as to how much more effective German armaments production might have been without this Nazi proclivity for miraculous thinking.

Nazi Werewolves and Partisan Vampires

Just a couple of years after the Second World War, the historian Robert Eisler gave a lecture entitled 'Man into Wolf: An Anthropological Interpretation of Sadism, Masochism, and Lycanthropy', to the Royal Society of Medicine in London. A belief in lycanthropy, Eisler began, was prevalent across ancient and medieval Germany. Many Germans believed that a magical change from man into wolf could be brought about 'by donning a wolf's pelt just as the 'Isawiyya and the Bacchic maenads wrap themselves in animals' skins by taking to the woods'.[98]

This belief in lycanthropy, Eisler argued, had been resuscitated in Nazi Germany. He noted that the Third Reich employed the 'uncanny word' *werewolf* to designate the secret terrorist and para-military 'Organisation Werewolf'. The term was employed again in 'Himmler's rabid speech on the new Volkssturm [people's militia] of 1945', whom the Reichsführer encouraged to 'harass "like were-wolves" the allied lines of communication in occupied Germany'.[99] Hitler himself hoped that wartime necessity might eradicate 'thousands of years of human domestication'. Nothing could be more thrilling, the Führer suggested, than 'to see once more in the eyes of a pitiless youth the gleam of pride and independence of the beast of prey', who, organized in 'wolf packs', might hunt down and murder Germany's enemies in the dead of night.[100]

Eisler's lecture, delivered only two years after Germany's surrender, hit upon a salient aspect of supernatural thinking in the Third Reich: the remarkable persistence of werewolves and vampires in the wartime imagination. For just as the Nazis modelled their guerrilla attacks on werewolves, ethnic Germans fleeing the Soviets accused Slavic partisans of vampiric tendencies, as noted earlier. These strange accounts, collected by the SS folklorist Alfred Karasek, confirm the contemporary impression of a wartime resurgence in occultism and popular superstition across the population.[101] Ethnic Germans' conviction that their enemies transformed into vampires, like the hopes Nazi leaders pinned to werewolves, are emblematic of the final phase of the war.

Long before 1945 the Nazis, along with many Germans, had imbibed folk tales as a central feature of popular consciousness, linked not to formal religious faith (*Glaube*) but popular superstition (*Aberglaube*).[102] It might seem implausible that ordinary Germans, much less Nazi leaders, put any authentic stake in these traditions. And yet 'folklore and oral tales', in the words of Monica Black, 'need not have an internal logic' to make sense to the people who reproduced them.[103] The widespread preoccupations with Nazi werewolves and Slavic vampires provide rather an important window into the 'psychology of violence and its legacies in the wake of war', essential to our larger argument about 'taking fantasy and the monstrous seriously' in coming to terms with the Third Reich.[104]

Nazi Werewolves

The Nazi idea of organizing German soldiers and partisans in bands of werewolves did not emerge for the first time in the winter of 1944. Hitler, whose first name derives from 'father wolf', enthusiastically appropriated the (were) wolf metaphor throughout his life.[105] He compared himself to a wolf on more than one occasion, claiming that 'I don't need to be afraid of wolves, I myself am the wolf.'[106] Hitler also employed the (were)wolf metaphor in praising the Hitler Youth as well as his Stormtroopers, who 'flung themselves upon the enemy in packs of eight and ten', like 'wolves'.[107] Hitler referred to his headquarters in the Ukraine between 1942 and 1943 as his 'Werewolf' compound and christened his better-known headquarters near Rastenburg in East Prussia the 'Wolf's Lair' (*Wolfschanze*).[108] Eisler even speculates that Hitler 'suffered from a cyclothymic manic-depressive psychosis', which explained his 'lycanthropic' transformation into an 'accursed state of a blood-stained predatory werewolf or lion-man'.[109]

There were precursors to the Werewolf Organization outside the ambit of Hitler's own supernatural imaginary.[110] The Ahnenerbe chief Walther Wüst noted that the 'incarnation of the Werewolf runs through Aryan and German fairy tales and naming conventions', as one of the Ur-Germanic characteristics of the German racial spirit.[111] The archetype of the Ur-Germanic partisan could be found in tales of werewolves, who like wild hunters, protected Germans against their enemies.[112] There was no connection between the 'werewolf and slavic vampire', according to the Nazi folklorist Mackensen. While vampires were evil, werewolves belonged to that rare group of heroes who could change into animals, such as the hero Sigmund.[113] The belief that human beings could turn into wolves at will and do so for noble reasons was common in German-speaking lands.[114] Werewolves only ate animals and could never 'serve the devil', Mackensen added. As the 'dogs of God', they were forces for good, a counterweight to the devil in defending the people against evil and protecting their soul.[115]

Another example of the Nazi fascination with werewolves is a dissertation written by one of Alfred Rosenberg's subordinates, 'The Essence and History of the Werewolf'.[116] The Catholic Church may have associated werewolves with witchcraft and Satanism, the author observed, but lycanthropy had a very different connotation in the 'old North'.[117] In order to defend their kith and kin, Odin's soldiers turned into wild dogs or wolves with the strength of bears ('berserkers') and nigh invulnerability.[118] German werewolves – in contrast to Slavic vampires – were viewed as positive figures in German literature, the author concluded.[119] Many Germans (and Nazis) likewise recalled the Free Corps units raised by General Lützow against Napoleon in 1813. Lützow's 'wild hunters' were named after the ghostly revenants who emerged at night to avenge themselves on Germany's enemies, often accompanied by Wotan and his wolves. Both the SS 'Death's Head' and the insignia of the Weimar-era Werewolves bore similarities to these 'wild hunters'.[120]

Equally important in popularizing the link between werewolves and partisan resistance in the Third Reich was Hermann Löns' aforementioned novel, *Wehrwolf* (1910). Harassed and terrorized by roving soldiers, who murder his family, Löns's protagonist Harm Wulf organizes a band of 'Wehrwolf' partisans in the surrounding forests and successfully repels the invaders.[121] The Weimar-era Werewolf (*Wehrwolf*) paramilitary organization, to which many Nazis belonged, was inspired by Löns's book.[122] So were the Nazis, who announced with considerable excitement in 1934 that 'The grave of the poet [Löns] had been found' in France and that the regime would make every effort to bring his remains back to Germany.[123] So effective was the Third Reich's promotion of Löns's work that a new edition sold a half million copies.[124]

Given these many cultural antecedents, it is hardly surprising that the werewolf would emerge with renewed vigour during the Second World War. In 1941 the German intelligence service (*Abwehr*) created a special forces group, code-named 'Wehrwolf', for training spies to operate behind enemy lines.[125] In 1943, Himmler and Globocnik christened their racial resettlement project in the Ukraine, 'Werewolf'.[126] We'll also recall Hitler's invocation of the werewolf in naming his wartime headquarters. By the time they initiated Operation Werewolf in late 1944, Hitler, Himmler, and Goebbels were clearly drawing on a wide range of native paramilitary and supernatural traditions.[127]

In choosing their name for the operation, however, there was a small though important difference in nomenclature that distinguished the Nazi Werewolf from its paramilitary predecessors. Löns's *Wehrwolf* and the interwar 'Wehrwolf' movement both employed the term 'Wehr', a play on the German word for 'defence', in their title. Hitler and Himmler nevertheless chose the more overtly supernatural derivation of the word, *Werwolf* – as they had previously in naming their respective headquarters and Ukrainian resettlement operations. In making this subtle break with paramilitary tradition, Peter Longerich observes, there can be no doubt that Hitler and Himmler wanted to invoke 'the creature of folklore, a human being who under cover of night transforms into an animal'.[128] Himmler in particular envisioned a 'program for these werewolves out of Germanic mythology and vulgar occultism', encouraging the use of a black armband with skull and crossbones and silver SS insignia drawn from Lützow's 'wild hunters'.[129]

For Hitler, Himmler, and Goebbels, Operation Werewolf was much more than a last-ditch military operation. It constituted a core element in their Wagnerian vision of total victory or apocalypse.[130] The timing of Operation Werewolf was linked, after all, to the impending Allied invasion of the Reich proper and the rise of local militia movements in the East, where Communist partisans carried out increasingly effective guerrilla warfare, assassinations, and sabotage against German occupiers.[131] Himmler believed his Werewolves would somehow rescue the Reich from the jaws of defeat while providing the basis for armed peasant 'outposts' in the tradition of the Artamanen.[132] He alluded to this supernaturally inspired vision of political, military, and racial rebirth in an October 1944 radio broadcast: 'even in the territory [the Allies] believe they have conquered,' he announced, the Germans will 'constantly spring to life again, and, like werewolves, death-defying volunteers will damage and destroy the enemy from the rear'.[133]

Goebbels too embraced the Werewolf as a central feature in his end of times propaganda. The Propaganda Minister even created his own 'Radio Werewolf' station. Many Werewolf broadcasts began with the sound of a wolf howling and a song, sung by a woman named Lily, which included the lyrics, 'I am so savage. I am filled with rage ... Lily the werewolf is my name. I bite, I eat, I am not tame ... My werewolf teeth bite the enemy/And then he's done and then he's gone/Hoo, hoo hoo.'[134] 'The members of the Werewolf organization use any means good enough to harm the enemy,' declared another Radio Werewolf broadcast. 'Woe to the enemies of the country, but thrice woe to the traitors of our won people who put themselves at their disposal!'[135]

The burden of these (unrealistic) expectations fell on two widely renowned SS officers, Hans-Adolf Prützmann and Otto Skorzeny, which indicates the importance that Hitler and Himmler placed on Operation Werewolf. From June to October 1941, Prützmann was the Higher SS and Police Leader (*Höhere SS- und Polizeiführer* or HSSPF) for Russia-North, playing a decisive role in initiating the Holocaust in Latvia. By 1944 he was HSSPF for Russia-South and SS Director for Special Intelligence, leading combat forces against the Russians.[136] Stationed in the Ukraine, Prützmann had studied Soviet partisan tactics up close, which he both admired and feared.[137] Like the Soviet partisans, according to Prützmann, Werewolf trainees were to be recruited for their ideological fanaticism and battle-hardened brutality. Due to the unavailability of seasoned fighters, however, many Werewolf recruits were culled from the Hitler Youth instead.[138]

The Werewolf trained in secret locations in Berlin and the Rhineland under the purview of Skorzeny, a famed Special Forces leader, best known for his efforts leading Operation Oak to rescue Mussolini. The guerrilla training was similar to that of Special Forces in Allied countries, including techniques for survival in harsh conditions, sabotage, hand-to-hand combat, and assassination.[139] There is also some evidence that Himmler and Prützmann welcomed women into the Werewolves, due to the fact that the Soviets used them, that manpower was short, and that they fit the Wagnerian trope of fighting Valkyrie within the Nazi supernatural imaginary.[140]

The Werewolves carried out bold acts of terrorism, blowing up captured planes, planting bombs, and setting military installations on fire.[141] Werewolves were also given orders to assassinate collaborators, shoot retreating Wehrmacht troops, and murder hostile Poles and Russians. Hence Werewolf groups were more dangerous – and caused greater anxiety – among local German 'collaborators' and Slavs than among Allied forces.[142]

The Werewolves were also better organized and more widely feared by local populations in eastern Germany, where it was easier to recruit refugees fleeing the Russians.[143] Radio Werewolf, according to Skorzeny, was also more active and effective in the eastern zones, reflecting both the greater urgency of partisan warfare and the resonance of the werewolf concept in the East.[144] For similar reasons the Werewolves were popular among the ethnic German populations in the Sudetenland, Silesia, and South Tyrol, where they could portray themselves more legitimately as a German 'self-defence' force against Slavic interlopers.[145]

Certainly some French and British soldiers were killed by Werewolves in southwestern and northern Germany respectively.[146] The Americans were still fighting Werewolves in the Austrian Tyrol until late May 1945, two weeks after Germany's surrender.[147] But even in regions where their political and military influence was negligible, the mere idea of the Werewolf, combined with Himmler and Goebbels' propaganda efforts, encouraged Nazi diehards and scared German collaborators. The Werewolves left portentous messages on houses and public buildings, writing on the graves of fallen comrades: 'We shall avenge you. The wolves are awaiting their chance to spring.'[148] There were also reports of female Werewolves in Leipzig that would 'pour scalding water from the windows on troops passing below them'.[149] Even when the Werewolves were not responsible for a particular death, Prützmann or Goebbels often claimed responsibility in order to create anxiety among the local populations.[150]

Goebbels' Radio Werewolf was especially effective in creating a myth of thousands of vicious partisans, a number out of all proportion with reality, marshalling their strength across Germany.[151] These rumors, fuelled by native Germans, generated consternation among Allied invaders, who feared widespread guerrilla actions, coordinated from a rumoured 'National redoubt' or 'Alpine fortress' in the mountains of southern Germany.[152] Although no Alpine redoubt materialized, General Eisenhower was concerned enough about the Munich-based Werewolf resistance to order the detention and internment of thousands of potential partisans as well as reprisals against guerrillas. The Soviets were even more ruthless and indiscriminate.[153]

Ultimately, the Werewolves were an omnipresent and widely feared guerrilla movement, which had a significant psychological impact on both anxious Germans and Nazi fanatics roving the countryside in the final months of the war.[154] To be sure, the Werewolves never enjoyed the full support of the German population. Nor did they have a significant political or military impact. They did capture the popular imagination, however, constituting the epitome of what the Third Reich hoped to create through its last-gasp exploitation of the supernatural imaginary: ruthless Nazi Werewolves as the heroic German counterpoise to Slavic-Communist monsters flooding in from the East.[155]

Partisan Vampires

Whereas the werewolf was the 'good' monster in Ur-Germanic folklore, the vampire was the evil 'other'.[156] We have seen how the Slavic and Jewish vampire, as blood-sucking colonizer and progenitor of racial miscegenation, functioned as a prop in justifying Nazi anti-Semitism and genocide.[157] In the final months of the war this image of the Slav as vampiric interloper resurfaced in accounts collected by the infamous SS folklorist, Alfred Karasek.[158]

Karasek assembled reports of Slavic blood-drinkers from Banat Germans (also called 'Danube Swabians'). The Danube Swabians were a small group among the millions of ethnic Germans flooding west in a wave of forced emigration known as the *Vertriebung*. Still, unlike many ethnic Germans evacuated during the last months of the war, thousands of Banat Germans remained stranded in the east for a longer period of time, exposed to ethnopolitical violence and retribution.[159] Their position was all the more precarious due to Soviet fears of Nazi 'Werewolves', whose attacks were especially vicious on the frontiers of the Reich.[160]

According to Germans fleeing the Banat, the Tito Partisans – anti-German insurgents led by the Yugoslavian Communist leader Josip Tito – had become vampires.[161] Thousands of eyewitnesses confirmed these observations, reporting on an 'epilepsy-like attack, in which the body of the victim, possessed like a demon, was thrown violently to the ground'. Then 'animalistic noises came forth, foam spurted from the mouth and nose, until the body was worked into a fury'. The vampiric partisans 'tortured their victims before murdering them in the most fantastical fashion, in which they cut off their ears or nose, poked out their eyes, ripped off their faces'. Other partisans stood by watching, expressing 'with bloodshot eyes, in predatory fashion', their 'desire to drink "fascist" blood'.[162] Partisans also felt compelled to shout obscenities and disturbing details about the violent acts they committed or were about to commit. In a frenzied state, one woman claimed 'to have killed 70 Swabians', which she began to 'describe in the most horrific detail'.[163]

Even when the partisans were unarmed, another witness reported, ethnic Germans were defenceless because Slavs overcome by the 'partisan sickness' developed 'unnatural physical powers and exterminated everything around them ... In a demonic state they called and screamed [for] Swabian blood and carried out murder and threats of terror'. Sometimes they would 'stop quietly for short moments and with an empty and soulless look' mutter the words, 'Oh, how sweet is this Swabian blood'. Once sated, the partisans would sink into exhaustion and gradually regain their senses, which is why it was called 'partisan sickness'.[164]

Indicating the racialized character of these attacks, German witnesses claimed the 'transformation' was triggered by chance encounters with Germans.[165] One partisan officer had an attack while eating in an ethnic German restaurant.[166] Another Serbian civilian transformed suddenly after discovering a passerby was German.[167] Many witnesses also relate the contagious nature of the partisan sickness, if only among Serbians. According to Bertha Sohl, who witnessed three separate attacks, the sickness could 'easily befall many and spread in contagious fashion'.[168] Many witnesses confirmed that only the Slavs turned into monsters, whereas 'German soldiers, who were also in the woods and in the thick of the fighting, have never caught the disease and no German prisoner of war or captive Swabian has had it.'[169]

These reports were not confined to the Banat. Stefan Apazeller, who fled the Banat in 1944, reported on rumours of Slavic blood-drinkers among the Serbs, Croats, and even ethnic Germans in other parts of Yugoslavia.[170] In fact, many Serbian civilians appeared equally wary of the partisans – occasionally corroborating the Germans' stories – which suggests the attacks were quite real, even if their supernatural causes were not.[171]

Fantastical accounts of Communist atrocities emerged from Poland, Ukraine, and the Baltic as well. But the theme of vampirism and blood-drinking was peculiar to the Balkans.[172] Part of this might be related to regional mythology, as Serbia was the centre of modern vampire legends.[173] Certainly, Catholic Swabians were more prone to viewing the drinking of blood in the sacrificial sense of (dark) communion than German Protestants.[174] At the same time, however, we must recall the extent to which a *völkisch* preoccupation with the biomystical power of the blood and the Slavic-Jewish vampire was prevalent across interwar Germany.[175] Hence the equation of partisan warfare – or warfare more generally – with Jewish/Slavic vampires (or Nazi 'Werewolves') should not be surprising.

Moreover, much like the Jewish vampires in the Nazi supernatural imaginary, Slavic partisans did not have to rise from the grave to spread vampirism. Slavic blood-drinkers were, like Jews, both biological enemies infected by (and capable of spreading) disease and vampiric monsters, cursed with the 'mark of Cain'.[176] Also similar to Nazi images of Jewish vampires, Banat Germans perceived Slavic partisans in biomystical fashion. Partisans desired only Swabian (*svabi*) blood (*krev*), because that is how they might consume or destroy ethnic German purity and power.[177]

Interestingly, reports suggest that the Slavic partisans often emerged from the forests, which tended to bring on a particularly wild and monstrous form of 'partisan sickness'.[178] The ethnic German Philipp Ungar observed the relapse of a 'wild devil' who had lived in the woods during the 'time of struggle' and repeatedly captured and shot German prisoners. The Serb would experience 'attacks' every now and then during which he gained superhuman strength, fantasized about 'Swabian blood', and babbled uncontrollably about the atrocities he committed in the forest.[179] Three partisans experienced an attack when encountering German civilians while walking through the park, which must have triggered memories of being a 'partisan in the woods'. All three fell to the ground, feverishly 'trying to dig holes with their bare hands and biting into the grass with their teeth'.[180] The similarities to a wild dog or wolf are unmistakable.

The idea of wild Slavic partisans roaming the forest and transforming into blood-drinking animals that sound a lot like werewolves is fascinating. It also indicates the importance of distinctive folkloric traditions in defining supernatural thinking across the Reich. For whereas the werewolf (*Werwolf*) and vampire (*vampir*) were both ethnically and linguistically distinct in the Nazi supernatural imaginary – with the werewolf viewed much more positively – the two concepts were closely intertwined in the eastern European imagination. The old Slavonic word for vampire (*varkolak* or *vrykolak*; Serbian *vukodlak*) could also mean werewolf, after all – and in both cases the creature is evil.[181] Similar to the werewolf myth, many witnesses noted the unhappy nature of the partisans' transformation and the terrible violence and sexual mutilation that accompanied their bouts of partisan fever.[182]

Here the image of 'wild', blood-drinking monsters, emerging from the forests to carry out partisan warfare against German soldiers and civilians, becomes the mirror image of the German Werewolf movement that preceded reports of blood-drinking partisans by just a few months. Except that ethnic Germans' positive image of the 'werewolf', in contrast to the hybrid 'vrykolak' of Slavic folklore, seemingly precluded the Donau Swabians from employing the werewolf trope to describe Slavs. No matter what their manifestation or provenance, wild, forest-roaming Slavic partisans were repeatedly associated with vampires.

The image of the blood-drinking Slavic partisan was also gendered. Women, according to many witnesses, were particularly susceptible to becoming man-eating monsters.[183] A group of Swabian high-school students described one female partisan who 'walked around the camp completely normally and was then stricken, pulled her hair and started to shriek, "I want blood!"' ... During the time of struggle, when many partisans were still in the woods, she was one of the worst ... if this partisan captured a German prisoner [she] slaughtered her in the worst fashion'.[184] Barbara Prumm observed a Serbian woman who, after an attack of 'partisan sickness' in the middle of Belgrade, began foaming at the mouth and shouted 'Hurray, forwards against the Swabians.'[185] Another female partisan suffered attacks that 'always came at night', resulting in her moniker, 'The Black Nada' (Der Schwarze Nada).[186] The Black Nada had an extremely 'evil' visage 'which could terrify anyone'. When a refugee mocked her, 'she immediately had an attack'. 'Foam spurted from her mouth' and in 'her immense rage and with all her strength' she attacked the individual who had shouted at her.[187]

This perception of Slavic women being more susceptible to partisan sickness comports with a broader German fear of the Slavic Flintenweib ('gun-toting wench') among the 'sub-human' Bolsheviks, who frequently recruited women in military roles.[188] It is no coincidence that Germans labelled the women in the Soviets' 588th Night Bomber Regiment the 'Night Witches', a regiment that Germans feared more than any Soviet bombers. Although certainly as effective as their male counterparts, there is no evidence that the 'Night Witches' were consistently more accurate in their sorties. Rumours of the Night Witches' ruthlessness were linked primarily to gendered ideas of Slavic (Bolshevik) women as particularly monstrous and unnatural.[189] Nazi Werewolves, in contrast to Slavic blood-drinkers, were almost always male, indicating their Ur-Germanic racial power and masculinity.

Chauvinist and racist elements in these accounts are certainly subordinate to the very real fear of Serbian partisans qua partisans.[190] According to Magdalena Jerich, a number of Swabian men, many sick with typhus, were isolated in a single house, ostensibly for 'recovery'. They were then led out one night by drunken partisans, forced to undress, and murdered in the most brutal fashion – skulls cracked, brains torn out, bodies hung from the ceiling and burned. The Danube Swabians from the camp were forced to load the muti-lated bodies onto a wagon in such a way that dismembered arms and legs wouldn't fall on the ground.[191] In July 1946 a local Bosnian political candidate is reported to have said: 'We have exterminated [vernichtet] the trunk and the branches, but the roots unfortunately remain; however, we will also ensure that these are no longer a threat.'[192] The refugees further claimed that 'the graves they had to leave behind [were] desecrated in their absence ... the gold being extracted from the teeth of their abandoned dead' – reminiscent of the crimes that the Nazis visited upon the Jews.[193]

Indeed, there is some evidence that the Banat Germans' expressions of terror were 'spawned *both* by real violence *and* by fantasies and anxieties about Swabians' own guilt or crimes or transgressions committed by their group.'[194] Accounts of Slavic vampirism and monstrosity helped to sublimate ethnic Germans' guilt, facilitate their self-fashioning as victims, and even justify in turn the actions of German soldiers (or Werewolves) against Slavs.[195] They represent what John Horne and Alan Kramer call a 'legend' or 'myth-complex', which feature common elements: an emphasis on women partisans, transgressive violence, bouts of ill conscience, and a desire to drink blood.[196]

A strong regional history of vampirism and ethnic Germans' minority status in the region may have magnified the supernatural lens through which the Donau Swabians viewed their Slavic neighbours.[197] Nevertheless, stories about blood-drinking partisans cannot be attributed 'exclusively to an eruption of irrationality in a moment of chaos and distress'.[198] These reports had a history in the German (and Nazi) supernatural imaginary stretching back many decades. They spoke to the 'phantasmagorical elements of a war of conquest and extermination' in central Europe and provided the idiom in which many Germans 'explained violent wartime and post-war encounters to themselves and others'.[199]

The End of the Third Reich

The 20 July 1944 assassination attempt on Hitler represents a watershed moment. On the one hand it signalled that ordinary Germans had finally begun to break Hitler's spell. Millions recognized that the Führer and his coterie, driven by megalomaniacal fantasies and a belief in their divine mission, were leading the Third Reich toward catastrophe. Of course, many continued to honour Goebbels' call for 'fanatical resistance', envisioning 'all manner of apocalyptic scenarios' if Germany lost the war.[200] But as the 'euphoria of victory began to yield to the grim realities of mass, violent death', images of the Third Reich were changing.[201]

Unable to discard a proclivity for supernatural thinking that helped make sense of the Nazi racial and imperial project, ordinary Germans 'groped in the dark for points of comparison, linking what was happening to a natural catastrophe or a biblical end times'.[202] The supernatural imaginary, replete with images of violent floods, earthquakes, and ice ages, helped prepare Germans for global conflagration. Just as the moon hitting the earth had destroyed Atlantis

10,000 years earlier, so would the Second World War result in a new apocalypse.[203] For millions of ordinary Germans, however, whose preoccupations
had long ago shifted toward mere everyday survival, the mythology of Ragnarok
likewise held out the promise of rebirth and redemption.

For many Nazis who could not abide the collapse of their thousand-year
Reich, such images represented a kind of wish fulfilment. Weaned on Nordic
mythology, Wagner, and the Edda, ariosophy and World Ice Theory, Nazi
leaders 'began to imagine a war unlike any ever before witnessed and to chore-
ograph its denouement'. 'Even if the war was lost, which became increasingly
likely over time', the Nazis 'dreamed that future generations would look
back and revere Germany for its unending will to fight, its will to death'. The
Nazis, as suggested above, 'had always fantasized about a specifically German
enthusiasm for death; that illusion now became a matter of war policy'.[204] For
ordinary Germans and Nazis alike, these widespread images of annihilation
and rebirth reflected the everyday devastation that defined the final months
of the war.

Nazi Twilight

The Third Reich was fascinated by the cult of death, which often merged with
the cult of the warrior in the Nazi supernatural imaginary. For fascist thinkers
in the wake of the First World War, 'the field of wheat suggest[ed] collective
destiny-death, resurrection, and growing strength . . . a common death in battle,
whole rows of men mown down together'.[205] *Völkisch* and right-wing thinkers
subsumed their inchoate feelings of 'humiliation, anxiety, hatred, and fear . . .
[into] a mythology of patriotic sacrifice and national resurrection'. Through
this psychological process, writes Peter Fisher, the 'intellectually and morally
crippled products of a disastrous war' transformed 'themselves into the
vanguard of an even more catastrophic future'.[206]

These feelings, filtered through the supernatural imaginary, resonated
beyond the *völkisch* right. A liberal journalist described his 'disbelief at the
population's impressionability and the local government's inability to quell the
alarm' inherent in fantasy literature. This 'psychosis through a book' also
revealed itself in exaggerated public reactions to the noise of a transport car
or a plane flying overhead, and anxiety that every activity involving public
construction augured the prelude to another devastating war.[207]

Nazi folklorists and politicians described similar phenomena.[208] 'The white
races are in the stage of decline', wrote the Nazi fellow traveller Gottfried Benn,
whether by 'the moon crashing into Earth or atomic destruction, freezing or
[incineration]'.[209] Hitler's Wagnerian vision of politics manifested itself from
the early years of the Third Reich, as he instructed Goebbels to purchase an

original draft of the prelude to Wagner's *Meisterwerk* – the *Götterdämmerung Vorspiel*.[210]

This millennial vision of political, military, and racial cataclysm became exaggerated during the final years of the Second World War.[211] For Nazi true believers, the assassination attempt of 20 July 1944 reinforced the conviction that the Third Reich was beset by inner enemies who lacked faith in the Führer. Only a firm commitment to 'total war' could overcome the global conspiracy of Jews, Bolsheviks, and Freemasons that had now infiltrated even the upper echelons of the Wehrmacht. Either Germany would achieve final victory (*Endsieg*) or total annihilation.[212] The entire Reich infrastructure was now going to be devoted to waging total war.[213]

In support of total war, the Nazi propaganda machine embraced the mythology of 'final struggle' (*Endkampf*), of Ragnarok, which prophesied 'the doom of the gods ... The strife of man against man ... The Great Winter will fall, three years long ... The wolf Skoll will swallow the sun, and Hati will devour the moon; their gore will splatter the earth and heavens.'[214] In his 1943 work *Indogermanisches Bekenntnis* (*Indo-Germanic Confessions*), Wüst utilized the Ragnarok myth, lamenting the historical failure of Indo-Germanic culture to achieve final victory against repeated attacks on its racial, spiritual, and geographical core. The Second World War represented another such moment in which the 'racially alien' civilizations carried out an 'exterminatory attack' against the foundations of 'Germanic essence'.[215] As the Reich crumbled in the winter of 1945, the German Indologist, Jakob Wilhelm Hauer, offered a course at Tübingen along similar lines, entitled 'Death and Immortality in Indo-Germanic Faith and Thought 1944–45'.[216]

By early 1945 the East Prussian Gauleiter and murderous SS administrator, Erich Koch, was speaking in apocalyptic terms about the coming defeat. So too was Rudolf Hess, who compared himself to a witch soon to be burnt at the stake.[217] The correspondence between Martin and Gerda Bormann took on an equally apocalyptic tone. Gerda reported that her discussions with the children had turned to 'folk songs, which led us to the *Nibelungenlied* and hence to the struggle between Light and Darkness in fairy tales, myths, history, and daily life, and that our stuggle against Bolshevism and the British is no other than the fight of Good against Evil ... That the principle of Light, of the Good, always emerges triumphantly after all, and that no sacrifice is too great for the final victory of Light'.[218] Koch, Hess, and the Bormanns were typical, according to Hugh Trevor-Roper, of many Nazis who swallowed wholesale the Nordic metaphysics of 'Nazi theology – Charlemagne and the Nibelungs, the virus of Christianity and the Wagnerian Twilight'.[219]

As a young man Himmler too read the Nibelungen stories of Werner Jansen, who manipulated the sagas in order to bolster German national feeling.[220]

Decades later, as the Third Reich was collapsing around him, Himmler and his SS colleagues pursued their investigations into Nordic and Indo-Aryan mythology in maniacal fashion, desperate to locate symbols of Germany's death and resurrection.[221] Ernst Schäfer and Bruno Beger ruminated on the 'glorious war dance' of the Tibetans, attracted as both were 'to the destructive, horrible, morbid and macabre side of Tibetan culture'. The Tibetan gods, according to Schäfer, hungered for real and imaginary blood, offering 'blood sacrifices' for 'the purposes of satisfying the Tantric gods'.[222] Ostensibly inspired by the 'Death's-Head Crown' of the Demon of Protection, Mahakala, a poem appeared in *Das Schwarze Korps*, with the line: 'The symbol of the skull, on the cap, says to you, how little life means. Reminds you, to be ready, at every hour.'[223]

Like the Third Reich more generally, Himmler's Ahnenerbe experienced a crisis during the last years of the war, reflecting the endemic contradiction between pursuing border scientific fantasies and channelling any last resources toward the war effort.[224] Himmler squandered time and energy consulting the defrocked Karl Maria Wiligut on the appropriate life or death runes with which to adorn the proliferating number of SS graves – favouring runes that would honour the Norse god of war, Tyr.[225] In 1944, Himmler even encouraged Wolfgang Krause and his folklore-obsessed colleagues to produce 'rune fables' in order to improve German morale.[226]

The Nazis resented the way in which the German cemetery before 1933 had become corrupted and desacralized, 'the playground of foreign races and worldviews'. Now, in the wake of mass death, cemeteries and burial rituals needed to match Nazi values by invoking Nordic mythology or the Führer ('on my gravestone will be Adolf Hitler, nothing more').[227] At the same time Nazi soldiers wore the symbol of the bird of prey, the Totenvögel, becoming a 'uniform-wearing version of the ancient beasts of battle', who 'foretold the carnage of war in medieval sagas'.[228] Inspired by this apocalyptic, Wagnerian symbolism of death and rebirth, diehard Nazis, like the Werewolves, kept fighting long after the war was lost.[229]

Although most Werewolves would surrender within a couple of years, the esoteric death cult around Himmler and the Wewelsburg echoed long after 1945.[230] Rumours persisted that the SS had removed an object from the Wewelsburg – possibly what they thought was the Holy Grail – and buried it on the Hochfeiler glacier in Zillertal, Austria, waiting for a time when the Third Reich might be reborn.[231]

That so many earlier prophecies had proved false did not stop Nazis from doubling down on astrology.[232] By the final weeks of the war, the astrologer Wilhelm Wulff was virtually unable to leave Himmler's side. The Reichsführer consulted him on virtually every matter, from military strategy and the Jewish Question to when and how Hitler would die. It got to the point that Walter

Schellenberg was debriefing Wulff just to find out what Himmler – by then the second most powerful figure in the Reich – might do next.[233] Gerda Bormann and other Nazi wives were excited in late 1944 about rumours of a 'Swedish clairvoyant who speaks of a great battle in the West in November, but forecasts for us a favourable end of the war in 1946'.[234]

Even Goebbels appears to have revisited astrology at this time. Alexander Centgraf claims to have been called to Berlin in the summer of 1944 to help Goebbels produce interpretations of Nostradamus which would reassure Germans that the Soviets would *not* conquer Berlin.[235] Centgraf's recollections are circumstantial. But Goebbels did write in his diary on 25 July 1944 – only five days after the attempt on Hitler's life – that a new Nostradamus brochure was being prepared for distribution over England. Five days later Goebbels mentioned that Nostradamus might still be useful for domestic propaganda as well, since his prophecies 'could be related to the German present and future in very positive fashion'.[236] 'We know that the idea lives on,' Goebbels announced in the final weeks of the war, 'even if all its bearers have fallen.'[237]

Alfred Rosenberg, true to form, continued to believe that Germany's troubles were linked to a global conspiracy of Jews, Masons, and shadowy esoteric groups. In the wake of the D-Day landings on 6 June 1944, Rosenberg's staff in France forwarded a detailed report on an obscure occult-Masonic group called the 'Synarchy'.[238] According to the report, the Synarchy were a neo-Rosicrucian order that presented a threat because they supported the idea of a 'Monarchy without a fatherland' based on a 'federative French Empire'.[239] Rumours also circulated that a German aircraft flew over the runes of Montségur – the Grail Mountain – on the 700th anniversary of its fall. Witnesses claimed that Rosenberg was on board and that the plane traced 'a Celtic cross in the sky'.[240]

In terms of his own 'fatalism and attraction to a Wagnerian Götterdämmerung', Hitler was very much a product of his times. There was a 'peculiar, apocalyptic dimension' to his thinking, which he shared with other Nazis, embedded in the notion that the 'life of the nation is lodged in an unalterable cycle of rise and fall'.[241] Before 1939, Hitler had acted as a prophet whose war aims were 'motivated in no small measure by apocalyptic visions of purity, by an existential battle between good and evil, and by the promise of creating a new and (for the chosen few) utopian world'.[242] As the war took a bleaker turn, Hitler became obsessed by this 'interplay of destruction and creativity', articulating a grandiose vision of Germany consumed by fire.[243]

Hitler's scorched-earth policy during the last months of the war was linked to a personal obsession with 'his own immolation' and a broader Nazi belief that Germans had to die in order for Germany to be reborn.[244] His many references to the 'Final Solution' and decision to destroy Germany's infrastructure are only the most conspicuous examples of Hitler's attempt to force the end of times.[245] In ordering a *Götterdämmerung* for this world, observes Robert Waite, Hitler saw himself as 'fulfilling ancient myth ... a darkly brooding Teutonic God enthroned in Valhalla, the shadowed Hall of the Dead'.[246] No surprise that Albert Speer, in planning Hitler's final birthday concert, 'ordered Brünnhilde's last aria and the finale of *Götterdämmerung* – a rather bathetic and also melancholy gesture pointing to the end of the Reich'.[247] For even Hitler's suicide on 30 April 1945 was a 'grand magical' act consistent with the myth of Ragnarok, when the world would be destroyed by 'fire followed by the renewal of life'.[248]

Rebirth

The reality that Germans confronted at the end of the war was so 'fantastic and gruesome', observed Konrad Heiden, that it surpassed in 'dreadfulness anything the most vivid imagination can evoke'.[249] Facing unprecedented mass death and catastrophic defeat, Germans were forced 'to wrestle with their losses in an atmosphere of acute existential crisis'.[250] And yet many did so in ways that hardly represent a break from Nazi supernatural thinking. The Nazi runologist Bernhard Kummer invoked the Edda to capture his feelings in the wake of defeat, observing that 'the concussive Ragnarök poem could have a new and direct meaning for the understanding of our own days', helping the Germans negotiate their psychological distress.[251] Hauer reflected similarly on the 'meaning of Ragnarök', which, after so much destruction, helped one come to terms with the 'Germanic-German view' of divinity in Old Norse and Hindu tradition.[252]

In his last will and testament, Robert Ley made an explicit attempt to rescue the 'positive side' of Nazism, the biomystical synthesis of race and spirit that 'was one of the greatest things people ever thought'.[253] Walther Darré extolled the 'positive' virtues of *völkisch*-organicist thinking as well, which, he claimed, had nothing to do with Hitler's nihilistic attitude toward Jews. Instead of distancing himself from blood-and-soil fantasies, Darré burnished his *völkisch*-esoteric mysticism. The positive attempt to build an organic racial community (*Volksgemeinschaft*), Darré argued, had always been distinct from the brutal race war spearheaded by Hitler and Himmler.[254]

The SS Dean of the University of Strasbourg, Ernst Anrich, declaimed proudly after 1945 that he 'be recognized as a National Socialist' in contrast to the 'traitors to National Socialism' such as Hitler.[255] 'That the party, that Hitler had led the people and army falsely' was undeniable, Anrich conceded. This did not mean that all true National Socialists were 'thereby complicit', however, or that 'the ideas, which one actually believed they were serving', were false.[256] Here Anrich tried to defend a 'pure' form of National Socialism whose racialism was more spiritual and mystical than biopolitical, and might therefore be rehabilitated.[257]

True National Socialism could not flourish under Western occupation, Anrich argued, because the materialist Allies undermined the 'spiritual-intellectual weight of the people' (*seelisch-geistigen Gewicht eines Volkes*). The Allies needed to understand that a 'pure faith in the idea of national Socialism, of ethnicity and the duty-bound power of the whole', was worth rehabilitating.[258]

Some Nazi thinkers claimed to reject the Third Reich outright. The defrocked Hermann Wirth, once Himmler's right-hand man, now argued that his departure from the Ahnenerbe had to do with profound 'ideological' differences with the regime. But the December 1938 letter to Himmler that Wirth cited to indicate his differences with the regime was, according to most experts, a forgery – like the Ura Linda chronicle on which he based his Nordic fantasies. Wirth remained in fact a devoted proponent of Nordic race and culture, founding a *völkisch*-esoteric prehistorical museum and delivering papers to major academic conferences with picturesque titles such as 'The Formation of Military Leaders' Religions during the Indo-European Migration and the End of Cult Matriarchy'.[259]

Though obviously disingenuous, the claims of Wirth and other border scientists that they opposed the regime apparently worked.[260] How else to explain the fact that Hermann Wirth and Franz Altheim were invited to the eighth annual International Congress for the History of Religions in Rome in 1955? Or that the SS esotericists Julius Evola and Hermann Grabert became leading figures of the post-war far right?[261]

Carl Jung agreed that impressions of German contrition masked, in some cases, 'the most pronounced Nazi psychology ... still alive with all its violence and savagery'.[262] When questioned why Germans had got themselves into this 'psychic mess', Jung explained that they had projected their 'demons' – their insecurities and resentments – onto others, be they the Jews or the Allies, and 'steadily loaded [their] unconscious with them'.[263] For Germans living in the Third Reich, all these conspiratorial fantasies, insecurities, and resentments, the 'pressure of the demons' in Jung's words, became 'so great that they got human beings into their power', first Hitler, who 'then infected the rest'. 'All the Nazi leaders were possessed in the truest sense of the word.'[264]

And yet, many Germans, Jung admitted, were ready to exorcise Hitler and his demons. As the SD dutifully reported in early 1945, most Germans had begun questioning the regime's apocalyptic propaganda. Others remarked that the Allied troops – at least in the West – hardly fit the monstrous depictions spread by official propaganda. If any individuals were monsters, some Germans reasoned, they were members of the SS who had committed atrocities in the East.[265]

The ideological investment of Germans in the supernatural imaginary did not immediately disappear in the last months of the war. Nor can we ignore the role of the Allied denazification process in uprooting the Third Reich's commitments to 'the glories of war and sacrificial battlefield death'.[266] Still, the search for *völkisch*-spiritual wholeness could be channelled into less racist, less imperialist, more productive avenues. 'Anyone who falls so low has depth,' Jung suggested, making it likely that 'positive forces will emerge from the catastrophe'.[267]

On the one hand Germans sought comfort in their churches and alternative forms of Christianity.[268] The Catholic stigmatist, Thérèse Neumann von Konnersreuth, for example, reemerged in 1945 to take advantage of a 'new wave of miracles, both religious and otherwise, that expressed the anxiety of a war-torn population'. Her annual visitors ranged into the tens of thousands, including hundreds of American soldiers, who helped make Neumann 'an ideal symbol to overcome tensions in the German-American relationship'.[269]

Not all such prophecies occurred within a Christian idiom. In the chaos and confusion of defeat there proliferated numerous 'prophecies and folk legends' percolating through the German supernatural imaginary.[270] Some promised more apocalyptic wars. Others helped reassure Germans that their suffering was not in vain, that they might return to their villages and live in harmony with other nationalities.[271]

Many Germans began to envision the Nazis themselves as 'beasts, devils, [and] fiends ... utterly depraved, only masquerading as human' and prone to 'corpse desecration'.[272] As the famous line from the Book of Revelation circulated amongst the ruins ('let anyone with understanding calculate the number of the beast'), some Germans portrayed their former messiah Hitler, whose name ostensibly spelled 666, as the Beast.[273]

Yet the process of 'denazifying consciousness' was complex. Germans 'clung to certain beliefs rooted in the recent past concerning death even as they distanced themselves from Nazism'. They viewed the Allies' putative mishandling of the German dead as 'a signal theme in postwar discourses of German victimization' and 'compared it with the mishandling of the bodies of the Nazis' victims in the concentration camps'.[274]

With millions missing, many Germans also turned to 'supernatural explanations' reminiscent of Nazi-era thinking in order to 'illuminate the otherwise unfathomable deaths of loved ones'.[275] An emphasis on fate drawn from Germanic religious tradition served after 1945 'to link the horrors of National Socialism and World War II to a transcendental concept ... into an integral metaphor for coping, repression, and justification'.[276] The immensely popular faith healer Bruno Groening emerged, like Neumann, in the late 1940s, attracting millions of Germans, Catholic and Protestant alike. Some viewed him as a post-Hitlerian messiah, helping to exorcise Nazi demons. Others worried that Groening, a former Nazi Party member with no real ties to Christian tradition (he was compared to an 'Indian yogi'), represented 'another Hitler'.[277]

Bourgeois Germans less prone to the *Volksreligion* of Groening had recourse to the border scientific mysticism of Ernst Kallmeyer and Willy Hellpach. Kallmeyer's book *Do our Dead Live? A World View as Answer* (1946) reflects the persistence of 'this worldly' religiosity propagated by the Nazis before 1945.[278] Employing esoteric metaphors redolent of Bormann or Himmler, Kallmeyer compared the human soul to atoms that could not be extinguished through physical death. There was scientific evidence, he claimed, that the dead still live in the everyday 'supernatural' (*übersinnliche*) realm that stands opposite the 'empirical' (*sinnliche*) world, a 'beyond' (*Jenseits*) that lives alongside the 'here and now [*Diesseits*] . . . Already for these reasons we may be certain that our dead live!'[279] Humanity only had meaning 'from the standpoint of the teaching of reincarnation, otherwise it would be nonsensical and not worth living.'[280]

We find the same *völkisch*-esoteric mélange of science and religion in the post-war scholarship of Willy Hellpach.[281] Before 1945, the erstwhile Rector of the University of Heidelberg had contributed to the field of *Völkerpsychologie* that helped justify Nazi *Volksgemeinschaft* and empire.[282] With the collapse of the Third Reich, Hellpach turned to a less *völkisch* form of parapsychology.[283] In the spring of 1946 he completed *Magethos: An Investigation into Magical Thinking and Magical Service in Connection to the Powers of the Beyond with this-worldly Duties for the Creation and Securing of Values and Principles, Custom and Law, Conscience and Practices, Morals and Religions.*[284] *Magethos* was hardly a dispassionate scientific analysis. 'Perhaps seldom has the fundamental problem of otherwordly powers and this-worldly duties been so burning,' Hellpach explained in his preface, 'as in the terrible experience of recent years.'[285]

One of Goebbels and Himmler's favourite occult collaborators, H. H. Kritzinger, found a receptive audience after 1945. In a 1951 book, *On the Philosophy of the Supernatural World*, Kritzinger reiterated his belief in the need to recognize the mystical antimonies in the world. Except the Nazi border scientist was careful, this time around, not to dismiss the 'Jewish science' of relativity which, in its alternative view of the space-time continuum, helped confirm esotericist insights from the Near East.[286] In this respect Kritzinger attempted to reinscribe a universalism into his occult thinking that had gradually been lost in Germany – at least in regard to Jews – after the First World War.

Many other Nazi astrologers landed on their feet. The long-time Goebbels collaborator Alexander Centgraf resuscitated his career as a Nostradamus scholar, asserting that he opposed Nazism and that nearly all his wartime predictions had come true.[287] With his tell-all account of astrology in the Third Reich, *Zodiac and Swastika*, Wilhelm Wulff became a minor celebrity.[288] Other pro-Nazi occultists, including many anthroposophists, distanced themselves from Nazism, joining the German Green Party or (re)directing their efforts into Waldorf schools and progressive, New Age pursuits.[289]

The erstwhile SS folklorist Alfred Karasek managed to transition seamlessly from folklore-fuelled imperialism to respected academic. Karasek's repeated declarations in support of European reconciliation helped to mask his continued belief in German ethno-linguistic purity and his subtle academic contributions to the revanchist field of 'expellee folklore' (*Vertriebenenvolkskunde*).[290] Typical of this revisionist history, Karasek's analysis of *Folk Tales of the Carpathian Germans* recounted the terrible events that had befallen expellees since 1944.[291] Karasek continued to insist on his ability to glean German ethnic feeling through folklore – especially in the case of ethnic Germans who had lost their Heimat.[292] These thinly veiled revanchiste sentiments, grounded in a quasi-mystical emphasis on the ethno-national purity of German folklore, would persist in Karasek's work until his death in 1970.[293]

Sitting in an American internment camp, Hans Bender dealt with the hard reality of loss, defeat, and complicity by abandoning any remaining semblance of critical distance to border science. In notes collected by American interrogators, Bender criticized the materialist West's tendency toward too much 'thinking'. 'Thinking is an indication of the decay of the brain. Every serious thought is a tombstone of a brain cell. Every time a person thinks it is a sign that a brain cell has died and deteriorated (decomposed) and the result is a decomposition of thought.' While humans 'poison' themselves with thoughts and therefore lose sight of nature, a 'panther is too clever to think'. Like a panther, 'whose blood stream . . . [isn't] poisoned by those gaseous products of the degeneration of the brain which we call thoughts . . . [we must] destroy thinking, killing it in its very beginning so thoroughly that it destroys the multiplication of micro-organisms as in an infected wound; the sun makes our brain asceptic and free of thoughts.'[294]

Unsurprisingly, given its SS funding and Nazi provenance, Bender's 'Paracelsus' Institute was immediately closed by the French government. Only in 1954, when German law changed to allow the reappointment of former Nazi officials, was Bender reinstated as 'associate professor for frontier areas of psychology at the University of Freiburg'.[295] Within a decade the 'spook professor' resumed his place as Germany's leading (para)psychologist, founding his own institute for esoteric research. He became a nationally recognized media figure, attracting a new generation of those seeking alternative answers to questions that neither mainstream science nor traditional religion could resolve.

With his 'experiments' now broadcast on television game shows and popular radio programmes, Bender's research shifted from receiving official government sponsorship in the Third Reich to becoming harmless TV entertainment in the Federal Republic. Emblematic of the depoliticized (deracialized) nature of occultism in the Federal Republic is the fact that one of Bender's chief onscreen collaborators was the Israeli-Jewish magician, Uri Geller.[296]

***

For most Nazis and millions of Germans during the first half of the twentieth century, the line between natural and supernatural, empirical and border science, was always porous. Once the Third Reich entered a period of total war after the battle of Stalingrad, these elements within the Nazi supernatural imaginary found all the more fantastical and violent expression.[297] 'We can hardly expect the cultural history of violence in the wake of a war of such fantastic, apocalyptic and pathological dimensions, a war that unleashed so many wild demons,' observes Monica Black, 'to come down to us in the unadorned language of the crop report or the bank statement.'[298]

It is unlikely Germany could have won the war even had the Nazi leadership shed their supernatural thinking and committed to more rational, pragmatic decision-making processes. But the material, human, and psychological investment in miracle weapons and border scientific technologies certainly did not help the war effort. Rather, such projects attest to the impact of the supernatural imaginary even in areas where twentieth-century historians have become most accustomed to the 'unadorned language of the crop report or the bank statement.'[299]

As the *Endkampf* took on especially violent, monstrous, apocalyptic dimensions, the Nazis revived the idea of a final battle, a twilight of the gods, in which every German must take part.[300] A widely shared supernatural imaginary operated before the outbreak of the war to marginalize Slavic and Jewish enemies of the Reich. The exterminatory zeal toward the monstrous other that we find after 1939 was exacerbated, however, by 'the cataclysm of ethnic war and defeat', which unleashed 'phantasms, wild rumors and uncanny stories' that verified 'events that seem to lie outside our reality.'[301] The final stage of the Second World War, epitomized by the battle between German Werewolves and Slavic vampires, highlights both the remarkable resonance and inherent dangers of the supernatural imaginary.

If most of the German population did not follow the Werewolves and rise up, as Hitler, Goebbels, and Himmler intended, they certainly conceived of the final years of the war, like the Nazis themselves, in supernatural terms.[302] But the myriad stories, prophecies, and conspiracy theories shared by ordinary Germans were less likely to excoriate Jews or Masons than peddle visions of retribution and redemption that helped Germans work through the outcome of the war.[303] Their final recourse to the supernatural imaginary was no longer about political domination, ethnic cleansing, or empire. It was much more the expression of 'bodily insecurity' and 'fears of annihilation', of 'repressed guilt' and the dissolution of their 'community and its place in the world' – namely the dissolution of the Third Reich.[304]

EPILOGUE

Supernatural thinking is but one element in understanding Nazism. To explain the rise, popularity, and character of the Third Reich, we must take into account a range of factors. These include the devastating outcome of the First World War, popular resentment toward the Versailles Treaty, and the challenging dynamics (and breakdown) of global capitalism in the wake of hyperinflation and the Great Depression. In terms of domestic policy after 1933, we need to pay particular attention to Hitler's distinctive ruling style, his desire for popular assent, and the complex dynamics between party, state, labour, industry, and the churches. The Nazis' manipulation of mass culture and the media is significant, as is the integrative role of 'racial community' (*Volksgemeinschaft*) in policy and propaganda. In foreign policy and military decision-making, any analysis must begin with the Nazi obsessions over obtaining 'living space' and eliminating 'Judeo-Bolshevism' in eastern Europe, even as we acknowledge the important roles played by domestic political and economic pressures and wartime circumstances.[1]

In coming to terms with the arguments in this book, we also need to recognize that supernatural alternatives to traditional religion and mainstream science emerged elsewhere in Europe and the United States. Rarely did such ideas and practices contribute to the rise of fascist movements or racist imperialism as they did in Nazi Germany.

The particular interplay of supernatural thinking and sociopolitical reality, however, was hardly identical in content and character across interwar Europe. In comparison to Germany, British and French occultism and border science didn't contain the same level and mix of biomystical racism, Indo-Aryan paganism, or anti-Semitism. Nor did a supernatural way of thinking find analogous political and ideological – much less sociocultural, religious, and scientific – expression in the mass parties that dominated interwar politics in France, Great Britain, or the United States.[2] The same holds, to a lesser extent, for fascist Italy and Falangist Spain.[3]

Even in a specifically Austro-German context, the Nazi movement had closer ties to occult, border scientific, and pagan-mythological ideas and doctrines than any mass political party. There is simply no equivalent relationship between popular occultism, paganism, or border science, on the one hand, and German liberalism, Socialism, Communism, political Catholicism or mainstream conservatism on the other. To be sure, Hitler and the Nazi Party may have broken with the Thule Society that helped inspire National Socialism. Yet the Society's *völkisch*-esoteric ideas and border scientific doctrines persisted within the Nazi (and broader German) supernatural imaginary long after individuals such as Sebottendorff and Karl Harrer lost their influence.

Not all Germans who shared elements of this supernatural imaginary were fascists, racist imperialists, or anti-Semites. But that is precisely why the Nazis' exploitation of the supernatural imaginary was so effective in attracting and maintaining support from a broad cross section of the German population. The NSDAP's appeal to such ideas helped the party transcend the thorny social and political reality of Depression-era Germany. It allowed a party with no clear political or economic programme to supersede the materialist, class-based rhetoric of the left, the pragmatic, incremental republicanism of the liberal centre, and the more traditional, nationalist conservatism of the Catholic and Protestant centre right.[4]

***

Although the Nazi supernatural imaginary did not disappear overnight, its more overtly racist and imperialist elements receded in the final months of the war.[5] Forced to confront the destructive reality of Hitler's foreign and domestic policy, Germans became wary of relying on occult, mythological, pagan religious, and border scientific reasoning in addressing social or political problems. For these reasons the Germans would likely 'recover', Carl Jung observed, and shed their historical 'demons'.[6]

But other nations, Jung continued, 'will become victims of possession if, in their horror at the German guilt, they forget [that] they can just as suddenly become a victim of the demonic powers'. 'Every man who loses his shadow, every nation that falls into self-righteousness, is their prey. We love the criminal and take a burning interest in him because the devil makes us forget the beam in our own eye.'[7] Indeed, 'The power of the demons is immense, and the most modern media of mass suggestion – press, radio, film, etc. – are at their service,' Jung concluded. This 'general suggestibility plays a tremendous role in America today'.[8]

Jung wrote these words more than seventy years ago. Whether we look at Europe or the United States, however, Germany is no longer the country in which supernatural thinking, in the service of right-wing politics, appears the most dangerous to democracy.[9] With the end of the Cold War we have seen a 'paranormal turn' in the 'Anglo-American cultural sphere', according to Annette Hill, 'a response to anxiety and uncertainty, allowing for a possibility to play with ideas of mortality, death, and afterlife, or to deal with both individual and national trauma'.[10] Widespread rumours of UFOs and reports of alien abduction are merely contemporary responses to the 'artificial barrier between the spirit and material worlds in the West'.[11]

This return of the repressed in terms of supernatural thinking has been aided by the internet, argues the historian Sabine Doering-Manteuffel, which has created an 'occult structure' and discursive space where various conspiracy theories, apocalyptic claims, and border scientific arguments can challenge empirical reality.[12] Much like supernatural thinking in interwar Germany a century ago, millions of Europeans and Americans are convinced that their 'spiritual science' is true and that 'their vision of another reality [is] securely anchored in the higher worlds, far removed from the demeaning world below'.[13]

None of this would be particularly remarkable were the proclivity for supernatural thinking confined to matters of religion and the private sphere, as it appears to have been during much of the Cold War era. But those who engage in supernatural thinking today, by applying it to the political and social sphere, are potentially just as susceptible as interwar Germans to 'the distorting and harmful effects of viewing political events through an occult prism'.[14]

As in Germany a century ago, a renaissance in supernatural reasoning, shadowy conspiracy theories, extraterrestrial powers, and the omnipresence of a hostile ethno-religious other has begun to correlate with illiberal political and ideological convictions, influencing national elections, domestic social policies, and matters of war and peace.[15] This phenomenon is evident globally, whether in the emergence of nativist and neo-fascist ('alt-right') groups across Europe and the United States or in the exponential spread and politicization of fundamentalist Islam.[16] The history of the Third Reich, both real and imagined, has helped to inspire these neo-folk and neo-fascist movements, which have resuscitated in turn fantasies of a racially pure, immigrant (Islam)-free Europe.[17]

Still, the greatest danger is not that Americans and Europeans will become preoccupied by the same border scientific ideas and doctrines, the mythological utopias and racial fantasies, so eagerly consumed by Germans in the interwar period and exploited by the Third Reich between 1919 and 1945. The reality is that every culture has its own supernatural imaginary which can, in times of crisis, begin to displace more empirically grounded, nuanced arguments about the challenges that define our sociopolitical and geopolitical reality. That the supernatural imaginary is always more malleable, accessible, and open to border scientific reasoning than both traditional religion and modern science makes it all the more dangerous and easier to exploit.

We must remember that the links between Nazism and the supernatural were 'neither concealed nor surprising'. They can be explained, in the words of Peter Staudenmaier, 'not through the apparent deviance and strangeness of esotericism, but through its commonness and popularity, through its participation in and influence by central cultural currents of the era'.[18] For people immersed in a supernatural way of thinking, Adorno reminds us, facts 'which differ from what is the case only by not being facts are trumped up as a fourth dimension'. 'With their blunt, drastic answers to every question, the astrologists and spiritualists' – and here Adorno meant the Nazis as well – 'do not so much solve problems as remove them by crude premises from all possibility of solution.'[19] It is only by acknowledging the persistence and potential dangers of this kind of supernatural thinking that we might comprehend 'its development in the Nazi era and its implications for today'.[20]

NOTES

Introduction

1. Alfred Rosenberg, as quoted in BAB: NS 8/185, pp. 49–50.
2. Ernst Schertel, *Magic: History, Theory, Practice*, Boise: Cotum, 2009 (1923), p. 130.
3. Nicholas Goodrick-Clarke, *Black Sun: Aryan Cults, Esoteric Nazism, and the Politics of Identity*, London/New York: I. B. Tauris, 2003, p. 107.
4. Corinna Treitel, *A Science for the Soul: Occultism and the Genesis of the German Modern*, Baltimore, MD: Johns Hopkins University Press, 2004, pp. 56–8.
5. See, for example, Uwe Schellinger, Andreas Anton, and Michael Schetsche, eds, Zwischen Szientismus und Okkultismus. Grenzwissenschaftliche Experimente der deutschen Marine im Zweiten Weltkrieg, in *Zeitschrift für Anomalistik* 10 (2010), pp. 287–321.
6. Timothy Ryback, 'Hitler's Forgotten Library', *Atlantic Monthly*; http://www.theatlantic.com/doc/200305/ryback; Timothy Ryback, *Hitler's Private Library: The Books that Shaped his Life*, New York: Random House, 2008, pp. 159–62; Schertel, *Magic: History, Theory, Practice*.
7. Nicholas Goodrick-Clarke, *The Occult Roots of Nazism*, London: I. B. Tauris, 2003, pp. 202–4; Nigel Pennick, *Hitler's Secret Sciences*, Sudbury, Suffolk: Neville Spearman, 1981, pp. 1–2.
8. See Eric Kurlander, 'Hitler's Monsters: The Occult Roots of Nazism and the Emergence of the Nazi Supernatural Imaginary', *German History* 30:4 (2012), pp. 528–49.
9. H. R. Knickerbocker, *Is Tomorrow Hitler's*, New York: Penguin, 1942; http://www.oldmagazinearticles.com/pdf/Carl_Jung_on_Hitler.pdf; Raymond L. Sickinger, 'Hitler and the Occult: The Magical Thinking of Adolf Hitler', *Journal of Popular Culture* 34:2 (Fall 2000), pp. 107–25.
10. Hermann Rauschning, *Gespräche mit Hitler*, Zürich: Europa Verlag, 2005, p. 208.
11. Michael Burleigh, 'National Socialism as a Political Religion', *Totalitarian Movements and Political Religions* 1:2 (Autumn 2000), pp. 1–26, here pp. 2–3; Klaus Vondung, 'Von der völkischen Religiösität zur politischen Religion', in Uwe Puschner and Clemens Vollnhals, eds, *Die völkisch - religiöse Bewegung im Nationalsozialismus*. Göttingen: Vandenhoeck & Rupprecht, 2012, pp. 30–3.
12. IfZG: ED 386, Gerhard Szczesny, 'Die Presse des Okkultismus, Geschichte und Typologie der okkultistischen Zeitschriften' (diss 1940, Munich, under Karl d'Ester), pp. 48–65, 119–32.
13. Willy Ley, 'Pseudoscience in Naziland', *Astounding Science Fiction* 39:3 (1947), p. 90; William McGuire and R. F. C. Hull, eds, *C. G. Jung Speaking: Interviews and Encounters*, Princeton, NJ: Princeton University Press, 1993, p. 142.
14. Peter Staudenmaier, 'Nazi Perceptions of Esotericism: The Occult as Fascination and Menace', in Ashwin Manthripragada, Emina Musanovic, and Dagmar Theison, eds, *The Threat and Allure of the Magical*, Cambridge: Cambridge Scholars Publishing, 2013, pp. 26–7.
15. Lewis Spence, *The Occult Causes of the Present War*, London: Kessinger, 1940, pp. 172–4.
16. Treitel, *Science*, p. 210.
17. To take a few prominent examples, which vary greatly in scholarly quality, see Ernst Bloch, *Erbschaft dieser Zeit*, Frankfurt am Main: Suhrkamp, 1962; Spence, *The Occult Causes of the Present War*; Siegfried Kracauer, *From Caligari to Hitler: A Psychological History of the German Film*, Princeton,

NJ: Princeton University Press, 2004; George Mosse, *The Crisis of German Ideology*, New York: Fertig, 1999 (orig. pub. Grosset & Dunlap, 1964); Theodor Adorno, *The Stars Down to Earth and Other Essays on the Irrational in Culture*, New York: Routledge, 1994 (1974); Fritz Stern, *The Politics of Cultural Despair*, Berkeley, CA: University of California Press, 1974; Cary J. Nederman and James Wray, 'Popular Occultism and Critical Social Theory: Exploring Some Themes in Adorno's Critique of Astrology and the Occult', *Sociology of Religion* 42:4 (1981), pp. 325–32.

18. See Kracauer, *From Caligari to Hitler*; see also Jared Poley, 'Siegfried Kracauer, Spirit, and the Soul of Weimar Germany', in Monica Black and Eric Kurlander, eds, *Revisiting the Nazi Occult: Histories, Realities, Legacies*, Rochester, NY: Camden House, 2015, pp. 86–100.

19. Through its 'irrational rationalization of what advanced industrial society cannot itself rationalize' and 'ideological mystification of actual social conditions', Adorno argued, occultism facilitated Nazism. Nederman and Wray, 'Popular Occultism and Critical Social Theory', pp. 325–32. See also Adorno, *The Stars Down to Earth*.

20. Lotte Eisner, *The Haunted Screen*, Berkeley, CA: University of California Press, 1969, pp. 8–9, 95–7. The book was originally published in French (1952) and then German (1955) under the title *The Demonic Screen*.

21. Treitel, *Science*, p. 25; see also Mosse, *The Crisis of German Ideology*, 1999; Stern, *The Politics of Cultural Despair*, Berkeley, CA: University of California Press, 1974; Ellic Howe, *Nostradamus and the Nazis*, London: Arborfield, 1965; James Webb, *Flight from Reason*, London: MacDonald & Co., 1971; Goodrick-Clarke, *The Occult Roots of Nazism*.

22. Michael Rißmann, *Hitler's Gott*, Munich: Pendo, pp. 144–8. For only a few examples, see Trevor Ravenscroft, *The Spear of Destiny*, New York: Weiser, 1982; Louis Pauwels and Jacques Bergier, *The Morning of the Magicians*, London: Souvenir, 2007; Michael Baigent, Richard Leigh, and Henry Lincoln, *Holy Blood, Holy Grail*, New York: Dell, 1983; Pauwels and Bergier, *Morning of the Magicians*; Peter Orzechowski, *Schwarze Magie – Braune Macht*, Ravensburg: Selinka, 1987; Jean-Michel Angebert, *The Occult and the Third Reich: The Mystical Origins of Nazism and the Search for the Holy Grail*, New York, Macmillan, 1974; Francis King, *Satan and Swastika*, St Albans: Mayflower, 1976; Michael Fitzgerald, *Stormtroopers of Satan: An Occult History of the Second World War*, New York: Robert Hale, 1990; Peter Levenda, *Unholy Alliance: A History of Nazi Involvement with the Occult. With a Foreword by Norman Mailer*. New York/London: Continuum, 2002; Dusty Sklar, *Gods and Beasts: The Nazis and the Occult*, New York: Thomas Crowell, 1977; Stephen Flowers and Michael Moynihan, *The Secret King: The Myth and Reality of Nazi Occultism*, London: Feral House, 2007.

23. Rißmann, *Hitler's Gott*, pp. 139–40; Detlev Rose, *Die Thule-Gesellschaft: Legende-Mythos-Wirklichkeit*, Tübingen: Grabert, 1994, pp. 159–72. See also Isrun Engelhardt, 'Nazis of Tibet: A Twentieth Century Myth', in Monica Esposito, ed., *Images of Tibet in the 19th and 20th Centuries*, Paris: Ecole française d'Extrême-Orient (EFEO), coll. Etudes thématiques 22, vol. 1 (2008), pp. 63–96; Michael Howard, *The Occult Conspiracy*, Rochester, VT: Destiny Books, 1989; Pauwels and Bergier, *Morning of the Magicians*; Dietrich Bronder, *Bevor Hitler kam*, Geneva: Lüha, 1975; Michel-Jean Angebert, *Les mystiques du soleil*, Paris: Robert Lafont, 1971; Herbert Brennan, *Occult Reich*, New York: Signet Classics, 1974; Alan Baker, *Invisible Eagle. The History of Nazi Occultism*, London: Virgin Books, 2000; E. R. Carmin, *Das schwarze Reich: Geheimgesellschaften und Politik im 20. Jahrhundert*, Munich: Nikol, 1997; Pennick, *Hitler's Secret Sciences*; Paul Roland, *The Nazis and the Occult: The Esoteric Roots of the Third Reich*, London: Foulsham, 2007; Franz Wegener, *Heinrich Himmler. Deutscher Spiritismus – Französischer Okkultismus und der Reichsführer SS*, Gladbeck: KFVR, 2004; Franz Wegener, *Der Alchemist Franz Tausend. Alchemie und Nationalsozialismus*, Gladbeck: KFVR, 2006.

24. Goodrick-Clarke, *Occult Roots*.

25. Ibid.

26. Treitel, *Science*, pp. 26, 52.

27. Ibid., pp. 50–2.

28. Ibid., pp. 209–10; as Marco Pasi argues, 'the mutual attraction of esotericism and right-wing radicalism appear to be a contingent reorientation of the political color of esotericism, rather than an inherent structural necessity . . . the occultist organizations such as the Theosophical Society and the Golden Dawn offered, among other things, a virtual space for social and cultural experimentation and innovation . . . This of course clashes with the opinion we have seen expressed by such authoritative thinkers as Adorno. The idea put forward by Orwell immediately after the Second World War, according to which esotericists must necessarily "dread the prospect of universal suffrage, popular education, freedom of thought, emancipation of women" can no longer convince anyone who has studied the history of 19th-century esotericism.' Marco Pasi, 'The Modernity of Occultism: Reflection on Some Crucial Aspects', in Wouter J. Hanegraaff and Joyce Pijnenburg, eds, *Hermes in the Academy*, Amsterdam: Amsterdam University Press, 2009, pp. 62, 67–8. See also Thomas

Laqueur, 'Why the Margins Matter: Occultism and the Making of Modernity', *Modern Intellectual History* 3:1 (2006), pp. 111–35; Heather Wolffram, *The Stepchildren of Science*, Amsterdam: Rodopi, 2009; Kevin Repp, *Reformers, Critics, and the Paths of German Modernity: Anti-Politics and the Search for Alternatives, 1890–1914*, Cambridge, MA: Harvard University Press, 2000; Anson Rabinbach, *In the Shadow of Catastrophe: German Intellectuals Between Apocalypse and Enlightenment*, Berkeley, CA: University of California Press, 2001; Frederick Gregory, *Nature Lost: Natural Science and the German Theological Traditions of the Nineteenth Century*, Cambridge, MA: Harvard University Press, 1992; Anne Harrington, *Reenchanted Science: Holism in German Culture from Wilhelm II to Hitler*, Princeton, NJ: Princeton University Press, 1996.

29. Laqueur, 'Why the Margins Matter', pp 111–35.

30. See Black and Kurlander, eds, *Revisiting*; Peter Staudenmaier, *Between Occultism and Nazism*, Boston, MA: Brill, 2014; Eric Kurlander, 'The Nazi Magician's Controversy: Enlightenment, "Border Science", and Occultism in the Third Reich', *Central European History* 48:4 (December 2015), pp. 498–522; Eric Kurlander, 'Hitler's Supernatural Sciences: Astrology, Anthroposophy, and World Ice Theory', in Monica Black and Eric Kurlander, eds, *The Nazi Soul Between Science and Religion: Revisiting the Occult Roots of Nazism*, Elizabethtown, NY: Camden House, 2015, pp. 132–56; 'Liberalism in Imperial Germany, 1871–1918', in Black and Kurlander, eds, *Revisiting*; Matthew Jefferies, ed., *Ashgate Research Companion to Imperial Germany*, London: Ashgate, 2015, pp. 91–110; Eric Kurlander, 'Between Weimar's Horrors and Hitler's Monsters: The Politics of Race, Nationalism, and Cosmopolitanism in Hanns Heinz Ewers Supernatural Imaginary', in Rainer Godel, Erdmut Jost, and Barry Murnane, eds, *Zwischen Popularisierung und Ästhetisierung? Hanns Heinz Ewers und die Moderne*, Bielefeld: Moderne Studien (Aisthesis), 2014, pp. 229–56; Eric Kurlander, 'The Orientalist Roots of National Socialism? Nazism, Occultism, and South Asian Spirituality, 1919–1945', in Joanne Miyang Cho, Eric Kurlander, and Douglas McGetchin, eds, *Transcultural Encounters between Germany and India: Kindred Spirits in the Nineteenth and Twentieth Centuries*, New York and London: Routledge, 2014, pp. 155–69; Kurlander, 'Hitler's Monsters', pp. 528–49.

31. James Dow and Hannjost Lixfeld, eds, *The Nazification of an Academic Discipline: Folklore in the Third Reich*, Bloomington, IN: Indiana University Press, 1994; Michael Fahlbusch, *Wissenschaft im Dienst der nationalsozialistischen Politik? Die Volksdeutschen Forschungsgemeinschaften von 1931– 1945*, Baden-Baden: Nomos, 1999; Ingo Haar, *Historiker im Nationalsozialismus*, Göttingen: Vandenhoeck & Rupprecht, 2000; Michael Burleigh, *Germany Turns Eastwards: A Study of Ostforschung in the Third Reich*, Cambridge: Cambridge University Press, 1988; Michael Burleigh, *Sacred Causes: The Clash of Religion and Politics from the Great War to the War on Terror*, New York: HarperCollins, 2007.

32. Black and Kurlander, eds, *Revisiting the Nazi Occult*; Staudenmaier, *Between Occultism and Nazism*; Staudenmaier, 'Nazi Perceptions of Esotericism', pp. 26–7; Uwe Schellinger, Andreas Anton, and Michael T. Schetsche, 'Pragmatic Occultism in the Military History of the Third Reich', in Black and Kurlander, eds, *Revisiting*, pp. 157–80; see Uwe Schellinger, Andreas Anton, and Michael Schetsche, 'Zwischen Szientismus und Okkultismus. Grenzwissenschaftliche Experimente der deutschen Marine im Zweiten Weltkrieg', *Zeitschrift für Anomalistik Band* 10 (2010), pp. 287–321; Eric Kurlander, 'Supernatural Science', in Black and Kurlander, eds, *Revisiting the Nazi Occult*; Uwe Werner, *Anthroposophen in der Zeit des Nationalsozialismus (1933–1945)*, Munich: Oldenbourg, 1999, pp. 287–336; Kurlander, 'Hitler's Monsters'; Uwe Schellinger, 'Sonderaktion Heß', in Viertes Hannoverisches Symposium, NS-Raubgut in Museen, Bibliotheken und Archiven, Frankfurt 2012, p. 318; Rißmann, *Hitler's Gott*; See Mosse, *Crisis*; Stern, *Politics of Cultural Despair*; Goodrick-Clarke, *Occult Roots*. See also Peter Staudenmaier, 'Occultism, Race and Politics in Germany, 1880– 1940: A Survey of the Historical Literature', *European History Quarterly* 39:1 (January 2009), pp. 47–70.

33. Michael Saler, 'Modernity and Enchantment: A Historiographic Review', *American Historical Review* 11:3 (June 2006), pp. 692–716; Treitel, *Science*; Goodrick-Clarke, *Occult Roots*; Diethard Sawicki, *Leben mit den Toten: Geisterglauben und die Entstehung des Spiritismus in Deutschland 1770–1900*, Paderborn: Schöningh, 2002; Helmut Zander, *Anthroposophie in Deutschland: Theosophische Weltanschauung und gesellschaftliche Praxis 1884–1945*, Göttingen: Vandenhoeck & Ruprecht, 2007; Christoph Meinel, 'Okkulte und exakte Wissenschaften', in August Buck, ed., *Die okkulten Wissenschaften in der Renaissance*, Wiesbaden: Harrassowitz, 1992.

34. As Konrad Jarausch and Michael Geyer put it, 'mass consumption is increasingly presented as the destiny of German history, its refuge and redemption. The emergence of a consumer-oriented society is becoming the narrative of the age.' Konrad H. Jarausch and Michael Geyer, *Shattered Past: Reconstructing German Histories*, Princeton: Princeton University Press, 2003, p. 269; Bryan Ganaway, 'Consumer Culture and Political Transformations in Twentieth-Century Germany', *History Compass* 1:1 (2005), pp. 1–5; Treitel, *Science*, pp. 57–62, 75–7; Sabine Doering-Manteuffel,

Das Okkulte. Eine Erfolgsgeschichte im Schatten der Aufklärung. Von Gutenberg bis zum World Wide Web, Munich: Siedler, 2008.

35. Treitel, *Science*, 73–5; George Mosse, *Masses and Man: Nationalist and Fascist Perceptions of Reality*, Detroit, IL: Wayne State University Press, 1987, pp. 199–200, 205–8; Dirk Rupnow, Veronika Lipphardt, Jens Thiel, and Christina Wessely, eds, *Pseudowissenschaft: Konzeptionen von Nichtwissenschaftlichkeit in der Wissenschaftsgeschichte*, Frankfurt am Main: Suhrkamp, 2008.

36. Occultism may have originated in a 'religious way of thinking, the roots of which stretch back into antiquity and which may be described as the Western esoteric tradition'. Goodrick-Clarke, *Occult Roots*, p. 17; George Williamson, *The Longing for Myth in Germany*, Chicago, IL: University of Chicago Press, 2004, p. 289.

37. Erich Voegelin, *Political Religions*, Lewiston, NY: E. Mellen, 2003; Stanley Payne, *Fascism: Comparison and Definition*, Madison, WI: University of Wisconsin Press, 1980, pp. 3–13; Robert Paxton, *The Anatomy of Fascism*, New York: Knopf, 2004, pp. 13–15; Roger Griffin, ed., *International Fascism*, London: Oxford University Press, 1998; Hans Maier, *Politische Religionen: Die totalitären Regime und das Christentum*, Freiburg: Herder, 1995; Hans Maier, 'Political Religion: A Concept and its Limitations', *Totalitarian Movements and Political Religions* 1:2 (Autumn 2000), pp. 1–26; Richard Steigmann-Gall, *The Holy Reich: Nazi Conceptions of Christianity, 1919–1945*, Cambridge: Cambridge University Press, 2003. See the Discussion Forum, 'Richard Steigmann-Gall's *The Holy Reich*', *Journal of Contemporary History* 42:1 (January 2007); Michael Burleigh, *The Third Reich*, London: Hill and Wang, 2001, pp. 252–5; Jürgen Schreiber, *Politische Religion. Geschichtswissenschaftliche Perspektiven und Kritik eines interdisziplinären Konzepts zur Erforschung des Nationalsozialismus*, Marburg: Tectum, 2009; Emilio Gentile, *Politics as Religion*, Princeton, NJ: Princeton University Press, 2006; Michael Ley and Julius Schoeps, *Der Nationalsozialismus als politische Religion*, Bodenheim b. Mainz: Philo, 1997; Claus-Ekkehard Bärsch, *Die Politische Religion des National Sozialismus*, Munich: Fink, 1998; Werner Reichelt, *Das braune Evangelium: Hitler und die NS-Liturgie*, Wuppertal: P. Hammer, 1990; Klaus Vondung, *Magie und Manipulation: Ideologischer Kult und Politische Religion des Nationalsozialismus*, Göttingen: Vandenhoeck & Ruprecht, 1971; Hans-Jochen Gamm, *Der braune Kult: Das Dritte Reich und seine Ersatzreligion. Ein Beitrag zur politischen Bildung*, Hamburg: Rütten & Loening, 1962.

38. George Mosse, *The Nationalization of the Masses: Political Symbolism and Mass Movements in Germany, from the Napoleonic Wars Through the Third Reich*, New York: H. Fertig, 2001, p. 2; Mosse, *Masses and Man*, pp. 76–7.

39. Mosse, *Masses and Man*, p. 14; see also Eduard Gugenberger and Roman Schweidlenka, *Die Faden der Nornen*, Vienna: Verlag für Gesellschaftskritik, 1993, pp. 23–4, 73–97; the 'importance of myth and symbol was not confined to anti-Semitism or racism,' Mosse reminds us: 'During the first part of the twentieth century, men and women increasingly perceived the world in which they lived through myth, symbol, and stereotype . . . The longing for totality was accompanied by a strong urge to appropriate immutabilities: the landscape, national traditions, history, and even the sky. All of these were thought to stand outside the rush of time, helping men to keep control, introducing something of the sacred into individual lives.' Mosse, *Masses and Man*, pp. 11–12.

40. See Puschner and Vollnhals, eds, *Bewegung*; Mark Edward Ruff, 'Review Essay: Integrating Religion into the Historical Mainstream: Recent Literature on Religion in the Federal Republic of Germany', *Central European History* 42 (2009), p. 311. Dagmar Herzog, 'The Death of God in West Germany: Between Secularization, Postfascism, and the Rise of Liberation Theology', in Michael Geyer and Lucian Hölscher, eds, *Die Gegenwart Gottes in der modernen Gesellschaft: Transzendenz und religiöse Vergemeinschaftung in Deutschland*, Göttingen: Wallstein, 2006, p. 428. See also Benjamin Ziemann, *Katholische Kirche und Sozialwissenschaften 1945–1975*, Göttingen: Vandenhoeck & Ruprecht, 2007; Benjamin Ziemann, 'Religion and the Search for Meaning, 1945–1990', in Helmut Walser Smith, ed., *The Oxford Handbook of Modern German History*, Oxford: Oxford University Press, 2011. Yet 'Theories about fascism itself have tended to ignore the importance of those myths and cults which eventually provided the essence of fascist politics,' according to Mosse, *Nationalization of the Masses*, p. 3; Mosse, *Masses and Man*, pp. 77–9; Robert Darnton, 'Peasants Tell Tales', in *Great Cat Massacre*, New York: Basic Books, 1984, pp. 21–2, 50–63; Jack Zipes, *Fairy Tale as Myth/Myth as Fairy Tale*, Lexington, KY: University Press of Kentucky, 1994.

41. Anna Lux, 'On all Channels: Hans Bender, the Supernatural, and the Mass Media', in Black and Kurlander, eds, *Revisiting*, pp. 223–4; see, e.g., Eric Kurlander, 'The Orientalist Roots of National Socialism?'; Kris Manjapra, *Age of Entanglement: German and Indian Intellectuals across the Empire*, Cambridge, MA: Harvard University Press, 2014; Suzanne Marchand, *German Orientalism in the Age of Empire: Religion, Race, and Scholarship*, Washington DC: Cambridge University Press, 2009; Treitel, *Science*; Wolffram, *Stepchildren of Science*; Alex Owen, *The Place of Enchantment: British Occultism and the Culture of the Modern*, Chicago, IL: University of Chicago Press, 2004; Repp, *Reformers, Critics, and the Paths of German Modernity*; Michael Saler, 'Clap if You Believe in Sherlock

Holmes: Mass Culture and the Re-Enchantment of Modernity, c.1890–c.1940', *The Historical Journal* 46:3 (2003), pp. 599–622; Edward A. Tiryakian, 'Dialectics of Modernity: Reenchantment and Dedifferentiation as Counterprocesses', in Hans Haferkamp and Neil J. Smelser, eds, *Social Change and Modernity*, Berkeley, CA: University of California Press, 1992, pp. 78–83; Michael Simon, '"Volksmedizin" im frühen 20. Jahrhundert: Zum Quellenwert des Atlas der deutschen Volkskunde', *Studien zur Volkskultur* 28. Mainz: Gesellschaft für Volkskunde in Rheinland-Pfalz, 2003, pp. 147–8, n. 459; Owen Davies, *Grimoires: A History of Magic Books*, Oxford: Oxford University Press, 2009, p. 11.

42. http://www.mpiwg-berlin.mpg.de/en/research/projects/deptIII-ChristinaWessely-Welteislehre; see also (from the same) Christina Wessely, 'Cosmic Ice Theory – Science, Fiction and the Public, 1894–1945'; Christina Wessely, 'Welteis, Die "Astronomie des Unsichtbaren" um 1900', in Rupnow et al., eds, *Pseudowissenschaft*, pp. 163–93; ibid., p. 166; David Redles, *Hitler's Millennial Reich: Apocalyptic Belief and the Search for Salvation*, New York: New York University Press, 2005, p. 13; Saler, 'Modernity and Enchantment', pp. 692–716; Lorraine Daston and Katherine Park, *Wonders and the Order of Nature*, New York: Zone, 2001; Owen, *The Place of Enchantment*, p. 25; Daniel Pick, *Faces of Degeneration: A European Disorder c. 1848–1918*, New York: Cambridge University Press, 1959.

43. Treitel, *Science*; Saler, 'Modernity and Enchantment', pp. 692–716; Mitchell G. Ash, 'Pseudowissenschaft als historische Größe; Ein Abschlusskommentar', in Alexander C. T. Geppert and Till Kössler, eds, *Wunder – Poetik und Politik des Staunens im 20. Jahrhundert*, Berlin: Suhrkamp, 2011, pp. 422–5, 457–8.

44. The last thirty years have seen a 'dethroning [of] positivist narratives about the progress of science' within the field of history, anthropology, sociology, and even the natural sciences. In this new paradigm, border science is merely another form of 'non-hegemonial knowledge production', no more or less valid than any other. See 'Gesellschaftliche Innovation durch "Nichthegemoniale" Wissensproduktion. "Okkulte" Phänomene zwischen Mediengeschichte, Kulturtransfer und Wissenschaft', 1770 bis 1970; http://www.uni-siegen.de/mediaresearch/nichthegemoniale_innovation. As Anna Lux reminds us, moreover, science, then as now, is 'not only determined in the arena of scientific practice, but also in the public'; Lux, 'On all Channels', p. 224.

45. Adorno as cited in Denis Dutton, 'Theodor Adorno on Astrology', *Philosophy and Literature* 19:2 (1995), pp. 424–30; these 'semi-erudite' occultists, Adorno argued, were 'driven by the narcissistic wish to prove superior to the plain people', but were 'not in a position to carry through complicated and detached intellectual operations'. See also Egil Asprem, *The Problem of Disenchantment: Scientific Naturalism and Esoteric Discourse 1900–1939*, Leiden: Brill, 2014; Bruno Latour, *Science in Action: How to Follow Scientists and Engineers through Society*, Cambridge, MA: Harvard University Press, 1987; Bruno Latour, *Reassembling the Social: An Introduction to Actor-Network-Theory*, Oxford: Oxford University Press, 2005.

46. See Michael Hagner, 'Bye Bye Science, Welcome Pseudoscience?', in Rupnow et al., eds, *Pseudowissenschaft*, p. 50; Saler, 'Modernity and Enchantment'; many might find it 'mind-boggling' that so many otherwise educated people might 'seem willing to ignore the facts … if the facts conflict with their sense of what someone like them believes'. And yet a number of scholars have begun to show scientifically the ways in which 'people process evidence differently when they think with a factual mind-set rather than with a religious mind-set'; C. H. Legare and A. Visala, 'Between Religion and Science: Integrating Psychological and Philosophical Accounts of Explanatory Coexistence', in *Human Development* 54 (2011), pp. 169–84; C. H. Legare and S. A. Gelman, 'Bewitchment, Biology, or Both: The Co-existence of Natural and Supernatural Explanatory Frameworks across Development', *Cognitive Science* 32 (2008), pp. 607–42.

47. See Mosse, *Crisis*; Stern, *Politics*; see also Peter Laslett, *The World We Have Lost*, New York: Routledge, 2004; Peter Fritzsche, *Stranded in the Present: Modern Time and the Melancholy of History*, Cambridge, MA: Harvard University Press, 2004; H. Stuart Hughes, *Consciousness and Society: The Reorientation of Social Thought, 1890–1930*, New York: Vintage, 1961; Mark J. Sedgwick, *Against the Modern World: Traditionalism and the Secret Intellectual History of the Twentieth Century*, New York/Oxford: Oxford University Press, 2004; Russell Berman, *The Reenchantment of the* World, Ithaca, NY: Cornell University Press, 1981; Keith Thomas, *Religion and the Decline of Magic*, New York: Scribner's, 1971; Robert Darnton, *Mesmerism and the End of the Enlightenment in France*, Cambridge, MA: Harvard University Press, 1986.

48. Horkheimer and Adorno, 'For the scientific temper, any deviation of thought from the business of manipulating the actual … is no less senseless and self-destructive than it would be for the magician to step outside the magic circle drawn for his incantation; and in both cases violation of the taboo caries a heavy price for the offender. The mastery of nature draws the circle in which the critique of pure reason holds thought spellbound.' as quoted in Max Horkheimer and Theodor Adorno, *Dialectic of Enlightenment: Philosophical Fragments*, Stanford, CA: Stanford University Press, 2002, p. 19; ibid., p. 5; Staudenmaier, 'Nazi Perceptions of Esotericism', pp. 49–50.

49. 'Dort sollte ein Weg gefunden werden, um archaisch-religiöse Weltbilder mit der "Modernen" zu kombinieren: Bauernromantik und Grossindustrie, die Rückkehr der Götter und technische Hochleistung, Magie und Wissenschaft', in Victor and Victoria Trimondi, *Hitler, Buddha, Krishna*, Vienna: Ueberreuter, 2002, p. 17; see also Saler, 'Modernity and Enchantment', pp. 704–5. Christoph Asendorf, *Batteries of Life: On the History of Things and Their Perception in Modernity*, trans. Don Reneau, Berkeley, CA: University of California Press, 1993; Erik Davis, *TechGnosis: Myth, Magic, and Mysticism in the Age of Information*, New York: Harmony, 1998; Erik Larson, *The Devil in the White City: Murder, Magic, and Madness at the Fair That Changed America*, New York: Crown, 2003; David Nye, *Electrifying America: Social Meanings of New Technology, 1880–1940*, Cambridge, MA: Harvard University Press, 1992; Vanessa R. Schwartz, *Spectacular Realities: Early Mass Culture in Fin-de-Siècle Paris*, Berkeley, CA: University of California Press, 1999; Barbara Maria Stafford and Frances Terpak, *Devices of Wonder: From the World in a Box to Images on a Screen*, Los Angeles, CA: Getty, 2001; Robin Walz, *Pulp Surrealism: Insolent Popular Culture in Twentieth-Century France*, Berkeley, CA: University of California Press, 2000.

50. George Steinmetz, 'The notion of imaginary identification can also be connected to the overarching psychoanalytic conception of fantasy, which has been used to great avail by theorists of nationalism, communism, totalitarianism, and postfascism. Fantasy scenarios express a conscious or unconscious wish. Imaginary identification is one site for such wishful scenarios.' in his *The Devil's Handwriting: Precoloniality and the German Colonial State in Qingdao, Samoa, and Southwest Africa*, Chicago, IL: University of Chicago Press, 2007, p. 60.

51. Charles Taylor, *Modern Social Imaginaries*, Durham, NC: Duke University Press, 2004, pp. 23–4. Whereas Taylor's concept of an 'imaginary' has some important affinities with Jacques Lacan's, it is far broader in its implications and obviously transcends the 'mirror stage' of early childhood development. See Jacques Lacan, *The Seminar of Jacques Lacan: The Psychoses* (Book III), New York: Norton, 1997, pp. 143–60.

52. Taylor, *Modern Social Imaginaries*, p. 25.

53. Ibid., pp. 185–7.

54. Ibid.

55. 'Sacred values may even have different neural signatures in the brain', according to T. M. Luhrmann, 'Faith vs. Facts', *The New York Times*, 18 April 2015.

56. Ibid.

57. See Martin Baumeister, 'Auf dem Weg in die Diktatur: Faschistische Bewegungen und die Krise der europäischen Demokratien', in Dietmar Süß and Winfried Süß, eds, *Das 'Dritte Reich': Eine Einführung*, Munich: Pantehon, 2008. p. 31.

58. Steinmetz, *Devil's Handwriting*, pp. 62, 66; see also Uwe Puschner and Hubert Cancik, eds, *Antisemitismus, Paganismus, Völkische Religion / Anti-Semitism, Paganism, Voelkish Religion*, Munich: K. G. Saur, 2004; Christina von Braun, Wolfgang Gerlach, and Ludger Heid, eds, *Der ewige Judenhaß. Christlicher Antijudaismus, Deutschnationale Judenfeindlichkeit, Rassistischer Antisemitismus*, Berlin: Philo Verlag, 2000; Olaf Blaschke, *Katholizismus und Antisemitismus im deutschem Kaiserreich*, Göttingen: Vandenhoeck & Ruprecht, 1997; Adolf Leschnitzer, *The Magic Background of Modern Antisemitism*, New York: International Universities Press, 1956; Wolfgang Heinrichs, *Das Judenbild im Protestantismus des deutschen Kaiserreichs*, Pulheim: Theinland-Verlag, 2000; Walter Stephens, *Demon Lovers: Witchcraft, Sex, and the Crisis of Belief*, Chicago, IL: University of Chicago Press, 2001; Daniel Pick, *Svengali's Web: The Alien Enchanter in Modern Culture*, New Haven, CT: Yale University Press, 2000; Nazi intellectuals were given to invoking the power of the Norse gods against 'foreign demons' or the mythical demonization of the foreign and domestic enemy. Gugenberger and Schweidlenka, *Die Faden der Nornen*, pp. 112–13.

59. Because monsters 'embody social anxieties and form the discourse in which people talk about those anxieties. Each time the monster reappears, he or she becomes something new and specific – expressing the anxieties of that moment.' Monica Black, 'Refugees Tell Tales', in *History & Memory* 25:1 (Spring/Summer 2013), pp. 97–8.

60. Frantz Fanon, *The Wretched of the Earth*, New York: Grove Press, 2004, pp. 54–7.

61. See Jared Poley, *Decolonization in Germany*, Bern: Peter Lang, 2005.

62. Steinmeitz, *Devil's Handwriting*, pp. 59– 61.

63. In their preoccupation with witchcraft trials, for example, Himmler and other SS researchers repeatedly lamented the medieval Church's barbaric murder of women for expressing an alternative worldview, grounded in nature and folk traditions. See Wolfgang Behringer and Jürgen Michael Schmidt, *Himmlers Hexenkarthotek. Das Interesse des. Nationalsozialismus an der Hexenverfolgung*, Bielefeld: Verlag für Regionalgeschichte, 1999; Hugh Trevor-Roper, ed., *Hitler's Secret Conversations, 1941–1944*, New York: Farrar, Straus and Young, 1953; Felix Kersten, *The Kersten Memoirs 1940– 1945*, New York: Howard Fertig, 1994; Hugh Trevor-Roper, ed., *The Bormann Letters*, London: Weidenfeld and Nicolson, 1954; Wilhelm Wulff, *Zodiac and Swastika*, New York: Coward, 1973.

64. See Susanne Zantop, *Colonial Fantasies: Conquest, Family, and Nation in Precolonial Germany, 1770–1870*, Durham, NC: Duke University Press, 1997.

65. See Russell Berman, *Enlightenment or Empire: Colonial Discourse in German Culture*, Lincoln, NB: University of Nebraska Press, 1998.

66. Matthew Gibson, *Dracula and the Eastern Question*, New York: Palgrave, 2006; Wilfried Kugel, *Der Unverantwortliche. Das Leben des Hanns Heinz Ewers*, Düsseldorf: Grupello, 1992; Poley, *Decolonization*; Zantop, *Colonial Fantasies*; Andrew Zimmerman, *Anthropology and Antihumanism in Imperial Germany*, Chicago, IL: University of Chicago Press, 2001; Sara Friedrichsmeyer, Sarah Lennox, and Susanne Zantop, eds, *The Imperialist Imagination*, Ann Arbor, MI: Michigan, 1998; Lutz Mackensen, *Sagen in Wartheland*, Posen: Hirt Reger, 1943.

67. Theodor Schieder, *Hermann Rauschnings 'Gespräche mit Hitler' als Geschichtsquelle*, Opladen: Westdeutscher Verlag, 1972, p. 16.

68. Ibid., p. 18.

69. Ibid., p. 62.

70. In employing Trevor-Roper's sometimes problematic English translation of Hitler's table talk, edited by Martin Bormann (trans. Trevor-Roper, *Hitler's Secret Conversations 1941-1944*), I have made an effort only to include passages that are corroborated by the German originals from Picker's text: Henry Picker, ed., *Hitlers Tischgespräche im Führerhauptquartier*, Munich: Propyläen, 2003.

71. Wolfgang Kaufmann, *Das Dritte Reich und Tibet*, Ludwigsfeld: Ludwigsfelder, 2009, pp. 87–8.

72. Ibid., pp. 82–5.

73. Treitel, *Science*, pp. 24–38, 243–8.

74. Williamson, *The Longing for Myth in Germany*; for more examples of the relationship between the supernatural and racial or 'imperial imaginary', see Steinmetz, *The Devil's Handwriting*; Gibson, *Dracula and the Eastern Question*; Poley, *Decolonization*; Zantop, *Colonial Fantasies*; Zimmerman, *Anthropology and Antihumanism in Imperial Germany*; Friedrichsmeyer, Lennox, and Zantop, eds, *The Imperialist Imagination*; Norman Cohn, *The Pursuit of the Millennium*, Oxford: Oxford University Press, 1970; Redles, *Hitlers Millennial Reich*; Anton Grabner-Haider and Peter Strasser, *Hitlers mythische Religion. Theologische Denklinien und NS-Ideologie*, Vienna: Böhlau, 2007.

Chapter 1

1. Cited in *The Month: An Illustrated Magazine of Literature, Science and Art* 610 (April 1915), p. 354.

2. Mosse, *Masses and Man*, p. 213.

3. Goodrick-Clarke, *Occult Roots*, pp. 194–6; *Ostara* 39 (1915).

4. Wilfried Daim, *Der Mann der Hitler die Ideen Gab*, Vienna: Böhlau, 1985, pp. 25–7.

5. Goodrick-Clarke, *Occult Roots*, pp. 194–8.

6. *Ostara* 39 (1915); Goodrick-Clarke, *Occult Roots*, pp. 193–4; Daim, *Der Mann*, pp. 160–75.

7. For more detail on the broader concept of *völkisch* (racialist) ideology, see Uwe Puschner, 'The Notions *Völkisch* and *Nordic*', in Horst Junginger and Andreas Ackerlund, eds, *Nordic Ideology Between Religion and Scholarship*, Frankfurt: Peter Lang, 2013, pp. 21–32.

8. Mosse, *Masses and Man*, p. 69; see also Max Weber, *Science as a Vocation*, Indianapolis, IN: Bobbs-Merrill, 1959 (1918); Rodney Stark, *Discovering God*, New York: HarperCollins, 2004; James Webb, *The Occult Underground*, London: Open Court, 1974; Thomas Luckmann, *The Invisible Religion*, New York: Macmillan, 1967, pp. 44–9; Williamson, *Longing*, pp. 12–18; Geppert and Kössler, eds, *Wunder*, pp. 9–12; Steigmann-Gall, *Holy Reich*, pp. 112–13.

9. See 'Introduction', in Black and Kurlander, *Revisiting*, p. 9; see also Staudenmaier, 'Esoteric Alternatives in Imperial Germany: Science, Spirit, and the Modern Occult Revival', in Black and Kurlander, *Revisiting*; see Treitel, *Science*; Pasi, 'The Modernity of Occultism', in Hanegraaff and Pijnenburg, eds, *Hermes*, pp. 62, 67–8.

10. See Williamson, *Longing*, pp. 1–6, 294–8; Brigitte Hamann, *Hitlers Wien: Lehrjahre eines Diktators*, Munich: Piper, 1996, pp. 7–9, 285–323; Ellic Howe, *Urania's Children*, London: Kimber, 1967, p. 4; Thomas Weber, *Hitler's First War*, Oxford: Oxford University Press, 2010, pp. 255–60; Mosse, *Masses and Man*, pp. 178–80.

11. Mosse, *Masses and Man*, p. 69.

12. H. H. Gerth and C. Wright Mills (trans. and ed.), *From Max Weber: Essays in Sociology*, New York: Oxford University Press, 1946, pp. 153–4.

13. Ibid.

14. See Weber, *Science*; Stark, *Discovering God*; Webb, *Occult Underground*; Eva Johach, 'Entzauberte Natur? Die Ökonomien des Wunder(n)s im naturwissenschaftlichen Zeitalter', in Geppert and Kössler, eds, *Wunder*, p. 181; Harrington, *Reenchanted Science*, xx.

15. See Mosse, *Masses and Man*; Rupnow et al., eds, *Pseudowissenschaft*. As Monica Black reminds us, the 'decades before the First World War already saw a flourishing of religious movements outside the

conventional Protestant–Catholic confessional divide.' Monica Black, 'Groening', in Black and Kurlander, *Revisiting*, p. 212.

16. Christian Voller, 'Wider die "Mode heutiger Archaik": Konzeptionen von Präsenz und Repräsentation im Mythosdiskurs der Nachkriegszeit', in Bent Gebert and Uwe Mayer, *Zwischen Präsenz und Repräsentation*, Göttingen: De Gruyter, 2014, pp. 226–7.

17. 'Germany, but where is it? I don't know how to find such a country', in James J. Sheehan, 'What is German History? Reflections on the Role of the *Nation* in German History and Historiography', *Journal of Modern History* 53 (March 1981), p. 1.

18. http://www.virtualreligion.net/primer/herder.html.

19. Gugenberger and Schweidlenka, *Die Faden*, pp. 97–9.

20. Mosse, *Nationalization*, pp. 7–8, 14–15, 40–3; Bernard Mees, 'Hitler and Germanentum', *Journal of Contemporary History* 39:2 (2004), pp. 255–70.

21. Darnton, 'Peasants Tell Tales', in *Great Cat Massacre*, pp. 35–41.

22. Louis L. Snyder, 'Nationalistic Aspects of the Grimm Brothers' Fairy Tales', *The Journal of Social Psychology* 33:2 (1951), pp. 209–23; Maria Tatar, 'Reading the Grimms' Children's Stories and Household Tales', in Maria Tatar, ed., *The Annotated Brothers Grimm*, New York: Norton, 2012 pp. xxvii–xxxix.

23. Gugenberger and Schweidlenka, *Die Faden*, pp. 103–5.

24. Goodrick-Clarke, *Occult Roots*, p. 193.

25. Mosse, *Masses and Man*, pp. 76–7; see also Hannjost Lixfeld, *Folklore and Fascism: The Reich Institute for German Volkskunde*, Bloomington, IN: Indiana University Press, 1994, pp. 21–2; Woodruff D. Smith, *Politics and the Sciences of Culture in Germany, 1840–1920*, Oxford: Oxford University Press, 1991, pp. 162–3; Ellic Howe, *Rudolph Freiherr von Sebottendorff*, Freiburg: [private publisher], 1989, pp. 25–7.

26. Debora Dusse, 'The Edda Myth Between Academic and Religious Interpretations', in Junginger and Ackerlund, eds, *Nordic Ideology*, pp. 73–8.

27. Uwe Puschner, *Die völkische Bewegung im wilhelminischen Kaiserreich*, Darmstadt: Wissenschaftliche Buchgesellschaft, 2001, pp. 29–51, 125–41.

28. Williamson, *Longing*, pp. 12–18; Luckmann, *Invisible Religion*, pp. 43–4.

29. Mosse, *Masses and Man*, pp. 199–208.

30. Treitel, *Science*, p. 217.

31. Puschner, *Die völkische Bewegung*, pp. 207–52.

32. Willibald Alexis, *Der Werwolf*, Berlin: Jahnke, 1904 (1848); Hermann Löns, *Der Wehrwolf*, Jena: Diederichs, 1910.

33. K. F. Koppen, *Hexen und Hexenprozesse; zur geschichte des aberglaubens und des inquisitorischen prozesses*, Leipzig: Wigand, 1858; Wilhelm Pressel, *Hexen und hexenmeister; oder, Vollständige und getreue schilderung dex hexenwesens*, Stuttgart: Belser, 1860; Joseph Hansen, *Zauberwahn, Inquisition und Hexenprozess im Mittelalter: und die Entstehung der grossen Hexenverfolgung*, Munich: Oldenbourg, 1900; Hugo Gering, *Über weissagung und zauber im nordischen altertum*, Kiel: Lipsius, 1902; Paul Ehrenreich, 'Götter und Heilbringer. Eine ethnologische Kritik', *Zeitschrift für Ethnologie* 38:4/5 (1 January 1906), pp. 536–610; Alfred Lehmann, *Aberglaube und Zauberei von den ältesten Zeiten an bis in die Gegenwart*, Stuttgart: Enke, 1908; Hans Kübert, *Zauberwahn, die Greuel der Inquisition und Hexenprozesse; dem Ultramontanismus ein Spiegel, kulturhistorischer Vortrag, gehalten am 28. April 1913 im lib. Verein Frei-München*, Munich: Nationalverein, 1913; Oswald Kurtz, *Beiträge zur Erklärung des volkstümlichen Hexenglaubens in Schlesien*, Anklam: Pottke, 1916; Ernst Maass, 'Hekate und ihre Hexen', *Zeitschrift für vergleichende Sprachforschung auf dem Gebiete der Indogermanischen Sprachen* 50:3/4 (1 January 1922), pp. 219–31.

34. Spence, *Occult Causes*, pp. 40–1, 72–3.

35. Ibid., pp. 81–2; Eduard Jacobs, *Der Brocken in Geschichte und Sage*, Halle: Pfeffer, 1879; Michael Zelle, *Externsteine*, Detmold: Lippischer Heimatbund, 2012.

36. Andrew McCall, *The Medieval Underworld*, New York: Barnes and Noble, 1972, pp. 110–12; Spence, *Occult Causes*, pp. 92–6; P. Wigand, *Das Femgericht Westfalens*, Hamm: Schulz and Wundermann, 1825, 2nd ed., 1893; L. Tross, *Sammlung merkwurdiger Urkunden für die Geschichte der Femgerichte*, Hanover, Schultz, 1826; F. P. Usener, *Die frei- und heimlichen Gerichte Westfalens*, Frankfurt: Archiv der freien Stadt Frankfurt, 1832; O. Wächter, *Femgerichte und Hexenprozesse in Deutschland*, Stuttgart: Spemann, 1882; T. Lindner, *Die Feme*, Münster and Paderborn: Ferdinand Schöningh, 1888; F. Thudichum, *Femgericht und Inquisition*, Giessen: J. Ricker, 1889; T. Lindner, *Der angebliche Ursprung der Femgerichte aus der Inquisition*, Münster and Paderborn: Ferdinand Schöningh, 1890.

37. Emil Julius Gumbel, Berthold Jacob, and Ernst Falck, eds, *Verräter verfallen der Feme: Opfer, Mörder, Richter 1919–1929: Abschliessende Darstellung*. Berlin: Malik-Verlag, 1929; Arthur D. Brenner, 'Feme Murder: Paramilitary "Self-Justice" in Weimar Germany', in Bruce D. Campbell and Arthur D.

Brenner, eds, *Death Squads in Global Perspective: Murder With Deniability*, New York: Palgrave Macmillan, 2002, pp. 57–84.

38. Black, 'Expellees', p. 94; see also Paul Barber, *Vampires, Burial, and Death: Folklore and Reality*, New Haven, CT: Yale University Press, 1988, pp. 5–14, 90–101; Thomas M. Bohn, 'Vampirismus in Österreich und Preussen: Von der Entdeckung einer Seuche zum Narrativ der Gegenkolonisation', *Jahrbücher für Geschichte Osteuropas* 56:2 (2008), pp. 2–5; Raymond McNally and Radu Florescu, *In Search of Dracula: A True History of Dracula and Vampire Legends*, Greenwich, CT: New York Graphic Society, 1972, p. 197.

39. Bohn, 'Vampirismus', pp. 1–2, 5–6; J. Striedter, 'Die Erzahlung vom walachischen vojevoden Drakula in der russischen und deutschen überlierferung', *Zeitscrift für Slawische Philologie* 29 (Heidelberg, 1961–2), pp. 12–20, 32–6, 107–20.

40. Bohn, 'Vampirismus', p. 8.

41. Mosse, *Masses and Man*, p. 66; Hamann, *Hitlers Wien*, pp. 39–45; Goodrick-Clark, *Occult Roots*, p. 193; August Kubizek, *The Young Hitler I Knew* (trans. E. V. Anderson), London: Paul Popper and Co., 1954, pp. 117, 179–83, 190–8; Picker, *Hitlers Tischgespräche*, p. 95.

42. Kurlander, 'Orientalist Roots', in Cho, Kurlander, and McGetchin, eds, *Transcultural Encounters*, pp. 155–69; Mosse, *Masses and Man*, pp. 69, 213, 178–80; Williamson, *Longing*, pp. 1–6; Nicholas Goodrick-Clarke, *Hitler's Priestess: Savitri Devi, the Hindu-Aryan Myth and Neo-Nazism*, New York: New York University Press, 1998, pp. 30–5; Nicholas Germana, *The Orient of Europe: The Mythical Image of India and Competing Images of German National Identity*, Newcastle: Cambridge Scholars, 2009; Sylvia Horsch, ' "Was findest du darinne, das nicht mit der allerstrengsten Vernunft übereinkomme?": Islam as Natural Theology in Lessing's Writings and in the Enlightenment', in Eleoma Joshua and Robert Vilain, eds, *Edinburgh German Yearbook* 1 (2007), pp. 45–62; Christian Moser, 'Aneignung, Verpflanzung, Zirkulation: Johann Gottfried Herders Konzeption des interkulturellen Austauschs', *Edinburgh German Yearbook* 1 (2007), pp. 89–108.

43. Puschner, *Die völkische Bewegung*, pp. 79–87; Mees, 'Hitler and Germanentum', pp. 255–70; Houston Stewart Chamberlain, *The Foundations of the Nineteenth Century*, London: Ballantyne, 1910, vol. 1, pp. 264–6, 403–36; vol. 2, pp. 18–25, 62–70.

44. Samuel Koehne, 'Were the National Socialists a Völkisch Party? Paganism, Christianity and the Nazi Christmas', *Central European History* 47 (December 2014), p. 763.

45. Puschner, *Die völkische Bewegung*, pp. 139–43; Kaufmann, *Das Dritte Reich*, pp. 103–4.

46. Vishwa Adluri and Joydeep Bagchee, *The Nay Science: A History of German Indology*, Oxford: Oxford University Press, 2014, pp. 31–2, 107.

47. Ibid. See also Goodrick-Clarke, *Hitler's Priestess*, pp. 30–5; Germana, *Orient of Europe*; Horsch, ' "Was findest Du darinne . . ." ', in Joshua and Vilain, eds, *Edinburgh German Yearbook*, pp. 45–62; Moser, 'Aneignung', pp. 89–108; Williamson, *Longing*, pp. 294–5; Marchand, *German Orientalism*, pp. 252–91; Kaufmann, *Das Dritte Reich*, pp. 143–4, 381–2.

48. David Motadel, *Islam and Nazi Germany's War*, Cambridge, MA: Belknap Press, 2014, pp. 18–28.

49. See Kurlander, 'Orientalist Roots', in Cho, Kurlander, and McGetchin, eds, *Transcultural Encounters*, pp. 156–7; Mosse, *Masses and Man*, pp. 69, 213, 178–80; Williamson, *Longing*, pp. 1–6, 294–5; Goodrick-Clarke, *Hitler's Priestess*, pp. 30–5; Germana, *Orient of Europe*; Horsch, ' "Was findest Du darinne . . ." ', pp. 45–62; Moser, 'Aneignung', pp. 45–62.

50. Myers, 'Imagined India', p. 619; Kaufmann, *Das Dritte Reich*, pp. 145–6.

51. Adluri and Bagchee, *Nay Science*, pp. 26–7, 72–3.

52. Hauer's scholarship was little different from 'all other [German] Indologists' in being 'placed entirely in the service of religious, nationalist or ethnocentric needs . . . because [Hauer] was drawing on a broad continuity in German Gita scholarship . . . essentially an amalgam of Jacobi's and Otto's views'. Adluri and Bagchee, *Nay Science*, p. 277; Kaufmann, *Das Dritte Reich*, pp. 100–1, 143–51; Myers, 'Imagined India', pp. 631–62.

53. Mosse, *Masses and Man*, pp. 213, 178–80; Puschner, *Die völkische Bewegung*; see also Klaus Vondung, 'Von der völkischen Religiosität zur politischen Religion des Nationalsozialismus: Kontinuität oder neue Qualität?', in Puschner and Vollnhals, eds, *Bewegung*, pp. 29–30.

54. Mosse, *Masses and Man*, pp. 76–7; Hermann Bausinger, 'Nazi Folk Ideology and Folk Research', in Dow and Lixfeld, eds, *Nazification*, pp. 13–14.

55. Goodrick-Clarke, *Occult Roots*, p. 193.

56. Manjapra, *Age of Entanglement*, p. 210.

57. Ibid., p. 210; see also Berman, *Enlightenment or Empire*; Zantop, *Colonial Fantasies*; Williamson, *Longing*, p. 4; Motadel, *Islam*.

58. Leschnitzer, *Magic Background*, pp. 155–8.

59. Stern, *Politics of Cultural Despair*.

60. Junginger and Ackerlund, eds, *Nordic Ideology*, p. 30; see also Repp, *Reformers*.

61. See Stern, *Politics of Cultural Despair*, pp. 5–16.

62. See ibid., pp. 13–25; Mosse, *Masses and Man*, pp. 199–200, p. 13; Mees, 'Hitler and Germanentum'; Ulrich Sieg, *Deutschlands Prophet. Paul de Lagarde und die Ursprünge des modernen Antisemitismus*, Munich: Carl Hanser, 2007.

63. Stern, *Politics of Cultural Despair*, pp. 108–21.

64. Mosse, *Masses and Man*, pp. 199–200.

65. Puschner, *Die völkische Bewegung*, pp. 146–51; for more on the ambivalent role of Heimat in the German social and political imaginary, see Mack Walker, *German Home Towns*, Ithaca, NY: Cornell University Press, 1971, and Celia Applegate, *A Nation of Provincials*, Berkeley, CA: University of California Press, 1990.

66. Puschner, *Die völkische Bewegung*, pp. 66–75; Hildegard Chatellier, 'Friedrich Lienhard', in Uwe Puschner, Walter Schmitz, and Justus H. Ulbricht, eds, *Handbuch zur 'Völkischen Bewegung' 1871–1918*, Munich: K. G. Saur, 1996, pp. 121–7.

67. Franz Wegener, *Alfred Schuler, der letzte Deutsche katharer*, Gladbeck: KFVR, 2003, pp. 50–73.

68. Mosse, *Masses and Man*, p. 201; Puschner and Vollnhals, 'Zur Abbildung auf dem Umschlag', in Puschner and Vollnhals, eds, *Bewegung*, pp. 11–12; 'Germanentum als Überideologie', in Puschner, ed., *Die völkisch-religiöse Bewegung*, pp. 266–80; Wegener, *Schuler*, pp. 30–49, 74–81; see also Cornelia Essner, *Die 'Nürnberger Gesetze' oder die Verwaltung des Rassenwahns 1933–1945*, Paderborn: Schöningh, 2002, pp. 37–8.

69. Stern, *Politics of Cultural Despair*, pp. 185–202.

70. Peter S. Fisher, *Fantasy and Politics: Visions of the Future in the Weimar* Republic, Madison, WI: University of Wisconsin Press, 1991, p. 3.

71. See Eric Kurlander, 'Between Völkisch and Universal Visions of Empire: Liberal Imperialism in *Mitteleuropa*, 1890–1918', in Matthew Fitzpatrick, ed., *Liberal Imperialism in Europe*, London: Palgrave, 2012, pp. 141–66.

72. Smith, *Politics*, pp. 223–4.

73. Ibid., pp. 226–8.

74. Puschner, *Die völkische Bewegung*, pp. 153–5.

75. Manjapra, *Age of Entanglement*, p. 200.

76. Smith, *Politics*, pp. 229–32.

77. Puschner, 'The Notions *Völkisch* and Nordic', pp. 29–30; Jackson Spielvogel and David Redles, 'Hitler's Racial Ideology: Content and Occult Sources', *Simon Wiesenthal Center Annual* 3 (1986), pp. 227–46.

78. Mees, 'Hitler and Germanentum', pp. 259–61; Puschner, *Die völkische Bewegung*, pp. 92–9. It is no surprise that Günther's first publication was a bizarre 1919 pamphlet titled *Knights, Death, and the Devil: The Heroic Idea*, which merged pagan religion, folklore, and mythology with biological nationalism and eugenics. See H. K. Günther, *Ritter, Tod und Teufel*, Munich: J. F. Lehmanns, 1920.

79. Kaufmann, *Das Dritte Reich*, pp. 388–9; Mees, 'Hitler and Germanentum', pp. 267–8.

80. Mees, 'Hitler and Germanentum', p. 268; Puschner, *Die völkische Bewegung*, pp. 100–2.

81. Klaus Vondung, 'Von der völkischen Religiosität zur politischen Religion des Nationalsozialismus: Kontinuität oder neue Qualität?', in Puschner and Vollnhals, eds, *Bewegung*, p. 29; Kaufmann, *Das Dritte Reich*, pp. 390–1.

82. Kaufmann, *Das Dritte Reich*; Mees, 'Hitler and Germanentum', pp. 268–9.

83. Howe, *Urania's Children*, pp. 5–6.

84. Spence, *Occult Causes*, pp. 59–60.

85. Treitel, *Science*, pp. 57–8.

86. Ibid., p. 71.

87. Webb, *Flight from Reason*; Owen, *Place of Enchantment*; Christopher McIntosh, *Eliphas Lévi and the French Occult Revival*, London: Rider, 1972; David Allen Harvey, 'Beyond Enlightenment: Occultism, Politics, and Culture in France from the Old Regime to the Fin-de-Siècle', *The Historian* 65:3 (March 2003), pp. 665–94; John Warne Monroe, *Laboratories of Faith: Mesmerism, Spiritism, and Occultism in Modern France*, Ithaca, NY: Cornell University Press, 2008.

88. Treitel, *Science*, pp. 58–9; Hamann, *Wien*, pp. 7–9, 285–323; Howe, *Urania's Children*, p. 4.

89. Treitel, *Science*, pp. 73–4.

90. Pasi, 'The Modernity of Occultism', pp. 62–8.

91. See Stern, *Politics of Cultural* Despair; Mosse, *Masses and Man*, pp. 199–200.

92. Goodrick-Clarke, *Occult Roots*, pp. 59–60.

93. Howe, *Urania's Children*, 78–90.

94. Helena Blavatsky, *The Secret Doctrine*, New York: Theosophical Society, 1888.

95. Ibid; Ley, 'Pseudoscience in Naziland', p. 93; see also Julian Strube, *Vril. Eine okkulte Urkraft in Theosophie und esoterischem Neonazismus*, Paderborn/Munich: Wilhelm Fink, 2013, pp. 55–74; Alexander Berzin, 'The Berzin Archives: The Nazi Connection with Shambhala and Tibet', May 2003.

96. Blavatksy, *Secret Doctrine*, pp. 150–200, 421; Treitel, *Science*, pp. 85–6.
97. Webb, *Flight from Reason*.
98. Hans J. Glowka, *Deutsche Okkultgruppen 1875–1937*, Munich: Arbeitsgemeinschaft für Religions- und Weltanschauungen, 1981, pp. 7–15; Treitel, *Science*, pp. 82–3.
99. Glowka, *Okkultgruppen*, pp. 8–10.
100. Treitel, *Science*, pp. 85–6.
101. Ibid., pp. 84–5; Bruce Campbell, *Ancient Wisdom Revived: History of the Theosophical Movement*, Berkeley, CA: University of California Press, 1980.
102. Treitel, *Science*, p. 103.
103. Ibid., pp. 106–7.
104. Ibid., p. 84.
105. Engelhardt, 'Nazis of Tibet', pp. 131–4.
106. Kaufmann, *Das Dritte Reich*, pp. 133–5.
107. Goodrick-Clarke, *Occult Roots*, pp. 100–1; Rose, *Die Thule-Gesellschaft*, pp. 37–9; see also Rudolf von Sebottendorff's history of the Thule Society in *Thule-Bote*, Munich: Thule-Gesellschaft, 1933, p. 28.
108. Südwestrundfunk SWR2 Essay, 'Manuskriptdienst Zivilisation ist Eis. Hanns Hörbigers Welteislehre?'.
109. Treitel, *Science*, pp. 90–1.
110. Ibid., pp. 90–3.
111. Ibid., pp. 92–4.
112. Ibid., pp. 84–9.
113. Goodrick-Clarke, *Occult Roots*, pp. 24–6, 58–61.
114. Treitel, *Science*, pp. 94–5; Goodrick-Clarke, *Occult Roots*, pp. 25–6.
115. Treitel, *Science*, pp. 95–7.
116. Goodrick-Clarke, *Occult Roots*, pp. 27–9, 44–5.
117. Treitel, *Science*, pp. 99–100.
118. Helmut Zander, 'Esoterische Wissenschaft um 1900. "Pseudowissenschaft" als Produkt ehemals "hochkultureller" Praxis', in Rupnow et al., eds, *Pseudowissenschaft*, pp. 78–9.
119. Goodrick-Clarke, *Occult Roots*, 26–30.
120. Zander, 'Esoterische Wissenschaft um 1900', pp. 81–4.
121. Treitel, *Science*, pp. 99–102; Staudenmaier, *Between Occultism and Nazism*, pp. 24–7.
122. Zander, 'Esoterische Wissenschaft um 1900', pp. 89–94.
123. See Rudolf Steiner, 'Christ in Relation to Lucifer and Ahriman', in Kaufmann, *Das Dritte Reich*, pp. 134–5.
124. Treitel, *Science*, p. 103; Staudenmaier, *Between Occultism and Nazism*, p. 39.
125. Staudenmaier, 'Race and Redemption: Racial and Ethnic Evolution in Rudolf Steiner's Anthroposophy', pp. 20–1; Staudenmauer, *Between Occultism and Nazism*, pp. 45–55.
126. Staudenmaier, *Between Occultism and Nazism*, pp. 164–5.
127. Goodrick-Clarke, *Occult Roots*, pp. 24–30, 58–61; Treitel, *Science*, pp. 98–9; Helmut Zander, *Rudolf Steiner. Die Biografie*, Munich: Piper Verlag, 2011.
128. Staudenmaier, *Between Occultism and Nazism*, pp. 264–5.
129. Peter Staudenmaier, 'Rudolf Steiner and the Jewish Question', *Leo Baeck Institute Yearbook* (2005), pp. 127–47, 128–9.
130. Staudenmaier, 'Rudolf Steiner', pp. 127–47.
131. Treitel, *Science*, pp. 84–5.
132. Black and Kurlander, 'Introduction', in *Revisiting*, p. 10.
133. Goodrick-Clarke, *Occult Roots*, pp. 33–40; Mosse, *Masses and Man*, p. 201.
134. Treitel, *Science*, pp. 104–7.
135. Mosse, *Masses and Man*, pp. 103–4, 207–12; Treitel, *Science*, pp. 74–5; Goodrick-Clarke, *Occult Roots*, pp. 28–30, 59–61.
136. Goodrick-Clarke, *Occult Roots*, pp. 49–50, 157–60; Puschner, *Die völkische Bewegung*, pp. 138–9.
137. Mosse, *Masses and Man*, p. 209; see also Winfried Mogge, 'Wir lieben Balder, den Lichten . . ', in Puschner and Vollnhals, eds, *Bewegung*, pp. 45–52.
138. Mosse, *Masses and Man*, pp. 103–4, 207–12; Treitel, *Science*, pp. 74–5; Goodrick-Clarke, *Occult Roots*, pp. 28–30, 59–61.
139. Goodrick-Clarke, *Occult Roots*, pp. 33–48; Treitel, *Science*, pp. 104–6; Mosse, *Masses and Man*, p. 209.
140. Jörg Lanz von Liebenfels, *Die Theozoologie oder die Kunde von den Sodoms-Äfflingen und dem Götter-Elektron*, Vienna: Ostara, 1905; Puschner, *Die völkische Bewegung*, pp. 180–2, 191–3; Daim, *Der Mann*, pp. 23–74; Goodrick-Clarke, *Occult Roots*, pp. 196–9.
141. Daim, *Der Mann*, pp. 142–4.
142. Ibid., pp. 144–6.

143. Ley, 'Pseudoscience in Naziland', pp. 91–2.

144. Ibid., pp. 91–2; Ernst Hiemer, *Der Giftpilz*, Nüremberg: Stürmer, 1938.

145. Lanz von Liebenfels, *Die Theozoologie oder die Kunde*; David Luhrssen, *Hammer of the Gods: The Thule Society and the Birth of Nazism*, Washington, DC: Potomac, 2012, pp. 40–1; Daim, *Der Mann*, pp. 23–74; Goodrick-Clarke, *Occult Roots*, pp. 196–9.

146. Goodrick-Clarke, *Occult Roots*, pp. 196–8; Ernst Issberner-Haldane, *Mein eigener Weg*, Zeulenroda: Bernhard Sporn, 1936, p. 276.

147. Kurlander, 'Orientalist Roots', in Cho, Kurlander, and McGetchin, eds, *Transcultural Encounters*; Manfred Ach, *Hitlers Religion: Pseudoreligiose Elemente im nationalsozialistischen Sprachgebrauch*, Munich: ARW, 1977, pp. 8–19; Glowka, *Okkultgruppen*, pp. 14–24; Mosse, *Masses and Man*, p. 209; Goodrick-Clarke, *Occult Roots*, pp. 90–105; Douglas McGetchin, *Indology, Indomania, Orientalism: Ancient India's Rebirth in Modern Germany*, Madison, WI: Fairleigh Dickinson University Press, 2009, pp. 171–6.

148. Koehne, 'Were the National Socialists a Völkisch Party?', pp. 778–80.

149. Goodrick-Clarke, *Occult Roots*, pp. 177–8.

150. Puschner, *Die völkische Bewegung*, pp. 173–8; Mosse, *Masses and Man*, pp. 165–71, 204–5; Goodrick-Clarke, *Occult Roots*, pp. 59–60; Redles, *Hitler's Millennial Reich*, pp. 35–57.

151. Treitel, *Science*, pp. 103–4; Kaufmann, *Das Dritte Reich*, pp. 134–8.

152. Treitel, *Science*, pp. 104–7; Goodrick-Clarke, *Occult Roots*, pp. 192–4; Essner, *Die 'Nürnberger Gesetze'*, p. 43; Paul Weindling, *Health, Race and German Politics between National Unification and Nazism, 1870–1945*, Cambridge/New York: Cambridge University Press, 1989, p. 74.

153. Treitel, *Science*, pp. 71–4; Howe, *Urania's Children*, pp. 84–7.

154. Leo Pammer, *Hitlers Vorbilder: Dr. Karl Lueger*, pp. 3–4, 9–11; Bruce F. Pauley, *From Prejudice to Persecution: A History of Austrian Anti-Semitism*, Chapel Hill, NC: University of North Carolina Press, 1992, pp. 42–5.

155. Goodrick-Clarke, *Occult Roots*, pp. 194–8.

156. Christina Wessely, *Cosmic Ice Theory: Science, Fiction and the Public, 1894–1945*; http://www.mpiwg-berlin.mpg.de/en/research/projects/deptIII-ChristinaWessely-Welteislehre.

157. As Michael Saler reminds us, 'The German scientific tradition in the nineteenth century consisted of a mix of empiricism and idealism that was hospitable to the metaphysical preoccupations of modern occultists', in 'Modernity and Enchantment', pp. 38–51.

158. Geppert and Kössler, eds, *Wunder*, p. 26.

159. Ernst Issberner-Haldane, *Mein eigener Weg. Werdegang, Erinnerungen von Reisen und aus der Praxis eines Suchenden*, Zeulenroda: Sporn, 1936, p. 271.

160. Treitel, *Science*, pp. 8–10, 16–18, 72–4.

161. Harrington, *Reenchanted Science*, p. 4; see also Treitel, *Science*, pp. 165–209; Owen, *Enchantment*; McIntosh, *Eliphas Lévi*; Harvey, 'Beyond Enlightenment'; Monroe, *Laboratories of Faith*.

162. Harrington, *Reenchanted Science*, p. 4; see also Treitel, *Science*, pp. 8–10, 16–18, 72–4.

163. Geppert and Kössler, eds, *Wunder*, p. 26; Ley, 'Pseudoscience in Naziland', pp. 90–1.

164. Harrington, *Reenchanted Science*, pp. 4, 19–20.

165. Treitel, *Science*, pp. 22–5, 30–8.

166. Wolfram, *Stepchildren*, pp. 264–7.

167. Ibid., pp. 271–2.

168. Tomas Kaiser, *Zwischen Philosophie und Spiritismus: Annäherungen an Leben und Werk des Carl du Prel*, Saarbrücken: VDM Verlag, 2008, pp. 39–54.

169. Kaiser, *Zwischen Philosophie*, pp. 61–2; Andreas Sommer, 'From Astronomy to Transcendental Darwinism: Carl du Prel (1839–1899)', *Journal of Scientific Exploration* 23:1 (2009), pp. 59–60.

170. Treitel, *Science*, pp. 43–4.

171. Ibid., pp. 15–16.

172. *The Sphinx* merged with Steiner's occult journal, *Lucifer*, in 1908; Treitel, *Science*, pp. 53–4.

173. Wolfram, *Science*, pp. 273–4.

174. Susanne Michl, 'Gehe hin, dein Glaube hat dir geholfen. Kriegswunder und Heilsversprechen in der Medizin des 20. Jahrhunderts', in Geppert and Kössler, eds, *Wunder*, p. 216; Wolfram, *Science*, pp. 279–82.

175. Manjapra, *Age of Entanglement*, pp. 218–19.

176. Wolfram, *Science*, pp. 282–4.

177. Michl, 'Gehe hin, dein Glaube hat dir geholfen', p. 217; Ellic Howe, *Urania's Children*, pp. 2–3.

178. Manjapra, *Age of Entanglement*, pp. 231–3; Hamann, *Wien*, pp. 7–9, 285–323; Howe, *Urania's Children*, p. 4; Weber, *Hitler's First War*, pp. 255–60.

179. Wolfram, *Science*, pp. 263–4.

180. Jay Gonen, *The Roots of Nazi Psychology: Hitler's Utopian Barbarism*, Lexington, KY: University Press of Kentucky, 2013, p. 92.

181. Wolfram, *Science*, pp. 273–7.
182. Gonen, *Roots*, pp. 92–3.
183. Howe, *Urania's Children*, pp. 8–12.
184. Ibid., pp. 78–80.
185. Treitel, *Science*, p. 141; Johach, 'Entzauberte Natur?', p. 181.
186. Howe, *Urania's Children*, pp. 78–83.
187. Ibid., pp. 83–8; Howe, *Sebottendorff*.
188. Treitel, *Science*, pp. 138–41.
189. Ibid., p. 190; Howe, *Urania's Children*, pp. 84–6.
190. Howe, *Urania's Children*, pp. 84–90; Szczesny, 'Die Presse des Okkultismus', pp. 55–6, 119–20; Karl Heimsoth, *Charakter-Kontsellation*, Munich: Barth, 1928; Treitel, *Science*, pp. 44–5.
191. Treitel, *Science*, p. 154.
192. See Kaufmann, *Das Dritte Reich*, p. 367; Solco Walle Tromp, *Psychical Physics: A Scientific Analysis of Dowsing Radiesthesia and Kindred Divining Phenomena*. New York: Elsevier, 1949; H. H. Kritzinger, *Erdstrahlen, Reizstreifen und Wünschelrute: Neue Versuche zur Abwendung krank-machender Einflüsse auf Grund eigener Forschungen volkstümlich dargestellt*, Dresden: Talisman, 1933; H. H. Kritzinger, *Todesstrahlen und Wünschelrute: Beiträge zur Schicksalskunde*, Leipzig: Grethlein, 1929, pp. 65–72; Letter from Sturmbannführer Frenzolf Schmid, 21 March 1937. BAB: NS 19/3974, pp. 10–11.
193. See Kaufmann, *Das Dritte Reich*, pp. 363–8; Howe, *Nostradamus and the Nazis*, p. 127.
194. Treitel, *Science*, pp. 133–4.
195. Kritzinger, *Erdstrahlen*, pp. 8–22, 25–39.
196. Kaufmann, *Das Dritte Reich*, p. 368.
197. Gerard P. Kuiper, 'German Astronomy During the War', *Popular Astronomy* 54:6 (June 1946), p. 278; Ley, 'Pseudoscience in Naziland', p. 93.
198. Goodrick-Clarke, *Occult Roots*, pp. 22–3; Anna Bramwell, *Blood and Soil: Richard Walther Darré and Hitler's 'Green Party'*, Abbotsbrook: Kensal, 1985, pp. 172–4; Puschner, *Die völkische Bewegung*, pp. 164–73.
199. Treitel, *Science*, pp. 75, 154–5. See also Ulrich Linse, 'Das "natürliche" Leben. Die Lebensreform', in Richard van Dülmen, *Die Erfindung des Menschen. Schöpfungsträume und Körperbilder 1500–2000*, Vienna: Böhlau, 1998; Uwe Heyll, *Wasser, Fasten, Luft und Licht. Die Geschichte der Naturheilkunde in Deutschland*, Frankfurt am Main: Campus, 2006; Wolfgang R. Krabbe, *Gesellschaftsveränderung durch Lebensreform. Strukturmerkmale einer sozialreformerischen Bewegung im Deutschland der Industrialisierungsperiode*, Göttingen: Vandenhoeck & Ruprecht, 1974.
200. Bramwell, *Blood and Soil*, pp. 174–7.
201. Piers Stephens, 'Blood, not Soil: Anna Bramwell and the Myth of "Hitler's Green Party"', *Organization and Environment* 14 (2001), p. 175.
202. Puschner, *Die völkische Bewegung*, pp. 119–23.
203. Treitel, *Science*, pp. 153–4.
204. Ibid., pp. 154–5; Puschner, *Die völkische Bewegung*, pp. 131–8.
205. Treitel, *Science*, pp. 153–4.
206. Harrington, *Reenchanted Science*, pp. 23–33; Ley, 'Pseudoscience in Naziland', pp. 93–4; Kuiper, 'German Astronomy During the War', pp. 263–80.
207. Goodrick-Clarke, *Occult Roots*, pp. 22–3; Mees, 'Hitler and Germanentum', pp. 255–70.
208. Treitel, *Science*, p. 107.
209. Staudenmaier, *Between Occultism and Nazism*, pp. 146–7, 153–4, 159.
210. Ibid., pp. 161–2.
211. Ibid., pp. 163–5.
212. Eva Johach, 'Entzauberte Natur? Die Ökonomien des Wunder(n)sim naturwissenschaftlichen Zeitalter', in Geppert and Kössler, eds, *Wunder*, pp. 189–95; Harrington, *Reenchanted Science*, p. xx.
213. Mogge, 'Wir lieben Balder', pp. 46–8; Puschner, 'The Notions *Völkisch* and Nordic', pp. 29–30; Puschner, *Die völkische Bewegung*, pp. 145–63, 178–9.
214. Puschner, *Die völkische Bewegung*, pp. 189–201.
215. Heike Jestram, *Mythen, Monster und Maschinen*, Cologne: Teiresias Verlag, 2000.
216. Ibid., pp. 55–62, 89–92.
217. Alongside radical *völkisch*-esotericists and eugenicists like Fritsch and List, supporters of holistic theories included reputable Wilhelmine scientists such as Ernst Haeckel, Alfred Ploetz, and Hans Driesch. Harrington, *Reenchanted Science*, p. xx.
218. Willy Ley, *Watchers of the Skies: An Informal History of Astronomy from Babylon to the Space Age*, New York: Viking Press, 1966, p. 515; Christina Wessely, 'Welteis, die "Astronomie des Unsichtbaren" um 1900', in Rupnow et al., *Konzeptionen*, pp. 163–4; Martin Halter, 'Zivilisation ist Eis. Hanns Hörbigers Welteislehre – eine Metapher des Kältetods im 20. Jahrhundert', Südwestrundfunk

SWR2 Essay (Redaktion Stephan Krass). Dienstag, 15.7.2008, 21.33 Uhr, SWR2. In developing his theory, Hörbiger, like Blavatsky, was inspired more by science fiction than science – in this case the above-mentioned *Planet Fire* by the Munich writer Max Haushofer. In Haushofer's novel a futuristic Munich society that has become hopelessly liberal and decadent is awakened from its cycle of degeneration and inspired toward rebirth by a violent shower of frozen meteors.

219. Ley, 'Pseudoscience in Naziland', pp. 95–6; Robert Bowen, *Universal Ice: Science and Ideology in the Nazi State*, London: Belhaven, 1993, pp. 5–6.
220. Halter, *Zivilisation*.
221. Christina Wessely, 'Welteis, die "Astronomie des Unsichtbaren" um 1900', p. 171; Ley, 'Pseudoscience in Naziland', pp. 96–7.
222. Halter, *Zivilisation*, p. 83.
223. Wessely, 'Welteis, die "Astronomie des Unsichtbaren" um 1900', pp. 186–7; Ley, 'Pseudoscience in Naziland', pp. 95–6.
224. http://www.mpiwg-berlin.mpg.de/en/research/projects/deptIII-ChristinaWessely-Welteislehre; Fisher, *Fantasy*, pp. 3–4.
225. As Christina Wessely puts it, 'the popularity of the Welteislehre was to a large extent the result of its subversive attraction based on an unsettling and fascinating amalgam of scientific terminology and methodology with popular images and clichés'; http://www.mpiwg-berlin.mpg.de/en/research/projects/deptIII-ChristinaWessely-Welteislehre.
226. Wessely, 'Welteis, die "Astronomie des Unsichtbaren" um 1900', pp. 182–6.
227. Ibid., pp. 174–8.
228. http://www.mpiwg-berlin.mpg.de/en/research/projects/deptIII-ChristinaWessely-Welteislehre.
229. Wessely, 'Welteis, die "Astronomie des Unsichtbaren" um 1900', p. 166; Halter, *Zivilisation*.
230. http://www.mpiwg-berlin.mpg.de/en/research/projects/deptIII-ChristinaWessely-Welteislehre.
231. Treitel, *Science*, p. 190.
232. Ibid., pp. 25–6.
233. Goodrick-Clarke, *Occult Roots*, pp. 177–93; Mosse, *Masses and Man*, pp. 210–12.
234. Wessely, *Cosmic Ice Theory*.
235. Williamson, *Longing*, pp. 294–8.
236. Rupnow et al., eds, *Pseudowissenschaft*.
237. Geppert and Kössler, eds, *Wunder*, p. 26; Saler, 'Modernity and Enchantment'.
238. Treitel, *Science*, p. 217.

Chapter 2

1. Mees, 'Hitler and Germanentum', p. 255.
2. Rudolf von Sebottendorff, *Bevor Hitler kam: Urkundlich aus der Frühzeit der Nationalsozialistischen Bewegung*, Munich: Deukula-Grassinger, 1933, p. 8.
3. Hermann Gilbhard, *Die Thule-Gesellschaft: vom okkulten-Mummenschanz zum Hakenkreuz*, Munich: Kiessling, 1994, pp. 15–18.
4. Goodrick-Clarke, *Occult Roots*, pp. 143–4.
5. Gilbhard, *Thule-Gesellschaft*, pp. 10–15; Goodrick-Clarke, *Occult Roots*, pp. 195–7.
6. Goodrick-Clarke, *Occult Roots*, p. 192; Daim, *Der Mann*, pp. 17–48; Sebottendorff, *Bevor Hitler kam*.
7. Puschner and Vollnhals, 'Forschungs- und problemgeschichtliche Perspektiven', in Puschner and Vollnhals, eds, *Bewegung*, pp. 18–20.
8. Ibid., pp. 22–3; Goodrick-Clarke, *Occult Roots*, pp. 196–204; Treitel, *Science*, pp. 210–42; Staudenmaier, 'Occultism, Race and Politics', pp. 47–70.
9. Howe, *Urania's Children*, pp. 84–7; Gilbhard, *Thule-Gesellschaft*, pp. 40–4; Reginald Phelps, 'Before Hitler Came: The Thule Society and German Order', *Journal of Modern History* 35:3 (September 1963), pp. 245–61; Mosse, *Masses and Man*, pp. 165–71.
10. Reginald Phelps, 'Theodor Fritsch und der Antisemitismus', in *Deutsche Rundschau* 87 (1961), pp. 442–9; Gilbhard, *Thule-Gesellschaft*, pp. 44–5.
11. Phelps, 'Before Hitler Came', pp. 248–50.
12. Puschner, *Die völkische Bewegung*, pp. 57–8; Robert Gellately, *The Politics of Economic Despair: Shopkeepers and German Politics 1890–1914*, London: Sage Publications, 1974, pp. 163, 176–83.
13. Puschner, *Die völkische Bewegung*, pp. 58–9; Gilbhard, *Thule-Gesellschaft*, pp. 44–6.
14. Goodrick-Clarke, *Occult Roots*, pp. 114–16; Puschner, *Die völkische Bewegung*, pp. 52–4; Gilbhard, *Thule-Gesellschaft*, p. 45.
15. Howe, *Sebottendorff*, pp. 26–7; Gilbhard, *Thule-Gesellschaft*, pp. 45–7; Franz Wegener, *Weishaar und der Geheimbund der Guoten*, Gladbeck: Kulturförderverein Ruhrgebiet (KVFR), 2005, pp. 35–6; Goodrick-Clarke, *Occult Roots*, pp. 64–5.

16. Phelps, 'Before Hitler Came', pp. 247–8.
17. Ibid., pp. 248–50; Gilbhard, *Thule-Gesellschaft*, pp. 45–7; Wegener, *Weishaar*, p. 36.
18. Winfried Mogge, 'Wir lieben Balder, den Lichten . . .', in Puschner and Vollnhals, eds, *Bewegung*, pp. 49–50.
19. Howe, *Sebottendorff*, pp. 26–7; Goodrick-Clarke, *Occult Roots*, p. 45.
20. Sebottendorff, *Bevor Hitler kam*, pp. 33–5.
21. Egbert Klautke, 'Theodor Fritsch: The "Godfather" of German Antisemitism', in Rebbeca Haynes and Martin Rady, eds, *In the Shadow of Hitler*, London: Tauris, 2011, p. 83; Wegener, *Weishaar*, p. 36.
22. Phelps, 'Before Hitler Came', pp. 248–9.
23. Howe, *Sebottendorff*, p. 25.
24. Goodrick-Clarke, *Occult Roots*, p. 128; Gilbhard, *Thule-Gesellschaft*, p. 45.
25. Phelps, 'Before Hitler Came', pp. 248–50.
26. Puschner and Vollnhals, 'Forschungs- und problemgeschichtliche Perspektiven', pp. 22–3; Gilbhard, *Thule-Gesellschaft*, pp. 45–7.
27. Rose, *Thule-Gesellschaft*, p. 20.
28. Phelps, 'Before Hitler Came', pp. 249–50.
29. Szczesny, 'Die Presse des Okkultismus', p. 119.
30. Staudenmaier, *Occultism*, pp. 64–5.
31. Richard J. Evans, 'The Emergence of Nazi Ideology', in Jane Caplan, ed., *Nazi Germany*, Oxford: Oxford University Press, 2008, p. 43.
32. Egbert Klautke, 'Theodor Fritsch (1852–1933): The "Godfather" of German Anti-Semitism', in Rebecca Haynes and Martyn Rady, eds, *In the Shadow of Hitler: Personalities of the Right in Central and Eastern Europe*, London: I. B. Tauris, 2011, p. 83.
33. Gilbhard, *Thule-Gesellschaft*, pp. 47–8; Goodrick-Clarke, *Occult Roots*, pp. 131–2.
34. Howe, *Sebottendorff*, pp. 5–7.
35. Ibid., pp. 11–13; Rose, *Thule-Gesellschaft*, pp. 26–32; Goodrick-Clarke, *Occult Roots*, pp. 135–9.
36. Goodrick-Clarke, *Occult Roots*, pp. 139–40; Phelps, 'Before Hitler Came', pp. 246–7.
37. Peter Staudenmaier, 'Esoteric Alternatives in Imperial Germany: Science, Spirit, and the Modern Occult Revival', in Black and Kurlander, eds, *Revisiting*, pp. 23–41; and Staudenmaier, *Between Occultism and Nazism*.
38. Staudenmaier, *Between Occultism and Nazism*, pp. 73–93.
39. Howe, *Sebottendorff*, pp. 16–17.
40. Howe, *Urania's Children*, pp. 86–9; Howe, *Nostradamus*, pp. 126–7.
41. Howe, *Sebottendorff*, pp. 17–23.
42. Goodrick-Clarke, *Occult Roots*, pp. 141–3; Gilbhard, *Thule-Gesellschaft*, pp. 47–51; Rose, *Thule-Gesellschaft*, pp. 32–3.
43. Rose, *Thule-Gesellschaft*, p. 20.
44. Howe, *Sebottendorff*, pp. 24–7, 32–4; Sebottendorff, *Bevor Hitler kam*, pp. 20–3.
45. Howe, *Sebottendorff*, pp. 33–4.
46. Ibid., pp. 28–9.
47. Rose, *Thule-Gesellschaft*, pp. 34–5; Sebottendorff, *Bevor Hitler kam*, pp. 41–3.
48. Gilbhard, *Thule-Gesellschaft*, pp. 10–15; Arn Strohmeyer, *Von Hyperborea ach Auschwitz: Wege eines antiken Mythos*, Witten: PapyRossa, 2005; Rose, *Thule-Gesellschaft*, pp. 37–9; BAB: NS 26/865a, 'Zur 1000 – Jahr – Verfassungsfeier Islands (930–1930) am 26.–28. Juni liegt abgeschlossen vor Thule: Altnordische Dichtung und Prosa', 24 vols, eds Felix Miedner, P. Herrmann, A. Heusler, R. Meißner, G. Meckel, F. Rancke, and W. H. Vogt, Jena: Eugen Diederichs Verlag, 1930.
49. Rose, *Thule-Gesellschaft*, pp. 37–9; Sebottendorff, *Bevor Hitler kam*, pp. 35–42.
50. Howe, *Sebottendorff*, p. 35.
51. Ibid., pp. 33–4.
52. Howe, *Sebottendorff*, pp. 33–4.
53. Sebottendorff, *Bevor Hitler kam*, pp. 23–5; Gilbhard, *Thule-Gesellschaft*, pp. 15–18; Redles, *Hitler's Millennial Reich*, pp. 54–5.
54. Sebottendorff, *Bevor Hitler kam*, pp. 47–56.
55. Goodrick-Clarke, *Occult Roots*, p. 149.
56. See Howe, *Sebottendorff*, p. 31; Phelps, 'Before Hitler Came', pp. 253–61; Sebottendorff, *Bevor Hitler kam*, pp. 7–8.
57. Redles, *Hitler's Millennial Reich*, pp. 56–7.
58. Howe, *Sebottendorff*, pp. 36–7.
59. Sebottendorff, *Bevor Hitler kam*, pp. 47–9.
60. Rose, *Thule-Gesellschaft*, p. 211.
61. Black, 'Groening', in Black and Kurlander, eds, *Revisiting*, p. 213.

62. Redles, *Hitler's Millennial Reich*, pp. 41–2.
63. Phelps, 'Before Hitler Came', pp. 245–61.
64. Redles, *Hitler's Millennial Reich*, pp. 54–5. See also Hartwig von Rheden in BAK: N 1094I/77, pp. 24–6.
65. Sebottendorff, *Bevor Hitler kam*, pp. 52–62; Howe, *Sebottendorff*, pp. 1–2, 60–6.
66. Ian Kershaw, *Hitler: Hubris*, London: Allen Lane, 1998, pp. 170–3.
67. Sebottendorff, *Bevor Hitler kam*, pp. 105–9; Redles, *Hitler's Millennial Reich*, pp. 56–7; Kershaw, *Hubris*, pp. 172–4.
68. Kershaw, *Hubris*, pp. 116–22.
69. Sebottendorff, *Bevor Hitler kam*, p. 105; Kershaw, *Hubris*, pp. 119–20.
70. Goodrick-Clarke, *Occult Roots*, pp. 143–6; Gilbhard, *Thule-Gesellschaft*, pp. 60–6.
71. Sebottendorff, *Bevor Hitler kam*, pp. 90–1.
72. Ibid.
73. Ibid.
74. Ibid., pp. 93–102.
75. Ibid., pp. 111–13.
76. Gilbhard, *Thule-Gesellschaft*, pp. 76–87, 136–47.
77. Phelps, 'Theodor Fritsch', pp. 442–9.
78. Sebottendorff, *Bevor Hitler kam*, pp. 81–4; Gilbhard, *Thule-Gesellschaft*, pp. 148–51; Goodrick-Clarke, *Occult Roots*, pp. 149–50.
79. See police reports and newspaper articles regarding DAP and Dietrich Eckart, BAB: R 1507/545, pp. 319–32.
80. Kershaw, *Hubris*, pp. 138–9; Goodrick-Clarke, *Occult Roots*, pp. 151–2; Sebottendorff, *Bevor Hitler kam*, pp. 103–25; material on right-wing associations, BAB: R 1507/2034, pp. 101–3, 111–12.
81. Phelps, 'Before Hitler Came', pp. 252–4; Mosse, *Masses and Man*, pp. 204–5; Sebottendorff, *Bevor Hitler kam*, pp. 7–8, 171–81.
82. Phelps, 'Before Hitler Came', pp. 252–4; Thomas Weber, *Hitler's First War*, Oxford: Oxford University Press, 2010, pp. 257–9; Sebottendorff, *Bevor Hitler kam*, pp. 7–8.
83. Richard J. Evans, 'The Emergence of Nazi Ideology', in Caplan, ed., *Nazi Germany*, pp. 42–3.
84. Howe, *Sebottendorff*, pp. 66–8; Almost 'all Hitler's early collaborators were connected with the Thule, even if they were not themselves members'. Gilbhard, *Thule-Gesellschaft*, pp. 71–5.
85. Howe, *Sebottendorff*, p. 14.
86. The combatants interpreted 'the battlefield bloodshed as a form of holy communion that had transformed them into the apostles of the nation'. Fisher, *Fantasy*, p. 220.
87. Ibid., p. 220.
88. Redles, *Hitler's Millennial Reich*, pp. 56–7.
89. Howe, *Nostradamus*, pp. 126–8.
90. Gilbhard, *Thule-Gesellschaft*, pp. 70–6; Rose, *Thule-Gesellschaft*, pp. 10–11; Michael Kellogg, *The Russian Roots of Nazism: White Emigrés and the Making of National Socialism, 1917–1945*, Cambridge: Cambridge University Press, 2005, p. 70.
91. Sebottendorff, *Bevor Hitler kam*, pp. 14–15.
92. https://www.historisches-lexikon-bayerns.de/Lexikon/Deutschsozialistische_Partei_ (DSP),_1920–1922.
93. Kershaw, *Hubris*, pp. 126–7.
94. Sebottendorff, *Bevor Hitler kam*, pp. 183–9.
95. As one Thule member recalled after the Nazi seizure of power: 'For me the interrelationship with occult matters was always uncomfortable, for they brought here and there questionable members into the Thule.' See also 'Vortrag Wilde über Okkultismus', 7 May 1919. BAB: NS 26/2233.
96. Puschner and Vollnhals, 'Forschungs- und problemgeschichtliche Perspektiven', pp. 22–3.
97. Sebottendorff, *Bevor Hitler kam*, pp. 9–10, 189–90; Goodrick-Clarke, *Occult Roots*, pp. 150–1; Howe, *Sebottendorff*, pp. 37–8; Darré biography in BAK: N 1094I/77, pp. 5–6.
98. Howe, *Sebottendorff*, pp. 37–8.
99. Goodrick-Clarke, *Roots*, pp. 221; Gilbhard, *Thule-Gesellschaft*, pp. 152–66.
100. Alan Bullock, *Hitler: A Study in Tyranny*, New York: Harper Perennial, 1991, p. 67.
101. Goodrick-Clarke, *Roots*, pp. 150–4; Howe, *Sebottendorff*, pp. 66–8, 190–6; Ernst Piper, *Alfred Rosenberg:Hitlers Chefideologe*, Munich: Blessing, 2005, pp. 19–42; Robert Cecil, *The Myth of the Master Race: Alfred Rosenberg and Nazi ideology*, New York: Dodd, Mead, and Co., 1972, pp. 34–5.
102. Puschner and Vollnhals, 'Forschungs- und problemgeschichtliche Perspektiven', pp. 22–3.
103. Phelps, 'Before Hitler Came', pp. 254–6; see also police reports from 22.2.24, BAB: R 1507/2022, pp. 112–14; 1.12.24, BAB: R 1507/2025.
104. Puschner, *Die völkische Bewegung*, pp. 57–8.

105. Essner, *Nürnberger Gesetze*, pp. 33–8; Samuel Koehne, 'Were the Nazis a völkisch Party? Paganism, Christianity, and the Nazi Christmas', *Central European History* 47:4 (2014), pp. 765–9.

106. Koehne, 'Paganism', pp. 765–9; police reports from 6.1.23, BAB: R 1507/2019, pp. 10–11; March 1927, BAB: R 1507/2032, pp. 60–3; 7.1.22, report on the *Bund Oberland*, BAB: R 1507/2016, p. 75. Michael Kater, *Das 'Ahnenerbe' der SS: 1935–1945*, Stuttgart: Deutsche Verlagsanstalt, 1974, pp. 17–18; 16.10.34, letter from Gauamtsleiter Graf praising Schmid; 10.12.34 letter; Frenzolf Schmid to RSK, 12.8.35, BAK: R 9361-V/10777.

107. Ibid., pp. 778–9.

108. Ibid., pp. 777–8.

109. Koehne, 'Paganism', pp. 781–3.

110. Ibid., pp. 783–4.

111. Ibid., pp. 786–7.

112. Hitler even honoured Dinter as the fifth-ranking party member upon the NSDAP's refoundation in 1925. See police report from 20.12.24, BAB: R 1507/2025, pp. 141–5; Nico Ocken, *Hitler's Braune Hochburg: Der Aufstieg der NSDAP im Land*, Thüriingen (1920–33), Hamburg: Diplomica, 2013, p. 65; Essner, *Nürnberger Gesetze*, pp. 33–5.

113. See police reports from 22.7.25, BAB: R 1507/2028, p. 14; report from 1.10.28, BAB: R 1507/2029, pp. 126–7; 1927 reports, BAB: R 1507/2032, p. 77; as late as 1939, however, the SS still encouraged Goebbels' Reich Literature Chamber to give Dinter preferential treatment since he was 'one of the oldest party members, the first Gauleiter of Thuringia'. See SD Report, 18.6.39, BAB: R 58/6217.

114. Fisher, *Fantasy*, pp. 5–6.

115. Sebottendorff, *Bevor Hitler kam*, pp. 14–15.

116. Treitel, *Science*, pp. 216–17; Koehne, 'Paganism', pp. 760–2.

117. The source: 'Erkenntnis und Propaganda', *Signale der neuen Zeit. 25 ausgewählte Reden von Dr. Joseph Goebbels*, Munich: Zentralverlag der NSDAP, 1934, pp. 28–52.

118. Puschner and Vollnhals, 'Forschungs- und problemgeschichtliche Perspektiven', pp. 22–3.

119. Ernst Anrich, Protokoll, IfZG 1536/54 (ZS Nr. 542), pp. 3–4.

120. Bernard Mees, 'Hitler and Germanentum', p. 268.

121. Koehne, 'Paganism', p. 764; see also Konrad A. Heiden, *A History of National Socialism*, New York: Alfred Knopf, 1935, pp. 66–9; Piper, *Rosenberg*, pp. 15–17; Samuel Koehne, 'The Racial Yardstick: "Ethnotheism" and Official Nazi Views on Religion', *German Studies Review* 37:3 (October 2014), p. 577. According to the Nazi theologian Ernst Anrich, 'Hitler's early statements against the völkisch movement were ignored by his supporters'. NL Ernst Anrich, IfZG: ZS 542 1536/54, pp. 3–4.

122. See John Ondrovcik, 'War, Revolution, and Phantasmagoria: The Visible and the Invisible in Germany, 1914–1921', in Black and Kurlander, eds, *Revisiting*.

123. Peter Longerich, *Himmler*, Oxford: Oxford University Press, 2013, pp. 77–8; Gilbhard, *Thule-Gesellschaft*, pp. 15–21, 67–9; Redles, *Hitler's Millennial Reich*, pp. 64–5; Szczesny, 'Die Presse des Okkultismus', pp. 119–22, 131–44; Fisher, *Fantasy*, pp. 11–12.

124. Claus E. Bärsch, *Die Politische Religion des* Nationalsozialismus, Munich: Fink, 1998, pp. 43–4.

125. Koehne, 'Paganism', p. 763; see also Bullock, *Hitler*, pp. 79–80; Goodrick-Clark, *Occult Roots*, pp. 169–70; Redles, *Hitler's Millennial Reich*, pp. 56–7; Bärsch, *Politische Religion*, pp. 79–83; Trimondi, *Hitler*, pp. 17–20.

126. Heiden, *History*, pp. 42, 66.

127. Fisher, *Fantasy*, p. 6.

128. Ryback, *Hitler's Private Library*, p. 30.

129. Bullock, *Hitler*, pp. 78–9.

130. Kellogg, *Russian Roots*, pp. 73–4; Alfred Rosenberg, *Dietrich Eckart: Ein Vermächtnis*, Munich: Eher, 1935, pp. 53–4.

131. Steigmann-Gall, *Holy Reich*, pp. 17–22, 142–3; Picker, *Hitlers Tischgespräche*, pp. 94–5.

132. Steigmann-Gall, *Holy Reich*, pp. 21–2; Dietrich Eckart, *Der Bolschewismus von Moses bis Lenin: Zwiegespräch zwischen Adolf Hitler und mir*, Munich: Hohenheichen, pp. 18–25.

133. Rosenberg, *Eckart*, pp. 23–4.

134. Ibid., pp. 26–8.

135. Bärsch, *Politische Religion*, pp. 58–9.

136. Kellogg, *Russian Roots*, pp. 70–3.

137. Steigmann-Gall, *Holy Reich*, pp. 17–22, 142–3; Picker, *Hitlers Tischgespräche*, pp. 94–5; Eckart, *Bolschewismus*, pp. 18–25; Heiden, *History*, pp. 66–9; Piper, *Rosenberg*, pp. 15–17.

138. Bärsch, *Politische Religion*, pp. 198–9, 206–8; Spence, *Occult Causes*, pp. 128–9, 144–6; Alfred Rosenberg, *Myth of the Twentieth Century*, Amazon, 2012 (1930), 1934, pp. 21–144; Bronder, *Bevor Hitler kam*, pp. 219–25.

139. Rosenberg, *Myth*, p. 4.

140. Ibid., pp. 5–7; Mees, 'Hitler and Germanentum', pp. 268–9.

141. Piper, *Rosenberg*, pp. 179–230; Williamson, *Longing*, pp. 290–2; Mosse, *Masses and Man*, pp. 71–5; Alfred Rosenberg, *Houston Stewart Chamberlain als Verkünder und Begründer einer deutschen Zukunft*, Munich: Bruckmann, 1927; Spence, *Occult Causes*, pp. 126–8; Kater, *Ahnenerbe*, pp. 32–3.

142. Bronder, *Bevor Hitler kam*, p. 94.

143. Monica Black, *Death in Berlin*, Cambridge: Cambridge University Press, 2013, p. 9.

144. Mosse, *Masses and Man*, p. 167.

145. Ibid., pp. 71–3.

146. Cecil, *Myth*, pp. 95–6; see also Steigmann-Gall, *Holy Reich*, p. 263.

147. Adolf Hitler, *Mein Kampf*, Boston, MA: Ralph Mannheim, 1943, pp. 402, 324, 327, 544, 665, 141; see also H. Schneider, *Der jüdische Vampyr Chaotisiert die Welt (Der Jude als Weltparasit)*, Lüneberg: Gauschulungsamt der NSDAP, 1943; Fred Karsten, *Vampyre des Aberglaubens*, Berlin: Deutsche Kulturwacht, 1935; Ernst Graf von Reventlow, *The Vampire of the Continent*, New York: Jackson, 1916.

148. Roger Griffin, ed., *Fascism*, Oxford: Oxford University Press, 1995, pp. 121–2.

149. Hitler, *Mein Kampf*, pp. 63, 662, 480; Schneider, *Der jüdische Vampyr*; Karsten, *Vampyre des Aberglaubens*; Reventlow, *Vampire of the Continent*; Heiden, *National Socialism*, pp. 66–70.

150. Black, *Death in Berlin*, p. 76.

151. Ibid.

152. Hans-Adolf Jacobsen, ' "Kampf um Lebensraum": Zur Rolle des Geopolitikers Karl Haushofer im Dritten Reich', *German Studies Review* 4:1 (February 1981), pp. 79–104.

153. Wolf Heß, *Rudolf Heß, Briefe 1908–1933*, Munich/Vienna: Langen Müller, 1987 (25.6.19), p. 243; Joachim Fest, *The Face of the Third Reich: Portraits of the Nazi Leadership*, New York: Pantheon Books, 1970, pp. 4–5, 190–1.

154. Heß, *Rudolf Heß*, 13.11.18, 25.6.19, pp. 235, 243; Fest, *Face of the Third Reich*, pp. 190–1.

155. Smith, *Politics*, pp. 229–32; Ach, *Hitlers Religion*, pp. 31–49; Wolf Rüdiger Hess, ed., *Rudolf Hess: Briefe*, Munich: Lange, 1987, pp. 17–18; Glowka, *Okkultgruppen*, pp. 25–6; Treitel, *Science*, pp. 213–16; see also Bormann to Gauleiter, 7.5.41, BAB: NS 6/334; Bronder, *Bevor Hitler kam*, pp. 239–44.

156. Heinz Höhne, *Order of the Death's Head: The Story of Hitler's S.S.*, New York: Coward-McCann, 1970, pp. 43–4.

157. Longerich, *Himmler*, pp. 70–1, 78–9.

158. Heather Pringle, *The Master Plan: Himmler's Scholars and the Holocaust*, New York: Hyperion, 2006, p. 18.

159. Trimondi, *Hitler*, pp. 27–8.

160. Longerich, *Himmler*, pp. 77–8; see also Heinrich Himmler's reading list (4.9.19–19.2.27), BAK, NL Himmler, N 1126/9; Treitel, *Science*, pp. 214–15.

161. Trimondi, *Hitler*, p. 28.

162. Longerich, *Himmler*, p. 739.

163. *Wesen und Geschichte des Werwolfs*, BAB: R 58/7237, pp. 54–73.

164. Ibid., pp. 89–91.

165. Robert Eisler, *Man into Wolf*, London: Spring, 1948, p. 34.

166. Ibid., p. 35; also see 1927 pamphlet and Wehrwolf guidelines from Wehrwolf, no. 32 (November 1928), BAB: R 1501/125673b, pp. 69–76.

167. Kurt Frankenberger, *Fertigmachen zum Einsatz*, Halle: Wehrwolf-Verlag, 1931, pp. 3–5.

168. Karla O. Poewe, *New Religions and the Nazis*, New York: Routledge, 2006, pp. 98–100.

169. See police reports on Wehrwolf and other paramilitary organizations from March 1927, BAB: R 1507/2032, March 1927, pp. 60–6, 74, 101–4, 112, 126–9; see police report on Theodor Fritsch and the *Bund Oberland*, 16.3.25, BAB: R 1507/2026, pp. 45–51.

170. 'See Der Wehrwolf', 3.7.24, BAK: NL HImmler N 1126/17; see police report on paramilitary groups, BAB: R 1507/2028, pp. 18, 95, 151.

171. Ibid.

172. See report on Wolf Graf von Helldorff, BAK: R 1507/2027, pp. 37–8; see police report, 26.1.26, 19.3.26, BAB: R 1507/2029, pp. 40–1, 90.

173. See police reports from early 1926, BAB: R 1507/2028, p. 16, 158–9, 168; reports on Edmund Heines, BAB: R 1507/2027, p. 39; on Röhm, BAB: R 1507/2028, pp. 95–9, 158–9; on Heines and paramilitary groups, BAB: R 1507/2031, pp. 65–7; on Heines and paramilitary, BAB: R 1507/2032, p. 105; Fritz Kloppe speech, 16.3.30, BAB: R 1501/125673b Bund Wehrwolf, 31.10.28, BAB: R 1507/2029, pp. 114–17.

174. Dow and Lixfeld, eds, *Nazification*, pp. 13–21.

175. Kater, 'Artamanen', pp. 598–9, 602–3; Stefan Brauckmann, 'Artamanen als völkisch-nationalistische Gruppierung innerhalb der deutschen Jugendbewegung 1924–1935', in *Jahrbuch des Archivs der deutschen Jugendbewegung* 2:5. Wochenschau-Verlag, Schwalbach, 2006; Bramwell, *Blood and Soil*, p. 59.

176. Stefan Breuer and Ina Schmidt, eds, *Die Kommenden. Eine Zeitschrift der Bundischen Jugend (1926–1933)*, Schwalbach am Taunus: Wochenschau Verlag, 2010, pp. 26ff.

177. Paula Diehl, *Macht, Mythos, Utopie: Die Körperbilder der SS-Männer*, Berlin: Akademie, 2005, p. 59; Kater, 'Die Artamanen', pp. 577–80, 592–8.

178. Kater, 'Artamanen', pp. 592–8.

179. Ibid., p. 603.

180. Ibid., pp. 598–9, 602–3; Brauckmann, 'Artamanen'.

181. Kater, 'Artamanen', p. 600; Kater, *Ahnenerbe*, p. 31.

182. Kater, 'Artamenen', pp. 599–601.

183. Ibid., p. 597.

184. Höhne, *Order*, p. 53; Hans-Christian Brandenburg, *Die Geschichte der H. J. Wege und Irrwege einer Generation*, 2 vols, Cologne: Verlag Wissenschaft und Politik, 1982, pp. 77–80 (Die Artamanen); Julien Reitzenstein, *Himmlers Forscher: Wehrwissenschaft and Medizinverbrechen im "Ahnenerbe" der SS*. Paderborn: Schöningh, 2014, pp. 47–8.

185. Brandenburg, *Die Geschichte der H. J. Wege*.

186. Bramwell, *Blood and Soil*, pp. 41–3; see Steiner's 1923 speech 'Die Miterleben der Geistigkeit und Bildekräfte der Nature', N 1094I–33.

187. Rudolf Steiner, 'Westliche und östliche Weltgegensätzlichkeit', *Anthroposophie und Soziologie* 3. Die Zeit und ihre sozialen Mängel (Asien-Europa). N 1094I/33, pp. 1–7; BAK: N 1094I–77, pp. 107–13.

188. NL Darré, BAK: N1094I-77, pp. 94–7.

189. Ibid., pp. 107–13.

190. Black, *Death in Berlin*, p. 76.

191. Ibid.

192. NL Darré, BAK: N1094I-77, p. 57; see also Essner, *Nürnberger Gesetze*, pp. 78–9, 154–5.

193. Stefan Breuer, *Die Völkischen in Deutschland*, Darmstadt: Wissenschaftliche Buchgesellschaft, 2008, pp. 218–20.

194. http://www.zeit.de/1958/42/ueber-die-artamanen-zur-ss; August Kenstler: R 1507/2031, Lage-Bericht nr. 115 from 21.12.26, p. 71.

195. Sickinger, 'Hitler and the Occult', pp. 107–25.

196. Mosse, *Masses and Man*, p. 66; Hamann, *Hitlers Wien*, pp. 39–45; Goodrick-Clark, *Occult Roots*, pp. 192–3; August Kubizek, *Young Hitler*, pp. 117, 179–83, 190–8; Picker, *Hitlers Tischgespräche*, p. 95; see Repp, *Reformers*.

197. Kubizek, *Young Hitler*, pp. 117, 179–83, 190–8; http://www.telegraph.co.uk/culture/music/classical-music/8659814/Hitler-and-Wagner.html.

198. Pammer, *Hitlers Vorbilder*, pp. 10–11; see also Goodrick Clarke, *Occult Roots*, pp. 196–7; Susan Power Bratton, 'From Iron Age Myth to Idealized National Landscape: Human-Nature Relationships and Environmental Racism in Fritz Lang's *Die Nibelungen*', *Worldviews* 4 (2000), pp. 195–212.

199. Goodrick-Clarke, *Occult Roots*, pp. 192, 194–9; Daim, *Der Mann*, pp. 17–48; Sebottendorff, *Bevor Hitler kam*, pp. 188–90.

200. Martin Leutsch, 'Karrieren des arischen Jesus zwischen 1918 und 1945', in Puschner, *Die völkische Bewegung*, pp. 196–7; Essner, *Nürnberger Gesetze*, pp. 33–8.

201. http://www.theatlantic.com/magazine/archive/2003/05/hitlers-forgotten-library/302727.

202. Jörg Lanz von Liebenfels, *Das Buch der Psalmen Teutsch: das Gebetbuch der Ariosophen Rassen-mystiker und Antisemiten*, Vienna: Ostara, 1926; Robert G. L. Waite, *The Psychopathic God: Adolf Hitler*, New York: Basic Books, 1977.

203. Koehne, 'Paganism', pp. 773–4.

204. Mees, 'Hitler and Germanentum', p. 268.

205. Hermann Rauschning, *The Voice of Destruction*, New York: Putnam, 1941, p. 252.

206. Redles, *Hitler's Millennial Reich*, pp. 71–2; see C. M. Vasey, *Nazi Ideology*, Lanham, MD: University Press of America, 2006, p. 60; Koehne, 'The Racial Yardstick', pp. 589–90.

207. Hitler, *Mein Kampf*, pp. 402, 324; Redles, *Hitler's Millennial Reich*, pp. 67, 70–1.

208. See Spielvogel and Redles, 'Hitler's Racial Ideology'; see also Anson Rabinbach and Sander Gilman, *The Third Reich Sourcebook*, Berkeley, CA: University of California Press, 2013, p. 113; see also Goodrick-Clarke, *Occult Roots*, pp. 194–203; Mosse, *Masses and Man*, p. 66; Hamann, *Hitlers Wien*, pp. 39–45; Goodrick-Clarke, *Occult Roots*, p. 193; Kubizek, *Young Hitler*, pp. 117, 179–83, 190–8; Picker, *Hitlers Tischgespräche*, p. 95; Hamann, *Hitlers Wien*, pp. 7–9, 285–323; Howe, *Urania's Children*, p. 4.

209. Mees, 'Hitler and Germanentum', p. 267.

210. Ibid., pp. 267–8.

211. Vasey, *Nazi Ideology*, p. 59.

212. Mees, 'Hitler and Germanentum', pp. 267–8.

213. A 'product of Lueger and Schönerer', Hitler's supernatural thinking was 'rougher' and more prag-matic than 'effete exemplars' of the old *völkisch* movement. Burleigh, 'National Socialism as a Political Religion', pp. 2–3.

214. Hamann, *Hitlers Wien*, pp. 327–9; Mosse, *Masses and Man*, pp. 54–7, 65–7, 71–3; Ach, *Hitlers Religion*, p. 52.

215. Bronder, *Bevor Hitler kam*, pp. 219–28.

216. Ryback, *Hitler's Library*, pp. 159–62; Schertel, *Magic*; Picker, *Hitlers Tischgespräche*, p. 74.

217. Schertel, *Magic*, p. 37.

218. Ibid., pp. 42–3.

219. Ibid., p. 45.

220. Ibid., p. 70.

221. Ibid., p. 72.

222. Ibid., p. 73.

223. Ibid., pp. 74, 78–9.

224. Ibid., pp. 82–7; 'In order to completely fulfil his mission', Rauschning reports elsewhere, Hitler believed he 'must die a martyr's death', that in 'the hour of supreme peril' he needed to sacrifice himself. Rauschning, *Voice of Destruction*, p. 252.

225. Schertel, *Magic*, p. 92; Sickinger, 'Hitler and the Occult', p. 108; Mosse, *Masses and Man*, pp. 54–7, 71–3.

226. Rauschning, *Voice of Destruction*, p. 253.

227. Ibid., p. 240.

228. Redles, *Hitler's Millennial Reich*, pp. 64–5.

229. See Kurlander, 'Hitler's Monsters'.

230. Treitel, *Science*, pp. 73–96, 155–9; Williamson, *Longing*, pp. 285–7; Zander, *Anthroposophie*, pp. 218–49, 308–34.

231. Black, *Death in Berlin*, p. 71.

232. Fest, *Face of the Third Reich*, p. 188.

233. Fisher, *Fantasy*, p. 6.

234. Ibid., p. 6.

235. Ibid., pp. 5–6.

236. Treitel, *Science*, pp. 24–6, 243–8.

237. See Williamson, *Longing*; Steinmetz, *Devil's Handwriting*; see also Cohn, *Pursuit of the Millenium*; Redles, *Hitler's Millennial Reich*; Grabner-Haider and Strasser, *Hitlers mythische Religion*.

Chapter 3

1. MS Konrad Heiden, IfZG: ED 209/34, pp. 9–10.

2. Ley, 'Pseudoscience in Naziland', pp. 90–8.

3. Heiden, IfZG: ED 209/34, pp. 12–13.

4. Ibid.

5. Eisner, *Haunted Screen*, pp. 8–9.

6. Fisher, *Fantasy*, pp. 11–12.

7. Hans Mommsen, *The Rise and Fall of Weimar Democracy*, Chapel Hill, NC: University of North Carolina Press, 1998; Detlev Peukert, *The Weimar Republic: The Crisis of Classical Modernity*, New York: Hill and Wang, 1992; Eric Kurlander, 'Violence, Volksgemeinschaft, and Empire: Interpreting the Third Reich in the Twenty-First Century', *Journal of Contemporary History* 46:4 (2011), pp. 920–34.

8. See also Geoff Eley, 'The German Right from Weimar to Hitler: Fragmentation and Coalescence', *Central European History* 48:1 (March 2015), pp. 100–13; Peter Fritzsche, 'The NSDAP 1919–1934: From Fringe Politics to the Nazi Seizure of Power', in Caplan, ed., *Nazi Germany*, pp. 49–66; Peter Fritzsche, *Germans into Nazis*, Cambridge: Harvard University Press, 1998; Richard J. Evans, *The Coming of the Third Reich*, London: Penguin, 2005.

9. Fisher, *Fantasy*, pp. 11–12.

10. Ryback, 'Hitler's Forgotten Library', *Atlantic Monthly*; http://www.theatlantic.com/doc/200305/ryback; Ryback, *Hitler's Private Library*, pp. 146–7.

11. Robert E. Norton, *Secret Germany: Stefan George and his Circle*, Ithaca, NY: Cornell University Press, 2002, pp. 727–7.

12. After the war Schertel opened his own holistic, occult-infused dance academies. Gerd Meyer, *Verfemter Nächte blasser Sohn – Ein erster Blick auf Ernst Schertel*, in Michael Farin, ed., *Phantom Schmerz. Quellentexte zur Begriffsgeschichte des Masochismus*, Munich: Belleville Verlag, 2003, pp. 496–7.

13. Ibid., p. 498.
14. Ibid., pp. 497–8; Ernst Schertel, *Magie – Geschichte, Theorie, Praxis*, Prien: Anthropos-Verlag, 1923, and *Der Flagellantismus als literarisches Motiv*, 4 vols, Leipzig: Parthenon, 1929–32; see also Thomas Karlauf: *Stefan George. Die Entdeckung des Charisma*, Munich: Blessing, 2007.
15. Ryback, 'Hitler's Forgotten Library'; Ryback, *Hitler's Private Library*, pp. 146–7.
16. Ryback, *Hitler's Private Library*, pp. 159–62.
17. Treitel, *Science*, pp. 77–8, 122–5.
18. Oscar A. H. Schmitz, 'Warum treibt unsere Zeit Astrologie?', *Zeitschrift für kritischen Okkultismus und Grenzfragen des Seelenlebens (ZfKO)* 11 (1927), p. 28.
19. Szczesny, 'Presse', p. 119.
20. Ibid., p. 48.
21. Ibid., p. 55.
22. Ibid., p. 119.
23. Ibid.
24. Ibid., pp. 56–8.
25. Ibid.
26. Ibid., p. 94.
27. See Treitel, *Science*; Staudenmaier, 'Occultism'.
28. Heiden, 'Preface', IfZG: ED 209/34, pp. 10–11.
29. Ibid., pp. 11–12.
30. Treitel, *Science*, pp. 77–8.
31. Heiden, 'Preface', IfZG: ED 209/34, pp. 11–12.
32. Ibid., pp. 13–14; see Treitel, *Science*, pp. 244–8.
33. Ley, 'Pseudoscience in Naziland', p. 91. 'The conditions present in the years between 1920 and 1940 in Germany,' wrote the British journalist Lewis Spence, left 'Germany peculiarly open to the assaults and suggestions of the Satanist caucus.' Spence, *Occult Causes*, pp. 22–3.
34. 'Besides this reciprocal process of a weakening of established religion and a rising quantity of would-be prophets,' adds the historian Peter Fisher, 'the economic and political instability of the postwar years helped spread feelings of anxiety and frustration, especially throughout the middle class, that undermined any initial willingness it may have had to accommodate itself to democracy.' Fisher, *Fantasy*, pp. 11–12.
35. Kracauer, *Caligari*, p. 11.
36. 'However, the dependence of a people's mental attitudes upon external factors,' such as the profound political, socioeconomic, and psychological dislocations of the First World War, 'does not justify the frequent disregard [by scholars] of these attitudes.' Kracauer, *Caligari*, pp. 11–12.
37. Wolfram, *Stepchildren*, pp. 9–10, 21–2.
38. Richard Baerwald, ed., *Zeitschrift für kritischen Okkultismus* 1 (1926), pp. 1–2, 16–17, 22–41.
39. See, e.g., various articles in the *Zentralblatt für Okkultismus* 26 (1932/3).
40. Wolfram, *Stepchildren*, pp. 22–3, 263–4.
41. Richard Baerwald, 'Das Dämonische Unterbewusstsein', *Zeitschrift für kritischen Okkultismus* 1 (1926), pp. 99–103; Kracauer, *Caligari*, pp. 3–11.
42. Howard L. Philp, 'Interview', *The Psychologist* (May 1939), in McGuire and Hull, eds, *C. G. Jung Speaking*, pp. 134–9.
43. Mircea Eliade, 'Rencontre avec Jung', in *Combat: De la Resistance à la Revolution* (9.10.52), p. 226.
44. Ibid., p. 217.
45. Willy Hellpach, 'Völkerentwicklung und Völkergeschichte unter Walten und Wirken von bindenden Gesetz und schöpferischer Freiheit im Völkerseelenleben', *Schriftenreihe zur Völkerpsychologie* (1944), pp. 7–10, 107–8; Egbert Klautke, *The Mind of the Nation: Völkerpsychologie in Germany, 1851–1955*, Oxford: Berghahn Books 2013.
46. 'Rencontre avec Jung', p. 226.
47. Schertel, *Magic*, pp. 7–19.
48. Ibid., pp. 10–12.
49. Ibid., p. 17.
50. Ibid., p. 82.
51. Ibid., pp. 88–91; 'By awakening of a new basic attitude toward existence ... when this completely irrational, above-moral, and above-personal transformation has taken place inside of us will all instructions [from the magician] make sense'; ibid., p. 100.
52. Ibid., pp. 122–3.
53. Ibid., p. 128.
54. Ibid., pp. 30, 67.
55. Ibid., pp. 135–6.

56. 'Hitler was greatly influenced by Gustave Le Bon and followed the dictum *in La Psychologie des Foules* that the leader must be an integral part of the shared faith', Mosse, *Nationalization of the Masses*, pp. 201–2.
57. Wolfram, *Stepchildren*, pp. 274–5.
58. Ibid., pp. 275–7.
59. Rauschning, *Voice of Destruction*, pp. 222–3.
60. Mosse, *Nationalization of the Masses*, pp. 199–201.
61. Sickinger, 'Hitler and the Occult', p. 112; Rauschning, *Voice of Destruction*, p. 245.
62. NL Ley, BAK: N 1468/5, pp. 24–5; Prof. Dr Karl Brandt, pp. 87–8, in NL Hitler, BAK: N 1128/33.
63. Howe, *Nostradamus*, pp. 123–4.
64. Olden, 'Introduction', in Rudolf von Olden, ed., *Propheten in deutscher Krise. Das Wunderbare oder Die Verzauberten. Eine Sammlung*, Berlin: Rowohlt, 1932, pp. 18–19.
65. 'These qualities have nothing to do with the medium's own personality. The medium is possessed by them. In the same way undeniable powers enter into Hitler, genuinely daemonic powers, which make men his instruments', Rauschning, *Voice of Destruction*, pp. 258–9.
66. Carl Jung, 'The Psychology of Dictatorship', *The Observer* (18 October 1936), in McGuire and Hull, eds, *C. G. Jung Speaking*, p. 92; Hitler's penchant for devolving into more 'primitive' or 'manic lycan- thropic states', of being overcome by ecstasy and emotion, was further cited by contemporaries as evidence of shamanism or mediumism. Robert Eisler, *Man Into Wolf: An Anthropological Interpretation of Sadism, Masochism, and Lycanthropy*, London: Routledge, 1951: 'Hitler's anger, like the anger of the magical shaman, was notorious . . . the visions and magic formulae of the shaman become absolute commands. The shaman was now the leader who divined the future'. Sickinger, 'Hitler and the Occult', p. 116.
67. Ibid.
68. Ibid., p. 117.
69. Otto Strasser, *Hitler and I*, Boston, MA: Houghton Mifflin, 1940, pp. 65–6.
70. Sickinger, 'Hitler and the Occult', p. 118.
71. Heiden, 'Preface', IfZG: ED 209/34, pp. 15–16.
72. Pammer, *Hitlers Vorbilder*, p. 11.
73. Sickinger, 'Hitler and the Occult', p. 116.
74. Heiden, 'Preface', IfZG: ED 209/34, pp. 14–15.
75. Olden, ed., 'Introduction', in *Propheten*, p. 17.
76. 'Many cannot understand,' wrote one early supporter. 'Foreign peoples, the Jews and their deceivers hate him and tempt the desperate – but honest searching Volk hold off through lies and deceit, to follow the Summoner'. Redles, *Hitler's Millennial Reich*, pp. 83–4.
77. Sickinger, 'Hitler and the Occult', p. 118.
78. H. R. Knickerbocker, 'Diagnosing the Dictators' (1938), in McGuire and Hull, eds, *C. G. Jung Speaking*, pp. 114–22.
79. McGuire and Hull, eds, *C. G. Jung Speaking*, p. 138.
80. Ibid., p. 138.
81. Heiden, 'Preface', IfZG: ED 209/34, pp. 14–15.
82. McGuire and Hull, eds, *C. G. Jung Speaking*, p. 138.
83. 'He is the first man to tell every German what he has been thinking and feeling all along in his unconscious about German fate, especially since the defeat in the World War'. Knickerbocker, 'Diagnosing the Dictators', pp. 114–18.
84. Fisher, *Fantasy*, p. 219.
85. Redles, *Hitler's Millennial Reich*, pp. 81–2.
86. Rauschning, *Voice of Destruction*, pp. 221–2; Sickinger, 'Hitler and the Occult', p. 110.
87. Fisher, *Fantasy*, p. 219.
88. Redles, *Hitler's Millennial Reich*, p. 87.
89. Sickinger, 'Hitler and the Occult', p. 117.
90. Redles, *Hitler's Millennial Reich*, pp. 81–2.
91. Heiden, 'Preface', IfZG: ED 209/34, pp. 14–15.
92. Schertel, *Magic*, p. 41. 'Understanding the nature of this conversion experience,' David Redles observes, 'is essential for comprehending the astonishing rise of Hitler and Nazism'. Redles, *Hitler's Millennial Reich*, pp. 77–8; Heiden, 'Preface', IfZG: ED 209/34, p. 16.
93. Heiden, 'Preface', IfZG: ED 209/34, p. 16.
94. See, e.g., Fritzsche, 'The NSDAP 1919–1934', pp. 49, 59–63, 66.
95. Heiden, 'Preface', IfZG: ED 209/34, p. 16; Detlev Peukert, *Inside Nazi Germany*, New Haven, CT: Yale University Press, 1989, pp. 26–7.
96. Ibid.

97. Joseph Goebbels, 'Erkenntnis und Propaganda', in *Signale der neuen Zeit. 25 ausgewählte Reden von Dr. Joseph Goebbels*, Munich: Eher (Zentralverlag der NSDAP), 1934, pp. 28–52.

98. Ibid.

99. Ibid.

100. Ibid.: 'That is what happens the first time one hears one of Hitler's major speeches. I have met people who had attended a Hitler meeting for the first time, and at the end they said: "This man put in words everything I have been searching for for years. For the first time, someone gave form to what I want."'

101. Ibid.

102. Ibid.

103. Kugel, *Ewers*, pp. 8, 126; Klaus Gmachl, *Zauberlehrling, Alraune und Vampir: Die Frank Braun-Romane von Hanns Heinz Ewers*, Norderstedt: Books on Demand, 2005, pp. 57–5.

104. Kugel, Ewers, pp. 24–5, 81–2, 126–7.

105. Poley, *Decolonization*, pp. 19–20, 44–6; Otto Kriegk, *Der deutsche Film im Spiegel der Ufa*, Berlin: Ufa, 1943, p. 47; Eisner, *Haunted Screen*, p. 97.

106. See Kurlander, 'Orientalist Roots', in Cho, Kurlander, and McGetchin, eds, *Transcultural Encounters*; Timo Kozlowski, 'Wenn Nazis weltenbummeln und schreiben. Über die Nähe zwischen Künstlern und Nationalsozialismus. Dargestellt am Beispiel von Hanns Heinz Ewers', *Die Brücke. Zeitschrift für Germanistik in Südostasien* 5 (2004); Poley, *Colonization*, pp. 21–2; Hanns Heinz Ewers, 'Die Mamaloi', in Ewers, *Die Grauen: Seltsame Geschichte*, Munich: Müller, 1908, pp. 243–90.

107. See Hanns Heinz Ewers, *Alraune*, Düsseldorf: Grupello, 1998, pp. 31–85; Gmachl *Zauberlehrling*, pp. 166–222; Jestram, *Mythen*, pp. 43–5.

108. Hanns Heinz Ewers, *Vampir: Ein verwildeter Roman in Fetzen und Farben*, Munich: Georg Müller, 1922; Jestram, *Mythen*, pp. 6–9, 49–52; Poley, *Decolonization*, pp. 116–26; Kozlowski, 'Ewers'; Jestram, *Mythen*, pp. 43–7.

109. Fisher, *Fantasy*, pp. 6–7.

110. Clemens Ruthner, *Unheimliche Wiederkehr: Interpretationen zu den gespenstischen Romanfiguren bei Ewers, Meyrink, Soyka, Spunda und Strobl*, Meitingen: Corian-Verlag, 1993.

111. Treitel, *Science*, pp. 109–10.

112. Ibid.

113. Ibid., pp. 108–9.

114. Ibid., pp. 109–10.

115. Ibid., pp. 125–31.

116. Ibid.

117. Ofer Ashkenazi, *Weimar Film and Modern Jewish Identity*, New York and London: Palgrave, 2012.

118. Kracauer, *Caligari*.

119. Eisner, *Haunted Screen*, pp. 95–7.

120. Treitel, *Science*, p. 109.

121. Thomas Koebner, 'Murnau – On Film History as Intellectual History', in Dietrich Scheunemann, ed., *Expressionist Film: New Perspectives*, Rochester, NY: Camden House, 2003, pp. 111–23. There are those who see the *völkisch*, supernatural, and irrational elements intrinsic to Weimar film as less all-encompassing. See, e.g., Ofer Ashkenazi, *A Walk into the Night: Reason and Subjectivity in the Films of the Weimar Republic*, Tel Aviv: Am Oved, 2010.

122. Eisner, *Haunted Screen*, pp. 95–7.

123. Jestram, *Mythen*, pp. 45–57.

124. Ibid., pp. 55–61, 89–91; see also Maya Barzilai, *Golem: Modern Wars and Their Monsters*, New York: New York University Press, 2016.

125. Bratton, 'From Iron Age Myth', *Worldviews* 4, pp. 206–7.

126. Paul Coates, *The Gorgon's Gaze: German Cinema, Expressionism, and the Image of Horror*, Cambridge: Cambridge University Press, 2008; Jeffrey Herf, *The Jewish Enemy: Nazi Propaganda during World War II and the Holocaust*, Cambridge, MA: Belknap Press, 2006; Nina Auerbach, *Our Vampires, Ourselves*, Chicago, IL: University of Chicago Press, 1995, pp. 73–4; Eisner, *Haunted Screen*, pp. 96–7.

127. Koebner, 'Murnau', pp. 111–23.

128. Black, 'Expellees', p. 97; for a less pessimistic vision of these themes, see Ashkenazi, *Weimar Film*, pp. 88–101.

129. Kracauer, *Caligari*, pp. 3–11; Koebner, 'Murnau', pp. 111–23; Jared Poley, 'Siegfried Kracauer, Spirit, and the Soul of Weimar Germany', in Black and Kurlander, eds, *Revisiting*.

130. Fisher, *Fantasy*, pp. 120–1.

131. Linda Schulte-Sasse, *Entertaining the Third Reich*, Durham, NC: Duke University Press, 1996, p. 11; see also Stephan Schindler and Lutz Koepnick, *The Cosmopolitan Screen*, Ann Arbor, MI: Michigan,

2007, pp. 1–2; Anton Kaes, *From Hitler to Heimat: The Return of History as Film*, Cambridge, MA: Harvard University Press, 1989. Thomas Elsaesser, *Weimar Cinema and After: Germany's Historical Imaginary*, London: Routledge, 2000, pp. 420–37.

132. Dietrich Scheunemann, *Expressionist Film: New Perspectives*, Rochester, NY: Camden House, 2003, pp. ix–xi.

133. Mosse, *Nationalization*, pp. 114–15; see also David Stewart Hull, *Film in the Third Reich*, Berkeley, CA: University of California Press, 1969, pp. 8–12; see also correspondence in Amt Rosenberg, BAB: NS 15/399, pp. 207–18.

134. Lutz Koepnick, *The Dark Mirror: German Cinema Between Hitler and Hollywood*, Berkeley, CA: University of California Press, 2002, pp. 2–6.

135. Weimar's fantasy writers 'created an immensely popular mass literature . . . that was a potent ingredient in the simmering stew of resentment, frustrated nationalism, political irrationalism, and economic distress underlying the Nazi rise to power', Fisher, *Fantasy*, pp. 1–2.

136. http://uwpress.wisc.edu/books/0271.htm.

137. Treitel, *Science*, p. 109.

138. Fisher, *Fantasy*, pp. 6–7.

139. Ibid.

140. Ibid., pp. 9–10.

141. Poley, *Decolonization*, p. 48; Gmachl, *Zauberlehrling*, pp. 41–3.

142. Gmachl, *Zauberlehrling*, pp. 54–5, 257–71; Poley, *Decolonization*, pp. 91–4, 104–10, 127–40; Auerbach, *Our Vampires, Ourselves*, pp. 72–74; Eisner, *Haunted Screen*, p. 95.

143. Fritzsche, 'The NSDAP 1919–1934'; Eric Kurlander, *The Price of Exclusion: Ethnicity, National Identity, and the Decline of German Liberalism, 1898–1933*, New York: Berghahn, 2006; Gmachl, *Zauberlehrling*, pp. 37–45.

144. Andreas Dornheim, *Röhms Mann für Ausland*, Münster: LIT, 1998, pp. 108–9; Bernhard Sauer, 'Die Schwarze Reichswehr', in *Berlin in Geschichte und Gegenwart*. Jahrbuch des Landesarchivs Berlin (2008), pp. 57–8. Die Weltbühne Nr. 21, 1925, S. 565.

145. Hanns Heinz Ewers, *Reiter in deutscher Nacht*. Stuttgart/Berlin: Cotta, 1931.

146. Kugel, *Ewers*, pp. 296–7.

147. Ibid., pp. 297–9; Heimsoth, *Charakter-Konstellation*.

148. Susanne zur Nieden, 'Aufstieg und Fall des virilen Männerhelden. Der Skandal um Ernst Röhm und seine Ermordung', in Susanne zur Nieden, ed., *Homosexualität und Staatsräson. Männlichkeit, Homophobie und Politik in Deutschland 1900–1945*, Frankfurt: Campus Verlag, 2005, pp. 147–61; see Goodrick-Clarke, *Occult Roots*, p. 234; Kugel, *Ewers*, pp. 298–9; Karl Heimsoth, 'Homosexualität. Eine Kontroverse mit Johannes Lang (Weniger eine Berichtigung als eine Rückweisung und Selbstergänzung', *Zenit: Zentralblatt für astrologische Forschung* 3 (1931), p. 111.

149. See report on Wolf Graf von Helldorff, BAB: R 1507/2027, pp. 37–8; See Spring 1926 police reports on Wehrwolf, BAB: R 1507/2028, pp. 16, 40.

150. See reports on Edmund Heines, Hermann Eckhardt, Friedrich Weber, Ludendorff and other *völkisch*-esoteric paramilitary cooperation, BAB: R 1507/2027, p. 39; BAB: R 1507/2028, pp. 18, 95– 9, 65–9, 105–6, 158–9; BAB: R 1507/2032, p. 105.

151. Kugel, *Ewers*, pp. 296–7.

152. Puschner and Vollnhals, 'Forschungs- und problemgeschichtliche Perspektiven', in Puschner and Vollnhals, eds, *Bewegung*, pp. 23–4.

153. See 1927 reports on Wehrwolf, including articles from 2.2.27 and 3.2.27, police reports from Reichskommisar, 19.2.27, 8.2.27, 12.4.27, reports from Reichskommisar, 19.2.27, 8.2.27, 12.4.27, regarding leaders Ehlert, Kloppe, and voluntary dissolution of the Berlin *Ortsgruppen*; 26.4.27, report on 'Verhaftung einees Wehrwolfführers'; 13.12.27, *Vossische Ztg* article about the decline in meaning of *nationalen Verbände*; *Reichskommissr für Überwachung der öffentlichen Ordnung to Reichsminister des Innern*, 9.11.28; regarding split in Wehrwolf joining Stahlhelm or Jungdo, 17.12.28; 12.9.30, copy of *Berliner Volkszeitung* article criticizing 'Eine Werwolfrede' at the graves of those who murdered Rathenau. BAB: R 1501/125673b, pp. 69–76.

154. Kater, 'Artamanen', p. 618.

155. Ewers, *Rider*; Kugel, *Ewers*, pp. 299–301.

156. Kugel, *Ewers*, pp. 299–301.

157. Fisher, *Fantasy*, pp. 6–7; Poley, *Decolonization*, pp. 16–18, 93–8.

158. Wolfgang Emmerich, 'The Mythos of Germanic Continuity', in Dow and Lixfeld, eds, *Nazification*, p. 34.

159. Black, *Death in Berlin*, p. 272.

160. Fanon, *Wretched*, p. 55.

161. Kugel, *Ewers*, pp. 299–302, 311–12.

162. Ibid., pp. 303–8.

163. Ibid., pp. 322–3.

164. Ibid., pp. 307–9.

165. Hanns Heinz Ewers, *Stürmer! Ein deutsches Schicksal; Nach dem Buche 'Horst Wessel'*, Stuttgart/ Berlin: Cotta, 1934; Hanns Heinz Ewers, *Horst Wessel. Ein deutsches Schicksal*, Stuttgart/Berlin: Cotta, 1932; Kugel, *Ewers*, pp. 311–13.

166. Daniel Siemens, *Horst Wessel. Tod und Verklärung eines Nationalsozialisten*, Munich: Siedler, 2009, pp. 55–72, 90–110, 170–208; Kugel, *Ewers*, pp. 319–20; Horst Wessel, BAB: R 1507/2063, p. 87; BAB: R 1507/2058, pp. 193, 42, 45, 81; 'Denkschrift über Kampfvorbereitung und Kampfgrundsätze radikaler Organisationen' by Polizeimajor Ratcliffe, 30.11.31, BAB: R 1507/2059, p. 16.

167. Kugel, *Ewers*, pp. 320–2; Kozlowski, 'Ewers'.

168. Kugel, *Ewers*, p. 325.

169. Kozlowski, 'Ewers'; Kugel, *Ewers*, pp. 382–4.

170. Gmachl, *Zauberlehrling*, pp. 45–53; Michael Sennewald, *Hanns Heinz Ewers. Phantastikund Jugendstil*, Maisenhain: Hain, 1973, pp. 200–7; Wilfried Kugel, *Hanussen: Die wahre Geschichte des Hermann Steinschneider*, Düsseldorf: Grupello, 1998, p. 326; Fisher, *Fantasy*, pp. 19–20.

171. Kugel, *Ewers*, pp. 326–7; H. H. Ewers: BAK: R 9361–V/5138, letter from 11.7.34.

172. Kugel, *Ewers*, pp. 328–9.

173. Ibid., pp. 329–30.

174. Ibid., pp. 327–8.

175. Ibid., pp. 329–30.

176. Ewers' *Rider* and *Wessel* exemplified the 'stark antinomies' of the NSDAP's 'Manichean universe', drawing young Germans to 'a worldview in which reason was excoriated as the diseased outgrowth of Western civilization', where 'the *völkish* man' opposes '*ratio* with religion, the individual with the collectivity', Fisher, *Fantasy*, pp. 17–19.

177. Ibid., pp. 6–7.

178. Ibid.

179. Ibid.

180. Kugel, *Hanussen*, pp. 334–5.

181. Fisher, *Fantasy*, p 10.

182. See Rosenberg, BAB: NS 8/185, p. 50.

183. Olden, ed., 'Introduction', in *Propheten*, p. 16.

184. Treitel, *Science*, pp. 195–7.

185. Szczesny, 'Okkultismus', pp. 131–2; see also Gerda Walther, *Zum Anderen Ufer: Vom Atheismus zum Christentum*, Remagen: Der Leuchter Verlag, 1960, pp. 481–92.

186. Monica Black, 'A Messiah after Hitler, and His Miracles: Postwar Popular Apocalypticism', in Black and Kurlander, eds, *Revisiting*, p. 213.

187. Howe, *Urania's Children*, pp. 84–7, 95–103; Treitel, *Science*, pp. 192–4.

188. Howe, *Urania's Children*, pp. 102–3.

189. Treitel, *Science*, pp. 77–8.

190. Walter Stach, *Gemeingefährliche Mysterien: Eine astrologische Studie*, Graf. Carl v. Klinckowstroem, 'Rund um Nostradamus', in *ZfKO* II (1927), p. 40, pp. 93–4.

191. Schmitz, 'Warum treibt unsere Zeit Astrologie?', p. 33.

192. Albert Hellwig, 'Ein betrügerischer Kriminaltelepath', in *Zeitschrift für kritischen Okkultismus* II (1927), p. 130.

193. Graf Carl V. Klinckowstroem, 'Mein okkultistischer Lebenslauf: Bekenntnisse', *ZfKO* II (1927). p. 104; see also Klinckowstroem, 'Die Seele des Okkultisten', *ZfKO* II (1927), pp. 206–7.

194. 'Zum Geleit', in *Zenit* (January 1933); Buchbender, 'Die Gedankenübertragung. Eine objektive Betrachtung', *Zentralblatt für Okkultismus* 26 (1932/33), pp. 84–5.

195. After leaving politics in 1920, Sebottendorff even took over editing Germany's greatest astrological journal, the *Astrologische Rundschau*. Howe, *Urania's Children*, pp. 126–7.

196. Wulff, *Zodiac*, pp. 37–45; Howe, *Nostradamus*, pp. 126–7.

197. Heimsoth, 'Homosexualität'; Kugel, *Ewers*, pp. 295–8.

198. Howe, *Nostradamus*, p. 122; Howe, *Urania's Children*, pp. 87–9.

199. Howe, *Nostradamus*, pp. 123–4.

200. See various issues of the *ZfKO* (1926–8), *Zeitschrift fir Parapsychologie* (1927); *Astrologische Rundschau* (1924–9).

201. Howe, *Nostradamus*, pp. 127–8.

202. Karl Frankenbach and Graz-Gösting in 'Astrologische Portraits', *Zenit* 4 (April 1931), pp. 129–35.

203. 'Adolf Hitler', *Zenit* 4 (May 1931), pp. 198–9.

204. Fr. Sachs, 'Reichskanzler D. Brüning', *Zenit* 2:11 (November 1931), pp. 428–30.

205. Korsch, 'Erneuerung', *Zenit* (May 1933), pp. 177–9.

206. See article from, 2.5.33, in NL Herbert Frank, IfZG: 414/138.

207. Howe, *Nostradamus*, p. 129; see Heinz Noesselt, 'Schicksalsdeterminaten des Reichskanzlers Adolf Hitler', *Zenit* (May 1933), pp. 301–11, 378–82; George Sellnich, 'Der Nationalsozialismus und die Astrologie', *Zenit* (May 1933), pp. 363–7; Ernst Hentges, 'Zum Horoskop des Reichskanzlers Adolf Hitler', *Zenit* (May 1933), pp. 437–8; H. C. Dierst, 'Die astropolitische Tagespresse', *Zenit* (May 1933), pp. 180–4; Dr Hans Pietzke 'Das Hakenkreuz als Sternbild', *Zenit* (May 1933), pp. 443–9; J. Dietrich, 'Dietrich Eckart', *Zenit* (May 1933), pp. 456–63; Erich Carl Kuhr, 'Aussprache und Diskussion. Primär-Direktionen des Reichskanzlers Adolf Hitler', *Zenit* (May 1933), pp. 469–71; Staudenmaier, 'Nazi Perceptions of Esotericism', pp. 32–9.
208. Staudenmaier, *Between Occultism*, pp. 223–9.
209. Fritz Quade Speech, 'Occultism and Politics', 12.10.33, BAB: R 58/6218, pp. 1–39; Fritz Quade biography, BAB: R 58/7312; H. Fehr. von Breidenbach, 'Der XII. Astrologen-Kongress', *Zenit* (May 1933), pp. 331–3.
210. Szczesny, 'Presse', pp. 131–2.
211. Ibid., pp. 131–2.
212. Fisher, *Fantasy*, pp. 219–20, 223–6.
213. Redles, *Hitler's Millennial Reich*, pp. 83–4.
214. Fisher, *Fantasy*, pp. 221–3; see also Kurt Hesse correspondence from RSK, 1.27.37, letter from Hans Johst, 6.9.40; correspondence regarding pen name, 7.7.41, 17.7.41, BAB: R 9361–V/6199.
215. Redles, *Hitler's Millennial Reich*, p. 65.
216. Erik Jan Hanussen, *Meine Lebenslinie*, Berlin: Universitas, 1930, pp. 21–2, 36, 47–55, 78–83.
217. Ibid., pp. 103–16; Hitler, *Mein Kampf*, Munich: Eher, 1943, pp. 54–65.
218. Hanussen, *Lebenslinie*, pp. 136–8, 162–70, 222–9; Treitel, *Science*, p. 231.
219. Hanussen, *Lebenslinie*, pp. 184–208; Kugel, *Hanussen*, p. 37.
220. Szczesny, 'Presse', pp. 122–4; Treitel, *Science*, p. 231.
221. Kugel, *Hanussen*, pp. 33–6.
222. Ibid., pp. 46–8.
223. Ibid., pp. 61–7; Geza von Cziffra, *Hanussen Hellseher des Teufels: Die Wahrheit über den Reichstagsbrand*, Munich: F. A. Herbig, 1978, pp. 86–7.
224. Kugel, *Hanussen*, pp. 89, 93–5.
225. Cziffra, *Hanussen*, pp. 94–112; Kugel, *Hanussen*, pp. 106–7.
226. Cziffra, *Hanussen*, pp. 114–23.
227. Kugel, *Hanussen*, p. 165; Erik Jan Hanussen, 'Was bringt 1932?', *Die Andere Welt*, Berlin: Hanussen, 1931–2.
228. At large public events he would throw 'destiny balls' into the audience. Whoever caught the ball could get his autograph and ask Hanussen questions, offering 10,000 marks to anyone who could prove that he had preselected the recipients. Kugel, *Hanussen*, p. 207.
229. See various articles, for example, 'Du wirst verfolgt von diesen Augen', in Hanussen, *Die Andere Welt* (1931), as well as additional articles in Hanussen, *Die Andere Welt* (1932).
230. Cziffra, *Hanussen*, p. 143. After the stock market crash, Hanussen boasted of his ability to manipulate financial futures, giving economic tips on investing in a bear market. Kugel, *Hanussen*, pp. 155–6.
231. Wilfried Kugel and Alexander Bahar, *Der Reichstagsbrand. Wie Geschichte wird gemacht*, Berlin: Quintessenz, 2001, pp. 640–1.
232. Cziffra, *Hanussen*, p. 135; Szczesny, 'Presse', pp. 128–9.
233. Treitel, *Science*, p. 231.
234. Kugel, *Hanussen*, pp. 159–62, 45–7: 'Séance des Monates'. There are a number of headlines shown on page 47, such as 'Unwetter erschlägt Menschen!', 'Schicksalsstunde', 'Brüning noch einem Sieger', 'Die Krise ist beigelegt', and '24 Millionen Verlust!', all in *Die Andere Welt*, vol. 1 (1931); '1932: das Jahr der Generationen', in *Die Andere Welt*, vol. 2 (1931).
235. Kugel, *Hanussen*, p. 213.
236. Szczesny, 'Presse', p. 142.
237. Kugel, *Hanussen*, pp. 187–9.
238. Cziffra, *Hanussen*, p. 133.
239. Kugel, *Hanussen*, pp. 334–5; Dirk Walter, *Antisemitische Kriminalität und Gewalt: Judenfeindschaft in der Weimarer Republik*, Bonn: Dietz, 1999, pp. 215–16; Benjamin Hett, *Burning the Reichstag: An Investigation into the Third Reich's Enduring Mystery*, Oxford: Oxford University Press, 2014, p. 54.
240. Kugel, *Hanussen*, pp. 131–8.
241. Treitel, *Science*, p. 232.
242. Kugel, *Hanussen*, pp. 159–62.
243. Ibid., pp. 195–201; pp. 131–2: IfZG, ED 386, G. Szczesny, 'Die Presse des Okkultismus, Geschichte und Typologie der okkultistischen Zeitschriften' (diss. 1940, Munich under Karl d'Ester) CH3, CH5 Occult.

244. Cziffra, *Hanussen*, pp. 9–10.

245. Kugel, *Hanussen*, pp. 182–4.

246. Kugel and Bahar, *Reichstagsbrand*, pp. 640–1.

247. Kugel, *Hanussen*, pp. 186–7; see also Walter C. Langer, *The Mind of Adolf Hitler: The Secret Wartime Report*, New York: Basic Books, p. 40.

248. Cziffra, *Hanussen*, p. 135.

249. Kugel, *Hanussen*, pp. 334–5.

250. Hett, *Burning*, pp. 106–7; Benjamin Hett, '"This Story Is About Something Fundamental": Nazi Criminals, History, Memory, and the Reichstag Fire', *Central European History* 48/2 (2015), pp. 199–224. On earlier interpretations that de-emphasize the role of the Third Reich in setting the fire, see Fritz Tobias, *The Reichstag Fire*, New York: Putnam, 1964; Hans Mommsen, 'Der Reichstagsbrand und seine politischen Folgen', *Vierteljahrshefte für Zeitgeschichte* 12 (1964), pp. 351–413.

251. Kugel, *Hanussen*, p. 191.

252. Ibid., pp. 221–5; Kugel and Bahar, *Reichstagsbrand*, p. 642.

253. Kugel, *Hanussen*, pp. 230–1; Kugel and Bahar, *Reichstagsbrand*, pp. 15–16, 122, 644–52; Hett, '"This Story Is About Something Fundamental"'.

254. Kugel and Bahar, *Reichstagsbrand*, pp. 644–52.

255. Fisher, *Fantasy*, pp. 3–4, 15–18; Karl Frankenbach, 'Die Zeichen der Zeit. Die Gefahrenherde Europas', *Zenit* (March 1931), p. 52: H. C. Dierst, 'Astropolitsche Fehltreffer', *Zenit* (February 1933), pp. 43–52.

256. Cziffra 'Hanussen', p. 150.

257. Knickerbocker, 'Diagnosing the Doctors', pp. 114–22.

258. Ibid.

259. Olden, ed., 'Introduction', in *Propheten*, p. 20.

260. Ibid., p. 16.

261. Ibid., p. 19.

262. Ibid., pp. 19–20.

263. Ibid., p. 18.

264. Ibid., pp. 19–20.

265. Hans Maier, 'Political Religion: A Concept and its Limitations', *Totalitarian Movements and Political Religions* 1:2 (Autumn 2000), pp. 7–8.

266. Black, 'Groening', p. 213.

267. 'In order to be useful, the mythical presentation had to choose a middle road between vagueness and specificity, for either the intent of the mythos is too dark to be useful or it is too clear to be believed.' Wolfgang Emmerich, 'The Mythos of Germanic Continuity', in Dow and Lixfeld, eds, *Nazification*, pp. 36–7.

268. Fisher, *Fantasy*, pp. 7–8; see also Scheunemann, *Expressionist Film*, pp. 59–67.

Chapter 4

1. Heinrich Himmler, as quoted in Wolfgang Emmerich, 'The Mythos of Germanic Continuity', in Dow and Lixfeld, eds, *Nazification*, p. 43.

2. See report, 'Kampf für und gegen Astrologie und Okkultismus', BAB: NS 8/185, *Amt Rosenberg*, pp. 64–8.

3. Anrich, IfZG: 1867/56. ZS–542–6. 'Bemerkungen zur Niederschrift über die Unterredung mit Professor Dr. Ernst Anrich am 16. Februar 1960 (verfasst von Dr. Hans-Dietrich Loock)', pp. 5–6.

4. Bormann Circular to all Gauleiter, 7.5.1941, BAB: NS 6/334.

5. Ibid.

6. Ibid.

7. Uwe Schellinger, Andreas Anton, and Michael T. Schetsche, eds, 'Pragmatic Occultism in the Military History of the Third Reich', in Black and Kurlander, eds, *Revisiting*, p. 157.

8. Treitel, *Science*, pp. 209–10.

9. Ludendorff on Hanussen, from SV, 5.2.33, in NL Herbert Frank, IfZG: 414/38.

10. Kugel, *Hanussen*, pp. 159–62, 221–4; Kugel and Bahar, *Reichstagsbrand*, pp. 641–2.

11. Treitel, *Science*, p. 209.

12. Ibid., pp. 225–8; Wolffram, *Stepchildren*, pp. 203–6; See Hörmann to Neumann, 6.12.40, Neumann to Hörmann, 9.12.40, BAB: NS 18/497; Kersten, *Kersten Memoirs*, pp. 28–37.

13. Treitel, *Science*, p. 209.

14. Ibid., p. 201.

15. By the 1920s 'professional scientists, doctors, philosophers, and theologians' had 'begun to take a real interest in such occult sciences as parapsychology, graphology, and dowsing'. Treitel, *Science*, pp. 193–4.

16. Howe, *Nostradamus*, p. 129; Treitel, *Science*, pp. 226–8; Staudenmaier, 'Nazi Perceptions of Esotericism', pp. 32–9.

17. Karsten, *Vampyre*, pp. 62–4.

18. See BAB: R 58/6206, Carl Pelz Report to Kripo, 28.2.1937; Treitel, *Science*, p. 220.

19. Treitel, *Science*, pp. 205–6.

20. Ibid., pp. 147–8.

21. Ibid., pp. 201–3.

22. See *Schwarze Korps* article, 26.11.36, 'Über einen grünen Weg', BAB: NS 5–VI/16959: Kurlander, 'Supernatural Sciences', in Black and Kurlander, eds, *Revisiting*, pp. 132–56; Treitel, *Science*, pp. 206–7, 212–15.

23. See *Schwarze Korps* article, 26.11.36, 'Über einen grünen Weg'.

24. Schellinger et al., 'Pragmatic Occultism'.

25. Two of Germany's leading astrologers, for example, Leopold Korsch and Hugo Vollrath, took the occasion of the Nazi seizure of power to attack each other more vociferously than ever before, appealing to Goebbels' new League for the Protection of German Culture to settle the debate. Howe, *Urania's Children*, pp. 114–18; H. C. Dierst, 'Astropolitsche Fehltreffer', *Zenit* (1933), pp. 43–52. 'In their polemics,' observed one sceptic already in 1926, 'occultists have now developed the tactic of discrediting their opponents and then ascribing to them tendentious motives.' Graf Perovsky-Petrovo-Solovovo, 'Versuche zur Feststellung des sog. Hellsehens der Medien', *Zeitschrift für kritischen Okkultismus* (1926), pp. 51–4; C. Dierst, 'Die astropolitische Tagespresse', *Zenit* (1933), pp. 180–4; Howe, *Urania's Children*, pp. 114–19; Walther, *Zum Anderen Ufer*, pp. 568–82.

26. http://www.dorsten-unterm-hakenkreuz.de/2012/05/28/hubert-korsch-dorstener-petrinum-absolvent-jurist-verleger-und-begrunder-der-wissenschaftlichen-astrologie-wurde–1942–im-kz-ermordet. The telegram is all the more remarkable given the Gestapo's opinion that Korsch was a homosexual who was openly critical of the Nazi regime. On the Third Reich's views of Korsch's politics and private life, see BAB: R 9361V/7196. Correspondence regarding immorality, 23.1.40, 21.4.40, 9.9.37, 2.4.35.

27. See letters and documents from RSK, 10.11.34, 4.5.34, 5.9.34, 20.1.37, BAB: R 58/6207; Lux, 'On all Channels', in Black and Kurlander, eds, *Revisiting*, pp. 229–30.

28. Ibid., pp. 230–1.

29. Howe, *Sebottendorff*, pp. 64–5; Goodrick-Clarke, *Occult Roots*, p. 221.

30. Sebottendorff, 'Thule-Bote', 15. Hartung 1934, Nummer 1. t. Thule-Bote, BAB: NS 26/2232.

31. Phelps 'Before Hitler Came'; Howe, *Sebottendorff*, pp. 66–8.

32. Sebottendorff, 'Thule-Bote', 15. Hartung 1934, Nummer 1. t. Thule-Bote, BAB: NS 26/2232; Gilbhard, *Thule-Gesellschaft*, pp. 176–8; Phelps, 'Before Hitler Came'; Schriftleiter Rudolf von Sebottendorff. Erschienen 31. Gilbhart 1933, Nummer 1. Thule-Bote, BAB: NS 26/2232.

33. 'Völkischer Beobachter', 5.14.36. Abend der Thule-Gesellschaft, BAB: NS 26/2233; 'Lieber Thulebruder!', by Valentin Büchold, H. G. Grassinger, and Dr Kurz, Munich, 20.3.34; 'Betrifft: Austrittserklärung', by Valentin Büchold, H. G. Grassinger, and Dr Kurz, Munich, 3.19.34; to Herrn Franz Dannehl, Tondichter, Thule-Bote, BAB: NS 26/2232.

34. Kater, 'Artamanen', pp. 612–13.

35. Ibid., p. 618.

36. Ibid., pp. 619–21.

37. 'For reasons of tradition,' observed the *völkisch* periodical *Germania*, 'the Wehrwolf are permitted to retain its black banners with the death's head.' See Bund Wehrwolf. See also Wehrwolf to Frick, 15.7.33, Frick to Wehrwolf, 2.8.33, Verbindungsstab der NSDAP, 9.9.33, letter from Röhm, 25.8.33, allowing group to keep its flags; 10.10.33 article in *Germania*, 'Wehrwolf in SA. Eingegliedert', BAB: R 1501/125673b.

38. Treitel, *Science*, p. 220.

39. Ibid., p. 221; Okkultismus-Neue Salemsgesellschaft, BAB: R 58/6218.

40. Goodrick-Clarke, *Occult Roots*, pp. 118–19, 192–7; Bramwell, *Blood and Soil*, pp. 52–3, 95–6, 125–9; Goodrick-Clarke, *Occult Roots*, p. 170.

41. The SD did complain about the 'series of unacceptable errors' that infused ariosophic 'racial teachings', from the 'sexual perversity of Aryan heroes' to their use of 'oriental-antique sources' such as the 'Jewish kabbala'. See SD report on anthroposophy and ariosophy, BAB: R 58/64, pp. 45–8.

42. See BAB: R 58/6217: Himmler's office to DAF, 4.28.39, pp. 1–2.

43. See SD reports from 24.5.39, BAB: R 58/6217; see also Bramwell, *Blood and Soil*, pp. 95–6, 126.

44. Treitel, *Science*, pp. 204–5, 227–8; see also Staudenmaier, 'Nazi Perceptions of Esotericism', pp. 31–5; Werner, *Anthroposophen*, pp. 7–13; BAB: R 58/6203: 13.4.36, voluntary dissolution of Theosophischen Gesellschaft; Staudenmaier, *Between Occultism and Nazism*, pp. 113–19, 223–6.

45. See report on anthroposophy, BAB: R 58/64, pp. 2–18; Werner, *Anthroposophen*, pp. 47–50.

46. Werner, *Anthroposophen*, pp. 7–8, 32–50, 66–72, 143–7, 194–6, 212–21, 341; Staudemaier, *Between Nazism and Occultism*, pp. 101–16; Bramwell, *Blood and Soil*, p. 176; Peter Staudenmaier, 'Organic Farming in Nazi Germany: The Politics of Biodynamic Agriculture, 1933–1945', in *Environmental History* (2013), p. 14.

47. Rauschning reports Hitler as saying, 'Ourselves or the Freemasons or the Church.' Hitler ostensibly continued, 'there is room for one of the three and no more . . . and we are the strongest of the three and shall get rid of the other two', Rauschning, *Voice of Destruction*, pp. 240–1.

48. Kersten, *Memoirs*, pp. 29–36; Sebottendorff, *Bevor Hitler kam*, p. 23.

49. Treitel, *Science*, pp. 216–19; SS Spengler writes SS/SD, 1.10.41; Heydrich to organizations, 12.1.42, in R58/1029; Werner, *Anthroposophen*, p. 310.

50. Chris Thomas, 'Defining "Freemason": Compromise, Pragmatism, and German Lodge Members in the NSDAP', *German Studies Review* 35:3 (October 2012), pp. 587–605; Ralf Melzer, 'In the Eye of the Hurricane: German Freemasonry in the Weimar Republic and the Third Reich', *Totalitarian Movements and Political Religions* 4:2 (Autumn 2003), pp. 113–32.

51. SD report from 30.6.41, pp. 6–7. BAB: R 58/6517. Thomas, 'Defining "Freemason"', pp. 587–605; David Cesarani, *Becoming Eichmann: Rethinking the Life, Crimes, and Trial of a 'Desk Murderer'*, Cambridge: Da Capo Press, 2006, pp. 362, 44–5; see also Staudenmaier, 'Nazi Perceptions of Esotericism', pp. 32–40.

52. See SV, 2.5.33, in NL Herbert Frank, IfZG: 414/38; Kugel, *Hanussen*, p. 214; Treitel, *Science*, pp. 232–3.

53. Corroborating this explanation is the fact that his office was destroyed and phone lines were cut after his murder, while Karl Ernst had possession of Hanussen's receipts for money loaned to Helldorf when he was killed in 1934. Cziffra, *Hanussen*, pp. 180–2; Kugel and Bahar, *Reichstagsbrand*, pp. 647–53; Treitel, *Science*, p. 233; Kugel, *Hanussen*, pp. 247–8, 260.

54. Kugel, *Hanussen*, pp. 202–3, 214, 246, 290–328; NL Herbert Frank, IfZG: 414/138, Ludendorff on Hanussen, 2.5.33; Treitel, *Science*, pp. 233–4; Hett, *Burning the Reichstag*, pp. 106–7, 131–2; Treitel, *Science*, pp. 233–4; Kugel and Bahar, *Reichstagsbrand*, pp. 15–16, 644–9.

55. Treitel, *Science*, pp. 232–4; Sickinger, 'Hitler and the Occult'; Hanussen's friend Hanns Heinz Ewers was also marginalized after 1933, but his occult and supernatural beliefs played little part in this. Ewers remained active in the Third Reich, obtaining reinstatement into the RSK and the right to publish after 1934. H. Ewers: R 9361–V/5138, 6.8.38, RMVP agrees to change Verbot for *Ameisen* and *Augen*; 12.6.41 Karl Karsch: 11.7.34, Reichsminister für Wiss., Erziehung, und Volksbildung noting the success of Wessel; 24.7.41, note to publisher Englehardt; 13.8.41, letter to Ewers; 18.6.43, FrZtg positive nachruf; 15.6.36.

56. Treitel, *Science*, p. 221; Staudenmaier, 'Nazi Perceptions of Esotericism', pp. 35–7.

57. Treitel, *Science*, pp. 223–4; 25.7.38, letter from SD to RSHA; 23.7.38, Hauer forwards chain letter, BAB: R 58 6206.

58. Frank-Rutger Hausmann, *Hans Bender (1907–1991) und das 'Institut für Psychologie und Klinische Psychologie' an der Reichsuniversität Straßburg 1941–1944*, Würzburg: Ergon, 2006, pp. 46–8; see also reports, including letter from RFSS to Minister of Interior, February 1937, BAB: R 58/6207.

59. See Karsten, *Vampyre*; BAB: NS 18/497, Neumann to Hörmann, 12.9.40,

60. Treitel, *Science*, 219; see also Annika Spiker, *Geschlecht, Religion und völkischer Nationalismus: Die Ärztin und Antisemitin Mathilde von Kemnitz-Ludendorff*, Frankfurt: Campus, 2013, pp. 99–134.

61. Articles from 19.2.33, 3.3.33, and 28.3.33, in NL Herbert Frank, IfZG: 414/138; Karsten, *Vampyre*, pp. 5–11; Albert Stadthagen, *Die Raetsel des Spiritismus: Erklaerung der mediumistischen Phaenomene und Anletiung die Wunder der vierten Dimension ohne Medium und Geister ausfuehren zu koennen (mit Illustrationen)*, Leipzig: Ficker's, 1911, pp. 5–11; Carl Pelz, *Die Hellseherin*, Munich: Ludendorff, 1937.

62. Articles from 19.2.33, 26.3.33, 28.3.33, in NL Herbert Frank, IfZG: 414/138.

63. Karsten, *Vampyre*, pp. 3–4; Mathilde Ludendorff: BAB: R 1507/2091, pp. 178–80: 28.12.31 correspondence by Röhm with Ludendorff; Pelz to Rosenberg (January 1941); Stadthagen to Tietze, 1.26.41, BAB: NS 15/399, pp. 110–11.

64. Karsten, *Vampyre*, pp. 9–16, 53–4.

65. Ibid., pp. 62–4; Ludendorff, *Der Trug der Astrologie*, Munich: Ludendorff, 1932; Rehwaldt, *Religion*; Treitel, *Science*, 219; Spiker, *Geschlecht*, pp. 166–204.

66. Karsten, *Vampyre*; Ludendorff, *Trug der Astrologie*; Hermann Rehwaldt, *Die Kommendo Religion*, Munich: Ludendorff, 1936; Treitel, *Science*, pp. 219–20; Spiker, *Geschlecht*, pp. 166–204.

67. Karsten, *Vampyre*, pp. 69–70.

68. Ibid., pp. 64–9; Ludendorff, *Trug der Astrologie*; Rehwaldt, *Religion*.

69. Treitel, *Science*, p. 225.

70. Ludendorff, *Trug der Astrologie*, pp. 1–2.

71. Ibid., p. 2.

72. Ibid., pp. 5–18: 'Astrologers claiming to be an ancient faith and also a young science were inherently contradictory and damaging. But so long as mixing of blood made humans rootless,' Ludendorff concluded, these Semitic forms of occultism would dominate.

73. 'Die Astrologie – eine Wissenschaft?', IGPP: 10/5 AII56.

74. Kaufmann, *Tibet*, pp. 107–14; Isrun Engelhardt, 'Nazis of Tibet: A Twentieth-Century Myth', in Monica Esposito (ed.), *Images of Tibet in the 19th and 20th Centuries*, Paris: École française d'Extrême-Orient (EFEO), coll. Études thématiques 22:1 (2008), pp. 63–96.

75. Heiden, 'Preface', pp. 10–11.

76. Hermann Rehwaldt, *Geheimbuende in Afrika*, Munich: Ludendorff, 1941, pp. 55–6.

77. 'Reports contradict each other insofar as [one of Ludendorff's closest collaborators] is portrayed [both] hand as an occultist and a fanatical Ludendorff-enthusiast.' SD report on Ludendorff supporter, Küchenmeister, 23.6.39. 'Although a "fanatical supporter of Ludendorff"', Küchenmeister's 'books on "shadow men" and the unnatural death of Schiller' represent clearly esoteric tendencies, the SD report continued, concluding that 'It requires more research to grasp which occultist circles with which Küchenmeister is associated.' BAB: R 58/6217; Rehwaldt approved as member of Bund Reichsdeutscher Buchhandler, 11.8.36, RVDP to Rehwaldt, 5.6.39, BAB: R 9361–V; letter to Hermann Rehwaldt from the Führer des SD-Leitabschnittes, 12.12.40, BAB: R 58/7313.

78. Pelz, *Hellseherin*; Stadthagen, Leipzig: Ficker's, 1911, pp. 5–11.

79. Carl Pelz Report to Kripo, 28.2.37; Nebe to Himmler, 23.3.37, 24.4.37, BAB: R 58/6206.

80. Nebe to Himmler, 23.3.37, 24.4.37, BAB: R 58/6206.

81. Ibid.

82. See Robert Gellately, *Backing Hitler: Consent and Coercion in Nazi Germany*, Oxford: Oxford, 2001; Robert Gellately, *The Gestapo and German Society: Enforcing Racial Policy 1933–1945*, Oxford: Clarendon Press, 1990; Eric Johnson, *Nazi Terror: The Gestapo, Jews and Ordinary Germans*, New York: Basic Books, 1999.

83. According to Peter Staudenmaier, the SD's hostility was less related to ideology than occultism's lack of authority and 'search of an image and mission', namely an attempt to prove itself by identifying and subsequently exaggerating the danger of 'ideological enemies', in 'Nazi Perceptions of Esotericism', pp. 38–42. See also Staudenmaier, *Occultism*, pp. 214–22; see also Wolfgang Dierker, *Himmlers Glaubenskrieger: Der Sicherheitsdienst der SS und seine Religionspolitik, 1933–1941*, Paderborn: Ferdinand Schöningh, 2002.

84. See Adam Tooze, *The Wages of Destruction*, London: Penguin, 2006, pp. 238–9; Ian Kershaw, *Hitler: Nemesis*, London/New York: Norton, 2001, pp. 43–60.

85. See Kurlander, 'Supernatural Sciences', in Black and Kurlander, eds, *Revisiting*, pp. 135–43, 145–51; Treitel, *Science*, pp. 214–15.

86. Bernard Hörmann 'Gesundheitsfuehrung und geistige Infektionen', *Volksgesundheitswacht* (VGW) 10 (May 1937), IGPP 10/5 BIII (Bender-Hellwig); BAB: R 58/6207.

87. See Treitel, *Science*, pp. 210–11, 222–3; Sickinger, 'Hitler and the Occult'; Staudenmaier, 'Nazi Perceptions of Esotericism', pp. 39–44.

88. Treitel, *Science*, pp. 221–2; Otto Urbach, *Reich des Aberglaubens*, Bad Homburg: Siemens, 1938, pp. 4–20, 49–65; R58/6215b: attacks on sectariansism.

89. Howe, *Nostradamus*, p. 129; Treitel, *Science*, p. 224; Howe, *Urania's Children*, pp. 114–19; Treitel, *Science*, pp. 226–8; 13.6.37, Stellvertreter des Führers wants answer from SD as to request from Int. Astrologen Kongress 19–25 July 1937 for Devisiebgenehmigung; Congress in Baden, BAB: R 58/6207.

90. Treitel, *Science*, pp. 228–30; Howe, *Urania's Children*, pp. 114–18; SD letter from 23.8.38, BAB: R 58/6205.

91. Treitel, *Science*, pp. 238–9; see also reports from 4.8.38, 30.7.38, BAB: R 58/6207.

92. See Hörmann article, 'Schutz der ernsthaften Wissenschaft', July 1937, BAB: NS 5VI/16959; Bernhard Hörmann Report on Johannes Verweyen from 2.2.37 and letter to Reichsschrifttumskammer (RSK), 30.7 38, BAB: R 9361V/89324; Reports on occultism addressed to Hörmann from 2.9.38 and 13.12.938, BAB: R 58/6206; Herlbauer to Hörmann, 26.2.37; Herlbauer to Kittler, 3.12.37; Herlbauer to Hitler's Chancellery, 7.2.38, BAB: R 58/6217.

93. Hörmann, 'Gesundheitsfuehrung'.

94. 'In an important sense, the point of *weltanschauliche Gegnerforschung* was to construct its targets and its objects of study, to create a profile of occultist tendencies and shape an image of the enemy into the mold prepared for it, and then mobilize against this invented opponent.' Staudenmaier, 'Nazi Perceptions of Esotericism', pp. 49–50.

95. See articles in *Volksgesundheitswacht 1937* 14 (July), pp. 211–12, 213–22; Kurd Kisshauer, 'Die Astrologie – eine Wissenschaft'; VB, 5.10.38, publishes article 'Sterne und Schiksal. Kostproben astrologischer Propheziehungen', BAB: NS 5–VI/16959.

96. Schreiber to Stadthagen, 14.1.41, BAB: NS 15/399.

97. KdF report, 28.2.41, BAB: NS 15/399.

98. Gestapo writes DAF, KdF division, Amt Deutsches Volksbildungswerk, 7.2.41, BAB: NS 15/399.

99. As Treitel has put it, 'Even under the general rubric of hostility . . . the [Nazi] official response to occultism was multivalent, and not all forms of occult activity were treated in the same way.' Treitel, *Science*, p. 231; Schellinger, et al., 'Zwischen Szientismus und Okkultismus: Grenzwissenschaftliche Experimente der deutschen Marine im Zweiten Weltkrieg', *Zeitschrift für Anomalistik* 10 (2010), pp. 287–321.

100. Treitel, *Science*, pp. 228–30, 238–9; SS-Unterstrumführer and SD Unterabschnitt, Nils Klimsch, has connections to occultism and an occult library, 8.3.38; 12.3.38, Aktennotiz. 11.3.38, Zentralbibliothek, BAB: R 58/6206,

101. Hausmann, *Hans Bender*, pp. 46–8. See letters Hellwig to Bender in IGPP 10 – 5 BIII (Bender-Hellwig), pp. 155–8; report to DAF/Deutsches Volksbildungswerk, 5.6.39, BAB: NS 18/497, Rolf Sylvéro (Eduard Neumann) Experimental-Psychologe; Werner, *Anthroposophen*, pp. 56–7.

102. Evidence of Ausweis for RSK/RVDP permission to publish, 29.8.35; Korsch inquiry, 26.6.40; Anmeldung, 20.3.37; 13.8.37, 'Ersuchen aus dem Strafregister'; 16.7.34, letter from RVDP to board of 'Orga'; 21.6.34, letter from RSK; 19.7.38, response from RSK to letter from Korsch, 22.12.37; 3.2.38, letter from Metzner in RSK, 9.9.37, and later 23.1.40, discussing conviction for immorality and lying, which Korsch appeals (21.4.40), and which is rejected on 12.6.40. BAB: R 9361–V/7196.

103. Himmler to Heydrich, 10.1.39, BAB: R 58/6207; for more on the SD and Gestapo's careful attempts to differentiate between 'scientific occultism' and occult charlatanry, see Haselbacher to Gestapo, 29.3.37, Nebe to Himmler, 24.4.37, Aktennotiz, 12.3.38, Peer Review reports forwarded from Hörmann to Ehlich, 13.12.38, BAB: R 58/6206.

104. Report to Heydrich, 23.6.38, BAB: R 58/6207.

105. Report from 4.8.38; 29.9.38, Himmler agrees to endorse Geheimisse Mächte pamphlet; 10.1.39, Himmler to Heydrich, BAB: R 58/6207.

106. Himmler to Heydrich 1.10.39, BAB: R 58/6207.

107. Deutsche Arbeitsfront (okkultismus): *Volksgesundheitswacht 1947 Nr. 14 Juli*, pp. 211–12, Long article on Bernhard Hörmann's 'Schutz der ernsthaften Wissenschaft', BAB: NS 5–VI/16959.

108. Ibid., *Volksgesundheitswacht 1947*.

109. Report from Kiendl to Hörmann, 2.9.38, 13.12.38, BAB: R 58/6206; Herlbauer to Hörmann, 26.2.37; Herlbauer to Hitler's Chancellery, 7.2.38; Bayer to Kittler, 13.3.38; Rossnagel to Kittler, 21.5.38, Kittler to Herlbauer, 1.7.38; see also Staudenmaier, *Between Occultism and Nazism*, p. 126; Howe, *Urania's Children*, pp. 173–6, 178–81; Hans Frank, *Im Angesichts des Galgens: Deutung Hitlers und seiner Zeit auf Grund eigener Erlebnisse und Erkenntnisse. Geschrieben im Nürnberger, Justizgefängnis*, Munich: Beck, 1953, p. 15, BAB: R 58/6217.

110. Treitel, *Science*, pp. 238–9.

111. Pelz to Tietze, 1.26.41, BAB: NS 15/399, p. 111.

112. Attachment to Tietze's letter, 28.1.41; Stadthagen to Tietze, 26.1.41, BAB: NS 15/399, pp. 110–11, BAB: NS 15/399, pp. 90–1; Pelz to Tietze, 26.1.41, BAB: NS 15/399, p. 111.

113. Report from Kiendl to Hörmann, 2.9.38, 13.12.38, BAB: R 58/6206; Herlbauer to Hörmann, 26.2.37; Herlbauer to Hitler's Chancellery, 7.2.38; Bayer to Kittler, 13.3.38; Rossnagel to Kittler, 21.5.38; Kittler to Herlbauer, 1.7.38; Frank, *Im Angesichts des Galgens*, p. 15; SD letter from 2.8.38, 8.12.36 letter to Frick, BAB: R 58/6205.

114. VB, 29.4.37, 'Aus dem Lesebuch des Zauberlehrlings. Von Abracadabra bis zum Magischen Zirkel', Article honouring 8–10 May celebration of Magic circle, BAB: NS 5–VI/16959.

115. Treitel, *Science*, pp. 238–9.

116. *Gutachten* on Sternenmacht und Liebesleben: 5.1.38, RSK first writes to ban book; 16.2.38, RSK writes RMVP to request that book be banned, R 56–V/1150.

117. *Gutachten* on Sternenmacht und Liebesleben, RSK report from 21.12.37, describing the situation, BAB: R 56–V/1150.

118. Ibid.

119. 'Instead of comparing two horoscopes and multiple factors of importance inscribed therein,' Rosten observed, 'the author restricts herself merely to comparing two kinds of Zodiac signs. Since one can never find pure representations of types of Zodiac signs as a consequence of the many possible combinations of the constellations of the planets within a horoscope, the comparison of two types of Zodiac signs can never have practical meaning.' Ibid.

120. 'The exposition of the author regarding the position of the moon in individial signs appears just as grotesque.' 'Through this kind of advice lay people will only inculcate nonsense in a form that can only be harmful because it must produce a fully errroneous view of the actual effective laws of harmony between man and wife.' BAB: R 56–V/1150, *Gutachten* on Sternenmacht und Liebesleben: *Gutachten* from Rosten, 21.12.37.

121. *Gutachten* on Sternenmacht und Liebesleben, 10.5.38, BAB: R 56–V/1150.
122. See letters from 9.11.23, 20.4.37, 26.8.36, 13.11.37; 17.10.38, 18.10.38 letters, BAB: R 55/24198.
123. Dokument Abschriftlich, BAB: R 43 II/479. *Gutachten* Hugo Koch, RMVP, zu pro-Astrologie-Politik der PPK Berlin, 20.5.41; http://www.polunbi.de/archiv/41–05–20–01.html.
124. See letter from DAF, 30.1.40, BAB: NS 8/185, p. 53.
125. See Kittler report for PPK, 3.8.38; RMVP report from 10.5.41, BAB: R 43 II/479a; http://www.polunbi.de/archiv/39–11–29–01.html.
126. See Kiendl's support for Werner Kittler's 'original and useful method, in which he brought together natural scientists and astrologers' in work groups within the Reich Literary Chamber (RSK) and Reich Ministry of Propaganda (RMVP), report from Kiendl to Hörmann, 2.9.38, BAB: R 58/6206; Werner Kittler, 14.3.38, 13.6.38, BAB: R 9361V/1107.
127. Dokument Abschriftlich, BAB: R 43 II/ 479a, *Gutachten* Hugo Koch, RMVP, zu pro-Astrologie-Politik der PPK Berlin, 20.5.41; http://www.polunbi.de/archiv/41–05–20–01.html.
128. Ibid.
129. 'Confident in his own ability to divine the future direction of Germany, Hitler had no need of astrologers and others who claimed special insights. In fact, such people were a genuine threat to his own power.' Sickinger, 'Hitler and the Occult'.
130. Karl Heinz Hederich, PPK to RSK, Abt. Schrifttum – Stellungnahme gegen Verbot astrologischer Literatur Berlin, 14.10.39; Rosenberg to Bouhler, 29.11.39, BAB: R 43 II/ 479a; http://www.polunbi.de/archiv/39–10–14–01.html.
131. Not to mention the fact, Hederich concluded, that it was 'childish to think that the National Socialist movement could be endangered through astrological publications'. Rosenberg to Bouhler, 29.11.39, BAB: R 43 II/479a; http://www.polunbi.de/archiv/39–11–29–01.html.
132. Rosenberg to Joseph Goebbels 'gegen Unterstützung astrologischen Schrifttums durch die PPK' Berlin, 29.11.1939, BAB: R 43 II/479a; http://www.polunbi.de/archiv/39–11–29–01.html.
133. Ibid.
134. Goebbels was far more tolerant of the occult and superstition, for example, than he was of cabarets. Memo by Joseph Goebbels. 'Trotz meiner wiederholten Erlasse vom 8. Dezember 1937, 6 Mai 1939 und 11. Dezember 1940', BAB: R 2/4871.
135. Treitel, *Science*, p. 39.
136. Stadthagen to Hörmann, President of the German Assocation for Combating Negative Inluences in Public Health, 26.1.41, BAB: NS 15/399.
137. Pelz to Rosenberg (January 1941); Stadthagen to Tietze, 26.1.41, BAB: NS 15/399, pp. 110–11; see also Mauer to Deutsche Verlag, 27.12.39, Pelz to RSK, 1.1.40, RSK to Pelz, 17.1.40, discussion with Buhl, 20.12.39, letterhead with 'Carl Pelz, Vortragsredner des Reichsamtes Detusches Volksbildungswerk', BAB: R 9361–V/9000.
138. Schreiber to Stadthagen, 14.1.41; Stadthagen to Hörmann, 26.1.41, BAB: NS 15/399.
139. Schreiber to Stadthagen, 14.1.41, BAB: NS 15/399.
140. Schreiber to Stadthagen, 20.2.41, BAB: NS 15/399.
141. Stadthagen to Schreiber, 16.3.41, BAB: NS 15/399.
142. Ibid.
143. Stadthagen to Schreiber, 16.3.41, BAB: NS 15/399.
144. Ibid.
145. Ibid.
146. See Kershaw, *Hubris*, pp. 168–9; Eric Kurlander, 'Violence, Volksgemeinschaft, and Empire: Interpreting the Third Reich in the Twenty-First Century', *Journal of Contemporary History* 46:4 (2011), pp. 921–4.
147. Stadthagen to Hörmann, 26.1.41, BAB: NS 15/399; see Kershaw, 'Working towards the Führer: Reflections on the Nature of the Hitler Dictatorship', *Contemporary European History* 2:2 (July 1993), pp. 103–18.
148. Stadthagen to Hörmann, 26.1.41, BAB: NS 15/399.
149. Ibid.
150. Stadthagen to Hörmann, 19.2.41; Hörmann to Stadthagen, 3.2.41, BAB: NS 15/399.
151. Letter from Hitler's Chancellery to Kisshauer, 31.3.41, BAB: NS 15/399.
152. Stadthagen to Brümmel, 22.2.41, BAB: NS 15/399.
153. Pelz Enclosure, 6.2.41, BAB: NS 15/399.
154. Gestapo to DAF, 7.2.41, BAB: NS 15/399.
155. DAF notations on Gestapo letter, 7.2.41, BAB: NS 15/399.
156. KdF division III/Vortragswesen to Rosenberg, 28.2.41, BAB: NS 15/399.
157. Ibid.
158. Attachment to letter, including letter from Pelz to Rosenberg personally, 28.1.41, BAB: NS 15/399.

159. KdF division III/Vortragswesen (Tietze) to 'Beauftragten des Führers für die Überwachung der gesamten geistigen und weltanschaulichen Schulung und Erziehung der NSDAP, 28.2.41, BAB: NS 15/399.

160. Ibid.

161. See again attachment to letter, including letter from Pelz to Rosenberg personally, 28.4.4, BAB: NS 15/399.

162. Letter to Reichsminister und Chef der Reichskanzlei, 2.4.41, in Gutterer's Representative; http://www.polunbi.de/archiv/39-11-29-01.html.

163. Werner, Anthroposophen, pp. 248–9, 259–61.

164. Letter to Reinhard Heydrich requesting Heinrich Träncker's astrological library to be delivered to Himmler due to his great interest in such matters, 4.12.39; 5.12.39, another letter asking Heydrich for all these materials to be sent to Himmler; 6.1.40, Denkschrift zur Astrologie discussed; 16.2.40, RSHA letter reporting on Denkschrift and Himmler's request that SD reprint of Denkschrift from 6.7.38 discussion, BAB: R 58/6207; Treitel, Science, p. 230; Werner, Anthroposophen, pp. 302–3; 7.9.39, Kisshauer to SS Hartl, and 4.9.39, Kisshauer Denkschrift, 'Astrologie als Mittel zur Beeinflussung der Volksstimmung', BAB: R 58/6207.

165. When the war broke out, many astrological newspapers, anthroposophical institutions, professional dowsers, and practising 'cosmobiologists' were still in circulation. Treitel, Science, pp. 228–30; Goodrick-Clarke, Occult Roots, pp. 118–19, 192–7; Bramwell, Blood and Soil, pp. 95–6, 129; Glowka, Okkultgruppen, p. 28.

166. Rainer F. Schmidt, Rudolf Hess. Botengang eines Toren?, Düsseldorf: Econ, 1997, p. 198. Some observers still claim that Hess was murdered by British intelligence to prevent him revealing secrets about British misconduct in the war. Although some questions remain, the autopsy did appear to confirm the cause of death. See Roy Conyers Nesbitt and Georges van Acker, The Flight of Rudolf Hess: Myths and Reality, Stroud: History Press, 2007, pp. 83–97.

167. Ibid., pp. 197–8.

168. Howe, Urania's Children, pp. 192–5; Schellinger, 'Hess', pp. 321–2.

169. Schmidt, Hess, p. 198; Staudenmaier, Between Nazism and Occultism, p. 230; Bormann's hostility to occultism was not quite as intense as his 'absolutely diabolical hatred of Christianity'. But he viewed both belief systems as rivals to Nazi ideology. Trevor-Roper, ed., Bormann Letters, p. xvi.

170. The Hess Affair was 'a tragic comedy [about which] one could simultaneously laugh and cry . . . The whole thing arose from the atmosphere of his faith healing and grass eating. A thoroughly pathological affair.' Treitel, Science, pp. 216–17; Staudenmaier, 'Nazi Perceptions of Esotericism', p. 46; Werner, Anthroposophen, p. 304; Schellinger, 'Hess', p. 322.

171. On 14 May, four days after Hess's flight, Bormann reported gleefully to Heydrich that Hitler had finally decided to move against 'occultists, astrologers, natural healers and the like who seduce the people to stupidity and superstition'. Werner, Anthroposophen, p. 304; Peter Longerich, Hitlers Stellvertreter. Führung der Partei und Kontrolle des Staatsapparates durch den Stab Heß und die Partei-Kanzlei Bormann, Munich: K. G. Saur, 1992, p. 153; Staudenmaier, 'Nazi Perceptions of Esotericism', p. 46; Hitler ostensibly shortly after Hess's flight: 'to me this step seems to have been co-authored by these astrology cronies whom Heß allowed to influence him. It is thus high time to radically clear up this astrology rubbish.' Frank, Im Angesichts des Galgens, p. 401; Schellinger, 'Hess', p. 320.

172. Treitel, Science, p. 225.

173. Ibid., p. 225.

174. Even with Heydrich, the SD, and the Gestapo receiving carte blanche to arrest occultists, the Third Reich's 'Janus-faced attitude toward German occultism' persisted. Schellinger, 'Hess', pp. 323–5.

175. Staudenmaier, 'Occultism, Race and Politics', pp. 325–7.

176. Schmidt, Hess, 192–7.

177. Christopher Browning, The Origins of the Final Solution, Jerusalem: Yad Vashem, pp. 252–3.

178. Publishing an article in the Völkischer Beobachter on 14 May detailing Hess's occult proclivities and writing in his diaries two days later, 'The whole obscure swindle is now finally rooted out. The miracle men, Hess's darlings, are going under lock and key.' Treitel, Science, pp. 216–17; Schellinger et al., 'Pragmatic Occultism'.

179. Robert Gerwarth, Hitler's Hangman: The Life of Heydrich, New Haven, CT, and London: Yale University Press, 2011, pp. 86–93, 106–7, 185–6; Werner, Anthroposophen, p. 309; Schellinger, 'Hess', p. 322; Staudenmaier, Occultism, pp. 214–15. In a broader sense, Heydrich felt the SD was being marginalized within the SS police apparatus, as the shift had focused away from policing 'sectarian' tendencies to pursuing Jews, Poles, and other alien groups. In short, the Hess Action was an opportunity for the SD to assert its authority in designating and policing Nazism's ideological enemies. Staudenmaier, Between Occultism and Nazism, pp. 216–17.

180. Heydrich to Gauleiter, 4.6.41, BAB: R 58/1029.

181. Ibid.
182. Heydrich to Lohse, 21.6.41, BAB: R 58/1029; Schellinger, 'Hess', pp. 321–2.
183. Letter from 8.12.41, 14.1.42 to AMT VII; 27.1.42, another box sent to AMT VII, BAB: R 58/6204.
184. This included the German Society for Scientific Occultism (DGWO), for example. The group *had* changed its name to the 'German Metaphysical Society' in order to avoid the same level of surveillance. See BAB: R 58/6216a and R 58/6217. See extensive lists of individuals detained and materials confiscated across Germany and Austria in the wake of the June 1941 Hess Action; Schellinger et al., 'Pragmatic Occultism', pp. 160–1; Treitel, *Science*, pp. 211–12, 241–2; Schellinger, 'Hess'.
185. Howe, *Urania's Children*, pp. 194–7.
186. Werner, *Anthroposophen*, pp. 303–4, 335; BAK: N 1094II-1. Darré to Peuckert, 27.6.1941, Bartsch detained; Staudenmaier, 'Organic Farming', pp. 10–11.
187. Treitel, *Science*, p. 238; Howe, *Urania's Children*, pp. 196–203.
188. See various letters, BAB: R 9361–V/38599, R 9361–V/89324.
189. Treitel, *Science*, p. 238; Howe, *Urania's Children*, pp. 198–203.
190. Treitel, *Science*, p. 224; Schellinger, 'Hess', pp. 323–7; Staudenmaier, *Between Occultism and Nazism*, pp. 234–40; files on occult persecution, BAB: R 58/6216a.
191. Treitel, *Science*, p. 238. See also Hans Weinert, *Hellsehen und Wahrsagen ein uralter Traum der Menschheit*, Leipzig: Helingsche Verlagsanstalt, 1943.
192. Rosenberg to Bormann, 20.5.41, BAB: NS 8/185, pp. 47–8.
193. Ibid.
194. Ibid.
195. Ibid. See also Kurlander, 'Supernatural Sciences'.
196. See report 'Kampf für und gegen Astrologie und Okkultismus', BAB: NS 8/185 *Amt Rosenberg*, pp. 64–8.
197. Ibid.
198. 'Kampf für und gegen Astrologie und Okkultismus', pp. 66–8.
199. Bormann to Goebbels, 30.6.41, BAB: NS 18/211.
200. Ibid.
201. Goebbels directive, 15.5.41, BAB: NS 43/1650.
202. Goebbels to Bormann, 3.7.41, BAB: NS 18/211.
203. Schreiben Joseph Goebbels, RMVP, an Hans Lammers zu Kompetenzen des RMVP und der PPK bei der Buchzensur Berlin, 26.6.41; Goebbels to Bouhler, 7.7.41, Hugo Kochs, 20.5.1941: BAB: R 43 II/ 479a; http://www.polunbi.de/archiv/39–11–29–01.html.
204. See Pelz's affidavit, 'Verpflichtungserklärung', 7.7.41; Schreiber to Tietze (DAF), 16.7.41; Notice to Kisshauer of Propaganda Ministry Conference, 9.9.41; see the report declaring that 'Contributions on pseudo-occultism and related areas by Criminal Commissioner a.D. Carl Pelz amy once more be permitted', 9.9.41; DAF to Kisshauer, 9.9.41, BAB: NS 15/399.
205. Pelz, 'Verpflichtungserklärung', 7.7.41; Schreiber to Tietze (DAF), 16.7.41, BAB: NS 15/399.
206. Heydrich to Darré, 18.10.41, NL Darré, BAK: N1094II-1.
207. 'Given this, one could venture to think that Bender would have been vulnerable to similar actions against himself. There was, however, a standard delineated that scientific research concerning occult and paranormal phenomena was not prohibited – an important loophole, so to speak, for Bender.' Anna Lux, 'On all Channels', in Black and Kurlander, eds, *Revisiting*, p. 228; Werner, *Anthroposophen*, p. 306; Treitel, *Science*, p. 225; Schellinger et al., 'Pragmatic Occultism'.
208. SD report from AMT VII, 22.9.41; Murawski proposal, 14.5.41; letter from Spengler, 27.6.41; letter from Schick, 30.1.42, BAB: R 58/6517.
209. Letter to DAF/Deutsches Volksbildungswerk, 5.7.39, BAB: NS 18/497.
210. Pfriemer (Reichstelle gegen Mißstuande im Gesundheitswesen) to Tiessler, 24.1.42, BAB: NS 18/497.
211. Sylvéro to Gauring, local office of the Ministry for Public Enlightenment and Propaganda, 3.8.41, RMVP Bayreuth letter of inquiry, 9.8.41, RMVP to Sylvéro, 19.8.41, BAB: NS 18/497.
212. The official Reich ban on occultism in June hadn't caused Neumann undue stress, in fact, since as late as 1 August 1941, according to a local Bavarian RMVP official, he had given a performance in eastern Bavaria, insisting that he had the approval of Hitler's Reich Chancellery, which was the case. Letter from RMVP, 11.8.41, Neumann to Kremer, 19.8.41. BAB: NS 18/497.
213. Sylvéro to RMVP, 21.8.41, BAB: NS 18/497.
214. Ibid.
215. Sylvéro to Reichsring, 31.8.41; 11.9.41; RMVP to Sylvéro, 12.9.41, BAB: NS 18/497.
216. Ibid.
217. RMVP, 1.9.41, BAB: NS 18/497.
218. Report on Veranstaltung Sylvéro, 15.9.41, BAB: NS 18/497
219. Ibid.; RMVP to Reichsring, 24.9.41, DVB in KdF, 30.9.41, determining not to employ Sylvéro. BAB: NS 18/497.

220. Letter from KdF, 16.10.41, including report from 25.9.41, BAB: NS 18/497.

221. Munich KdF writes to Berlin KdF employee Tietze, 16.10.41, BAB: NS 18/497.

222. Ibid.

223. Sylvéro writes to Tiessler, 12.1.42, showing letter that he mentioned in conversations on 5 and 8 January that as of 9 December 1940 he had already agreed to conduct experimental presentations in connection with Hörmann, BAB: NS 18/497.

224. Sylvéro to Tiessler, 12.1.42, BAB: NS 18/497.

225. Tiessler to Hörmann, 16.1.42, BAB: NS 18/497.

226. Pfriemer to Tiessler, 24.1.42, referring to a report from 5.6.39 that his office had already sent to DAF/DVBW, BAB: NS 18/497.

227. Pfriemer to Tiessler, 24.1.42, BAB: NS 18/497.

228. In conclusion, Pfriemer noted that the compromising information had to do with an anti-occult speaker in Dresden, Bernhard Springer, who claimed that Sylvéro appeared under his name. Pfriemer to Tiessler, 24.1.42, BAB: NS 18/497.

229. Tiessler to Neumann, 28.1.42, BAB: NS 18/497.

230. Neumann to Reichsring (Tiessler), 17.2.42, BAB: NS 18/497.

231. Sylvéro to Tiessler, 29.4.42, to confirm the conversation on 20.4.42 and the next meeting in October 1942, BAB: NS 18/497.

232. Ibid.

233. Mueller to Tiessler, 8.7.42, asking for response to letter from 12.5.42; letter to Spangenberg in Reichsring, 29.12.42; Reichsring to RMVP, 26.8.41; Christiansen to RMVP, 26.8.41, BAB: NS 18/497; Propaganda reports, 30.4.43, BAB: R 58/210, pp. 13–14.

234. Hitler and Goebbels preferred to wait until after the war to settle scores with Galen and the rest of the Church. See Nathan Stoltzfus, *Hitler's Compromises: Coercion and Consensus in Nazi Germany*, New Haven, Ct: Yale University Press, 2016, p. 201.

235. See correspondence from Stellvertreter des Führers to Hauptamt für Volkswohlfahrt, 5.2.37; Janowitz in Personalabteilung writes to NSDAP Sstab des Stellvertrter des Führeres, 19.1.37; Daluege writes to Rachor in Brown Hause on 10.12.36, BAB: NS 37/3630.

236. See Kisshauer article (1937), 'Die Astrologie – eine Wissenschaft', BAB: NS 5VI/16959; Kisshauer to Kittler, 14.4.39, BAB: R 58/6206; Kisshauer *Denkschrift* and letter to Hartl, 7.9.39; Rudolph to Kittler, 4.6.40, BAB: R 58/6217.

237. 'Practical accuracy', Kisshauer wrote, 'is a necessary precondition, for otherwise the author can be easily dismissed as laughable in the circles of those who are well informed in occult matters, whose number is still very large.' Clearly the author failed to understand that 'the ascendant stemming from the sixth house' was 'astrologically impossible' while he confused Saturn and Jupiter. More exasperating for Kisshauer was the line 'Mercury and moon stand in a sixty-degree angle to the earth', since it is completely unastrological to speak of this facet in connection to the earth. See letters from 25.8.41, BAB: NS 15/399,.

238. See Schellinger et al., 'Pragmatic Occultism'; Schellinger, *'Szientismus'*; Kurlander, 'Supernatural Science', in Wulff, *Zodiac*, pp. 2–94.

239. Much better than opening a public discussion, Irkowsky suggested, was to assemble a local jury and deal with such issues on a case-by-case basis, through the police. BAB: NS 18/497, Irkowsky to Tiessler, 3.12.41.

240. Tiessler to Irkowsky, 5.12.41, BAB: NS 18/497; as Goebbels' representative in Bormann's Party Chancellery, Tiessler frequently advocated the importance of maintaining a positive morale over Bormann's efforts to attack occultism or Christianity. Steigmann-Gall, *Holy Reich*, pp. 249–50.

241. Tiessler to Rosenberg, 6.12.41, BAB: NS 18/497.

242. Irkowsky to Tiessler, 13.12.41, BAB: NS 18/497.

243. Christian Goepfert, *Immer noch Aberglaube!*, Zürich: Zwingli Verlag, 1943, pp. 3–11.

244. Werner, *Anthroposophen*, p. 341.

245. Schellinger, 'Hess', pp. 324–5; see letters from Bischof to RMVP, 8.8.40, to Loth, 5.12.42, Meyer to RSK, 30.6.41, Ewers to RSK, 10.6.40, Ewers to RSK, 13.2.42, RSK to Ewers, 15.4.41, Cotta to RSK, 12.2.42, 30.3.42, W. J. Becker to RSK, 18.6.43, BAB: R 9361-V/5138.

246. Only after 1933 did 'alternative culture became criminally deviant' and 'occultists, like so many others who belonged to suspect groups, face[d] state terror'. 'Although the occult may have played a minor part in the "fool's paradise" inhabited by top Nazi leaders,' Treitel concludes, 'the fact remains that escalating hostility was the dominant theme in the regime's response to the occult movement.' Treitel, *Science*, pp. 241–2.

247. Ibid., p. 209.

248. Ibid., pp. 241–2, 247–8.

249. See Kurlander, 'Supernatural Sciences'.

250. As Himmler's personal astrologer Wilhelm Wulff reported, the Reichsführer was convinced that one could 'bring the knowledge and the methods of traditional astrology into line with the Natural Sciences'. Wulff, *Zodiac*, pp. 92–4.

251. Trevor-Roper, ed., *Hitler's Secret Conversations*, p. 473; cf. Picker, ed., *Hitlers Tischgespräche*, pp. 444–5. The Nazis understood folk superstitions as a healthy part of popular consciousness, linked not to formal religion but to faith in the power of magic and the *Volk*; Gottfried Holtz, *Die Faszination der Zwange: Aberglaube und Okkultismus*, Göttingen: Vandenhoeck & Ruprecht, 1984, pp. 13–15; Sickinger, 'Hitler and the Occult'.

252. Staudenmaier, 'Nazi Perceptions of Esotericism', pp. 27–8.

Chapter 5

1. Burleigh, 'National Socialism as a Political Religion', pp. 10–11.

2. Theodor Adorno, *Minima Moralia*, trans. E. F. N. Jephcott, London: Verso, 2005, pp. 238–44.

3. Trimondi, *Hitler*, p. 120.

4. Ley admitted that the Third Reich had produced an impressive array of technological innovations – which he attributed to Hitler's 'shotgun technique; if you shoot enough holes in the unknown, something's apt to drop in your lap. And the Nazis tried everything – anything, no matter how wild!' Ley, 'Pseudoscience in Naziland', p. 91.

5. Ibid.

6. Ley, 'Pseudoscience', p. 90.

7. Ibid., p. 91; Treitel, *Science*, p. 22.

8. Dutton, 'Theodor Adorno on Astrology', pp. 424–44.

9. Heiden, *Preface*, MS Konrad Heiden (preface to Kersten), IfZG: ED 209/34, p. 12; The Third Reich's 'absurd adherence to something that was so obviously not natural scientific – from our [contemporary] perspective – is only explicable through the belief that unites religion and natural science'. Kater, *Ahnenerbe*, p. 226.

10. Lumir and M. K. Bardon, *Erinnerungen an Franz Bardon*. Wuppertal: Rüggeberg, 1992.

11. Geppert and Kössler, 'Einleitung: Wunder der Zeitgeschichte', in *Wunder*, p. 46.

12. Heiden, Preface to *Kersten Memoirs*, p. 12.

13. Krafft to Bender, 20.2.32, IGPP: 10/5 AII9 File 1 (Krafft – Walther).

14. Bender to Krafft, Krafft to Bender, 4.12.31, IGPP: 10/5 AII9 File 1 (Krafft – Walther).

15. Bender to Krafft, 10.11.36, IGPP: 10/5 AII9 File 2 (Krafft).

16. Ibid.

17. Bender to Krafft, 5.12.36, IGPP: 10/5 AII9 File 3 (Krafft).

18. Bender to Krafft, 10.11.36; Bender to Krafft, 5.12.36, IGPP: 10/5 AII9 File 2 (Krafft).

19. Walter Kröner, *Wiedergeburt des Magischen*, Leipzig: Hummel, 1938, pp. 12, 14–16.

20. Ibid., pp. 13–14.

21. Die Astrologie – eine Wissenschaft?', IGPP: 10/5 AII56 ('Wissenschaftliche Korrespondenz', 1942–9).

22. See speech, 10.12.33, Quade, 'Occultism and Politics', BAB: R 58/6218, pp. 37–9.

23. Howe, *Urania's Children*, pp. 103–19.

24. *Völkischer Beobachter*, 'Aus dem Lesebuch des Zauberlehrlings', 29.4.37, BAB: NS 5–VI/16959; Kurlander, 'Hitler's Monsters'; Howe, *Nostradamus*, p. 126; Treitel, *Science*, pp. 214–15; Kersten, *Memoirs*, p. 148; see Kurlander, 'Supernatural Sciences', in Black and Kurlander, eds, *Revisiting*, pp. 134–40.

25. Howe, *Nostradamus*, pp. 123–4; Rauschning, *Voice of Destruction*, p. 244.

26. Howe, *Urania's Children*, pp. 108–14; foreword by Walter Laqueur in Wulff, *Zodiac*.

27. Howe, *Urania's Children*, pp. 114–18.

28. 'Die Astrologie – eine Wissenschaft?', IGPP: 10/5 AII56; Otto Sigfrid Reuter, *Germanische Himmelskunde: Untersuchungen zur Geschichte des Geistes*, Munich: J. F. Lehmanns, 1934. When Hanns Fischer published a book that extolled 'Aryan' astrology, *The Ur-Symbols of Humanity*, the regime allowed its publication because of its roots in 'signs of Ur-Aryan natural science'. Dingler on Fischer, 'Die Ur-Symbole der Menschheit', 1.12.37, BAB: NS 21/1322; Ludendorff, *Trug*, pp. 2–5.

29. Gutachten on Sternenmacht und Liebesleben: 5.1.38, RSK first writes to ban book; 16.2.38, RSK writes to RMVP to request book be banned; 5.4.38, Gestapo official to RSK; Schlecht in RMVP finally responds to president of RSK, 10.5.38, RSK report from 21.12.37; Gutachten from Rosten on 21.12.37, BAB: R 56–V/1150.

30. Howe, *Urania's Children*, pp. 4–5, 99–102. Following Bender and Krafft, these scientfic astrologers sought to move beyond 'the intuitive methods favoured by occultists and theosophists ...

urging readers to think of astrology as an extension of the science of heredity, explaining that the arrangement of the heavens could affect one's fate and character in the same way as one's hereditary material'. Treitel, *Science*, pp. 22–41, 138–41; see also Karl Frankenbach, 'Die Zeichen der Zeit. Die grosse Konjunktion von 1842', *Zenit* 5 (May 1931).

31. Kritzinger, *Todesstrahlen*, pp. 328–34.

32. 'That the body is affected by atmospheric influences is evident', while 'the picture of the nervous system as medium to the outer world . . . the astral body' is clear. Kritzinger, *Todesstrahlen*, p 356; see also Ernst Kallmeyer, *Leben unsere Toten? Eine Weltanschauung als Antwort*, Stuttgart: Kulturaufbau, 1946, p. 9.

33. Comment on a book by Robert Henseling, *Umstrittenes Weltbild*: Bender to Krafft, 28.1.39, IGPP: 10/5 AII9 File 1 (Krafft – Walther); Kaufmann, *Tibet*, p. 139.

34. Kritzinger, *Erdstrahlen*; Heiden, 'Preface', pp. 10–12; Hans-Hermann Kritzinger, *Magische Kräfte: Geheimnisse der menschlichen Seele*, Berlin: Neufeld & Henius, 1922; ibid., *Mysterien von Sonne und Seele: Psychische Studien und Klärung der okkulten Probleme*, Berlin: Universitas Buch und Kunst, 1922; see Hans-Hermann Kritzinger and Friedrich Stuhlmann, eds, *Artillerie und Ballistik in Stichworten*, Berlin: Springer, 1939; Kritzinger, *Todesstrahlen*, pp. 192, 289–324; see also R58/6217: Frau Frieda Stein-Huch, 6.1.38, regarding Kittler's work.

35. Walther, *Zum Anderen Ufer*, pp. 261–9, 409–92, 509–43.

36. Alexander Centgraf, 3.4.37, RSK application, which shows him as Theol. Presse Referent, 1.4.37, the application including Gutachten from former employee, Rektor Schalck, 12.2.37, BAB: R 9361–V/4599.

37. Alexander Centgraf, 3.4.37, RSK application, 1.4.37; Gutachten from former employee, Rektor Schalck, 12.2.37; 21.5.35, another Gutachten from DAD Ortsgruppenwalter in Halle-Merseburg, 15.2.37; Aufnahme-Erklärkung in RSK; 19.4.41 update on AC and still a member, BAB: R 9361–V/4599.

38. See Krafft Horoscopes in Hans Bender, IGPP: 10/5 AII9 File 2.

39. Karl Krafft, 19.1.41 Gestapo RSK saying there is no record of anything 'politically disadvantageous', BAB: R 9361–V/25648; *Der Mensch und das All*, IGPP: 10/5 AII9 File 2 (Krafft); Howe, *Urania's Children*, p. 119; IfZG: 1867/56. ZS–542–6. Bemerkungen zur Niederschrift über die Unterredung mit Professor Dr. Ernst Anrich am 16. Februar 1960, verfasst von Dr. Hans-Dietrich Loock.

40. Howe, *Urania's Children*, pp. 164–72; Wulff, *Zodiac*, pp. 15–16; Walther, *Zum Anderen Ufer*, pp. 560–7.

41. Laqueur, foreword, in Wulff, *Zodiac*, pp. 6–7; ibid., pp. 19–32; Treitel, *Science*, pp. 216–17.

42. Letter from Hamburg Hauleitung RSK, 16.4.37; 16.4.37 letter about Wulff; 23.6.37 long letter from SD to RSK explaining Wulff's problematic work, which includes 10,000 horoscopes over 30 years at 50 to 300 RM, BAB: R 58/6207; 28.7.37 Wulff and wife interviewed, details from report 16.7.37; 15.7.37 Gestapo report on Wulff's wife; 16.7.37 Wulff goes to Gestapo, in Wilhelm Wulff, BAB: R 9361–V/40789.

43. Wulff, *Zodiac*, pp. 29–33; Kritzinger, *Todesstrahlen*, pp. 351–5; Urbach, *Reich*. pp. 33–8; Walther, *Zum Anderen Ufer*, pp. 568–82; Howe, *Urania's Children*, pp. 114–19.

44. See *Schwarze Korps* call for positive astrological work and Werner Kittler's desire to organize cosmobiological research group, BAB: R 58/6217.

45. Reprint of Denkschrift from 6.7.38 discussion, BAB: R 58/6207.

46. Letter from SD/SS Obersturmbannführer, 23.6.38; 4.8.38 to SS Obersturmbannführer Dr Ehlich 9, BAB: R 58/6207.

47. Himmler to Heydrich, 10.1.39, BAB: R 58/6207. Again in 1940 the SD reiterated the need to leave scientific research on astrology open; 16.2.40, RSHA letter, BAB: R 58/6207.

48. BAB: R 58/6206: 71938, 13.12.38, Hörmann writes to 'Parteigenoisse Dr. Ehlich!' and forwards reports from two Gutachter, one hostile (Karl Foltz), one friendly (Pg. Kiendl, a doctor).

49. 28.8.38 report from Foltz, pp. 18–19, BAB: R 58/6206; 14.7.37 report, BAB: R 58/6207.

50. 28.8.38 report from Foltz, pp. 1–2, BAB: R 58/6206.

51. Ibid., pp. 3–10, BAB: R 58/6206.

52. 2.9.38 report from Kiendl, R 58/6206 (71938), pp. 1–2, 6.

53. Ibid., pp. 4–7.

54. See Kiendl's support for Werner Kittler's 'original and useful method, in which he brought together natural scientists and astrologers' in work groups within the Reich Literary Chamber (RSK) and Reich Ministry of Propaganda (RMVP), BAB: R 58/6206. Report from Kiendl to Hörmann, 2.9.38, BAB: R 9361V/1107.

55. See dozens of letters from and to Kittler from late 1937 through early 1939, including Kittler to Poprowski, 16.3.38, inviting him to 'Mitarbeit innerhalb der Arbeitsgemeinschaft für kosmobiologische Forschung'; Kittler to Georg Wilhelm Haag, 22.7.38, in his 'Eigenschaft als Sacharbeiter des Referats Kosmobiologie der Reichsschrifttumskammer', BAB: R 58/6217.

56. Reinhold Ebertin to Kittler, 12.3.38; Kittler to Ebertin, 8.3.38; Kittler, as 'Sachbearbeiter für Kosmobiologische in der Reichsschrifttumskammer', to Rossnagel, 1.8.37, BAB: R 58/6217.
57. Kittler to Rossnagel, 10.3.38; Rossnagel to Kittler, 21.5.38; Kittler replies, 24.5.38; Kittler to Frau Frieda Stein-Huch, 4.5.38; 6.1.38 to Frieda Stein-Huch, BAB: R 58/6217.
58. Reinhold Ebertin to Kittler, 12.3.38; Kittler to Ebertin, 8.3.38; Kittler invites Julius Hartmann, 10.9.38; 14.11.38, writes to Professor Göschl; Kittler to Trusen, 18.1.39; 24.8.38, Kittler to Thomas Ring; Kittler to Hermann Jaeger, 13.7.38; Jaeger to Kittler, 11.7.38; 13.7.38, Kritzinger invitation; invitation from Kittler to Frau Elisabeth v. Brasch, 21.7.38, BAB: R 58/6217.
59. Heilpraktiker and cosmobiologist R. Herlbauer (Virusgo) writes to Kittler, 3.12.37; letter from Kittler to Karl Th. Bayer responding, 15.3.38; Herlbauer to Kanzlei des Führers, 7.2.38, BAB: R 58/6217.
60. Letter from Kittler to Herlbauer, 1.7.38; Herlbauer to Kittler, 28.6.38, BAB: R 58/6217.
61. Kisshauer to SD, 14.4.39; report from Foltz, 28.8.38, BAB: R 58 6206 (71938); Kisshauer to SS Hartl, 7.9.39; 4.9.39; Kisshauer Denkschrift, 'Astrologie als Mittel zur Beeinflussung der Volksstimmung', BAB: R 58/6207.
62. Gutachten Hugo Koch, RMVP, zu pro-Astrologie-Politik der PPK Berlin, 5.20.41, BAB (Reichskanzlei) R 43 II/479a.
63. Ibid.
64. Ibid.
65. BAB (Reichskanzlei) R 43 II/ 479a Rudolf Erckmann, RMVP, zu Karl Heinz Hederich und dessen Verhältnis zu Astrologie Berlin, 21.5.41.
66. So too was the conviction that there was ample scientific 'evidence of the accuracy of predictions based on cosmobiological basis', BAB (Reichskanzlei) R 43 II/ 479a Rudolf Erckmann, RMVP, zu Karl Heinz Hederich und dessen Verhältnis zu Astrologie Berlin, 21.5.41.
67. Rauschning, *Voice of Destruction*, p. 244.
68. Ibid.
69. Howe, *Urania's Children*, p. 7; Heiden, 'Preface', IfZG: ED 209/34, p. 3.
70. 'Physiologically', the magician 'appears as atavistic ... diving back into states, which are "overcome" by the dominating [present] time ... Only the magician is therefore able to also learn something from historical symbols, only he is able to interpret life forms which have faded away.' Schertel, *Magic*, p. 98.
71. Ibid., pp. 48–65.
72. Ibid., pp. 70–9.
73. Ibid., p. 61.
74. Ibid., p. 62; 'None of our perceptions, whether "imagination" or "observation"', wrote Schertel, 'can be related to any "thing". Since facts of consciousness do not originate in "things" ... So, no perception can per se be described as "true" or "wrong", as "right" or "false", as "real" or "illusory"'; ibid., p. 67.
75. The 'emerged imagination (subconscious)' might then be 'projected onto the outside world' and appear as either hallucination or reality, 'depending on whether it can be brought into accordance with our other world of consciousness or not'; ibid., pp. 69–70.
76. Ibid., pp. 135–6; Karl Kosegg, 'Okkulete Erscheinungen verstuandlich gemacht? Wege zu ihrer Deutung', in *Die Parapsychischen Erscheinungen* 1 (Graz: Leykam, 1936), pp. VII–XI.
77. Trimondi, *Hitler*, pp. 24–5.
78. Ibid., pp. 140–4.
79. Michael O'Sullivan, 'Disruptive Potential: Therese Neumann from Konnersreuth, National Socialism, and Democracy', in Black and Kurlander, eds, *Revisiting*, pp. 184, 195.
80. Hausmann, *Bender*, pp. 19–20.
81. Germany's most prominent psychologists, such as Willy Hellpach and Carl Jung, drew on parapsychology in their work while Nazi leaders encouraged attempts to establish parapsychology as a legitimate field. Lux, 'On All Channels', in Black and Kurlander, eds, *Revisiting the Nazi Occult*, p. 226; Willy Hellpach, *Einführung in die Völkerpsychologie*, Stuttgart: Ferdinand Enkel, 1938, pp. 104–5, 113–14; E. Klautke, 'Defining the Volk: Willy Hellpach's *Völkerpsychologie* between National Socialism and Liberal Democracy, 1934–1954', *History of European Ideas* (2012); Howe, *Urania's Children*, pp. 2–3; Manjapra, *Entanglement*, pp. 218–19, 231–3; http://archive.org/stream/MemoriesDreamsReflectionsCarlJung/carlgustavjung-interviewsandencounters-110821120821-phpapp02_djvu.txt, pp. 176–7, 180–2, 198.
82. Lux, 'On All Channels', p. 226.
83. Hausmann, *Bender*, pp. 41–51; Ernst Klee, *Das Personenlexikon zum Dritten Reich. Wer war was vor und nach 1945*, Frankfurt am Main: Fischer, 2005, p. 37.
84. Lux, 'On All Channels', pp. 229–31; *Volksgesundheitswacht (VGW)* 10 (May 1937), IGPP: 10/5 BIII (Bender-Hellwig).
85. Lux, 'On All Channels', pp. 232–3.

86. Ibid., pp. 227–8. A conversation with one official in the Propaganda Ministry, Bender reported, 'has us expecting that the scientific parapsychology will not be stymied'. Lux, 'On All Channels', p. 232; Hausmann, *Bender*, pp. 52–4. Meanwhile, in the spring of 1937, Bender received notice that the Nazi Education Ministry had approved his proposal for a research division on the border sciences. Krafft to Bender, 4.6.37, IGPP: 10/5 AII9 File 3 (Krafft).

87. Hausmann, *Bender*, pp. 84–6, 96–7; Briefe an Dr. Hans Buchheim vom 18.3.53, IfZG: 1867/56. ZS–542–6, pp. 5–6.

88. See his 'Habilitationschrift', *Experimentelle Visionen. Ein Beitrag zum Problem der Sinnestäuschung, des Realitätsbewusstseins und der Schichten der Persönlichkeit*, Bonn (Dissertation, University of Bonn), 1941; see also Lux, 'On All Channels', p. 226.

89. *Ansprache bei der ersten Fakultätssitzung im zweiten Semester der Reichsuniversität Strassburg am 22. April 1942*, 'Sondermappe Universität Straßburg', 1942–3; IGPP: Bestand 10/5, AII17, pp. 1–2.

90. Hausmann, *Bender*, p. 37.

91. Lux, 'On All Channels', p. 226; Heinz-Dietrich Loock, 'Der Hünenburg-Verlag Friedrich Spiesers und der Nationalsozialismus', in *Gutachten des Instituts für Zeitgeschichte 2* (1966), pp. 430–1; Hausmann, *Bender*, pp. 104–7; Thomas Ring to Bender, 23.10.42. 'Korrespondenz Hans Bender–Friedrich Spieser', 1942–68, IGPP: Bestand 10/5, AII17.

92. Spieser to Bender, 30.10.42, 'Korrespondenz Hans Bender–Friedrich Spieser', 1942–68, IGPP: Bestand 10/5 AII17; Hausmann, *Bender*, pp. 102–4.

93. Spieser to Bender, 30.10.42, 'Korrespondenz Hans Bender–Friedrich Spieser', 1942–68, IGPP: Bestand 10/5 AII17; Hausmann, *Bender*, pp. 45–8, 101.

94. Schellinger, 'Hess', p. 319, BAB: R 4901/2887, Internationaler Kongress fuer Kosmobiologie in Nizza and fuer Biophysik und Kosmobiologie in New York: Dr Franz Linke, Direktor des Universitäts-Institut für Meteorologie und Geophysik, to Herrn Minister für Wissenschaftlichen Fakultätder J. W. Goethe Universität, 12.5.38; Roth in Auswuartiges Amt, 27.5.38, 'Schnellbrief'; see Junginger, 'Nordic Ideology in the SS and SS Ahnenerbe', in Junginger and Ackerlund, eds, *Nordic Ideology*, pp. 49–53.

95. Lux, 'On All Channels', p. 226.

96. Spieser to Bender, 30.10.42, 'Korrespondenz Hans Bender–Friedrich Spieser', 1942–68, IGPP; Bestand 10/5 AII17; Hausmann, *Bender*, pp. 45–8, 101.

97. Schellinger, 'Hess Aktion', pp. 329–31; Walter Schellenberg, *Hitlers letzter Geheimdienstchef*, Wiesbaden: Limes Verlag, 1979, pp. 39–49; Kersten, *Memoirs*, p. 148; Lux, 'On All Channels', pp. 227–8; Anrich himself would assert after the war that Himmler envisioned 'an institute for the study of astrology'. Anrich, IfZG: 1536/54, ZS 542.

98. Anrich to Dr Hans Buchheim, 3.18.53, IfZG: 1867/56. ZS–542–6; Hausmann, *Bender*, pp. 91–5; see letters, including one from the Personal Staff of Reichsführer SS to Bender, 28.7.43, in NL Bender, IGPP: 10/5 AIII2.

99. Hausmann, *Bender*, pp. 108–9.

100. Dr Friedrich Spieser to Bender, 10.7.42 'Korrespondenz Hans Bender–Friedrich Spieser', 1942–68, IGPP: 10/5 AII17.

101. Anrich to Dr Hans Buchheim, 18.3.53, IfZG: 1867/56. ZS–542–6; Loock, 'Der Hünenburg-Verlag Friedrich Spiesers', pp. 430–1; Hausmann, *Bender*, pp. 104–7.

102. Hausmann, *Bender*, p. 37.

103. Ibid., pp. 109–10.

104. Ibid., pp. 56–9.

105. Ibid., pp. 109–10; Lux, 'On All Channels', p. 227.

106. Hausmann, *Bender*, pp. 77–84; Bender to Göring, 16.4.40, IGPP: 10/5 AII49.

107. Hausmann, *Bender*, pp. 118–22; for more detail, see Günther Nagel, *Wissenschaft für den Krieg, Die geheimen Arbeiten des Heereswaffenamtes*, Stuttgart: Steiner, 2012.

108. Ibid.; Schellinger, 'Szientismus'; Kurlander, 'Supernatural Sciences', pp. 133–38.

109. BAB: R 43 II/479a, Igez. Erckmann, 21.5.41; http://www.polunbi.de/archiv/41–05–21–01.html.

110. Krafft to Bender, 4.12.31, IGPP: 10/5 AII9 File 2 (Krafft).

111. Bender to Krafft, 1940, 'Siebenjahr-Rhythmus', IGPP: 10/5 AII9 File 1 (Krafft–Walther).

112. Even the pagan-mysticist Ludendorff circle and erstwhile Nazi occultists, J. W. Hauer and Schwarz-Bostunitsch, issued mordant criticism of anthroposophy's scientific claims. IfZG: 414/138 (Frank): *Ludendorffs Volkswarte* (LVW), *Der Schaffende Volk*, 27.3.32; LVW, 13.11.32; M. Lud attacking 'Wachssuggestion und Wahnideen als Mittelzur Priesterherrschaft, seelenärztliche Erkenntnisse', LVW, 11.12.32; M. Lud, 'Christliche Suggestivebehandlung als Wegbereiter zum künstlichen Irresein', LVW, 18.12.32; 'Der Trug der Astrologie', LVW, 8.1.33; Ludendorffs 'Vor'm Volksgericht'. 31.12.32; 'Astronomie und Astrologie', SV, 5.2.33.

113. Werner, *Anthroposophen*, pp. 7–8, 38–46, 75–6, 83, 93–4; Treitel, *Science*, p. 159.

114. Helmut Zander, 'Esoterische Wissenschaft um 1900', in Rupnow et al., *Pseudowissenschaft*, eds, pp. 88–9, 95–6; Staudenmaier, *Between Occultism and Nazism*, pp. 30–2.

115. Ibid.
116. Treitel, *Science*, pp. 212–13; see also Staudenmaier, *Between Between Occultism and Nazism*, pp. 32–8; Bramwell, *Blood and Soil*, p. 176; Staudenmaier, 'Organic Farming', pp. 1–29 (14).
117. Treitel, *Science*, pp. 212–13.
118. Kritzinger, *Erdstrahlen*; Walther to Bender, 30.11.38, IGPP: 10/5 AII9 File 1 (Krafft–Walther); Wulff, *Zodiac*, pp. 40–5; Armin Mohler, *Die Konservative Revolution in Deutschland 1918–1932. Ein Handbuch*, Darmstadt: Wissenschaftliche Buchgesellschaft, 1989, p. 447; Wilhelm Th. H. Wulff, *Tierkreis und Hakenkreuz. Als Astrologe an Himmlers Hof*, Bertelsmann, 1968, p. 43; Jörg Vollmer, *Imaginäre Schlachtfelder. Kriegsliteratur in der Weimarer Republik*. Dissertation, FU Berlin 2003, p. 420.
119. Stephens, 'Blood, not Soil', p. 178.
120. Harrington, *Reenchanted Science*, p. xx. The *völkisch* ariosophist Friederich Bernhard Marby, a natural-healing specialist and occultist, published these ideas in Dietz's 1935 book, *Die Ausstrahlungen des Menschens im Lichte neuer Forschung*, in Jens Henkel, 'Wie ich lerne pendeln?', pp. 114–15; Bramwell, *Blood and Soil*, p. 172.
121. Harrington, *Science*, pp. 207–8; *Zum Thema der Arbeitsgemeinschaft des Amtes Wissenschaft des NSD – Dozentenbundes der Reichsuniversität Strassburg. 'Lebensgesetze von Volkstum und Volk' von Ernst Anrich. 30. September 1942*, 'Sondermappe Universität Straßburg', 1942–3; Archiv des IGPP, 10/5, pp. 10–13.
122. Harrington, *Science*, pp. 103–7.
123. Ibid., pp. 36–7, 61–5.
124. Ibid., pp. 188–92; Kröner, *Wiedergeburt* (introduction from Driesch), pp. 84–99; http://heterodox-ology.com/2012/07/17/parapsychology-in-germany-review-of-heather-wolfframs-stepchildren-of-science-2009; Szczesny, *Presse*.
125. See Uwe Schellinger, 'Trancemedien und Verbrechensaufklärung', in Marcus Hahn and Erhard Schüttpelz, eds, *Transmedien und Neue Medien um 1900: Ein anderer Blick auf die Moderne*, Bielefeld: Transcript Verlag, 2009, pp. 327–9.
126. Kröner, *Wiedergeburt*; Walter Kröner, *Der Untergang des Materialismus und die Grundlegung des biomagischen Weltbildes*, Leipzig: Hummel, 1939.
127. Kröner, *Wiedergeburt*, pp. 20–1, 24.
128. Ibid., pp. 14–18.
129. A. Usthal, 'Pendeltelepathie – eine Tatsache', *Zentralblatt für Okkultismus* (1932/3).
130. Treitel, *Science*, pp. 153–4; Winzer, H. Th. and W. Melzer, 'Cancer in the Light of Geophysical Radiation. Aeiologie und Pathogenese', *Zeitschrift für Krebsforschung* 26:3 (1928), pp. 33–5; Henkel, 'Wie ich lerne pendeln?', p. 112.
131. Treitel, *Science*, pp. 158–9.
132. Kaufmann, *Tibet*, pp. 368–9.
133. Kritzinger, *Erdstrahlen*, pp. 8–22, 25–39.
134. Ibid., pp. 42–87.
135. Kritzinger, *Erdstrahlen*, pp. 1–7.
136. Ibid., pp. 28–38. In the words of Kritzinger, 'how right were are ancestors when they employed a trusted diviner to dowse the area before building a house in order not to find out after the fact through chronic diseases that they had not built on healthy ground'. Kritzinger, *Todesstrahlen*, p. 62.
137. Ibid., pp. 40–7.
138. Ludwig Straniak, *Das Siderische Pendel als Indikator der achten Naturkraft*, Rudolstadt: Gesundes Leben, 1937.
139. Ibid., 5–16.
140. Henkel, 'Wie ich lerne pendeln?', p. 113.
141. Report on Divining Rods, pp. 1–10; Rickmers to Hedwig Winzer 11.3.33, 22.4.33, 4.9.33, 11.10.33, 13.11.33; Max Stehle to Winzer, 29.3.34, 10.4.34; Winzer to Stehle, 13.3.37, 25.5.34, responds and praises his work and attacks 'dogmatic' scientists; 10.4.34, Stehle to Winzer; Winzer to Stehle, 13.4.37; 25.5.34; 10.2.40, 22.7.40, Rickmers writes to Winzer, BAB: R 58/6206.
142. Ley, 'Pseudoscience in Naziland', p. 93; Henkel, 'Gesundes Leben', pp. 114–18, BAB: R 58/7383.
143. Treitel, *Science*, pp. 133–4.
144. Alick Bartholomew, *Hidden Nature: The Startling Insights of Viktor Schauberger*, Edinburgh: Floris Books, 2004, pp. 73–104, 215–40; see correspondence, including Schauberger to Hitler, 10.7.34; report from Dr Willuhn, 13.7.34, IFZG: ED 458/1, pp. 80–6, 99–100, 104–5; Michael Derrich, *Geheimwaffen des Dritten Reiches*, Greiz (Thuringia): König, 2000, p. 192; letter from Reichskanzlei, 7.7.34; 10.7.34, signed promise from Schauberger; Schauberger to Lammers, 10.7.34; 10.7.34, Schauberger to Hitler, explaining why he's not approaching Mussolini, pp. 102–03; 14.7.34, Roselius to Lammers, BAB: R 43–II/342.
145. Treitel, *Science*, pp. 213–16.
146. Trimondi, *Hitler*, p. 109.

147. Schäfer to Brandt, 25.6.40, BAB: N19/2709, pp. 3–6; letter from Sturmbannführer Frenzolf Schmid, 21.3.37, BAB: NS 19/3974, pp. 10–11; letter from SS on Schmid's behalf, 11.1.37; 4.5.40 RSK; 10.12.34, letter from Graf, BAB: R 9361–V/10777; Kaufmann, *Tibet*, pp. 368–71.

148. Longerich, *Himmler*, p. 266.

149. Pringle, *Plan*, p. 11; Fritz Bose, 'Law and Freedom in the Interpretation of European Folk Epics', *Journal of the International Folk Music Council* 10 (1958), p. 31.

150. Pringle, *Plan*, p. 90.

151. 'Mees, 'Hitler and Germanentum', *Journal of Contemporary History* 39:2 (2004), pp. 255–70; Schertel, *Magie*, pp. 87–97; Henkel, 'Wie ich lerne pendeln?', p. 116; Treitel, *Science*, pp. 132–4; 212–16.

152. E. Ernst, ' "Neue Deutsche Heilkunde": Complementary/Alternative Medicine in the Third Reich', *Complementary Therapies in Medicine* 9:1 (March 2001), pp. 49–51; Treitel, *Science*, pp. 213–14.

153. http://www.info3.de/ycms/artikel_1775.shtml. The print version is in the July–August 2007 issue of Peter Staudenmaier, 'Anthroposophen und Nationalsozialismus – Neue Erkenntnisse', *Info3* 32 (2007), pp. 42–3.

154. Kater, *Ahnenerbe*, pp. 214–15; Frenzolf Schmid, 21.3.37, BAB: NS 19/3974, p. 10; Ernst, ' "Neue Deutsche Heilkunde" ', pp. 49–51, Treitel, *Science*, pp. 213–14.

155. Staudenmaier, *Nazism*, pp. 124–6.

156. 'Neue Deutsche Heilkunde'; Treitel, *Science*, pp. 213–16; Staudenmaier, *Between Occultism and Nazism*, p. 123.

157. Merkel to Darré, 27.5.41; letter/*Gutachten*, 14.5.34; 11.3.35 Merkel; 3.9.43, based on Hitler's request to simplify administration; 15.11.39, Head of Reichsnährstand, BAB: R16/12437.

158. Merkel to Darré, 27.5.41, BAB: R16/12437 (Reichsnahrstand), p. 1.

159. Ibid.

160. Ibid., p. 2.

161. Ibid., p. 3.

162. Staudenmaier, 'Anthroposophen und Nationalsozialismus'; http://www.info3.de/ycms/artikel_1775.shtml; Treitel, *Science*, pp. 213–14.

163. Bramwell, *Blood and Soil*, pp. 174–7.

164. Ohlendorf's brother and doctor were Anthroposophists and his funeral in 1951 another pro-Anthroposophic SS leader and 'Christian Community' priest, Werner Haverbeck, conducted his funeral in 1951. Staudenmaier, 'Anthroposophen und Nationalsozialismus'.

165. IfZG: ED 498/23 NL Otto Ohlendorf, (1945), pp. 1–2, 5–6; see also Staudenmaier, 'Nazi Perceptions of Esotericism', pp. 42–4.

166. Staudenmaier, 'Anthroposophen und Nationalsozialismus', http://www.info3.de/ycms/artikel_1775.shtml; Merkel to Darré, 27.5.41, R16/12437 (Reichsnahrstand), p. 3.

167. Staudenmaier, 'Nazi Perceptions of Esotericism', pp. 45–50; Bramwell, *Blood and Soil*, pp. 173–177; Staudenmaier, *Nazism*, pp. 115–118; Staudenmaier, 'Anthroposophen und Nationalsozialismus'; http://www.info3.de/ycms/artikel_1775.shtml.

168. Helmut Zander, 'Esoterische Wissenschaft um 1900. "Pseudowissenschaft" als Produkt ehemals "hochkultureller" Praxis', in Rupnow et al., eds, *Pseudowissenschaft*, pp. 77–81; Staudenmaier, 'Nazi Perceptions of Esotericism', pp. 27–30, 39–45.

169. Treitel, *Science*, p. 212.

170. Staudenmaier, 'Organic Farming'; Staudenmaier, *Between Occultism and Nazism*, pp. 129–30.

171. Stephens, *Blood, Not Soil*, p. 175.

172. Staudenmaier, 'Organic Farming', p. 14; Kritzinger, *Todesstrahlen*, pp. 99–140; Kritzinger, *Todesstrahlen*, pp. 99–140; Staudenmaier, *Between Occultism and Nazism*, pp. 131–3.

173. Staudenmaier, 'Organic Farming', p. 14; Stephens, *Blood, Not Soil*, p. 188; Staudenmaier, *Between Occultism and Nazism*, pp. 101–6, 144–5.

174. NL Otto Ohlendorf (1945), IfZG: ED 498/23, pp. 2–3; Werner, *Anthroposophen*, pp. 85–91; Staudenmaier, *Between Occultism and Nazism*, pp. 138–40.

175. Staudenmaier, 'Organic Farming', pp. 6–7; Werner, *Anthroposophen*, pp. 89–91.

176. NL Otto Ohlendorf, (1945), IfZG: ED 498/23, pp. 2–3.

177. Gutachten Dr Hugo Koch, 20.5.41, Abteilung Schrifttum der RSK, gegen Engagement für die Astrologie in seiner Arbeit für die PPK. BAB: R 43 II/479a.

178. Werner, *Anthroposophen*, p. 93.

179. Pringle, *Plan*, pp. 40–1; Diehl, *Macht*, p. 59.

180. See Darré's correspondence and articles in NL Darré, BAK: N 1094/16.

181. Darré to Lübbemeier, 26.4.53, BAK: N 1094/11; Bramwell, *Blood Soil*, pp. 172–7.

182. Darré to Backe, 1.6.41, BAK: N1094II/1.

183. Darré to Himmler, 5.6.39, in NL Darré, BAK: N 1094II/58; Darré, 'Zur Geschichte des SS-Rasse-Und-Siedlungshauptames', in NL Darré, BAK: N 1094I/3, pp. 2–5.

184. NL Otto Ohlendorf (1945), IfZG: ED 498/23, p. 6; Werner, *Anthroposophen*, p. 306.

185. Staudenmaier, 'Organic Farming'; Werner, *Anthroposophen*, pp. 49–51, 279–83; Erhard Bartsch, 31.5.38, R 9361-V/13284; Staudenmaier, 'Nazi Perceptions of Esotericism', pp. 45–6.

186. Werner, *Anthroposophen*, pp. 279–82; Kurlander, 'Supernatural Sciences', p. 141.

187. NL Otto Ohlendorf (1945), IfZG: ED 498/23, pp. 4–7.

188. Ibid., p. 5.

189. As Heydrich explained Bartsch's subsequent arrest to Darré, the 'essence of anthroposophic teaching' could provide 'no ideology for the entire people, but dangerous sectarian teachings for a narrowly confined circle of people'. Heydrich to Darré, 18.10.41, in NL Darré, BAK: N1094II/1; Werner, *Anthroposophen*, p. 310.

190. Heydrich to Darré, 18.10.41, in NL Darré, BAK: N 1094II/1.

191. Darré to Peuckert, 27.6.41, in NL Darré, BAK: N 1094II/1; IfZG: ED 498/23 NL Otto Ohlendorf (1945), p. 7; Werner, *Anthroposophen*, pp. 303–5; Bramwell, *Blood and Soil*, p. 124; letter to Darré, 10.6.41, BAK: N 1094II-1 Kiel to Darré, 10.6.41, N 1094II-1; see also correspondence in NL Darré, BAK: N 1094/14.

192. Werner, *Anthroposophen*, p. 284.

193. Ibid., pp. 26–7, 59, 66, 72, 301–2.

194. Halter, 'Zivilisation'; Pringle, *Plan*, p. 180.

195. Ibid., p. 79.

196. Ibid.

197. Kaufmann, *Tibet*, pp. 139–40.

198. Kater, *Ahnenerbe*, p. 50.

199. http://www.mpiwg-berlin.mpg.de/en/research/projects/DeptIII-ChristinaWessely-Welteislehre.

200. Ibid.

201. Wessely, *Welteis*, pp. 165, 215–22; Wessely, 'Welteis, die "Astronomie des Unsichtbaren" um 1900', in Rupnow et al., eds, *Pseudowissenschaft*, pp. 178–88.

202. Halter, 'Welteislehre'; Wessely, *Welteis*, pp. 165–96, 226–33.

203. Wessely, *Welteis*, pp. 223–6, 233–7; Halter, 'Welteislehre'; Kater, *Ahnenerbe*, p. 151.

204. http://www.mpiwg-berlin.mpg.de/en/research/projects/DeptIII-ChristinaWessely-Welteislehre; Willy Ley, 'Pseudoscience in Naziland', p. 98.

205. Bowen, *Universal Ice*, pp. 3–6.

206. Trimondi, *Hitler*, p. 12.

207. Goodrick-Clarke, *Black Sun*, p. 133; see letter, 'Der Führer äusserte im Frühjjahr dieses Jares im Gespräch den Reichsführer gegenüber', from 4.8.42, IfZG: MA 3/8; von Hase to Hitler, 11.7.36; Hitler to von Hase, 14.7.37, BAB: NS 21/714.

208. Goodrick-Clarke, *Black Sun*, p. 133.

209. Bowen, *Universal Ice*, p. 7.

210. See SD report from 30.6.41; Hess's request for evaluation of Dacque on 13.7.40, 5.9.40, BAB: R 58/6517.

211. Kater, *Ahnenerbe*, p. 51.

212. Ley, 'Pseudoscience in Naziland', p. 98.

213. Wessely, *Welteis*, pp. 238–9; Kater, *Ahnenerbe*, p. 51.

214. Hess's request for evaluation of Dacque on 13.7.40 by 5.9.40, pp. 1–3, BAB: R 58/6517, pp. 6–10, BAB: R 58/6517.

215. Bowen, *Universal Ice*, p. 16.

216. Kater, *Ahnenerbe*, p. 50; Himmler to Wüst, 6.3.38, IfZG: MA 3/8.

217. Kater, *Ahnenerbe*, pp. 51–2.

218. Ibid., p. 51.

219. Ibid., p. 52.

220. Halter, 'Welteislehre'.

221. Ibid.; Bowen, *Universal Ice*, p. 149.

222. Bowen, *Universal Ice*, pp. 130–46; Kaufmann, *Tibet*, pp. 139–40; as a devout Nazi, Elmayer – also author of a 1942 biography, *Georg Ritter von Schönerer: Der Vater des politischen Antisemitismus. Von einem, der ihm selbst erlebt hat*, Munich: Franz Eher, 1942; Scultetus to Elmayer, 21.12.36, BAB: N S21/699 (WEL); Halter, 'Welteislehre'.

223. Kater, *Ahnenerbe*, pp. 52–3.

224. Robert Hauke, 25.1.38, Scultetus to Herr Hauke, 19.1.37, BAB: NS 21/770.

225. 'Forschungsreise Abessinien' (October 1936); Hörbiger letter, 9.9.36, in Hans Robert Hörbiger: BAB: NS 21/1606;Scultetus to Galke, 10.18.36, BAB: NS 21/770.

226. See Goodrick-Clarke, *Black Sun*, pp. 132–3; Kater, *Ahnenerbe*, p. 52.

227. Pringle, *Plan*, pp. 179–82; Kaufmann, *Tibet*, pp. 140–2.

228. Kaufmann, *Tibet*, pp. 140–1; Trimondi, *Hitler*, p. 111. The first such novel, *The Crystal Sea* (1930), told the story of an ancient Nordic race that was forced south after the fall of the 'Tertiary Moon', surviving by stealing Aryan women and subjecting the 'darker races' to slavery. *Spring in Atlantis* (1933) portrayed the ancient Aryan golden age, when two million Nordic 'Asen' ruled over 60 million sub-human

'darks'. *The Last Queen of Atlantis* (1931) chronicled the decline of Atlantis due to the capture of our present moon 14,000 years ago, after which the remnants of the Aryan population fled to the Andes, where they practised strict eugenics to preserve the race. Finally, *The Swan Song of the Thule* (1939) discussed how the Nordics tried to return to the north, but, forced south by the cold, founded Greek civilization instead. See Goodrick-Clarke, *Black Sun*, pp. 132–3; Wessely, *Welteis*, pp. 163, 256–7.

229. Wessely, *Welteis*, pp. 223–6.
230. Kater, *Ahnenerbe*, pp. 7–11.
231. Ibid., pp. 7–8.
232. Junginger, 'Nordic Ideology', p. 52; Kater, *Ahnenerbe*, pp. 11–16; Reitzenstein, *Himmlers Forscher*, pp. 25–37.
233. Ibid., pp. 17–35; Hans-Christian Harten, *Himmlers Lehrer: Die Weltanschauliche Schulung in der SS 1933–1945*, Paderborn: Schöningh, 2014, p. 18.
234. Kater, *Ahnenerbe*, pp. 37–43; Junginger, 'Nordic Ideology', pp. 51–2.
235. Ibid., pp. 12–18, 58–69.
236. Himmler followed just one goal: 'he wanted only to see his genius reflected in its projects, to find his ... thoughts confirmed', Kater, *Ahnenerbe*, p. 226.
237. Ibid., pp. 37–57, 59–61, 72–89.
238. Ibid., pp. 87–9; Reitzenstein, *Himmlers Forscher*, pp. 149–51.
239. Trimondi, *Hitler*, p. 110.
240. Kater, *Ahnenerbe*, p. 50; Pringle, *Plan*, p. 277.
241. Kater, *Ahnenerbe*, p. 110; Ley, 'Pseudoscience in Naziland', p. 98.
242. Kater, *Ahnenerbe*, pp. 51–2.
243. Ibid.; Pringle, *Plan*, pp. 277–9; Ley, 'Pseudoscience in Naziland', p. 98.
244. Ley, 'Pseudoscience in Naziland', pp. 98–9.
245. Urbach, *Das Reich des Aberglaubens*; see articles from 19.2.33 and 26.3.32, IfZG: 414/138.
246. Kaufmann, *Tibet*, p. 139; Wessely, *Welteis*, pp. 248–9; see also letter from Berlin-Bablesberg Sternwarte, 10.6.38, to Ahnenerbe, IfZG: MA 3/8; Scultetus to Galke, 17.2.37, BAB: NS 21/770.
247. Scultetus to Galke, 12.12.36, BAB: NS 21/770; Scultetus to Galke, 10.18.36; Scultetus to Galke, 12.12.36; Scultetus to Herr Hauke, 19.1.37, BAB: NS 21/770.
248. Himmler letter from 22.6.38, IfZG: MA 3/8; Halter, 'Welteislehre'.
249. Ibid.; Junginger, 'Nordic Ideology', p. 52.
250. On Heisenberg's willingness to compromise with the regime politically, see Paul Lawrence Rose, *Heisenberg and the Nazi Atomic Bomb Project: A Study in German Culture*, Berkeley, CA: University of California Press, 1998, pp. 302–9.
251. Kater, *Ahnenerbe*, p. 52.
252. Scultetus to Hörbiger, 19.5.38, BAB: NS 21/1604; Longerich, *Himmler*, pp. 279–80; Wessely, 'Welteis', p. 190; Kater, *Ahnenerbe*, p. 52.
253. Kater, *Ahnenerbe*, pp. 118–19; Wessely, *Welteis*, pp. 236–7.
254. Wessely, *Welteis*, pp. 224–6; Kater, *Ahnenerbe*, p. 52; Hans Robert Scultetus, 1.2.43; promoted 19.3.36; Galke to Scultetus, 14.7.36; Scultetus to Galke, 14.8.36; Scultetus to Kiss, 30.1.37; 28.6.37, Wolff records Milch allowing Scultetus to leave the Luftwaffe for the SS; letter from Milch to Wolff, 22.12.36, BAB: NS 21/2547 (B.1); Kater, *Ahnenerbe*, pp. 214–15.
255. Fauth to Hummel, 13.2.38, BAB: NS 21/770.
256. See Hörbiger to Scultetus, 14.4.37; Hörbiger to Scultetus, 13.4.37; Sievers to Hinzpeter, 19.4.37, BAB: NS 21/770; Fauth to Hummel, 13.2.38, BAB: NS 21/770.
257. Hörbinger to Scultetus, 15.4.37; Hörbiger to Scultetus, 13.4.37; Sievers to Hinzpeter, 19.4.37, BAB: NS 21/770.
258. Elmayer, *Schönerer*; Scultetus to Elmayer, 21.12.36, BAB: NS 21/699 (WEL).
259. Scultetus to Elmayer, 6.12.36, Scultetus to Elmayer, 4.1.37, Scultetus to Fauth, 17.3.37, BAB: NS 21/699 (WEL).
260. Scultetus to Fauth, 17.3.37, BAB: NS 21/699. Meanwhile, Scultetus urged Sievers to produce, in contrast to SS literature, a simplified introduction to World Ice Theory for propagation among the SA. Scultetus to Sievers, 27.5.37, BAB: NS 21/770.
261. Kunze to Loder, 6.2.37, BAB: NS 21/699.
262. Lautner to Loder, 28.1.37, BAB: NS 21/699.
263. 'Such publications are capable of damaging the reputation of state institutions and consequently the state itself.' Hoffmeyer to Franz Eher Verlag, 29.1.37, BAB: NS 21/699.
264. Scultetus to Elmayer, 30.1.37, BAB: N S21/699.
265. 'You have worked for the *Reichsführung* [Himmler] for the whole year. Moreover, you have signed the Pyrmonter Protocol and thereby contracted yourself to loyal work ... If we want to be able to achieve anything for the World Ice Theory, these kind of special endeavours cannot occur.' Scultetus to Hinzpeter, 22.3.37, BAB: NS 21/770; Wessely, *Welteis*, pp. 257–8.

266. Hinzpeter to Sievers, 25.4.37, BAB: NS 21/770.

267. Sievers to Hinzpeter, 30.4.37; Himmler to Hinzpeter, 30.4.37, BAB: NS 21/770.

268. Hörbinger to Hinzpeter, including 'open letter', 25.5.13; see also Hörbinger to Scultetus, 25.5.37; Scultetus to Hörbinger, 27.5.37; Scultetus to Sievers, 27.5.37, BAB: NS 21/770.

269. Hörbinger to Haenichen, 13.1.38, BAB: NS 21/770.

270. Kiss to Reichsgeschäftsführer der Ahnenerbe, 4.10.38, BAB: NS 21/770. Despite Hinzpeter's attempt to get the support of the GFW's rank and file, he could not overcome the opposition of Scultetus, Kiss, and the Ahnenerbe. See various letters from members to Scultetus, 11.1.38, 6.1.38, 7.1.38, BAB: NS 21/770.

271. K. Hummel, 'Wissenschaft und Welteislehre', Zeitschrift der Deutschen Geologischen Gesellschaft 90 (January 1938), pp. 46–50.

272. It was 'no coincidence that Hörbiger's World Ice Theories, which were developed before the war, achieved their first major success in the German public in the post-war years'. Ibid.

273. That 'the followers and representatives of World Ice Theory were not proletarians, but largely representative of thoroughly bourgeois social groups (especially from technical fields)', Hummel opined, 'shows just how far the mental confusion and alienation among the different strata then thrived'. Hummel, 'Wissenschaft'.

274. Ibid.

275. Scultetus to Wüst, 9.2.38; Fauth to Hummel, 7.2.38, BAB: NS 21/770.

276. Hummel to Fauth, 11.2.38, BAB: NS 21/770.

277. Ibid.

278. Fauth denied that his belief in World Ice Theory was 'faith-based', though he conceded that 'Certainly I "believe" that next to the World Ice Theory there has never existed another worldview of such coherence, such breadth and such consistency'. Fauth to Hummel, 13.2.38, BAB: NS 21/770.

279. Fauth Denkschrift, February 1938, BAB: NS 21/770.

280. See Protocol, 19–21.7.39, BAB: NS 21/458.

281. 'Allgemein verstaendliche Darstellungen der Welteislehre', July 1939; Sievers to Forschungstätte für Geophysik, 21.8.39, BAB: NS 21/458 (WEL).

282. Ibid. Fauth, 24.4.38, BAB: NS 21/1342 (B.2).

283. Wessely, 'Welteis', in Rupnow et al., eds, Pseudowissenschaft, p. 190; Wessely, Welteis, pp. 251–9; Pringle, Himmler, p. 280.

284. Treitel, Science, p. 248. If 'Nazis like Hess, Himmler, and even, on occasion, Hitler, dabbled in occultism to varying degrees,' writes Treitel, these 'dabblings were essentially private, part of their more general embrace of natural medicine'. 'There is no evidence to suggest,' Treitel concludes, that the Nazis' 'occult interests ever factored into major policy decisions. Moreover, their selective affinity for occultism was dwarfed by the enormity of their regime's hostility toward the occult movement more generally.' Treitel, Science, pp. 239–40; Saler, 'Modernity and Enchantment'; Geppert and Kössler, Wunder, pp. 455–8.

285. Even 'under the general rubric of hostility,' Trietel concedes, 'the official [Nazi] response to occultism was multivalent, and not all forms of occult activity were treated in the same way'. Treitel, Science, pp. 216–17.

286. http://www.mpiwg-berlin.mpg.de/en/research/projects/DeptIII-ChristinaWessely-Welteislehre.

287. Harrington, Reenchanted Science, pp. 175–85; see also Treitel, Science, pp. 132–3.

288. '[It] is immaterial how objectively false' Nazi border scientists' 'original premises were and how unmethodological and illogical' their theses might have been. The success of these ideas 'from a National Socialist point of view cannot be written off with historical hindsight; it defined a generation of fanatics'. Kater, Ahnenerbe, p. 358.

Chapter 6

1. Kersten, Memoirs, p. 149.

2. Trevor-Roper, ed., Conversations, p. 319; Picker, Tischgespräche, p. 184.

3. Otto Rahn, Luzifers Hofgesind, Dresden: Zeitwende, 2006, p. 8.

4. http://www.telegraph.co.uk/culture/film/starsandstories/3673575/The-original-Indiana-Jones-Otto-Rahn-and-the-temple-of-doom.html.

5. Brandt to Best, April 1943, BAB: NS 19/688.

6. Richard Evans, 'Nazism, Christianity and Political Religion: A Debate', Journal of Contemporary History 42 (January 2007), p. 5; see essays in Puschner and Vollnhals, eds, Bewegung.

7. Steigmann-Gall, Holy Reich; Derek Hastings, Catholicism and the Roots of Nazism: Religious Identity and National Socialism, Oxford: Oxford University Press, 2009; Richard Steigmann-Gall, 'Rethinking Nazism and Religion: How Anti-Christian Were the "Pagans"?', Central European

History 36:1 (2003), p. 104; Derek Hastings, 'How "Catholic" Was the Early Nazi Movement? Religion, Race, and Culture in Munich, 1919-1923', *Central European History* 36:3 (2003), pp. 383-7; Junginger and Ackerlund, eds, *Nordic Ideology*, pp. 39-40; see also essays in Manfred Gailus and Armin Nolzen, eds, *Zerstrittene 'Volksgemeinschaft'. Glaube, Konfession und Religion im Nationalsozialismus*, Göttingen: Vandenhoeck & Ruprecht, 2011.

8. Michael Burleigh, 'National Socialism as a Political Religion', *Totalitarian Movements and Political Religions* 1:2 (Autumn 2000), pp. 4-5; Klaus Vondung, 'Religiösität', in Puschner and Vollnhals, eds, *Bewegung*, pp. 29-41; Klaus Vondung, 'National Socialism as a Political Religion: Potentials and Limits of an Analytical Concept', *Totalitarian Movements and Political Religions* 6:1 (2005), pp. 87-90; see also Klaus Vondung, *Deutsche Wege zur Erlösung: Formen des Religiösen im Nationalsozialismus*, Munich: Wilhelm Fink Verlag, 2013, pp. 24-8; see also Maier, 'Political Religion', p. 39.

9. See Junginger and Ackerlund, eds, *Nordic Ideology*, pp. 39-58; Maier, 'Political Religion', pp. 10-11; Doris L. Bergen, 'Nazism and Christianity: Partners and Rivals? A Response to Richard Steigmann-Gall, *The Holy Reich*: Nazi Conceptions of Christianity, 1919-1945', *Journal of Contemporary History* 42 (January 2007), pp. 25-33; Stanley Sowers, 'The Concepts of "Religion", "Political Religion", and the Study of Nazism', *Journal of Contemporary History* 42:1 (January 2007), pp. 9-24; Uwe Puschner, 'Weltanschauung und Religion, Religion und Weltanschauung. Ideologie und Formen völkischer Religion', *Zeitenblicke* 5:1 (2006); George Williamson, 'A Religious Sonderweg? Reflections on the Sacred and the Secular in the Historiography of Modern Germany', *Church History* 75:1 (2006), pp. 139-56; Mosse, *Nationalization*, pp. 202-5; Michael Burleigh, *The Third Reich*, London: Hill and Wang, 2001, pp. 261-5; Trevor-Roper, ed., *Conversations*, p. 173; Grabner-Haider and Strasser, *Hitlers mythische Religion*; Koehne, 'Paganism', p. 760; Goodrick-Clarke, *Occult Roots*, pp. 29-31.

10. Burleigh, 'National Socialism', pp. 11-12. For more on Hitler's 'ethics', see Richard Weikart, *Hitler's Ethic: The Nazi Pursuit of Evolutionary Progress*, London: Palgrave, 2009.

11. Junginger, 'Intro', in Junginger and Ackerlund, eds, *Nordic Ideology*, pp. 7-8; Goodrick-Clarke, *Occult Roots*, p. 177.

12. Koehne, 'Paganism', pp. 777-8.

13. In December 1922 the 'night of the winter solstice' and of the 'divine sun-hero' was again celebrated by the NSDAP. And again, Christ's death and rebirth took a back seat to discussions of Nordic mythology and the 'resurrection of our people'. Koehne, 'Paganism', pp. 782-3.

14. In the wake of extensive research on German Protestant and Catholic support for Nazism, some historians have begun to argue that the Nazi movement itself might be fundamentally Christian. See Guenter Lewy, *The Catholic Church and Nazi Germany*, New York: Da Capo, 2000; Georg Denzler, *Die Kirchen im Dritten Reich*, Frankfurt am Main: Fischer Taschenbuch Verlag, 1984; Shelley Baranowski, *The Confessing Church, Conservative Elites, and the Nazi State*, Lewiston, NY: Edwin Mellen, 1986; Ian Kershaw, *Popular Opinion and Political Dissent in the Third Reich, Bavaria 1933-1945*, Oxford: Oxford University Press, 2002; Kevin P. Spicer, *Resisting the Third Reich: The Catholic Clergy in Hitler's Berlin*, DeKalb, IL: University of Northern Illinois Press, 2004; see also Evans, 'Nazism, Christianity and Political Religion', pp. 5-7; Maria Anna Zumholz, *Volksfrömmigkeit und Katholisches Milieu: Marienerscheinungen in Heede 1937-1940*, Cloppenburg: Runge, 2004; Steigmann-Gall, *Holy Reich*, pp. 2-7, 84-5, 153-6, 216-49; Hastings, *Catholicism*.

15. Kaufmann, *Tibet*, p. 165.

16. Steigmann-Gall, *Holy Reich*, p. 259; Manfred Gailus, 'A Strange Obsession with Nazi Christianity: A Critical Comment on Richard Steigmann-Gall's The Holy Reich', *Journal of Contemporary History* 42 (January 2007), pp. 35-46; Ernst Piper, 'Steigmann-Gall, The Holy Reich', *Journal of Contemporary History* 42 (January 2007), pp. 47-57; Irving Hexham, 'Inventing "Paganists": A Close Reading of Richard Steigmann-Gall's The Holy Reich', *Journal of Contemporary History* 42 (January 2007), pp. 59-78; Treitel, *Science*, pp. 199-200.

17. Gerhard Schormann, 'Wie entstand die Karthotek, und wem war sie bekannt?', in Dietrich R. Bauer, Sönke Lorenz, Wolfgang Behringer, and Jürgen Schmidt, eds, *Himmlers Hexenkartothek: Das Interesse des Nationalsozialismus an der Hexenverfolgung*, Bielefeld: Verlag für Regionalgeschichte, 1999, pp. 135-42; Rudolf, 'Geheime Reichskommando-Sache!', in Bauer, Lorenz, Behringer, and Schmidt, eds, *Himmlers Hexenkartothek*, pp. 86-94; http://www.dailymail.co.uk/news/article-3498908/Heinrich-Himmler-s-stash-books-witchcraft-discovered-Czech-library-hidden-50-years.html.

18. Rudolf, 'Geheime Reichskommando-Sache!', pp. 64-8, 70-9; see letter to Personal Staff and accompanying Ahnenerbe summary analysis and translation of documents from Gauamtsleiter Walter Steinecke (Lemgo), 11.7.38, BAB: R 58/1599, pp. 4-5; Rudolf, 'Geheime Reichskommando-Sache!', pp. 58-9.

19. Wolfgang Brückner, 'Hauptströmungen nationalsozialistischer Volksunde-Arbeit', in Bauer et al., *Hexenkartothek*, pp. 30-1.

20. Rudolf, 'Geheime Reichskommando-Sache!', pp. 86–94.

21. Schormann, 'Wie entstand die Karthotek, und wem war sie bekannt?', pp. 135–42.

22. 'Introduction', in Bauer et al., *Hexenkartothek*, p. xiii; Walter Rummel, 'Die Erforschung der spon-heimischen und kurtrierischen Hexenprozessakten durch Mitglieder des H-Sonderauftrags-Anspruch und Wirklichkeit', in Bauer et al., *Hexenkartothek*, pp. 143–8.

23. See report by Gauamtsleiter Walter Steinecke (Lemgo), BAB: R 58/1599, pp. 7–9; Schier, 'Hexenwahn-Interpretationen', in Bauer et al., *Hexenkartothek*, p. 9; letters and reports requesting witch records and bibliography, BAB: R 58/7484 (Teufelsaustreibung).

24. Rudolf, 'Geheime Reichskommando-Sache!', p. 51; see also Brandt to Wolfram Sievers, BAB: R 58/1599, pp. 9–10, 19–26; Walther Wüst, *Indogermanisches Bekenntnis*, Berlin-Dahlem: Ahnenerbe-Stiftung, 1942, p. 12; Bärsch, *Politische Religion*, p. 333.

25. Gugenberger and Schweidlenka, *Faden der Norne*, pp. 142–3, 162–77.

26. Anton Mayer, *Erdmutter und Hexe*, Munich: Datterer & CIE, 1936, pp. 11–14.

27. Ibid., pp. 15–28, 32–9.

28. Ibid., pp. 40–7.

29. Gustav Lassen, *Hexe Anna Schütterlin*, Bodensee: Heim-Verlag Dressler, 1936, pp. 10–33, 35–45, 51–4, 72–84.

30. Mathilde Ludendorff, *Christliche Grausamkeit an Deutschen Frauen*, Munich: Ludendorff, 1934; see also Bettina Amm, 'Die Ludendorff-Bewegung im Nationalsozialismus', in Puschner and Vollnhals, eds, *Bewegung*, pp. 127–48; Bettina Amm, *Die Ludendorff-Bewegung. Vom nationalistischen Kampfbund zur völkischen Weltanschauungssekt*, Hamburg: Ad Fontes, 2006.

31. Schormann, 'Wie entstand die Karthotek, und wem war sie bekannt?', pp. 177–8.

32. Rudolf, 'Geheime Reichskommando-Sache!', pp. 53–4.

33. Kaufmann, *Tibet*, p. 166.

34. Rudolf, 'Geheime Reichskommando-Sache!', pp. 53–4.

35. Longerich, *Himmler*, p. 225.

36. Pringle, *Plan*, p. 56.

37. Longerich, *Himmler*, pp. 219–21, 271–2; Stoltzus, *Hitler's Compromises*, pp. 178–83; Spence, *Occult Causes*, p. 146; Piper, 'Steigmann-Gall, *The Holy Reich*', pp. 51–2; BAB: R 58/6217: Entwurf: für ein 'Jahrbuch der Nordischen Aktion'; Hans H. Reinsch to Gengler, vertraulich, 6.7.38; 26.8.36, letter from Schriftleiter of Hammer Verlag to Reinsch.

38. Trevor-Roper, ed., *Bormann Letters*, pp. xvi–xviii, pp. 51–2; Steigmann-Gall, *Holy Reich*, p. 259.

39. NL Robert Ley, BAK: N 1468/5, pp. 24–5; Thomas Kühne, *Belonging and Genocide: Hitler's Community, 1918–1945*, New Haven, CT: Yale University Press, 2010, p. 131.

40. Piper 'Steigmann-Gall, *The Holy Reich*', *Journal of Contemporary History* 42 (January 2007), pp. 53–4.

41. To salvage Christianity, Goebbels suggested, one needed to 'destroy' the priests. Hexham, 'Inventing "Paganists"', pp. 63–4; Manfred Gailius, 'A Strange Obsession with Nazi Christianity', *Journal of Contemporary History* 42 (January 2007), p. 40.

42. Rudolf, 'Geheime Reichskommando-Sache!', pp. 58–9.

43. Picker, *Tischgespräche*, p. 355; Trevor-Roper, ed., *Conversations*, p. 255; cf. Picker, *Tischgespräche*, pp. 104–6; Ach, *Hitlers Religion*, pp. 67–84.

44. Rosenberg, ed., *Eckart*, pp. 23–4.

45. Kaufmann, *Tibet*, p. 165.

46. Trevor-Roper, ed., *Conversations*, p. 255; cf. Picker, *Tischgespräche*, pp. 106, 305.

47. Picker, *Tischgespräche*, p. 104; Hitler, *Mein Kampf*, p. 268; see also Ach, *Hitlers Religion*, pp. 113–14, 156–7; Hexham, 'Inventing "Paganists"', p. 65.

48. Prof. Dr von Hasselbach, 'Hitlers Mangel an Menschenkenntnis', 26.9.45, in NL Adolf Hitler, BAK: N 1128–33, p. 7. Frustrated Catholic bishops such as Sproll and Galen openly confronted what they perceived as 'the paganism of the state'. Stoltzfus, *Hitler's Compromises*, p. 129.

49. Trevor-Roper, ed., *Bormann Letters*, pp. xvi–xviii; Christa Schroeder interview with Albert Zoeller in NL Hitler, and BAK: N 1128/33, p. 141. As the Austrian ambassador in Berlin observed, the Third Reich's 'attack on the churches . . . is a war of attrition which begins with the soul of the child and aims slowly and by degrees to do away with Catholic schools, and to drive the faithful away from the churches, religious houses, and other church institutions, so that these become, over decades, redundant'. Stoltzfus, *Hitler's Compromises*, p. 177.

50. Kersten, *Memoirs*, p. 155; Piper, 'Steigmann-Gall, *The Holy Reich*', pp. 50–1; 'After the war,' Himmler claimed elsewhere, 'the German gods will be restored.' Pringle, *Plan*, p. 56.

51. Koehne, 'The Racial Yardstick', SR 37/3 (2014), p. 584.

52. Christa Schroeder interview with Albert Zoeller in NL Hitler, and BAK: N 1128/33, p. 141; Ach, *Hitlers Religion*, pp. 94, 112, 118.

53. Hexham, 'Inventing "Paganists"', p. 65; see also Koehne, 'The Racial Yardstick', p. 587.

54. Trevor-Roper, ed., *Conversations*, p. 49; Picker, *Tischgespräche*, pp. 73, 267. On the Nazis' enduring hostility to but also fear of antagonizing the Church during war, see Stoltzfus, *Hitler's Compromises*, pp. 188–206.

55. Schroeder interview in NL Hitler, and BAK: N 1128/33, p. 141; Steigmann-Gall, *Holy Reich*, pp. 96–101, 153–6, 245–59.

56. Vondung, 'National Socialism', p. 94; Junginger and Ackerlund, eds, *Nordic Ideology*, pp. 44–52; Robert A. Pois, *National Socialism and the Religion of Nature*, New York: St Martin's Press, 1986, p. 3; Koehne, 'Paganism', pp. 788–90.

57. Hastings, *Catholicism*; Oded Heilbronner, 'From Ghetto to Ghetto: The Place of German Catholic Society in Recent Historiography', *Journal of Modern History* 72:2 (2000), pp. 453–95; Goodrick-Clarke, *Occult Roots*, pp. 192–3; Wulff, *Zodiac*, pp. 32–8; Longerich, *Himmler*, pp. 739–40.

58. Bärsch, *Politische Religion*, pp. 133–4; Koehne, 'Paganism', pp. 788–9.

59. Steigmann-Gall, *Holy Reich*, p. 261; Eckart, *Der Bolschewismus*, pp. 24–5; Bergen on Steigmann-Gall, 'Nazism and Christianity: Partners and Rivals? A Response to Richard Steigmann-Gall, *The Holy Reich*. Nazi Conceptions of Christianity, 1919–1945', *Journal of Contemporary History* 42 (January 2007), pp. 25–30.

60. Redles, *Hitler's Millennial Reich*, pp. 8–9; Maier, 'Political Religion', p. 12; Goodrick-Clarke, *Occult Roots*, pp. 192–3; Wulff, *Zodiac*, pp. 32–8.

61. Koehne, 'Paganism', pp. 784–6; Koehne, 'The Racial Yardstick', pp. 587–8.

62. Schormann, 'Wie entstand die Karthotek, und wem war sie bekannt?', pp. 177–8; see reports BAB: R 58/1599, pp. 9–10, 19–26; Wüst, *Indogermanisches Bekenntnis*, p. 12; Bärsch, *Politische Religion*, p. 333; Rudolf, 'Geheime Reichskommando-Sache!', pp. 82–3; Longerich, *Himmler*, pp. 266–7.

63. Piper, 'Steigmann-Gall', p. 56; see also Maier, 'Political Religion', p. 14; Steigmann-Gall, *Holy Reich*, pp. 261–2.

64. NL Darré, BAK: N 1094I/77, pp. 94–5, 124.

65. Hasselbach, 'Hitlers Mangel an Menschenkenntnis', p. 7.

66. His private secretary Traudl Junge recalls how a throwaway comment or question might cause Hitler to launch into 'interesting discussions over the Church and development of humanity'. Traudl Junge, Bis zur Letzten Stunde; Hitlers Sekretarin Erzahlt ihr Leben, Berlin: Ullstein, 2003, p. 122.

67. Trevor-Roper, ed., *Conversations*, pp. 49–51, 473; Picker, *Tischgespräche*, pp. 444–5; Jörgen Hansen, *Volkskunde und völkische Schule*, Braunschweig: Westermann, 1935, p. 71.

68. Trevor-Roper, ed., *Conversations*, p. 473; Picker, *Tischgespräche*, pp. 444–5; Holtz, *Die Faszination der Zwange*, pp. 13–15.

69. Kaufmann, *Tibet*, p. 168.

70. Kersten, *Memoirs*, p. 148.

71. Longerich, *Himmler*, p. 281.

72. Rosenberg *Denkschrift*, BAB: NS 15/447, p. 2.

73. Ibid., p. 3; see also Rosenberg *Denkschrift*, BAB: NS 15/447, pp. 9–11; Ach, *Hitlers Religion*, pp. 132–3.

74. Goebbels, 'Knowledge and Propaganda'; Hermann Rauschning, *Hitler Speaks*, London: Thornton Butterworth, 1939, pp. 239–40; Longerich, *Himmler*, p. 256; Goodrick-Clarke, *Occult Roots*, pp. 192–3; Wulff, *Zodiac*, pp. 32–8.

75. Pois, *National Socialism*, p. 3; for more on the Nazi 'pantheistic religion of nature', see Weikart, *Hitler's Religion*.

76. Pois, *National Socialism*, pp. 10–11.

77. Spence, *Occult Causes*, pp. 122–3; see also Pois, *National Socialism*, pp. 10–11; Ach, *Hitlers Religion*, pp. 63–6; Pois, *Religion of Nature*, p. 10; Hansen, *Volkskunde*, pp. 75–6; Treitel, *Science*, p. 194; Walther, *Zum Anderen Ufer*, pp. 294–311, 321–41, 568–82; Bärsch, *Politische Religion*, p. 57; Spence, *Occult Causes*, p. 146; see also Quade, 'Occultism', 12.10.33, pp. 33–4, BAB: R 58/6218 (SD RSHA).

78. Pois, *National Socialism*, pp. 5–10; Hansen, *Volkskunde*, pp. 88–9; Ach, *Hitlers Religion*, pp. 77–8, 83–4, 89–93, 106–9.

79. Hitler, as quoted in Ach, *Hitlers Religion*, p. 68; cf. Trevor-Roper, ed., *Conversations*, pp. 229–30.

80. Rosenberg *Denkschrift*, BAB NS 15/447, p. 12.

81. NL Ley, BAK: N 1468/5, pp. 24–5.

82. Koehne, 'Paganism', pp. 785–6.

83. Vondung, 'National Socialism', p. 90.

84. Koehne, 'The Racial Yardstick', pp. 585–6; This 'ethnotheism', in the words of Samuel Koehne, meant a religion 'defined by race and the supposed moral or spiritual characteristics that the Nazis believed were inherent in race'. Koehne, 'The Racial Yardstick', p. 576; see also Koehne, 'Paganism', pp. 785–6; Steigmann-Gall, *Holy Reich*, pp. 112–13, 261–2; see a series of work on 'mythological' aspects of Nazi religion, for example Grabner-Haider and Strasser, *Hitlers mythische Religion*; Cecil, *Myth*, pp. 36–41.

85. Schertel, *Magic*, p. 45.

86. Ibid., pp. 81–2. Many of Hitler's citations in Schertel's *Magic* focus on the Gnostic, symbiotic relationship between good and evil, the latter bring 'destructive-creative' and therefore essential in exercising power. 'Evil is the dark-violent, irrational, destructive-creative, which eternally appears as inconceivable, unfamiliar and therefore gruesome.' Schertel, *Magic*, p. 116.

87. Ibid., p. 100.

88. Spence, *Occult Causes*, pp. 40–1; see also Piper, 'Steigmann-Gall, *The Holy Reich*', pp. 51–2.

89. Koehne, 'The Racial Yardstick', p. 586.

90. Gailius, 'A Strange Obsession', p. 46.

91. Hexham, 'Inventing "Paganists"', p. 75; see also Kühne, *Belonging and Genocide*, p. 5; BAB: R 58/6217: SD Report on Hauer, 5.6.39; Longerich, *Himmler*, pp. 265–7; Kersten, *Memoirs*, pp. 148–50; Evans, 'Nazism', p. 5; Ach, *Hitlers Religion*, pp. 66–72, 96–7, 103, 122; Rosenberg *Denkschrift*, BAB NS 15/447, p. 13; Rauschning, *Voice of Destruction*, pp. 248–51.

92. Burleigh, 'National Socialism', pp. 8–9.

93. Angela Kurtz, 'God, not Caesar: Revisiting National Socialism as "political religion"', *History of European Ideas* 35:2 (June 2009), pp. 236–52; Evans, 'Nazism', p. 5.

94. McGuire and Hull, eds, *C. G. Jung Speaking*, pp. 121–2.

95. Piper, 'Steigmann-Gall', p. 50. As we saw in Chapter Three, the 'magician' might also abandon his people were they not 'reactive enough' to his will and authority. Schertel, *Magic*, p. 82.

96. Black, *Death in Berlin*, pp. 71, 75.

97. Memorandum to Party Comrade Knopfel, *17.2.44*, in Trevor-Roper, ed., *Bormann Letters*, pp. 51–2.

98. Mosse, *Masses and Man*, pp. 71–2.

99. Ibid., pp. 71–2; Cecil, *Myth*, pp. 36–41, 95–6, 111, 119, 163; Steigmann-Gall, *Holy Reich*, p. 263.

100. Black, *Death in Berlin*, p. 74.

101. Kühne, *Belonging and Genocide*, p. 19.

102. See Hansen, *Volkskunde*, pp. 89–92, 100–1; Hartmann, *Trollvorstellungen*, pp. 4–5, 6–9.

103. Schertel, *Magic*, pp. 122–3, and p. 114; Rauschning, *Voice of Destruction*, p. 253.

104. NL Darré, BAK: N1094I-77, pp. 99–106.

105. Copy of letter M. B. sent G. B, 21.2.44, in Trevor-Roper, ed., *Bormann Letters*, pp. 54–5.

106. Fisher, *Fantasy and Politics*, p. 3.

107. Black, *Death in Berlin*, p. 75; see also Gailius, 'A Strange Obsession', pp. 41–2; Vondung, 'National Socialism', p. 91; see also Die Kommenden, 'Vererbung und Wiederverkörperung', Seite 8, Nummer 18, 25. September 1949; BAB: N 1094I-33.

108. Anrich, IfZG: 1536/54, ZS Nr. 542, pp. 3–4.

109. Steigmann-Gall, *Holy Reich*, p. 14.

110. Koehne, 'The Racial Yardstick', pp. 784–5; Rosenberg *Denkschrift*, BAB: NS 15/447, p. 8; Hitler, as quoted in Ach, *Hitlers Religion*, p. 59; Trevor-Roper, ed., *Conversations*, pp. 100, 277–9; cf. Picker, *Tischgespräche*, p. 76; Koehne, 'The Racial Yardstick', pp. 581–5; Sowers on Steigmann-Gall, 'The Concepts of "Religion", "Political Religion" and the Study of Nazism', *Journal of Contemporary History* 42 (January 2007), pp. 21–6.

111. Spence, *Occult Causes*, pp. 40–1.

112. Ibid., pp. 72–3. As thousands of Germans rejected the imposition of Catholic orthodoxy, according to Spence, they sunk 'back into their ancient paganism. Here the Luciferians recognized a typical opportunity for sowing the seeds of devil worship and anarchy and irreligion and licence soon claimed the region for their own.' Spence, *Occult Causes*, pp. 73–6; see also Klaus Dede, *Stedingen Ein Land, das nicht sein durfte*, Fischerhude: Verlag Atelier, 1976; 'Stedinger Crusade', *Encyclopædia Britannica Online Academic Edition*, 2013.

113. Spence, *Occult Causes*, pp. 92–6, 101, 104–6, 116.

114. Ibid., p. 144.

115. Ibid., p. 27; 'Nazism was not initiated by Satanism,' Spence was careful to say, 'but annexed it' for political purposes in following a proclivity toward 'inverted Jesuitism'. Spence, *Occult Causes*, pp. 22–5.

116. Black, *Death in Berlin*, p. 273; Michael Burleigh agrees that National Socialism was reminiscent of medieval, 'Satanic' cult-based movements promising salvation, often associated with 'negative Christians' in a 'state of revolt' against Christian tenets. Burleigh, 'National Socialism', p. 4.

117. Redles, *Reich*, pp. 53–7; Spence, *Occult Causes*, pp. 40–1; Michael Rißmann, *Hitlers Gott*, Munich: Pendo, 2001, pp. 198–206.

118. Spence, *Occult Causes*, pp. 59–60, 66; see also Pringle, *Plan*, p. 79.

119. Black, *Death in Berlin*, p. 273.

120. Hans-Jurgen Lange, *Otto Rahn. Leben und Werk*, Arun: Engerda, 1995, pp. 14–15.

121. Ibid., pp. 12–14.

122. Pennick, *Hitler's Secret Sciences*, pp. 56–7, 163–6; Treitel, *Science*, pp. 227–8; Lange, *Otto Rahn*, pp. 14–15; Levenda, *Unholy Alliance*, pp. 203–5.

123. Kaufmann, *Tibet*, pp. 173–4; Wegener, *Alfred Schuler*, pp. 68–9; Lange, *Otto Rahn*, pp. 12–19.

124. Wegener, *Schuler*, pp. 67–9; Wegener, *Himmler*, pp. 103–4; Lange, *Otto Rahn*, pp. 19–21, 39–42.

125. Lange, *Otto Rahn*, pp. 22–4; Kaufmann, *Tibet*, p. 175; Goodrick-Clarke, *Occult Roots*, p. 189; Wegener, *Himmler*, pp. 17–18. Rahn argued further that Esclarmonde, a famous Cathar saint, was the 'real Satan' and he embraced the theosophic-ariosophic myth of Shambala. Wegener, *Schuler*, pp. 67–8; Wegener, *Himmler*, p. 90; Michael Hesemann, *Hitlers Religion: Die fatale Heilslehre des Nationalsozialismus*, Munich: Pattloch Verlag, 2004, pp. 345–8; Otto Rahn, *Kreuzzug gegen den Gral*, Freiburg: Urban Verlag, 1934, p. 137.

126. Lange, *Otto Rahn*, pp. 23–8, 48–54; Kaufmann, *Tibet*, p. 175; Goodrick-Clarke, *Occult Roots*, p. 189; Goodrick-Clarke, *Black Sun*, pp. 134–5. As Rahn noted, his first book, 'accords with the National Socialist way of thinking and ... initiated my invitation to join the staff of the Reichsführer SS'. Lange, *Otto Rahn*, p. 27.

127. Letters from Rahn to Weist, 19.10.36; Bergmann to Brandt, 4.11.36, NL Himmler, BAK: NS 1126/21; Lange, *Otto Rahn*, pp. 55–6.

128. Otto Rahn, *Luzifers Hofgesind*. Dresden, Zeitwende, 2006, p. 8.

129. Rahn, *Luzifers Hofgesind*, p. 9; Joscelyn Godwin, *Arktos. Der polare Mythos zwischen NS-Okkultismus und moderner Esoterik*, Graz: Ares 2007, pp. 110–11; Lange, *Otto Rahn*, pp. 21–2, 26, 42.

130. Spence, *Occult Causes*, pp. 40–1, 80–2; Steven C. Weisenburger, *A Gravity's Rainbow Companion: Sources and Contexts for Pynchon's Novel*, Athens, GA: University of Georgia, 2011, p. 203.

131. Lange, *Otto Rahn*, p. 29.

132. Jung himself kept a 'book of spells for making magic in the name of Baldur'; http://archive.org/stream/MemoriesDreamsReflectionsCarlJung/carlgustavjung-interviewsandencounters-110821120821-phpapp02_djvu.txt, p. 177; Koehne, 'National Socialists', pp. 770–3; Susannah Heschel, *The Aryan Jesus: Christian Theologians and the Bible in Nazi Germany*, Princeton, NJ: Princeton University Press, 2008, pp. 21–8.

133. Frenzolf Schmid, 21.3.37, BAB: NS 19: 3974, p. 9; see also Sievers to Schmid, 31.3.42; Schmid to Himmler, 17.1.39, 23.7.40, BAB: NS 21/2294; Reichstein to Schmid, 8.7.43, letter from SS to Reichstein, 21.6.43, Schmid to Languth, 11.1.37, 24.1.37, 10.3.39, in R 9361–V/10777; Kaufmann, *Tibet*, pp. 172–4.

134. Goodrick-Clarke, *Black Sun*, pp. 134–5.

135. Horst Junginger, 'From Buddha to Adolf Hitler: Walther Wüst and the Aryan Tradition', in Junginger, ed., *The Study of Religion under the Impact of Fascism*, Leiden: Brill, 2007, p. 143; Kaufmann, *Tibet*, pp. 173–4, 348–9; Kersten, *Memoirs*, pp. 152–4; Redles, *Reich*, pp. 53–7; Lange, *Otto Rahn*, p. 16; Longerich, *Himmler*, pp. 294–6.

136. Gugenberger and Schweidlenka, *Faden der Nornen*, p. 175.

137. Letters, 5.437, 7.4.37, BAB: NS 19/688; Lange, *Otto Rahn*, pp. 28–9, 56–63.

138. Lange, *Otto Rahn*, pp. 19–21; Moynihan and Flowers, *Secret King*, pp. 57–8; Lange, *Otto Rahn*, pp. 39–40.

139. Lange, *Otto Rahn*, pp. 27–8, 56–63; Goodrick-Clarke, *Occult Roots*, p. 189.

140. Letter, 5.4.37, regarding Himmler's office of Luzifers Hofgesind from the publisher; 7.4.37, a response by Himmler's office ordering the five special copies in parchment, and that the pricing be put in writing to Berlin, BAB: NS 19/688; Lange, *Otto Rahn*, pp. 28–9, 56–63.

141. After getting transferred to guard duty at Dachau as a form of penance, Rahn chose to resign from the SS rather than experience continued disciplinary action. But Himmler tried to rehabilitate his star religious scholar by urging him to stop drinking and to marry a close female friend in early 1939. Rahn chose suicide instead, dying of exposure in the Alps. Nigel Graddon, *Otto Rahn and the Quest for the Grail: The Amazing Life of the Real Indiana* Jones, Kempton, IL: Adventures Unlimited Press, 2008, pp. 159–62; Moynihan and Flowers, *Secret King*, pp. 57–8; Lange, *Otto Rahn*, pp. 30–5, 70–1; letters from 10.2.38; 17.11.40 request for fifty new copies of *Kreuzzug*, followed by a letter from the publisher fulfilling a request on 3.1.41; 6.4.38, more financial issues with the firm Spamer, in which RSK under Hanns Johst is involved; 3.11.37, Rahn to Johst, BAB: R 9361–V/9665 (Otto Rahn).

142. Lange, *Otto Rahn*, pp. 37–9; Rahn, *Luzifers Hofgesind*, BAB: NS 19/688.

143. Letter to SS Brigadefuhrer Dr Naumann, 2.11.43, BAB: NS 19/688.

144. Webendörfer to Brandt, 15.2.44; Himmler's personal staff to Webendörfer, 26.6.44, BAB: NS 19/688; Lange, *Otto Rahn*, p. 35; Rahn, *Luzifers Hofgesind*, pp. 6–10, 72–86.

145. Junginger, 'From Buddha to Adolf Hitler', pp. 127–8; Kaufmann, *Tibet*, pp. 349–50; positive reports on speeches, 13.7.38, 16.3.38; positive view by Langsdorff in his essay, 'Gralsmysterium und Reichsgedanke', 16.3.38, NS 21/1333.

146. April 1939 SD Report on Julius Evola, pp. 1–2; Evola to Six, 15.6.39; Evola to Six, 20.8.39; BAB: R 58/6517; Junginger, 'From Buddha to Adolf Hitler', pp. 132–5.

147. April 1939 SD Report on Julius Evola, pp. 1–2, BAB: R 58/6517, pp. 2–3.

148. Goodrick-Clarke, *Occult Roots*, pp. 189–91.

149. Ibid., pp. 178–9, 182–3; Longerich, *Himmler*, pp. 284–5; Treitel, *Science*, p. 214; Lange, *Otto Rahn*, p. 25; Moynihan and Flowers, *Secret King*, pp. 44–6.

150. Goodrick-Clarke, *Occult Roots*, p. 182; Treitel, *Science*, p. 214; Hans-Jürgen Lange, *Weisthor: Karl-Maria Wiligut, Himmlers Rasputin und seine Erben*, Arun-Verlag: Engerda, 1998, p. 6.

151. Goodrick-Clarke, *Occult Roots*, pp. 182–4; Treitel, *Science*, p. 214; Lange, *Otto Rahn*, p. 25; Pringle, *Plan*, pp. 46–8; Longerich, *Himmler*, p. 284; Junginger and Ackerlund, eds, *Nordic Ideology*, p. 55.

152. Goodrick-Clarke, *Occult Roots*, p. 180.

153. Pringle, *Plan*, pp. 46–7.

154. Longerich, *Himmler*, pp. 285–6; Goodrick-Clarke, *Occult Roots*, p. 177; Kaufmann, *Tibet*, pp. 124–6. Dozens of Nazi and SS researchers took mediumistic and visionary abilities seriously, which included conducting an ongoing investigation into the powers of the Catholic religious visionary and stigmatic Therese Neumann. Michael O'Sullivan, 'Disruptive Potential: Therese Neumann of Konnersreuth, National Socialism, and Democracy', in Black and Kurlander, eds, *Revisiting*, pp. 188–93.

155. Pringle, *Plan*, p. 100.

156. Trimondi, *Hitler*, p. 107.

157. Kaufmann, *Tibet*, p. 174; Goodrick-Clarke, *Occult Roots*, pp. 180–1; Junginger and Ackerlund, eds, *Nordic Ideology*, pp. 55–6.

158. Goodrick-Clarke, *Occult Roots*, pp. 285–6.

159. Kaufmann, *Tibet*, pp. 173, 368–70; Trimondi, *Hitler*, pp. 107–9; Longerich, *Himmler*, p. 266.

160. Treitel, *Science*, p. 214; Felix Wiedemann, 'Altes Wissen', in Puschner and Vollnhals, eds, *Bewegung*, pp. 463–4; Goodrick-Clarke, *Occult Roots*, pp. 177–8, 186–7; Longerich, *Himmler*, pp. 285–6, 293–4.

161. Bernard Mees, *The Science of the Swastika*, Budapest: Central European University Press, 2008, pp. 180–1; see Fritz Paul, *History of the Scandinavian Languages at the Georg-August-Universität Göttingen: A Preliminary Sketch*, Göttingen, 1985; http://www.uni-goettingen.de/de/91592.html; http://www.dhm.de/lemo/html/nazi/innenpolitik/ahnenerbe/index.html; Kater, *Das 'Ahnenerbe'*, pp. 196–7; Wolfgang Krause, *Runeninschriften im älteren Futhark*, Halle: Niemeyer, 1937; Ulrich Hunger, *Die Runenkunde im Dritten Reich. Ein Beitrag zur Wissenschafts- und Ideologiegeschichte des Nationalsozialismus*, Frankfurt am Main: Lang, 1984; also letters to and from Karl Theodor Weigel, article on 'Zur Frage der Sinnbildforschung', 21.10.42, Sievers sends the book to Himmler; 16.12.41, Weigel sends his book on *In Sand gestreute Sinnbilder* to Plassmann, BAB: NS 21/2649; Wolfgang Krause writes to Wüst, 15.5.42, about Rune institutes; Wüst to Himmler, 5.2.43; 10.2.43, Wüst to Krause confirming he is now 'Leiter der Lehr- und Forschungsstätte für Runen- und Sinnbildkunde'; 10.9.41, letter from Sievers extolling Krause's work regarding 'Speerblatt von Wolfsburg'; more material on lance in Wolhynien; 25.6.40, Krause writes to Sievers about the famous Lance of Kowel, BAB: NS 21/1784.

162. Junginger, 'From Buddha to Adolf Hitler', pp. 116–18; Kaufmann, *Tibet*, pp. 127–8, 173–4.

163. Kater, *Das 'Ahnenerbe'*, pp. 12–13; see also Pringle, *Plan*, pp. 54–7; Dow and Lixfeld, eds, *Nazification*, pp. 100–5; Junginger, 'Intro', in Junginger and Ackerlund, eds, *Nordic Ideology*, pp. 8–9; ibid., pp. 47–50.

164. Pringle, *Plan*, pp. 73–5; Longerich, *Himmler*, p. 224; Kaufmann, *Tibet*, pp. 173–4; Rudolf, 'Geheime Reichskommando-Sache!', pp. 55–8; Mees, 'Hitler and Germanentum', pp. 262–3; Junginger and Ackerlund, eds, *Nordic Ideology*, pp. 50–1.

165. Longerich, *Himmler*, pp. 293–5.

166. Pringle, *Plan*, pp. 48–9; Kaufmann, *Tibet*, pp. 371–2; Longerich, *Himmler*, p. 294; Lange, *Otto Rahn*, p. 25; Junginger and Ackerlund, eds, *Nordic Ideology*, p. 56. For more on SS castle research, see Fabian Link, *Burgen und Burgenforschung in Nationalsozialismus*, Cologne: Böhlau, 2014; Link, 'Der Mythos Burg im Nationalsozialismus', in Ulrich Grossmann and Hans Ottomeyer, eds, *Die Burg*. Dresden: Sandstein, 2010, pp. 302–11; Harten, *Himmlers Forscher*, pp. 160–71.

167. Pringle, *Plan*, p. 49; Longerich, *Himmler*, pp. 294–6; Goodrick-Clarke, *Occult Roots*, pp. 186–8; Moynihan and Flowers, *Secret King*, pp. 47–51.

168. Kaufmann, *Tibet*, pp. 371–2; Goodrick-Clarke, *Occult Roots*, p. 187.

169. Longerich, *Himmler*, p. 294.

170. Ibid., pp. 296–7; Junginger, 'From Buddha to Adolf Hitler', p. 121; a letter 'Über SS-Sturmbannführer Galke an das "Ahnenerbe"', BAB: NS 19 1163; Mees, 'Hitler and Germanentum', pp. 255–70; Kater, *Das 'Ahnenerbe'*, pp. 81–2.

171. Lawrence Hare, *Excavating Nations: Archaeology, Museums, and the German-Danish Borderlands*, Toronto: University of Toronto Press, pp. 146–7; Lawrence Hare and Fabian Link, '"Pseudoscience" Reconsidered', in Black and Kurlander, eds, *Revisiting*; Kater, *Das 'Ahnenerbe'*, pp. 54–5; Mees, 'Hitler

and Germanentum', pp. 255–70; Reinerth to DFG, 23.4.37, asking for money to support his Reichsbund für Deutsche Vorgeschichte and Rosenberg's project of creating an Atlas der Deutsche Vorgeschichte; 14.4.38, Reinerth reporting on research on RfDV letterhead, BAB: NS 21/2136; Wilhelm Teudt: NS 21/2528, Teudt article on Detmold, 4.6.38; Teudt speech, 10.6.38 speech; Teudt speech from Vienna, 14.4.37; reports, 4.11.37, 12.2.38, suggesting conflict between Teudt, Pohl, and Steinecke (witch studies) in Ahnenerbe, in which Himmler has to intervene.

172. Wüst, *Indogermanisches Bekenntnis*, pp. 3–7.
173. Goodrick-Clarke, *Occult Roots*, pp. 188–90; Treitel, *Science*, pp. 214–15; Rudolf J. Mund, *Der Rasputin Himmlers: Die Wiligut Saga*, Bochum: Zeitreisen, 2014, pp. 284–7; Lange, *Otto Rahn*, p. 25; Goodrick-Clarke, *Occult Roots*, p. 190; see letters from Wiligut to Brandt, Galke, etc., from July 1940, BAB: NS 19/1573; Piper, 'Steigmann-Gall, *The Holy Reich*', p. 50; Paul, *History of the Scandinavian Languages*.
174. Treitel, *Science*, p. 214; Mund, *Der Rasputin Himmlers*; Longerich, *Himmler*, p. 285; Moynihan and Flowers, *Secret King*, pp. 27–8.
175. Kershaw, *Hubris*, pp. 142–4.
176. Koehne, 'Paganism', pp. 766–8; Kaufmann, *Tibet*, p. 170.
177. Koehne, 'Paganism', pp. 778–80.
178. Ibid., pp. 787–8.
179. Ibid., pp. 784–6; Kaufmann, *Tibet*, pp. 359–61.
180. Kater, *Das 'Ahnenerbe'*, pp. 35–7, 320–5; Peter Bahn, *Friedrich Hielscher, 1902–1990: Einführung in Leben und Werk*, Schnellbach: Biblies, 1999, pp. 71–4, 81–2; letter showing Hielscher accepted into RSK, 9.9.39, in R 9361–V/22175; Koehne, 'Paganism', pp. 780–1.
181. Koehne, 'Paganism', pp. 788–90.
182. Darré diary, NL Darré, BAK: N 1094I-65a, pp. 31–4; Bramwell, *Blood and Soil*, pp. 75–7, 80–90, 133.
183. Rheden biography in NL Darré, BAK: N 1094I/77, pp. 94–7, 113–21; see also entries in NL Darré, BAK: N 1094I/65a, p. 44; Rheden biography in NL Darré, BAK: N 1094I-77, pp. 107–8, 121.
184. Darré diary in NL Darré, BAK: N 1094I-65a, p. 33; see also Bramwell, *Blood and Soil*, pp. 54–55, 60–61; Vortrag von Rudolf Steiner, *Das Miterleben der Geistigkeit und Bildekräfte der Natur*; Dornach 20. Januar 1923; Forschungsring für Biologisch-Dynamische Wirtschaftsweise Juni 1948; in NL Darré, BAK: N 1094I/33, p. 1–5. BAK: N1094I-33.
185. Bärsch, *Politische Religion*, pp. 198–9, 202–8, 263–4; Gugenberger and Schweidlenka, *Faden der Nornen*, pp. 154–61.
186. Gugenberger and Schweidlenka, *Faden der Norne*, pp. 116–17; Spence, *Occult Causes*, pp. 158–9, 178.
187. Koehne, 'Paganism', pp. 788–9; Cecil, *Myth*, p. 95; Gugenberger and Schweidlenka, *Faden der Nornen*, pp. 166–7.
188. Gugenberger and Schweidlenka, *Faden der Nornen*, pp. 129–32, 163–6; Steigmann-Gall, *Holy Reich*, p. 263; Cecil, *Myth*, pp. 36–41, 111–19; Bronder, *Bevor Hitler kam*, pp. 261–3.
189. Koehne, 'Paganism', pp. 789–90; Spence, *Occult Causes*, p. 141.
190. Mees, 'Hitler and Germanentum', pp. 263–5. In 1934, Rosenberg recruited the *völkisch* religious theorist (and anthroposophist) Werner Haverbeck to lead his Reich Association for Ethnicity and Homeland (*Reichsbund Volkstum und Heimat*), which subsequently organized *völkisch*-pagan religious festivals. Letter to Reichs und Preussische Ministerium für Wissenschaft Erziehung und Volksbilding, indicating Himmler's desire to employ Werner Haverbeck, 9.4.36; Haverbeck to University of Berlin, 14.4.36, BAB: NS 21/1539.
191. Longerich, *Himmler*, pp. 286–7.
192. Ibid., pp. 742–3; see also Kater, *Das 'Ahnenerbe'*, pp. 567; Longerich, *Himmler*, pp. 288–90; Pringle, *Plan*, p. 84; Kersten, *Memoirs*, pp. 151–3.
193. Pringle, *Plan*, p. 84; Longerich, *Himmler*, p. 291; Kater, *Das 'Ahnenerbe'*, pp. 80–1.
194. Longerich, *Himmler*, p. 287; Junginger, 'From Buddha to Adolf Hitler', p. 122; Richard Wolffram, 'Leiter der Kulturkommission beim Deutschen Umsiedlungsbevollmächtigten für die Provinz Laibach' (1941); Plassmann to Wolfram, 23.10.40, sending Roman de Fauvel; 21.3.40, Prödinger to Sievers over new 'Jünglingsweihen' for HY and DM; 31.3.43, Sievers letter trying to transfer Wolfram, noting his work for the 'volkskundlichen Sektor bei der Umsiedlung der Südtiroler im Mai 1940'. See file 'Richard Wolffram', BAB (signature unknown).
195. Longerich, *Himmler*, p. 294.
196. Ibid., p. 298.
197. Pringle, *Plan*, pp. 77, 87–90; Fritz Bose, 'Law and Freedom in the Interpretation of European Folk Epics', *Journal of the International Folk Music Council* 10 (1958), p. 31.
198. See Lutz Hachmeister, 'Der Gegnerforscher. Die Karriere des SS-Führers Franz Alfred Six, München', and Jörg Rudolf, 'Geheime Reichskommando-Sache!' – Hexenjäger im Schwarzen Orden. Der H-Sonderauftrag des Reichsführers-SS, 1935–1944', in Bauer et al., *Hexenkartothek*, pp. 84–5, 177–8.

199. Longerich, *Himmler*, pp. 289–92; Piper, 'Steigmann-Gall', p. 56.

200. Pringle, *Plan*, p. 80, Longerich, *Himmler*, p. 225.

201. Longerich, *Himmler*, pp. 266–7.

202. Pennick, *Secret Sciences*, pp. 42–3; Treitel, *Science*, p. 214; Goodrick-Clarke, *Occult Roots*, pp. 177–8, 186–7; Longerich, *Himmler*, pp. 285–6, 293–4; Werner Haverbeck (Christian Community priest and friend of Ohlendorff) to Sievers, 16.4.36; Plassman to Sievers, 20.11.36; request to Lembke for *Gutachten*, 20.11.36; Lembke to Plassman, 21.11.36; Sievers to Wolff, 23.11.36; Wirth to Sievers, 13.1.38, 19.1.38; letter on Haverbeck's acceptance into Ahnenerbe, 30.4.38; BAB: NS 21/1539.

203. Weisenburger, *A Gravity's Rainbow Companion*, pp. 20, 203.

204. Schertel, *Magic*, pp. 118–19.

205. Ibid., p. 80.

206. Bärsch, *Politische Religion*, pp. 293–6, 354–7; Ach, *Hitlers Religion*, pp. 52–4; Goodrick-Clarke, *Occult Roots*, pp. 200–2; Koehne, 'Paganism', pp. 789–90.

207. Gugenberger and Schweidlenka, *Faden der Nornen*, pp. 146–50; Spence, *Occult Causes*, pp. 66–9; Ach, *Hitlers Religion*, pp. 76–7; Maier, 'Political Religion', pp. 7–8.

208. Ach, *Hitlers Religion*, pp. 108, 140–3.

209. Mees, 'Hitler and Germanentum', pp. 267–9; Vondung, *Deutsche Wege*, pp. 82–6.

210. Koehne, 'Paganism', pp. 772–3.

211. Ach, *Hitlers Religion*, pp. 37, 104–7, 142–3; Steigmann-Gall, *Holy Reich*, pp. 96–101, 112–13.

212. Rauschning, *Voice of Destruction*, p. 245; Schertel, *Magic*, p. 46.

213. Koehne, 'Paganism', pp. 773–4; see also Spence, *Occult Causes*, pp. 142–3; H. R. Knickerbocker, 'Diagnosing the Dictators', *Hearst's International Cosmopolitan* (January 1939), in McGuire and Hull, eds, *C. G. Jung Speaking*, pp. 114–22.

214. Koehne, 'Were the National Socialists a Völkisch Party?', pp. 789–90; Bronder, *Bevor Hitler kam*, pp. 205–9, 213–17; Piper 'Steigmann-Gall', pp. 51–3; Koehne, 'Paganism', pp. 789–90; Heschel, *Aryan Jesus*, pp. 68–81.

215. Poewe, *New Religions*, p. i.

216. Junginger and Ackerlund, eds, *Nordic Ideology*, pp. 43–6; see also Horst Junginger and Martin Finkberger, eds, *Im Dienste der Lügen. Herbert Grabert (1901–1978) und seine Verlage*, Aschaffenburg: Alibri, 2004; Ulrich Nanko, *Die Deutsche Glaubensbewegung. Eine historische und soziologische Untersuchung*, Marburg: Diagonal, 1993; Schaul Baumann, *Die Deutsche Glaubensbewegung und ihr Gründer Jakob Wilhelm Hauer (1881–1962)*, Marburg: Diagonal, 2005.

217. Poewe, *New Religions*, pp. 10–11; Karla Poewe and Irving Hexham, 'Surprising Aryan Mediations between German Indology and Nazism: Research and the Adluri/Grünendahl Debate', *International Journal of Hindu Studies* 19:3 (September 2015), p. 14; Poewe, *New Religions*, pp. 10–14, 57–65; see also Horst Junginger, 'Die Deutsche Glaubensbewegung als ideologisches Zentrum der völkisch-religiösen Bewegung', in Puschner and Vollnhals, eds, *Bewegung*, pp. 65–102.

218. Junginger, 'Glaubensbwegung', pp. 83–5; Junginger and Ackerlund, eds, *Nordic Ideology*, p. 40–3; Kaufmann, *Tibet*, p. 176; see also Juninger and Finkberger, eds, *Im Dienste der Lügen*.

219. Junginger and Ackerlund, eds, *Nordic Ideology*, pp. 43–4.

220. Gailius, 'A Strange Obsession', p. 38

221. Indeed, members of the Nazi Party very clearly 'promoted the ideas of Liebenfels, List, Dinter, and Fritsch' Koehne, 'Paganism', pp. 786–7. As Horst Junginger notes, this was a disproportionate number of the nearly three million unaffiliated 'God-believing' Germans in 1939 – a category created by Hess in 1936 to encourage religious-minded but pagan-inclined Germans to leave the traditional churches. Junginger also speculates that the NSDAP and SS had a disproportionate number of 'God-believing' individuals. Junginger and Ackerlund, eds, *Nordic Ideology*, pp. 63–4.

222. http://www.guardian.co.uk/world/2012/sep/28/nazi-buddha-statue-carved-from-meteorite/print.

223. Engelhardt, 'Nazis of Tibet'.

224. Kaufmann, *Tibet*, pp. 19–31.

225. Koehne, 'Paganism', pp. 784–6.

226. Goepfert, *Immer noch Aberglaube!*, pp. 3–11; Junginger, 'From Buddha to Adolf Hitler', pp. 125–43; Kröner, *Wiedergeburt des Magischen*, p. 24.

227. Kaufmann, *Tibet*, p. 754.

228. Quade speech, 'Occultism and Politics', pp. 34–6; Kaufmann, *Tibet*, pp. 347–9; Ach, *Hitlers Religion*, pp. 50–1.

229. Junginger, 'From Buddha to Adolph Hitler', p. 143; Engelhardt, 'Nazis of Tibet'; Graddon, *Otto Rahn*, pp. 210–19; Longerich, *Himmler*, pp. 281–2; Kaufmann, *Tibet*, pp. 130–9; Christopher Hale, *Himmler's Crusade: The Nazi Expedition to Find the Origins of the Aryan Race*, London: Wiley, 2003, pp. 19–27.

230. Kaufmann, *Tibet*, pp. 392–4.

231. Hans F. K. Günther, *The Racial Elements of European History*, London: Methuen, 1927; Hans F. K. Günther, *Die nordische Rasse bei den Indogermanen Asiens*, Munich: J. F. Lehmanns, 1934, pp. 3–11

232. Poewe and Hexham, 'Surprising Aryan Mediations', p. 15; Junginger, 'From Buddha to Adolf Hitler', pp. 147–9; Piper, 'Steigmann-Gall, *The Holy Reich*', pp. 52–3; Staudenmaier, 'Nazi Perceptions of Esotericism', pp. 32–6; SD report on Hauer, 5.6.39, BAB: R 58/6217; Hauer letter to SD on occult religious sects, 23.7.38, BAB: R 58/6206.

233. SD report from 30.6.41, pp. 7–10, BAB: R 58/6517.

234. Poewe and Hexham, 'Surprising Aryan Mediations', p. 15.

235. Trimondi, *Hitler*, pp. 61–3.

236. Buddha did not want to ignore terrestrial matters, as theologians traditionally argued, but inspired his followers to influence the world through 'passive heroism'. Trimondi, *Hitler*, pp. 77–9.

237. Poewe and Hexham, 'Surprising Aryan Mediations', p. 15.

238. SD report from 30.6.41, BAB: R 58/6517, pp. 6–10.

239. Vishwa Adluri and Joydeep Bagchee, eds, *When the Goddess was a Woman*, Leiden: Brill, 2011, p. xxx.

240. See Kater, *Das 'Ahnenerbe'*, pp. 43–6; Junginger, *Nordic Ideology*, p. 177; Junginger and Ackerlund, eds, *Nordic Ideology*, pp. 51–2.

241. Wüst, *Indogermanisches Bekenntnis*, pp. 10–12, 19–20.

242. Here 'the Buddha ends up in the mind of Hitler'. Poewe and Hexham, 'Surprising Aryan Mediations', p. 10; Junginger, 'From Buddha to Adolf Hitler', pp. 125–6.

243. Junginger, 'From Buddha to Adolf Hitler', pp. 105–78.

244. Wüst, *Indogermanisches Bekenntnis*, pp. 46–50; Junginger, 'From Buddha to Adolf Hitler', pp. 109–10.

245. Wüst, *Indogermanisches Bekenntnis*, pp. 29–39, 86–7, 103; Walther Wüst, *Japan und Wir*, Berlin-Dahlem: Ahnenerbe-Stiftung, 1942, pp. 3–29.

246. Kater, *Das 'Ahnenerbe'*, pp. 51–2; Reinhard Greve, 'Tibetforschung im SS Ahnenerbe', in Thomas Hauschild, ed., *Lebenslust durch Fremdenfurcht*, Frankfurt am Main: Suhrkamp, 1995, pp. 168–209; Glowka, *Okkultgruppen*, pp. 111–15.

247. Ingo Wiwjorra, 'Herman Wirth – Ein gescheiterter Ideologe zwischen "Ahnenerbe" und "Atlantis" ', in Barbara Danckwortt, ed., *Historische Rassismusforschung. Ideologen, Täter, Opfer*, Hamburg: Argument, 1995; see also Franz Wegener, *Das atlantidische Weltbild: Nationalsozialismus und Neue Rechte auf der Suche nach der versunkenen Atlantis*, Gladbeck: Kulturförderverein Ruhrgebiet, 2003.

248. Trimondi, *Hitler*, pp. 37–8.

249. Kaufmann, *Tibet*, pp. 131–2.

250. Rolf Wilhelm Brednich, 'The Weigel Symbol Archive and the Ideology of National Socialist Folklore', in Dow and Lixfeld, eds, *Nazification*, pp. 97–111.

251. Memo by Wiligut, 13.1.37, letter to Wiligut (Weisthor), 9.3.37, BAB: NS 19 3974; Wegener, *Himmler*, pp. 78–81.

252. Frenzolf Schmid to RSK, 12.8.35; RSK, 27.4.40; 4.5.40, on *Last Ramadan*, R 9361–V/10777.

253. Memo by Weisthor, 9.3.37; memo by Weisthor, 23.4.37, BAB:NS 19 3974; Schmid was 'certain that de Mengel's conclusions', whether 'consciously or unconsiously', were indebted to the traditions of the 'Atlanteans, Germans and Indo-Germans … recalling the Aryan-Atlantean world circle that was taken over not only by Germans but other Aryan peoples. These Atlantean-Aryan Holy numbers led to the German triangle and pentagram' – a magic Atlantean-German world triangle or 'axis' that connects the Nordic countries with France, South Asia and Tibet. Letter by Frenzolf Schmid, 21.3.37, BAB: NS 19 3974, p. 10; Schmid, *Urtexte-der-Ersten-Goettlichen-Offenbarung: Attalantinische Ur-Bibel.Das Goldene Buch der Menschheit, Mit den ersten offenbarungen aus der Paradieseszeit zurückreichend auf 85000 Jahre vor Christi geburt (Nach attalantinische Überlieferungen und altindischen Aufzeichnungen aus den Urtexten wiederhergestellt*, Pforzheim: Reichstein, 1931; see also Kaufmann, *Tibet*, pp. 371–2.

254. Trimondi, *Hitler*, pp. 110–11; Kaufmann, *Tibet*, pp. 368–70.

255. To achieve its goals, Sievers argued, National Socialism needed to appropriate the qualities of 'innerness', 'transcendence', and 'faith' embodied by the SS and 'religions of the east'.Trimondi, *Hitler*, pp. 67–8; Kaufmann, *Tibet*, pp. 141–3.

256. Longerich, *Himmler*, pp. 280–1; Kaufmann, *Tibet*, pp. 172–4.

257. Pringle, *Plan*, p. 150; Carol Otto, *Hitler's Japanese Confidant*, Lawrence, KS, 1993; Oshima and Himmler, 31.1.39, International Military Tribunal Nuremberg, *Trial of Major German War Criminals*, vol. 2, IMT Nuremberg, 1947, p. 135.

258. Junginger, 'From Buddha to Hitler', p. 143; Kater, *Das 'Ahenenerbe'*, pp. 51–3; Longerich, *Himmler*, pp. 280–2; Greve, 'Tibetforschung im SS Ahnenerbe', pp. 168–209.

259. Berzin, 'The Nazi Connection with Shambhala and Tibet'.

260. Ernst Schäfer, *Fest der weissen Schleier: Eine Forscherfahrt durch Tibet nach Lhasa, der heiligen Stadt des Gottkönigtums* (*Festival of the White Gauze Scarves: A Research Expedition through Tibet to Lhasa, the Holy City of the God Realm*), Wiesbaden: Vieweg & Teubner, 1950; Berzin, 'The Nazi Connection with Shambhala and Tibet'; Longerich, *Himmler*, p. 282; Engelhardt, 'Nazis of Tibet'.

261. Kaufmann, *Tibet*, p. 192.

262. Ibid., pp. 204–9; Pringle, *Plan*, pp. 149–50; Kater, *Das 'Ahnenerbe'*, pp. 75–9; Junginger, 'From Buddha to Adolf Hitler', p. 143.

263. Kaufmann, *Tibet*, pp. 141–2, 212–18.

264. Pringle, *Plan*, pp. 150–1; Kater, *Das 'Ahenenerbe'*, pp. 51–2.

265. Pringle, *Plan*, pp. 151–2; Engelhardt, 'Nazis of Tibet'; Kenneth Hite, *The Nazi Occult*, Oxford: Osprey, 2013, p. 44; Kaufmann, *Tibet*, pp. 198–200.

266. Trimondi, *Hitler*, p. 130.

267. 'In the darkness of the world the Aryans brought light.' 'We believe in [the Führer] because he is Germany, because he is Germania. His light illuminates everything.' Trimondi, *Hitler*, p. 127.

268. Ibid., p. 128; Pringle, *Plan*, p. 171.

269. Trimondi, *Hitler*, pp. 143–4.

270. Pringle, *Plan*, p. 173.

271. Trimondi, *Hitler*, pp. 150–5.

272. Ibid., pp. 137–40.

273. Schäfer to Brandt, 25.6.40, pp. 3–6, BAB: N 19/2709.

274. Ibid., pp. 11–12, BAB: N 19/2709.

275. Manjapra, *Age of Entanglement*, pp. 244, 261, 266–7.

276. Schäfer to Brandt, 25.6.40, pp. 3–6, 16, BAB: N19/2709

277. Kaufmann, *Tibet*, pp. 193, 232–49; Junginger, 'Intro', in Junginger and Ackerlund, eds, *Nordic Ideology*, pp. 11–12; ibid., p. 53.

278. Kaufmann, *Tibet*, pp. 178–80.

279. Pringle, *Plan*, p. 79.

280. Eckart, *Der Bolschewismus*, p. 7.

281. Picker, *Tischgespräche*, pp. 74, 94.

282. Perry Myers, 'Leopold von Schroeder's Imagined India: Buddhist Spirituality and Christian Politics During the Wilhelmine Era', *German Studies Review* 32:3 (October 2009), p. 619.

283. Schertel, *Magic*, pp. 80–7, 97–101, 128; Trimondi, *Hitler*, pp. 107–9; Bronder, *Bevor Hitler kam*, pp. 219–20.

284. Kaufmann, *Tibet*, pp. 116–19, 176–7.

285. Ach, *Hitlers Religion*, pp. 109–10, 141–3, 148; Gailius, 'A Strange Obsession', p. 40.

286. Trevor-Roper, ed., *Conversations*, pp. 339–40; Picker, *Tischgespräche*, pp. 209–11, 267, 355; Kaufmann, *Tibet*, pp. 179–80.

287. Trevor-Roper, ed., *Conversations*, p. 319; Picker, *Tischgespräche*, p. 184.

288. Motadel, *Islam*, p. 65; Jeffrey Herf, 'Nazi Germany's Propaganda Aimed at Arabs and Muslims During World War II and the Holocaust: Old Themes, New Archival Findings', *Central European History* 42 (2009), pp. 709–36; Herf, 'Nazi Germany's Propaganda', pp. 199–202.

289. Spence, *Occult Causes*, pp. 142–4.

290. McGuire and Hull, eds, *C. G. Jung Speaking*, pp. 122–3.

291. Kaufmann, *Tibet*, pp. 100–1; Berzin, 'The Nazi Connection with Shambhala and Tibet'; Dow and Lixfeld, eds, *Nazification*, pp. 21–2; Engelhardt, 'Nazis of Tibet'.

292. NL Darré, in BAK N 1094I-65a, p. 31; Kaufmann, *Tibet*, pp. 101–2.

293. Gugenberger and Schweidlenka, *der Nornen*, pp. 116–20.

294. Trevor-Roper, ed., *Bormann Letters*, pp. 51–4.

295. Ibid., pp. xix–xx.

296. Ibid., pp. 47–8.

297. Berzin, 'The Nazi Connection with Shambhala'.

298. Bronder, *Bevor Hitler kam*, pp. 239–45; Bruno Hipler, *Hitlers Lehrmeister: Karl Haushofer als Vater der NS-Ideologie*, St Ottilien: EOS, 1996, pp. 54–63.

299. Motadel, *Islam*, p. 62; see Walther Darré, *Tagebuch*, p. 43, NL Darré, BAK: N 1094I-65a; Darré notes and articles on Steiner and 'biodynamic' agricultural practices in BAK: N 1094I-33; Werner, *Anthroposophen*, pp. 74–94.

300. SD report on Dacqué, 30.6.41, BAB: R 58/6517, pp. 21–6.

301. Rheden biography, NL Darré, BAK: N 1094I-77, p. 62.

302. Ibid., pp. 62, 86; Steiner, 'Westliche und östliche Weltgegensätzlichkeit', in Darré, BAK: N 1094I-33, pp. 1–4.

303. Rheden biography, NL Darré, BAK: N 1094I-77, p. 86.
304. Ibid., p. 96.
305. Diary in NL Darré, BAK: N 1094I-65a, p. 43.
306. Trimondi, *Hitler*, p. 32.
307. Wulff, *Zodiac*, pp. 103–8.
308. Trimondi, *Hitler*, p. 90; Kersten, *Memoirs*, pp. 148–54.
309. Trimondi, *Hitler*, pp. 81–2; see Vishwa Adluri and Joydeep Bagchee, *The Nay Science: A History of German Indology*, Oxford: Oxford University Press, 2014, pp. 69–76, 81–3, 131–2.
310. Kersten, *Memoirs*, pp. 149–54; Kaufmann, *Tibet*, p. 170; Manvell and Frankel, Longerich, *Himmler*, pp. 181–2; Ach, *Hitlers Religion*, pp. 23–6.
311. Longerich, *Himmler*, p. 285.
312. Kersten, *Memoirs*, p. 151; see also Longerich, *Himmler*, pp. 268–9.
313. Kersten, *Memoirs*, pp. 10–11; Wulff, *Zodiac*, pp. 103–5.
314. Treitel, *Science*, pp. 213–14; Kersten, *Memoirs*, pp. 10–11; Wulff, *Zodiac*, pp. 105–8.
315. Longerich, *Himmler*, pp. 269–70.
316. Ibid., pp. 268–9; Kaufmann, *Tibet*, pp. 359–60.
317. Longerich, *Himmler*, pp. 281–2.
318. Pringle, *Plan*, p. 145.
319. Motadel, *Islam*, pp. 60–1; Herf, 'Nazi Germany's Propaganda'; Rehwaldt, *Geheimbuende in Africa*, pp. 14–24.
320. Motadel, *Islam*, pp. 61–2; Herf, 'Nazi Germany's Propaganda'.
321. Herf, 'Nazi Germany's Propaganda', pp. 6, 90, 121, 157, 199–202.
322. Koehne, 'Paganism', pp. 768–72.
323. Marchand, *German Orientalism*, pp. xxii, 495. See also Zantop, *Colonial Fantasies*; see Berman, *Enlightenment or Empire*; Goodrick-Clarke, *Hitler's Priestess*, pp. 36–62.
324. Trimondi, *Hitler*, p. 20; see also Kaufmann, *Tibet*, pp. 179–82, 358–60; Herf, 'Nazi Germany's Propaganda', pp. 154–62, 194–204; Kater, *Das 'Ahnenerbe'*, pp. 320–5.
325. Trimondi, *Hitler*, p. 19; Junginger, 'From Buddha to Adolf Hitler', pp. 149–62.
326. Longerich, *Himmler*, p. 285.
327. Robert Soucy, 'Fascism in France', in Brian Jenkins, ed., *France in the Era of Fascism*, New York and Oxford, Berghahn, pp. 60–70; Peter Davies and Derek Lynch, *The Routledge Companion to the Far Right*, London: Routledge, 2002.
328. Piper, 'Steigmann-Gall, *The Holy Reich*', p. 56.
329. Ach, *Hitlers Religion*, pp. 78–84, 89–93; Koehne, 'Paganism', pp. 762–3; Treitel, *Science*, pp. 196–7.
330. Mosse, *Nationalization*, pp. 202–5; Burleigh, *The Third Reich*, pp. 261–5; Trevor-Roper, ed., *Conversations*, p. 173; Grabner-Haider and Strasser, *Hitlers mythische Religion*; Schier in Lorenz et al., 'Introduction', in Bauer et al., *Hexenkartothek*, pp. 3–17.
331. Junginger and Ackerlund, eds, *Nordic Ideology*, pp. 58–64.
332. Horst Heldt, 'Die Astrologie – eine Wissenschaft?', IGPP: 10 5 AII56.
333. Trimondi, *Hitler*, p. 40.
334. Williamson, *Longing for Myth*, pp. 291–6.

Chapter 7

1. Ingo Eser, *'Volk, Staat, Gott!' Die deutsche Minderheit in Polen und ihr Schulwesen 1918–1939*, Wiesbaden, 2010, p. 235.
2. 23.11.39, Goebbels, *Tagebücher*, as quoted in Maichle, 'Die Nostradamus-Propaganda'.
3. Bender to Krafft, 22.3.40, IGPP: 10/5 AII9 File 1 (Krafft – Walther).
4. Krafft to Bender, 27.3.40, IGPP: 10/5 AII9 File 2 (Krafft).
5. Bender to Schenz, 16.2.40, IGPP: 10/5 AII9 File 1 (Krafft – Walther); Goepfert, *Immer noch Aberglaube!*, pp. 3–16; Susanne Michl, 'Das wundersame 20. Jahrhundert?', in ibid., p. 236.
6. See, among others, A. J. P. Taylor, *Origins of the Second World War*, New York: Simon & Schuster, 1996; Tim Mason, 'Some Origins of the Second World War', in Caplan, ed., *Nazism;* Richard Overy, 'Germany, "Domestic Crisis" and War in 1939', in Christian Leitz, ed., *The Third Reich*, Oxford: Blackwell, 2006, pp. 95–128; Tooze, *Wages*.
7. See Sebastian Conrad, *Globalisation and the Nation in Imperial Germany*, Cambridge: Cambridge Univesity Press, 2010; Lora Wildenthal, *German Women for Empire, 1884–1945*, Durham, NC: Duke University Press, 2001; Zantop, *Colonial Fantasies*; Smith, *Politics and the Sciences*; Lixfeld, *Folklore and Fascism*; Gugenberger and Schweidlenka, *Faden der Nornen*, pp. 16–23; Darnton, 'Peasants Tell Tales', pp. 21–2, 50–63. See also Zipes, *Fairy Tale as Myth*.
8. Mosse, *Masses and Man*, pp. 76–7.

9. Fahlbusch, *Wissenschaft*; Haar, *Historiker im Nationalsozialismus*; Conrad, *Globalisation*; Wildenthal, *German Women*; Steve Attridge, *Nationalism, Imperialism and Identity in Late Victorian Culture: Civil and Military Worlds*, New York: Palgrave Macmillan, 2003; Zantop, *Colonial Fantasies*; Smith, *Politics and the Sciences*, pp. 163–5.

10. Dow and Lixfeld, eds, *Nazification*, pp. 21–2; Smith, *Politics and the Sciences*, pp. 162–3.

11. The 'secret of Hitler's power' is 'that his unconscious has exceptional access to his consciousness, and second, that he allows himself to be moved by it', in McGuire and Hull, eds, *C. G. Jung Speaking*, p. 118.

12. Alfred Karasek-Langer, 'Vom Sagengute der Vorkarpathendeutschen', in *Volk und Rasse: Illustrierte Vierteljahreshefte für deutsches Volkstum*, Munich: J. F. Lehmanns, 1930, pp. 96–111.

13. Ibid., pp. 98, 100–2, 106–8.

14. Ibid., pp. 103–5.

15. Ibid., pp. 98, 100–2, 106–8.

16. Halter, 'Zivilisation'; www.swr.de/swr2/programm/. . ./essay/-/. . ./swr2–essay–20080715.rtf?.

17. Black, 'Expellees', pp. 81–2.

18. Helge Gerndt, 'Folklore and National Socialism: Questions for Further Investigation', in Dow and Lixfeld, eds, *Nazification*, pp. 7–8.

19. Smith, *Politics and the Sciences*, pp. 226–7; Dow and Lixfeld, eds, *Nazification*; Max Weinreich, *Hitler's Professors: The Part of Scholarship in Germany's Crimes Against the Jewish People*, Oxford: Oxford University Press, 1946; Steven Remy, *The Heidelberg Myth: The Nazification and Denazification of a German University*, Cambridge, MA: Harvard University Press, 2002; Michael Prosser-Schell, 'Zum Wandel der Funktion und des Traditionswertes vom Sagen-Texten', *Jahrbuch für deutsche und osteuropäische Volkskunde* 51 (2010), pp. 47–8, 60–2.

20. Rose, *Thule-Gesellschaft*, pp. 176–7; Kater, 'Die Artamanen', pp. 602–4.

21. Smith, *Politics and the Sciences*, pp. 226–8; Wolfgang Brückner, 'Hauptströmungen nationalsozialistischer Volkskunde-Arbeit Klaus Graf: Eine von Himmler angeregte antikirchliche Kampfschrift Arnold Ruges (1881–1945) über die Hexenprozesse (1936)', in Bauer et al., eds, *Hexenkartothek*, pp. 20–31.

22. Staudenmaier, *Between Occultism and Nazism*, pp. 91–2; Kaufmann, *Tibet*, p. 364.

23. This 'glorified picture of Germanic antiquity promoted in academic theatres and halls, in the offerings of the Aryan Grub Street, and after 1933, increasingly with the imprimatur of the state as well, for some seemed to provide a legitimizing intellectual foundation for many of the often grimmer discourses which grew up about the project of völkisch renewal'. Mees, 'Germanentum', pp. 268–9; Kaufmann, *Tibet*, pp. 392–3; Lixfeld, *Folklore and Fascism*, pp. 31–3; Harten, *Himmlers Lehrer*, pp.18–19.

24. Gustav Jungbauer and Herbert Horntrich, eds, Die Volkslieder der Sudetendeutschen, Reichenberg: Roland, 1943.

25. Helge Gerndt, 'Folklore and National Socialism', in Dow and Lixfeld, eds, *Nazification*, pp. 8–9.

26. Kater, 'Artamanen', pp. 592–4, 634–5; Kater, *Das 'Ahnenerbe'*, pp. 31–2.

27. Lixfeld, *Folklore and Fascism*; Dow and Lixfeld, eds, *Nazification*; Mees, 'Hitler and Germanentum'. See also Karen Schönwälder, *Historiker und Politik. Geschichtswissenschaft im Nationalsozialismus*, Frankfurt am Main: Campus, 1992; Ursula Wolff, *Litteris et Patriae. Das Janusgesicht der Historie*, Stuttgart: Franz Steiner, 1996; Peter Schöttler, ed., *Geschichtsschreibung als Legitimationswissenschaft 1918–1945*, Frankfurt am Main: Suhrkamp, 1997; Winfried Schulze and Otto Gerhard Oexle, eds, *Deutsche Historiker im Nationalsozialismus*, Frankfurt am Main: Fischer, 1999; Fahlbusch, *Wissenschaft*; Brückner, 'Hauptströmungen', pp. 19–31.

28. Mees, 'Hitler and Germanentum', pp. 263–4.

29. BAB: R 58/6517, Long SD report from 30.6.41 expressing immense frustration at Edgar Dacqué, pp. 1–7, 25–7.

30. The SD complained about Dacqué's 'one-sided and exaggerated emphasis of the occult life of the soul', but recognized the value of his other ideas. SD report from 30.6.41, pp. 7–10, BAB: R 58/6517.

31. Lixfeld, *Folklore and Fascism*, pp. 21–2; Kater, *Das 'Ahnenerbe'*, p. 113; Junginger, 'Nordic Ideology', p. 66.

32. See James R. Dow and Ulrike Kammerhofer-Aggermann, 'Austrian *Volkskunde* and National Socialism: The Case of Karl Hauding, Born Paganini', *The Folklore Historian* 22 (2005), pp. 35–58; Kater, *Das 'Ahnenerbe'*, pp. 12–14; Richard Bollmus, *Das Amt Rosenberg und seine Gegner. Zum Machtkampf im nationalsozialistischen Herrschaftssystem*, Stuttgart: Deutsche Verlags-Anstalt, 1970, pp. 360, 9, 55.

33. Kater, *Das 'Ahnenerbe'*, pp. 22–5; Reinerth, 23.4.37, asking DFG for money; 14.4.38, Reinerth reporting on winter research on RfDV letterhead; Reinerth writing all related Vereine und Gesellschaften of the RfDV, 20.12.41; 1.5.42, Sievers to Willvonseder, Hans Reinerth, BAB: NS 21/2136.

34. Pringle, *Plan*, pp. 38, 50–7; see also Bausinger, 'Folk-National Work during the Third Reich', in Dow and Lixfeld, eds, *Nazification*, pp. 76–87; Kater, *Das 'Ahnenerbe'*, pp. 29–30; Kater, 'Artamanen', pp. 622–7, 634–5.

35. Himmler, as quoted in Wolfgang Emmerich, 'The Mythos of Germanic Continuity', in Dow and Lixfeld, eds, *Nazification*, p. 48.
36. Kater, *Das 'Ahnenerbe'*, pp. 38–40.
37. Ibid., pp. 21–3; Junginger, 'From Buddha to Adolf Hitler', p. 112. And yet, even Rosenberg argued, in the context of the *Generalplan Ost*, that Germany should 'recall that Siberia *until Lake Baikal* was an old European sphere of settlement'. Kaufmann, *Tibet*, p. 605.
38. See correspondence from 6.11.42 and *Gutachten* over Carl von Spiess and Edmund Mudrak, pp. 24–41. See also Dow and Lixfield, eds, *Nazification*, pp. 199–200; 4.8.38, letter from Rosenberg to Himmler complaining about Himmler's incursions, BAB: NS 21/2136.
39. 'We prehistorians, from the ground up almost entirely SA- and SS leaders,' wrote one SS folklorist, 'are the first front in the battle for the Germanic Empire.' 'Instead of helping us in the fight, Reinerth shoots us in the back' with his fraudulent work. Walter von Stokar to RfDV, 30.12.42, regarding Reinerth; 20.2.43; Reinerth to Professor Dr Walter von Stokar, 20.2.43; 11.11.42, Sievers writes to Himmler, BAB: NS 21/2136 (Reinerth). On Reinerth's dubious efforts elsewhere, see Lawrence Hare, *Excavating Nations: Archaeology, Museums, and the German-Danish Borderlands*, Toronto: University of Toronto Press, pp. 146–7, 151–3.
40. Pringle, *Plan*, p. 3.
41. Emmerich, 'The Mythos of Germanic Continuity', pp. 31–7.
42. Hermann Bausinger, 'Folk-National Work During the Third Reich', in Dow and Lixfeld, eds, *Nazification*, pp. 88–9.
43. Pringle, *Plan*, p. 3.
44. Kater, *Das 'Ahnenerbe'*, pp. 21, 118; Kaufmann, *Tibet*, pp. 374–5.
45. Bausinger, 'Folk-National Work', pp. 89–93.
46. Mees, 'Hitler and Germanentum', pp. 264–5; Bramwell, *Blood and Soil*, pp. 91–3, 121–4.
47. Kater, *Das 'Ahnenerbe'*, pp. 145–52.
48. Mees, 'Hitler and Germanentum', pp. 262–3.
49. Kater, *Das 'Ahnenerbe'*, pp. 118–19.
50. Junginger, 'From Buddha to Adolf Hitler', p. 159.
51. Black, *Death in Berlin*, 91.
52. Mees, 'Hitler and Germanentum', pp. 259–63.
53. Wüst, *Indogermanisches Bekenntnis*, p. 3.
54. Mees, 'Hitler and Germanentum', pp. 262–3; Weinreich, *Hitler's Professors*, p. 6; Wilhelm Teudt, *Germanische Heiligtümer*, Jena: Diederichs, 1929; Kater, *Das 'Ahnenerbe'*, pp. 22–3; Teudt article on Detmold, 4.6.38; Teudt speech, 10.6.38 speech; Teudt speech from Vienna, 14.4.37, BAB: NS 21/2528; Kaufmann, *Tibet*, pp. 392–3.
55. Kater, *Das 'Ahnenerbe'*, p. 75; Heinrich Harmjanz writes to Plassmann, 14.11.38; 20.11.39, 20.1.40, letters securing Hitler's permission to collect artefacts, 22.11.39; 23.2.40, Göring agrees to pay Harmjanz and Sievers 100 deutschmark for their help, BAB: NS 21/1495; on the important role of geography and cartography in *völkisch* and pan-German conceptions of race and space, see Jason Hansen, *Mapping the Germans: Statistical Science, Cartography, and the Visualization of the German Nation, 1848–1914*, Oxford: Oxford University Press, 2015.
56. Peter Assion, 'Eugen Fehrle and "The Mythos of our Folk"', in Dow and Lixfeld, eds, *Nazification*, pp. 112–21; Bruce Lincoln, 'Hermann Güntert in the 1930s: Heidelberg, Politics, and the Study of Germanic/Indogermanic Religion', in Horst Junginger, *The Study of Religion under the Impact of Fascism*, Leiden: Brill, 2008, p. 118.
57. Mees, 'Hitler and Germanentum'; for more detail, see Peter Schöttler, 'Die historische Westforschung zwischen Abwehrkampf und territorialer Offensive', in Schöttler, *Geschichtsschreibung*, pp. 204–61; Peter Schöttler, 'Von der rheinischen Landesgeschichte zur nazistischen Volksgeschichte oder Die unhörbare Stimme des Blutes', in Schulze and Oexle, eds, *Deutsche Historiker*, pp. 89–113; Burkhard Dietz, 'Die interdisziplinäre Westforschung der Weimarer Republik und NS-Zeit als Gegenstand der Wissenschafts- und Zeitgeschichte. Überlegungen zu Forschungsstand und Forschungsperspektiven', in *Geschichte im Westen* 14 (1999), pp. 189–209.
58. Hansen, *Volkskunde*, pp. 4–7, 10–11.
59. Ibid., pp. 64–6.
60. Pringle, *Plan*, pp. 187–90; see Fehrle's 1939–42 correspondence and Swedish cliff pictures, BAB: NS 21/1295; see also Hartmann, *Trollvorstellungen*, p. 2; Rheden biography of Darré, BAK: N 1094I/77, p. 35.
61. Heinrich Pudor wants Ahnenerbe stipend. Letter from Brandt to Galke, 7.12.37; Pudor letter, 7.11.41 asking for money for Helgoland research; Sievers to Pudor, 11.11.41; Pudor book with anti-Semitic and Atlantis material, p. 23, BAB: NS 21/2215.
62. Pringle, *Plan*, pp. 11–12, 90–1; Fritz Bose, 'Law and Freedom in the Interpretation of European Folk Epics', *Journal of the International Folk Music Council* 10 (1958), p. 31.

63. John Randolph Angolia, David Littlejohn, and C. M. Dodkins, *Edged Weaponry of the Third Reich*, San Jose, CA: R. J. Bender, 1974, pp. 132–5.

64. Junginger, 'Nordic Ideology', pp. 53–4.

65. Pringle, *Plan*, p. 11; Herman Wirth, 'Bericht über die Hällristningar-Expedition des Deutschen Ahnenerbe', 27.8.35 to 3.9.35; Kater, *Das 'Ahnenerbe'*, pp. 58–9; Harten, *Himmlers Lehrer*, pp. 388–409.

66. Ernst Anrich, 'Zum Thema der Arbeitsgemeinschaft des Amtes Wissenschaft des NSD – Dozentenbundes der Reichsuniversität Strassburg', Lebensgesetze von Volkstum und Volk. 30 September 1942, Sondermappe Universität Straßburg, 1942–3; Archiv des IGPP, Bestand 10/5.

67. Pringle, *Plan*, pp. 123–35.

68. Kater, *Das 'Ahnenerbe'*, p. 108; Hans Derks, *Deutsche Westforschung: Ideologie und Praxis im 20. Jahrhundert*. Leipzig: AVA-Akademische Verlagsanstalt, 2001.

69. Derks, *Deutsche Westforschung*, pp. 86–92.

70. Pringle, *Plan*, pp. 105–18, 306–7; Franz Altheim and Erika Trautmann, 'Nordische und italische Felsbildkunst', *Die Welt als Geschichte* 3 (1937), pp. 1–82.

71. Kater, *Das 'Ahnenerbe'*, p. 118.

72. Alexander Laban Hinton, ed., *Annihilating Difference: The Anthropology of Genocide*, Berkeley, CA: University of California Press, 2002, p. 105; see Walther Gehl, *Geschichte*, Breslau: Hirt, 1940, pp. 72–122; Kater, *Das 'Ahnenerbe'*, p. 301.

73. Olaf Bockhorn, 'The Battle for the "Ostmark": Nazi Folklore in Austria', in Dow and Lixfeld, eds, *Nazification*, pp. 135–42; Kater, *Das 'Ahnenerbe'*, pp. 108–9.

74. Pringle, *Plan*, p. 301.

75. Junginger, 'From Buddha to Adolf Hitler', pp. 137–9.

76. Kater, *Das 'Ahnenerbe'*, p. 109; Burleigh, *Germany Turns Eastwards*; Mechthild Rössler, '*Wissenschaft und Lebensraum': Geographische Ostforschung im Nationalsozialismus. Ein Beitrag zur Disziplingeschichte der Geographie*, Berlin: Reimer, 1990; Haar, *Historiker*; Black, 'Expellees', pp. 81–8.

77. Lutz Mackensen, *Sagen der Deutschen im Wartheland*, Posen: Hirt-Reger, 1943, foreword.

78. Heinrich Harmjanz late-1940 Warthegau and Poland instructions as to what is 'Kulturgut', 28.10.40; 18.5.40, discussion of genealogical work in Latvia, 17.11.39, more work on cultural commission, which shows negotations with Latvian and Estonian authorities; 18.6.40, negotiations successful with Estonia and Latvia, BAB: NS 21/1495.

79. Karasek, 'Vom Sagengute der Vorkarpathendeutschen', pp. 96–7.

80. Jungbauer, *Sudetenland*, pp. 468–9, 472–3.

81. Ibid., pp. 467, 472–3, 488.

82. Kater, *Das 'Ahnenerbe'*, pp. 292–4; BAB: NS 21/2676 Willvonseder, 25.11.40, archaeological digs in Slovakia.

83. Krause to Wüst, 15.5.42, about Rune institutes in absurdly sycophantic way; Wüst to Himmler, 5.2.43; Wüst to Krause, 10.2.43; 10.9.41, letter extolling Krause's work on the spearhead of Kowel; 25.6.40, Krause to Sievers; 29.7.43, sycophantic thanks to Wüst; 8.7.43, Sievers to Brandt; 6.4.44, Brandt (Himmler) to Sievers and copying Wüst; 17.11.41, Krause wants to follow up on 1932 research in Polish/Ukrainian 'Vandal' site, where the *Lanzenspitze von Kowel* was found; 26.11.43, BAB: NS 21/1784. See also Gustav Must, 'The Inscription on the Spearhead of Kovel', *Language* 31:4 (October–December 1955), pp. 493–8.

84. Hans Reinerth, 11.6.42, *VB*, 'Forschungsauftrag für Professor Reinerth: Vor- und Frühgeschichtsforschung im besetzten Ostgebiet', BAB: NS 21/2136.

85. https://homepages.uni-tuebingen.de//gerd.simon/ChrKarasek.pdf.

86. Black, *Expellees*, pp. 81–2; Alfred Karasek, 'Sprachinselvolkstum', *Deutsche Blätter in Polen. Monatshefte für den geistigen Aufbau des Deutschtums in Polen* 3 (1926), pp. 569–94; Alfred Karasek-Langer, 'Das Schrifttum überdie Deutschen in Wolhynien und Polen', *Deutsche wissenschaftliche Zeitschrift für Polen* (1931), vol. 22, pp. 124–36; Alfred Karasek-Langer, 'Ostschlesische Volkskunde', in Viktor Kauder, ed., *Das Deutschtum in Polnisch-Schlesien. Ein Handbuch über Land und Leute* (Deutsch Gaue im Osten, vol. 4), Plauen: Wolff, 1932; Alfred Karasek-Langer, 'Grundsätzliches zur Volkskunde der Deutschen in Polen, in *Monatshefte für den geistigen Aufbau des Deutschtums in Polen* 2:12 (1935/36), pp. 126–33; Alfred Karasek-Langer, 'Die deutsche Volkskundeforschung im heutigen Ungarn', in *Deutsches Archiv für Landes- und Volksforschung* 1 (1937), pp. 287–308, 959–89; Alfred Karasek-Langer and Josef Strzygowski, *Vom Sagengute der Vorkarpathendeutschen. Ein Beitrag zur Sagenforschung in den deutschen Sprachinseln des Ostens*, Munich: J. F. Lehmanns, 1930; Alfred Karasek-Langer, *Die deutschen Siedlungen in Wolhynien. Geschichte, Volkskunde, Lebensfragen* (Deutsche Gaue im Osten, vol. 3), Leipzig: Hirzel, 1931.

87. An empire was 'an administrative area of rather unified size, with definite borders, with inhabitants who are opposed to foreign races, with provinces and major cities, with taxes and other imperial institutions'. Wüst, *Indogermanisches Bekenntnis*, pp. 16–17.

88. Ibid., p. 19.
89. Wüst explained, 'This is the legacy, the law', the history 'of the Empires of the old Aryans'. Wüst, *Indogermanisches Bekenntnis*, p. 20; Kaufmann, *Tibet*, pp. 364–5.
90. Kater, *Das 'Ahnenerbe'*, p. 29.
91. Wüst, *Indogermanisches Bekenntnis*, pp. 17–18.
92. Trimondi, *Hitler*, pp. 49–50; see also Manjapra, *Entanglement*, p. 204; Kaufmann, *Tibet*, pp. 600–1; Conrad, *Globalisation*; Wildenthal, *Empire*.
93. See Kurlander, 'Orientalist Roots'; Manjapra, *Entanglement*, pp. 195–6, 203–8; hence the *völkisch*-nationalist Association for German Cultural Relations Abroad supported the Indian nationalist struggle in the 1920s. Manjapra, *Entanglement*, p. 203.
94. Manjapra, *Entanglement*, p. 91; see also Marchand, *German Orientalism*, pp. 495–8; Kaufmann, *Dritte Reich*, pp. 67–70.
95. Manjapra, *Entanglement*, p. 210.
96. Christian Spang, *Karl Haushofer und Japan: Die Rezeption seiner geopolitischen Theorien in der deutschen und japanischen Politik*, Munich: Ludicum, 2013, p. 414.
97. Pringle, *Plan*, pp. 135–6.
98. Kaufmann, *Tibet*, pp. 601–4.
99. Pringle, *Plan*, pp. 146–7.
100. Ibid., p. 150. In 'distant times the people in the Far East had the same code of honour as our fathers had long ago', Himmler argued, giving 'a nation eternal life in earthly terms'. Longerich, *Himmler*, pp. 281–2.
101. Pringle, *Plan*, pp. 145–6.
102. Kaufmann, *Tibet*, p. 601.
103. Ibid., pp. 178–9; Steinmetz, *Devil's Handwriting*, p. 61; Smith, *Politics and the Sciences*, pp. 162–3; Pringle, *Plan*, pp. 135–6; see also Marchand, *German Orientalism*, pp. 483–4; Ekkehard Ellinger, *Deutsche Orientalistik zur Zeit des Nationalsozialismus, 1933–1945*, Edingen-Neckarhausen: Deux Mondes, 2006; Douglas McGetchin, *Indology, Indomania, and Orientalism: Ancient India's Rebirth in Modern Germany*, Danvers, MA: Rosemont, 2009; Ursula Woköck, *German Orientalism: The Study of the Middle East and Islam from 1800 to 1945 – Culture and Civilization in the Middle East*, London: Routledge, 2009; Johannes Fück, *Die arabischen Studien in Europa bis in den Anfang des 19. Jahrhunderts*, Leipzig: Harrassowitz, 1955; Ludmila Hanisch, *Die Nachfolger der Exegeten: Deutschsprachige Erforschung des Vorderen Orients in der ersten Hälfte des 20. Jahrhunderts*, Wiesbaden: Harrassowitz, 2003; Sabine Mangold, *Eine 'weltbürgerliche Wissenschaft': Die deutsche Orientalistik im 19. Jahrhundert*, Stuttgart: Steiner, 2004.
104. Baron Julius Evola positive reports; 16.3.38, Professor Langsdorff's favourable view of Evola's essay, 'Gralsmysterium und Reichsgedanke', BAB: NS 21/1333, 13.7.38.
105. Junginger, 'From Buddha to Adolf Hitler', pp. 128–9.
106. Ibid., pp. 131–3.
107. Trimondi, *Hitler*, p. 69.
108. Edmund Kiss, BAB: NS 21/1751, letter from Sievers, 5.5.38, confirming Kiss should go to South America – Tihuanaka; *Denkschrift* over WEL in Abyssinia, 2.8.35; 7.3.38, letter from Galke to Himmler over his results; 30.1.39, Kiss ordered to undertake a trip to Tripoli and Sardinia.
109. Pringle, *Plan*, pp. 185–6.
110. Kaufmann, *Tibet*, pp. 368–71; Frenzolf Schmid: BAB: NS 21/2294, 31.3.42, Sievers sends Schmid material; 17.1.39, Schmid writes Himmler a long letter recommending *völkisch stichworter*; 23.7.40, Schmid returns some old silver to Himmler, ist prehistorical meaning 'Teufelsee'; Anrich, IfZG 542: 1536/54, p. 5.
111. Treitel, *Science*, pp. 87–8.
112. Trimondi, *Hitler*, p. 73; Kaufmann, *Tibet*, pp. 392–3.
113. Trimondi, *Hitler*, pp. 54–6; see also Kater, *Das 'Ahnenerbe'*, pp. 30–1, 33–8.
114. Trimondi, *Hitler*, p. 93.
115. Manjapra, *Entanglement*, pp. 207–8; Marchand, *German Orientalism*, pp. 495–8; Rehwaldt, *Indien*, pp. 92–100.
116. Trimondi, *Hitler*, pp. 93–5.
117. Kaufmann, *Tibet*, pp. 412–23; Berzin, 'The Berzin Archives'; Longerich, *Himmler*, pp. 282–3.
118. Kaufmann, *Tibet*, p. 11.
119. Engelhardt, 'Nazis of Tibet'; Kaufmann, *Tibet*, pp. 217–24, 457–61.
120. Kater, *Das 'Ahnenerbe'*, p. 211; Kaufmann, *Tibet*, pp. 434–9, 471–535.
121. Longerich, *Himmler*, pp. 281–2; Himmler to Schäfer, 7.9.39, BAB: N 19/2709. Schäfer had the impression that the Tibetans were greatly interested in political developments in Germany, citing the Panchen Lama's expression of support for Hitler, the peaceful 'King of the Germans'. Kaufmann, *Tibet*, pp. 119–20.

122. Schäfer to Brandt, 25.6.40, BAB: N19/2709, pp. 3–6; Manjapra, *Entanglement*, pp. 261–2, 266–7; Junginger, 'Nordic Ideology', p. 54; Kaufmann, *Tibet*, pp. 254–8, 553–73.

123. Trimondi, *Hitler*, pp. 145–6; also Kaufmann, *Tibet*, pp. 608–10; Berzin, 'The Berzin Archives'.

124. Trimondi, *Hitler*, p. 130.

125. Wüst, *Japan und Wir*, pp. 9–11.

126. François Genoud, as quoted in Trevor-Roper, ed., *Bormann Letters*, pp. xix–xx.

127. Kaufmann, *Tibet*, p. 609.

128. Spang, *Karl Haushofer und Japan*, p. 414; Kaufmann, *Tibet*, p. 638.

129. Hipler, *Hitlers Lehrmeister*, p. 43.

130. Ibid., pp. 6, 50–1, 63; Spang, *Karl Haushofer und Japan*. As Haushofer's son Albrecht put it in 1945, 'My dad has broken the seal' and let 'demons . . . escape into the world'. Hipler, *Hitlers Lehrmeister*, p. 18; Rose, *Thule-Gesellschaft*, pp. 176–7.

131. Spang, *Karl Haushofer und Japan*, p. 423.

132. Hipler, *Hitlers Lehrmeister*, p. 51.

133. Kaufmann, *Tibet*, pp. 634–5.

134. Pringle, *Plan*, p. 150.

135. Kaufmann, *Tibet*, pp. 179–80, 610–34.

136. Ibid., pp. 642–8.

137. Herf, 'Nazi Germany's Propaganda', pp. 715–17.

138. Kater, *Das 'Ahnenerbe'*, pp. 30–3, 33–8; Pringle, *Plan*, p. 183.

139. Pringle, *Plan*, pp. 110–20, 301–2.

140. Ibid., pp. 90–1, 306–7.

141. Herf, 'Nazi Germany's Propaganda', pp. 722–3.

142. Ibid., pp. 718–20; Barry Rubin and Wolfgang G. Schwanitz, *Nazis, Islamists, and the Making of the Modern Middle East*, New Haven, CT: Yale University Press, 2014, p. 178.

143. Herf, 'Nazi Germany's Propaganda', pp. 718–19.

144. Kaufmann, *Tibet*, p. 609; the SD had more ambitious plans to found an 'Asian Institute' to investigate the racial and political character of 'Japan, China, India, Tibet, Turkestan, Mongolia, etc.', but was ultimately dissuaded due to its overlap with Schäfer's Central Asian Institute. Kaufmann, *Tibet*, pp. 677–9.

145. Herf, 'Nazi Germany's Propaganda', pp. 711, 718–19.

146. Ibid., p. 736; Rubin and Schwanitz, *Nazis, Islamists*, pp. 156–7, 182–5.

147. See Herf, 'Nazi Germany's Propaganda', pp. 3–8, 51–9, 154–62; 194–204.

148. Rubin and Schwanitz, *Nazis, Islamists*, pp. 127–34, 142–3, 181–2.

149. Kater, *Das 'Ahnenerbe'*, p. 113.

150. Kaufmann, *Tibet*, pp. 67–9.

151. Kater, *Das 'Ahnenerbe'*, pp. 113–15; Ach, *Hitlers Religion*, p. 48; see also Mark Mazower, *Hitler's Empire: Nazi Rule in Occupied Europe*, London: Allen Lane, 2008; Shelley Baranowski, *Nazi Empire: German Colonialism and Imperialism from Bismarck to Hitler*, Cambridge: Cambridge University Press, 2011; Manjapra, *Entanglement*; Kurlander, 'Orientalist Roots', in *Transnational Encounters*; Conrad, *Globalisation*; Wildenthal, *German Women*; Zantop, *Colonial Fantasies*.

152. McGuire and Hull, eds, *C. G. Jung Speaking*, pp. 115–17; see also Ian Kershaw, *The Hitler Myth: Image and Reality*, Oxford: Oxford University Press, 2001.

153. Goepfert, *Aberglaube!*, pp. 85–95.

154. Staudenmaier, *Between Occultism and Nazism*, pp. 65–6.

155. Fisher, *Fantasy and Politics*, p. 3; Goepfert, *Aberglaube!*, pp. 38–71.

156. Fisher, *Fantasy and Politics*, pp. 1–2.

157. On the less rosy and uncritical assessment of German morale during the war, see Richard Bessel, *Germany 1945: From War to Peace*, New York: Harper, 2010; Tooze, *Wages*; Mazower, *Hitler's Empire*; Johannes Steinhoff, Peter Pechel, and Dennis Showalter, eds, *Voices from the Reich: An Oral History*, Boston, MA: Da Capo Press, 1994.

158. Fisher, *Fantasy and Politics*, p. 3; see also Spence, *Occult Causes*, pp. 22–3.

159. Fisher, *Fantasy and Politics*, pp. 6–7.

160. See in particular Poley, *Decolonization*; see also Manjapra, *Entanglement*.

161. Fanon, *Wretched of the Earth*, p. 54.

162. Ibid., pp. 54–5.

163. Fisher, *Fantasy and Politics*, p. 6.

164. Not yet strong enough to engage the enemy physically, German nationalists therefore fantasized 'about a war of revenge that would erase the reality of Versailles'. Fisher, *Fantasy and Politics*, pp. 11–13.

165. Fisher, *Fantasy and Politics*, pp. 9–11; German bookstores were replete with novels and political pamphlets that 'blended politics and wish-fulfilling fantasies . . . popular authors and hack writers

imagined great technological discoveries, political upheavals, and cataclysmic wars that would overthrow the Versailles order'. Fisher, *Fantasy and Politics*, pp. 1–2.

166. Kurt Hesse, *Der Feldherr Psychologos: Ein Suchen Nach dem Führer der Deutschen Zukunft*, Berlin: E. S. Mittler, 1922; see also Fisher, *Fantasy and Politics*, p. 221.

167. Fanon, *Wretched of the Earth*, pp. 54–5.

168. Spence, *Occult Causes*, p. 124.

169. Fisher, *Fantasy and Politics*, p. 19. According to Kersten, Himmler 'adapted what he regards as his enemies' method and the basis of their power and has turned it to logical use as the basis of the dominant position occupied in the state by the SS. From this point of view the SS is nothing but an anti-Masonry – though the Reichsführer does not admit it – with whose help ... he is trying to occupy the leading position in the Government and the Party'. Kersten, *Memoirs*, pp. 28–32. See also SS Schüler to SS Stabsführung Netherlands, Southeast, Middle, Italy, etc., 19.7.44; report from 9.6.44, pp. 20–21; 5.5.41, Henry Chavin, *Rapport confidentiel sur la société secrète polytechnicienne dite Mouvement synarchique d'Empire (MSE) ou Convention synarchique révolutionnaire*, 1941, BAB: NS 51/186; Richard F. Kuisel, 'The Legend of the Vichy Synarchy', *French Historical Studies* 6:3 (Spring 1970). Olivier Dard, *La synarchie, le mythe du complot permanent*, Paris : Perrin, 1998, pp. 237–8; Project 'Bibliographie zur nationalsozialistischen Bewegung [1919–1933]', in Lorenz, Bauer, Behringer, and Schmid, *Hexenkartothek,*, pp. 60–9; William Langer, *Our Vichy Gamble*, New York: Knopf, 1947.

170. Heiden, 'Preface', pp. 10–12. Himmler dutifully sent SS officers to visit the Masonic Museum in Berlin in order for them to understand this 'superior national power', Kersten, *Memoirs*, pp. 23–5.

171. Heiden, 'Preface', pp. 4–7; Spence, *Occult Causes*, pp. 12–13, 22–3.

172. Fisher, *Fantasy and Politics*, p. 6.

173. McGuire and Hull, eds, *C. G. Jung Speaking*, pp. 120–1.

174. Goepfert, *Aberglaube!*, pp. 30–7.

175. Fisher, *Fantasy and Politics*, pp. 11–12; Alfred Rosenberg, as quoted in BAB: NS 8/185, pp. 49–50.

176. Fisher, *Fantasy and Politics*, p. 3; see Michl, 'Das wundersame 20. Jahrhundert?', in Geppert and Kössler, eds, Wunder, p. 236; Mackensen, *Sagen*, pp. xii–xiv; Sickinger, 'Hitler and the Occult', p. 118.

177. McGuire and Hull, eds, *C. G. Jung Speaking*, pp. 123–4.

178. Ibid., pp. 115–17; see also Kershaw, *Hitler Myth*.

179. McGuire and Hull, eds, *C. G. Jung Speaking*, pp. 134–5; see also Heiden, 'Preface', pp. 13–14.

180. Fisher, *Fantasy and Politics*, p. 220.

181. Heiden, 'Preface', pp. 14–15.

182. Draft of Quade speech, 'Occultism and Politics', R 58/6218 (SD RSHA), pp. 1–2, 34–6.

183. McGuire and Hull, eds, *C. G. Jung Speaking*, pp. 131–2.

184. Ibid., p. 118.

185. Ibid., pp. 134–5. Because Hitler's unconscious was 'the receptacle of the souls of seventy-eight million Germans, he is powerful,' Jung added, 'and with his unconscious perception of the true balance of political forces at home and in the world, he has so far been infallible'. McGuire and Hull, eds, *C. G. Jung Speaking*, p. 119.

186. Based 'on his magical belief that he could divine the future', Hitler 'thought that he could lead the German people ... if they would only listen to and obey him'. Sickinger, 'Hitler and the Occult', p. 118.

187. McGuire and Hull, eds, *C. G. Jung Speaking*, pp. 119–20.

188. Sickinger, 'Hitler and the Occult', p. 119.

189. McGuire and Hull, eds, *C. G. Jung Speaking*, pp. 119–20.

190. Ibid.

191. 'Germany stands today on the threshold,' Jung wrote in 1939, 'he has just begun and if his Voice tells him that the German people are destined to become the lords of Europe and perhaps of the world, and if his Voice continues always to be right, then we are in for an extremely interesting period, aren't we?' McGuire and Hull, eds, *C. G. Jung Speaking*, pp. 120–1.

192. Sickinger, 'Hitler and the Occult', p. 119.

193. John Toland, *Adolf Hitler*, New York: Anchor, 1992.

194. Sickinger, 'Hitler and the Occult', p. 120.

195. 7.9.39, Kisshauer to SS Hartl; 4.9.39, Kisshauer *Denkschrift*, 'Astrologie als Mittel zur Beeinflussung der Volksstimmung'; 31.8.39, Hans Hagemeyer in RMVP asking PPK to ban astrological calendars, BAB: R 58/6207.

196. http://www.nostradamus-online.de/index1.htm.

197. Boris von Borresholm and Karena Niehoff, *Dr. Goebbels nach Aufzeichnungen aus seiner Umgebung*, Berlin: Journal, 1949, pp. 146–7; see Howe, *Urania's Children*, pp. 168–72; Ulrich Maichle, Die verlorene Welt der Planetenengel und die Prophezeiungen des Michel Nostradamus, Berlin: Rhombus, 2004; Howe, *Urania's Children*, pp. 168–72; Krafft to Reichskanzlei Berlin, 9.11.39, IGPP: 10/5 AII9;

letter to Heydrich requesting Heinrich Träncker's astrological library to be delivered to Himmler, 4.12.39; 5.12.39, letter to Heydrich; 6.4.40, discussion of Denkschrift zur Astrologie, BAB: R 58/6207. On an interesting sidenote, Goebbels and his colleagues seemed to accept the convenient claims of earlier occultists that Nostradamus was 'no racial Jew' despite clear documentation that he was born into a Jewish family that converted to Catholicism. See Stéphanie Gerson, *Nostradamus: How an Obscure Renaissance Astrologer Became the Modern Prophet*, New York: Macmillan, 2012, pp. 19–20.

198. 24.11.39, Goebbels, *Tagebücher*, as quoted in Maichle, 'Die Nostradamus-Propaganda'.

199. Howe, *Urania's Children*, pp. 164–7, 170–2; Maichle, 'Die Nostradamus-Propaganda'; Wulff, *Zodiac*, pp. 16–18, 92–8, 112–13; Willi A. Boelcke, ed., *Kriegspropaganda 1939–1941: Geheime Ministerkonferenzen in Reichstpropagandaministerium*, Stuttgart: DVA, 1966 [PdGMK], as quoted in Maichle, 'Die Nostradamus-Propaganda', pp. 230–1; Borresholm, *Goebbels*, pp. 148–9.

200. He made the curious remark that the brochures 'should have propagandistic not scientific character' – as if scientific astrology was indeed possible. PdGMK, 5.12.39, pp. 236–8.

201. Howe, *Urania's Children*, pp. 164–7; Schellinger et al., 'Pragmatic Occultism', p. 162.

202. Howe, *Nostradamus*, pp. 115–16; Howe, *Urania's Children*, pp. 175–7.

203. Howe, *Nostradamus*, pp. 116–17; Howe, *Urania's Children*, pp. 175–7.

204. Howe, *Urania's Children*, pp. 178–81.

205. 9.1.40, Goebbels, *Tagebücher*, as quoted in Maichle, 'Die Nostradamus-Propaganda'; Howe, *Urania's Children*, pp. 168–72; Alexander Centgraf claims someone from the regime – most likely the RMVP or SD – approached him already in late 1939 to ask his opinion of a lightning strike against France in the spring of 1940; http://www.nostradamusresearch.org/en/ww2/Centgraaf-info.htm.

206. See Van Berkel, http://www.nostradamusresearch.org/en/ww2/bittenfeld-info.htm#02; 25.11.39, *Gutterer berichtet über die Flugblattbroschüren für Frankreich*, PdGMK, as quoted in Willi A. Boelcke, ed., *Kriegspropaganda 1939–1941: Geheime Ministerkonferenzen in Reichstpropagandaministerium*, Stuttgart: DVA, 1966, pp. 232–3. Bittenfeld was a prominent and respected journalist and foreign-policy expert who had worked as a military attaché in Washington, DC, lending all the more legitimacy to his work on astrological propaganda. Hans Wolfgang Herwarth von Bittenfeld articles from Berliner Borsen Zeitung 'Verkehrszersplitterung', from 5.7.31; article, 'Vom Weltpostverein zum Weltverkehrsverein', 28.3.31; 22.10.38, letter to RSK from Bittenfeld; 20.2.39, letter to RSK from Bittenfeld, BAB: R 9361–V/6162.

207. Der Bericht von Martin H. Sommerfeld, RMVP, Maichle, 'Die Nostradamus-Propaganda'.

208. Ibid., pp. 55–7.

209. See Van Berkel, http://www.nostradamusresearch.org/en/ww2/bittenfeld-info.htm#02; 25.11.39, in Boelcke, ed., *Kriegspropaganda 1939–1941*, pp. 232–3; 5.12.39, PdGMK, pp. 236–8; 13.12.39, PdGMK, p. 241; 14.12.39, Goebbels, *Tagebücher*, as quoted in Maichle, 'Die Nostradamus-Propaganda'.

210. 23.2.40, Goebbels, *Tägebücher*, as quoted in Maichle, 'Die Nostradamus-Propaganda'; Schellinger et al., 'Pragmatic Occultism', p. 162.

211. Goebbels diary entries, 23.2.40, 12.3.40, 27–28.3.40, PdGMK, as quoted in Maichle, 'Die Nostradamus-Propaganda', pp. 303–5.

212. Goebbels diary entries, 24.4.40, PdGMK, as quoted in Maichle, 'Die Nostradamus-Propaganda', pp. 328–31, and 25.4.40, Goebbels, *Tagebücher*, as quoted in ibid.

213. 30.3.40, Goebbels, *Tagebücher*, as quoted in Maichle, 'Die Nostradamus-Propaganda'.

214. 26.3.40, in ibid.; see also 24.5.40, PdGMK, as quoted in Maichle, 'Die Nostradamus-Propaganda', p. 363; 25.5.40, Goebbels, *Tagebücher*, as quoted in ibid.

215. 26.5.40, PdGMK, p. 365; 27.5.40, PdGMK, p. 366, as quoted in Maichle, 'Die Nostradamus-Propaganda'.

216. Im Antrag auf Mit-gliedschaft vom 9.7.40. Maichle, 'Die Nostradamus-Propaganda'.

217. Howe, *Urania's Children*, pp. 173–4.

218. Ibid., pp. 182–6; 1.2.41, Karl Krafft writes to RSK to explain the purpose of translation; 15.3.41, Maurer in RSK to Krafft; 18.12.40, letter from Maurer to Krafft; 27.8.40, Krafft handwritten note to RSK; 3.9.40, follow-up by Krafft to RSK, BAB: R 9361–V/25648. According to Alexander Centgraf, it was Goebbels' insistence that Krafft 'reinterpret' this passage that led to his final falling out with the RMVP. *Nostradamus, Der Prophet der Weltgeschichte*, p. 128; *Die großen Weissa-gungen des Nostradamus*, p. 177; http://www.nostradamus-online.de/index1.htm.

219. Maichle, 'Die Nostradamus-Propaganda'; Howe, *Urania's Children*, pp. 178–81.

220. See the brochure, *Comment Nostradamus a-t-il l'avenir de l'Europe* (October 1940); Alexander Centgraf, 'Nostradamus, Der Prophet der Weltgeschichte', 1955, p. 128.

221. Karl Krafft, 19.1.41, Gestapo to RSK; 27.3.41, Maurer writing to get decision on Krafft; 27.1.41, Maurer to Krafft; 27.1.41, letter to NSDAP Party Office Gau Berlin, 'Politischer Urteilung'; 12.2.41, Krafft receives permission from Maurer in RSK to translate Nostradamus; 7.2.41, Maurer asks Krafft to come discuss with RSK, BAB: R 9361–V/25648; Howe, *Urania's Children*, pp. 186–91.

222. Karl Loog, Die Weissagungen des Nostradamus, Pfullingen: J. Baum, 1921.
223. 9.6.40. *2. Herr Raskin soll im Geheimsender Nostradamus anklingen lassen*, PdGMK, pp. 383–5.
224. 22.7.40, PdGMK, p. 434.
225. 12.7.40, 16.1.40, Goebbels, *Tagebücher*, as quoted in Maichle, 'Die Nostradamus-Propaganda'.
226. Howe, *Urania's Children*, pp. 204–18; Wulff, *Zodiac*, pp. 95–8; 'British Used Astrologer in Fight Against Hitler', AP: 3/03/2008; http://www.nbcnews.com/id/23456119; Walter Laqueur, 'Foreword', in Wulff, *Zodiac*; ibid., pp. 95–8.
227. Howe, *Urania's Children*, pp. 204–18; Wulff, *Zodiac*, pp. 95–8.
228. Walter Schellenberg, *Hitler's Secret Service*, New York: Harper, 1974, p. 116; 'Das Urmanuskript *"Nostradamus sieht die Zukunft Europas"* entstand spätestens in der zweiten Jahreshälfte 1940, wurde jedoch im deutschsprachigen Raum nie zur Publikation zugelassen'. Maichle, 'Die Nostradamus-Propaganda'.
229. Such as Karl Loog's 1921 book reading Nostradamus' *Centuries* with an eye to 'France's rise and fall'. Maichle, 'Die Nostradamus-Propaganda'.
230. 10.9.40: 1. PdGMK, Maichle, 'Die Nostradamus-Propaganda', pp. 498–9.
231. See Alexander Centgraf, 3.4.37, RSK application; 1.4.37, application includes *Gutachten* from former employee, Rektor Schalck, 12.2.37; 15.2.37, Aufnahme-Erklärkung in RSK; 19.4.41, update on AC and still a member; article on 'Nostradamus und Berlin' by Alexander Centgraf in Sonntag Beilag der Kurier, BAB: R 9361–V/4599; Alexander Centgraf, *Eine Jude Treibt Philosophie*, Berlin: Hochmuth, 1943, pp. 3–25.
232. Alexander Centgraf, *Voorspellingen die uitgekomen zijn – Michael Nostradamus spreekt in 1558 over het verloop en het einde van dezen oorlog*, Arnhem: Hijman, Stenfert Kroese & Van de Zande, 1941.
233. Also problematic was the mention of the Prince of Armenia making it to 'Cologne'. Were the prince still Stalin – a native of Georgia, which shared a border with Armenia – this might suggest the conquest of all Germany by the Bolsheviks. Alexander Centgraf, *Nostradamus, Der Prophet der Weltgeschichte*, p. 128. Maichle, 'Die Nostradamus-Propaganda'.
234. See comment from 22.6.41, Maichle, 'Die Nostradamus-Propaganda'.
235. Centgraf, *Voorspellingen*; Maichle, 'Die Nostradamus-Propaganda'.
236. 19.4.42, Goebbels, *Tagebücher*, as quoted in Maichle, 'Die Nostradamus-Propaganda'.
237. Maichle, 'Die Nostradamus-Propaganda'; Howe, *Urania's Children*, pp. 204–18. 'British Used Astrologer in Fight Against Hitler', AP: 3/03/2008; http://www.nbcnews.com/id/23456119; Laqueur, 'Foreword', in Wulff, *Zodiac*.
238. http://www.ubka.uni-karlsruhe.de/; https://portal.dnb.de/; Maichle, 'Die Nostradamus-Propaganda'.
239. See exchange between Alfred Rosenberg's expert in occult matters, Kurd Kisshauer, and Goebbels' Reichspropaganda Ministry, 23.7.41, 25.8.41, BAB: NS 15/399; Wulff, *Zodiac*, pp. 92–5; Laqueur, 'Foreword', in ibid.
240. See also files on Operation Eiche, BAM: N 756/329b, 'Sonderlehrgang z.b.V. Oranienburg, SS-Sonderverband z.b.V. Friedenthal, SS-Jäger-Bataillon 502 Unternehmen "Eiche"' (Mussolini-Befreiung, 12.9.43); Schellenberg, *Memoirs*, pp. 301–2.
241. Wulff, *Zodiac*, pp. 92–4; Treitel, *Science*, p. 214; Schellinger et al., 'Pragmatic Occultism', pp. 168–71; Walther, *Zum Anderen Ufer*, pp. 583–601; Howe, *Nostradamus*, pp. 130–1.
242. Walther, *Zum Anderen Ufer*, pp. 599–602.
243. Howe, *Nostradamus*, pp. 130–1; Walther, *Zum Anderen Ufer*, pp. 599–601; Schellinger et al., 'Zwischen Szientismus'; Uwe Schellinger, 'Sonderaktion Heß: Beschlagnahmung und "Verwertung" von Buchbeständen der "Grenzwissenschaften"', in Viertes Hannoverisches Symposium, NS-Raubgut in Museen, Bibliotheken und Archiven, Frankfurt, 2012; http://www.gwlb.de/projekte/ns-raubgut/Symposium_2011/22Schellinger.pdf; Walther, *Zum Anderen Ufer*, pp. 583–99.
244. Schellinger et al., 'Pragmatic Occultism', p. 159.
245. Howe, *Urania's Children*, pp. 235–43; Howe, *Nostradamus*, p. 131; Schellinger et al., 'Pragmatic Occultism', pp. 160–2.
246. Schellinger et al., 'Pragmatic Occultism', pp. 161–6; Howe, *Urania's Children*, pp. 237–43; Walther, *Zum Anderen Ufer*, pp. 599–602.
247. http://www.skyscript.co.uk/wulff3.html; 'Strahlen zu denken', August 1938, IGPP: 10/5 AII49.
248. For further development see the report by Gerard P. Kuiper on 'German Astronomy During the War', *Popular Astronomy* 54:6 (June 1946), p. 278; Ley, 'Pseudoscience in Naziland', p. 94.
249. Schellinger et al., 'Pragmatic Occultism', pp. 163–4; Jens Henkel, 'Der Verlag "Gesundes Leben" Mellenbach Rudolstadt: Von den lebensreformerischen Ideen des Wilhelm Hotz zu den Pendelforschungen von Karl Dietz', *Blätter der Gesellschaft für Buchkultur und Geschichte* 6 (2002), pp. 83–144.
250. Wulff, *Zodiac*, pp. 75–7; Schellinger et al., 'Zwischen Szientismus'; Ley, 'Pseudoscience in Naziland', pp. 92–3; Howe, *Nostradamus*, p. 131; Schellinger et al., 'Pragmatic Occultism', pp. 160–1.

251. Schellinger et al., 'Pragmatic Occultism', p. 163; see also Ley, 'Pseudoscience in Naziland', pp. 92–9.

252. Schellinger et al., 'Pragmatic Occultism', p. 161; Howe, *Nostradamus*, p. 131.

253. Schellinger et al., 'Pragmatic Occultism', p. 161; Howe, *Nostradamus*, pp. 130–2; Wulff, *Zodiac*, pp. 74–7.

254. Wulff, *Zodiac*, pp. 6–7; Schellinger et al., 'Pragmatic Occultism', pp. 161–2.

255. Schellinger et al., 'Pragmatic Occultism', pp. 160–3.

256. Ibid., p. 164.

257. Ley, 'Pseudoscience in Naziland in Naziland', p. 93.

258. Schellinger et al., 'Pragmatic Occultism', p. 164.

259. Ibid., p. 165.

260. Ibid., p. 166.

261. Ibid., pp. 166–7.

262. Wulff, *Zodiac*, pp. 19–33, 81–5.

263. Ibid., pp. 86–8; Schellinger et al., 'Pragmatic Occultism', p. 167.

264. According to Münch, on 1 August 1943 he had been taken from the concentration camp of Sachsenhausen to Berlin, together with other seers. Schellinger et al., 'Pragmatic Occultism', pp. 170–1; 26.6.41, Wulff's wife writes to Loth in allowing Wulff to stay in RSK; 23.6.41, longer letter regarding his work; 27.5.41, RKK Ihde complains to RSHA that there is a move to take Wulff off allowed writers; 30.6.41, letter from Ihde explaining that the emphasis on astrology makes his renewal impossible until RSK allows it. BAB: R 9361–V/40789.

265. Schellenberg, *Memoirs*, pp. 301–2; see also Schellinger et al., 'Pragmatic Occultism', pp. 169–70.

266. Schellinger et al., 'Pragmatic Occultism', pp. 169–70; Wulff, *Zodiac*, pp. 77–80, 86–7; see also files on Operation Eiche in BAF: N 756/329b, 'Sonderlehrgang z.b.V. Oranienburg', 12.9.43; Howe, *Urania's Children*, pp. 235–43.

267. Schellinger et al., 'Pragmatic Occultism'.

268. On 12 September 1943, Mussolini was liberated by a German commando of paratroopers from the Hotel Campo Imperatore on the Gran Sasso. Schellinger et al., 'Pragmatic Occultism', pp. 170–1.

269. Ibid., pp. 169–70.

270. Ibid.

271. Schellenberg, *Memoirs*, p. 301.

272. Schellinger et al., 'Pragmatic Occultism', pp. 169–70. For Otto Skorzeny one thing was clear: 'It was Himmler who was said to believe in these always somewhat disputed sciences. I was never told about any positive result of these "investigations". Otto Skorzeny, *Geheimkommando Skorzeny*, Hamburg: Toth, 1950, p. 116.

273. Schellinger et al., 'Pragmatic Occultism', pp. 169–70.

274. Ibid., p. 168.

275. Ibid., pp. 170–1.

276. Ibid., p. 168.

277. Fisher, *Fantasy and Politics*, pp. 10–11.

278. Ibid., pp. 11–12. These mystical ideas fed the 'urge to fantasize a war of revenge that would erase the reality of Versailles' and confirm the idea that 'the nation's strivings were invincible'. Fisher, *Fantasy and Politics*, pp. 12–13; Gugenberger and Schweidlenka, *Faden der Nornen*, pp. 111–13.

279. Fisher, *Fantasy and Politics*, pp. 12–13; Gugenberger and Schweidlenka, *Faden der Nornen*, pp. 111–13.

280. Sievers to Wolfram, 6.11.42, BAB: NS Richard Wolfram.

281. Kater, 'Artamanen', p. 607.

282. Ibid., pp. 622–5, 631–4.

283. Rauschning, *Hitler Speaks*, p. 247; Eisler, *Man Into Wolf*, pp. 169–70.

284. Black, *Death in Berlin*, p. 9. More generally, the Nordic folk hero Siegfried became a symbol of the Wehrmacht, whereas Jews and Bolsheviks were portrayed as Hagen. Gugenberger and Schweidlenka, *Faden der Nornen*, pp. 133–41.

285. 'Wesen und Geschichte des Werwolfs', dissertation by Amt Rosenberg co-worker, with detailed analysis of maps and histories, BAB: R 58/7237, pp. 54–66.

286. Roderick H. Watt, 'Wehrwolf or Werwolf? Literature, Legend, or Lexical Error into Nazi Propaganda?', *Modern Language Review* 87:4 (October 1992), pp. 879–83; Antony Beevor, *Downfall*, London: Penguin, 2002, p. 173; Longerich, *Himmler*, p. 705; Klaus Neumann, *Shifting Memories: The Nazi Past in the New Germany*, Ann Arbor, MI: University of Michigan Press, 2000, p. 50; 'Unternehmen Werwolf', 'Werwolf' Raum Propoisk-Dowsk-Merkulowitschi-Korma, 5–15.7.41, BAM: RH 26–221/63; see report on the tasks of the Werewolf organization, 12.7.41, BAM: RH 20/11–334.

287. Adluri and Bagchee, *Nay Science*, pp. 46–53, 60–5, 80–1, 91–6; Trimondi, *Hitler*, pp. 31–2, 82; Junginger, 'From Buddha to Adolf Hitler', p. 135.

288. Since the Indra of the Vedas drank, was sexually prolific and undisciplined, Himmler and Wüst preferred to cite the *Bhagavad Gita*, where 'discipline, emotional control, willingness to sacrifice, obedience' were the norm. Trimondi, *Hitler*, pp. 91–2; see also Junginger, 'From Buddha to Adolf Hitler', pp. 154–5.
289. Trimondi, *Hitler*, pp. 79–80.
290. Ibid., pp. 49–51.
291. Ibid., p. 68.
292. Ibid., pp. 82, 148–9.
293. Ibid., p. 150.
294. Ibid., p. 32.
295. Ibid., pp. 86–9.
296. Junginger, 'From Buddha to Adolf Hitler', pp. 129–30.
297. Longerich, *Himmler*, pp. 268–9.
298. Herf, 'Nazi Germany's Propaganda', pp. 6, 90, 121, 157, 199–202.
299. Kaufmann, *Tibet*, p. 644.
300. Longerich, *Himmler*, pp. 281–2; see also Bill Maltarich, *Samurai and Supermen: National Socialist Views of Japan*, Oxford: Peter Lang, 2005, pp. 156–8.
301. This recalled 'Franz von Sickingen or Ulrich Butten – Co-creators of the [Holy Roman] Empire', Wüst, *Japan und Wir*, pp. 13–14.
302. Kaufmann, *Tibet*, p. 179.
303. Ibid., p. 180.
304. Ibid., p. 642.
305. Aufbau Werwolf: Similar address, 'Angelegenheit Indische Legion. Anruf SS-Ostubaf. Grothmann am 23.12.1944', BAB: NS 34/47; Günther Lewy, *The Nazi Persecution of the Gypsies*, Oxford: Oxford University Press, 2000, pp. 138–9.
306. Motadel, *Islam*, pp. 230–42.
307. Kaufmann, *Tibet*, p. 694.
308. Ibid., pp. 694–7.
309. Pringle, *Plan*, p. 79
310. Kaufmann, *Tibet*, pp. 370–1.
311. Wulff, *Zodiac*, pp. 78–82; http://www.skyscript.co.uk/wulff4.html; Levenda, *Unholy Alliance*, pp. 230–3.
312. Kater, *Das 'Ahnenerbe'*, pp. 193–4; see also Laurence Hare and Fabian Link, 'Pseudoscience Reconsidered: SS Research and the Archaeology of Haithabu', in Black and Kurlander, eds, *Revisiting*, pp. 105–31.
313. Longerich, *Himmler*, p. 266.
314. Ibid., p. 266.
315. Kaufmann, *Tibet*, pp. 727–30.
316. Kater, *Das 'Ahnenerbe'*, pp. 208–10; Kaufmann, *Tibet*, pp. 731–2; see Beger and Wienert biographies, letter about Rassen im Kampf, 'Denkschrift über Tibet-Expedition'; 22.5.43 letter about studying Russian POWs, per Eichmann. Bruno Beger, BAB: NS 21/869.
317. 30.1.45, Wessely promoted as of September 1944; 5.1.45, Sievers sends Wessely letter about working for IWZ; 19.12.44, reports to Sievers on his research; 1.10.44, Wessely to Sievers; 15.7.44, Brandt writes to Heiss over Sievers' recommendation that Wessely study 'die sogenannten militärgrenze'; articles from Wessely, 5.9.41; 15.4.42, RMVP agrees to support him with funds; 13.6.42, Stephan to Wessely to agree to help him finish his research on military borders by placing him with his future company commander, Hauptmann Miketta, including naming him an officer due to his service. BAB: NS 21/2652.
318. Kater, *Das 'Ahnenerbe'*, pp. 236–7.
319. Junginger, 'Nordic Ideology', p. 54; Pringle, *Plan*, pp. 248–9; Kater, *Das 'Ahnenerbe'*, pp. 255–7; Reitzenstein, *Himmlers Forscher*, pp. 71–7.
320. Junginger, 'From Buddha to Adolf Hitler', p. 159.
321. Wulff, *Zodiac*, pp. 78–81; Longerich, *Himmler*, p. 281.
322. These experiments included teaching a soldier how to 'kill without regard for his personal safety' and then forgetting 'who had programmed him to kill, and why'. Wulff, *Zodiac*, pp. 77–8; Levenda, *Unholy Alliance*, pp. 232–8.
323. Wulff, *Zodiac*, pp. 79–81; Longerich, *Himmler*, pp. 281–2.
324. Schellinger et al., 'Pragmatic Occultism', p. 166.
325. Kater, *Das 'Ahnenerbe'*, pp. 145–6.
326. Heiden, 'Preface', pp. 10–12.
327. 'Reichserziehungsministeriums', Göring to Bender, 28.5.40, 8.6.40, IGPP: 10/5 AII49.
328. Bender to Luther, 2.8.40, IGPP:10/5 AII49.
329. 'Korrespondenz Hans Bender – Friedrich Spießer', IGPP: 10/5 AII17.

330. Ibid.
331. Bender–Spießer', IGPP: 10/5 AII17.
332. *Astroligisches 1943*, 'Betr.: Astrologisches Buch und Aktenmaterial Bezug.: Ihr Schreiben vom 12.7.1943'; see also letter from 8.12.41 acknowledging receipt of the last of nine boxes originally ordered in August (see 23.9.41 letter); 14.1.42, another letter to AMT VII with list of occult books taken from Chemnitz; 27.1.42, another box sent to AMT VII from Frankfurt, BAB: R 58/6204; see files in Bender papers, IGPP: 10/5 AII51, IGPP: 10/5 AIII2.
333. 'Der Führer hat dem Regiment den Namen "Thule" verleihen', letter from 24.7.42, BAM: N 756/133a.
334. Aktenvermerk, Himmler: 28.8.42, letter from SS, BAM: N 756/133a; see also BAM: RH 21/2/621.
335. Pennick, *Hitler's Secret Sciences*, pp. 170–2; Jürgen Obmann and Derk Wirtz, 'Orte der Kraft? Bodendenkmalpflege im Spannungsfeld zwischen Archäologie und Esoterik', *Kölner Jahrbuch* 27 (1994), p. 572; Josef Heinsch, 'Grundsätze vorzeitlicher Kultgeographie', *Comptes Rendus du Congrès International de Geographie* (1938), section V, pp. 90–108. http://www.cantab.net/users/michael.behrend/repubs/ggw/heinsch_gvkg/pages/gvkg_en.html.
336. Wessely, *Welteis*, pp. 257–261; Scultetus to Sievers, 10.14.41; 10.25.41 Sievers to Scultetus; 1.09.42, Scultetus to Sievers, BAB: NS 21/2547.
337. Christina Wessely, *Welteis: Ein wahre Geschichte*, Berlin: Matthes & Seitz, 2013, pp. 258–9; Ley, 'Pseudoscience in Naziland', p. 98; Goodrick-Clarke, *Black Sun*, p. 133.
338. Wessely, *Welteis*, p. 259.
339. Kater, *Das 'Ahnenerbe'*, pp. 113–15.
340. Sickinger, 'Hitler and the Occult', p. 119.
341. Schellinger et al., 'Pragmatic Occultism', pp. 169–70.
342. According to sources as disparate as Schellenberg and Wulff, the Hess Action did absolutely nothing to quell the regime's border scientific agenda. Wulff, *Zodiac*, p. 112; Schellenberg, *Memoirs*, p. 160.
343. Schellinger et al., 'Pragmatic Occultism', p. 172.
344. Wulff, *Zodiac*, pp. 112–13.
345. Schellinger et al., 'Pragmatic Occultism', pp. 29–33, 171–2; see the exchange between Kisshauer and the Reich Propaganda Ministry, 23.7.41, 25.8.41, BAB: NS 15/399.
346. Schellinger et al., 'Pragmatic Occultism', pp. 171–2.

Chapter 8

1. Adorno, *Minima Moralia*, pp. 238–44.
2. Hitler, *Mein Kampf*, pp. 309, 327.
3. http://biographien.kulturimpuls.org/detail.php?&id=544; Staudenmaier, *Between Occultism and Nazism*, p. 103.
4. Staudenmaier, *Between Occultism and Nazism*, p. 319.
5. Zygmunt Baumann, *Modernity and the Holocaust*, Ithaca, NY: Cornell University Press, 1989; Georgio Agamben, *Homo Sacer: Sovereign Power and Bare Life*, Stanford, CA: Stanford University Press, 1998; Detlev Peukert, 'The Genesis of the "Final Solution" from the Spirit of Science', in Thomas Childers and Jane Caplan, eds, *Reevaluating the Third Reich*, New York: Holmes & Meier, 1994, pp. 234–52; Michel Foucault, *The Birth of Biopolitics: Lectures at the Collège de France, 1978–79*, New York: Palgrave Macmillan, 2008; Michael Burleigh and Wolfgang Wippermann, *The Racial State: Germany 1933–1945*, Cambridge: Cambridge University Press, 1991; Michael Freeman, 'Genocide, Civilization, and Modernity', *The British Journal of Sociology* 46:2 (June 1995), pp. 207–3; see also Saler, 'Modernity'.
6. Matthew P. Fitzpatrick, 'The Pre-History of the Holocaust? The Sonderweg and Historikerstreit Debates and the Abject Colonial Past', *Central European History* 41:3 (2008), pp. 500–3.
7. Levenda, *Unholy Alliance*, p. 363; see also Fitzpatrick, 'The Pre-History of the Holocaust?', pp. 500–3.
8. Jonathan Steinberg, 'Types of Genocide? Croatians, Serbs and Jews, 1941–5', in David Cesarani, ed., *Final Solution: Origins and Implementation*, London: Routledge, 1996, p. 190; see see Kater, *Das 'Ahnenerbe'*, pp. 194–5.
9. Veronika Lipphardt, 'Das "schwarze Schaf" der Biowissenschaften: Marginalisierungen und Rehabilitierungen der Rassenbiologie im 20. Jahrhundert', in Rupnow et al., eds, *Pseudowissenschaft*, p. 227.
10. Wüst, *Indogermanisches Bekenntnis*, p. 4.
11. Ibid., p. 6.
12. Ibid., pp. 11–12; Junginger, 'From Buddha to Adolf Hitler', pp. 157–9.
13. Poewe and Hexham, 'Surprising Aryan Mediations', p. 12; see also Junginger, 'From Buddha to Adolf Hitler', pp. 159–60; BAB: R 58/64, pp. 45–52.

14. Gugenberger and Schweidlenka, *Faden der Nornen*, pp. 112–13; see also Darnton, 'Peasants Tell Tales', pp. 9–74.
15. Gugenberger and Schweidlenka, *Faden der Nornen*, pp. 135–6.
16. Black, *Death in Berlin*, p. 10; for more on the mystical role of Heimat in this period, see Mack Walker, *German Home Towns*, Ithaca, NY: Cornell University Press, 1971; Karlheinz Rossbacher, *Heimatkunstbewegung und Heimatroman: Zu einer Literatursoziologie der Jahrhundertwende*, Stuttgart: Ernst Klett, 1975; Applegate, *Nation of Provincials*, Berkeley, CA: University of California Press, 1990.
17. Steinmetz, *Devil's Handwriting*, pp. 62–6.
18. Fitzpatrick, 'The Pre-History of the Holocaust?, pp. 500–3.
19. Gugenberger and Schweidlenka, *Faden der Nornen*, pp. 137–9.
20. Staudenmaier, *Between Occultism and Nazism*, p. 149; Kater, 'Artamanen', pp. 598–604; Gilbhard, *Thule-Gesellschaft*, pp. 17–18.
21. Mees, 'Hitler and Germanentum', pp. 262–3; Bramwell, *Blood and Soil*, pp. 54–5, 64–5, 130–1; Rheden biography in NL Darré, BAK: N 1094I/77, p. 35.
22. Heinrich Himmler, *Die Schutzstaffel als antibolschewistische Kampforganisation*, Munich: Franz Eher (Zentralverlag der NSDAP), 1937, p. 6.
23. Poewe and Hexham, 'Surprising Aryan Mediations', p. 12; see also Kaufmann, *Tibet*, pp. 363–4; Pringle, *Plan*, p. 5; Wüst, *Indogermanisches Bekenntnis*, pp. 23–7; 21.3.37, cover letter to Schmid's report on de Mengel's work, BAB: NS 19/3974, p. 8; Greve, 'Tibetforschung', pp. 168–209.
24. Kater, *Das 'Ahnenerbe'*, p. 50.
25. Longerich, *Himmler*, pp. 264–5.
26. Ibid., pp. 512–20; Clemens Hütter, *Gruselwanderen in Salzburg*, Salzburg: Pustet, 1999, p. 211; Jörg Rudolf, 'Geheime Reichskommando-Sache!', in Bauer et al., *Hexenkartothek*, pp. 48–51.
27. Bramwell, *Blood and Soil*, pp. 167–70; Trimondi, *Hitler*, pp. 66–70.
28. Kersten, *Memoirs*, p. 299; Wüst, *Indogermanisches Bekenntnis*, pp. 12–17; Himmler, *Schutzstaffel*, pp. 6–11, 14–15.
29. Bockhorn, 'The Battle for the "Ostmark"', pp. 143–50; Ernst Anrich, 'Zum Thema der Arbeitsgemeinschaft', 30.9.42, and 'Sondermappe Universität Straßburg', 1942–3; IGPP: 10/5, AIII13, pp. 3–5.
30. Bramwell, *Blood and Soil*, pp. 151–2, 157.
31. Longerich, *Himmler*, pp. 258–60; Kater, *Das 'Ahnenerbe'*, pp. 305–6; Nanko, *Deutsche Glaubensbewegung*, pp. 110–12.
32. Kater, 'Artamanen', pp. 592–6, 601–2.
33. Pringle, *Plan*, pp. 142–4, 150–60; Kater, *Das 'Ahnenerbe'*, pp. 291–5; for more on Nazi breeding of 'aurochs' and other prehistoric animals, see http://www.newyorker.com/magazine/2012/12/24/recall-of-the-wild; Cis van Vuure, *Retracing the Aurochs*, Moscow: Pensoft, 2005, p. 345.
34. Pringle, *Plan*, pp. 228–9.
35. Mees, 'Hitler and Germanentum', p. 263.
36. Kater, 'Artamanen', p. 607.
37. Bramwell, *Blood and Soil*, pp. 169–70; Wüst, *Indogermanisches Bekenntnis*, pp. 10–11.
38. Bramwell, *Blood and Soil*, pp. 130–1.
39. Trimondi, *Hitler*, pp. 64–5; Kaufmann, *Tibet*, pp. 579–85; Longerich, *Himmler*, pp. 262–3.
40. Wüst, *Indogermanisches Bekenntnis*, p. 4; Kater, 'Artamanen', pp. 625–6.
41. Junginger, 'From Buddha to Adolf Hitler', p. 160.
42. Ibid., p. 159.
43. Trimondi, *Hitler*, p. 78.
44. Ibid., p. 107.
45. Black, 'Expellees'.
46. Trimondi, *Hitler*, pp. 88–9.
47. Ibid., pp. 86–7.
48. Himmler, *Schutzstaffel*, pp. 16–17.
49. Kater, 'Artamanen', pp. 630–4.
50. Kater, *Das 'Ahnenerbe'*, p. 47.
51. Kater, 'Artamanen', pp. 628–9.
52. Ibid., p. 628; see also Gugenberger and Schweidlenka, *Faden der Nornen*, pp. 145–7.
53. See 20.10.39 entry in Darré's diary, NL Darré, BAK: N 1094I/65a, v. 15.
54. Poewe and Hexham, 'Surprising Aryan Mediations', p. 12.
55. Kater, *Das 'Ahnenerbe'*, pp. 201, 104–5.
56. Wolfgang Behringer, 'Der Abwickler der Hexenforschung im Reichssicherheitshauptamt (RSHA)', in Bauer et al., *Hexenkartothek*, pp. 116–17; Günther Franz, promotion and reviews, BAB: NS 21/1279.

57. Poewe and Hexham, 'Surprising Aryan Mediations', pp. 274–5; Kater, *Das 'Ahnenerbe'*, pp. 39–41; Longerich, *Himmler*, pp. 595–600.
58. The Third Reich set out to 'purify newly conquered *Heimat* by extinguishing the lives of those who had no place in the new order'. Black, *Death in Berlin*, p. 275; Kater, *Das 'Ahnenerbe'*, p. 152; Mees, 'Hitler and Germanentum', pp. 253–4; Longerich, *Himmler*, pp. 425–7.
59. Black, *Death in Berlin*, p. 91.
60. Gugenberger and Schweidlenka, *Faden der Nornen*, pp. 135–6.
61. See Dow and Lixfeld, eds, *Nazification*, p. 137; Kater, *Das 'Ahnenerbe'*, pp. 145–9, 153–4; Longerich, *Himmler*, pp. 640–1.
62. Kater, *Das 'Ahnenerbe'*, pp. 152–3.
63. Burleigh, *Germany Turns Eastwards*, pp. 28–31, 75–6; Kater, *Das 'Ahnenerbe'*, pp. 146–7.
64. Bramwell, *Blood and Soil*, p. 157; Nanko, *Deutsche Glaubensbewegung*, pp. 114–15.
65. Kaufmann, *Tibet*, pp. 590–1, 696–8.
66. Kater, *Das 'Ahnenerbe'*, pp. 152–4; see correspondence between Sievers, Harmjanz, and other SS officials from 17.11.39, 22.11.39, 20.1.40, and 23.2.40, BAB: NS 21/1496.
67. Burleigh, *Germany Turns Eastwards*, pp. 7–8; Longerich, *Himmler*, p. 263.
68. Longerich, *Himmler*, p. 446.
69. Kater, *Das 'Ahnenerbe'*, pp. 152–3; Longerich, *Himmler*, pp. 640–1; see various articles in Alfred Lattermann, ed., *Deutsche Wissenschaftliche Zeitschrift im Wartherland*, Posen: Historischen Gesellschaft im Wartheland, 1940.
70. Wolfgang Krause: see letters to Wüst, 15.5.42; Wüst to Himmler, 5.2.43; Wüst to Krause, 10.2.43; Sievers on Krause's work, 10.9.41; Krause to Sievers, 25.6.40; Krause to Wüst, 29.7.43; Sievers to Brandt, 8.7.43; Brandt (Himmler) to Sievers, copying Wüst, regarding runes by Weigel and Krause, 6.4.44; Krause and Weigel on 'Runenfibel', 26.11.43, BAB: NS 21/1784; for more on Nazi resettlement policy in the Warthegau see Christopher Browning, *Nazi Policy, Jewish Workers, German Killers*, Cambridge: Cambridge University Press, 2000, pp. 8–20.
71. Monica Black, 'Expellees', pp. 81–2; 'Der grosse Treck. Aus dem Tagebuch Alfred Karasek-Langers, eines Gebietsbevollmachtigten des wolhyniendeutschen Umsiedlungskommandos', in Kurt Lück, ed., *Deutsche Volksgruppen aus dem Osten kehren heim ins Vaterland* (Tornisterschrift des Oberkommandos der Wehrmacht/Abt. Inland 19), Berlin: Tornisterschrift des Oberkommandos der Wehrmacht/Abt. Inland 19, 1940.
72. Mackensen, *Sagen*, pp. 1–4; 'Whether a matter of faith or custom ... one thing is certain,' Mackensen argued. 'The stories contain within and emanate from an ancient consciousness of ethnicity.' Ibid., pp. 5–6.
73. Ibid., pp. 6–10.
74. Ibid., p. 11.
75. Ibid., pp. 4–11.
76. See Fahlbusch, *Wissenschaft*, pp. 19–20.
77. Kater, *Das 'Ahnenerbe'*, pp. 155–8, 294–5; see also Fahlbusch, *Wissenschaft*, pp. 227–35.
78. Kater, *Das 'Ahnenerbe'*, p. 294.
79. Ibid., pp. 170–1.
80. Ibid., pp. 155–7, 188; Harten, *Himmlers Lehrer*, pp. 310–15.
81. See extensive correspondence between Wessely, Sievers, and Wolff, BAB: NS 21/2652.
82. Kater, *Das 'Ahnenerbe'*, pp. 207–8; Kaufmann, *Tibet*, pp. 399–403; see also Beger letters, BAB: NS 21/869.
83. See Globocnik report in BAB: NS 19/2234, pp. 20–4; see also Michael Marrus, *The Nazi Holocaust*, Berlin: De Gruyter, 2011, pp. 1,023–5.
84. Behringer, 'Der Abwickler der Hexenforschung', p. 122.
85. Kater, *Das 'Ahnenerbe'*, pp. 185–8; Mazower, *Hitler's Empire*, pp. 461–5.
86. Kater, *Das 'Ahnenerbe'*, p. 194.
87. Ibid. See correspondence between Sievers, Brandt, and Wessely, 15.7.44, 27.7.44, BAB: NS 19/3060.
88. Staudenmaier, 'Organic Farming', p.11; Werner, *Anthroposophen*, pp. 279–82.
89. Staudenmaier, 'Organic Farming', pp. 11–12.
90. Werner, *Anthroposophen*, p. 283; Staudenmaier, *Between Nazism and Occultism*, pp. 139–41; Treitel, *Science*, p. 213; Staudenmaier, 'Organic Farming', pp. 11–12.
91. Werner, *Anthroposophen*, pp. 279–86; Staudenmaier, 'Organic Farming', pp. 3–4, 9–13; Darré to Blankemeyer, 21.5.41, NL Darré, BAK: N1094II/1; Gayl to Darré, BAK: N1094II/1.
92. Staudenmaier, 'Organic Farming', p. 12.
93. Ibid., p. 13.
94. Staudenmaier, *Between Occultism and Nazism*, pp. 136–42; Staudenmaier, 'Organic Farming', pp. 12–13; Werner, *Anthroposophen*, pp. 284–6.
95. Werner, *Anthroposophen*, p. 348.

96. Staudenmaier, 'Organic Farming', 12–13; Staudenmaier, *Between Occultism and Nazism*, p. 141; see also Werner, *Anthroposophen*, pp. 280–6; Kaufmann, *Tibet*, pp. 302–3.

97. Darré to Blankemeyer, 21.5.41, NL Darré, BAK: N 1094II/1; Gayl to Darré, BAK: N1094II/1; Werner, *Anthroposophen*, pp. 283–6; Staudenmaier, *Between Occultism and Nazism*, p. 143.

98. Staudenmaier, 'Organic Farming', pp. 3–4, 9–10; Merkel to Buettner, 1951, NL Darré, BAK: N 1094/14.

99. Staudenmaier, 'Organic Farming', pp. 13–14; IfZG ED 498/23, NL Otto Ohlendorff (1945), p. 7. In 1943 Himmler was also sending Waffen-SS expeditions from Schäfer's Central Asia Institute in search of 'rumoured' super specimens of rye in Russia. Kaufmann, *Tibet*, pp. 264–5.

100. Staudenmaier, 'Organic Farming', pp. 13–14; IfZG: ED 498/23, NL Otto Ohlendorff (1945), p. 7; Kaufmann, *Tibet*, pp. 296–301.

101. Staudenmaier, 'Organic Farming', pp. 12–13; Hansen, *Volkskunde*, pp. 64, 88–9.

102. Burleigh, 'National Socialism', pp. 10–11.

103. Harrington, *Reenchanted Science*, p. 175.

104. Rauschning, *Voice of Destruction*, p. 245.

105. See Ernst Anrich, *Zeugenschrifttum*, IfZG: 1536/54, ZS Nr. 542.

106. Treitel, *Science*, pp. 216–17.

107. Heiko Stoff, 'Verjüngungsrummel: Der Kampf um Wissenschaftlichkeit in den 1920er Jahren', in Rupnow et al., eds, *Pseudowissenschaft*, pp. 196–7.

108. Robert Proctor, *The Nazi War on Cancer*, Princeton, NJ: Princeton University Press, 2000.

109. See Young-sun Hong, 'Neither Singular nor Alternative: Narratives of Modernity and Welfare in Germany, 1870–1945', *Social History* 30:2 (May 2005), pp. 133–53.

110. Kaufmann, *Tibet*, pp. 358–62; Hale, *Himmler's Crusade*, pp. 24–7; Staudenmaier, *Between Occultism and Nazism*, pp. 84–93.

111. Lipphardt, 'Das "schwarze Schaf"', pp. 233–4.

112. Trimondi, *Hitler*, p. 48; Staudenmaier, *Between Nazism and Occultism*, pp. 159–61. Hauer claimed that the Indian caste order derived from racial categories, since 'the word for caste is *varna*; and *varna* means 'color''. This Aryan racial purity, per Hauer, was corrupted by the Mongol invasions. Trimondi, *Hitler*, p. 79.

113. Lipphardt, 'Das "schwarze Schaf"', pp. 233–4.

114. Ibid., pp. 228–9, 236–47; see also Alexa Geisthovel, *Intelligenz und Rasse Franz Boas' psychologischer Antirassismus zwischen Amerika und Deutschland, 1920–1942*, New York: Transcript, 2013, pp. 131–8; Junginger, 'From Buddha to Adolf Hitler', pp. 151–3.

115. Lewy, *Gypsies*, pp. 136–42. Nor were many German eugenicists willing to acknowledge empirical studies, most famously by the German-American emigré Franz Boas, indicating the difficulty of assigning an essential character to entire races or groups. See Geisthövel, *Intelligenz*, pp. 140–8; Lipphardt, 'Das "schwarze Schaf"', pp. 223–5.

116. Harrington, *Science*, pp. 207–8.

117. Geisthövel, *Intelligenz*, pp. 151–5; Harrington, *Reenchanted Science*, p. 175; Horst Junginger, 'Die Deutsche Glaubensbewegung als ideologisches Zentrum der völkisch-religiösen Bewegung', in Puschner and Vollnhals, eds, *Bewegung*, pp. 79–80; Ernst Anrich, 'Lebensgesetze von Volkstum und Volk', 30.9.42, and 'Sondermappe Universität Straßburg', 1942–3; IGPP: 10/5 AIII13, pp. 6–7.

118. Kröner, *Untergang*, p. 42.

119. Ibid., pp. 10–11, 22.

120. Harrington, *Science*, p. 175.

121. Ibid., p. 177.

122. Ibid., p. 185.

123. Trimondi, *Hitler*, p. 40. See also Burleigh, *Germany Turns Eastwards*, pp. 7–8, 26–7; Kater, *Das 'Ahnenerbe'*, pp. 51–2; Wüst, *Indogermanisches Bekenntnis*, pp. 35–45; Bramwell, *Blood and Soil*, pp. 8–9.

124. Pringle, *Plan*, 134–5.

125. Longerich, *Himmler*, pp. 279–81; Pringle, *Plan*, p. 281; Kaufmann, *Tibet*, pp. 363–5.

126. Wüst, *Indogermanisches Bekenntnis*, p. 18.

127. Bramwell, *Blood and Soil*, p. 60.

128. Pringle, *Plan*, p. 150; see also Longerich, *Himmler*, pp. 261–2; Koehne, 'The Racial Yardstick', pp. 582–5; Schertel, *Magic*, p. 79; Bowen, *Universal Ice*, p. 164; Stephens, *Blood, not Soil*, p. 181. On Nazi theories of evolution, see also Richard Weikart, *From Darwin to Hitler: Evolutionary Ethics, Eugenics, and Racism in Germany*, London: Palgrave, 2004; Weikart, *Hitler's Ethic*.

129. Kater, *Das 'Ahnenerbe'*, p. 50; see also Junginger, 'From Buddha to Adolf Hitler', pp. 158–9.

130. Trimondi, *Hitler*, p. 107; report from Frenzolf Schmid, 21.3.37, BAB: NS 19/3974, pp. 10–11.

131. Gugenberger und Schweidlenka, *Faden der Nornen*, pp. 138–43.

132. Rauschning, *Voice of Destruction*, p. 246.

133. Ibid., pp. 246–7.

134. Ibid., pp. 247–8; see also Harrington, *Science*, pp. 175–6.

135. Kater, *Das 'Ahnenerbe'*, pp. 323–9.

136. Gugenberger and Schweidlenka, *Faden der Nornen*, pp. 138–43; Rudolf, 'Geheime Reichskommando-Sache!, pp. 58–9; Barbara Schier, 'Hexenwahn Interpretationen im "Dritten Reich"', in Bauer et al., eds, *Hexenkarthotek*, p. 9; Felix Wiedemann, 'Hexendeutungen im Nationalsozialismus', in Puschner and Vollnhals, eds, *Bewegung*, pp. 452–5; Junginger, 'Die Deutsche Glaubensbewegung', pp. 77–8.

137. Pringle, *Plan*, p. 7.

138. Kater, *Das 'Ahnenerbe'*, p. 205; see also Kaufmann, *Tibet*, pp. 363–5.

139. Nanko, *Deutsche Glaubensbewegung*, pp. 115–23; Pringle, *Plan*, pp. 277–8.

140. Behringer, 'Der Abwickler der Hexenforschung', pp. 127–8; Kaufmann, *Tibet*, pp. 698–9; Wiedemann, 'Wissen', p. 437; Reitzenstein, *Himmlers Forscher*, pp. 117–28.

141. Kaufmann, *Tibet*, pp. 363–5, 404–5; Trimondi, *Hitler*, pp. 139–44; Pringle, *Plan*, p. 169.

142. Kater, *Das 'Ahnenerbe'*, pp. 214–15; Kaufmann, *Tibet*, pp. 250–6.

143. Kater, 'Artamanen', p. 626; Redles, *Hitler's Millennial Reich*, pp. 12–13.

144. Report on Eduard May, 30.9.42, IfZG: MA 141/8, pp. 2–5

145. Ibid.; Reitzenstein, *Himmlers Forscher*, pp. 87–92.

146. Kater, *Das 'Ahnenerbe'*, p. 227.

147. Mees, 'Hitler and Germanentum'; Kater, *Das 'Ahnenerbe'*, pp. 229–30.

148. Anrich, 'Zum Thema'; IGPP: 10/5 AII13, pp. 3–4, 10–13.

149. IGPP: 10/5 AII51, letter from Büchner to Anthony 19.7.41; Hausmann, *Bender*, pp. 19–20; Bender to Herrn Regierungsrat Dr Bosch, 29.8.40, IGPP: 10/5 AII49; Bender also worked with Göring's cousin Matthias Heinrich Göring, who ran the Deutsches Institut für Psyzchologische Forderung und Psychotherapie, and co-edited the journal, *Central Journal for Psychotherapy and its Border Areas (Zentralblattes für Psychotherapie und ihre Grenzgebiete)* with the esoterically inclined Carl Jung. Matthias Göring showed clear interest in Bender's occult work, including delivering a lecture at the institute entitled 'Mental Illnesses in the Course of "Occult" Practices'. M. H. Göring to Bender, 22.1.40; Bender to Göring, 15.2.40, regarding 'Seelische Erkrankungen im Gefolge "okkulter" Praktiken (mit Vorführung von Schallfilmen)'; Bender to Göring, 16.4.41, IGPP: 10/5 AII49.

150. Hausmann, *Bender*, pp. 118–20; Junginger and Ackerlund, eds, *Nordic Ideology*, pp. 54–5.

151. Hausmann, *Bender*, pp. 121–2; Pringle, *Plan*, pp. 273–4.

152. Steinmetz, *Devil's Handwriting*, pp. 62–6.

153. Kater, *Das 'Ahnenerbe'*, pp. 229–31.

154. Ibid.; John J. Michalczyk, *Medicine, Ethics, and the Third Reich: Historical and Contemporary Issues*, London: Rowman & Littlefield, 1994, p. 95; see also correspondence, including 4.5.42 letter and 3.5.42 remark from Sievers; 11.10.39, Rascher accepted into SS; 27.3.41, Rascher wants to work full time for Ahnenerbe and Sievers discusses ways of promoting him if he can be released from the Luftwaffe; 9.11.42, Rascher promoted by Himmler to Hauptsturmführer; 15.11.43, Rascher to Sievers; 2.12.43, Himmler facilitates Rascher being released from the Luftwaffe and into the Waffen-SS, BAB: NS 21/2120; Reitzenstein, *Himmlers Forscher*, pp. 55–6.

155. Weltz had been experimenting with methods aimed at 'rescuing pilots from great heights' pioneered by Dr Siegfried Ruff in Berlin. Since Ruff lacked human subjects, Weltz needed technical support, and Rascher could bring plenty of 'volunteers' from Dachau, the three scientists agreed to work together. Kater, *Das 'Ahnenerbe'*, pp. 231–2; see letters regarding details of setting up the laboratory and experiments, including Sievers' comments, 3.5.42, 13.14.42, and letter of transfer, 4.5.42, BAB: NS 21/2120.

156. Sievers comments on obtaining the appropriate 'Ariflex camera' and filming equipment for Rascher, 3.5.42, BAB: NS 21/2120.

157. Kater, *Das 'Ahnenerbe'*, p 234; see also Pringle, *Plan*, p. 242.

158. Kater, *Das 'Ahnenerbe'*, p. 235.

159. Ibid., pp. 233–4.

160. Trimondi, *Hitler*, p. 124; Kater, *Das 'Ahnenerbe'*, pp. 232–4; confidential letters, including a copy of Rascher's orders from Hippke to the air force indicating that Rascher's experiments in Dachau between 16.3.42 and 16.4.42 should continue because of their success, but emphasizing Rascher's delicate nature. BAB: NS 21/2120.

161. Kater, *Das 'Ahnenerbe'*, pp. 236–7; Kaufmann, *Tibet*, pp. 320–1; Junginger, 'From Buddha to Adolf Hitler', p. 145.

162. Pringle, *Plan*, pp. 248–9; Kater, *Das 'Ahnenerbe'*, pp. 255–7.

163. Pringle, *Plan*, pp. 248–9.

164. Kühne, *Belonging and Genocide*, pp. 90–1.

165. Kater, *Das 'Ahnenerbe'*, pp. 103–4, 228–31, 257–60.

166. There were limits to how much responsibility the IWZ could take on. While the IWZ conducted signicant research on a blood coagulant, 'Polygal', Oswald Pohl indicated an unwillingess to allow

them to fabricate it as well, preferring to preserve Dachau inmates for other labour (see BDW). Kater, *Das 'Ahnenerbe'*, pp. 256–8; 18.1.44, report on Rascher's visit to Polygal factory; 21.1.44, Rascher to Sievers; 29.2.44, Sievers remarks that on 23.2.44 Rascher received a research contract from IWZ to produce Polygal; Sievers to Grawitz, 21.3.44, issues with the publication of Rascher and Haferkamp on Polygal because it didn't go through the proper channels; 13.4.44, letter indicating Rascher's approval from Göring, Himmler, and others to build a laboratory for working with Polygal; BAB: NS 21/2120; Junginger and Ackerlund, eds, *Nordic Ideology*, p. 54; Reitzenstein, *Himmlers Forscher*, pp. 216–44.

167. Kater, *Das 'Ahnenerbe'*, pp. 214–15.
168. Ibid., p. 235; see also Junginger and Ackerlund, eds, *Nordic Ideology*, p. 54; Junginger, 'From Buddha to Adolf Hitler', p. 145; Reitzenstein, *Himmlers Forscher*, pp. 129–31, 167–8.
169. Kater, *Das 'Ahnenerbe'*, pp. 237–8; Pringle, *Plan*, pp. 272–3.
170. Kater, *Das 'Ahnenerbe'*, pp. 240–4; Reitzenstein, *Himmlers Forscher*, pp. 202–11.
171. Junginger and Ackerlund, eds, *Nordic Ideology*, pp. 54–5.
172. Pringle, *Plan*, pp. 272–3; Kater, *Das 'Ahnenerbe'*, pp. 246–9; 3.1.42, letter from Sievers to Hirt about experiments on criminals and inmates; Hirt to Sievers, 20.1.42, on experiments with insects, parasites, diseases, etc.; Sievers, 22.12.44, BAB: NS 21/1532; Reitzenstein, *Himmlers Forscher*, pp. 149–51.
173. Trimondi, *Hitler*, p. 132.
174. Kater, *Das 'Ahnenerbe'*, pp. 207–9; Pringle, *Plan*, pp. 245–7; Beger letters, BAB: NS 21/869; Ludwig F. Clauss, *Rasse und Seele. Eine Einführung in die Gegenwart*, Munich: J. F. Lehmanns, 1926; Ludwig F. Clauss, *Rasse und Charakter – das lebendige Antlitz*, Frankfurt am Main: M. Diesterweg, 1936; Ludwig F. Clauss, *Die Nordische Seele: Eine Einführung in die Rassenseelenkunde*, Munich: J. F. Lehmanns, 1932; Peter Weingart, *Doppel-Leben. Ludwig Ferdinand Clauss: Zwischen Rassenforschung und Widerstand*, Frankfurt am Main: Campus, 1995.
175. Kater, *Das 'Ahnenerbe'*, pp. 207–8.
176. 'Subject: Securing Skulls of Jewish-Bolshevik Commissars for the Purpose of Scientific Research at the Strassburg Reich University', February 1942, National Archives (Washington, DC), Records of the U.S. Nuremberg War Crimes Trials: United States of America v. Karl Brandt et al. (Case 1), 21.11.46–20.8.47, RG 238, M 887/16/Jewish Skeleton Collection.
177. Kater, *Das 'Ahnenerbe'*, pp. 249–50; Pringle, *Plan*, p. 246.
178. Pringle, *Plan*, p. 247. The location appears all the more absurd given its location on the western-most frontier of the Reich when virtually all its research 'material' would be arriving from Poland and the Eastern Front.
179. Kater, *Das 'Ahnenerbe'*, pp. 245–6; Pringle, *Plan*, pp. 242–3, 246–9.
180. Kater, *Das 'Ahnenerbe'*, pp. 251–2; Kaufmann, *Tibet*, pp. 258–9; Pringle, *Plan*, pp. 246–7, 251–3; see also Richard Wetzell, 'Eugenics and Racial Science in Nazi Germany: Was There a Genesis of the "Final Solution" from the Spirit of Science?', in Devin Pendas, Mark Roseman, and Richard F. Wetzell, eds, *Beyond the Racial State: Rethinking Nazi Germany*, Cambridge: Cambridge University Press, 2017.
181. Trimondi, *Hitler*, p. 124; Kaufmann, *Tibet*, pp. 258–9.
182. Kater, *Das 'Ahnenerbe'*, pp. 252–4; Kaufmann, *Tibet*, pp. 258–9.
183. Kaufmann, *Tibet*, pp. 260–1, 702–4.
184. Kater, *Das 'Ahnenerbe'*, pp. 249–54; Kaufmann, *Tibet*, pp. 700–2; Junginger, 'From Buddha to Adolf Hitler', pp. 144–5; Pringle, *Plan*, pp. 259–67; see also Beger letters from BAB: NS 21/869; Reitzenstein, *Himmlers Forscher*, pp. 111–28.
185. While some institutes managed to avoid this request, others were incorporated directly into the killing process, including the anthroposophic Healing and Nursing Institute at Pirna, where thousands of disabled and older patients were murdered. Werner, *Anthroposophen*, p. 344.
186. Kater, *Das 'Ahnenerbe'*, pp. 216, 230–1. Sievers subsequently facilitated experiments by the Strasbourg virologist Dr Eugen Haage on concentration-camp inmates with fatal viruses as well. Kater, *Das 'Ahnenerbe'*, p. 261.
187. Ibid., p. 100.
188. Kersten, *Memoirs*, pp. 115–18.
189. Kater, *Das 'Ahnenerbe'*, p. 237.
190. Ibid., pp. 261–3.
191. Kater, *Das 'Ahnenerbe'*, pp. 231–3; Burleigh, 'National Socialism', p. 15.
192. Kater, *Das 'Ahnenerbe'*, pp. 245–6; Pringle, *Plan*, pp. 242–3, 246–9.
193. Kater, *Das 'Ahnenerbe'*, p. 256; Sabine Schleiermacher and Udo Schlagen, 'Medizinische Forschung als Pseudowissenschaft', in Rupnow et al., eds, *Pseudowissenschaft*, p. 259.
194. Kater, *Das 'Ahnenerbe'*, p. 260.
195. Ibid., p. 263.
196. Schäfer to Brandt, 25.6.40, pp. 1–2, BAB: N19/2709; Pringle, *Plan*, pp. 322–3.
197. Pringle, *Plan*, p. 228; Wendy Lower, *Hitler's Furies: German Women in the Nazi Killing Fields*, New York: Houghton Mifflin, 2013, pp. 239–40.

198. See letter from 14.1.42 and manuscript 'Aberglaube in Film', BAB: NS 15/399, pp. 194–220; Redles, *Hitler's Millennial Reich*, pp. 68–9.

199. See Christopher Browning and Jürgen Matthäus, *The Origins of the Final Solution: The Evolution of Nazi Jewish Policy, September 1939–March 1942*, Lincoln, NB: University of Nebraska Press, 2004; Christopher Browning, *The Path to Genocide: Essays on Launching the Final Solution*, Cambridge: Cambridge University Press, 1998; Jürgen Matthäus, 'Historiography and the Perpetrators of the Holocaust', in Dan Stone, ed., *The Historiography of the Holocaust*, London: Palgrave, pp. 197–215.

200. Tooze, *Wages*; Götz Aly, *Hitler's Beneficiaries: Plunder, Racial War, and the Nazi Welfare State*, London: Metropolitan, 2007; Christian Gerlach, *Krieg, Ernährung, Völkermord. Deutsche Vernichtungspolitik im Zweiten Weltkrieg*, Zürich: Pendo, 2001.

201. Baranowski, *Nazi Empire*; Mazower, *Hitler's Empire*; Wendy Lower, *Nazi Empire-Building and the Holocaust in the Ukraine*, Chapel Hill, NC: University of North Carolina Press, 2007; Richard King and Dan Stone, eds, *Hannah Arendt and the Uses of History: Imperialism, Nation, Race, and Genocide*, New York: Berghahn, 2007; A. Dirk Moses and Dan Stone, eds, *Colonialism and Genocide*, London: Routledge, 2007; Jürgen Zimmerer and Joachim Zeller, eds, *Völkermord in Deutsch-Südwestafrika: Der Kolonialkrieg (1904–1908) in Namibia und seine Folgen*, Berlin: Christoph Links Verlag, 2003.

202. Alon Confino, *A World Without Jews: The Nazi Imagination from Persecution to Genocide*, New Haven, CT: Yale University Press, 2014, p. 10.

203. A. Dirk Moses, 'Redemptive Anti-Semitism and the Imperialist Imaginary', in Christian Wiese and Paul Betts, eds, *Years of Persecution, Years of Extermination*, London: Continuum, 2010, pp. 233–54.

204. Seminal works in this regard were: Robert Lifton, *Nazi Doctors*, New York: Basic Books, 1986; Detlev Peukert, *Inside the Third Reich*, New Haven, CT: Yale University Press, 1987; Gisela Bock, *Zwangssterilisation im Nationalsozialismus: Studien zur Rassenpolitik und Frauenpolitik*, Opladen: Westdeutscher, 1987; Claudia Koonz, *Mothers in the Fatherland: Women, the Family and Nazi Politics*, New York: St Martin's Press, 1987; and Burleigh and Wippermann, *Racial State*.

205. Saul Friedländer, *Nazi Germany and the Jews*, vol. 1, New York: Orion, 1998, p. 87; Alon Confino, *Foundational Pasts: The Holocaust as Understanding*, Cambridge: Cambridge University Press, 2011, p. 158; see also Herf, *Jewish Enemy*.

206. Steinberg, 'Types of Genocide?', p. 190.

207. Rupnow et al., eds, *Pseudowissenschaft*, p. 292; Hale, *Himmler's Crusade*, pp. 11, 19–27; Trevor-Roper, ed., *Conversations*, p. 116. Cf. Picker, *Tischgespräche*, pp. 78–9; Hitler, *Mein Kampf*, p. 305.

208. 'When it came to Jews, the proneness to wild, "magical thinking" – by the Nazi leadership and the perpetrators – and their incapacity for "reality testing" generally distinguishes them from the perpetrators of other mass slaughters.' Daniel Goldhagen. *Hitler's Willing Executioners*, New York: Random House, 1997, p. 412.

209. Staudenmaier, *Between Occultism and Nazism*, pp. 166–73.

210. Gugenberger and Schweidlenka, *Faden der Nornen*, pp. 137–9; Jestram, *Mythen*, p. 200; http://motlc. wiesenthal.com/site/pp.asp?c=gvKVLcMVIuG&b=395043; Staudenmaier, *Between Occultism and Nazism*, pp. 93–4, 100–1.

211. F. W. Murnau, director, *Nosferatu, eine Symphonie des Grauens*, Germany Prana-Film, 1922, re-release on DVD Kino-International 2007. Film/DVD. Not Rated. B/W. Silent with German intertitles, English subtitles, or English intertitles. Running time: 94 min.

212. Coates, *Gorgon's Gaze*; Jeffrey Herf, *Jewish Enemy*.

213. Auerbach, *Our Vampires*, pp. 72–4; see also Bohn, 'Vampirismus', p. 8; Fitzpatrick, 'The Pre-History of the Holocaust?', pp. 500–3; Leschnitzer, *Magic Background*, pp. 164–5.

214. Brenda Gardenour, 'The Biology of Blood-Lust: Medieval Medicine, Theology, and the Vampire Jew', *Film & History* 41:2 (Fall 2011), pp. 51–8; Black, 'Expellees', pp. 94–6; see also Eisner, *Haunted Screen*, p. 97.

215. Hitler, *Mein Kampf*, pp. 305, 544.

216. Ibid., pp. 309–10.

217. Ibid., p. 327.

218. Ibid., p. 544.

219. Redles, *Hitler's Millennial Reich*, pp. 62–3.

220. Sebottendorff, *Bevor Hitler kam*, pp. 29–40; see letters, including Hinkel to Theodor Fritsch, Jr., 16.6.36, BAB: R 9361–V/5404.

221. Kater, 'Artamanen', pp. 599–601.

222. Junginger, 'From Buddha to Adolf Hitler', pp. 129–31, 136–9; Redles, *Hitler's Millennial Reich*, pp. 58–9, 66; Sebottendorff, *Bevor Hitler kam*, p. 23; Burleigh, 'National Socialism', p. 13.

223. Himmler, *Schutzstaffel*, pp. 4–6; Alfred Rosenberg, *Die Spur des Juden im Wandel der Zeiten*, Munich: Druck, 1937, p. 84. Rheden biography in NL Darré, BAK: N 1094I/77, pp. 5–6, 24.

224. Trimondi, *Hitler*, p. 107.

225. Trevor-Roper, ed., *Bormann Letters*, pp. xix–xx.

226. Koehne, 'The Racial Yardstick', pp. 586–9.

227. Gardenour, 'The Biology of Blood-Lust', pp. 59–60.

228. Ibid., pp. 60–1; Auerbach, *Our Vampires*, pp. 15–21, 75–89; Kater, 'Artamanen', pp. 599–600.

229. Gregor Schwartz-Bostunitsch, *Jüde und Weib: Theorie und Praxis des jüdischen Vampyrismus, der Ausbeutung und Verseuchung der Wirtsvölker*, Berlin: Theodor Fritsch Verlag, 1939; Goodrick-Clarke, *Occult Roots*, pp. 169–71.

230. Sickinger, 'Hitler and the Occult'.

231. Leschnitzer, *Magic Background*, pp. 113–14; Cecil, *Myth*, pp. 12–13.

232. For the Nazis, the 'story of Cain and Abel and the language of martyrdom and the monstrous also helped ... describe the shock of inversion, a dramatic reversal of fortunes epitomized by the First and later Second World War'. Black, 'Expellees', pp. 97–8; see also Bärsch, *Politische Religion*, p. 88; Fitzpatrick, 'The Pre-History of the Holocaust?', pp. 502–3.

233. Ach, *Hitlers Religion*, pp. 123–7; Bärsch, *Politische Religion*, pp. 106–7, 124–7; Redles, *Hitler's Millennial Reich*, pp. 58–9, 66.

234. Redles, *Hitler's Millennial Reich*, p. 63.

235. Ibid., p. 61.

236. Eckart, *Der Bolschewismus*, p. 7.

237. Koehne, 'Were the National Socialists a Völkisch Party?', pp. 775–6.

238. Trevor-Roper, ed., *Conversations*, pp. 63–4.

239. Kersten, *Memoirs*, p. 35.

240. Himmler, *Schutzstaffel*, pp. 3–4.

241. Gregor Schwartz-Bostunitsch, *Jüdischer Imperialismus: 3000 Jahre hebräischer Schleichwege zur Erlangung der weltherrschaft*, Leipzig: Theodor Fritsch Verlag, 1935, pp. 39–62.

242. Ibid., pp. 26–42.

243. Trevor-Roper, ed., *Conversations*, p. 229.

244. Behringer, 'Der Abwickler der Hexenforschung', pp. 117–21, 127–8; Rudolf, 'Geheime Reichskommando-Sache!', pp. 53–54; Wiedemann, 'Wissen', pp. 449–452.

245. Behringer, 'Der Abwickler der Hexenforschung', pp. 109–34.

246. Ibid., pp. 125–9; Junginger, 'From Buddha to Adolf Hitler', pp. 144–5.

247. Behringer, 'Der Abwickler der Hexenforschung', pp. 122–3.

248. Kaufmann, *Tibet*, pp. 678–9; Junginger, 'From Buddha to Adolf Hitler', pp. 133–5.

249. Behringer, 'Der Abwickler der Hexenforschung', pp. 109–17, 128–9; see also Longerich, *Himmler*, pp. 464–5, 509–11.

250. Alexander Centgraf, *Eine Jude Treibt Philosophie*, Berlin: Hochmuth, 1943, pp. 3, 15.

251. Ibid., p. 21.

252. Harrington, *Reenchanted Science*, p. 281.

253. Rauschning, *Voice of Destruction*, p. 242.

254. Trimondi, *Hitler*, p. 107.

255. Vondung, 'National Socialism', pp. 87–95.

256. Burleigh, 'National Socialism', p. 12.

257. Lewy, *Gypsies*, p. 67.

258. Yehuda Bauer, 'The Holocaust and Genocide: Some Comparisons', in Peter Hayes, ed., *Lessons and Legacies*, Evanston, IL: Northwestern University Press, 1991, p. 42.

259. Lewy, *Gypsies*, p. 136.

260. Ibid., pp. 138–9.

261. Yehuda Bauer, 'Holocaust and Genocide: Some Comparisons', in Hayes, ed., *Lessons and Legacies*, p. 42.

262. See Trimondi, *Hitler*, pp. 64–5; see also Longerich, *Himmler*, pp. 262–3; 'All these far-fetched claims for Nordic overlords in Asia made a deep impression on Himmler. He was keen to unearth the hard archaeological proof of these gold-haired conquerors.' Pringle, *Plan*, pp. 136–47.

263. Trimondi, *Hitler*, p. 146.

264. Goldhagen, *Executioners*, p. 28.

265. Hütter, *Gruselwandern*, p. 211; Dirk Rupnow, ' "Pseudowissenschaft" als Argument und Ausrede', in Rupnow et al., eds, *Pseudowissenschaft*, p. 285.

266. Goldhagen, *Executioners*, p. 28.

267. Kater, 'Artamanen', p. 627.

268. H. Schneider, *Der jüdische Vampyr chaotisiert die Welt (Der Jude als Weltparasit)*, Lüneberg: Stern (Gauschulungsamt der NSDAP), 1943.

269. Ibid., p. 7.
270. Ibid., p. 8.
271. Ibid., p. 9.
272. Ibid., p. 8.
273. Ibid., pp. 37–48; Maichle, 'Die Nostradamus-Propaganda der Nazis'; http://www.nostradamus-online.de/index1.htm.
274. See the foreword, Gauschulungsamt der NSDAP, *Der jüdische Vampyr.*
275. Gauschulungsamt der NSDAP, *Der jüdische Vampyr*; see also Kaufmann, *Tibet*, pp. 583–8.
276. Black, 'Expellees', p. 95; Harten, *Himmlers Lehrer*, pp. 139–41.
277. Gerda to Martin Bormann, 10.7.44, in Trevor-Roper, ed., *Bormann Letters*, p. 136.
278. Redles, *Millennial Reich*, pp. 69–70.
279. Trevor-Roper, ed., *Conversations*, p. 116. Cf. Picker, *Tischgespräche*, pp. 78–9.
280. Mees, 'Hitler and Germanentum', p. 263.
281. Trevor-Roper, ed., *Conversations*, p. 269.
282. Kater, *Das 'Ahnenerbe'*, p. 205.
283. Burleigh, 'National Socialism', pp. 13–14.
284. Yitzhak Arad, *The Holocaust in the Soviet Union*, Lincoln, NB: University of Nebraska Press, pp. 56–7.
285. Rupnow et al., eds, *Pseudowissenschaft*, p. 280.
286. Kater, 'Artamanen', pp. 628–9; Vondung, 'National Socialism', p. 92.
287. Christoph Daxelmuller, 'Nazi Conceptions of Culture and the Erasure of Jewish Folklore', in Dow and Lixfeld, eds, *Nazification*, pp. 73–7; see also Kater, *Das 'Ahnenerbe'*, pp. 118–19.
288. Behringer, 'Der Abwickler der Hexenforschung', pp. 125–9; Junginger, 'From Buddha to Adolf Hitler', pp. 144–5.
289. Rudolf, 'Geheime Reichskommando-Sache!', pp. 53–4.
290. Jürgen Matthäus, 'Kameraden im Geist: Himmlers Hexenforscher im Kontext des nationalsozialistischen Wissenschaftsbetriebs', in Bauer et al., *Hexenkarthotek*, pp. 102–7.
291. Hütter, *Gruselwandern*, p. 211; see also Wiedemann, 'Wissen', pp. 449–55.
292. Schleiermacher and Schagen, 'Medizinische Forschung', pp. 254–6, 276–8. For more on the unscientific premises behind the 'Final Solution', see Wetzell, 'Eugenics and Racial Science'.
293. Herf, 'Nazi Germany's Propaganda'; Rubin and Schwanitz, *Nazis, Islamists*, pp. 125–9, 164–5, 181.
294. Herf, 'Nazi Germany's Propaganda'.
295. Although Bormann criticized Himmler's plans 'as overblown ... [a] fundamental departure from presently applied measures for fighting the Gypsy plague', Hitler appeared to have sided with Himmler and his border scientific colleagues, leading to Bormann's chancellery conceding to the Ministry of Justice in 1943 that 'New research has shown that among the Gypsies are racially valuable elements.' Lewy, *Gypsies*, pp. 140–1; Gugenberger and Schweidlenka, *Faden der Nornen*, p. 155.
296. Lewy, *Gypsies*, pp. 138–9.
297. Burleigh, 'National Socialism', p. 3. In comparison to other cases of ethnic cleansing, the 'Final Solution' had a more obviously 'pseudo-religious motivation that brought Jew-hatred into the center of Nazi ideology'. Bauer, 'Holocaust', p. 43.
298. Confino, *World Without Jews*, p. 6. The entire war was perceived in 'starkly existential but also religious terms ... Nazi anti-Jewish apocalypticism and the genocide that grew out of it were about clearing the slate of time, reestablishing and purifying origins, rewriting history to suit a revolutionary, millennial age.' Black, 'Groening', p. 213; The 'construction of the Jewish Other' within the Third Reich was 'thoroughly apocalyptic ... [and] ultimately gave impetus to what the Nazis termed ... the Final Solution'. Redles, *Hitler's Millennial Reich*, pp. 12–13.
299. Confino, *World Without Jews*, p. 10; That is, in the words of Michael Burleigh, 'Lower-key moral transformations' were occurring long before the Holocaust, which helped provide the deeper metaphysical context by which this extraordinary level of violence was made possible; Burleigh, 'National Socialism', p. 13.
300. Hale, *Himmler's Crusade*, pp. 11, 19–27; Trevor-Roper, ed., *Conversations*, p. 116. Cf. Picker, *Tischgespräche*, pp. 78–9; Hitler, *Mein Kampf*, p. 305; Engelhardt, 'Nazis of Tibet', pp. 63–96.
301. Rupnow et al., eds, *Pseudowissenschaft*, pp. 301–2.
302. Harrington, *Reenchanted Science*, p. 208.
303. Burleigh, 'National Socialism', pp. 4–5.
304. Kater, *Das 'Ahnenerbe'*, p. 236; Kater, 'Artamanen', p. 627.
305. Hale, *Himmler's Crusade*, pp. 11, 19–27; Trevor-Roper, ed., *Conversations*, p. 116. Cf. Picker, *Tischgespräche*, pp. 78–9; Hitler, *Mein Kampf*, p. 305; Kater, *Das 'Ahnenerbe'*, pp. 261–4; Schleiermacher and Schagen, 'Medizinische Forschung', pp. 276–8.
306. Kater, *Das 'Ahnenerbe'*, pp. 227–8.
307. Lipphardt, 'Das "schwarze Schaf"', pp. 241–4.

308. Schleiermacher and Schagen, 'Medizinische Forschung', pp. 251–63, 271–5; Kater, *Das 'Ahnenerbe'*, pp. 265–6.
309. Fitzpatrick, 'The Pre-History of the Holocaust?', pp. 477–503.
310. Vondung, 'National Socialism', pp. 92–3.
311. I do not mean to suggest, of course, that all cases of ethnic cleansing or political murder, for example Mao's Great Leap Forward or Stalin's purges, are a product of supernatural thinking.

Chapter 9

1. Speer speech, 31.8.44, to leading armaments producers, 'Aktenauszüge über die Wunderwaffen 4 Sept. 1945', IfZG: ED 99–9, p. 102.
2. Report from Elisabeth Kowitzki, 18.5.52, in Sammlung Karasek, 04/02–144, NSG 297.
3. Bormann, as quoted in Trevor-Roper, ed., *Bormann Letters*, p. xxi.
4. Hitler attempted to buy an original copy of the score of *Götterdämmerung* as Reich Chancellor. 'Ankauf eines Autographs von Richard Wagner durch Hitler (Götterdämmerung Vorspiel)': Herbert Bittner to 'Sekretariat des Herrn Reichskanzlers', 19.4.34; 'Sekretariat' to Bittner, 28.6.34; 30.4.34, Bittner sends the MS to the RKK; 6.7.34, RKK Meerwald sends MS to RMVP; personal referent in RMVP to Personlichen Referent des Reichskanzlers, 11.7.34, 14.7.34, Bittner to Meerwald; 17.7.34, Meerwald to Bittner; 16.7.34, RMVP (von Keudell) returns MS; 14.7.34, Wolf *Gutachten* to Keudell; 19.7.34, Meerwald to Bittner. BAB: R 43II/1245, Bd. 6.
5. Haraldur Bernharðsson, 'Old Icelandic *Ragnarök* and *Ragnarökkr*', in Alan Nussbaum, ed., *Verba Docenti*, Ann Arbor, MI: Beech Stave Press, 2007, pp. 25–38; Carolyne Larrington (trans.), *The Poetic Edda*, Oxford: Oxford University Press, 2014; Snorri Sturlson (trans. Jesse Byock), *The Prose Edda*, New York: Penguin, 2006.
6. Kellogg, *Russian Roots*, p. 23.
7. Terje Emberland, 'Im Zeichen der Hagal-Rune', in Puschner and Vollnhals, eds, *Bewegung*, pp. 520–1; Cornelia Schmitz-Berning, *Vokabular des Nationalsozialismus*, Berlin: De Gruyter, 1998, pp. 176–7; David Welch, 'Goebbels, Götterdämmerung and the Deutsche Wochenschau', in K. M. Short and Stephen Dolezel, eds, *Hitler's Fall: The Newsreel Witness*, London: Routledge, 1988, pp. 80–93.
8. Kater, *Das 'Ahnenerbe'*, p. 220. In times of war, supernatural thinking, whether in terms of faith (*Glaube*) or superstition (*Aberglaube*) often experiences a resurgence; Goepfert, *Immer noch Aberglaube!*, p. 92; see also Darnton, 'Peasants Tell Tales', pp. 21–2, 50–63; Zipes, *Fairy Tale*.
9. Kater, *Das 'Ahnenerbe'*, p. 220.
10. Perry Biddiscombe, *The Last Nazis: SS Werewolf Guerrilla Resistance in Europe 1944-1947*, London: Tempus, 2006.
11. Sammlung Karasek, 02/04–66, NSG 219, 13.5.51; Black, 'Expellees', p. 78.
12. Goepfert, *Immer noch Aberglaube!*, pp. 17–21, 30–7, 72–3.
13. Perry Biddiscombe, *Werwolf! The History of the National Socialist Guerrilla Movement, 1944-1946*, Cardiff: University of Wales Press, 1998, pp. 289–91; Beevor, *Downfall*; Stephen Fritz, *Endkampf: Soldiers, Civilians, and the Death of the Third Reich*, Lexington, KY: University Press of Kentucky, 2004, pp. 7–8, 196–204; Bessel, *Germany 1945*, pp. 16–17, 299–300.
14. Biddiscombe, *Last Nazis*, pp. 252–74; Petra Weber, *Justiz und Diktatur: Justizverwaltung und politische Strafjustiz in Thüringen 1945-1961. Veröffentlichungen zur SBZ-/DDR -Forschung im Institut für Zeitgeschichte*, Oldenbourg: Wissenschaftsverlag, 2000, p. 99.
15. Speer, 'Aktenauszüge über die Wunderwaffen 4 Sept. 1945', IfZG: ED 99/9, p. 100.
16. Ibid.
17. Unfortunately, little academic work has been done on the nature of miraculous thinking, technological or otherwise, in the Third Reich. Much of the popular or crypto-history that we do have suffers from a highly speculative, poorly documented approach. And yet this literature has suggested, more consistently than mainstream scholarship, that the Nazi quest for miracle weapons was a product of 'occult beliefs and practices' allied 'with certain very "German" advances in physics' – also noting the connection between the Nazi quest for a 'barbarous arsenal of prototypical "smart weapons" and weapons of mass destruction' and the 'machinery, bureaucracy, and technologies of mass death and slavery'. Joseph Farrell, *Reich of the Black Sun: Nazi Secret Weapons and the Cold War Allied Legend*, Kempton, IL: Adventures Unlimited Press, 2015, pp. v–vi; Derrich, *Geheimwaffen*, p. 6.
18. Indeed, while 'magic realism' in regard to technology played a marginal role in fascist Italy, 'in Germany it was officially approved and furthered'. Mosse, *Masses and Man*, pp. 179–83; see also Alexander Geppert and Till Kössler, 'Einleitung: *Wunder der Zeitgeschichte*', in Geppert and Kössler, eds, *Wunder*, pp. 9–12, 46; Jeffrey Herf, *Reactionary Modernism*, Cambridge: Cambridge University Press, 1986, pp. 70–8.
19. Geppert and Kössler, 'Einleitung', p. 46.

20. 'Weimar's science fiction,' writes Peter Fisher, 'helped keep the embers of *ressentiment* burning' by providing 'cheap compensation to the discontented individual by implying that German Geist – manifested by revolutionary inventions – was bound, at sometime in the near future, to bring about a new age of superiority, of individual and collective achievement'. Fisher, *Fantasy*, pp. 220–1; Halter, 'Zivilisation'. ?

21. Herf, *Reactionary Modernism*, pp. 202–3; Ach, *Hitlers Religion*, pp. 35–7.

22. Adam Tooze, 'The Economic History of the Nazi Regime', in Caplan, ed., *Nazi Germany*, pp. 185–94.

23. Kater, *Das 'Ahnenerbe'*, pp. 218–19.

24. Ibid., p. 219. Already in late 1942, as a response to Stalingrad, miracle-weapon underground facilities were built near Mauthausen and KZ Gusen in Austria, where all available inmates were ordered to work on war-related projects. Derrich, *Geheimwaffen*, pp. 154–5; see also project reports in BAB: R 3/1626, 'Wunderwaffen Propaganda'; BAB: R 26–III/52, 'Wunderwaffen', pp. 3–227.

25. Kater, *Das 'Ahnenerbe'*, p. 219; Reitzenstein, *Himmlers Forscher*, p. 43.

26. See Mark Walker, *German National Socialism and the Quest for Nuclear Power*, Cambridge: Cambridge University Press, 1993, pp. 160–76, 216–17; Pringle, *Plan*, pp. 282–3; Kater, *Das 'Ahnenerbe'*, p. 219.

27. Or that the scientists Fritz Houtermann and Baron Manfred von Ardenne were involved in experiments in turning uranium–235 into plutonium. Farrell, *Reich*, pp. 8–13, 18–23, 26–49, 67–72, 81–7, 130–6, 154–7; Nagel, *Wissenschaft für den Krieg*, pp. 189–208; http://www.dailymail.co.uk/news/article-2014146/Nazi-nuclear-waste-Hitlers-secret-A-bomb-programme-mine.html.

28. Rainer Karlsch, *Hitlers Bombe*, Stuttgart: Deutsche Verlags-Anstalt, 2005, pp. 216–27; Farrell, *Reich*, pp. 35–48, 55–63, 118–28, 149–53; http://www.dailymail.co.uk/news/article-2014146/Nazi-nuclear-waste-Hitlers-secret-A-bomb-programme-mine.html.

29. http://www.forbes.com/sites/paulrodgers/2014/02/11/search-is-on-for-hitlers-secret-atom-bomb-lab-under-death-camp.

30. Pringle, *Plan*, pp. 282–3.

31. Kater, *Das 'Ahnenerbe'*, p. 220.

32. As well as Andreas Epp and Otto Habermohl. Heiner Gehring and Klaus Rothkugel, *Der Flugscheiben Mythos*, Schleusingen: Amun, 2001, pp. 36–41.

33. Derrich, *Geheimwaffen*, pp. 13–14, 123–32; Werner Keller in *Welt am Sonntag: Erste 'Flugscheibe' flog 1945 in Prag*, 26.4.53; Gehring and Rothkugel, *Flugscheiben Mythos*, pp. 31–5, 44–5; http://www.welt.de/geschichte/zweiter-weltkrieg/article133061716/Die-Ufos-des-Dritten-Reiches-kamen-bis-in-die-USA.html.

34. Gehring and Rothkugel, *Flugscheiben Mythos*, pp. 36–41; Derrich, *Geheimwaffen*, p. 13.

35. 31.1.45, 'Massnahmen zur Bomberbekämpfung auf dem Gebiete der Hochfrequenz', which suggests methods, in consultation with Dr Roessler, including 1. Entdüppelung, 2. Störung feindlicher Navigationsverfahren, 3. Reflektionsbeseitigung; 26.2.45, report, 'Vergleich der Erfolgsausrichten der verschiedenen Möglichkeiten zur Brechung des Luftterrors', concluding with 'Planeten', p. 222; letter from Wist in Institut für elektrische Anlagen to Planungsamt des Reichsforschungrates Osenberg, 2.3.45. BAB: R 26–III/52, Wunderwaffen.

36. Derrich, *Geheimwaffen*, pp. 84–5.

37. Hermann Oberth, 'They Come from Outer Space', *Flying Saucer Review* 1:2 (May–June 1955), pp. 12–14; Hermann Oberth, 'Dr. Hermann Oberth Discusses UFOs', *Fate Magazine* (May 1962), pp. 36–43; see also https://www.youtube.com/watch?v=OQkJqAA268o; https://en.wikipedia.org/wiki/Hermann_Oberth; http://www.telegraph.co.uk/technology/5201410/Are-UFOs-real-Famous-people-who-believed.html; Pennick, *Hitler's Secret Sciences*, pp. 141–2.

38. Neufeld, *Rocket*, pp. 41–72, 197–266; Nagel, *Wissenschaft für den Krieg*, pp. 228–38; Derrich, *Geheimwaffen*, pp. 86–7.

39. Kater, *Das 'Ahnenerbe'*, p. 219.

40. Neufeld, *Rocket*, p. 201; Derrich, *Geheimwaffen*, p. 94–5.

41. Neufeld, *Rocket*, pp. 201–3; Bernhard Kroener, *Wartime Administration, Economy, and Manpower Resources 1942–1944/5*, Oxford: Oxford University Press, 2003, p. 390; Nick Cook, *The Hunt for Zero Point: Inside the Classified World of Antigravity Technology*, New York: Broadway Books, 2002, pp. 169–72; Rainer Karlsch, 'Was wurde aus Hans Kammler?', *Zeitschrift für Geschichtswissenschaft* 6 (2014).

42. Derrich, *Geheimwaffen*, pp. 88–90; Cook, *Hunt*, pp. 170–2.

43. Cook, *Hunt*, pp. 163–8; see also 'Wunderwaffen'. First folder, 'Kammler, Geheime Kommandosache, 6,2.45, BAB: R 26–III/52, pp. 189–95.

44. Cook, *Hunt*, pp. 153–8, 170–2; http://www.forbes.com/sites/paulrodgers/2014/02/11/search-is-on-for-hitlers-secret-atom-bomb-lab-under-death-camp; http://www.dailymail.co.uk/news/article-2014146/Nazi-nuclear-waste-Hitlers-secret-A-bomb-programme-mine.html.

45. Speer, 3.8.44, aus der Rede vor den Gauleitern in Posen (excerpted from the speech before the Gauleiter in Posen), 'Aktenauszüge über die Wunderwaffen 4 Sept. 1945', IfZG: ED 99–9, p. 101.

46. Ibid.

47. Speer, 29.8.44, Rede vor der Reichspropagandaleitung, den Leitern der Reichspropagandaämter im Propagandaministerium (speech before the Reich Propaganda Leadership, the leaders of the Reich Propaganda Offices in the Propaganda Ministry), 'Aktenauszüge über die Wunderwaffen 4 Sept. 1945', IfZG: ED 99/9, pp. 101–2.

48. Ibid., p. 101.

49. Ibid.

50. 'So we have the question whether the V-2, which has a truly terrible effect, now is in some form psychologically decisive in terms of the outcome of the war. Purely in technical terms it cannot be.' Ibid.

51. 'Wunderwaffen', BAB: R 26–III/52, quote from 12.11.44, The Observer, p. 35.

52. 15.9.44, aus einem Reisebericht an A. H. 10 (excerpt from a travel report to A. H. [Adolf Hitler]), 'Aktenauszüge über die Wunderwaffen 4 Sept. 1945', IfZG: ED 99–9, p. 103.

53. Ibid., pp. 103–4.

54. Ralf Schnabel, Die Illusion der Wunderfwaffen, Oldenbourg: DeGruyter, 1994, pp. 285–6.

55. 1.12.44, Schlussrede in Rechlin vor Vorsitzer der Rüstungskommisionen, Hauptausschussleitern, Ringleitern, Kommissionsvorsitzern (closing speech to the Chairmen of the Armaments Commission, Main Committee Leaders, Ring Leaders, and Commission Chairmen), 'Aktenauszüge über die Wunderwaffen 4 Sept. 1945', IfZG: ED 99/9, p. 104.

56. Kater, Das 'Ahnenerbe', pp. 219–20; Cook, Hunt, pp. 163–8.

57. Monica Black, 'A Messiah after Hitler, and his Miracles: Bruno Groening and Popular Apocalypticism in Early West German History', in Black and Kurlander, eds, Revisiting, p. 217.

58. 'Aktenauszüge über die Wunderwaffen 4 Sept. 1945', IfZG: ED 99–9, p. 105. As Jeremy Noakes observes, over the course of the war, Hitler increasingly delegated power over regional administration to ideologically committed Nazi Party Gauleiter, such as Hellmuth, as opposed to state experts and industry leaders. This shift in power favoured the faith-based thinking that pervaded the Nazi Party leadership. See Jeremy Noakes, 'Hitler and the Nazi State: Leadership, Hierarchy, and Power', in Caplan, ed., Nazi Germany, pp. 93–8.

59. Kater, Das 'Ahnenerbe', p. 220.

60. Ibid.

61. Cook, Hunt, pp. 163–8; see also 'Kammler, Geheime Kommandosache, 6.2.45, BAB: R 26–III/52, pp. 189–95; https://www.welt.de/geschichte/article128873148/Versteckten-die-USA-den-Chef-Ingenieur-der-SS.html.

62. Kater, Das 'Ahnenerbe', pp. 219–20; Farrell, Reich, pp. 67–9, 82–7, 103–7.

63. Cook, Hunt, pp. 159–62; Farrell, Reich, pp. 103–7; Kammler ostensibly had concentration-camp inmates from Buchenwald dig twenty-five tunnels into the Jonastal near Ohrdruf (see above), which may have been the location for additional electromagnetic experiments and nuclear-based technologies. Derrich, Geheimwaffen, pp. 145–7, 151–3; http://www.dailymail.co.uk/news/article-2014146/Nazi-nuclear-waste-Hitlers-secret-A-bomb-programme-mine.html.

64. Kater, Das 'Ahnenerbe', p. 220.

65. Ibid.; Kaufmann, Tibet, pp. 318–19.

66. Kater, Das 'Ahnenerbe', p. 220.

67. Ibid., pp. 220–1.

68. Ibid.; Kaufmann, Tibet, pp. 314–16; see also the Wienert biography and Beger Denkschrift on the Tibet expedition, BAB: NS 21/869.

69. See correspondence between Joseph Wimmer and SS, 26.7.38, 29.1.42, 13.2.42, BAB: NS 21/2669; Kater, Das 'Ahnenerbe', p. 222.

70. Hans Robert Scultetus: BAB: NS 21/2547. Scultetus named Oberregierungsrat in Munich, 12.1.43; 29.6.43, transferred back as part of the Luftwaffe administration; 15.2.44, Scultetus back to Geophysics Institute and Himmler confirms desire to keep it open, but no new workers or publications due to war situation; Kater, Das 'Ahnenerbe', pp. 214–15, 222; Kaufmann, Tibet, pp. 315–17.

71. See letter to Wimmer, 13.6.42, BAB: NS 21/2669; Kater, Das 'Ahnenerbe', pp. 214–15, 222.

72. Kater, Das 'Ahnenerbe', p. 222.

73. Pringle, Plan, pp. 283–4; Derrich, Geheimwaffen, p. 153.

74. Kater, Das 'Ahnenerbe', pp. 51–2; see also Longerich, Himmler, pp. 266–7.

75. Pringle, Plan, pp. 283–4; Derrich, Geheimwaffen, p. 153.

76. A. G. Shenstone, 'The Brocken Spectre', Science 119 (1994), pp. 511–12; Derrich, Geheimwaffen, pp. 13–15; Pennick, Hitler's Secret Sciences, pp. 169–70.

77. Jakob Sporrenberg (a member of the SS police regiment SD in Warsaw, Radom, and Galicia, the SS training camp Trawniki and SS battalion Streibel), 21.7.44, as well as other July 1944 letters, giving awards from RSHA to SD men (KVK 2. Klasse mit Schwertern; into September, more 'Verleihung von Kriegsauszeichnungen'), BAB: R 70–Polen/783 (B. 9); 6.9.44 (Krakau), Sporrenberg to Koppe; BAB: R 70–Polen/784 (B. 10).

78. Led by SS-Obersturmbannführer Otto Neumann; Cook, *Hunt*, pp. 182–8, 192–4; http://www.welt. de/geschichte/zweiter-weltkrieg/article133061716/Die-Ufos-des-Dritten-Reiches-kamen-bis-in-die-USA.html.

79. Cook, *Hunt*, pp. 188–93; Henry Stevens, *Hitler's Suppressed and Still-Secret Weapons, Science and Technology*, Kempton, IL: Adventures Unlimited, 2007, pp. 250–5; Derrich, *Geheimwaffen*, pp. 13–15.

80. Bartholomew, *Hidden Nature*, pp. 73–104, 215–40.

81. Willuhn to Pietzsch, 13.7.34, explaining that Schauberger had not been honest in his letter, BAB: R 43–II/342; see also copies of correspondence, including Schauberger to Hitler, 10.7.34, and to Roselius; report from Dr Willuhn, 13.7.34, in IfZG: ED 458/1, pp. 80–6, 99–100, 104–5; Bartholomew, *Hidden Nature*, pp. 241–3; Derrich, *Geheimwaffen*, p. 192.

82. 7.7.34, Dr Roselius writes to the Chancellery; 10.7.34, telegram and letter reporting on meeting with Keppler and how Hitler thought Schauberger was a deceiver; 10.7.34, signed promise from Schauberger, BAB: R 43–II/342.

83. 10.7.34, letter signed by Willuhn, indicating evidence that Schauberger was not sharing his secret methods for purifying water; Willuhn to Pietzsch, 13.7.34, explaining that Schauberger had not been honest; 13.7.34, Roselius to Staatsekretar Lammers regretting Schauberger's coyness and attitude about revealing his 'Erfinder-Geheimnis', when he had promised to reveal it, and hopes this doesn't dissuade Hitler from pursuing his ideas, BAB: R 43–II/342; see also copies of correspondence, including Schauberger to Hitler, 10.7.34, letter to Roselius; report from Dr Willuhn, 13.7.34, IfZG: ED 458/1, pp. 80–6, 99–100, 104–5; Bartholomew, *Hidden Nature*, pp. 241–3; Derrich, *Geheimwaffen*, p. 192.

84. Schauberger to Lammers, 10.7.34, enclosing another letter for Himmler; 10.7.34, Schauberger to Hitler, explaining why he's not approaching Mussolini, whom he had already met, and why he wants Hitler's support, as an Austro-German who wants to make his discoveries for Germany, BAB: R 43–II/342, pp. 102–3.

85. Willuhn to Pietzsch, 13.7.34, explaining that Schauberger had not been honest in his letter; 17.7.34, copying Keppler and noting that Schauberger had every opportunity to prove the validity of his theories, but failed, reinforcing the idea that 'Autodidakten' rarely contribute 'bahnbrechende Erfindungen'; 14.7.34, Roselius to Lammers; 18.7.34, Pietzsch to Willuhn. BAB: R 43–II/342.

86. !7.7.34, Lammers, copying Keppler, not wanting Hitler, like Franz Josef in the 1860s, to be repeatedly swindled by alchemists claiming to turn lead into gold, BAB: R 43–II/342.

87. Martina Rodier: *Viktor Schauberger – Naturforscher und Erfinder*, Frankfurt: Zweitausendeins, 1999, pp. 183–4.

88. Cook, *Hunt*, pp. 50–1, 210–14; Bartholomew, *Hidden Nature*, pp. 241–2.

89. Cook, *Hunt*, pp. 212–16; Bartholomew, *Hidden Nature*, pp. 242–3; Derrich, *Geheimwaffen*, p. 192.

90. Cook, *Hunt*, pp. 217–23; Bartholomew, *Hidden Nature*, pp. 251–4; http://www.forbes.com/sites/paulrodgers/2014/02/11/search-is-on-for-hitlers-secret-atom-bomb-lab-under-death-camp.

91. Cook, *Hunt*, p. 206; Bartholomew, *Hidden Nature*, pp. 251–4.

92. Cook, *Hunt*, pp. 206–8, 223–5; Bartholomew, *Hidden Nature*, pp. 15–24, 244–7.

93. Bartholomew, *Hidden Nature*, pp. 251–4; http://www.forbes.com/sites/paulrodgers/2014/02/11/search-is-on-for-hitlers-secret-atom-bomb-lab-under-death-camp.

94. Farrell, *Reich*, pp. 103–7; Cook, *Hunt*, pp. 187–8, 219–25; Bartholomew, *Hidden Nature*, pp. 244–63.

95. 'In Stalingrad brauchte man zuverlässige Wetterberichte und winterfeste Uniformen, nicht kosmologische Spekulationen und Horoskope aus dem Eis.' (In Stalingrad people needed dependable weather reports and winter-ready uniforms, not cosmological speculations and horoscopes derived from [WEL].) Halter, 'Welteislehre'.

96. Kater, *Das 'Ahnenerbe'*, p. 225.

97. Ibid., p. 226; see also report from 3.4.45, pp. 137–44, BAB: R 26–III/52, 'Wunderwaffen'.

98. Once transformed, these werewolves experienced 'a nocturnal hunter's and killer's wild and blood-stained vampire life'. Eisler, *Man into Wolf*, p. 34; interestingly, many of these assertions were anticipated by a dissertation written by a functionary in Rosenberg's office, BAB: R 58/7237, 'Wesen und Geschichte des Werwolfs'.

99. Eisler, *Man into Wolf*, p. 165.

100. Ibid., pp. 34–5.

101. The Karasek archive is rife with ethnic German reports on apparitions of the Virgin Mary and other supernatural occurrences. Sammlung Karasek, 2.4.52, NSG 205, 21.5.52; 4.2.53, NSG 206, 19.5.51; see also Zoran Janjetović, *Between Hitler and Tito: The Disappearance of the Vojvodina Germans*, Belgrade: SD Publik, 2005; Valdis O. Lumans, *Himmler's Auxiliaries: The Volksdeutsche Mittelstelle and the German National Minorities of Europe, 1939–1945*, Chapel Hill, NC: University of North Carolina Press, 1993, p. 235; Goepfert, *Immer noch Aberglaube!*, pp. 38–56, 64–5; for an earlier analysis of similar phenomena, see David Blackbourn, *Marpingen: Apparitions of the Virgin Mary in Bismarckian Germany*, Oxford: Clarendon Press, 1995.

102. Holtz, *Faszination*, pp. 13–15.
103. Black, 'Expellees', p. 95.
104. Ibid., p. 77.
105. Eisler, *Man into Wolf*, p. 141. 'When I closed the meeting, I was not alone in thinking that now a wolf had been born, destined to burst upon the herd of seducers of the people.' Toland, *Hitler*, p. 98.
106. Robert Waite, *Psychopathic God*, New York: Basic Books, 1977, p. 166.
107. Sklar, *Gods and Beasts*, p. 61.
108. Wendy Lower, *Nazi Empire-Building and the Holocaust in the Ukraine*, Chapel Hill, NC: University of North Carolina Press, 2007, pp. 62, 151–5, 172; Walter Warlimont, *Inside Hitler's Headquarters, 1939–45*, New York: Praeger, 1964, p. 246; Eisler, *Man into Wolf*, p. 169.
109. Were there 'a reliable eyewitness account of the story of Hitler "biting the carpet" in his accesses of rage, the problem would arise whether these carpets represented for him the hairy coat of the living animals into which the "Isawiyya "lions" put their teeth or the grass which the despondent king Nebuchadnezzar ate. If the stories about Hitler's rages are true, they would appear to have been manic lycanthropic states.' Eisler, *Man into Wolf*, p. 165.
110. Ibid., p. 141.
111. Wüst, *Indogermanisches Bekenntnis*, p. 46.
112. Mackensen, *Sagen*, pp. 4–6, 10–11, 14–15.
113. Ibid., pp. 15–16.
114. Ibid., pp. 119–23; Goepfert, *Immer noch Aberglaube!*, p. 65.
115. Mackensen, *Sagen*, p. 10. Here the German werewolf contrasts with 'the werewolf superstition' in Scandinavia, which 'acted more than any other popular belief as a cover for criminals and dark undertakings, and also therefore certainly many stories have originated that strengthen the belief and keep the terror alive'. Odstedt, *Varulven*, pp. 227–8.
116. 'Wesen und Geschichte des Werwolfs', dissertation by Amt Rosenberg co-worker, BAB: R 58/7237, pp. 2–11.
117. Ibid., pp. 12–22.
118. Ibid., pp. 54–70; Odstedt, *Varulven*, pp. 220–2, 227–8.
119. The works of Max Fehring, Willibald Alexis, Christian Morgenstern, and others had reinforced a link in the popular mind between werewolves and national defence. See again 'Wesen und Geschichte des Werwolfs', pp. 88–91, 112–21. Weimar reprints of Max Fehring's *Der Werwolf* (1924) and Willibald Alexis's *Werwolf* (1925) illustrated positive attitudes toward the figure of the werewolf as well. Fehring's book emphasized the werewolf coming in the night and punishing those who had sinned. Alexis's *Werwolf* extolled the animal's power, freedom, and tie to nature. Scarce are images of the tragically cursed werewolf typical of Anglo-American fiction and film, working to hide his afflication from loved ones. Nor are werewolves in German folklore and popular culture the scion of Slavs or gypsies, as were vampires, but Ur-Germanic archetypes of nature and blood.
120. Eisler, *Man into Wolf*, p. 169.
121. Neumann, *Shifting Memories*, p. 50; Bronder, *Bevor Hitler kam*, p. 94.
122. See letter from 3.7.24 and additional correspondence, BAK: N 1126/27; see also police report on Helldorff, member of the Werewolves, BAB: 1507/2027, pp. 37–8; Eisler, *Man into Wolf*, p. 168.
123. 8.5.34, 'VB announces with great pleasure that "Das Grab des Dichters Hermann Loens Aufgefunden" in France', BAB: R 43II/1245, Bd. 6.
124. Roderick H. Watt, 'Wehrwolf or Werwolf? Literature, Legend, or Lexical Error into Nazi Propaganda?', *Modern Language Review* 87:4 (October 1992), pp. 879–83; Beevor, *Downfall*, p. 173; Longerich, *Himmler*, p. 705; Neumann, *Shifting Memories*, p. 50; Biddiscombe, 'Review of Volker Koop, *Himmlers letztes Aufgebot*'.
125. See report on tasks of Werewolf organization, 12.7.41, BAM: RH 20/11–334.
126. See report on 'Behandlung Fremdvölkischer' Vermerk from Globocnik: 1.7.43, 15.3.43, BAB: NS 19/2234; 'Unternehmen Werwolf', 'Werwolf' Raum Propoisk-Dowsk-Merkulowitschi-Korma, 5–15.7.43, BAM: RH 26–221/63; Globus (Globocnik) to Himmler, 4.11.43, BAB: NS 19/2234, pp. 20–3; Lower, *Nazi Empire-Building*, pp. 62, 151–5, 172.
127. These 'Werewolves' were resuscitated by Dr Goebbels (see *The Times*, 28 May 1945, p. 5, last col., by 'Military Correspondent lately in Germany') as an underground resistance movement after the Second World War. Eisler, *Man into Wolf*, p. 168; Neumann, *Shifting Memories*, p. 50; Beevor, *Downfall*, pp. 134–5, 174–5.
128. Longerich, *Himmler*, p. 714; see also Perry Biddiscombe, 'Review of Volker Koop, *Himmlers letztes Aufgebot: Die Organisation des Werwolf*, in *Gutachten des Instituts für Zeitgeschichte*. Munich: IfZG, 1958, pp. 11–12; Wessely promoted as of September 1944; 5.1.45, Sievers sends Wessely letter about working for IWZ; 19.12.44, Wessely reports to Sievers; 19.12.44, Wessely sends Wolff suggestion; 1.10.44, Wessely to Sievers; 11.11.44, letter to Wessely about work on people's army/arming the people/Volkssturm. BAB: NS 21/2652.

129. Hutter, *Gruselwandern*, p. 67; see also Eisler, *Man into Wolf*, pp. 168–9.
130. Watt, 'Wehrwolf or Werwolf?', pp. 892–5; Artur Ehrhardt, *Werwolf: Winke für Jagdeinheiten*, Ubstadt-Weiher: Enforcer Pülz, 2007, p. 1.
131. Neumann, *Shifting Memories*, pp. 50–1; Biddiscombe, 'Review of Volker Koop, *Himmlers letztes Aufgebot*'; Biddiscombe, *Werwolf!*, p. 2; Zur Erfüllung besonderer Aufgaben hinter der feindlichen Front ist unter Führung des 'Generalinspekteure für Spezialabwehr' (Obergruppenführer Prützmann) die Organisation 'Werwolf' (abgekürzt 'W-Organisation'), BAM: RH 2/1186, 6.2.45; 'Rheinische Post', 27.4.85, BAM: N 756–28 (Werwolf), 68.
132. See letters from Voigh to Rose, Vopersal, etc., BAM: N756–28 (Werwolf), pp. 177–8.
133. Longerich, *Himmler*, pp. 704–5.
134. 'Hoo, Hoo, Hoo, Lily the Werewolf Sings on Radio', *The Washington Post*, 6 April 1945, p. 1; Biddiscombe, 'Review of Volker Koop, *Himmlers letztes Aufgebot*': BAM: N 756–28 (Werwolf), pp. 354–5; Beevor, *Downfall*, pp. 261, 285.
135. Robert Eisler, *Man into Wolf*, p. 34; Biddiscombe, *Werwolf!*, pp. 115–30, 150–97.
136. Longerich, *Himmler*, p. 705; see article 'Wir kämpften, wir verloren', p. 106, BAM: N 756–28 (Werwolf); Aufbau Werwolf, 19.9.44; 'AMT I Betr. SS-Gruf. Sporrenberg', 19.9.44, 'Betr. SS-Ogruf. Prutzmann', BAB: NS 34/47.
137. Biddiscombe, *Last Nazis*; 3. Der 'Sonderstab Prützmann', 6.2.45, BAM: RH 2/1186; Eisler, *Man into Wolf*, pp. 168–9; 'AMT I Betr. SS-Gruf. Sporrenberg', 19.9.44, 'Betr. SS-Ogruf. Prutzmann'. BAB: NS 34/47; Biddiscombe, *Werwolf!*, pp. 57–63.
138. *Rheinische Post*, 27.4.85, p. 68, BAM: N 756/28 (Werwolf); Longerich, *Himmler*, p. 705.
139. Oberstleutnant Hobe, 'Fernschreiben', 2.22.45, directed at 9. VGD, 79. VGD, and 352. VGD. RH24–53–133; Biddiscombe, *Werwolf!*, pp. 57–63; ibid., pp. 12–14, 20–3.
140. Gugenberger and Schweidlenka, *Faden der Nornen*, pp. 140–1; Eisler, *Man into Wolf*, pp. 168–9.
141. Longerich, *Himmler*, p. 705; Eisler, *Man into Wolf*, pp. 168–9; Biddiscombe, 'Review of Volker Koop, *Himmlers letztes Aufgebot*'.
142. Ibid.; *Rheinische Post*, 27.4.85, BAM: N 756–28.
143. Biddiscombe, 'Review of Volker Koop, *Himmlers letztes Aufgebot*'.
144. Skorzeny, 'Wir kämpften, wir verloren', BAM: N 756/28 (Werwolf), p. 106.
145. Biddiscombe, *Werwolf!*, p. 7; Hutter, *Gruselwandern*, p. 67.
146. Biddiscombe, 'Review of Volker Koop, *Himmlers letztes Aufgebot*'.
147. Longerich, *Himmler*, p. 705; Eisler, *Man into Wolf*, pp. 168–9.
148. Eisler, *Man into Wolf*, p. 168.
149. A considerable number of soldiers of the French occupation army were killed by 'Werewolves' in the Grand Duchy of Baden (*Daily Mail*, 29 August 1945); *Picture Post*, 18 May 1946, p. 168.
150. Rheinische Post', 27.2.85, BAM: N 756/28 (Werwolf), p. 69; Robert Eisler, *Man into Wolf*, p. 34.
151. Biddiscombe, *Werwolf!*, pp. 135–50; Eisler, *Man into Wolf*, p. 168.
152. 'Die Motivation der Werwölfe war jedoch eine politische und keine heimatschützende oder freiheitskämpferische. Als Ergebnis dieser Bemühungen wurde dann im Januar 1945 eine Kleinkriegsanleitung unter dem Titel Werwolf-Winke für Jagdeinheiten herausgegeben'. Biddiscombe, *Werwolf!*, pp. 2; Beevor, *Downfall*, pp. 131–5, 174–5.
153. Hutter, *Gruselwandern*, p. 67; Biddiscombe, *Werwolf!*, pp. 252–74; Beevor, *Downfall*, pp. 160, 174–5; Petra Weber, *Justiz und Diktatur: Justizverwaltung und politische Strafjustiz in Thüringen 1945–1961*, Oldenbourg: Wissenschaftsverlag, p. 99.
154. Biddiscombe, *Werwolf!*, pp. 115–30, 150–97; 'Die Werwolforganisation wurde auf deutscher und alliierter Seite für gefährlicher gehalten als sie in Wirklichkeit war. Sie diente NS-Fanatiker als Droh- und Schreckmittel', *Rheinische Post*, 27.4.85, p. 68. BAM: N 756/28 (Werwolf). See also Frederick Taylor, *Exorcising Hitler: The Occupation and Denazification of Germany*, London: Bloomsbury, 2012, pp. 24–5; Antony Beevor, *Downfall*, pp. 412–416.
155. *Rheinische Post*, 27.4.85, BAM: N 756/28 (Werwolf), pp. 68–9; Biddiscombe, *Werwolf!*, pp. 8–9, 259–74; Hutter, *Gruselwandern*, p. 66.
156. Bohn, 'Vampirismus', pp. 5–8; Wüst, *Indogermanisches Bekenntnis*, pp. 63–80; Goepfert, *Immer noch Aberglaube!*, p. 42; Steinmetz, *Devil's Handwriting*, p. 61.
157. Steinmetz, *Devil's Handwriting*, p. 61.
158. Black, 'Expellees', p. 78.
159. Ibid.; Hans-Ulrich Wehler, *Nationalitätenspolitik in Jugoslawien: Die deutsche Minderheit 1918–1978*, Göttingen: Vandenhoeck & Ruprecht, 1980, pp. 45–72.
160. Biddiscombe, *Werwolf!*, p. 7; Biddiscombe, 'Review of Volker Koop, *Himmlers letztes Aufgebot*'; Black, 'Expellees', pp. 85–6.
161. Black, 'Expellees', p. 77.
162. Sammlung Karasek, 2.4.50, NSG 269; A. K. Gauß, 'Unser Schicksal wird Sagen', *Neuland* (12–13 April 1951), p. 9.

163. Report from Bertha Sohl, 10.5.52, in Sammlung Karasek, 04/02–115, NSG 284.

164. Sammlung Karasek, 04/02–115, NSG 268, 9.4.49.

165. Reports from Marie Schmidt, Rosa Dolak, Peter Deschner, and Katharine Engel, 30.5.52, 8.5.52, 18.5.52, 10.5.52, 22.6.52, in Sammlung Karasek, 04/02–137–8, 140–1, 143, 145, NSG 290–1, 293–4, 296, 298; Black, 'Expellees', p. 85.

166. Report from Philipp Ungar, 30.5.52, in Sammlung Karasek, 04/02–128–130, NSG 281–3.

167. Report from Elisabeth Kowitzki, 18.5.52, in Sammlung Karasek, 04/02–144, NSG 297.

168. Report from Bertha Sohl, 10.5.52, in Sammlung Karasek, 04/02–131, NSG 284.

169. Report from Bertha Sohl, 10.5.52, in Sammlung Karasek, 04/02–121, NSG 274.

170. Report from Stefan Apazeller, 17.12.50, in Sammlung Karasek, 04/02–124, NSG 277; Black, 'Expellees', p. 83.

171. Report from Herr Ringel, 22.6.52, in Sammlung Karasek, 04/02–146, NSG 299. Cases of 'partisan fever' were recorded by professional psychologists as well, who attributed them to involuntary psychosis or post-traumatic stress disorder. The Slovenian-Jewish psychoanalyst Paul Parin claimed to have witnessed attacks on an everyday basis between 1944 and 1946. Black, 'Expellees', pp. 82–5; see also reports from Marie Schmidt, Rosa Dolak, Peter Deschner, and Katharine Engel, 30.5.52, 8.5.52, 18.5.52, 10.5.52, 22.6.52, in Sammlung Karasek, 04/02–137–8, 140–1, 143, 145, NSG 290–1, 293–4, 296, 298.

172. Black, 'Expellees', pp. 80–1, 92–3; Jurij Striedter, 'Die Erzahlung vom walachischen vojevoden Drakula in der russischen und deutschen überlierferung', Zeitschrift für Slawische Philologie 29 (1961–2); Sammlung Karasek, 04/02–52, NSG 205, 21.5.52; 04/02–53, NSG 206, 19.5.51; see also Janjetović, Between Hitler and Tito; Lumans, Himmler's Auxiliaries, p. 235.

173. Bohn, 'Vampirismus', pp. 2–3; Black, 'Expellees', p. 93. Some reports, for example, indicate that the Slavs believed 'the fascists drank the blood of our people in a particular kind of glass' because 'they wanted to become strong from it'. Report from Katharine Engel, 10.5.52, in Sammlung Karasek, 04/02–127, NSG 280; Black, 'Expellees', pp. 95–6; see also McNally and Florescu, In Search of Dracula; Michael Bell, Food for the Dead: On the Trail of New England's Vampires, New York: Carroll and Graf, 2001; Barber, Vampires; Dagmar Burkhart, 'Vampir glaube und Vampirsage auf dem Balkan', in Alois Schuams, ed., Beiträge zur Südosteuropa-Forschung, Munich: Rudolf Troefenik, 1966, pp. 211–52; Margaret Carter, The Vampire in Literature: A Critical Bibliography, Ann Arbor, MI: UMI Research Press, 1989. Alan Dundes, The Vampire: A Casebook, Madison, WI: University of Wisconsin Press, 1998.

174. Black, 'Expellees', p. 95.

175. Report from Michael Kuhn, 1.4.51, in Sammlung Karasek, 04/02–123, NSG 276; Black, 'Expellees', p. 94.

176. Black, 'Expellees', pp. 97–8.

177. Report from Yugoslavian German refugees, 8.5.52, in Sammlung Karasek, 04/02–139, NSG 292; Black, 'Expellees', pp. 86–7.

178. Report from one Herr Ringel, 22.6.52, in Sammlung Karasek, 04/02–146, NSG 299; Black, 'Expellees', pp. 90–1, 97.

179. Report from Philipp Ungar, 30.5.52, in Sammlung Karasek, 04/02–134, NSG 287.

180. Report from Peter Deschner, 18.5.52, in Sammlung Karasek, 04/02–141, NSG 294.

181. Barber, Vampires, p. 26.

182. Black, 'Expellees', p. 84.

183. Judit Prohaska and another witness, Ingrid Sachradik, confirmed that the disease appeared to affect women more than men, which she attributed to the fact that 'women lacked the inner robustness and tough will of the men and therefore everything had affected their nerves most . . . It is certain that these attacks and nervous episodes affected the partisans more than the effects of war on the regular military. That must have something to do with the lawlessness of the partisan war and with all the gruesome events.' Report from Judit Prohaska, 9.5.52, in Sammlung Karasek, 04/02–119, NSG 272; Report from Ing. Sachradnik, 22.6.52, in Sammlung Karasek, 04/02–122, NSG 275.

184. Report from Swabian high-school students, 14.11.51, in Sammlung Karasek, 04/02–132, NSG 285.

185. Report from Barbara Prumm, 8.5.52, in Sammlung Karasek, 04/02–133, NSG 286.

186. Report from Philipp Ungar, 30.5.52, in Sammlung Karasek, 04/02–134, NSG 287.

187. Only the rapid intervention of the guard prevented her from 'biting through his neck with her teeth; he was bloody enough already'. The camp commandant then arrived and forbade her from walking in close proximity to the camp, since 'she already had enough on her conscience . . . during [attacks] she had often exclaimed that she had killed 150 [German soldiers] and [committed] still worse atrocities'. Report from Yugoslav Germans, 22.6.52, in Sammlung Karasek, 04/02–136, NSG 289.

188. Black, 'Expellees', pp. 89–90.

189. Megan Garber, 'The Night Witches: The Female Fighter Pilots of World War II', *The Atlantic* (15 July 2013). http://www.theatlantic.com/technology/archive/2013/07/night-witches-the-female-fighter-pilots-of-world-war-ii/277779; Anne and Christine White, *A Dance with Death: Soviet Airwomen in World War II*, College Station, TX: Texas A&M University Press, 2001, pp. 20–5; Garber, 'Night Witches'; 'Nadezhda Popova, WWII "Night Witch", Dies at 91', http://www.nytimes.com/2013/07/15/world/europe/nadezhda-popova-ww-ii-night-witch-dies-at-91.html?_r=1.

190. Black, 'Expellees', pp. 88–9. The 'so-called Tito-Youth marched out with red handkerchief and wooden rifles and sang a marching song', which included the words (translated from Serbo-Croatian), 'Who would have thought in 1942 that the Swabians would be our servants . . . During the time of struggle the partisans drink no water, no wine or vodka, only blood'. Report from Peter Schneider, 16.5.51, in Sammlung Karasek, 04/02–126, NSG 279.

191. Report from Magdalena Jerich, 9.5.52, in Sammlung Karasek, 04/02–125, NSG 278.

192. Report from Peter Schneider, 16.5.51, in Sammlung Karasek, 04/02–126, NSG 279.

193. Black, 'Expellees', pp. 85–6, 99.

194. These reports 'excluded all discussion of German aggression and violence in the Balkans during World War II', including 'mass killings of Jews, Serbs, Sinti, Roma and anyone else the Wehrmacht decided was in league with the Partisans. The fact that most Banat Swabian leaders had thrown their lot in with the Nazis was also excluded from narratives about Partisan blood drinkers'. Black, 'Expellees', p. 99; Kater, *Das 'Ahnenerbe'*, pp. 291–4.

195. Ethnic Germans claimed, for example, that the partisans would cry 'out in pain . . . asking for the burden to be taken away . . . and to confess to expiate his sins'. A. E. Gauß, 'Unser Schicksal wird Sagen', *Neuland* 4:12–13 (1951), p. 9, in Sammlung Karasek, 04/02–119, NSG 270; report from Michael Kuhn, 1.4.51, in Sammlung Karasek, 04/02–118, NSG 271; report from Ing. Sachradnik, 22.6.52, in Sammlung Karasek, 04/02–120, NSG 273.

196. Black, 'Expellees', p. 83; John Horne and Alan Kramer, *German Atrocities, 1914: A History of Denial*, New Haven, CT: Yale University Press, 2001, pp. 90–104.

197. He 'was a vampire: a predator; a fearsome, transgressive extractor; a product of local culture that distilled disembodied and generalized anxieties and displaced guilt. She was also an irremediable composite of reality, memory and fantasy – an unkillable, lurking enemy who infects by telling and confessing and biting, and whose crazed desires can be slaked only by consuming her victims, by taking things away'. Black, 'Expellees', p. 95; Goepfert, *Immer noch Aberglaube!*, pp. 72–84.

198. Black, 'Expellees', p. 79.

199. Ibid., p. 79.

200. Black, 'Groening', p. 213

201. For most Germans, 'whatever tenuous links to the ancient or to the recent past still obtained by 1943 . . . were severed by the sheer destructive power of the air war and the Battle of Berlin'. Black, *Death in Berlin*, p. 275.

202. Ibid.

203. Halter, 'Welteislehre'.

204. Black, *Death in Berlin*, p. 275.

205. Fisher, *Fantasy*, p. 223.

206. Ibid., p. 226.

207. Ibid., pp. 8–9.

208. Jungbauer, *Kriegsgefangene*, p. 12.

209. Halter, 'Welteislehre'.

210. See correspondence, 19.4.34, 30.4.34, 6.7.34, 14.7.34, 16.7.34, 28.6.34, BAB: R 43II/1245 Bd. 6 1934–5, Ankauf eines Autographs von Richard Wagner druch Hitler (Götterdämmerung Vorspiel).

211. Redles, *Hitler's Millennial Reich*, p. 9; Jungbauer, *Kriegsgefangene*, p. 12.

212. Fritz, *Endkampf*, pp. xi–iii.

213. See report 25.7.44, BAB: N 1118/100.

214. Meanwhile, the 'stars will flicker and die. The earth will shake and quake, and all Yggdrasill will tremble . . . Fenrir the wolf will burst free . . . Surt will lead the fire demons from Muspell . . . fire will encompass them'. David Leeming, *From Olympus to Camelot: The World of European Mythology*, Oxford: Oxford University Press, 2003, pp. 120–1; Fritz, *Endkampf*, p. 9.

215. Wüst, *Indogermanisches Bekenntnis*, pp. 4–6.

216. Deborah Dusse, 'The Eddic Myth Between Academic and Religious Interpretations', in Junginger, *Nordic Ideology*, p. 79.

217. Levenda, *Unholy Alliance*, p. 276.

218. Gerda Bormann to Martin Bormann in Trevor-Roper, ed., *Bormann Letters*, p. 37.

219. Ibid., pp. xix–xx; Bormann, 2.4.45, in ibid., p. xxi; see also Fritz, *Endkampf*, p. 66.

220. Longerich, *Himmler*, p. 80.

221. Kater, *Das 'Ahnenerbe'*, pp. 290–1, 354–5; Longerich, *Himmler*, pp. 742–3.

222. Trimondi, *Hitler*, p. 150.
223. Ibid., pp. 151–2.
224. Kater, *Das 'Ahnenerbe'*, pp. 302–4.
225. See letters from Wiligut to Brandt, Galke, etc., from July 1940; 12.7.40, letter to SS Gruppenführer Eicke; 18.7.40, letter from Wiligut/Weisthor to R. Brandt, NS 19/1573; see also Treitel, *Science*, p. 215; Longerich, *Himmler*, pp. 286–7; Goodrick-Clarke, *Occult Roots*, p. 190; Kater, *Das 'Ahnenerbe'*, pp. 291–2.
226. Yet the rune fables – like so many other Ahnenerbe projects – never came to fruition; 26.11.43, Krause and Weigel encouraged to write popular Runenfibel; 22.5.44, letter to Krause from Ahnenerbe, BAB: NS 21/1784.
227. Black, *Death in Berlin*, p. 80.
228. Ibid., p. 275.
229. Biddiscombe, *Werwolf!*, pp. 3–4; Biddiscombe, *Last Nazis*.
230. See Heilbronner, 'The Wewelsburg Effect: Nazi Myth and Paganism in Postwar European Popular Music', in Black and Kurlander, eds, *Revisiting*.
231. Goodrick-Clarke, *Black Sun*, p. 122.
232. Howe, *Urania's Children*, pp. 219–34; Howe, *Nostradamus*, p. 115; Maichle, 'Die Nostradamus-Propaganda der Nazis, 1939–1942'.
233. Wulff, *Zodiac*, pp. 118–25, 172–4, 191–2, 298–9.
234. 'There has never yet been a prophecy which was bad for us, they all have spoken of a hard struggle but final victory.' Excerpt of letter from Gerda Bormann to Martin Bormann, Obersalzberg, 26.10.44, in Trevor-Roper, ed., *Bormann Letters*, pp. 140–1.
235. Dorfes Hölkewiese ums Leben. Seine sterblichen Überreste, insbesondere seine Erkennungsmarke, wurden am 18.10.2002 vom '*Verein zur Bergung Gefallener in Osteu-ropa*' geborgen; Maichle, 'Die Nostradamus-Propaganda der Nazis, 1939–1942'; T. W. M. van Berkel, Information on dr. phil. Alexandrer Max Centgraf alias dr. N. Alexander Centurio (1893–1970), http://www.nostradamus-research.org/en/ww2/centgraf-info.htm; see also Alexander Centurio (aka Centgraf), '*Nostradamus und das jüngste Weltgeschehen*', in *Schweizer Monatshefte – Zeitschrift für Politik Wirtschaft Kultur* (August 1959).
236. Centgraf's story can be contested. See Berkel, *Nostradamus*, http://www.nostradamusresearch.org/en/ww2/centgraf-info.htm; '25. Juli 1944/ Gestern … 30. Juli 1944', *Die Tagebücher* von Joseph Goebbels Online, as quoted in Maichle, 'Die Nostradamus-Propaganda'.
237. Fritz, *Endkampf*, p. xii.
238. SS Schüller to SS Stabsführung Netherlands, Southeast, Middle, Italy, etc., 19.7.44; Henry Chavin, 'Rapport confidentiel sur la société secrète polytechnicienne dite Mouvement synarchique d'Empire (MSE) ou Convention synarchique révolutionnaire', 1941, BAB: NS 51/186; Annie Lacroix-Riz, *Le choix de la défaite: Les élites françaises dans les années 1930*, Paris: Armand Collin, 2006; Richard F. Kuisel, 'The Legend of the Vichy Synarchy', *French Historical Studies* 6 :3 (Spring 1970); Olivier Dard, *La synarchie, le mythe du complot permanent*, Paris: Perrin, 1998.
239. Report from 9.6.44, pp. 3–19, BAB: NS 51/186.
240. Richard Barber, *The Holy Grail: Imagination and Belief*, London: Penguin, 2004, p. 316; http://www.theguardian.com/books/2000/oct/07/books.guardianreview.
241. Fisher, *Fantasy*, pp. 222–3; Spr. 1: Bloch erwähnte in diesem Zusammenhang auch den Paläontologen. Spr. 2: Max Bense, Leiter der Kölner Ortsgruppe der Kosmotechnischen Gesellschaft,– www.swr.de/swr2/programm/.../essay/-/.../swr2-essay-20080715.rtf?;
242. Black, 'Groening', pp. 207–8, 211.
243. MS Konrad Heiden (preface to Kersten) IfZG: ED 209/34, pp. 26–8; Sickinger, 'Hitler and the Occult', pp. 120–1.
244. Ibid., p. 122.
245. Redles, *Hitler's Millennial Reich*, p. 9.
246. Waite, *Psychopathic God*, pp. 432–3.
247. Albert Speer, *Inside the Third Reich*, New York: Simon and Schuster, 1970, p. 463.
248. Sickinger, 'Hitler and the Occult', p. 122.
249. MS Konrad Heiden, IfZG: ED 209/34, p. 35.
250. Black, *Death in Berlin*, p. 11.
251. Dusse, 'Myth', p. 79.
252. Ibid., p. 82.
253. Robert Ley, 'Mein Politisches Testament!', 25.8.45, in NL Ley, BAK: N 1468/2.
254. Bramwell, *Blood and Soil*, pp. 184–7.
255. Anrich, IfZG: 1867/56, ZS–542–6. Dr Hans-Dietrich Loock, 'Bemerkungen zur Niederschrift über die Unterredung mit Professor Dr. Ernst Anrich am 16. Februar 1960', in NL Ernst Anrich, IfZG: 1867/56, ZS–542–6, p. 7.

256. Ibid., p. 19.
257. Loock, 'Bemerkungen', p. 21.
258. Ibid., p. 23.
259. Wiwjorra, 'Hermann Wirth', pp. 414–16; Junginger, 'From Buddha to Adolf Hitler', pp. 163–4.
260. Bernd Wedemeyer-Kolwe, 'Völkisch-religôse Runengymnastiker', in Puschner and Vollnhals, eds, *Bewegungen*, pp. 459–72.
261. Junginger, 'From Buddha to Adolf Hitler', pp. 163–8.
262. Carl Jung, 'Werden die Seelen Frieden finden?' ('Will the Souls Find Peace?'), *PM* (New York), 10.5.45, in McGuire and Hull, eds, *C. G. Jung Speaking*, pp. 147–9.
263. Germans, Jung explained, displayed 'a specific weakness in the face of these demons because of their incredible suggestibility' and history of 'psychic catastrophe', from the wars of religion to the First World War, a 'result of their precarious position between East and West'. Ibid., p. 151.
264. Ibid., p. 152; see also Goepfert, *Immer noch Aberglaube!*, pp. 72–84.
265. Fritz, *Endkampf*, pp. 46–7.
266. Black, *Death in Berlin*, p. 11.
267. McGuire and Hull, eds, *C. G. Jung Speaking*, pp. 152–3.
268. Black, *Death in Berlin*, p. 11.
269. O'Sullivan, 'Neumann', pp. 196–7.
270. Black, 'Groening', p. 214. As many as 70,000 Croatians and Danube Swabians, as well as some Serbs, gathered one day to see an appearance of the Virgin between three Linden trees in the Croatian city of Koprivnica in 1947; Sammlung Karasek, 04/02–66, NSG 219, 13.5.51.
271. Black, 'Groening', p. 214; Sammlung Karasek, 04/02–66, NSG 219, 13.5.51.
272. Black, *Death in Berlin*, p. 153.
273. Black, 'Groening', pp. 213–14.
274. Black, *Death in Berlin*, p. 11.
275. Ibid., p. 174.
276. Dusse, 'Myth', p. 79.
277. Black, 'Groening', in Black and Kurlander, eds, *Revisiting*, pp. 207–8, 211.
278. Kallmeyer, *Leben unsere Toten?*, pp. 8–9.
279. '[T]hat the dead live is then … no longer a question, but something completely evident!' This world and the beyond were 'only poles of the same world, divided and differentated only through the diversity of the spheres'. Ibid., pp. 9–10, 13; 'Dying in this world is nothing other than being born in that world, from which we came, for that, what we so commonly call life', Kallmeyer continued, 'is only a snapshot of our actual life, of which we know neither the beginning nor the end.' Ibid., p. 21.
280. Ibid., p. 32.
281. Ibid., pp. 36–7, 42–6.
282. Eric Kurlander, *Living with Hitler: Liberal Democrats in the Third Reich, 1933–1945*, New Haven, CT, and London: Yale University Press, 2009, pp. 14, 69.
283. See Egbert Klautke, 'Defining the Volk: Willy Hellpach's *Völkerpsychologie* between National Socialism and Liberal Democracy, 1934–1954', *History of European Ideas* 39:5 (September 2013), pp. 693–708.
284. Willy Hellpach, *Das Magethos: Eine Untersuchung über Zauberdenken und Zauberdienst als Verknüpfung von jenseitigen Mächten mit diesseitigen Pflichten für die Entstehung und Befestigung von Geltungen und Setzungen, Brauch und Rech, Gewissen und Gesittung, Moralen und Religionen*, Stuttgart: Hippokarates, 1947.
285. Ibid., p. 5.
286. H. H. Kritzinger, *Zur Philosophie der Überwelt*, Tübingen: Mohr, 1951, pp. 6–12, 17–18.
287. Maichle, 'Die Nostradamus-Propaganda der Nazis, 1939–1942'; Centgraf, *Prophetische Weltgeschichte*.
288. See Thomas Laqueur, 'Foreword', in Wulff, *Zodiac*.
289. Anthroposophy is still associated with far-right, neo-Nazi activities. Staudenmaier, *Between Occultism and Nazism*, pp. 321–4.
290. Black, 'Expellees', p. 81; Alfred Cammann and Alfred Karasek, 'Volkserzählung der Karpartendeutsche', in Cammann and Karasek, *Volkserzählung der* Karpartendeutsche, Marburg: Elwer, 1981, pp. 13–15, 18.
291. The fate of these Germans was tragic, Karasek insisted, since they always got along with their Slovak neighbours ('Nowhere did the Germans feel superior as is often claimed today'). 'In diesem Werk versuchen Karasek und Cammann, die Geschichte neu zu schreiben, in dem sie durch vielerlei Beweise behaupten, dass Deutsche und Slowaken während des 2 Weltkrieg ebenbürtig waren.' ('In this work Karasek and Cammann attempt to write a new history in which they claim,

through diverse evidence, that Germans and Slovakians treated each other equally during the Second World War.') Cammann and Karasek, 'Volkserzählung der Karpartendeutsche', pp. 11–13.

292. 'The picture of a small Danube Swabian Marian lady is only one of many stages of a long, often lamentable wandering,' Karasek wrote. 'It indicates where the heart of every East German lies: in a lost Heimat.' Cammann and Karasek, 'Ungarndeutsche Volkserzählungen, pp. 19–22, 32–3, 40–5.

293. The Johannes-Künzig Institute for East German Folklore, with which Karasek was affiliated and where his extensive archives may be consulted, has long since moved away from its founder's emphasis on (re)claiming ethnic German territory in eastern Europe. http://www.jkibw.de/?Das_Institut:Institutsgeschichte.

294. Dokumente aus der amerikanischen Internierung (1944–45) (Bender Internierung), IGPP: A I 20.

295. Lux, 'On all Channels', p. 227.

296. Ibid., pp. 223–41. Although Bender's Institute for Border Areas in Psychology and Psychological Health (IGPP) persists to this day, it is now thoroughly devoid of any links to Bender's Nazi past. http://igpp.de/german/about.htm.

297. Steigmann-Gall, Holy Reich, pp. 3–11, 261–2; Cecil, Myth, p. 163.

298. Black, 'Expellees', pp. 99–100.

299. Cook, Hunt, pp. 217–25; Farrell, Reich, pp. 35–49, 55–97, 118–57.

300. Biddiscombe, Werwolf!, pp. 289–91; Beevor, Downfall; Fritz, Endkampf, pp. 7–8, 196–204; Bessel, Germany 1945, pp. 16–17, 299–300.

301. Black, 'Expellees', p. 79; see also John Ondrovcik, 'Max Holz', in Black and Kurlander, eds, Revisiting; Jungbauer, Kriegsgefangene, p. 12.

302. Mosse, Masses and Man, pp. 78–9.

303. Black, 'Expellees', p. 78.

304. These visions took shape from 'collective memories of war, their legends and religious practices'. Black, 'Expellees', p. 100.

Epilogue

1. For a summary of recent trends in the historiography, see chapters in Caplan, ed., Nazi Germany; Geoff Eley, Nazism as Fascism, New York: Routledge, 2013; Eric Kurlander, 'Violence, Volksgemeinschaft, and Empire: Interpreting the Third Reich in the Twenty-First Century', Journal of Contemporary History 46:4 (2011), pp. 920–4.

2. See again, Owen, Enchantment; Harvey, 'Beyond Enlightenment'.

3. Despite attempts to subordinate religion to the state, the Catholic Church and 'clerical fascists' remained significantly more powerful in Mussolini's Italy and Franco's Spain than in Hitler's Germany. See David Kertzer, The Pope and Mussolini, New York: Random House, 2014; Roger Griffin, 'The "Holy Storm": "Clerical Fascism" through the Lens of Modernism', Totalitarian Movements and Political Religions 8:2 (June 2007), pp. 213–27; Stanley Payne, A History of Fascism, 1914–1945, Madison, WI: University of Wisconsin Press, 1995, pp. 261–2.

4. Treitel, Science, p. 244.

5. Rauschning, Voice of Destruction, p. 254; Kater, Das 'Ahnenerbe', p. 360; Black and Kurlander, eds, Revisiting, p. 214.

6. McGuire and Hull, eds, C. G. Jung Speaking, pp. 153–4.

7. Ibid.

8. Ibid.

9. See, for example, Theodor Adorno, 'The Stars Down to Earth: The Los Angeles Times Astrology Column', Telos 19 (Spring 1974).

10. Lux, 'On all Channels', p. 224.

11. Walter Stephens, Demon Lovers: Witchcraft, Sex, and the Crisis of Belief, Chicago, IL: University of Chicago Press, 2001, pp. 367–9.

12. Sabine Doering-Manteuffel, Das Okkulte: Eine Erfolgsgeschichte im Schatten der Aufklärung – Von Gutenberg bis zum World Wide Web, Munich: Siedler, 2008.

13. Staudenmaier, Between Occultism and Nazism, p. 326. A recent survey by National Geographic finds that three-quarters of Americans believe that the government is hiding evidence of UFOs; nearly 40 per cent believe that aliens have already visited; http://www.usnews.com/news/articles/2012/06/28/most-americans-believe-government-keeps-ufo-secrets-survey-finds. According to a 2005 Gallup poll, three-quarters of Americans believe in at least one paranormal (occult) phenomenon, whether ESP, haunted houses or ghosts, telepathy, clairvoyance, witchcraft, communication with the dead, or reincarnation. More than 20 per cent believe in every one of the

above-mentioned occult and border scientific phenomena; http://www.gallup.com/poll/16915/three-four-americans-believe-paranormal.aspx. Fundamentalist religious beliefs have also risen in the past three decades, with more Americans (nearly 50 per cent) believing that God created humans in their current form and nearly 80 per cent believing that Jesus was resurrected from the dead; http://www.gallup.com/poll/21814/evolution-creationism-intelligent-design.aspx.

14. Ibid., p. 326.

15. Indeed, there was little correlation between the degree of religious devotion and party membership in the 1970s and early 1980s. There has been a high correlation, however, in the first two decades of the twenty-first century. See Robert Putnam, David E. Campbell, and Shaylyn Romney Garrett, *American Grace: How Religion Divides and Unites Us*, New York: Simon and Schuster, 2012, pp. 371–4; http://archives.politicususa.com/2011/07/09/poll-bible-literally.html.

16. A decade after 9/11 nearly the same number of Americans believed in the link between Saddam Hussein and the World Trade Center bombing (66 per cent) as in 2003 (70 per cent); http://themoderatevoice.com/ten-years-later-belief-in-iraq-connection-with-911-attack-persists; Stephens, *Demon Lovers*, pp. 369–71.

17. See Cynthia Miller-Idris, *Blood and Culture: Youth, Right-Wing Extremism, and National Belonging in Contemporary Germany*, Durham, NC: Duke University Press, 2009; Oded Heilbronner, 'The Wewelsburg Effect', in Black and Kurlander, eds, *Revisiting*, pp. 269–86.

18. Staudenmaier, 'Nazi Perceptions of Esotericism', p. 50.

19. Adorno, *Minima Moralia*, pp. 238–44.

20. Staudenmaier, 'Nazi Perceptions of Esotericism', p. 50.

BIBLIOGRAPHY

Primary Sources

Archival Sources

Bundesarchiv Berlin (BAB)
NS 5-VI/16959; NS 6/334x; NS 5-VI/16959; NS 8/185; NS 15/34; NS 15/399; NS 15/405; NS 15/408; NS
15/409; NS 15/415; NS 15/421; NS 15/426; NS 15/428; NS 15/441; NS 15/447; NS 15/448; NS 15/452;
NS 15/474; NS 15/485; NS 15/531; NS 15/558; NS 15/697; NS 15/734; NS 15/737; NS 15/738; NS
18/211; NS 18/444; NS 18/494; NS 18/497; NS 19/250; NS 19/397; NS 19/455; NS 19/527; NS 19/552;
NS 19/562; NS 19/595; NS 19/634; NS 19/641; NS 19/658; NS 19/688; NS 19/696; NS 19/700; NS
19/707; NS 19/954; NS 19/1023; NS 19/1025; NS 19/1052; NS 19/1053; NS 19/1124; NS 19/1138; NS
19/1146; NS 19/1149; NS 19/1163; NS 19/1295; NS 19/1329; NS 19/1332; NS 19/1356; NS 19/1362;
NS 19/1388; NS 19/1389; NS 19/1419; NS 19/1573; NS 19/1631; NS 19/1659; NS 19/1705; NS 19/1853;
NS 19/1860; NS 19/1942; NS 19/2212; NS 19/2234; NS 19/2239; NS 19/2241; NS 19/2244; NS 19/2398;
NS 19/2709; NS 19/2841; NS 19/2891; NS 19/2906; NS 19/2914; NS 19/2945; NS 19/3042; NS 19/3046;
NS 19/3052; NS 19/3060; NS 19/3074; NS 19/3082; NS 19/3356; NS 19/3633; NS 19/3634; NS 19/3656;
NS 19/3671; NS 19/3683; NS 19/3933; NS 19/3944; NS 19/3974; NS 19/4045; NS 19/4047; NS 19/4103;
NS 19/4106; NS 21/167; NS 21/682; NS 21/699; NS 21/739; NS 21/767; NS 21/770; NS 21/869; NS
21/1279; NS 21/1295; NS 21/1322; NS 21/1333; NS 21/1341; NS 21/1495; NS 21/1496; NS 21/1528;
NS 21/1532; NS 21/1539; NS 21/1604; NS 21/1606; NS 21/1751; NS 21/1784; NS 21/2120; NS 21/2136;
NS 21/2215; NS 21/2227; NS 21/2294; NS 21/2528; NS 21/2547; NS 21/2548; NS 21/2648; NS 21/2649;
NS 21/2652; NS 21/2669; NS 21/2676; NS 26/865a; NS 26/2232; NS 26/2233; NS 26/2234; NS
26/2235; NS 27/458; NS 27/465; NS 27/676; NS 27/699; NS 27/714; NS 27/715; NS 27/769; NS 27/875;
NS 27/902; NS 27/916; NS 27/939; NS 34/47; NS 34/69; NS 37/3630; NS 43/1650; NS 51/186.
R 2/4871; R 3/1626; R 901/59143; R 1501/125673b; R 1507/545; R 1507/2022; R 1507/2025; R 1507/2026;
R 1507/2027; R 1507/2028; R 1507/2029; R 1507/2031; R 1507/2032; R 1507/2034; R 1507/2091; R
16/12437; R 43-II/342; R 43-II/479a; R 43-II/1245; R 55/24198; R 56-V/924; R 56-V/1150; R 58/64; R
58/210; R 58/405; R 58/717; R 58/1029; R 58/1599; R 58/6203; R 58/6204; R 58/6205; R 58/6206; R
58/6207; R 58/6215b; R 58/6216a; R 58/6217; R 58/6218; R 58/6509; R 58/6517; R 58/7222; R 58/7237;
R 58/7312; R 58/7313; R 58/7383; R 58/7484; R 901/13034; R 1507/2016; R 1507/2025; R 1507/2028;
R 1507/2029; R 1507/2032; R 1507/2063; R 1507/2397; R 4901/2887; R 9361-V/1107; R 9361-V/4599;
R 9361-V/5138; R 9361-V/6162; R 9361-V/6199; R 9361-V/7196; R 9361-V/10777; R 9361-V/22175;
R 9361-V/25648; R 9361-V/40789; R 9361V/89324.

Bundesarchiv Koblenz (BAK)
N 756/28; N 756/329b; N 1110/4; N 1075/3; N 1094/11; N 1094/12; N 1094/14; N 1094/16; N 1094I/1; N
1094I/3; N 1094I/6; N 1094I/10; N 1094I/18; N 1094I/19; N 1094I/20; N 1094I/33; N 1094I/36; N
1094I/65a; N 1094I/68; N 1094I/70; N 1094I/71; N 1094I/77; N 1094II/1; N 1094II/42; N 1094II/43;
N 1094II/58; N 1118/100; N 1118/113; N 1126; N 1126/21; N 1128; N 1128/5; N 1128/3; N 1468.

Bundesmilitärarchiv Freiburg (BAM)
N 756/28; N 756/133; N 756/133a.

RH 2/1186; RH 2/1523; RH 2/1930; RH 2/2129; RH 20/11/334; RH 21/2/621; RH 24-52/133; RH
    26-221/63.
Institut für Zeitgeschichte-Munich (IfZG)
ED 99-9; ED 209/34; ED 386; ED 414/38; ED 414/41; ED 414/138; ED 414/174; ED 458/1; ED 498/23.
    MA 3/8; MA 43/1; MA 141/3; MA 141/6; MA 141/8; MA 141/9; MA 253/1; MA 254; MA 292/1; MA
    309/1; MA 322; MA 330/1; MA 331; MA 545/1; MA 596; MA 609/1; MA 610/1; MA 667; MA 744/1.
    ZS 542.
Institut für Grenzgebiete der Psychologie und Psychohygiene (IGPP)
10/5 AIA; 10/5 AI21; 10/5 AII2; 10/5 AII9; 10/5 AII12; 10/5 AII13; 10/5 AII14; 10/5 AII15; 10/5 AII16;
    10/5 AII17; 10/5 AII19; 10/5 AII20; 10/5 AII21; 10/5 AII27; 10/5 AII28; 10/5 AII29; 10/5 AII48; 10/5
    AII49; 10/5 AII51; 10/5 AV5; 10/5 BV; 10/5 BII; 10/5 BIII.

Published Primary Sources

Åberg, Nils. 'Herman Wirth: En germansk kulturprofet', *Fornvännen* 28 (1933), pp. 247–9.
Alexis, Willibald. *Der Werwolf*. Berlin: Janke, 1904.
Altheim, Franz. *Die Araber in der alten Welt*, 6 vols. Berlin: De Gruyter, 1964–6.
—— *Geschichte der lateinischen Sprache*. Frankfurt: Klostermann, 1951.
—— *Goten und Finnen im dritten und vierten Jahrhundert*. Berlin: Ranke, 1944.
—— *Griechische Götter im alten Rom*. Giessen: Töpelmann, 1930 (1980).
—— *Italien und die dorische Wanderung*. Amsterdam: Pantheon, 1940.
Altheim, Franz and Erika Trautmann. 'Nordische und italische Felsbildkunst', *Die Welt als Geschichte* 3
    (1937), pp. 1–82.
Andreas-Friedrich, Ruth. *Aberglauben in der Liebe*. Leipzig: J. J. Weber, 1933.
Bellamy, H. S. *Moons, Myths and Man: A Reinterpretation*. London: Faber & Faber, 1936.
Blavatksy, Helena. *The Secret Doctrine*. New York: Theosophical Society, 1888.
Bloch, Ernst. *Erbschaft dieser Zeit*. Frankfurt am Main: Suhrkamp, 1962.
Blumhardt, Johann. *Krankheitsgeschichte der Gottlieben Dittus in Möttlingen*. Neudietendorf (Thuringia):
    Friedrich Jansa, 1934.
Bormann, Martin, ed. (tr. Hugh Trevor-Roper). *Hitler's Secret Conversations 1941–1944*. New York:
    Farrar, Straus and Young, 1953.
Breidenbach, H. Fehr. 'Von Der XII. Astrologen-Kongress', *Zenit* (1933).
Breuer, Stefan and Schmidt, Ina, eds. *Die Kommenden. Eine Zeitschrift der Bundischen Jugend (1926–
    1933)*. Schwalbach am Taunus: Wochenschau Verlag, 2010.
Buttersack, Felix. *Zu den Pforten des Magischen*. Stuttgart: Kröner, 1941.
Byloff, Stitz. *Hexenglaube und Hexenverfolgung in den Österreichischen Alpenländern*. Berlin: de Gruyter,
    1934.
Chamberlain, Houston Stewart. *The Foundations of the Nineteenth Century*. London: Ballantyne, 1910.
Crowley, Aleister. *The Confessions of Aleister Crowley: An Autohagiography*. London: Routledge & Kegan
    Paul, 1969.
Cziffra, Geza von. *Hanussen Hellseher des Teufels: Die Wahrheit über den Reichstagsbrand*. Munich: F. A.
    Herbig, 1978.
Darré, R. Walther. *Das Bauerntum als Lebensquell der Nordifshen Rasse*. Berlin: J. S. Lehmanns, 1940.
—— *Neuadel aus Blut und Boden*. Berlin: J. S. Lehmanns, 1939.
—— *Um Blut und Boden. Reden u. Aufsätze*. Munich: Eher, 1940.
Dierst, H. C. 'Die Astropolitische Tagespresse', *Zenit* (1933).
Dietrich, Christoff. *Die Wahrheit über das Pendel*. Diessen: Huber, 1936.
—— *Pendel und Alltag*. Rudolstadt: Gesundes Leben, 1938.
Dietrich, J. 'Dietrich Eckart', *Zenit* (1933).
Dingler, Hugo. *Max Planck und die Begründung der sogenannten modernen theoretischen Physik*. Berlin:
    Ahnenerbe, 1939.
Driesch, Hans. *Alltagrätsel des Seelenlebens*. Stuttgart: Deutsche Verlags-Anstalt, 1938.
—— *Die Überwindung des Materialismus*. Zürich: Rascher & CIE, 1935.
—— *Lebenserinnerungen*. Munich: Ernst Reinhardt, 1951.
—— *Parapsychologie*. Zürich: Rascher Verlag, 1945.
—— 'Schopenhauers Stellung zur Parapsychologie', in *Schopenhauer Jahrbuch* 15:99 (1936).
—— *Selbstbesinnung und Selbsterkenntnis*. Leipzig: Rudolf Birnbach, 1942.
Ebertin, Elsbeth. *Was bringt mir Glück?* Altona: Dreizach-Verlag, 1935.
Ebertin, Reinhold. *Durchschaut dürch deine Handschrift*. Erfurt: Ebertin-Verlag, 1934.
Eckart, Dietrich. *Der Bolschewismus von Moses bis Lenin: Zwiegespräch zwischen Adolf Hitler und mir.*
    Munich: Hohenheichen, 1924.

Eisler, Robert. *Man into Wolf*. London: Spring, 1948.

Ewers, Hanns Heinz. *Alraune*. Düsseldorf: Grupello, 1998.

—— *Das Grauen. Seltsame Geschichten*. Munich/Leipzig: G. Müller, 1907.

—— *Horst Wessel. Ein deutsches Schicksal*. Stuttgart/Berlin: Cotta, 1932.

—— *Reiter in deutscher Nacht*. Stuttgart/Berlin: Cotta, 1931.

—— *Vampir*. Berlin: Sieben Stäbe, 1928.

Fankhauser, Alfred. *Magie*. Zürich: Orell Füssli, 1934.

Frank, Hans. *Im Angesichts des Galgens: Deutung Hitlers und seiner Zeit auf Grund eigener Erlebnisse und Erkenntnisse. Geschrieben im Nürnberger Justizgefängnis*. Munich: Beck, 1953.

Frankenberger, Kurt. *Fertigmachen zum Einsatz*. Halle: Wehrwolf-Verlag, 1931.

Fritsche, Herbert. *Kleines Lehrbuch der Weissen Magie*. Prague: Verlag Neubert & Söhne, 1934.

Geymüller, H. *Swedenborg und die übersinnliche Welt*. Stuttgart: Deutsche Verlags-Anstalt, 1936.

Goebbels, Joseph. 'Erkenntnis und Propaganda', in *Signale der neuen Zeit. 25 ausgewählte Reden von Dr. Joseph Goebbels*. Munich: Eher (Zentralverlag der NSDAP), 1934, pp. 28–52.

—— (Fred Taylor, ed.). *The Goebbels Diaries, 1939–1941*. New York: Putnam's, 1983.

—— (Louis Lochner, ed.). *The Goebbels Diaries, 1942–1945*. London: Praeger, 1970.

—— *Tagebücher, 1924–1925*. Munich: Piper, 2000.

—— *Wesen und Gestalt des Nationalsozialismus*. Berlin: Junker und Dünnhaupt, 1934.

Goepfert, Christian. *Immer noch Aberglaube!* Zürich: Zwingli Verlag, 1943.Gumbel, Emil Julius, Berthhold Jacob, and Ernst Falck, eds. *Verräter verfallen der Feme: Opfer, Mörder, Richter 1919–1929: Abschliessende Darstellung*. Berlin: Malik-Verlag, 1929.

Günther, Hans F. K. *Die nordische Rasse bei den Indogermanen Asiens*. Munich: J. F. Lehmanns, 1934.

—— *Herkunft und Rassengeschichte der Germanen*. Munich: J. F. Lehmanns, 1935.

—— *Rassenkunde des jüdischen Volkes*. Munich: J. F. Lehmanns, 1932.

—— *The Racial Elements of European History*. London: Methuen, 1927.

Hanussen, Erik Jan. *Berliner Wochenschau*. Berlin: Hanussen, 1932 (self-published).

—— *Die Andere Welt*. Berlin: Hanussen, 1931–2 (self-published).

—— *Meine Lebenslinie*. Berlin: Universitas, 1930.

Heiden, Konrad A. *A History of National Socialism*. New York: Alfred Knopf, 1935.

Heimsoth, Karl. *Charakter-Kontsellation*. Munich: Barth, 1928.

Hellpach, Willy. *Das Magethos: Eine Untersuchung über Zauberdenken und Zauberdienst als Verknüpfung von jenseitigen Mächten mit diesseitigen Pflichten für die Entstehung und Befestigung von Geltungen und Setzungen, Brauch und Rech, Gewissen und Gesittung, Moralen und Religionen*. Stuttgart: Hippokarates, 1947.

—— *Einführung in die Völkerpsychologie*. Stuttgart: Ferdinand Enkel, 1938.

—— *Schriftenreihe zur Völkerpsychologie*. Stuttgart: Hippokrates, 1944.

Hentges, Ernst. 'Zum Horoskop des Reichskanzlers Adolf Hitler', *Zenit* (1933).

Heuss, Eugen. *Rationale Biologie und ihre Kritik*. Leipzig: Gerhardt, 1938.

Hiemer, Ernst. *Der Giftpilz*. Nüremberg: Stürmer, 1938.

Himmler, Heinrich. *Die Schutzstaffel als antibolschewistische Kampforganisation*. Munich: Franz Eher (Zentralverlag der NSDAP), 1937.

—— *Rede des Reichsführers im Dom zu Quedlinburg*. Magdeburg: Nordland, 1936.

—— (Bradley F. Smith and Agnes F. Peterson, eds). *Geheimreden 1933 bis 1945*. Frankfurt am Main: Propyläen, 1974.

Hitler, Adolf. *Mein Kampf*. Boston, MA: Ralph Mannheim, 1943.

—— (Gerhard Weinberg, ed.). *Hitler's Second Book*. New York: Enigma, 2006.

Hoermann, Bernard. 'Gesundheitsfuehrung und geistige Infektionen', *Volksgesundheitswacht* (VGW) 10, May 1937.

Hoffmann, Hans. *Der Hexen - und Besessenenglaube des 15. und 16. Jahrhunderts im Spiegel des Psychiaters*. Greifswald: Universitätsverlag Ratsbuchhandlung L. Bamberg, 1935.

Hübner, Arthur. *Herman Wirth und die Ura-Linda-Chronik*. Berlin: De Gruyter, 1934.

Hummel, K. 'Wissenschaft und Welteislehre', *Zeitschrift der Deutschen Geologischen Gesellschaft*, vol. 90 (January 1938).

Jung, Carl (http://www.archive.org/stream/MemoriesDreamsReflectionsCarlJung/carlgustavjung-interviewsandencounters-110821120821-phpapp02_djvu.txt).

Kallmeyer, Ernst. *Leben unsere Toten? Eine Weltanschauung als Antwort*. Stuttgart: Kulturaufbau, 1946.

Karasek-Langer, Alfred. 'Das Schrifttum überdie Deutschen in Wolhynien und Polen', *Deutsche wissen-schaftliche Zeitschrift für Polen* (1931), vol. 22, pp. 124–36.

—— *Die deutschen Siedlungen in Wolhynien. Geschichte, Volkskunde, Lebensfragen* (Deutsche Gaue im Osten, vol. 3). Leipzig: Hirzel 1931.

—— 'Die deutsche Volkskundeforschung im heutigen Ungarn', in *Deutsches Archiv für Landes- und Volksforschung* 1 (1937), pp. 287–308, 959–89.

—— 'Grundsätzliches zur Volkskunde der Deutschen in Polen', in *Monatshefte für den geistigen Aufbau des Deutschtums in Polen* 2:12 (1935/6), pp. 126–33.

—— 'Ostschlesische Volkskunde', in Viktor Kauder, ed., *Das Deutschtum in Polnisch-Schlesien. Ein Handbuch über Land und Leute* (Deutsch Gaue im Osten, vol. 4). Plauen: Wolff, 1932.

—— 'Vom Sagengute der Vorkarpathendeutschen', in *Volk und Rasse: Illustrierte Vierteljahreshefte für deutsches Volkstum*. Munich: J. F. Lehmanns, 1930, pp. 96–111

—— and Josef Strzygowski. *Vom Sagengute der Vorkarpathendeutschen. Ein Beitrag zur Sagenforschung in den deutschen Sprachinseln des Ostens*. Munich: J. F. Lehmanns, 1930.

Karsten, Fred. *Vampyre des Aberglaubens*. Berlin: Deutsche Kulturwacht, 1935.

Kersten, Felix. *The Kersten Memoirs: 1940–1945*. New York: Howard Fertig, 1994.

Kiessling, Edith. *Zauberei in den Germanischen Volksrechten*. Jena: Gustav Fischer, 1941.

Klinckowstroem, Graf Carl V. 'Mein okkultistischer Lebenslauf: Bekenntnisse', *ZfKO* II (1927).

—— 'Die Seele des Okkultisten', *ZfKO* II (1927).

Koch, Hugo. *Hexenprozesse und Reste des Hexenglaubens in der Wetterau*. Giessen: Verlag von Münchowische Universitäts-Druckerei, 1935.

Kossegg, Karl. *Okkulte Erscheinungen verständlich gemacht?* Graz: Leykam-Verlag, 1936.

Kriegk, Otto. *Der deutsche Film im Spiegel der Ufa*. Berlin: Ufa, 1943.

Kritzinger, H. H. *Erdstrahlen, Reizstreifen und Wünschelrute: Neue Versuche zur Abwendung krank-machender Einflüsse auf Grund eigener Forschungen volkstümlich dargestellt*. Dresden: Talisman, 1933.

—— *Magische Kräfte: Geheimnisse der menschlichen Seele*. Berlin: Neufeld & Henius, 1922.

—— *Mysterien von Sonne und Seele: Psychische Studien zur Klärung der okkulten Probleme*. Berlin: Universitas Buch und Kunst, 1922.

—— *Spaziergänge durch den Weltenraum*. Berlin: Buchgemeinde, 1927.

—— *Todesstrahlen und Wünschelrute: Beiträge zur Schicksalskunde*. Leipzig: Grethlein, 1929.

—— *Zur Philosophie der Überwelt*. Tübingen: Mohr, 1951.

Kröner, Walter. *Der Untergang des Materialismus und die Grundlegung des biomagischen Weltbildes*. Leipzig: Hummel, 1939.

—— *Die Wiedergeburt des Magischen*. Leipzig: Hummel, 1938.

Kubizek, August. *The Young Hitler I Knew* (trans. E. V. Anderson). London: Paul Popper, 1954.

Kuhr, Erich Carl. 'Aussprache und Diskussion. Primär-Direktionen des Reichskanzlers Adolf Hitler', *Zenit* (1933).

Kuiper, Gerard P. 'German Astronomy During the War', *Popular Astronomy* 54:6 (June 1946).

Kummer, Bernhard. *Brünhild und Ragnarök*. Lübeck: Dittmer, 1950.

Kurd, Kisshauer. *Sternenlauf und Lebensweg*. Leipzig: Reclam, 1935.

Langer, Walter C. *The Mind of Adolf Hitler: The Secret Wartime Report*. New York: Basic Books, 1972.

Lanz von Liebenfels, Jörg. *Abriß der ariosophischen Rassenphysiognomik*. Pforzheim: Reichstein, 1927.

—— *Bibliomystikon oder Die Geheimbibel der Eingeweihten*. Pforzheim: Bibliomystikon, 1931.

—— *Das wiederentdeckte Vineta-Rethra und die arisch-christliche Urreligion der Elektrizität und Rasse*. Prerow-Pommern: Hertesburg, 1934.

—— *Der elektrische Urgott und sein grosses Heiligtum in der Vorzeit*. Prerow-Pommern: Hertesburg, 1933.

—— *Jakob Lorbeer, das größte ariosophische Medium der Neuzeit*. Pforzheim: Reichstein, 1926.

—— *Ostara*. Rodaun: Ostara, 1907–30.

—— *Praktisch-empirisches Handbuch der ariosophischen Astrologie*, vol. 1. Düsseldorf: Reichstein, 1926.

—— *Schrecken und Herrlichkeiten des elektrotheonischen Logos im Uranusmenschen*. Berlin: Manserie Szt. Balázs, 1930.

—— *Theozoologie oder Naturgeschichte der Götter. 1. Der 'alte Bund' und alte Gott*. Vienna: Johann Walther, 1928.

Lassen, Gustav. *Hexe Anna Schütterlin*. Bodensee: Heim-Verlag Dressler, 1936.

Ley, Willy. 'Pseudoscience in Naziland', *Astounding Science Fiction* 39:3 (1947), pp. 90–8.

Libenstoeckl, Hans. *Die Geheimwissenschaften im Lichte unserer Zeit*. Zürich: Amalthea, 1952.

Lindner, Thomas. *Der angebliche Ursprung der Femgerichte aus der Inquisition*. Münster and Paderborn: Ferdinand Schöningh, 1890.

—— *Die Feme*. Münster and Paderborn: Ferdinand Schöningh, 1888.

Löns, Hermann. *Der Wehrwolf*. Jena: Diederichs, 1910.

—— (trans. Robert Kvinnesland). *The Warwolf*. Yardley, PENN: Westholme, 2006.

Ludendorff, Mathilde. *Christliche Grausamkeit an Deutschen Frauen*. Munich: Ludendorff, 1934.

—— *Das Geheimnis der Jesuitenmacht und ihr Ende*. Munich: Ludendorff, 1929.

—— *Der Trug der Astrologie*. Munich: Ludendorff, 1932.

—— *Die Judenmacht ihr Wesen und Ende*. Munich: Ludendorff, 1939.

—— *Ein Blick in die Dunkelkammer der Geisterseher*. Munich: Ludendorff, 1937.

—— *Europa den Asiatenpriestern*. Munich: Ludendorff, 1938.

Lück, Kurt, ed. *Deutsche Volksgruppen aus dem Osten kehren heim ins Vaterland*, vol. 19. Berlin: Abt. Inland, 1940.

Mayer, Anton. *Erdmutter und Hexe*. Munich: Datterer & CIE, 1936.

McGuire, William and R. F. C. Hull, eds. *C. G. Jung Speaking: Interviews and Encounters*. Princeton, NJ: Princeton University Press, 1993.Mudrak, Edmund. *Grundlagen des Hexenwahnes*. Leipzig: Adolf Klein, 1936.

Müller, Wilhelm. *Jüdsiche und Deutsche Physik*. Leipzig: Helingsche, 1941.

Noesself, Heinz. 'Schicksalsdeterminaten des Reichskanzlers Adolf Hitler', *Zenit* (1933).

NSDAP. *Tatsachen und Lügen um Hitler*. Munich: Franz Eher, 1932.

Oberth, Hermann. 'They Come from Outer Space', *Flying Saucer Review* 1:2 (May–June 1955).

Olden, Rudolf von, ed. *Propheten in deutscher Krise. Das Wunderbare oder Die Verzauberten. Eine Sammlung*. Berlin: Rowohlt, 1932.

Pelz, Carl. *Die Hellseherin*. Munich: Ludendorff, 1937.

—— *Hellseher–Medien–Gespenster*. Freiburg: Hohe Warte, 1952.

Perovsky-Petrovo-Solovovo, Graf. 'Versuche zur Feststellung des sog. Hellsehens der Medien', *Zeitschrift für kritischen Okkultismus* (1926).

Peuckert, Will-Erich. *Pansophie: Ein Versuch zur Geschichte der weißen und schwarzen Magie*. Stuttgart: Verlag von W. Kohlhammer, 1936.

Piaschewski, Gisela. *Der Wechselbalg: Ein Beitrag zum Aberglauben der nordeuropäischen Wölfer*. Breslau: Maruschke und Berendt, 1935.

Pick, Daniel. *Faces of Degeneration: A European Disorder c. 1848–1918*. New York: Cambridge University Press, 1959.

Picker, Henry, ed. *Hitlers Tischgespräche im Führerhauptquartier*. Munich: Propyläen, 2003.

Pietzke, Dr Hans. 'Das Hakenkreuz als Sternbild', *Zenit* (1933).

Rahn, Otto. *Crusade Against the Grail* (trans. Christopher Jones). New York: Inner Traditions, 1934/2006.

—— *Kreuzzug gegen den Gral*. Freiburg: Urban Verlag, 1934.

—— *Luzifers Hofgesind*. Dresden: Zeitwende, 2006.

Rauschning, Hermann. *Gespräche mit Hitler*. Zürich: Europa Verlag, 2005.

—— *Hitler Speaks*. London: Thornton Butterworth, 1939.

—— *The Voice of Destruction*. New York: Putnam, 1941.

Rehwaldt, Hermann. *Das Schleichende Gift*. Munich: Ludendorff, 1934.

—— *Der Kollektivstaat – das Ziel Rom-Judas: einige Beispiele aus der Geschichte*. Munich: Ludendorff, 1934.

—— *Die Kommendo Religion*. Munich: Ludendorff, 1936.

—— *Die Kriegshetzer von heute*. Munich: Ludendorff, 1938.

—— *Geheimbuende in Afrika*. Munich: Ludendorff, 1941.

—— *Indien, die Schönste Perle der Krone Britanniens*. Munich: Ludendorff, 1940.

—— *Weissagungen*. Munich: Ludendorff,1939.

Reimann, Günter (aka Hans Steinicke). *The Vampire Economy: Doing Business under Fascism*. New York: Vanguard, 1939.

Rosenberg, Alfred. *Der Kampf um die Weltanschauung*. Munich: Eher, 1938.

—— *Diary* (http://www.ushmm.org/information/exhibitions/online-features/special-focus/the-alfred-rosenberg-diary).

—— *Dietrich Eckart: Ein Vermächtnis*. Munich: Eher, 1935.

—— (Eric Posselt, trans.). *Memoirs*. Chicago, IL: Ziff-Davis, 1949.

—— *Myth of the Twentieth Century*. Amazon, 2012 (1930).

Rüsslein, Heinrich. *Was Menschen bindet*. Erfurt: Ebertin-Verlag, 1935.

Schäfer, Ernst. *Geheimnis Tibet*. Munich: Verlag F. Bruckmann, 1938.

Schertel, Ernst. *Der Flagellantismus als literarisches Motiv*, 4 vols. Leipzig: Parthenon, 1929–32.

—— *Die Sünde des Ewigen oder Dies ist mein Leib*. Berlin: Die Wende, 1918.

—— *Erotische Komplex: Untersuchungen zum Problem der Paranormalen Erotik im Leben, Literatur und Bilderei*. Berlin: Pergamon, 1930.

—— *Magic: History, Theory, Practice*. Boise: Cotum, 2009.

—— *Magie – Geschichte, Theorie, Praxis*. Prien: Anthropos-Verlag, 1923.

Schmitz, Oscar A. H. 'Warum treibt unsere Zeit Astrologie?', *Zeitschrift für kritischen Okkultismus und Grenzfragen des Seelenlebens (ZfKO)* 11 (1927), p. 28.

Schwarz-Bostunitsch, Gregor. *Die Freimaurerei*. Weimar: Ulerander Dunder Verlag, 1928.

Sebottendorff, Rudolf von. *Bevor Hitler kam: Urkundlich aus der Frühzeit der Nationalsozialistischen Bewegung*. Munich: Deukula-Grassinger, 1933.

—— *Thule-Bote*. Munich: Thule-Gesellschaft, 1933.

Sellnich, George. 'Der Nationalsozialismus und die Astrologie', *Zenit* (1933).

Spence, Lewis. *The Occult Causes of the Present War*. London: Kessinger, 1940.

Stadthagen, Albert. *Die Raetsel des Spiritismus: Erklaerung der mediumistischen Phaenomene und Anletiung die Wunder der vierten Dimension ohne Medium und Geister ausfuehren zu koennen (mit Illustrationen)*. Leipzig: Ficker's, 1911.

Strasser, Otto. *Hitler and I*. Boston, MA: Houghton Mifflin, 1940.

Szczesny, Gerhard. 'Die Presse des Okkultismus, Geschichte und Typologie der okkultistischen Zeitschriften' (diss 1940, Munich, under Karl d'Ester).Teudt, Wilhelm. *Germanische Heiligtümer*. Jena: Diederichs, 1929.

Thudichum, F. *Femgericht und Inquisition*. Giessen: J. Ricker, 1889.

Tross, L. *Sammlung merkwurdiger Urkunden für die Geschichte der Femgerichte*. Hanover: Schultz, 1826.

Uexkull, J. von. *Bedeutungs Lehre*. Leipzig: Johann Ambrosius Barth, 1940.

—— *Staatsbiologie: Anatomie, Physiologie, Pathologie des Staates*. Berlin: Gebruder Vaetel, 1920.

Unger, Edhard. *Das antike Hakenkreuz als Wirbelsturm*. Berlin: Witting, 1937.

Urbach, Otto. *Reich des Aberglaubens*. Bad Homburg: Siemens, 1938.

Usener, F. P. *Die frei- und heimlichen Gerichte Westfalens*. Frankfurt: Archiv der freien Stadt Frankfurt, 1832.

Voegelin, Erich. *Political Religions*. Lewiston, NY: E. Mellen, 2003.

Voigt, Heinrich. *Eis: Ein Weltenbaustoff*. Leipzig: R. Voigtlaenders Verlag, 1928.

Wächter, O. *Femgerichte und Hexenprozesse in Deutschland*. Stuttgart: Spemann, 1882.

Wagner, Kurt. *Aberglaube, Volksglaube und Erfahrung*. Halle/Saale: Max Niemeyer Verlag, 1941.

Walter, Don. *Die Hexengreuel*. Paderborn: Bonifacius-Druckerei, 1934.

Walther, Gerda. *Zum Anderen Ufer: Vom Atheismus zum Christentum*. Remagen: Der Leuchter Verlag, 1960.

Warlimont, Walter. *Inside Hitler's Headquarters, 1939–45*. New York: Praeger, 1964.

Weber, Max. *Science as a Vocation*. Indianapolis, IN: Bobbs-Merrill, 1959 (1918).

Wehrhan, Karl. *Der Aberglaube im Sport*. Breslau: M & H Marcus, 1936.

Weishaar, H. A. *Rote Erde – Das Weltgericht*. Ragnit: Guoten, 1932.

Wüst, Walther. *Indogermanisches Bekenntnis*. Berlin-Dahlem: Ahnenerbe-Stiftung, 1942.

—— *Japan und Wir*. Berlin-Dahlem: Ahnenerbe-Stiftung, 1942.

Wulff, Wilhelm. *Zodiac and Swastika*. New York: Coward, 1973.

Secondary Sources

Ach, Manfred. *Hitlers Religion: Pseudoreligiose Elemente im nationalsozialistischen Sprachgerbrauch*. Munich: ARW, 1977.

Adorno, Theodor. *Minima Moralia*, trans. E. F. N. Jephcott. London: Verso, 2005.

—— *The Stars Down to Earth and Other Essays on the Irrational in Culture*. New York: Routledge, 1994 (1974).

Adorno, Theodor and Horkheimer, Max. *Dialectic of Enlightenment: Philosophical Fragments*. Stanford, CA: Stanford University Press, 2002.

Agamben, Georgio. *Homo Sacer: Sovereign Power and Bare Life*. Stanford, CA: Stanford University Press, 1998.

Aly, Götz. *Hitler's Beneficiaries: Plunder, Racial War, and the Nazi Welfare State*. London: Metropolitan, 2007.

Ambelain, Robert. *Les Arcanes Noirs de l'Hitlérisme*. Paris: Editions Robert Laffont, S.A, 1990.

Angebert, Jean-Michel, *The Occult and the Third Reich: The Mystical Origins of Nazism and the Search for the Holy Grail*. New York: Macmillan, 1974.

Applegate, Celia. *A Nation of Provincials*. Berkeley, CA: University of California Press, 1990.

Appleyard, James and Casterline, Lee. 'Misusing Archaeology and Manipulating History', *The World & I* 15:5 (May 2000), pp. 328–41.

Arnold, Bettina. '"Arierdämmerung": Race and Archaeology in Nazi Germany', *World Archaeology* 38:1 (2006), pp. 8–31.

Ashkenazi, Ofer. *A Walk into the Night: Reason and Subjectivity in the Films of the Weimar Republic*. Tel Aviv: Am Oved, 2010.

—— *Weimar Film and Modern Jewish Identity*. New York and London: Palgrave, 2012.

Asprem, Egil. *The Problem of Disenchantment: Scientific Naturalism and Esoteric Discourse 1900–1939*. Leiden: Brill, 2014.

Assion, Peter. *Eugen Fehrle and 'The Mythos of our Folk'*, in Dow and Lixfeld, eds, *The Nazification of an Academic Discipline: Folklore in the Third Reich*. Bloomington, IN: Indiana University Press, 1994.

Attridge, Steve. *Nationalism, Imperialism and Identity in Late Victorian Culture: Civil and Military Worlds*. New York: Palgrave Macmillan, 2003.

Auerbach, Nina. *Our Vampires, Ourselves*. Chicago, IL: University of Chicago Press, 1995.

Bärsch, Claus E. *Die Politische Religion des Nationalsozialismus*. Munich: Fink, 1998.

Baier, Lothar. *Die große Ketzere*. Berlin: Klaus Wagenbach, 1984.

Baigent, Michael, Richard Leigh, and Harry Lincoln. *Holy Blood, Holy Grail*. New York: Dell, 1983.

Bailey, Peter. *Popular Culture and Performance in the Victorian City*. Cambridge: Cambridge University Press, 1998.

Baranowski, Shelley. *Nazi Empire: German Colonialism and Imperialism from Bismarck to Hitler*. Cambridge: Cambridge University Press, 2011.

—— *The Confessing Church, Conservative Elites, and the Nazi State*. Lewiston, NY: Edwin Mellen Press, 1986.

Barber, Paul. *Vampires, Burial, and Death: Folklore and Reality*. New Haven, CT: Yale University Press, 1988, pp. 5–14, 90–101.

Barber, Richard. *The Holy Grail: Imagination and Belief*. London: Penguin, 2004.

Bartholomew, Alick. *Hidden Nature: The Startling Insights of Viktor Schauberger*. Edinburgh: Floris Books, 2004.

Barzilai, Maya. *Golem: Modern Wars and Their Monsters*. New York: New York University Press, 2016.

Bauer, Dietrich R., Lorenz, Sönke, Behringer, Wolfgang and Schmidt, Jürgen, eds. *Himmlers Hexenkartothek: Das Interesse des Nationalsozialismus an der Hexenverfolgung*. Bielefeld: Verlag für Regionalgeschichte, 1999.

Bauer, Eberhard. *German Parapsychology During the Third Reich*. Freiburg: Institut für Grenzgebiete der Psychologie und Psychohygiene, 2007.

Baumann, Schaul. *Die Deutsche Glaubensbewegung und ihr Gründer Jakob Wilhelm Hauer (1881–1962)*. Marburg: Diagonal, 2005.

Baumann, Zygmunt. *Modernity and the Holocaust*. Ithaca, NY: Cornell University Press, 1989.

Baumeister, Martin. 'Auf dem Weg in die Diktatur: Faschistische Bewegungen und die Krise der europäischen Demokratien', in Dietmar Süß and Winfried Süß, eds, *Das 'Dritte Reich': Eine Einführung*. Munich: Pantheon, 2008.

Baumgartner, Raimund. *Weltanschauungskampf im Dritten Reich: Die Auseinandersetzung de Kirchen mit Alfred Rosenberg*. Mainz: Matthias-Grunewald, 1977.

Beevor, Antony. *Downfall*. London: Penguin, 2002.

Bergen, Doris L. 'Nazism and Christianity: Partners and Rivals? A Response to Richard Steigmann-Gall, *The Holy Reich: Nazi Conceptions of Christianity, 1919–1945*', *Journal of Contemporary History* 42 (January 2007), pp. 25–33.

Berman, Russell. *Enlightenment or Empire: Colonial Discourse in German Culture*. Lincoln, NB: University of Nebraska Press, 1998.

—— *The Reenchantment of the World*. Ithaca, NY: Cornell University Press, 1981.

Bernadac, Christian. *Le Mystère Otto Rahn*. Paris: Editions France-Empire, 1978.

Berzin, Alexander. 'The Berzin Archives: The Nazi Connection with Shambhala and Tibet', May 2003 (http://www.berzinarchives.com/web/en/archives/advanced/kalachakra/ shambhala/nazi_connection_shambhala_tibet.html).

Bessel, Richard. *Germany 1945: From War to Peace*. New York: Harper, 2010.

Biddiscombe, Perry. 'Review of Volker Koop, *Himmlers letztes Aufgebot: Die Organisation des Werwolf*, in *Gutachten des Instituts für Zeitgeschichte*. Munich: IfZG, 1958.

—— *The Last Nazis: SS Werewolf Guerrilla Resistance in Europe 1944–1947*. London: Tempus, 2006.

—— *Werwolf! The History of the National Socialist Guerrilla Movement, 1944–1946*. Cardiff: University of Wales Press, 1998.

Black, Monica. *Death in Berlin*. Cambridge: Cambridge University Press, 2013.

—— 'Expellees Tell Tales: Partisan Blood Drinkers and the Cultural History of Violence after World War II', *History and Memory* 25:1 (2013), pp. 77–110.

—— *Revisiting the Nazi Occult: Histories, Realities, Legacies*. Rochester, NY: Camden House, 2015.

Blackbourn, David. *Marpingen: Apparitions of the Virgin Mary in Bismarckian Germany*. Oxford: Clarendon Press, 1995.

Bock, Gisela. *Zwangssterilisation im Nationalsozialismus: Studien zur Rassenpolitik und Frauenpolitik*. Opladen: Westdeutscher, 1987.

Bockhorn, Olaf. 'The Battle for the "Ostmark": Nazi Folklore in Austria', in Dow and Lixfeld, eds, *The Nazification of an Academic Discipline: Folklore in the Third Reich*. Bloomington, IN: Indiana University Press, 1994, pp. 135–42.

Bohn, Thomas M. 'Vampirismus in Österreich und Preussen: Von der Entdeckung einer Seuche zum Narrativ der Gegenkolonisation', *Jahrbücher für Geschichte Osteuropas* 56:2 (2008), pp. 161–77.

Bollmus, Reinhard. *Das Amt Rosenberg und seine Gegner. Zum Machtkampf im nationalsozialistischen Herrschaftssystem*. Stuttgart: Deutsche Verlags-Anstalt, 1970.

Bose, Fritz. 'Law and Freedom in the Interpretation of European Folk Epics', *Journal of the International Folk Music Council* 10 (1958).

Bowen, Robert. *Universal Ice: Science and Ideology in the Nazi State*. London: Belhaven, 1993.

Bramwell, Anna. *Blood and Soil: Richard Walther Darré and Hitler's 'Green Party'*. Abbotsbrook: Kensal, 1985.

Bratton, Susan Power. 'From Iron Age Myth to Idealized National Landscape: Human-Nature Relationships and Environmental Racism in Fritz Lang's *Die Nibelungen*', *Worldviews* 4, pp. 195–212.

Brauckmann, Stefan, 'Artamanen als völkisch-nationalistische Gruppierung innerhalb der deutschen Jugendbewegung 1924–1935', *Jahrbuch des Archivs der deutschen Jugendbewegung* 2:5. Wochenschau-Verlag, Schwalbach, 2006, pp. 176–96.

Breitman, Richard. *The Architect of Genocide: Himmler and the Final Solution*. Waltham, MA: Brandeis, 1992.

Brennan, Herbert. *Occult Reich*. New York: Signet Classics, 1974.

Brenner, Arthur D. 'Feme Murder: Paramilitary "Self-Justice" in Weimar Germany', in Bruce D. Campbell and Arthur D. Brenner, eds, *Death Squads in Global Perspective: Murder With Deniability*. New York: Palgrave Macmillan, 2002, pp. 57–84.

Bronder, Dietrich. *Bevor Hitler kam*. Geneva: Lüha, 1975.

Browning, Christopher. *Nazi Policy, Jewish Workers, German Killers*. Cambridge: Cambridge University Press, 2000.

—— and Jürgen Matthäus. *The Origins of the Final Solution: The Evolution of Nazi Jewish Policy, September 1939–March 1942*. Lincoln, NB: University of Nebraska Press, 2004.

—— *The Path to Genocide: Essays on Launching the Final Solution*. Cambridge: Cambridge University Press, 1998.

Buechner, Col. Howard A. *Emerald Cup – Ark of Gold*. Metairie, LO: Thunderbird Press, Inc. 1991.

Bullock, Alan. *Hitler: A Study in Tyranny*. New York: Harper Perennial, 1991.

Burleigh, Michael. *Germany Turns Eastwards: A Study of Ostforschung in the Third Reich*. Cambridge: Cambridge University Press, 1988.

—— 'National Socialism as a Political Religion', *Totalitarian Movements and Political Religions* 1:2 (Autumn 2000), pp. 1–26.

—— *Sacred Causes: The Clash of Religion and Politics from the Great War to the War on Terror*. New York: HarperCollins, 2007.

—— *The Third Reich*. London: Hill and Wang, 2001.

—— and Wolfgang Wippermann, *The Racial State: Germany 1933–1945*. Cambridge: Cambridge University Press, 1991.

Carmin, E. R. *Das schwarze Reich: Geheimgesellschaften und Politik im 20. Jahrhundert*. Munich: Nikol, 1997.

Cecil, Robert. *The Myth of the Master Race: Alfred Rosenberg and Nazi Ideology*. New York: Dodd, Mead, 1972.

Cesarani, David. *Becoming Eichmann: Rethinking the Life, Crimes, and Trial of a 'Desk Murderer'*. Cambridge: Da Capo Press, 2006.

Cho, Joanne, Eric Kurlander, and Douglas McGetchin, eds. *Transcultural Encounters between Germany and India*. New York: Routledge, 2014.

Coates, Paul. *The Gorgon's Gaze: German Cinema, Expressionism, and the Image of Horror*. Cambridge: Cambridge University Press, 2008.

Cohn, Norman. *The Pursuit of the Millennium*. Oxford: Oxford University Press, 1970.

Confino, Alon. *A World Without Jews: The Nazi Imagination from Persecution to Genocide*. New Haven, CT: Yale University Press, 2014.

Conrad, Sebastian. *Globalisation and the Nation in Imperial Germany*. Cambridge: Cambridge University Press, 2010.

Cook, Nick. *The Hunt for Zero Point: Inside the Classified World of Antigravity Technology*. New York: Broadway Books, 2002.

Dahrendorf, Ralf. *Society and Democracy in Germany*. New York: Doubleday, 1967.

Daim, Wilfried. *Der Mann der Hitler die Ideen gab*. Vienna: Böhlau, 1985.

Darnton, Robert. *Mesmerism and the End of the Enlightenment in France*. Cambridge, MA: Harvard University Press, 1986.

—— 'Peasants Tell Tales', in *The Great Cat Massacre*. New York: Basic Books, 1984.

Daston, Lorraine and Katherine Park. *Wonders and the Order of Nature*. New York: Zone, 2001.

Davies, Owen. *Grimoires: A History of Magic Books*. Oxford: Oxford University Press, 2009.

Denzler, Georg. *Die Kirchen im Dritten Reich*. Frankfurt am Main: Fischer Taschenbuch Verlag, 1984.

Derks, Hans. *Deutsche Westforschung: Ideologie und Praxis im 20. Jahrhundert*. Leipzig: AVA-Akademische Verlagsanstalt, 2001.

Derrich, Michael. *Geheimwaffen des Dritten Reiches*. Greiz (Thuringia): König, 2000.

Diehl, Paula. *Macht, Mythos, Utopie: Die Korperbilder der SS-Männer*. Berlin: Akademie, 2005.

Dierker, Wolfgang. *Himmlers Glaubenkrieger: Der Sicherheitsdienst der SS und seine Religionspolitik, 1933–1941*. Paderborn: Ferdinand Schöningh, 2002.

Dow, James R. and Ulrike Kammerhofer-Aggermann. 'Austrian *Volkskunde* and National Socialism: The Case of Karl Hauding, Born Paganini', *The Folklore Historian* 22 (2005).

—— and Hannjost Lixfeld, eds. *The Nazification of an Academic Discipline: Folklore in the Third Reich.* Bloomington, IN: Indiana University Press, 1994.

Dutton, Denis. 'Theodor Adorno on Astrology', *Philosophy and Literature* 19:2 (1995), pp. 424–30.

Eisler, Robert. *Man Into Wolf: An Anthropological Interpretation of Sadism, Masochism, and Lycanthropy.* London: Routledge, 1951.

Eisner, Lotte. *The Haunted Screen.* Berkeley, CA: University of California Press, 1969.

Eley, Geoff. *Nazism as Fascism.* New York: Routledge, 2013.

—— and Bradley Naranch, eds. *German Colonialism in a Global Age.* Durham, NC: Duke University Press, 2015.

Elsaesser, Thomas. *Weimar Cinema and After: Germany's Historical Imaginary.* London: Routledge, 2000.

Engelhardt, Isrun. 'Nazis of Tibet: A Twentieth Century Myth', in Monica Esposito, ed., *Images of Tibet in the 19th and 20th Centuries',* Paris: Ecole française d'Extrême-Orient (EFEO), coll. Etudes thématiques 22, vol. 1 (2008), pp. 63–96.

Evans, Richard. 'Nazism, Christianity and Political Religion: A Debate', *Journal of Contemporary History* 42:1 (2007), pp. 5–7.

—— *The Coming of the Third Reich.* London: Penguin, 2005.

—— *The Third Reich in Power.* London: Penguin, 2006.

—— *The Third Reich at War.* London: Penguin, 2010.

Fahlbusch, Michael. *Wissenschaft im Dienst der nationalsozialistischen Politik? Die Volksdeutschen Forschungsgemeinschaften von 1931–1945.* Baden-Baden: Nomos, 1999.

Fanon, Frantz. *The Wretched of the Earth.* New York: Grove Press, 2004.

Farrell, Joseph. *Reich of the Black Sun: Nazi Secret Weapons and the Cold War Allied Legend.* Kempton, IL: Adventures Unlimited Press, 2015.

Fest, Joachim, *The Face of the Third Reich: Portraits of the Nazi Leadership.* New York: Pantheon Books, 1970.

Fischer, Fritz. *Griff Nach der Weltmacht: Die Kreigszielpolitik des kaiserlichen Deutschland 1914/1918.* Düsseldorf: Droste, 1961.

Fisher, Peter S. *Fantasy and Politics: Visions of the Future in the Weimar Republic.* Madison, WI: University of Wisconsin Press, 1991.

Fitzgerald, Michael. *Stormtroopers of Satan: An Occult History of the Second World War.* London: Robert Hale, 1990.

Fitzpatrick, Matthew P. 'The Pre-History of the Holocaust? The Sonderweg and Historikstreit Debates and the Abject Colonial Past', *Central European History* 41:3 (2008), pp. 477–503.

Flowers, Stephen and Michael Moynihan. *The Secret King: The Myth and Reality of Nazi Occultism.* London: Feral House, 2007.

Foucault, Michel. *The Birth of Biopolitics: Lectures at the Collège de France, 1978–79.* New York: Palgrave Macmillan, 2008.

François, Stéphane. *Le Nazisme revisité: L'occultisme contre l'histoire.* Paris: Berg International éditeurs, 2008.

Freeman, Michael. 'Genocide, Civilization, and Modernity', *The British Journal of Sociology* 46:2 (June 1995), pp. 207–23.

Friedländer, Saul. *Nazi Germany and the Jews,* vol. 1. New York: Orion, 1998.

Friedrichsmeyer, Sara, Sarah Lennox, and Susanne Zantop, eds. *The Imperialist Imagination.* Ann Arbor, MI: Michigan, 1998.

Fritz, Stephen. *Endkampf: Soldiers, Civilians, and the Death of the Third Reich.* Lexington, KY: University Press of Kentucky, 2004.

Fritzsche, Peter, *Germans into Nazis.* Cambridge, MA: Harvard University Press, 1998.

—— *Life and Death in the Third Reich.* Cambridge, MA: Belknap Press, 2008.

—— *Stranded in the Present: Modern Time and the Melancholy of History.* Cambridge, MA: Harvard University Press, 2004.

—— 'The NSDAP 1919–1934: From Fringe Politics to the Nazi Seizure of Power', in Jane Caplan, ed., *Nazi Germany.* Oxford: Oxford University Press, 2008, pp. 48–72.

Gadal, Antonin. *De Triomf van de Universele Gnosis.* Amsterdam: Bibliotheca Philosophica Hermetica, 2004.

Gailus, Manfred. 'A Strange Obsession with Nazi Christianity: A Critical Comment on Richard Steigmann-Gall's *The Holy Reich', Journal of Contemporary History* 42 (January 2007), pp. 35–46.

—— and Armin Nolzen, eds. *Zerstrittene 'Volksgemeinschaft'. Glaube, Konfession und Religion im Nationalsozialismus.* Göttingen: Vandenhoeck & Ruprecht, 2011.

Ganaway, Bryan. 'Consumer Culture and Political Transformations in Twentieth-Century Germany', *History Compass,* vol. 1 (2005).

Gans, Herbert J. *Popular Culture and High Culture: An Analysis and Evaluation of Taste*. New York: Basic Books, 1975.

Gardenour, Brenda. 'The Biology of Blood-Lust: Medieval Medicine, Theology, and the Vampire Jew', *Film & History* 41:2 (Fall 2011), p. 51.

Gates, Donald K. and Peter Steane. 'Political Religion: The Influence of Ideological and Identity Orientation', in *Totalitarian Movements and Political Religions*, vol. 10, nos 3–4 (2009), pp. 303–25.

Gehring, Heiner. *Abenteuer 'Innere Erde'*. Schleusingen: AMUN-Verlag, 2001.

—— and Peter Bahn. *Der Vril-Mythos*. Düsseldorf: Omega, 1997.

Gellately, Robert. *Backing Hitler: Consent and Coercion in Nazi Germany*. Oxford: Oxford University Press, 2001.

—— *The Gestapo and German Society: Enforcing Racial Policy 1933–1945*. Oxford: Clarendon Press, 1990.

—— *The Politics of Economic Despair: Shopkeepers and German Politics 1890–1914*. London: Sage, 1974.

Gentile, Emilio. *Politics as Religion*. Princeton, NJ: Princeton University Press, 2006.

Geppert, Alexander C. T. and Till Kössler, eds. *Wunder – Poetik und Politik des Staunens im 20. Jahrhundert*. Berlin: Suhrkamp, 2011.

Gerlach, Christian. *Krieg, Ernährung, Völkermord. Deutsche Vernichtungspolitik im Zweiten Weltkrieg*. Zürich: Pendo, 2001.

Germana, Nicholas. *The Orient of Europe: The Mythical Image of India and Competing Images of German National Identity*. Newcastle: Cambridge Scholars, 2009.

Gerth, H. H. and C. Wright Mills (trans. and ed.). *From Max Weber: Essays in Sociology*. New York: Oxford University Press, 1946.

Gerwarth, Robert. *Hitler's Hangman: The Life of Heydrich*. New Haven, CT, and London: Yale University Press, 2011.

Gibson, Matthew. *Dracula and the Eastern Question*. New York: Palgrave, 2006.

Gilbhard, Hermann. *Die Thule-Gesellschaft: von okkulten-Mummenschanz zum Hakenkreuz*. Munich: Kiessling, 1994.

Glowka, Hans J. *Deutsche Okkultgruppen 1875–1937*. Munich: Arbeitsgemeinschaft für Religions- und Weltanschauungen, 1981.

Gmachl, Klaus. *Zauberlehrling, Alraune und Vampir: Die Frank Braun-Romane von Hanns Heinz Ewers*. Norderstedt: Books on Demand, 2005.

Godwin, Joscelyn. *Arktos. Der polare Mythos zwischen NS-Okkultismus und moderner Esoterik*. Graz: Ares 2007.

Gonen, Jay. *The Roots of Nazi Psychology: Hitler's Utopian Barbarism*. Lexington, KY: University Press of Kentucky, 2013.

Goodrick-Clarke, Nicholas. *Black Sun: Aryan Cults, Esoteric Nazism, and the Politics of Identity*. London/ New York: I. B. Tauris, 2003.

—— *Hitler's Priestess: Savitri Devi, the Hindu-Aryan Myth and Neo-Nazism*. New York: New York University Press, 1998.

—— *The Occult Roots of Nazism*. London: I. B. Tauris, 2003.

Gordon, Mel. *Erik Jan Hanussen: Hitler's Jewish Clairvoyant*. London: Feral House, 2001.

Grabner-Haider, Anton and Peter Strasser. *Hitlers mythische Religion. Theologische Denklinien und NS-Ideologie*. Vienna: Böhlau, 2007.

Graddon, Nigel. *Otto Rahn and the Quest for the Grail: The Amazing Life of the Real Indiana Jones*. Kempton, IL: Adventures Unlimited Press, 2008.

Gregory, Frederick. *Nature Lost: Natural Science and the German Theological Traditions of the Nineteenth Century*. Cambridge, MA: Harvard University Press, 1992.

Greve, Reinhard. 'Tibetforschung im SS Ahnenerbe', in Thomas Hauschild, ed., *Lebenslust durch Fremdenfurcht*. Frankfurt am Main: Suhrkamp, 1995, pp. 168–209.

Griffin, Roger, ed. *Fascism*. Oxford: Oxford University Press, 1995.

Gugenberger, Eduard. *Hitlers Visionäre: Die okkulten Wegbereiter des Dritten Reichs*. Vienna: Ueberreuter, 2001.

—— and Roman Schweidlenka. *Die Faden der Nornen*. Vienna: Verlag für Gesellschaftskritik, 1993.

Günther, H. K. *Ritter, Tod und Teufel*. Munich: J. F. Lehmanns, 1920.

Haar, Ingo (and Michael Fahlbusch), eds. *German Scholars and Ethnic Cleansing, 1920–1945*. New York: Berghahn, 2005.

—— *Historiker im Nationalsozialismus*. Göttingen: Vandenhoeck & Rupprecht, 2000.

Hale, Christopher. *Himmler's Crusade: The Nazi Expedition to Find the Origins of the Aryan Race*. London: Wiley, 2003.

Halle, Uta. 'Archaeology in the Third Reich: Academic Scholarship and the Rise of the "Lunatic Fringe"', *Archaeological Dialogues* 12:1 (2005), pp. 91–102.

Halter, Martin. 'Zivilisation ist Eis. Hanns Hörbigers Welteislehre – eine Metapher des Kältetods im 20. Jahrhundert', SWR2 Essay (Redaktion Stephan Krass). Südwestrundfunk. Dienstag, 15.07.2008, 21.03 Uhr, SWR 2.

Hamann, Brigitte. *Hitlers Wien: Lehrjahre eines Diktators.* Munich: Piper, 1996.

Hanegraaff, Wouter J. and Joyce Pijnenburg, eds. *Hermes in the Academy: Ten Years' Study of Western Esotericism at the Univesity of Amsterdam.* Amsterdam: Amsterdam University Press, 2009.

Harrington, Anne. *Reenchanted Science: Holism in German Culture from Wilhelm II to Hitler.* Princeton, NJ: Princeton University Press, 1996.

Harten, Hans-Christian. *Himmlers Lehrer: Die Weltanschauliche Schulung in der SS 1933–1945.* Paderborn: Schöningh, 2014.

Harvey, David Allen. 'Beyond Enlightenment: Occultism, Politics, and Culture in France from the Old Regime to the Fin-de-Siècle', *The Historian* 65:3 (March 2003), pp. 665–94.

Hastings, Derek. *Catholicism and the Roots of Nazism: Religious Identity and National Socialism.* Oxford: Oxford University Press, 2009.

—— 'How "Catholic" Was the Early Nazi Movement? Religion, Race, and Culture in Munich, 1919–1923', *Central European History* 36:3 (2003), pp. 383–7.

Hausmann, Frank-Rutger. *Hans Bender (1907–1991) und das 'Institut für Psychologie und Klinische Psychologie' an der Reichsuniversität Straßburg 1941–1944.* Würzburg: Ergon, 2006.

Heer, Friedrch. *Gottes Erste Liebe.* Munich: Bechtle, 1967.

Heilbronner, Oded. 'From Ghetto to Ghetto: The Place of German Catholic Society in Recent Historiography', *JMH* 72:2 (2000), pp. 453–95.

Henkel, Jens. 'Der Verlag "Gesundes Leben" Mellenbach Rudolfstadt: Von der lebensreformerischen Ideen des Wilhelm Hotz zu den Pendelforschungen von Karl Dietz, *Blätter der Gesellschaft für Buchkultur und Geschichte* 6 (2002), pp. 83–144.

Herf, Jeffrey. 'Nazi Germany's Propaganda Aimed at Arabs and Muslims During World War II and the Holocaust: Old Themes, New Archival Findings', *Central European History* 42 (2009), pp. 709–36.

—— *Nazi Propaganda for the Arab World.* New Haven, CT, and London: Yale University Press, 2009.

—— *Reactionary Modernism.* Cambridge: Cambridge University Press, 1986.

—— *The Jewish Enemy: Nazi Propaganda during World War II and the Holocaust.* Cambridge, MA: Belknap Press, 2006.

Herzog, Dagmar. 'The Death of God in West Germany: Between Secularization, Postfascism, and the Rise of Liberation Theology', in Michael Geyer and Lucian Hölscher, eds, *Die Gegenwart Gottes in der modernen Gesellschaft: Transzendenz und religiöse Vergemeinschaftung in Deutschland.* Göttingen: Wallstein, 2006.

Hesemann, Michael. *Hitlers Religion: Die fatale Heilslehre des Nationalsozialismus.* Munich: Pattloch Verlag, 2004.

Hett, Benjamin. *Burning the Reichstag: An Investigation into the Third Reich's Enduring Mystery.* Oxford: Oxford University Press, 2014.

Heyll, Uwe. *Wasser, Fasten, Luft und Licht. Die Geschichte der Naturheilkunde in Deutschland.* Frankfurt am Main: Campus, 2006.

Hexham, Irving. 'Inventing "Paganists": A Close Reading of Richard Steigmann-Gall's The Holy Reich', *Journal of Contemporary History* 42 (January 2007), pp. 59–78.

Hieronimus, Ekkehard. *Lanz von Liebenfels: Eine Bibliographie.* Toppenstedt: Uwe Berg-Verlag, 1991.

Hinton, Alexander Laban, ed. *Annihilating Difference: The Anthropology of Genocide.* Berkeley, CA: University of California Press, 2002.

Höhne, Heinz. *Order of the Death's Head: The Story of Hitler's S.S.* New York: Coward-McCann, 1970.

Holtz, Gottfried. *Die Faszination der Zwange: Aberglaube und Okkultismus.* Göttingen: Vandenhoeck & Ruprecht, 1984.

Horsch, Sylvia. '"Was findest du darinne, das nicht mit der allerstrengsten Vernunft übereinkomme?": Islam as Natural Theology in Lessing's Writings and in the Enlightenment', in Eleoma Joshua and Robert Vilain, eds, *Edinburgh German Yearbook* 1 (2007), pp. 45–62.

Howe, Ellic. *Nostradamus and the Nazis.* London: Arborfield, 1965.

—— *Rudolph Freiherr von Sebottendorff.* Freiburg: [private publisher], 1989.

—— *Urania's Children.* London: Kimber, 1967.

Hughes, H. Stuart. *Consciousness and Society: The Reorientation of Social Thought, 1890–1930.* New York: Vintage Books, 1961.

Hull, David Stewart. *Film in the Third Reich.* Berkeley, CA: University of California Press, 1969.

Hunger, Ulrich. *Die Runenkunde im Dritten Reich. Ein Beitrag zur Wissenschafts- und Ideologiegeschichte des Nationalsozialismus.* Frankfurt am Main: Lang, 1984.

Hutchinson, Roger. *Aleister Crowley: The Beast Demystified.* Edinburgh: Mainstream Publishing Company, 1998.

Hutton, J. Bernard. *Hess: The Man and His Mission.* Ann Arbor, MI: University of Michigan, 2008.

Jacobsen, Hans-Adolf. '"Kampf um Lebensraum": Zur Rolle des Geopolitikers Karl Haushofer im Dritten Reich', *German Studies Review* 4:1 (February 1981), pp. 79–104.

Janjetović, Zoran. *Between Hitler and Tito: The Disappearance of the Vojvodina Germans.* Belgrade: SD Publik, 2005.

Jarausch, Konrad and Michael Geyer. *Shattered Past: Reconstructing German Histories.* Princeton, NJ: Princeton University Press, 2003.

Jenkins, Jennifer. *Provincial Modernity: Local Culture and Liberal Politics in Fin-de-Siècle Hamburg.* Ithaca, NY: Cornell University Press, 2003.

Jestram, Heike. *Mythen, Monster und Maschinen.* Cologne: Teiresias Verlag, 2000.

Johnson, Eric. *Nazi Terror: The Gestapo, Jews and Ordinary Germans.* New York: Basic Books, 1999.

Jung, Emma. *Die Graalslegende.* Zürich: Rascher & Cie, 1960.

Junginger, Horst. 'From Buddha to Adolf Hitler: Walther Wüst and the Aryan Tradition', in Junginger, ed., *The Study of Religion under the Impact of Fascism.* Leiden: Brill, 2007, pp. 105–78.

—— and Andreas Ackerlund, eds. *Nordic Ideology Between Religion and Scholarship.* Frankfurt: Peter Lang, 2013.

—— and Martin Finkberger, eds. *Im Dienste der Lügen. Herbert Grabert (1901–1978) und seine Verlage.* Aschaffenburg: Alibri, 2004.

Kaes, Anton. *From Hitler to Heimat: The Return of History as Film.* Cambridge, MA: Harvard University Press, 1989.

Kaiser, Tomas. *Zwischen Philosophie und Spiritismus: Annäherungen an Leben und Werk des Carl du Prel.* Saarbrücken: VDM Verlag, 2008.

Kammen, Michael. *American Culture, American Tastes: Social Change in the Twentieth Century.* New York: Random House, 1999.

Kater, Michael. *Das 'Ahnenerbe' der SS: 1935–1945.* Stuttgart: Deutsche Verlagsanstalt, 1974.

—— 'Die Artamanen – Volkische Jugend in der Weimarer Republik', *Historische Zeitschrift* 213 (1971), pp. 577–638.

Kaufmann, Wolfgang. *Das Dritte Reich und Tibet.* Ludwigsfeld: Ludwigsfelder, 2009.

Kellogg, Michael. *The Russian Roots of Nazism: White Emigrés and the Making of National Socialism, 1917–1945.* Cambridge: Cambridge University Press, 2005.

Kershaw, Ian. *Hitler: Hubris.* London: Allen Lane, 1998.

—— *Hitler: Nemesis.* London/New York: Norton, 2001.

—— *Popular Opinion and Political Dissent in the Third Reich, Bavaria 1933–1945.* Oxford: Oxford University Press, 2002.

King, Francis. *Satan and Swastika.* St Albans: Mayflower, 1976.

King, Richard and Dan Stone, eds. *Hannah Arendt and the Uses of History: Imperialism, Nation, Race, and Genocide.* New York: Berghahn, 2007.

Klautke, Egbert. 'Defining the Volk: Willy Hellpach's *Völkerpsychologie* between National Socialism and Liberal Democracy, 1934–1954', *History of European Ideas* 39:5 (September 2013), pp. 693–708.

Klee, Ernst. *Das Personenlexikon zum Dritten Reich. Wer war was vor und nach 1945.* Frankfurt am Main: Fischer, 2005.Koebner, Thomas. 'Murnau – On Film History as Intellectual History', in Dietrich Scheunemann, ed., *Expressionist Film: New Perspectives.* Rochester, NY: Camden House, 2003, pp. 111–23.

Koehne, Samuel. 'The Racial Yardstick: "Ethnotheism" and Official Nazi Views on Religion', *German Studies Review* 37:3 (October 2014), pp. 575–96.

—— 'Were the National Socialists a Völkisch Party? Paganism, Christianity and the Nazi Christmas', *Central European History* 47 (December 2014), pp. 760–90.

Koepnick, Lutz. *The Dark Mirror: German Cinema Between Hitler and Hollywood.* Berkeley, CA: University of California Press, 2002.

Koonz, Claudia. *Mothers in the Fatherland: Women, the Family and Nazi Politics.* New York: St Martin's Press, 1987.

Kostermann, Vittorio. *NS- Raubgut in Museen, Bibliotheken und Archiven.* Hamburg: GmbH Frankfurt am Main, 2012.

Krabbe, Wolfgang R. *Gesellschaftsveränderung durch Lebensreform. Strukturmerkmale einer sozialrefor-merischen Bewegung im Deutschland der Industrialisierungsperiode.* Göttingen: Vandenhoeck & Ruprecht, 1974.

Kracauer, Siegfried. *From Caligari to Hitler: A Psychological History of the German Film.* Princeton NJ: Princeton University Press, 2004.

Kozlowski, Timo. 'Wenn Nazis weltenbummeln und schreiben. Über die Nähe zwischen Künstlern und Nationalsozialismus.' Dargestellt am Beispiel von Hanns Heinz Ewers', *Die Brücke. Zeitschrift für Germanistik in Südostasien* 5 (2004).

Kugel, Wilfried. *Der Unverantwortliche. Das Leben des Hanns Heinz Ewers.* Düsseldorf: Grupello, 1992.

—— *Hanussen: Die wahre Geschichte des Hermann Steinschneider.* Düsseldorf: Grupello, 1998.

—— and Alexander Bahar. *Der Reichstagsbrand. Wie Geschichte wird gemacht.* Berlin: Quintessenz, 2001.

Kühne, Thomas. *Belonging and Genocide: Hitler's Community, 1918–1945.* New Haven, CT: Yale University Press, 2010.

Kundrus, Birthe, ed. *Phantasiereiche: Zur Kulturgeschichte des deutschen Kolonialismus.* Frankfurt: Campus, 2003.

Kurlander, Eric. 'Between Völkisch and Universal Visions of Empire: Liberal Imperialism in *Mitteleuropa*, 1890–1918', in Matthew Fitzpatrick, ed., *Liberal Imperialism in Europe*, London: Palgrave, 2012, pp. 141–66.

—— 'Between Weimar's Horrors and Hitler's Monsters: The Politics of Race, Nationalism, and Cosmopolitanism in Hanns Heinz Ewers Supernatural Imaginary', in Rainer Godel, Erdmut Jost, and Barry Murnane, eds, *Zwischen Popularisierung und Ästhetisierung? Hanns Heinz Ewers und die Moderne.* Bielefeld: Moderne Studien (Aisthesis), 2014, pp. 229–56.

—— 'Hitler's Monsters: The Occult Roots of Nazism and the Emergence of the Nazi Supernatural Imaginary', *German History* 30:4 (2012).

—— *Living with Hitler: Liberal Democrats in the Third Reich, 1933–1945.* New Haven, CT, and London: Yale University Press, 2009.

—— 'The Nazi Magician's Controversy: Enlightenment, "Border Science", and Occultism in the Third Reich', *Central European History* 48:4 (December 2015), pp. 498–522.

—— 'The Orientalist Roots of National Socialism? Nazism, Occultism, and South Asian Spirituality, 1919–1945', in Joanne Miyang Cho, Eric Kurlander, and Douglas McGetchin, eds, *Transcultural Encounters between Germany and India: Kindred Spirits in the Nineteenth and Twentieth Centuries.* New York and London: Routledge, 2014, pp. 155–69.

Lachman, Alfred. *Rudolf Steiner: An Introduction to His Life and Work.* New York: Penguin, 2007.

Lange, Hans-Jurgen. *Otto Rahn. Leben und Werk.* Arun: Engerda, 1995.

—— *Otto Rahn und die Suche nach dem Gral.* Arun: Engerda, 1999.

—— *Weisthor: Karl-Maria Wiligut, Himmlers Rasputin und seine Erben.* Arun: Engerda, 1998.

Laqueur, Thomas. 'Why the Margins Matter: Occultism and the Making of Modernity', *Modern Intellectual History* 3:1 (2006), pp. 111–35.

Larson, Erik. *The Devil in the White City: Murder, Magic, and Madness at the Fair that Changed America.* New York: Crown, 2003.

Laslett, Peter. *The World We Have Lost.* New York: Routledge, 2004.

Latour, Bruno. *Reassembling the Social: An Introduction to Actor-Network-Theory.* Oxford: Oxford University Press, 2005.

—— *Science in Action: How to Follow Scientists and Engineers through Society.* Cambridge, MA: Harvard University Press, 1987.

Lechler, Volker. *Die ersten Jahre der Fraternitas Saturni.* Stuttgart: Lechler, 2014.

—— . *Heinrich Tränker als Theosoph, Rosenkreuzer und Pansoph.* Stuttgart: Lechler, 2013.

Leeming, David. *From Olympus to Camelot: The World of European Mythology.* Oxford: Oxford University Press, 2003, pp. 120–1.

Leschnitzer, Adolf. *The Magic Background of Modern Antisemitism.* New York: International, 1969.

Levenda, Peter. *Unholy Alliance: A History of Nazi Involvement with the Occult. With a Foreword by Norman Mailer.* New York/London: Continuum, 2002.

Levine, Lawrence. *Highbrow/Lowbrow: The Emergence of Cultural Hierarchy in America.* Cambridge, MA: Harvard University Press, 1988.

Ley, Michael and Julius Schoeps. *Der Nationalsozialismus als politische Religion.* Bodenheim B. Mainz: Philo, 1997.

Ley, Willy. *Watchers of the Skies: An Informal History of Astronomy from Babylon to the Space Age.* New York: Viking Press, 1966, p. 515.

Lifton, Robert. *Nazi Doctors.* New York: Basic Books, 1986.

Lincoln, Bruce. 'Hermann Güntert in the 1930s: Heidelberg, Politics, and the study of Germanic/ Indogermanic Religion', in Horst Junginger, ed., *The Study of Religion Under Fascism.* Leiden: Brill, 2007, pp. 179–204.

Link, Fabian. *Burgen und Burgenforschung in Nationalsozialismus.* Cologne: Böhlau, 2014.

—— 'Der Mythos Burg im Nationalsozialismus', in Ulrich Grossmann and Hans Ottomeyer, eds, *Die Burg.* Dresden: Sandstein, 2010, pp. 302–11.

—— 'The Internationalism of German Castle Research: Bodo Ebhardt, his European Network, and the Construction of "Castle Knowledge"', *Public Archaeology* 8:4 (2009), pp. 325–50.

—— 'Walter Hotz und das Handbuch der Kunstdenkmaler im Elsaß und in Lothringen', in Michael Fahlbusch and Ingo Haar, eds, *Wissenschaftliche Politikberatung im 20. Jahrhundert.* Paderborn: Ferdinand Schöningh, 2010, pp. 255–73.

Linse, Ulrich. 'Das "natürliche" Leben. Die Lebensreform', in Richard van Dülmen, ed., *Die Erfindung des Menschen. Schöpfungsträume und Körperbilder 1500–2000.* Vienna: Böhlau, 1998.

— *Geisterseher und Wunderwirker. Heilssuche im Industriezeitalter.* Frankfurt: Fischer, 1996.

Lixfeld, Hannjost. *Folklore and Fascism: The Reich Institute for German Volkskunde.* Bloomington, IN: Indiana University Press, 1994.

—— 'The Deutsche Forschungsgemeinschaft and the Umbrella Organizations of German "Volkskunde" during the Third Reich', *Asian Folklore* 50:1 (1991), pp. 95–116.

Longerich, Peter. *Himmler.* Oxford: Oxford University Press, 2013.

—— *Hitlers Stellvertreter. Führung der Partei und Kontrolle des Staatsapparates durch den Stab Heß und die Partei-Kanzlei Bormann.* Munich: K. G. Saur, 1992.

Lönnecker, Harald. 'Zwischen Esoterik und Wissenschaft – die Kreise des "völkischen Germanenkundlers" Wilhelm Teudt', in *Einst und jetzt. Jahrbuch des Vereins für corpsstudentische Geschichtsforschung* 49 (2004), pp. 265–94.

Lower, Wendy. *Nazi Empire-Building and the Holocaust in the Ukraine.* Chapel Hill, NC: University of North Carolina Press, 2007.

Luckmann, Thomas. *The Invisible Religion.* New York: Macmillan, 1967, pp. 44–9.

Luhrssen, David. *Hammer of the Gods: The Thule Society and the Birth of Nazism.* Lincoln, NB: Potomac, 2012.

Lumans, Valdis O. *Himmler's Auxiliaries: The Volksdeutsche Mittelstelle and the German National Minorities of Europe, 1939–1945.* Chapel Hill, NC: University of North Carolina Press, 1993.

Maier, Hans. 'Political Religion: A Concept and its Limitations', *Totalitarian Movements and Political Religions* 1:2 (Autumn 2000), pp. 1–26.

—— *Politische Religionen: Die totalitären Regime und das Christentum.* Freiburg: Herder, 1995.

Manjapra, Kris. *Age of Entanglement: German and Indian Intellectuals across the Empire.* Cambridge, MA: Harvard University Press, 2014.

Marchand, Suzanne. *German Orientalism in the Age of Empire: Religion, Race, and Scholarship.* Washington DC: Cambridge University Press, 2009.

Mazower, Mark. *Hitler's Empire: Nazi Rule in Occupied Europe.* London: Allen Lane, 2008.

McCall, Andrew. *The Medieval Underworld.* New York: Barnes and Noble, 1972.

McGetchin, Douglas. *Indology, Indomania, Orientalism: Ancient India's Rebirth in Modern Germany.* Madison, WI: Fairleigh Dickinson University Press, 2009.

McIntosh, Christopher. *Eliphas Lévi and the French Occult Revival.* London: Rider, 1972.

McNally, Raymond and Radu Florescu. *In Search of Dracula: A True History of Dracula and Vampire Legends.* Greenwich, CT: New York Graphic Society, 1972.

Mees, Bernard. 'Hitler and Germanentum', *Journal of Contemporary History* 39:2 (2004).

—— *The Science of the Swastika.* Budapest: Central European University Press, 2008.

Melzer, Ralf. 'In the Eye of the Hurricane: German Freemasonry in the Weimar Republic and the Third Reich', *Totalitarian Movements and Political Religions* 4:2 (Autumn 2003).

Michalczyk, John J. *Medicine, Ethics, and the Third Reich: Historical and Contemporary Issues.* London: Rowman & Littlefield, 1994.

Mizrach, Steve. *The Occult and Nazism Re-Examined* (http://www.www2.fiu.edu/~mizrachs/occult-reich.html).

Mocek, Reinhard. *Wilhelm Roux and Hans Driesch.* Jena: Gustav Fischer Verlag, 1974.

Mohler, Armin. *Die Konservative Revolution in Deutschland 1918–1932: Ein Handbuch.* Darmstadt: Wissenschaftliche Buchgesellschaft, 1989.

Mommsen, Hans. 'Der Reichstagsbrand und seine politischen Folgen', *Vierteljahrshefte für Zeitgeschichte* 12 (1964).

Monroe, John Warne. *Laboratories of Faith: Mesmerism, Spiritism, and Occultism in Modern France.* Ithaca, NY: Cornell University Press, 2008.

Moser, Christian. 'Aneignung, Verpflanzung, Zirkulation: Johann Gottfried Herders Konzeption des interkulturellen Austauschs', *Edinburgh German Yearbook* 1 (2007), pp. 89–108.

Moses, A. Dirk and Dan Stone, eds. *Colonialism and Genocide.* London: Routledge, 2007.

Mosse, George L. *Masses and Man: Nationalist and Fascist Perceptions of Reality.* Detroit, IL: Wayne State University Press, 1987.

—— *The Crisis of German Ideology.* New York: Fertig, 1999 (orig. pub. Grosset & Dunlap, 1964).

—— *The Nationalization of the Masses: Political Symbolism and Mass Movements in Germany, from the Napoleonic Wars Through the Third Reich.* New York: H. Fertig, 2001.

Motadel, David. *Islam and Nazi Germany's War.* Cambridge, MA: Belknap Press, 2014.

Mullern-Schonhausen, Johannes von. *Die Lösung des Rätsels Adolf Hitler.* Vienna: Verlag zur Förderung der wissenschaftlichen Forschung, 1959.

Myers, Perry. 'Leopold von Schroeder's Imagined India: Buddhist Spirituality and Christian Politics During the Wilhelmine Era', *German Studies Review* 32:3 (October 2009), pp. 619–36.

Nagel, Brigitte. *Die Welteislehre.* Stuttgart: Geschichte der Naturwissenschaften und der Technik, 1991.

Nagel, Günther. *Wissenschaft für den Krieg, Die geheimen Arbeiten des Heereswaffenamtes.* Stuttgart: Steiner, 2012.

Nanko, Ulrich. *Die Deutsche Glaubensbewegung. Eine historische und soziologische Untersuchung.* Marburg: Diagonal, 1993.

Nederman, Cary J. and James Wray. 'Popular Occultism and Critical Social Theory: Exploring Some Themes in Adorno's Critique of Astrology and the Occult', *Sociology of Religion* 42:4 (1981), pp. 325–32.

Neufeld, Michael. *The Rocket and the Reich: Peenemünde and the Coming of the Ballistic Missile Era.* New York: The Free Press, 1995.

Neumann, Klaus. *Shifting Memories: The Nazi Past in the New Germany.* Ann Arbor, MI: University of Michigan Press, 2000.

Norton, Robert E. *Secret Germany: Stefan George and his Circle.* Ithaca, NY: Cornell University Press, 2002.

Orzechowski, Peter. *Schwarze Magie – Braune Macht.* Ravensburg: Selinka, 1987.

Owen, Alex. *The Place of Enchantment: British Occultism and the Culture of the Modern.* Chicago, IL: University of Chicago Press, 2004.

Padfield, Peter. *Himmler.* London: Thistle Publishing, 2013.

Palmowski, Jan. *Urban Liberalism in Imperial Germany, 1866–1914: Frankfurt am Main.* Oxford: Oxford University Press, 1999.

Pammer, Leo. *Hitlers Vorbilder: Dr. Karl Lueger* (http://www.antifa.co.at/antifa/PAMMER2.PDF).

Pasi, Marco. 'The Modernity of Occultism: Reflection on Some Crucial Aspects', in Wouter J. Hanegraaff and Joyce Pijnenburg, eds, *Hermes in the Academy.* Amsterdam: Amsterdam University Press, 2009, pp. 62– 8.

Paul, Fritz. *History of the Scandinavian Languages at the Georg-August-Universität Göttingen: A Preliminary Sketch.* Göttingen 1985 (http://www.uni-goettingen.de/de/91592.html).

Pauley, Bruce F. *From Prejudice to Persecution: A History of Austrian Anti-Semitism.* Chapel Hill, NC: University of North Carolina Press, 1992.

Louis Pauwels and Jacques Bergier. *The Morning of the Magicians.* London: Souvenir, 2007.

Pendas, Devin, Mark Roseman, and Richard F. Wetzell, eds. *Beyond the Racial State: Rethinking Nazi Germany.* Cambridge: Cambridge University Press, 2017.

Pennick, Nigel. *Hitler's Secret Sciences: His Quest for the Hidden Knowledge of the Ancients.* Sudbury, Suffolk: Newille Spearman, 1981.

Peukert, Detlev. *Inside Nazi Germany.* New Haven, CT: Yale University Press, 1987.

—— 'The Genesis of the "Final Solution" from the Spirit of Science', in Thomas Childers and Jane Caplan, eds, *Reevaluating the Third Reich.* New York: Holmes & Meier, 1994, pp. 234–52.

Phelps, Reginald. 'Before Hitler Came: Thule Society and Germanen Orden', *Journal of Modern History* 35:3 (September 1963), pp. 245–61.

—— 'Theodor Fritsch und der Antisemitismus', in *Deutsche Rundschau* 87 (1961), pp. 442–9.

Piper, Ernst. *Alfred Rosenberg: Hitlers Chefideologe.* Munich: Blessing, 2005.

—— 'Steigmann-Gall, The Holy Reich', *Journal of Contemporary History* 42 (January 2007), pp. 47–57.

Poewe, Karla, O. *New Religions and the Nazis.* New York: Routledge, 2006.

Pois, Robert A. *National Socialism and the Religion of Nature.* New York: St Martin's Press, 1986.

Poley, Jared. *Decolonization in Germany.* Bern: Peter Lang, 2005.

Pringle, Heather. *The Master Plan: Himmler's Scholars and the Holocaust.* New York: Hyperion, 2006.

Prosser-Schell, Michael. 'Zum Wandel der Funktion und des Traditionswertes vom Sagen-Texten', *Jahrbuch für deutsche und osteuropäische Volkskunde* 51 (2010), pp. 47–62.

Puschner, Uwe. *Die völkische Bewegung im wilhelminischen Kaiserreich.* Darmstadt: Wissenschaftliche Buchgesellschaft, 2001.

—— 'Weltanschauung und Religion, Religion und Weltanschauung. Ideologie und Formen völkischer Religion', *Zeitenblicke* 5:1 (2006).

—— and Clemens Vollnhals, eds. *Die völkisch-religiöse Bewegung im Nationalsozialismus: Eine Beziehungs- und Konfliktgeschichte.* Göttingen: Vandenhoeck & Ruprecht, 2012.

—— and Hubert Cancik, eds. *Antisemitismus, Paganismus, Völkische Religion / Anti-Semitism, Paganism, Voelkisch Religion.* Munich: K. G. Saur, 2004.

Rabinbach, Anson. *In the Shadow of Catastrophe: German Intellectuals Between Apocalypse and Enlightenment.* Berkeley, CA: University of California Press, 2001.

Ramaswamy, Sumathi. *The Lost Land of Lemuria.* Berkeley, CA: University of California Press, 2004.

Ravenscroft, Trevor. *The Spear of Destiny.* New York: Weiser, 1982.

Redles, David. *Hitler's Millennial Reich: Apocalyptic Belief and the Search for Salvation.* New York: New York University Press, 2005.

Reichelt, Werner. *Das Braune Evangelium: Hitler und die NS-Liturgie.* Wuppertal: P. Hammer, 1990.

Reitzenstein, Julien. *Himmlers Forscher: Wehrwissenschaft und Medizinverbrechen im "Ahnenerbe" der SS.* Paderborn: Schöningh, 2014.

Remy, Steven P. *The Heidelberg Myth: The Nazification and Denazification of a German University.* Cambridge, MA: Harvard University Press, 2002.

Rentschler, Eric. *Ministry of Illusion.* Cambridge, MA: Harvard University Press, 1996.

Repp, Kevin. *Reformers, Critics, and the Paths of German Modernity: Anti-Politics and the Search for Alternatives, 1890–1914.* Cambridge, MA: Harvard University Press, 2000.

Rißmann, Michael. *Hitlers Gott.* Munich: Pendo, 2001.

Robin, Jean. *Hitler L'Elu du Dragon.* Paris: Editions de la Maisnie, 1987.

Roland, Paul. *The Nazis and the Occult: The Esoteric Roots of the Third Reich.* London: Foulsham, 2007.

Rose, Detlev. *Die Thule-Gesellschaft: Legende-Mythos-Wirklichkeit.* Tübingen: Grabert, 1994.

Rose, Paul Lawrence. *Heisenberg and the Nazi Atomic Bomb Project: A Study in German Culture.* Berkeley, CA: University of California Press, 1998.

Rossbacher, Karlheinz. *Heimatkunstbewegung und Heimatroman: Zu einer Literatursoziologie der Jahrhundertwende.* Stuttgart: Ernst Klett, 1975.

Rubin, Barry and Wolfgang G. Schwanitz. *Nazis, Islamists, and the Making of the Modern Middle East.* New Haven, CT: Yale University Press, 2014.

Rupnow, Dirk, Veronika Lipphardt, Jens Thiel, and Christina Wessely, eds. *Pseudowissenschaft: Konzeptionen von Nichtwissenschaftlichkeit in der Wissenschaftsgeschichte.* Frankfurt am Main: Suhrkamp, 2008.

Ruthner, Clemens. *Unheimliche Wiederkehr: Interpretationen zu den gespenstischen Romanfiguren bei Ewers, Meyrink, Soyka, Spunda und Strobl.* Meiten: Corian-Verlag, 1993.

Ryback, Timothy. 'Hitler's Forgotten Library', *Atlantic Monthly* (http://www.theatlantic.com/doc/200305/ryback).

—— *Hitler's Private Library: The Books that Shaped his Life.* New York: Random House, 2008.

Saler, Michael. 'Clap if You Believe in Sherlock Holmes: Mass Culture and the Re-Enchantment of Modernity, c.1890–c.1940', *The Historical Journal* 46:3 (2003).

—— 'Modernity and Enchantment: A Historiographic Review', *American Historical Review* 11:3 (June 2006), pp. 692–716.

Schellenberg, Walter. *Hitler's Secret Service.* New York: Harper, 1974.

Scheunemann, Dietrich. *Expressionist Film: New Perspectives.* Rochester, NY: Camden House, 2003.

Schieder, Theodor. *Hermann Rauschnings 'Gespräche mit Hitler' als Geschichtsquelle.* Opladen: Westdeutscher Verlag, 1972.

Schindler, Stephan and Lutz Koepnick. *The Cosmopolitan Screen.* Ann Arbor, MI: Michigan, 2007.

Schmidt, Rainer F. *Rudolf Hess. Botengang eines Toren?* Düsseldorf: Econ, 1997.

Schmitz-Berning, Cornelia. *Vokabular des Nationalsozialismus.* Berlin: De Gruyter, 1998.

Schmuhl, Hans-Walter. *The Kaiser-Wilhelm-Institute for Anthropology, Human Heredity and Eugenics, 1927–1945: Crossing Boundaries.* New York: Springer, 2008.

Schönwälder, Karen. *Historiker und Politik. Geschichtswissenschaft im Nationalsozialismus*, Frankfurt am Main: Campus, 1992.

Schöttler, Peter, ed. *Geschichtsschreibung als Legitimationswissenschaft 1918–1945.* Frankfurt am Main: Sührkamp, 1997.

Schormann, Gerhard. 'Wie entstand die Karthotek, und wem war sie bekannt?', in Bauer, Lorenz, Behringer, and Schmid, *Hexenkartothek*, pp. 135–42.

Schulte-Sasse, Linda. *Entertaining the Third Reich.* Durham, NC: Duke University Press, 1996.

Schulze, Winfried and Otto Gerhard Oexle. *Deutsche Historiker im Nationalsozialismus.* Frankfurt am Main: Fischer, 1999.

Sedgwick, Mark J. *Against the Modern World: Traditionalism and the Secret Intellectual History of the Twentieth Century.* New York/Oxford: Oxford University Press, 2004.

Sennewald, Michael. *Hanns Heinz Ewers. Phantastik und Jugendstil.* Maisenhain: Hain, 1973.

Shenstone, A. G. 'The Brocken Spectre', *Science* 119 (3094) (16 April 1954).

Sickinger, Raymond L. 'Hitler and the Occult: The Magical Thinking of Adolf Hitler', *Journal of Popular Culture* 34:2 (Fall 2000), pp. 107–25.

Sieg, Ulrich. *Deutschlands Prophet. Paul de Lagarde und die Ursprünge des modernen Antisemitismus.* Munich: Carl Hanser, 2007.

Siemens, Daniel. *Horst Wessel. Tod und Verklärung eines Nationalsozialisten.* Munich: Siedler, 2009.

Simon, Michael. '"Volksmedizin" im frühen 20. Jahrhundert. Zum Quellenwert des Atlas der deutschen Volkskunde', *Studien zur Volkskultur* 28. Mainz: Gesellschaft für Volkskunde in Rheinland-Pfalz, 2003.

Sklar, Dusty. *Gods and Beasts: The Nazis and the Occult.* New York: Thomas Crowell, 1977.

Smith, Helmut Walser. *The Continuities of German History.* Cambridge: Cambridge University Press, 2008.

Smith, Woodruff D. *Politics and the Sciences of Culture in Germany, 1840–1920.* Oxford: Oxford University Press, 1991.

Sommer, Andreas. 'From Astronomy to Transcendental Darwinism: Carl du Prel (1839–1899)', *Journal of Scientific Exploration* 23:1 (2009), pp. 59–68.

Spang, Christian. *Karl Haushofer und Japan: Die Rezeption seiner geopolitischen Theorien in der deutschen und japanischen Politik*. Munich: Ludicum, 2013.

Spicer, Kevin P. *Resisting the Third Reich: The Catholic Clergy in Hitler's Berlin*. DeKalb, IL: University of Northern Illinois Press, 2004.

Spielvogel, Jackson and David Redles. 'Hitler's Racial Ideology: Content and Occult Sources', *Simon Wiesenthal Center Annual* 3 (1986), pp. 227–46.

Spiker, Annika. *Geschlecht, Religion und völkischer Nationalismus: Die Ärztin und Antisemitin Mathilde von Kemnitz-Ludendorff*. Frankfurt: Campus, 2013.

Stach, Walter. *Gemeingefähliche Mysterien: Eine astrologische Studie*, Graf. Carl v. Klinckowstroem, 'Rund um Nostradamus', in ZfKO, vol. II (1927).

Stafford, Barbara Maria. *Artful Science: Enlightenment Entertainment and the Eclipse of Visual Education*. Cambridge, MA: MIT Press, 1996.

Standish, David. *Hollow Earth*. Boston, MA: Da Capo Press, 2006.

Stark, Rodney. *Discovering God*. New York: HarperCollins, 2004.

Staudenmaier, Peter. *Between Occultism and Nazism*. Boston, MA: Brill, 2014.

—— 'Nazi Perceptions of Esotericism: The Occult as Fascination and Menace', in Ashwin Manthripragada, Emina Musanovic, and Dagmar Theison, eds, *The Threat and Allure of the Magical: Selected Papers from the 17th Annual Interdisciplinary German Studies Conference*. Cambridge: Cambridge Scholars Publishing, 2013, pp. 24–58.

—— 'Occultism, Race and Politics in Germany, 1880–1940: A Survey of the Historical Literature', *European History Quarterly* 39:1 (January 2009), pp. 47–70.

—— 'Organic Farming in Nazi Germany: The Politics of Biodynamic Agriculture, 1933–1945', in *Environmental History* (2013), pp. 1–29.

—— 'Rudolf Steiner and the Jewish Question', *Leo Baeck Institute Yearbook* (2005).

Steegman, Robert. *Le Camp de Natzweiler Struthof*. Paris: Seuil, 2009.

Steigmann-Gall, Richard. *The Holy Reich: Nazi Conceptions of Christianity 1919–1945*. Cambridge: Cambridge University Press, 2003.

—— 'Rethinking Nazism and Religion: How Anti-Christian Were the "Pagans"?', *Central European History* 36:1 (2003), pp. 75–105.

Steinmetz, George. *The Devil's Handwriting: Precoloniality and the German Colonial State in Qingdao, Samoa, and Southwest Africa*. Chicago, IL: University of Chicago Press, 2007.

Stephens, Piers. 'Blood, not Soil: Anna Bramwell and the Myth of "Hitler's Green Party"', *Organization and Environment* 14 (2001), pp. 173–87.

Stern, Fritz. *The Politics of Cultural Despair*. Berkeley, CA: University of California Press, 1974.

Stoltzfus, Nathan. *Hitler's Compromises: Coercion and Consensus in Nazi Germany*. New Haven, CT: Yale University Press, 2016.

Stowers, Stanley. 'The Concepts of "Religion", "Political Religion" and the Study of Nazism', *Journal of Contemporary History* 42:1 (January 2007), pp. 9–24.

Strohmeyer, Arn. *Von Hyperborea nach Auschwitz: Wege eins antiken Mythos*. Witten: PapyRossa, 2005.

Strube, Julian. 'Nazism and the Occult', in Christopher Partridge, ed., *The Occult World*. London: Routledge, 2015, pp. 336–47.

—— *Vril. Eine okkulte Urkraft in Theosophie und esoterischem Neonazismus*. Paderborn/Munich: Wilhelm Fink, 2013.

Stutterheim, Kerstin D. *Okkulte Weltvorstellungen im Hintergrund dokumentarischer Filme des 'Dritten Reiches'*. Berlin: Weissensee Verlag, 2000.

Sutin, Lawrence. *Do What Thou Wilt: A Life of Aleister Crowley*. New York: St Martin's Press, 2000.

Taylor, Charles. *Modern Social Imaginaries*. Durham, NC: Duke University Press, 2004.

Thomas, Keith. *Religion and the Decline of Magic*. New York: Scribner's, 1971.

Tiryakian, Edward A. 'Dialectics of Modernity: Reenchantment and Dedifferentiation as Counterprocesses', in Hans Haferkamp and Neil J. Smelser, eds, *Social Change and Modernity*. Berkeley, CA: University of California Press, 1992.

Tooze, Adam. *The Wages of Destruction*. London: Penguin, 2006.

Treitel, Corinna. *A Science for the Soul: Occultism and the Genesis of the German Modern*. Baltimore, MD: Johns Hopkins University Press, 2004.

Trevor-Roper, Hugh, ed. *Hitler's Secret Conversations, 1941–1944*. New York: Farrar, Straus and Young, 1953.

—— *The Bormann Letters*. London: Weidenfeld and Nicolson, 1954.

Tromp, Solco Walle. *Psychical Physics: A Scientific Analysis of Dowsing Radiesthesia and Kindred Divining Phenomena*. New York: Elsevier, 1949.

Trimondi, Victor and Victoria Trimondi. *Hitler, Buddha, Krishna: An Unholy Alliance from the Third Reich to the Present Day*. Vienna: Ueberreuter, 2002.

Voller, Christian. 'Wider die "Mode heutiger Archaik": Konzeptionen von Präsenz und Repräsentation im Mythosdiskurs der Nachkriegszeit', in Bent Gebert and Uwe Mayer, *Zwischen Präsenz und Repräsentation*. Göttingen: De Gruyter, 2014, pp. 226–57.

Vondung, Klaus. *Deutsche Wege zur Erlösung: Formen des Religiösen im Nationalsozialismus*. Munich: Wilhelm Fink Verlag, 2013.

—— *Magie und Manipulation: Ideologischer Kult und Politsche Religion des Nationalsozialismus*. Göttingen: Vandenhoeck & Ruprecht, 1971.

—— 'National Socialism as a Political Religion: Potentials and Limits of an Analytical Concept', *Totalitarian Movements and Political Religions* 6:1 (2005), pp. 87–98.

Waite, Robert. *Psychopathic God*. New York: Basic Books, 1977.

Walker, Mack. *German Home Towns*. Ithaca, NY: Cornell University Press, 1971.

Watt, Roderick H. 'Wehrwolf or Werwolf? Literature, Legend, or Lexical Error into Nazi Propaganda?', *Modern Language Review* 87:4 (October 1992).

Webb, James. *Flight from Reason*. London: MacDonald, 1971.

—— *The Occult Underground*. London: Open Court, 1974.

Weber, Petra. *Justiz und Diktatur: Justizverwaltung und politische Strafjustiz in Thüringen 1945–1961*. Veröffentlichungen zur SBZ-/DDR -Forschung im Institut für Zeitgeschichte. Oldenbourg: Wissenschaftsverlag, 2000.

Wegener, Franz. *Alfred Schuler, der letzte Deutsche katharer*. Gladbeck: KFVR, 2003.

—— *Der Alchemist Franz Tausend. Alchemie und Nationalsozialismus*. Gladbeck: KFVR, 2006.

—— *Heinrich Himmler. Deutscher Spiritismus – Französischer Okkultismus und der Reichsführer SS*. Gladbeck: KFVR, 2004.

—— *Kelten, Hexen, Holocaust*. Gladbeck: KFVR, 2010.

Wehler, Hans-Ulrich. *Deutsche Gesellschaftsgeschichte*, vol. IV. Munich: Beck, 2003.

—— *The German Empire 1871–1918*. Providence, RI: Berg, 1993.

Weikart, Richard, *From Darwin to Hitler: Evolutionary Ethics, Eugenics, and Racism in Germany*. London: Palgrave, 2004.

—— *Hitler's Ethic: The Nazi Pursuit of Evolutionary Progress*. London: Palgrave, 2009.

—— *Hitler's Religion: The Twisted Beliefs that Drove the Third Reich*. Washington, DC: Regnery, 2016.

Weindling, Paul. *Health, Race and German Politics between National Unification and Nazism, 1870–1945*. Cambridge/New York: Cambridge University Press, 1989.

Weingart, Peter. *Doppel-Leben. Ludwig Ferdinand Clauss: Zwischen Rassenforschung und Widerstand*. Frankfurt: Campus, 1995.

Weinreich, Max. *Hitler's Professors: The Part of Scholarship in Germany's Crimes Against the Jewish People*. Oxford: Oxford University Press, 1946.

Weisenburger, Steven C. *A Gravity's Rainbow Companion: Sources and Contexts for Pynchon's Novel*. Athens, GA: University of Georgia, 2011.

Welch, David. 'Goebbels, Götterdämmerung and the Deutsche Wochenschau', in K. M. Short and Stephen Dolezel, eds, *Hitler's Fall: The Newsreel Witness*. London: Routledge, 1988, pp. 80–99.

Werner, Uwe. *Anthroposophen in der Zeit des Nationalsozialismus (1933–1945)*. Munich: Oldenbourg, 1999.

Wessely, Christina. *Welteis: Ein wahre Geschichte*. Berlin: Matthes & Seitz, 2013.

Wetzell, Richard. 'Eugenics and Racial Science in Nazi Germany: Was There a Genesis of the "Final Solution" from the Spirit of Science?', in Pendas et al., eds, *Beyond the Racial State: Rethinking Nazi Germany*.

Wildenthal, Lora. *German Women for Empire, 1884–1945*. Durham, NC: Duke University Press, 2001.

Williamson, George. 'A Religious Sonderweg? Reflections on the Sacred and the Secular in the Historiography of Modern Germany', *Church History* 75:1 (2006), pp. 139–56.

—— *The Longing for Myth in Germany*. Chicago, IL: University of Chicago Press, 2004.

Wiwjorra, Ingo. 'Herman Wirth – Ein gescheiterter Ideologe zwischen "Ahnenerbe" und "Atlantis"', in Barbara Danckwortt, ed., *Historische Rassismusforschung. Ideologen, Täter, Opfer*. Hamburg: Argument, 1995.

Wolff, Ursula. *Litteris et Patriae. Das Janusgesicht der Historie*. Stuttgart: Franz Steiner, 1996.

Wolffram, Heather. *The Stepchildren of Science*. Amsterdam: Rodopi, 2009.

Yenne, Bill. *Hitler's Master of the Dark Arts*. Minneapolis, MN: Zenith, 2010.

Zander, Helmut. *Anthroposophie in Deutschland: Theosophische Weltanschauung und gesellschaftliche Praxis 1884–1945*. Göttingen: Vandenhoeck & Ruprecht, 2007.

—— *Rudolf Steiner: Die Biografie*. Munich: Piper Verlag, 2011.

Zantop, Susanne. *Colonial Fantasies: Conquest, Family, and Nation in Precolonial Germany, 1770–1870*. Durham, NC: Duke University Press, 1997.

Ziemann, Benjamin. *Katholische Kirche und Sozialwissenschaften 1945–1975*. Göttingen: Vandenhoeck & Ruprecht, 2007.

—— 'Religion and the Search for Meaning, 1945–1990', in Helmut Walser Smith, ed., *The Oxford Handbook of Modern German History*. Oxford: Oxford University Press, 2011.

Zimmerer, Jürgen and Joachim Zeller, eds, *Völkermord in Deutsch-Südwestafrika: Der Kolonialkrieg (1904–1908) in Namibia und seine Folgen*. Berlin: Christoph Links Verlag, 2003.

Zimmerman, Andrew. *Anthropology and Antihumanism in Imperial Germany*. Chicago, IL: University of Chicago Press, 2001.

Zipes, Jack. *Fairy Tale as Myth/Myth as Fairy Tale*. Lexington, KY: University Press of Kentucky, 1994.

Zumholz, Maria Anna. *Volksfrömmigkeit und Katholisches Milieu: Marienerscheinungen in Heede 1937–1940*. Cloppenburg: Runge, 2004.

Websites

http://www.amazon.com/dp/B002IPG3YW/ref=rdr_kindle_ext_tmb%29

http://www.antifa.co.at/antifa/PAMMER2.PDF

http://www.archive.org/stream/MemoriesDreamsReflectionsCarlJung/carlgustavjung-interviewsand-encounters-110821120821-phpapp02_djvu.txt

http://www.biographien.kulturimpuls.org/detail.php?&id=544

http://www.bookline.hu/product/home.action?id=2100930525&type=10&_v=J_W_Hauer_Der_Yoga_Ein_ind ischer_Weg_zum_Selbst 324

http://www.books.google.com/books/about/Nostradamus_der_Prophet_der_Weltgeschich.html?id=aSknA

http://www.brainz.org/10-most-sinister-nazi-occultists/ 51 http://www.spiegel.de/fotostrecke/spuk-von-rosenheim-fotostrecke-110511-5.html

http://www.bruno-groening.org/english http://www.biographien.kulturimpuls.org/detail.php?&id=39

http://www.dailymail.co.uk/news/article-2014146/Nazi-nuclear-waste-Hitlers-secret-A-bomb-programme-mine.html

http://www.denisdutton.com/adorno_review.html

http://www.de.wikipedia.org/wiki/Alfred_Karasek

http://www.de.wikipedia.org/wiki/Jakob_Wilhelm_Hauer#/media/File:Deutscher_Glaube_November_1934.jpg

http://www.de.wikipedia.org/wiki/Lutz_Mackensenhttp://www.heterodoxology.com/2012/07/17/parapsychology-in-germany-review-of-heather-wolfframs-stepchildren-ofscience-2009

http://www.dhm.de/lemo/biografie/mathilde-ludendorff

http://www.dhm.de/lemo/html/biografien/HimmlerHeinrich/index.html

http://www.dhm.de/lemo/html/nazi/innenpolitik/ahnenerbe/index.html

http://www.dhm.de/lemo/html/nazi/innenpolitik/vwf/index.html

http://www.en.wikipedia.org/wiki/Ernst_Schäfer

http://www.en.wikipedia.org/wiki/Hans_F._K._Günther 64

http://www.en.wikipedia.org/wiki/Jakob_Wilhelm_Hauer

http://www.en.wikipedia.org/wiki/Otto_Ohlendorf#/media/File:Otto_Ohlendorf_at_the_Nuremberg_Trials.PNG

http://www.findagrave.com/cgi-bin/fg.cgi?page=gr&GRid=11369

http://www.forbes.com/sites/paulrodgers/2014/02/11/search-is-on-for-hitlers-secret-atom-bomb-lab-under-deathcamp

http://www.geschichte.hu-berlin.de/en/forschung-und-projekte-en-old/foundmed/dokumente/forschung-undprojekte/ns-zeit/ringvorlesung/teilIIordner/4februar

http://www.harunyahya.org/tr/Kitaplar/1599/yeni-masonik-duzen/chapter/121

http://www.historycooperative.org/journals/ahr/111.3/saler.html

http://www.h-net.org/reviews/showrev.php?id=345

http://www.holger-szymanski.de/wehrwolf.html

http://www.hsozkult.de/publicationreview/id/rezbuecher-10759

http://www.hsozkult.de/event/id/termine-10810

http://www.img.welt.de/img/zweiter-weltkrieg/crop133061778/7179566868-ci16x9-w780-aoriginal-h438- l0/Bildunterschrift-Eine-Theorie-besagt-d.jpg

http://www.indiana.edu/~beyond

http://www.info3.de/ycms/artikel_1775.shtmlhttp://www.kinoeye.org/03/11/gelbin11.php

http://www.interviewsandenconunters- 110821120821-phpapp02_djvu.txt

http://www.jkibw.de/?Archive_und_Sammlungen:Nachlass_Karasek http://www.ihr.org/jhr/v14/v14n2p-9_Montgomery.html

http://www.jstor.org/discover/10.2307/261215?sid=21105889929191&uid=2129&uid=70&uid=2 &uid=3739600 &uid=4&uid=3739456

http://www.motlc.wiesenthal.com/site/pp.asp?c=gvKVLcMVIuG&b=395043
http://www.mpiwg-berlin.mpg.de/en/research/projects/DeptIII-ChristinaWessely-Welteislehre
http://www.nbcnews.com/id/23456119
http://www.nostradamusresearch.org/en/ww2/bittenfeld-info.htm#0225
http://www.nostradamusresearch.org/en/ww2/centgraf-info.html
http://www.nytimes.com/2013/07/15/world/europe/nadezhda-popova-ww-ii-night-witch-dies-at-91.
    html?_r=1
http://www.nytimes.com/2015/04/19/opinion/sunday/t-m-luhrmann-faith-vs-facts.html
http://www.nyu.edu/pubs/anamesa/archive/fall_2005_culture/11_shull.pdf
http://www.occultforum.org/forum/viewtopic.php?t=29694
http://www.oldmagazinearticles.com/pdf/Carl_Jung_on_Hitler.pdf
http://www.pamelageller.com/2010/01/oh-what-an-enormous-slaughterhouse-the-world-is.html
http://www.peter-diem.at/Daim/Daim.html
http://www.philipcoppens.com/wewelsburg.html
http://www.polunbi.de/archiv/39-10-14-01.html
http://www.polunbi.de/archiv/39-11-29-01.html
http://www.polunbi.de/archiv/41-05-20-01.html
http://www.portal.dnb.de http://www.nostradamus-online.de/index1.html
http://www.queernations.de/de/wissenschaft_forschung/aufsaetze/zurnieden.html;jsessionid=144728
    269B4503D29BECD5C5587515 50?node:attribute=pdfattach_file&.pdf
http://www.readcube.com/articles/10.1111%2Fj.0022-3840.2000.3402_107.x?r3_referer=wol&tracking_
    action=preview_click&show_checkout=1&purchase_referrer=onlinelibrary.wiley.com&purchase_
    site_license=LICENSE_DENIED_NO_CUSTOMERhttp://www.science.orf.at/stories/1628033
http://www.seiyaku.com/customs/crosses/kabbalah.html
http://www.skyscript.co.uk/wulff4.html
http://www.ssp-exploration.de/raketen-in-thueringen.html
http://www.swr.de/swr2/programm/.../essay/-/.../swr2-essay-20080715.rtf 2
http://www.taringa.net/posts/info/9970514/Heinrich-Himmler-Personajes-2-guerra-mundial.html
http://www.telegraph.co.uk/culture/film/starsandstories/3673575/The-original-Indiana-Jones-Otto-
    Rahnand-the-temple-of-doom.html
http://www.theatlantic.com/doc/200305/ryback
http://www.theatlantic.com/magazine/archive/2003/05/hitlers-forgotten-library/302727
http://www.theatlantic.com/technology/archive/2013/07/night-witches-the-female-fighter-pilots-of-
    world-warii/277779
http://www.theguardian.com/books/2000/oct/07/books.guardianreview
http://www.theosociety.org/pasadena/hpb-tm/hpbtm-hp.html
http://www.theosophy-nw.org/theosnw/theos/wqj-selc.html
http://www.uboat.net/men/commanders/1016.html 306 http://www.history.com/news/history-lists/5-
    famous-wwii-covert-operations
http://www.uni-goettingen.de/de/91592.html
http://www.uni-siegen.de/mediaresearch/nichthegemoniale_innovation
http://www.utlib.ee/ekollekt/eeva/index.php?lang=en&do=autor&aid=594
http://www.visionsofjesuschrist.com/weeping1809.html
http://www.warhistoryonline.com/war-articles/hans-kammler-commit-suicide.html
http://www.web.utk.edu/~segsw/2013panels.html
http://www.welt.de/geschichte/zweiter-weltkrieg/article133061716/Die-Ufos-des-Dritten-Reiches-
    kamen-bis-in-dieUSA.html
http://www.wn.rsarchive.org/Lectures/19150518p01.html
http://www.worldscinema.org/2012/03/h-a-lettow-ernst-schafer-geheimnis-tibet-the-enigma-of
    -tibet-1943
http://www.youtube.com/watch?v=PbfMsd43HZE
http://www.zeit.de/1958/42/ueber-die-artamanen-zur-ss

ILLUSTRATION CREDITS

Uncredited illustrations lie in the public domain.

2. bpk / Bayerische Staatsbibliothek / Archiv Heinrich Hoffmann. 4. Technisches Museum Wien, Archive. 5. bpk. 7. bpk. 8. Alamy. 9. bpk / Bayerische Staatsbibliothek / Archiv Heinrich Hoffmann. 10. Getty Images. 11. bpk / Staatsbibliothek zu Berlin. 12. bpk / Bayerische Staatsbibliothek / Archiv Heinrich Hoffmann. 13. bpk / Bayerische Staatsbibliothek / Archiv Heinrich Hoffmann. 14. bpk. 15. Alamy. 16. Getty Images. 17. bpk / US-Army. 18. bpk / F. Bauer. 21. Getty Images. 22. bpk. 23. Getty Images. 24. Getty Images. 25. bpk / Siegmund Rascher. 30. bpk / Bayerische Staatsbibliothek / Archiv Heinrich Hoffmann. 31. bpk. 32. bpk / Hilmar Pabel.

INDEX